THE MIDLAND RAILWAY

— A CHRONOLOGY —

listing in geographical order the opening dates of
the lines and additional running lines of the company
(with the powers under which they were constructed)
together with the dates of
the opening, re-naming, and closing
of stations and signalboxes

Revised and expanded edition
illustrated with a set of line-diagrams

Compiled by
JOHN GOUGH

With a foreword by
Professor T. C. Barker

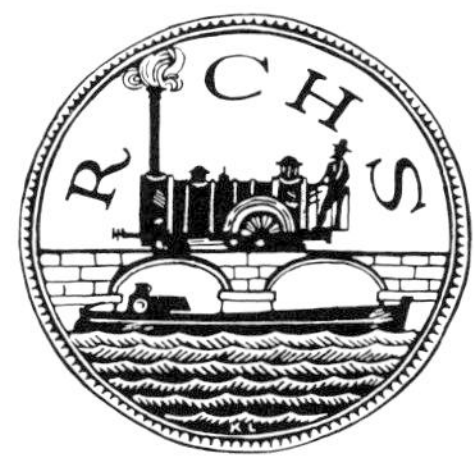

RAILWAY AND CANAL HISTORICAL SOCIETY

First published in 1989
by the
Railway and Canal Historical Society

Registered Office:
Fron Fawnog, Hafod Road, Gwernymynydd, Mold, Clwyd CH7 5JS

Printed by Hobbs the Printers Ltd, Southampton

British Library Cataloguing in Publication Data:
The Midland railway : a chronology. - 2nd ed
1. England. Railway services: London, Midland and Scottish Railway.
Midland lines, history
I. Gough, John, *1943-*
385'.0942

ISBN 0-901461-12-1

The main text is reproduced from typescript
in non-proportional Courier at 15 characters to the inch.
This layout is used to avoid the possibility of introducing errors
in a typesetting and proof-reading procedure.

Railway and Canal Historical Society

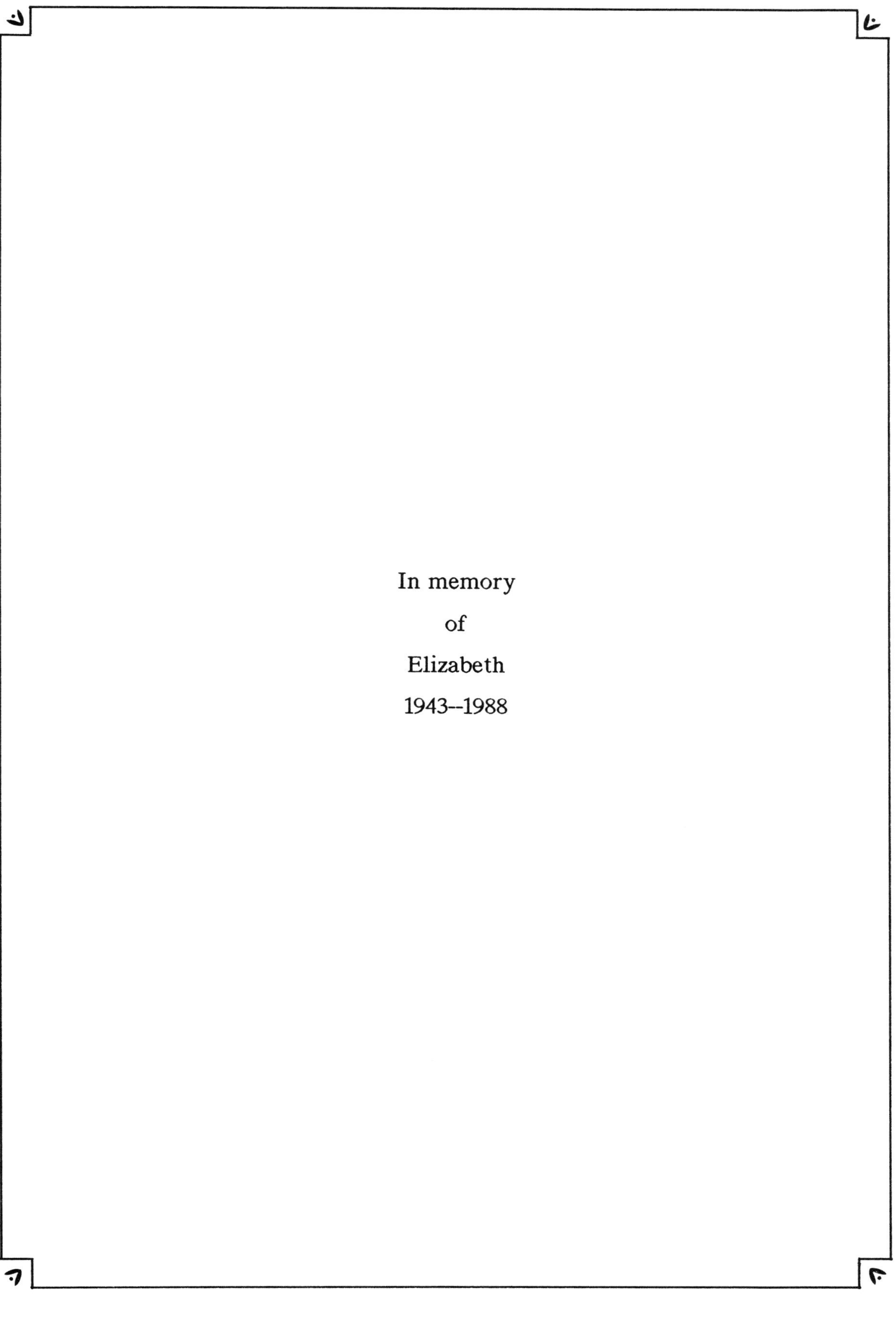

In memory

of

Elizabeth

1943--1988

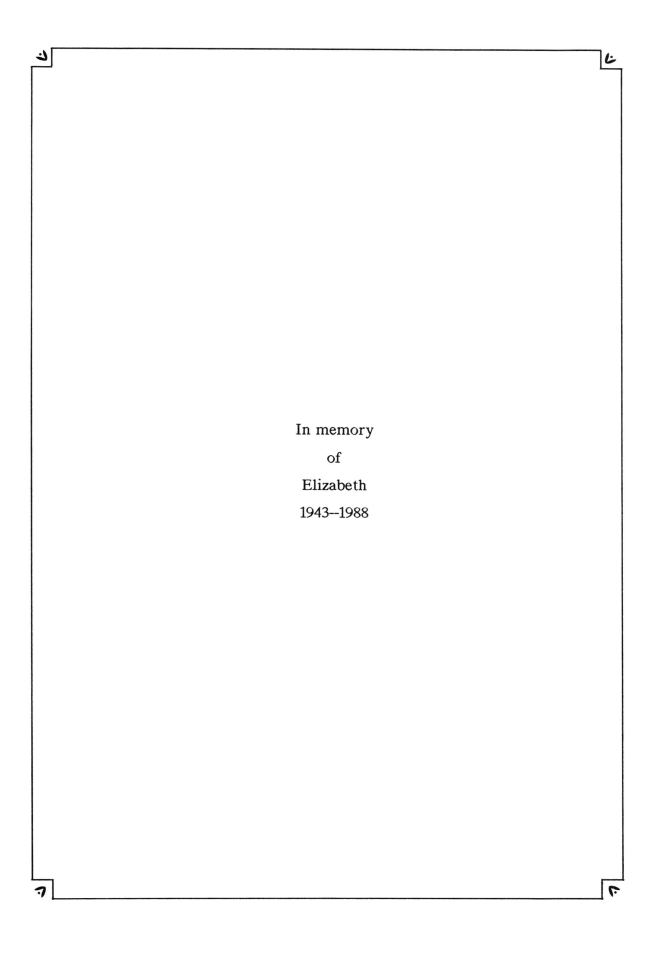

MIDLAND RAILWAY,
GENERAL MAP.

BELFAST & NORTHERN COUNTIES & DONEGAL SECTIONS OF THE MIDLAND RAILWAY.

LONDONDERRY
PORTRUSH
COLERAINE
LIMAVADY
BALLYMONEY
PARKMORE
LARNE
STRABANE
CLENTIES
STRANORLAR
DRAPERSTOWN
COOKSTOWN
BALLYMENA
ANTRIM
BELFAST
KILLYBEGS
DONEGAL
BALLYSHANNON

STANDARD - 5ft 3in GAUGE
Belfast & Northern Counties Committee
NARROW - 3ft GAUGE
Belfast & Northern Counties Committee
Donegal Lines (Midland Rly)
Do (Mid & G.N. of Ireland Joint)

Lines owned or leased, thus.
Lines jointly owned or leased, thus:
Lines projected or in course of construction, thus:

CARLISLE
APPLEBY
KIRKBY STEPHEN
HAWES JNC.
HAWES
TO BELFAST
BARROW
CARNFORTH
MORECAMBE
HEYSHAM
LANCASTER
SETTLE
SKIPTON
YORK
LEEDS
BRADFORD
HALIFAX
HUDDERSFIELD
CUDWORTH
BARNSLEY
KNOTTINGLEY
PONTEFRACT
DONCASTER
SOUTHPORT
AINTREE
LIVERPOOL
MANCHESTER
SHEFFIELD
RETFORD
CHESTER
CHESTERFIELD
LINCOLN
NOTTINGHAM
DERBY
BURTON
TRENT JUNC.
MANSFIELD
LEICESTER
PETERBOROUGH
WISBECH
NORWICH
YARMOUTH
CROMER
GORLESTON
LOWESTOFT
WOLVERHAMPTON
WALSALL
BIRMINGHAM
KETTERING
CAMBRIDGE
NORTHAMPTON
BEDFORD
HITCHIN
LUTON
HARPENDEN
ST ALBANS
HEMEL HEMPSTED
WORCESTER
CHELTENHAM
GLOUCESTER
SWANSEA
BRISTOL
BATH
WELLS
BURNHAM
BRIDGWATER
SHEPTON MALLET
TEMPLECOMBE
BLANDFORD
BOURNEMOUTH
Poole
ST PANCRAS
KENTISH TOWN
FENCHURCH ST
BARKING
ROMFORD
UPMINSTER
PITSEA
TILBURY
SOUTHEND
SHOEBURYNESS

FOREWORD

Contributions to the study of History come in many forms. At one extreme there are the broad, sweeping surveys which relate some particular aspect of the past to other events occurring contemporaneously; or the even more adventurous charges through whole centuries of time. Many valuable insights are often to be gained from such studies by talented generalisers. At the other extreme, and equally valuable, is the work of particularisers, those who study one little facet of the past in great detail, often with equal imagination and ingenuity. Those who apply the microscope to History can tell us as much as those who raise a telescope to their eye. In the hands of real scholars, both approaches can give us greater understanding.

Such scholars may be professionals or amateurs. Occasionally, like John Gough, a university teacher of English Language, they may be highly trained in a subject other than History. In Transport History (and in Railway History particularly) we are especially indebted to many who are fascinated by, and devoted to, the subject but do not earn their living by it. It is an absorbing hobby, often of greater concern to them than paid work itself. From their writings, professionals in other branches of History, Economic and Social History in particular, have much to learn. Their work is also of interest to geographers, urbanists in their many manifestations, and industrial archaeologists, as well as to engineers, civil and mechanical -- upon all of whom railway historians in their turn, if they are sensible, come to depend to some extent.

The specialist to whom we should all be particularly indebted is the devoted scholar like George Ottley who spends his life compiling a bibliography for the rest of us to use, or like John Gough who goes to enormous pains to collect, assess, and assemble source material in this other, most valuable, work of reference. Although this is the second edition of *The Midland Railway: A Chronology*, it is virtually a new work, for so much new detail has been added, including more recent information right down to 1989. All in all, this has occupied the author for over six years.

He deals with a significant subject, for the Midland Railway ranked third in importance, after the London & North Western and the Great Western, at the time of Grouping. It possessed running powers over other companies' lines and the reader will here find references to unexpected places, like Southend and Maidstone, as well as to others like Luton and Bedford on the Midland main line. Railway historians will find all they want to know about the dating of curves, additional lines, signal boxes, and the like. Urban specialists will discover exactly when stations were opened, their names changed, or even when platforms were added or subtracted. Economic historians and geographers may be encouraged to explore -- to take only one example -- the hitherto neglected history of the railway coal yard from its origins to its relatively recent closure, transformed, very often, into the station car park as the railways came to depend on commuters rather than on their staple goods traffic.

During his eight years as editor of the Railway and Canal Historical Society's *Journal*, John Gough has, by a judicious admixture of the general and the particular, the professional and the amateur, greatly improved its standard and its standing. Now, with this valuable compilation, he puts us further in his debt and sets an example to others in this specialised field of study.

T. C. Barker
London School of Economics

June 1989

INTRODUCTION

At the time of Grouping in 1922 the Midland Railway was second only to the Great Western in terms of its route-mileage, with 2,169 miles of railway. It came third in track-mileage, after the London & North Western and the Great Western, with 6,030 miles. With an issued capital of £204,140,713 and with an actual capital expenditure of £130,474,448 the company headed the list. On its ordinary shares it was paying a dividend of 8½%. In its last year of independence the company had gross receipts of £28,932,380 and expenditure of £23,114,278, to give a balance of £6,894,160 -- all these figures putting it in third place behind the London & North Western and the Great Western Railways. By most criteria the Midland tended to occupy this same third place -- behind the L&NWR and the GWR, and just ahead of the North Eastern Railway. It was a commercial organization of very considerable size and importance. Yet we have no full, modern history of the Midland Railway. Williams's work is very good indeed and the author clearly had access to official records, some of which are no longer available to use, but it is now a century since it was written. It is complemented by Stretton's book, but, as we all know, that is a work that must be used with care and it too is now long out of date. Barnes's account is highly selective in what it covers and thus does not present a full picture of the company's development or activities. We still await the detailed, modern business-history of the Midland Railway just as we also still await a similar work dealing with its neighbour, rival, and fellow-giant, the London & North Western.

'The first (though far from the only) duty of the railway historian is to establish a firm foundation for his story by means of an adequate chronology of the physical development of the lines he is concerned with.' So a reviewer more than thirty years ago began his survey of Charles Clinker's *Railways of the West Midlands: A Chronology, 1808-1954*. No such chronology was available for the Midland, and the first edition of this work was a first attempt to fill the gap. It developed from a desire to establish when and where the Midland provided additional running lines on its system, leading to a situation where major sections of the main lines had been quadrupled, and it is believed that the fullest available picture of this process is here given. All goods lines and slow/local lines are covered, together with the running crossovers linking those lines with one another, and wherever it has been possible to identify them, all lines available for through running (reception sidings, through sidings, coal lines, engine lines, etc) have been included. The decision to provide additional facilities was, of course, dictated by pressure of traffic. But what was provided where had to take account not only of what the company could afford at any given time but also of the engineering difficulties that the work might pose. For example, the main line was quadrupled north and south of Leicester in the mid-1870s, but although the company recognized at that time that it would eventually have to quadruple the line through Leicester itself because of the pressure of traffic, it put the work off for some fifteen years because of the cost and difficulty of carrying it out. When we consider the lines between Trent and Normanton we find an extremely complex picture of the work of widening emerging, leading at the end of the day to the apparently straightforward system of passenger lines and goods lines between Trent and Tapton Junction and passenger lines and goods/slow lines between Masborough and Altofts Junction (except through Chevet tunnel) which lasted until the changes of recent years.

In its coverage of the additional running lines the second edition does not expand greatly on the first, though in many cases it refines the information already given. However, in all other respects this counts as a new work -- not least in that coverage is carried forward beyond 31 December 1947 to the early summer of 1989. Details are provided of the parliamentary powers under which all sections of the railway were constructed. The relatively sketchy information given about the opening, closing, and re-naming of stations and goods depots in the first edition has been very greatly expanded, and information on marshalling sidings and exchange sidings appears. Details of signalboxes are given. Engine-sheds are also listed. Nevertheless, much has had to be omitted in order to keep within reasonable limits for publication: turntables, lie-bye sidings, other single sidings, and industrial lines other than actual Midland branches are not covered, and ground frames only appear when they came into use as the specific replacement for a signalbox. No details of control offices or train services are given.

It is hoped that all lines have been listed, even where no date of opening has so far been found, and that all stations are noted. Junctions of other companies with the Midland are given. The Midland Railway's interests in Scotland and in Northern Ireland are excluded, as are the three major joint railways in England: the Cheshire Lines Committee, the Midland & Great Northern, and the Somerset & Dorset. The geographical order of presentation chosen for the first edition has been retained. Its disadvantage of rendering it difficult to see what the company was doing at any one time -- although the Directors' Reports to

Shareholders give a generally adequate indication of that aspect -- seems to be outweighed by two advantages: what has happened in any given location can be ascertained at a glance, and it is also very easy to trace the information being sought without the need for elaborate cross-referencing systems.

Additional research, and information provided by users of the first edition in response to the appeal made in that work, have brought certainty to many of the doubtful areas of the earlier work, but inevitably, since choices -- some of which will prove wrong -- have once again had to be made where evidence conflicts, there will need to be a few corrections. No doubt a number of additions will be needed as well.

Any relevant information for inclusion or for the correction of errors, with a note of the authority for the date cited, or any comments on the work in general will be very much welcomed. It is hoped that it will be possible to make available to purchasers by publication in one form or another corrections to the content of the Chronology that prove to be required, thus ensuring that the information is as useful as possible to as many interested persons as possible. The reviewer quoted earlier went on later in his review to write that: 'This kind of work, though admittedly it does not constitute railway history but something a good deal short of that, is valuable and should be encouraged.' The compiler of this chronology hopes that others may find it valuable.

ACKNOWLEDGEMENTS

I am deeply grateful to Roger Newman both for putting at my disposal his records on the history of Midland signalboxes and for sharing with me my second reading of the weekly engineering notices held in the National Railway Museum at York and thereby not only making that lengthy task much more enjoyable than it might otherwise have been but also helping to ensure the completeness and accuracy of our notes. Especial thanks are also due to Messrs G. J. Aston and G. N. Webb for advice, information, and encouragement in the earlier stages of the work and for their continued support as revision has progressed, as well as to to Professor H. P. White and Peter Stevenson, who took on the thankless task of reading through the whole manuscript.

I have received particular assistance in the additional work leading towards this second edition from R. A. Cooke, Harry Paar, and Glynn Waite. Thanks are also due to Dr A. L. Barnett, the late H. V. Borley, S. L. Bragg, Dr Roger Brettle, the late C. R. Clinker, Colonel M. H. Cobb, the late George Dow, John Edgington, D. Edwards, Geoff Goslin, L. Hage, Mark Higginson, the late Ken Hoole, Laurence Knighton, J. P. McCrickard, Dr A. O. McDougall, Richard Maund, John Miller, Andrew Moore, J. E. Norris, Richard Pulleyn, Michael Robbins, K. P. Plant, P. L. Scowcroft, Professor J. Simmons, W. J. Skillern, Stephen Summerson, N. T. Wassell, B. D. J. Walsh, P. A. Witts, and John Wrottesley for information, as well as to the London Midland Region of British Rail. I have used the facilities of Brunel University Library, Leicester University Library, the British Library (Bloomsbury, Boston Spa, and Colindale), the Public Record Office (Kew), and the National Railway Museum, and to these institutions and their staffs -- particularly to Jane Elliott and Gwen Townend at the National Railway Museum -- I owe a debt of gratitude. Errors will no doubt remain, and for these I am alone responsible. Equally, since the work is an abbreviation of a much longer text, it may well be that some inconsistencies in the type of information given have slipped through. If this is so, it is my fault and I am sorry for it.

John Gough
12 Victoria Gardens
195 London Road
Leicester LE2 1ZH

June 1989

PRIMARY SOURCES

Board and Committee Minutes, Directors' Reports, Miscellaneous Documents, Public and Working Timetables, Appendices to the Working Timetable, and Weekly Notices of the Midland Railway Company have been the principal sources of information. Records of other railway companies have been consulted where relevant, as have records of the Railway Clearing House and of the Railway Department of the Board of Trade. Bradshaw's *Railway Guide* and Bradshaw's *Shareholder's Guide* have been extensively consulted. Periodicals referred to include *Herapath's Railway Journal, The Railway Gazette, The Railway Magazine, The Railway News, The Railway Times, The Illustrated London News,* and many local newspapers. *The London Gazette* and various Local & Personal Acts of Parliament have also been used. Various railway records in private hands have been most generously made available to me for consultation.

SECONDARY SOURCES

E. G. BARNES, *The Rise of the Midland Railway 1844-1874,* George Allen & Unwin 1966

E. G. BARNES, *The Midland Main Line 1875-1922,* George Allen & Unwin 1969

Peter E. BAUGHAN, *North of Leeds,* Roundhouse Books 1966

H. V. BORLEY, *Chronology of London Railways,* Railway & Canal Historical Society 1982

C. R. CLINKER, *The Birmingham & Derby Junction Railway,* Oxford: Dugdale Society 1956

C. R. CLINKER, *Clinker's Register of Closed Passenger Stations and Goods Depots in England, Scotland and Wales 1830-1977,* AvonAnglia Publications & Services 1978

C. R. CLINKER, *The Hay Railway,* David Charles, 1960

C. R. CLINKER, 'The Leicester & Swannington Railway', *Transactions of the Leicester Archaeological Society,* Vol. 30, 1954

C. R. CLINKER, *Railways of the West Midlands: a Chronology,* Stephenson Locomotive Society 1954

C. R. CLINKER, *The Railways of Northamptonshire, including the Soke of Peterborough, 1800 - 1960,* Rugby (privately published) 1960

R. A. COOK, *Lancashire & Yorkshire Railway Historical Maps,* 2edn, Railway & Canal Historical Society 1976

R. A. COOK & K. HOOLE, *North Eastern Railway Historical Maps,* Railway & Canal Historical Society 1975

Godfrey CROUGHTON, R. W. KIDNER, Alan YOUNG, *Private and Untimetabled Railway Stations, Halts, and Stopping Places,* The Oakwood Press 1982

George DOW, *Great Central,* 3 volumes, Locomotive Publishing Company 1959-65

M. D. GREVILLE, *Chronology of the Railways of Lancashire and Cheshire,* Railway & Canal Historical Society 1981

M. D. GREVILLE & Jeoffry SPENCE, *Closed Passenger Lines of Great Britain 1827-1947,* revised edition, Railway & Canal Historical Society 1974

Chris HAWKINS & George REEVE, *LMS Engine Sheds: Their History and Development, Vol. II The Midland Railway,* Wild Swan Publications, Berkshire 1981

David JOY, *South and West Yorkshire* (Volume 8: *A Regional History of the Railways of Great Britain,* general editors David St John Thomas and J. Allan Patmore), David & Charles 1975

H. Grote LEWIN, *The Railway Mania and its Aftermath,* reprinted by David & Charles with introduction and corrections by C. R. Clinker, 1968

H. W. PAAR, *The Severn & Wye Railway,* 2 edn, David & Charles 1973

Jeoffry SPENCE, 'Alterations to Names of Passenger Stations, Group C: London Midland & Scottish Railway, Section II: Midland Railway', *Journal of the Railway & Canal Historical Society,* Vol. XV No. 4, October 1969, pp. 77-82

Clement E. STRETTON, *The History of the Midland Railway,* Methuen 1901

Mike VINCENT, *Lines to Avonmouth,* Oxford Publishing Company 1979

F. S. WILLIAMS, *The Midland Railway: its Rise and Progress,* 3 edn., Bemrose 1877

John WROTTESLEY, *The Great Northern Railway,* 3 volumes, Batsford 1979-81

CONVENTIONS OF PRESENTATION

The Midland Railway divided its system into North, South, East, and West Lines. That pattern is followed here, with the exception that the main line between Derby and Nottingham is treated under the South Lines instead of under the East Lines. Sections I, II, and III cover the South Lines, Section IV covers the East Lines, Sections V, VI, and VII cover the North Lines, and Sections VIII, IX, X, and XI cover the West Lines.

Main lines appear in the units as built, which do not necessarily correspond to their final forms. Thus the main line from London to Derby, for example, appears in the sections St Pancras to Bedford, Hitchin to Wigston Junction, and Rugby to Derby. Curves and small, uncomplicated branches are inset into the entries for the line from which they diverge. Other branches are dealt with after the relevant main line and in the order of their departure from it. Branches of branches follow the main branch (if they have not been inset).

Parliamentary powers are given at the start of the section of line to which they refer, and they are set out in the same geographical order as is used for the line itself. Thus the earliest Act for a line may well not always occur first in the list.

The work is accompanied by a reproduction of the side-strip diagrams shewing the Midland system as it became during the inter-war years under the management of the London Midland & Scottish Railway. From these, it should be possible to locate accurately any feature in which the reader is interested. There is also an overview map of the Midland system. However, it is not possible to provide maps of the degree of detail that users of the chronology may well need, since the scale of the exercise would have been too large. The only fully satisfactory maps of the Midland system are the company's privately-produced *Distance Diagrams,* available for consultation in the Public Record Office at Kew, of which a set is soon to be published by Foxline. For most practical purposes, however, the Ian Allan *British Railways Pre-Grouping Atlas and Gazetteer* will prove satisfactory, especially if users can also refer to the relevant sheet of the Ordnance Survey maps on the One-Inch scale. For the detail of very complex areas there is no substitute for the Ordnance Survey Twenty-Five-Inch sheets, and these are generally available in Local Record Offices or Libraries. They are available in all editions for the whole of the country in the Map Room of the British Library in Bloomsbury. A good many early twenty-five-inch plans have been reprinted in slightly-reduced scale by Alan Godfrey.

Lines are named in the form most generally used by the Midland Railway, and all lines are followed in the DOWN direction as designated by the Midland except where otherwise stated by a note. This applies even where an UP facility is being listed. Thus, for example, Harlington to Flitwick: up goods line.

Where not otherwise stated, additional down lines were located on the down side of the railway and additional up lines were on the up side of the railway. A second additional up or down line should be assumed to lie outside a first additional up or down line and on the same side of the railway.

The names of stations, goods depots, and sorting/marshalling sidings are printed in capitals except when they are cited only as the points of location for running-line facilities. For stations, the usage of the relevant Public Time Table has been taken as standard, rather than the usage of tickets, station name-boards, or the Railway Clearing House. Where different forms appear in one Public Time Table, the form used in the main-line tables has been preferred to that of the branches. The ending '-boro" is rendered as '-borough'. The names of companies meeting the Midland are given in the form used at the time when the connection was provided.

Dates of openings of lines and stations are the dates on and from which a public service was available, the dates of ceremonial openings being ignored or separately cited. No attempt has been made to give opening dates for ticket-platforms, since it has proved well-nigh impossible to find this information. Indeed, it is certain that not all ticket-platforms are mentioned, and further information about these would be very much welcomed. Dates of openings of additional lines are the dates on which the facility was officially brought into use, as it is normally impossible to discover the date on which revenue-earning traffic first ran. Dates of opening of signalboxes are the dates on which the box was commissioned. Although this could often be the same date as that on which the box was erected, it was not always so.

'Opened by' dates mostly come from weekly engineering notices in which the actual day is not given but the work has apparently been done within the week, so day, month, and year appear. In some early cases the information is from monthly timetables, and the range is therefore within a month rather than a week. 'Open before' is used for vaguer dates. Where a date has been established from issues of timetables which are not consecutive, or from the Appendices to the Working Timetable (the first of which was issued in October 1872), a range is given. On one or two very early lines (especially the Birmingham & Gloucester) the opening dates for stations need to be treated with particular caution, as it has proved impossible so far to obtain the degree of precision the compiler would have wished. 'Open before' dates for signalboxes refer to the appearance of a box in the earliest lists that we have, those in the Appendixes for 1875 and 1876 listing boxes with restricted opening hours and that in 1877 listing all boxes. 'Open before 1872' for goods and mineral traffic at some stations refers to the evidence of the Midland's records of traffic and expenses at stations, which begin with 1872.

Dates of closures of stations and lines follow -- with some hesitation -- the normal modern practice of citing the date on and from which no public service was available, although in a number of cases the date on which a line was officially taken out of use has been preferred. The dates of closure of signalboxes are the official dates, which do not take account of the fact that some boxes could stand unused but in full working order for quite long periods of time before being formally closed. Only in the case of boxes burnt down or demolished in a mishap has this practice not been followed: for such boxes the formal closure date will be later than the date of the mishap which is given. In those cases where a box was closed 'until further notice' and apparently never re-opened, the date of the closure until further notice is given. Where major power signalling schemes have involved work carried out over a weekend, the date given for openings and closings has been taken as the Sunday.

ABBREVIATIONS

O	Opened
C	Closed
RO	Re-opened
(NA)	Unadvertised
(All)	Total closure (where a line/station has served goods or passenger traffic only)
t.o.u.	taken out of use
***	the current location
*	date inferred from timetables (Working, Public, or Bradshaw)
?	imples an element of doubt about the date given
M	Mineral traffic
G	Goods traffic
P	Passenger traffic
D	Down
U	Up
ML	Main Line
PL	Passenger Line
GL	Goods Line
FL	Fast Line
SL	Slow Line
LL	Local Line
R	Lie-bye
S	Siding
SB	Signalbox
BP	Block telegraph signal post
NBP	Not a block telegraph signal post
SF	Shunting frame
GF	Ground frame ('stage')
GB	Gate box
LC	Level crossing
AHBs	Automatic half barriers
CCTV	Closed circuit television
OLE	Overhead line equipment
LMS	London Midland & Scottish Railway
LNER	London & North Eastern Railway
GWR	Great Western Railway
RCH	Railway Clearing House
Approved	Approved by the Board of Trade
Inspected	Inspected by the Board of Trade
Dispensed	Board of Trade permitted the use of the facility before inspection

LIST OF PRINCIPAL ENTRIES

The first page-number given refers to the chronology, the second to the diagrams.

Some late corrections to the chronology are shown on page 392.

I. SOUTH OF BEDFORD

ST PANCRAS GOODS DEPOT

Powers: Midland Railway London Station Act 1860,
Midland Railway (New Lines and Additional Powers) Act 1865 (St Pancras Goods Branch)

ST PANCRAS GOODS DEPOT	OM	7.1862
***	OG	2.1.1865
***	CG	2.6.1975
Connection from the Great Northern line	Into use	7.1862
***	t.o.u.	23.3.1868
Connection with the North London Line	Into use	7.1862
***	t.o.u.	1.3.1868
Warehouse for Bass beer on the south side of the Regent's Canal	Into use	16.3.1865
***	Closed	....
Access over London & Bedford line via Luton	Commenced	9.9.1867
General goods service via Luton	Commenced	9.3.1868
St Pancras Goods Yard No. 2 SB	Opened	....
Replacement box	Opened	19.2.1893
***	Closed	20.3.1910
St Pancras Goods Yard No. 3 SB	Opened	12.1888-8.1893
***	Closed	20.3.1910

ST PANCRAS PASSENGER STATION

Powers: Midland Railway (Extension to London) Act 1863

St Pancras: Midland Grand Hotel	Opened	5.5.1873
***	Closed	by April 1935
***	Leased	....
St Pancras Station to St Paul's Road Jcn	Opened	1.10.1868
ST PANCRAS PASSENGER STATION	OP	1.10.1868
Temporary booking office	Opened	29.1.1980
Old booking office (removed to new site)	Re-opened	8.5.1983
Travel centre	Opened	10.7.1983
Additional platforms (Nos. 3 & 4)	Into use	15.5.1892
Platforms shortened by bomb damage	By	5.7.1941
Platform 5 restored to length	... ...	23.5.1942
Platforms 3 & 4 restored and lengthened by 8 feet	... ...	29.11.1942
Platform 2 restored to length	... ...	4.4.1943
Platform 1	t.o.u.	30.5.1982
St Pancras: connection from Platform 1 to down main line superseded by a new one 100 yards north	... ...	29.4.1900
St Pancras: most new track in the station area in place	By	8.7.1982

LONDON & BEDFORD LINE

Powers: Midland Railway (Extension to London) Act 1863
Midland Railway (Additional Powers) Act 1868 (St Pancras Connecting Line)
Midland Railway Act 1889 (widening at St Pancras)
Midland Railway Act 1897 (conversion of viaduct at St Pancras Gardens into embankment)
Midland Railway (Additional Powers) Act 1870 (removal of tunnel between St Paul's Road and Camden Mews South)
Midland Railway Act 1894 (Camden Road and Kentish Town widening)
Midland Railway (New Lines and Additional Powers) Act 1864 (Kentish Town to Cricklewood)
Midland Railway (Additional Powers) Act 1866 (extension of Belsize tunnel)
Midland Railway (Additional Powers) Act 1880 (Belsize second tunnel)
British Railways Act 1980 (decking gaps in the bridge at Cricklewood)
Midland Railway Act 1900 (Finchley Road and Welsh Harp widening)
Midland Railway (Additional Powers) Act 1881 (Hendon crossing)
Midland Railway Act 1892 (Elstree second tunnel)
Midland Railway (New Lines and Additional Powers) Act 1864 (Park Street to north of St Albans)
Midland Railway (New Lines and Additional Powers) Act 1864 (north of Harpenden to south of Chiltern Green)
Midland Railway Act 1906 (widening of a bridge at Luton)
Midland Railway (New Lines and Additional Powers) Act 1864 (Sundon to north of Ampthill)
Midland Railway Act 1892 (Ampthill second tunnel)
Midland Railway (New Lines and Additional Powers) Act 1864 (Millbrook to Bedford)

St Pancras Goods Depot to Bedford	OG	9.9.1867

Four tracks were provided between St Pancras Goods Depot and Brent North Junction. The up and down goods lines, which were gauntleted into the main lines through the Belsize tunnel, were on the down side. Brent North Junction was in the same position as the later Welsh Harp Junction. The goods lines between Brent South Junction and Brent North Junction became slow lines by August 1877 and reverted to goods lines before September 1956.

The line was worked by the block telegraph system from its opening.

King's Cross Jcn to Bedford	OP	13.7.1868
St Pancras to St Paul's Road Passenger Jcn	OP	1.10.1868
St Pancras to Dock Jcn: OLE	Energised	27.9.1982
Between St Pancras Station and Highgate Road Junction via Kentish Town Junction the Great Eastern Railway possessed running powers over the Midland line.		
St Pancras Departure SB	Opened	4.1883-11.1885
Re-named St Pancras West SB	... ...	22.5.1892
Replacement box	Opened	11.3.1900
Re-named St Pancras Station SB	... ...	25.3.1900
Replacement power signalbox	Opened	6.10.1957
***	Closed	6.7.1982
St Pancras Arrival SB	Opened	1867
Replacement box	Opened	1873 ?
Re-named St Pancras East SB	... ...	22.5.1892
***	Closed	25.3.1900

Brewer Street Coal Bays

Powers: -

BREWER STREET COAL BAYS	Opened	....
***	Closed	14.11.1898

St Pancras Junction SB	Open before	16.8.1877
Re-named St Pancras Passenger Station SB	... ...	8.1877-4.1878
Re-named St Pancras Passenger Junction SB	... ...	4.1883-11.1885
***	Closed	6.5.1900
New signalbox (without a name)	Opened	1.4.1900
Named St Pancras Junction SB and east frame brought into use	... ...	6.5.1900
***	Re-framed	8.6.1902
***	Closed	6.10.1957
St Pancras Passenger Jcn: facing crossover between main lines	Into use	22.5.1892
St Pancras Jcn: up goods line to passenger lines crossover	Into use	8.6.1902

St Pancras Road Coal Bays

Powers: -

ST PANCRAS ROAD COAL BAYS	Opened	18.5.1868
***	Closed	29.4.1968
Traverser and coal chutes	t.o.u.	29.11.1971

Somers Town Goods Depot

Powers: Midland Railway (Additional Powers) Act 1875

ST PANCRAS NEW GOODS DEPOT	O.Fish	1.4.1887
***	Opened	1.11.1887
ST PANCRAS NEW GOODS DEPOT altered to SOMERS TOWN GOODS DEPOT	... ...	1.8.1892
Low-level section	Closed	5.6.1967
High-level section	t.o.u.	4.6.1973
St Pancras Road SB (not a block post)	Opened	12.1888-8.1893
Re-named St Pancras Road South SB	... ...	31.7.1892
Re-named Somers Town Goods Yard SB	... ...	6.5.1900
Made a ground frame	... ...	1945-1960
Points converted to hand-operation	... ...	8.7.1957
St Pancras Road North SB	Opened	31.7.1892
***	Closed	1.4.1900
Somers Town Goods Yard to St Pancras Jcn: lines named goods arrival line and goods departure line respectively	... ...	6.5.1900
Somers Town Goods Depot: arrival and departure sidings	t.o.u.	17.1.1976

Phoenix Street Coal Depot

Powers: Midland Railway (Additional Powers) Act 1890

PHOENIX STREET COAL DEPOT	Opened	14.11.1898
***	Closed	23.4.1968
PHOENIX STREET COAL DEPOT: direct access from up goods line	Into use	22.6.1902

St Pancras Jcn to Cambridge Street: west departure line	Into use	6.5.1900
Line cut and made west departure neck, and east departure line made down fast line	... ...	24.6.1979
St Pancras to Cambridge Street: down passenger line named east departure line	... ...	6.5.1900
St Pancras to St Pancras Jcn: lines on eastern side named east arrival line and west arrival line respectively	... ...	6.5.1900
St Pancras to St Paul's Road Jcn: new pair of passenger lines in place of the former main lines, these being designated goods lines	Approved	9.3.1869
St Pancras Road bridge to St Paul's Road Jcn: up and down goods lines (to give access to the new goods depot)	Into use	31.7.1892
St Pancras to West Hampstead: goods lines made slow lines	... ...	1.5.1977
St Pancras to Cambridge Street: west departure line made west departure neck and east departure line made down fast line	... ...	24.6.1979
St Pancras to south end of Camden Road tunnel: down fast line taken out of use and up fast line re-named up & down local line	... ...	3.2.1980

St Pancras to south end of Camden Road tunnel: disused down fast line made up fast line, and joined at northern end to former up slow line, this line being taken out of use south of the slue	... ...	10.2.1980
St Pancras to Cambridge Street: west departure line slued into remains of up slow line (former up goods line) to provide a new shunting neck	... ...	26.7.1980
St Pancras to Engine Shed Jcn: down slow line made down fast line	... ...	19.10.1980
St Pancras to Finchley Road (throughout): slow lines re-named fast lines	... ...	19.10.1980
St Pancras to Camden Road tunnel: west departure neck extended and made down fast line; down fast line made Churchyard Siding No. 1	... ...	22.11.1981
St Pancras to Camden Road tunnel: local lines made slow lines	... ...	5.7.1982
Cambridge Street diesel depot	Opened	....
***	Closed	8.4.1984
Cambridge Street SB (signalling the passenger lines only)	Opened	31.7.1892
***	Closed	6.10.1957
Cambridge Street to Dock Jcn: down carriage line	Into use	15.12.1907
North London Incline SB (signalling the goods lines only)	Open before	1.11.1875
Replacement box	Opened	23.10.1892
Box closed and ground frame provided in lieu	... ...	31.12.1961
***	t.o.u.	21.12.1975

North London Incline

Powers: --

North London Incline SB to St Pancras Junction with the North London Railway	Into use	1867
North London Incline	Off. closed	31.12.1975

From 15 November 1909 the North London Incline was worked by train tablet, and on that day a new ground box was opened at the top of the incline, called the Midland Tablet Box.

Dock Junction SB	Open before	16.8.1877
Replacement box	Opened	31.7.1892
Replacement box 10 yards south	Opened	27.5.1956
Box ceased to signal up and down slow lines	... ...	27.6.1979
***	Closed	15.7.1979

Cambridge Street Coal Bays

Powers: Midland Railway (St. Pancras Branch) Act 1864

CAMBRIDGE STREET COAL BAYS	Opened	....
***	Closed	15.6.1963

Regent's Canal Branch

Powers: Midland Railway (St. Pancras Branch) Act 1864

Dock Jcn to St Pancras Dock	Into use	c.1870
***	t.o.u.	....

Dock Jcn to St Pancras Goods Depot: curve-line alongside North London Incline	Into use	31.7.1892
Dock Junction South (site of Dock Junction SB): ladder connection from up fast line to Churchyard Sidings and connections (facing to up trains) from the up & down slow line to the up fast line and to the up sidings	Into use	5.7.1982
Dock Jcn (and Moorgate) to Cricklewood: OLE	Energised	1.3.1982
Lomond Street SB (no signals for the goods lines)	Opened	1885
***	Closed	14.12.1902
St Paul's Road Goods Junction SB (goods lines only)	Open before	16.8.1877
Replacement box	Opened	7.8.1904
***	Closed	21.12.1975
St Paul's Road Passenger Junction SB (passenger lines only)	Opened	1868
Replacement box	Opened	6.1.1889
Replacement box	Opened	18.9.1898
***	Re-framed	7.9.1919
***	Closed	7.10.1956

St Pancras Branch

Powers: Midland Railway (St. Pancras Branch) Act 1864

St Paul's Jcn to King's Cross Jcn with the Metropolitan Railway	OP	13.7.1868
***	OG	16.11.1869
***	CP	11.9.1939
***	RO(P)	7.10.1946
***	CG	1968
***	CP	14.5.1979
OLE	Energised	1.3.1982
***	RO(P)	11.7.1983

Between King's Cross Junction and West Street Junction, Whitecross Street Junction, and Moorgate Street, the Midland Railway possessed running powers over the Metropolitan line. Between King's Cross Junction, Kentish Town Junction, and Hendon the London, Chatham & Dover Railway possessed running powers over the Midland line.

St Pancras tunnel: series of 11 marker lights	Into use	3.4.1944
Number of lights reduced to 9	... ...	8.10.1945
Remaining lights	Removed	....
St Pancras Tunnel SB	Opened	21.7.1889
***	Closed	2.2.1958

Midland Depots reached over the Metropolitan line

See page 28

Kings Cross LT to Carlton Road Jcn: up and down slow lines re-named up and down Moorgate lines	... ...	1.5.1977
St Paul's Road Passenger Jcn: double junction (DSL-DFL, UFL-USL)	Into use	13.11.1898
***	t.o.u.	....
St Paul's Road Passenger Jcn to Kentish Town Locomotive & Carriage Sidings: main lines re-named fast lines	... ...	6.11.1898
St Paul's Road Passenger Jcn to Kentish Town Locomotive & Carriage Sidings: up and down slow lines	Into use	13.11.1898
South end of Camden Road tunnel to Engine Shed Jcn: fast lines re-named local lines	... ...	3.2.1980
Up slow line made up fast line	... ...	10.2.1980
South end of Camden Road tunnel re-named Dock Junction North	... ...	....
Dock Junction North to Engine Shed Jcn: down local line re-named up & down slow line and up local line re-named up & down carriage line	... ...	5.7.1982
CAMDEN ROAD	OP	13.7.1868
***	CP(All)	1.1.1916
Camden Road SB	Open before	16.8.1877
Replacement box	Opened	5.6.1887
Replacement box	Opened	11.9.1898
Replacement box	Opened	13.11.1898
***	Closed	2.11.1919
Camden Road up slow line intermediate block signal	Into use	7.12.1978
***	t.o.u.	6.12.1981
Islip Street Jcn: double junction (DFL-DSL, USL-UFL)	Into use	13.11.1898
***	t.o.u.	23.12.1966
Islip Street SB	Open before	16.8.1877
Re-named Islip Street Junction SB	... ...	6.11.1898
Box demolished in mishap and not replaced	... ...	23.12.1966
***	Off. closed	21.1.1967
Islip Street Jcn: down goods line to down passenger line crossover	Into use	13.11.1892
***	t.o.u.	....
Kentish Town, south of: Moorgate line temporarily cut	... ...	13.5.1979
KENTISH TOWN	OP	13.7.1868
***	OG by	1895
***	CG	2.8.1971
old entrance and footbridge closed; new footbridge from LT station into use; tickets issued from LT office by LT staff	... ...	7.6.1981
Platform 4 temporarily closed	... ...	5.7.1982
Platform 4 brought back into use and platform 3 closed	... ...	3.2.1983
During the period of closure of platform No. 4 the up & down carriage line was used for passenger trains.		
Kentish Town Station SB (not a block post)	Opened	25.9.1898
***	Re-located	28.5.1899
Replacement box	Opened	27.5.1900
***	Closed	9.8.1908
Kentish Town Junction SB	Opened	1868
***	Alt.levers	17.8.1890
Replacement box	Opened	25.9.1898
***	Closed	16.3.1969

Kentish Town Curve or Tottenham South Curve

See page 28, and page 29 for the Tottenham & Hampstead Junction Railway

Kentish Town Jcn: up goods line to up fast line crossover	Into use	....
***	t.o.u.	22.11.1964
Kentish Town Jcn to Cattle Docks Jcn: siding between down fast line and up goods line made a running line worked in both directions	By w/e	30.4.1903
Connection from down fast line to middle line	Removed	30.10.1904
Extra running line (by now the up carriage line)	t.o.u.	18.11.1964
Kentish Town Sidings SB	Opened	....
Replacement box	Opened	3.7.1898
***	Closed	7.9.1969
Kentish Town Sidings SB ceased to signal the fast lines	... ...	26.7.1903
Kentish Town Sidings to Engine Shed Jcn: down slow line (up side)	Into use	23.4.1899
Kentish Town Sidings to Carlton Road Jcn: up slow line (up side)	Into use	23.4.1899

Kentish Town Sheds

Powers: Midland Railway (New Lines and Additional Powers) Act 1864

Kentish Town engine sheds (2)	Opened	1867-1868
Kentish Town engine sheds: old No. 1 shed closed, No. 2 shed became No. 1 shed, and new Nos. 2 and 3 sheds provided	... ...	1899
Kentish Town engine sheds	Closed	1963

ENGINE SHED SIDINGS	Opened	1.7.1868 *
***	Closed	....
Engine Shed Junction SB (no signals for the goods lines)	Opened	16.4.1899
***	Slued	28.10.1900
***	Re-framed	18.11.1900
***	Closed	6.12.1981

Engine Shed Curve
See page 28

Engine Shed Jcn to Carlton Road Jcn: down slow line (up side)	Into use	28.10.1900
Engine Shed Jcn (site of): ladder junction (south end in DFL)	Into use	8.7.1979
As the slow lines (the former goods lines) were actually out of use until 15 July 1979 (from January 1979) for work on the retaining wall, this opening date is hypothetical by one week.		
Engine Shed Jcn to Finchley Road Jcn: fast lines re-named local lines	... ...	19.10.1980
Engine Shed Jcn to Silk Stream Jcn: local lines re-named slow lines	... ...	26.4.1981
Engine Shed Jcn (site): up local line slued into up Moorgate line and made up Moorgate line from Carlton Road Jcn; junction laid in from down Moorgate line to future up & down local line; down local line made up & down local line	... ...	28.6.1981
Engine Shed Jcn to Carlton Road Jcn: Moorgate lines	t.o.u.	28.6.1981
Engine Shed Jcn to Carlton Road Jcn: up & down local line re-named up & down slow line	... ...	5.7.1982
Cattle Dock Junction SB	Open before	16.8.1877
Replacement box alongside down goods line	Opened	22.3.1903
Replacement box	Opened	23.5.1936
***	Closed	24.10.1964

Kentish Town Cattle Station
Powers: -

KENTISH TOWN CATTLE STATION	Opened	1.3.1868 *
***	Closed	....
Cattle Dock Sidings SB	Opened	11.1874-11.1875
Replacement box	Opened	12.6.1888
Replacement box	Opened	28.1.1894
***	Closed	22.3.1903
KENTISH TOWN CONTAINER SIDINGS (on the Cattle Dock site)	Opened	22.5.1966
TARTAN ARROW SIDING (on the Cattle Dock site)	t.o.u.	8.4.1978

Kentish Town (Spring Place) Coal Bays
Powers: Midland Railway (New Lines and Additional Powers) Act 1864, Midland Railway (Additional Powers) Act 1866

SPRING PLACE COAL BAYS	Opened	....
***	Closed	2.7.1970 ?

Carlton Road Junction SB	Opened	12.1882
Replacement bos	Opened	5.6.1898
Replacement box	Opened	25.10.1964
***	Closed	22.10.1978
Carlton Road Jcn: double junction	Recovered	25.6.1978
Carlton Road Jcn: ladder junction (south end in DGL)	Into use	9.12.1979
Carlton Road Jcn: Moorgate lines	t.o.u.	14.6.1981
Carlton Road Jcn to Finchley Road Jcn: main lines re-named fast lines	... ...	1.5.1977

Tottenham North Curve
See page 28

HAVERSTOCK HILL	OP	13.7.1868
***	CP(All)	1.1.1916
Haverstock Hill SB	Open before	16.8.1877
Replacement box	Opened	1882
***	Re-framed	11.2.1912
Ceased to signal passenger lines	... ...	30.12.1945
Box closed and up and down goods line IBS provided	... ...	20.10.1946
Down goods line IBS	t.o.u.	29.7.1972
Up goods line IBS	t.o.u.	....
Belsize tunnel: passenger and goods lines gauntleted	... ...	1867 -- 1884
Haverstock Hill to West End (south of): new passenger lines through the Belsize new tunnel	Into use	3.2.1884
FINCHLEY ROAD & ST JOHN'S WOOD	OP	13.7.1868
***	OM before	1872
***	OG	1874 ?
***	OG by	1883
Altered to FINCHLEY ROAD	... ...	1.9.1868 *
Old platforms closed and new ones opened	... ...	3.2.1884
***	CP	11.7.1927
***	CG	....
***	C.Coal	16.5.1983
Finchley Road: connection with Metropolitan Railway	Into use	1.10.1880
***	t.o.u.	8.3.1948

FINCHLEY ROAD EXCHANGE SIDINGS	Opened	....
***	Closed	....
Finchley Road SB	Opened by	1871
Replacement box	Opened	1884
Replacement box	Opened	21.5.1905
***	Closed	8.4.1978
***	Re-framed & re-opened	29.4.1978
***	Closed	26.4.1981
Finchley Road Jcn: fast lines diverted into old Belsize tunnel	... ...	18.10.1980
Finchley Road Jcn to West Hampstead: slow lines severed at Finchley Road and facing crossover at West Hampstead brought into use; up slow line re-named down Hendon line; up slow line made a run-round siding	... ...	19.10.1980
Finchley Road: ladder junction (south end in UFL)	Into use	25.4.1981
Junction re-named West Hampstead South Junction	... ...	....
Finchley Road to West End Station SB: block telegraph working on the goods lines	Discont'd	6.3.1905
***	Resumed	29.5.1905
Finchley Road to West End station (south end): existing goods lines taken out of use and replaced by new pair of goods lines	... ...	25.6.1905
Finchley Road to Watling Street Jcn: up and down local lines	Into use	3.12.1905
South of London & North Western overbridge to Watling Street Jcn: goods lines placed in their permanent position	... ...	2.4.1905
Passenger lines placed in their permanent position	... ...	9.4.1905
WEST END (FOR KILBURN & HAMPSTEAD)	OP&M	1.3.1871
***	OG	1877
Altered to WEST END	... ...	1.7.1903 *
Altered to WEST END & BRONDESBURY	... ...	1.4.1904
Altered to WEST HAMPSTEAD	... ...	1.9.1905
Altered to WEST HAMPSTEAD MIDLAND	Goods	1.7.1950
***	Passenger	25.9.1950
New booking office	Opened	11.1966
***	CG	3.8.1970
Altered to WEST HAMPSTEAD THAMESLINK	... ...	16.5.1988
West End: replacement up and down goods lines	Into use	27.11.1904
West End: double junction (DGL-DFL, UFL-UGL)	Into use	7.5.1905
Down slow line to down fast line crossover	t.o.u.	3.7.1977
Up fast line to up slow line crossover	t.o.u.	19.10.1980
West End Station: double junction (DGL-DPL, UPL-UGL)	Into use	15.7.1894
***	t.o.u.	....
West Hampstead to Cricklewood South Jcn: down goods line made down slow line	... ...	9.7.1977
Down slow line re-named down Hendon line	... ...	26.4.1981
West Hampstead to Silkstream Jcn: up goods line re-named up Hendon line	... ...	26.4.1981
West End Station SB	Open before	16.8.1877
Replacement box	Opened	15.7.1894
Replacement box	Opened	2.4.1905
Re-named West Hampstead Station SB	... ...	1.9.1905
***	Closed	29.4.1978
West Hampstead PSB:		
1. Harpenden and Luton	Into use	20-21.10.1979
1a. Cricklewood Depot	Into use	4.11.1979
2. Elstree to St Albans (including Mill Hill up IBS)	Into use	1-2.12.1979
3. Leagrave to Millbrook	Into use	31.5-1.6.1980
4. Bedford area	Into use	1-2.11.1980
5. Finchley Road to Hendon	Into use	25-26.4.1981
6. Sharnbrook to Irchester South (exc)	Into use	16-17.5.1981
7a. Moorgate to Engine Shed Jcn	Into use	5-6.12.1981
7b. St Pancras and Dock Jcn	Into use	3-6.7.1982
West Hampstead: ladder junction with goods lines (south end in UFL)	Into use	29.4.1978
Connection from second up goods line to up local line	Into use	3.12.1905
***	t.o.u.	....
West Hampstead to Watling Street Jcn: second up goods line	Into use	8.10.1905
***	t.o.u.	3.4.1977
The second up goods line lay between the slow lines and the fast lines.		
West Hampstead to Cricklewood South Jcn: down carriage line	Into use	29.4.1978
The down carriage line is on the site of the former second up goods line.		
West Hampstead to Cricklewood South Jcn: down goods line re-designated down slow line	... ...	3.7.1977
West End to West End North Jcn; Child's Hill Passenger Jcn to Brent Jcn No. 2: working by bell instead of by block telegraph	... ...	6.4.1902
West End Sidings South End: connection from sidings to up passenger line	t.o.u.	26.3.1905
WEST END SIDINGS (down side)	Opened	1868
***	t.o.u.	26.10.1970
West End North Junction SB (signalling the goods lines only)	Open before	16.8.1877
Replacement SB	Opened	16.2.1896
Replacement SB	Opened	1.4.1905
Re-named West End Sidings SB	... ...	3.9.1905
***	Closed	28.7.1968

West Hampstead to Watling Street Jcn:		
second up goods line placed in its permanent position	... ...	29.10.1905
West Hampstead to Cricklewood South Jcn:		
down goods line redesignated down slow line	... ...	3.7.1977
Down slow line re-named down Hendon line	... ...	26.4.1981
West Hampstead to Silkstream Jcn:		
up goods line re-named up Hendon line	... ...	26.4.1981
West Hampstead South Jcn to Cricklewood Jcn:		
slow lines closed temporarily on account of cutting instability at bridge No. 38	... ...	22.3.1985
Remedial works completed	... ...	7.7.1985
Mill Lane bridge to Cricklewood Jcn:		
up goods line placed in its permanent position	... ...	3.9.1905
Mill Lane bridge: passenger lines placed in their permanent position	... ...	15.10.1905
Watling Street SB (no signals for the passenger lines)	Opened	6.11.1892
Box commenced to signal the passenger lines	... ...	....
Re-named Watling Street Junction SB	... ...	....
Replacement box	Opened	25.6.1899
Replacement box	Opened	3.9.1905
Ceased to signal the goods lines	... ...	Early 1966
***	Closed	3.7.1977
Watling Street Jcn: double junction (DGL-DPL, UPL-UGL)	Into use	16.7.1899
***	t.o.u.	....
Double junction (DGL-DFL, UFL-UGL)	Into use	3.9.1905
***	t.o.u.	Early 1966
New junction between the up local and second up goods lines and the up passenger line	Into use	17.9.1905
Down passenger line to down local line crossover	Into use	....
Double junction (DFL-DLL, ULL-UFL)	t.o.u.	3.7.1977
Watling Street to Child's Hill Passenger Jcn:		
second down goods line	In use by	4.11.1892
Line made down reception line	... ...	....
***	t.o.u. by	9.1956
Watling St Jcn to Child's Hill South: second and third up goods lines	Into use	25.6.1899
Third up goods line	t.o.u.	2.10.1904
Watling Street Jcn to Child's Hill Passenger Jcn: up local line	Into use	2.10.1904
Down local line	Into use	24.9.1905
Watling Street Jcn to Cricklewood Jcn:		
goods lines placed in their permanent position	... ...	13.8.1905
Down local line	Into use	24.9.1905
Second up goods line	t.o.u.	3.4.1977
Cricklewood South Jcn (DGL-UGL-DFL, DFL/UFL-DSL/USL, DLL-ULL)	Into use	3.7.1977
Cricklewood South Jcn to Silk Stream Jcn:		
down goods line re-named down Hendon line	... ...	26.4.1981
Child's Hill South SB	Opened	25.6.1899
Re-named Cricklewood South SB	By	7.10.1903
***	Closed	2.10.1904
Cricklewood to Luton Hoo: OLE	Energised	28.9.1981
CHILD'S HILL & CRICKLEWOOD	OP	2.5.1870
***	OM before	1872
***	OG	1875
Altered to CRICKLEWOOD	... ...	1.5.1903
***	CG	6.10.1969
Child's Hill Goods Junction SB	Opened	2.1879-2.1880
***	Closed	6.11.1892
CHILD'S HILL DOWN SIDINGS	Opened	....
Re-named CRICKLEWOOD DOWN SIDINGS	... ...	....
***	Closed	....
Child's Hill Down Sidings SB (not a block post)	Opened	30.4.1893
Re-named Cricklewood Down Sidings SB	By	7.10.1903
Made a ground frame	... ...	1949-1953
***	t.o.u.	11.2.1967
Child's Hill Junction SB	Open before	16.8.1877
Re-named Child's Hill Passenger Junction SB	... ...	2.1879-2.1880
Replacement box	Opened	4.12.1892
Re-named Cricklewood Junction SB	By	7.10.1903
Replacement box	Opened	18.10.1903
***	Re-framed	1944
Cricklewood Junction SB closed and location re-named Cricklewood Curve Junction	... ...	26.4.1981

Cricklewood Curve

See page 40

Cricklewood Junction SB: ceased temporarily to signal goods lines	... ...	30.4.1977
Ceased temporarily to signal passenger lines	... ...	29.5.1977
Resumed control of both pairs of lines	... ...	3.7.1977
Cricklewood Jcn: double junction (DFL-DLL, ULL-UFL)	Into use	15.11.1903
Up local line to up fast line crossover	t.o.u.	4.3.1979
Down fast line to down local line crossover	t.o.u.	17.6.1979
Child's Hill Passenger Jcn: up and down carriage lines	Into use	9.6.1901

Cricklewood Jcn: carriage shed lines and junction closed, together with old depot, on opening of new depot	... ...	17.2.1980
Old carriage sidings	t.o.u.	19.11.1984
Cricklewood Jcn: bi-directional shunting line	Into use	28.2.1904
Cricklewood Jcn: facing connection from line to Dudding Hill into south end of Brent Empty Wagon Sidings	Into use	8.7.1912
Cricklewood Jcn: connection with Cricklewood Curve removed from the fast lines and connected to the goods lines	... ...	Early 1966
Cricklewood: facing connection between the up and down slow lines	Into use	18.7.1981
Connections between the up slow line and the reception and goods lines	Into use	5.7.1981
Child's Hill Passenger Jcn to Brent South Jcn: second and third up goods lines (on up side of passenger lines)	Into use	23.8.1885 ?
***	t.o.u. by	9.1956
Child's Hill Passenger Jcn to Brent Empty Wagon Sidings: second down goods line	Into use	28.9.1890
Line made down reception line	By	9.1956
***	t.o.u.	....
Cricklewood Jcn to Welsh Harp Jcn: up and down local lines	Into use	15.11.1903
Cricklewood Jcn to Brent No. 2 Jcn: down goods line	Slued	12.9.1921
Up goods line	Slued	14.9.1921
Cricklewood Jcn to Brent No. 2 Jcn: disused siding adjacent to the up local line made up & down no. 1 goods line and through siding made up & down no.2 goods line	... ...	20.8.1978
Nos. 1 and 2 up & down goods lines	t.o.u.	....
Cricklewood Curve Jcn to Cricklewood Depot Jcn: second up goods line	Into use	26.4.1981 ?
First up goods line	Into use	14.6.1981
Brent: connection from second down goods line to empty wagon sidings	Into use	16.3.1908
BRENT SIDINGS (down side)	Opened	1.5.1868 *
These sidings became Brent Empty Wagon Sidings and were later re-named Cricklewood Recess Sidings.		
Empty Wagon Sidings SB	Opened	....
Re-named Brent Empty Wagon Sidings SB	... ...	....
Replacement box	Opened	21.8.1888
Box closed and ground frame provided in lieu	... ...	4.9.1910
Ground frame re-named Cricklewood Recess Sidings SF	... ...	9.1979
***	t.o.u.	....
Brent Empty Wagon Sidings: shunting line	Into use	13.10.1901
Cricklewood Recess Sidings: wagon arrival line taken out of use and empty wagon departure line re-named arrival & departure line	... ...	16.7.1978
Brent Empty Wagon Sidings to Brent South Jcn: working of the arrival line by block telegraph	Commenced	16.4.1893
Brent Empty Wagon Sidings to Brent Junction No. 2: arrival and departure lines to be used for traffic in both directions	... ...	4.9.1910
Cricklewood diesel depot (up side)	Opened	1963
***	Closed	....
CHILD'S HILL NEW SIDINGS (up side)	Opened	23.8.1885
***	Closed	....
These sidings became the Loaded Wagon Sidings.		
Loaded Wagon Sidings SB, Child's Hill	Opened	4.1883-11.1885
Re-named Brent Loaded Wagon Sidings SB	... ...	....
Replacement box	Opened	27.9.1903
***	Re-framed	....
Box closed and ground frame provided in lieu	... ...	1945-1960
***	t.o.u.	8.12.1968
Brent Loaded Wagon Sidings to Brent South Jcn: first and second up outside lines	Into use	13.3.1892
***	t.o.u. by	9.1956
Cricklewood Depot PSB (not a block post -- depot lines only)	Opened	4.11.1979
Cricklewood EMU Depot (up side)	Opened	17.2.1980
***	Closed	....
Child's Hill new engine shed (down side)	Opened	1.11.1882
No. 2 engine shed	Opened	1893
Sheds re-named Cricklewood engine sheds	... ...	....
***	Closed	1965

Brent Engine Line

Powers: None

This line was a horse-shoe curve passing under the southernmost arch of Welsh Harp viaduct and terminating in the sidings on each side of the main line.

Brent engine line (worked by pilot guard)	In use by	26.7.1905
train tablet instead of pilot guard working	Commenced	16.8.1909
The tablets were in cabinets and were operated by enginemen.		
Brent engine line	Closed	9.12.1968

BRENT NEW SIDINGS (up side)	Opened	4.4.1892 ?
***	Closed	24.10.1977 ?
Brent South Junction SB	Open before	16.8.1877
***	Re-framed	1885
Replacement box	Opened	13.3.1892

Brent South Junction SB (continued)		
Re-named Brent Junction No. 1 SB	... ...	13.10.1901
***	Re-framed	1903
***	Closed	23.7.1978

Midland & South Western Junction line

See page 40

Brent South Sidings SB (not a block post)	Opened	4.1883-11.1885
Replacement block post signalbox named Brent Junction No. 2 SB	Opened	13.10.1901
***	Re-framed	1.6.1913
Box ceased to signal fast lines and took control of local lines	... ...	23.7.1978
Re-named Brent Junction SB and resumed control of fast lines	... ...	6.5.1979
Box closed and location re-named Brent Curve Junction	... ...	26.4.1981
Brent Junction No. 2: connection between Acton Branch and London & South Western sidings	Into use	21.10.1918
BRENT SOUTH SIDINGS (down side)	Opened	....
***	De-manned	17.4.1976
Converted to departmental use	... ...	1977
Brent Jcn No. 1: up fast line to up local line crossover	Into use	18.9.1904
***	t.o.u.	23.7.1978
Brent Jcn No. 1: up slow line to up fast line/up local line crossover	Into use	15.11.1903
***	t.o.u.	16.7.1978
Up goods line to up local line crossover	Restored	6.5.1979
***	t.o.u.	....
Brent Jcn: ladder connection from down Hendon line to down fast line provided and down Hendon line made reversible as far as the facing crossover south of Hendon station	... ...	25.4.1981
Brent: connection between slow lines and north end of new depot with a new 6-lever ground frame	Into use	24.1.1982
Brent North Junction SB	Open before	16.8.1877
***	Closed	1.6.1890
Welsh Harp Junction SB	Opened	1.6.1890
***	Re-framed	1.11.1903
***	Closed	30.4.1967
Welsh Harp Jcn: double junction (DGL-DFL, UFL-UGL)	Into use	13.7.1890
***	t.o.u.	30.4.1967
Double junction (DFL-DLL, ULL-UFL)	Into use	....
***	t.o.u.	30.4.1967
Welsh Harp Jcn to Hendon: up local line	Into use	22.6.1890
Down local line	Into use	13.7.1890
Welsh Harp Jcn to Mill Hill: widened lines	OG	12.10.1890

A new pair of lines was opened, situated on the down side between Welsh Harp Junction and a point just north of Hendon, there crossing above the existing lines and continuing on the up side to Mill Hill, where the existing goods lines on the up side were joined. The existing passenger/ main lines between Brent South Junction and Scratch Wood Junction were designated fast lines and the new lines became slow lines between the same points. The up and down local lines were extended from Hendon to a non-conflicting junction with the slow lines at Silk Stream Junction. One of the local lines was used previously between Hendon and Mill Hill as an up goods line. North of Silk Stream Junction the slow/goods lines were on the up side throughout to Glendon North Junction.

Welsh Harp Jcn to Scratch Wood Jcn: slow lines	Inspected	26.10.1890
Welsh Harp Jcn to Hendon: up and down fast lines	Slued	16-19.12.1917
WELSH HARP (side-platform station)	OP	2.5.1870
Up side of replacement island-platform station	Into use	22.6.1890
Down side of replacement island-platform station	Into use	13.7.1890
***	CP(All)	1.7.1903
Up local line slued to run parallel to down local line	... ...	8.1.1961
Hendon South SB	Open before	1.11.1875
***	Closed	10.1876-8.1877
HENDON	OG	9.3.1868
***	OP	13.7.1868
***	CG	1.1.1968
New station building	Opened	8.1980
Hendon North SB	Open before	1.11.1875
Replacement box named Hendon Station SB	Opened	10.1876-8.1877
Replacement box	Opened	13.7.1890
***	Re-framed	11.12.1949
***	Closed	26.4.1981
Hendon to Mill Hill: up goods line	Into use	14.9.1890
Hendon to Scratch Wood Jcn: up local/slow line	OP	2.5.1892
Down local/slow line	OP	23.6.1895
HENDON OLD SIDINGS (up side)	Opened	....
***	Closed	1.4.1892
HENDON NEW SIDINGS (between the fast lines and the goods lines)	Opened	12.10.1896
***	t.o.u.	....
HENDON DOWN SIDINGS	Opened	29.6.1931
***	t.o.u.	21.11.1971
Hendon: chord-line between fast lines and Hendon (goods) lines	Into use	17.4.1977
Chord-line (hitherto reversible) made an up line only	... ...	25.4.1981

Hendon Aircraft Factory Sidings SB	Opened	19.5.1918
***	Closed	28.1.1921
Hendon Factory Branch		
Powers: --		
Branch to Hendon Aircraft Factory	OP&G	19.5.1918
***	Closed	29.1.1921
HENDON FACTORY PLATFORM	OP(NA)	19.5.1918
***	CP	1919
Silk Stream Junction SB (no signals for the fast lines)	Opened	14.7.1890
***	Raised	1.10.1893
Altered to Silkstream Junction SB	... ...	....
Replacement box 40 yards nearer Hendon	Opened	16.3.1924
***	Closed	11.6.1978
Hendon aerodrome: emergency signals	Into use	23.7.1944
MILL HILL	OG	9.3.1868
***	OP	13.7.1868
Altered to MILL HILL (BROADWAY)	Goods	1.7.1950
***	Passenger	25.9.1950
***	CG	3.8.1964
Replacement subway and new ticket office at subway level	Into use	7.1966
Mill Hill SB	Open before	16.8.1877
Replacement box	Opened	23.2.1890
Box closed and up and down IBS provided in lieu	... ...	22.12.1968
Up fast line and up slow line IB signals	t.o.u.	2.12.1979
Down fast line and down slow line IB signals	t.o.u.	4.6.1978
Mill Hill: junction between the passenger lines and the goods lines	t.o.u.	....
Mill Hill to Scratch Wood Jcn: up and down goods lines	Into use	18.5.1890
These lines were designated slow lines on the opening of the widened lines between Welsh Harp Junction and Mill Hill.		
SCRATCHWOOD SIDINGS	Opened	26.11.1895 ?
***	Closed	....
Scratchwood Sidings SB (signalling slow lines only)	Opened	7.3.1897
***	Closed	4.4.1965
Scratch Wood Junction SB	Opened	22.9.1889
***	Closed	23.6.1895
Scratch Wood: junction between the passenger lines and the goods lines	t.o.u.	23.6.1895
Scratch Wood Jcn to Elstree South: up and down goods lines	Into use	23.6.1895
The second (eastern) Elstree tunnel was opened. The goods lines between Elstree South and St Albans became slow lines and the passenger lines between Scratch Wood Junction and St Albans became fast lines.		
Elstree South SB	Opened	1.9.1889
***	Alt.levers	23.4.1893
***	Re-framed	23.6.1895
***	Closed	2.11.1913
Elstree South: junction between the passenger lines and goods lines	t.o.u.	23.6.1895
Elstree South to Aldenham: up goods line	Into use	1.9.1889
Down goods line	Into use	23.4.1893
ELSTREE	OG	9.3.1868
***	OP	13.7.1868
Altered to ELSTREE & BOREHAM WOOD	... ...	1.6.1869
Altered to ELSTREE	... ...	1.4.1904
Altered to ELSTREE & BOREHAMWOOD	... ...	21.9.1953
Up-side entrance and ticket office	Opened	1959
Old (down-side) ticket office (open restricted hours from 1959)	Closed	22.5.1966
A fire in December 1967 caused the closing of the new ticket office and the re-opening of the old one. The new ticket office was not fully back in use until December 1968.		
***	CG	19.6.1967
Altered to ELSTREE	... ...	6.5.1974
Elstree Station SB	Open before	16.8.1877
***	Closed	1.9.1889
Elstree North SB	Opened	1.9.1889
***	Re-framed	9.6.1895
***	Re-framed	12.10.1913
Altered to Elstree Station SB	... ...	2.11.1913
***	Closed	2.12.1979
Elstree: double junction (UFL-USL, DSL-DFL)	Into use	2.11.1913
***	t.o.u.	2.12.1979
Aldenham SB	Opened	1873
Aldenham Junction SB (replacing Aldenham SB)	Opened	1.9.1889
***	Re-framed	23.4.1893
***	Closed	3.6.1894
Aldenham Junction	Closed	3.6.1894
Aldenham Jcn to St Albans South: up and down goods lines	Into use	3.6.1894
Radlett: double ladder junction between fast and slow lines	Into use	2.12.1979
Radlett SB (first site)	Open before	16.8.1877
Replacement box	Opened	9.11.1890
***	Closed	3.6.1894

ALDENHAM	OG	9.3.1868	
Altered to RADLETT	... ...	1.4.1868	*
Altered to ALDENHAM	... ...	1.5.1868	*
Altered to RADLETT	... ...	1.7.1868	*
***	OP	13.7.1868	
***	CG	25.3.1968	
New booking office	Into use	23.11.1979	
Rebuilt station officially re-opened	... ...	17.12.1979	
Radlett SB: replacement box (second site)	Opened	3.6.1894	
***	Closed	2.12.1979	
Harper Lane SB	Opened	8.7.1890	
***	Closed	3.6.1894	
NAPSBURY UP SIDINGS	Opened	....	
***	Closed	24.9.1967	
Park Street: laying in of points and crossings	... ...	10.11.1895	
Park Street: position of up slow line and siding altered	... ...	23.4.1905	
Up slow line placed adjacent to down slow line again	... ...	10.5.1981	
NAPSBURY	O.Formal	3.6.1905	
***	OP	19.6.1905	
***	CP(All)	14.9.1959	
Park Street Junction SB	Open before	1.11.1875	
***	Alt.levers	8.1.1893	
Replacement SB	Opened	3.6.1894	
Replacement SB	Opened	23.4.1905	
Re-named Napsbury SB	By	31.5.1905	
***	Closed	2.12.1979	
Napsbury: down fast to down slow crossover	Into use	14.9.1913	
Up slow to up fast crossover	Into use	8.3.1914	
Double junction	t.o.u.	2.12.1979	

Park Street Branch

Powers: Midland Railway (Extension to London) Act 1863
Midland Railway (New Lines and Additional Powers) Act 1864 (Deviated line)

Park Street to junction with the London & North Western Railway	Complete by	8.1868	
RCH distances for Park Street branch	Cancelled	20.11.1891	

This line, which was never opened to public traffic, joined the London & North Western's St Albans branch near Frogmore.

St Albans South SB	Open before	16.8.1877	
Replacement SB	Opened	12.6.1892	
***	Re-framed	15.4.1906	
***	Closed	2.12.1979	
St Albans South: first junction between main and goods lines	Removed	3.6.1894	
St Albans South: double junction (UFL-USL, DSL-DFL)	Into use	10.6.1894	
***	t.o.u.	2.12.1979	
St Albans South: up goods line to up fast line crossover	Into use	15.4.1906	
***	t.o.u.	5.10.1969	
St Albans South: facing crossover between the slow lines	Into use	6.5.1973	
***	t.o.u.	2.12.1979	
St Albans South to St Albans North: up and down goods lines	Into use	12.6.1892	
St Albans South to Harpenden Jcn: goods lines made slow lines; passenger lines designated fast lines	... ...	1.7.1906	
ST ALBANS	OG	9.3.1868	
***	OP	13.7.1868	
Altered to ST ALBANS CITY	... ...	2.6.1924	
***	CG	19.6.1967	
Rebuilt station	Opened	18.3.1973	
New entrance-building on up side of line	Opened	15.5.1973	
Altered to ST ALBANS	... ...	16.5.1988	*
St Albans: connection from back platform line to down goods line	Removed	9.4.1906	
St Albans (north of): up slow line	Slued	11.2.1979	
St Albans engine shed	Opened	1868	
***	Closed	11.1.1960	
St Albans: reversing siding	Into use	2.12.1979	
St Albans North SB	Open before	16.8.1877	
Replacement box	Opened	19.10.1890	
***	Re-framed	12.6.1892	
Replacement box	Opened	13.4.1906	
***	Closed	20.12.1970	
St Albans North SB: position of goods lines slightly altered	... ...	14.4.1906	
St Albans North to Sandridge: up goods line	Into use	27.12.1891	
St Albans North to Sandridge: up slow line made up goods line worked by telegraph bell	... ...	26.4.1914	
Up goods line became up slow line again	... ...	10.5.1914	
St Albans North (south of) to Harpenden Jcn: down goods line	Into use	9.10.1892	
Wheathampstead SB	Opened	26.10.1891	
***	Closed	9.10.1892	
Sandridge SB	Open before	1.11.1875	
Replacement box	Opened	20.12.1891	
Sandridge Goods Junction SB: replacement Sandridge SB	Opened	29.10.1893	
Box closed and up and down IBS provided in lieu	... ...	14.1.1962	
***	t.o.u.	21.10.1979	

Sandridge: up slow line to up fast line crossover	Into use	2.12.1900
***	t.o.u.	14.1.1962
SANDRIDGE SIDING	Opened	1893-1895
***	Closed	3.4.1967
Sandridge Goods Junction	t.o.u.	9.10.1892
Sandridge to Harpenden Jcn: up goods line	Into use	9.10.1892
Harpenden: up slow line to up fast line ladder crossover	Into use	17.10.1976
Additional crossovers to form double ladder junction	Into use	21.10.1979
Harpenden Station SB	Open before	1877
Replacement box	Opened	1877
Replacement box	Opened	4.9.1892
Re-named Harpenden South SB	... ...	21.4.1906
Replacement box named Harpenden SB	Opened	2.4.1933
***	Closed	21.10.1979
HARPENDEN	OG	12.1867
***	OP	13.7.1868
Altered to HARPENDEN (CENTRAL)	... ...	25.9.1950
***	CG	5.10.1964
Altered to HARPENDEN	... ...	18.4.1966
Harpenden: bay line	t.o.u.	2.4.1933
Harpenden North SB	Opened	21.4.1906
***	Closed	2.4.1933
Harpenden North: down passenger line to down goods line crossover	Into use	13.5.1906
***	t.o.u.	....
Harpenden Junction SB (new junction site)	Opened	13.3.1892
***	Re-framed	20.5.1906
Replacement box	Opened	24.11.1957
***	Closed	21.10.1979

Hemel Hempstead and London & North Western Junction Railway
See page 43

Harpenden Jcn: up passenger line to up goods line crossover	Removed	22.4.1894
***	Restored	20.5.1906
Double junction	t.o.u.	21.10.1979
The down goods line to down passenger line connection was retained when the goods lines were extended north to Chiltern Green on 22 April 1894.		
Harpenden Jcn to Chiltern Green Jcn: up and down goods lines	Into use	22.4.1894
Harpenden Jcn to Luton North: goods lines designated slow lines	... ...	28.6.1959
Local trains used the new slow lines (down direction at least)	... ...	20.7.1959
Harpenden Junction SB (old junction site)	Opened	16.7.1877
Replacement box	Opened	1.7.1888
***	Closed	13.3.1892
Hyde Mill SB	Opened	9.10.1892
***	Closed	22.4.1894
Chiltern Green Junction SB	Opened	c.8.1884
***	Closed	22.4.1894
Chiltern Green Junction	Removed	22.4.1894
Chiltern Green Jcn to Luton North: up goods line	Into use	10.8.1884
Down goods line	In use by	1.11.1885
CHILTERN GREEN	OG	12.1867
***	OP	13.7.1868
Altered to CHILTERN GREEN FOR LUTON HOO	... ...	1.12.1891
***	CP	7.4.1952
***	CG	6.3.1967
Chiltern Green Station SB	Open before	16.8.1877
Replacement box	Opened	24.10.1909
***	Closed	15.3.1959
Dumhills SB	Opened	1876
***	Closed	4.1883-11.1885
Luton Hoo to Bedford (Bromham Road bridge): OLE	Energised	12.1.1981
Luton: connection between former Midland and Great Northern lines	OG	3.1.1966
***	CG	30.4.1989
The 1863 Extension to London Act had provided for a connection with the Great Northern Railway at Luton, but the planned junction line had never been built.		
Luton South SB	Open before	16.8.1877
Replacement box	Opened	c.8.1884
Replacement box	Opened	6.7.1919
***	Closed	21.10.1979
LUTON CRESCENT ROAD GOODS DEPOT	Opened	....
***	C.Coal	1.8.1964
LUTON	OG	16.12.1867
***	OP	13.7.1868
Altered to LUTON MIDLAND ROAD	... ...	25.9.1950
Platform No. 3 made up & down platform line off the down slow line	... ...	20.7.1959
New up slow line platform (No. 4)	Into use	9.11.1959
Altered to LUTON	... ...	18.4.1966
No. 3 platform re-named down slow line, and down slow line through station taken out of use	... ...	5.11.1977

LUTON (continued)		
Up slow line diverted to new outer face of platform using track of former up siding	... ...	16.11.1977
Up slow line diverted to the new inner face of the platform, using site of disused down slow line	... ...	7.5.1978
Up slow line through station re-named up platform loop	... ...	18.6.1978
This line brought into use for terminating trains from London and re-named up & down platform loop	... ...	2.7.1978
Up slow line (on the outer face of the island)	Into use	10.9.1978
Luton North SB	Open before	16.8.1877
Replacement box	Opened	c.8.1884
Replacement box	Opened	19.12.1915
***	Closed	21.10.1979
Luton North: down goods line to down passenger line crossover	Into use	10.11.1889
***	t.o.u.	18.6.1978
Ladder junction between up slow line and down fast line	Into use	5.11.1977
Luton North to Leagrave: up goods line	Into use	13.10.1875
Down goods line	Into use	10.11.1889
Luton North to Millbrook: goods lines made slow lines and passenger lines made fast lines	... ...	28.9.1959
Work actually completed	... ...	9.11.1959
Limbury Road SB (no signals for the passenger lines)	Opened	21.9.1915
***	Closed	9.8.1959
LIMBURY ROAD GOODS DEPOT	Opened	1915 ?
***	Closed	4.3.1968
LUTON COAL CONCENTRATION DEPOT	Opened	1.7.1964
***	Closed	End 1986 ?
Limbury Road: new connections	Into use	8.7.1979
Leagrave SB	Open before	1.11.1875
Replacement box	Opened	6.10.1889
***	Re-framed	3.8.1913
Replacement box	Opened	17.6.1923
***	Closed	1.6.1980
Leagrave Goods Junction	t.o.u.	....
Leagrave: facing connection from up main line to up goods line in place of previous trailing connection between these two lines	Into use	7.1882
Up goods line to up passenger line crossover	Into use	13.1.1901
***	t.o.u.	8.12.1974
Down goods line to down passenger line crossover	Into use	10.1889
Up passenger line to up goods line crossover	Into use	3.8.1913
Double junction	t.o.u.	8.12.1974
Leagrave to Chalton Jcn: up goods line	Into use	6.10.1889
Leagrave: additional up goods line through the station	Into use	2.3.1890
Leagrave to Harlington: down goods line	Into use	3.8.1890
LEAGRAVE	OG	12.1867
***	OP	13.7.1868
Additional platforms (on the slow lines)	Into use	1959
***	C.Coal	4.1984
Leagrave: double ladder junction between fast lines and slow lines	Into use	15.12.1974
Leagrave to Chalton: down goods line	C.temp.	10.6.1894
Four-track working	Restored	2.9.1894
Toddington SB	Opened	1875
***	Closed	6.10.1889
Chorlton SB	Open before	1.11.1875
Replacement box	Opened	c.8.1883
Re-named Chorlton Junction SB	... ...	20.8.1883
Re-named Chalton Junction SB	... ...	11.1885-12.1888
***	Re-framed	3.8.1890
Re-named Chalton SB	... ...	1890
***	Closed	12.9.1897
Chorlton Jcn to Harlington: up goods line	Into use	20.8.1883
Sundon SB (this was the former Chalton box)	Opened	12.9.1897
Box ceased to signal the fast lines	... ...	22.6.1969
***	Closed	21.7.1974
Sundon: up passenger line to up goods line crossover	Into use	6.1.1901
***	t.o.u.	15.6.1969
Forder's Siding (south of) to Harlington: up goods line	Into use	14.7.1890
Harlington SB	Open before	1875
Replacement box	Opened	20.4.1890
Replacement box on down platform south of buildings	Opened	31.8.1913
Re-named Harlington (Beds.) SB	... ...	1.11.1927
***	Closed	1.6.1980
Harlington Station Jcn: up main line to up goods line connection	Removed	28.10.1894
Down goods line to down passenger line connection	Removed	28.7.1895
HARLINGTON	OG	12.1867
***	OP	13.7.1868
Altered to HARLINGTON (FOR TODDINGTON)	... ...	1.10.1889
Altered to HARLINGTON (BEDS.)	... ...	1.11.1927
Additional platforms (on the slow lines)	Into use	1959
***	CG	6.2.1967
Harlington to Flitwick: up goods line	Into use	28.10.1894
Harlington to Flitwick: replacement up goods line	Into use	18.3.1895

Harlington to Elstow: down goods line	Into use	28.7.1895
Harlington: double junction (DPL-DGL, UGL-UPL)	Into use	31.8.1913
***	t.o.u.	8.1.1978
Forder's Sidings North SB	Opened	5.2.1893
***	Closed	18.7.1895
Westoning SB	Opened	1875
Replacement box	Opened	5.2.1893
***	Closed	28.10.1894
FLITWICK	Opened	2.5.1870
Additional platforms (on the slow lines)	Into use	1959
***	CG	17.7.1967
Flitwick SB	Open before	1875
Replacement box	Opened	2.9.1894
***	Closed	1.6.1980
Flitwick to Ampthill: up goods line	Opened	15.10.1893
Flitwick: double ladder junction between fast lines and slow lines	Into use	21.11.1976
Ampthill Station SB	Opened	1868 ?
Replacement box	Opened	....
Replacement box	Opened	20.8.1893
***	Re-framed	16.6.1895
***	Closed	6.12.1964
Ampthill: South and North GFs	t.o.u.	23.2.1969
Ampthill Station SB: up main line to up goods line connection	Removed	16.6.1895
AMPTHILL	OG	12.1867
***	OP	13.7.1868
***	CP&G	4.5.1959
Ampthill to Ampthill Goods Jcn: up goods line	Into use	16.6.1895
The passenger lines were diverted to a new (western) tunnel at Ampthill and the old up main line became the new up goods line.		
Ampthill Goods Junction SB	Opened	c.7.1876
***	Re-framed	6.8.1893
***	Closed	16.6.1895
Ampthill Goods Jcn to Cow Bridge: up goods line	Into use	25.9.1876
Ampthill Goods Jcn: up goods line to up main line connection	Removed	16.6.1895
Millbrook SB (first box)	Open before	4.1874
***	Closed by	16.8.1877
Millbrook SB (second box)	Opened	8.10.1893
***	Raised	27.7.1913
***	Re-framed	17.8.1913
***	Closed	1.6.1980
Millbrook: up goods line to up passenger line crossover	Into use	30.10.1893
Down passenger line to down goods line crossover	Into use	17.8.1913
Double junction	t.o.u.	21.5.1978
Millbrook to Bedford South Jcn: down goods line made down slow line	... ...	6.5.1951
Millbrook to Kempston Road Jcn: up goods line made up slow line	... ...	30.6.1935
Houghton Conquest SB	Opened	30.6.1935
***	Closed	16.4.1973
Houghton Conquest: down goods loop	Into use	30.6.1935
***	t.o.u.	1956-1960
Wootton SB	Open before	1.10.1876
***	Closed	28.7.1895
Wilshamstead SB	Opened	3.8.1941
***	Closed	8.9.1968

Wilshamstead Branch

Powers: --

Wilshamstead SB to Wilshamstead Ordnance Factory	Into use	3.8.1941
Workmen's trains from Bedford	Commenced	18.8.1941
Workmen's trains from Luton	Commenced	6.10.1941
Passenger services withdrawn	By	5.1946
Wilshamstead Station SB	Opened	3.8.1941
***	Closed	8.9.1968
WILSHAMSTEAD PLATFORM	Into use	3.8.1941
***	CP by	5.1946

Elstow Junction SB	Opened	13.8.1893
Re-named Elstow SB	... ...	4.10.1896
Ceased to signal the fast lines	... ...	1950
***	Closed	5.11.1961
Elstow Jcn: up goods line to up passenger line crossover	Into use	13.8.1893
Down passenger line to down goods line crossover	Into use	28.7.1895
Double junction	Removed	4.10.1896
Elstow Jcn to Kempston Road Jcn: down goods line	Into use	13.8.1893
Cow Bridge SB	Open before	1.11.1875
***	Closed	28.7.1895
Cow Bridge to Bedford South SB: up goods line	Into use	29.5.1876
This line was gauntleted with the up passenger line across the Ouse bridge.		
Kempston Road Jcn: double junction (DFL-DSL, USL-UFL)	Into use	7.10.1894
Double junction (DSL-DFL, UFL-USL)	Into use	31.8.1902
Down fast line to down slow line crossover	Removed	24.8.1902
***	Restored	12.3.1967

Kempston Road Jcn (continued)		
Both double junctions	t.o.u.	3.9.1977
Ladder crossovers from USL to DFL, and double ladder junction (DFL-DSL, USL-UFL)	Into use	11.9.1977
Location re-named Bedford South Junction	... ...	2.11.1980
Kempston Road Junction SB	Opened	9.7.1893
Replacement box	Opened	30.9.1894
***	Re-framed	31.8.1902
***	Re-framed	....
***	Closed	2.11.1980

Bedford Curve

Powers: Midland Railway (Additional Powers) Act 1890

Section of new line over the Ouse bridge temporarily in use	30.7.1893 --	30.9.1894
Kempston Road Jcn to Bedford North: fast passenger lines	Into use	7.10.1894
Bedford Central SB (no signals for the slow lines)	Opened	7.10.1894
***	Closed	2.3.1930

Kempston Road Jcn to Bedford South SB: up goods line	Removed	9.7.1893
A new connection was provided at Kempston Road Junction.		
Ouse bridge (London & Bedford line): main lines diverted over new bridge to allow the reconstruction of the old one	... ...	30.7.1893
Main lines restored to their original location and designated slow passenger lines	... ...	30.9.1894
Bedford South SB	Opened	1867
Replacement box	Opened	....
Replacement box	Opened	30.7.1893
***	Re-framed	24.8.1902
Ceased to signal the slow lines, and replacement Bedford East GF provided in lieu	... ...	11.6.1967
Ceased to signal the fast lines, and replacement Bedford West GF provided in lieu	... ...	2.7.1967
Bedford West GF	t.o.u.	3.9.1977
Bedford East GF	t.o.u.	....
Bedford South: double junction (DFL-DSL, USL-UFL)	Into use	24.8.1902
Connection with up fast line	Removed	3.9.1977
Connection with down fast line	Removed	....
Bedford South SB to Bedford Jcn: up goods line	Into use	2.1880-6.1881
Re-named up through siding	... ...	8.1893-12.1896
Re-named reception line	... ...	....
Made a dead-end siding (and Bedford East GF taken out of use)	... ...	10.12.1978
Reception line	t.o.u.	11.6.1967 ?
Bedford engine shed	Opened	1868
Replacement engine shed to the west of the later fast lines	Opened	1886
All steam facilities withdrawn	... ...	12.10.1963
***	Closed	28.11.1971

MIDLAND TRAFFIC OVER THE METROPOLITAN RAILWAY

The Midland Railway possessed running powers:
- over the Metropolitan Railway between King's Cross Junction and Moorgate Street/West Street Junction;
- over the South Eastern & Chatham lines between West Street Junction and Bickley, Crystal Palace, Herne Hill Sorting Sidings, Lavender Hill Junction, Stewart's Lane Junction, and London Victoria, and also between Blackfriars Junction and Bricklayers Arms and Hither Green Sidings;
- over the London & South Western Railway between Lavender Hill Junction and Clapham Junction station;
- over the London, Brighton & South Coast Railway between Stewart's Lane Junction and Battersea Wharf.

King's Cross Jcn to Moorgate: track taken over from London Transport	... ...	7.1.1978
Modernisation work for Midland Suburban Electrification	Completed	6.12.1981
OLE	Energised	1.3.1982
Kentish Town Jcn (new junction) to Moorgate	RO(P)	11.7.1983
King's Cross SB (London Transport) ceased to signal Widened Lines	... ...	23.7.1978
KING'S CROSS (CITY WIDENED LINES) transferred from London Transport to British Railways Board	... ...	3.10.1977
Rebuilt station re-opened for passengers as KING'S CROSS MIDLAND	... ...	11.7.1983
Further alterations	... ...	1988
Altered to KING'S CROSS THAMESLINK	... ...	16.5.1988
MOORGATE STREET: replacement Midland booking office	Opened	16.2.1896
Working taken over by the Metropolitan Railway	... ...	1.7.1909

Farringdon Jcn to Snow Hill Tunnel north portal: OLE	Energised	2.11.1986
Farringdon to Ludgate Hill Jcn	Re-opened	26.4.1988

MIDLAND DEPOTS:

Whitecross Street Depot
Powers: Midland Railway (Additional Powers) Act 1873,
Midland Railway (New Works Etc) Act 1875

WHITECROSS STREET DEPOT	Opened	1.1.1878
***	Closed	1.3.1936
Whitecross Street Goods Depot SB	Opened	1878
***	Closed	17.5.1903

Walworth Road Depot
Powers: Midland Railway (Additional Powers) Act 1871,
Midland Railway (Additional Powers) Act 1874,
Midland Railway (Additional Powers) Act 1882

WALWORTH ROAD DEPOT	First trains	13.11.1871
***	Opened	16.11.1871
***	Closed	30.4.1973

Brixton Coal Depot
Powers: Midland Railway (Additional Powers) Act 1875

BRIXTON COAL DEPOT	Opened	19.7.1876
***	Closed	3.1947

Wandsworth Road Depot
Powers: Midland Railway (Additional Powers) Act 1873, Midland Railway Act 1897

WANDSWORTH ROAD DEPOT	Opened	19.1.1874
***	Closed	....

Stewart's Lane Sidings

STEWART'S LANE: Midland coal sidings and branch	Opened	19.1.1874
***	Closed	....

Peckham Rye Depot (Midland and London & North Western Joint)
Powers: London & North Western Railway Act 1888

PECKHAM RYE DEPOT	Opened	23.3.1891
***	Closed	8.1961

Maidstone Coal Depot
Powers: Midland Railway (Additional Powers) Act 1884

MAIDSTONE COAL DEPOT	Opened	1884-1885
***	Closed	8.5.1934

MIDLAND CURVES TO THE TOTTENHAM & HAMPSTEAD LINE

Tottenham South Curve

Powers: Tottenham & Hampstead Junction Railway Act 1862 (Land Powers only),
Midland Railway (Extension to London) Act 1863

Kentish Town Jcn to Highgate Road Jcn	OG	3.1.1870
***	OP	1.7.1870
***	CP	....
***	CG	....
***	t.o.u.	19.1.1964

Tottenham North Curve

Powers: Midland Railway (Additional Powers) Act 1880

Junction Road Jcn to Carlton Road Jcn	OG (up)	1.2.1883 *
***	OG (down)	2.4.1883
Earth Siding SB	Opened	3.5.1896
***	Closed	....
Mortimer Street SB	Opened	2.4.1883
Replacement box named Mortimer Street Junction SB	Opened	12.8.1900
***	Closed	22.10.1978
Mortimer Street Jcn to Junction Road Jcn	CP	5.1.1981

Kentish Town Curve

Powers: Midland Railway Act 1894

Engine Shed Jcn to Mortimer Street Jcn	Into use	16.12.1900
***	OP	17.12.1900
***	Closed	5.1.1981
HIGHGATE ROAD LOW LEVEL	OP	17.12.1900
***	CP(All)	1.3.1918

TOTTENHAM & HAMPSTEAD JUNCTION RAILWAY (Midland and Great Eastern Joint)

Powers: The Tottenham & Hampstead Junction Railway was incorporated by the Tottenham & Hampstead Junction Railway Act 1862. It was jointly worked by the Great Eastern and Midland Railways from 16 July 1866 and vested in the Tottenham & Hampstead Joint Committee from 1 July 1902 under the Midland Railway Act 1902.

Gospel Oak Spur

Gospel Oak to Highgate Road Jcn	Into use	27.5.1888
***	OP (GER)	4.6.1888
***	OG	30.1.1916
***	CG	7.1922
***	CP	6.9.1926
***	RO(G)	11.3.1940
***	RO(P)	5.1.1981
Gospel Oak Jcn with the London & North Western Railway	Into use	23.1.1916
***	Removed	3.9.1922
***	Restored	5.11.1939
***	First Tfc	11.3.1940
GOSPEL OAK	OP (GER)	4.6.1888
***	CP(All)	6.9.1926
Bank Holiday Monday use continued: last service ran	... ...	7.8.1939
Station re-opened using a new bay platform	Into use	13.12.1980
Gospel Oak SB	Opened	27.5.1888
***	Closed	1911

Main Line

Highgate Road to Tottenham North Jcn	OP (GER)	21.7.1868	
***	CP (GER)	31.1.1870	
Highgate Road Jcn to Tottenham West Jcn	OG (MR)	3.1.1870	
***	OP (GER)	1.7.1870	
Moorgate Street and Crouch Hill: Midland passenger services	Commenced	1.10.1870	
Highgate Road Jcns to Tottenham Jcns: block telegraph system	Installed by	1873	
Highgate Road SB	Opened by	16.8.1877	
Replacement box	Opened	27.5.1888	
Re-named Highgate Road Junction SB	By	1888	
***	Closed	5.9.1965	
HIGHGATE ROAD	OP	21.7.1868	
***	CP	31.1.1870	
***	RO(P)	1.10.1870	
Altered to HIGHGATE ROAD FOR PARLIAMENT HILL	... ...	11.1894	
Altered to HIGHGATE ROAD	... ...	1.7.1903	*
High-level platforms	CP (GER)	1.10.1915	
***	CP (MR)	1.3.1918	
Junction Road SB	Opened by	1.11.1875	
Replacement box named Junction Road Junction SB	Opened	c.4.1883	
***	Re-located	6.10.1912	
***	Re-framed	2.2.1913	
***	Closed	10.11.1985	
JUNCTION ROAD FOR TUFNELL PARK	OP	1.1.1872	
Altered to JUNCTION ROAD	... ...	1.7.1903	*
***	CP(All)	3.5.1943	
TUFNELL PARK GREAT EASTERN RAILWAY GOODS DEPOT	Opened	15.2.1886	
***	Closed	6.5.1968	
Junction Road to Upper Holloway: down reception line	Into use	2.2.1913	
Up reception line	Into use	23.1.1916	
Down reception line made down lie-by siding	... ...	10.11.1985	
Upper Holloway SB	Open before	1.11.1875	
Replacement box	Opened	5.3.1893	
Replacement PSB	Opened	10.11.1985	
UPPER HOLLOWAY	OP	21.7.1868	
***	CP	31.1.1870	
***	RO(P)	1.10.1870	
Altered to UPPER HOLLOWAY FOR ST JOHN'S PARK & HIGHGATE HILL	... ...	1.3.1871	*
***	OM	1.10.1873	*
Altered to UPPER HOLLOWAY FOR ST JOHN'S PARK	... ...	1.4.1875	*
Altered to UPPER HOLLOWAY	... ...	1.7.1903	*
***	CG	6.5.1968	
Goods -- as opposed to mineral -- traffic appears to have been handled between 1875 and 1878 only.			
Hornsey Road SB	Opened by	1.11.1875	
Hornsey Road SB: replacement box	Opened	9.2.1892	
HORNSEY ROAD	OP	1.1.1872	
Altered to HORNSEY ROAD FOR HORNSEY RISE	... ...	1.2.1880	*
Altered to HORNSEY ROAD	... ...	1.7.1903	*
Platform ground frames and signals	Removed	31.3.1937	
***	CP(All)	3.5.1943	

CROUCH HILL	OP	21.7.1868	
***	CP	31.1.1870	
***	RO(P)	1.10.1870	
Crouch Hill SB	Opened by	1.11.1875	
Replacement box	Opened	17.4.1888	
***	Closed	8.2.1959	
Midland passenger trains extended from Crouch Hill to South Tottenham	... ...	1.5.1871	
Crouch Hill to Tottenham section transferred from the Eastern Region to the London Midland Region	... ...	12.1.1948	
Harringay Junction SB (first box)	Opened	15.5.1916	
***	Closed	22.8.1920	
Harringay Junction SB (second box)	Opened	8.1.1940	
Replacement box	Opened	8.2.1959	

Harringay Curve

Harringay Jcn: curve to the Great Northern Railway	Completed	....	
***	Removed	1872	
Harringay: emergency curve to the Great Northern Railway	Into use	15.5.1916	
***	Removed	22.8.1920	
***	Restored	8.1.1940	

Green Lanes SB	Opened	c.6.1880	
Re-named Harringay Park, Green Lanes SB	... ...	30.8.1884	
***	Closed	8.2.1959	
GREEN LANES	OP	1.6.1880	
***	OM (MR)	1882	
Altered to HARRINGAY PARK, GREEN LANES	... ...	30.8.1884	
Altered to HARRINGAY PARK	By	4.1910	*
Altered to HARRINGAY PARK	... ...	18.6.1951	
Altered to HARRINGAY STADIUM	... ...	27.10.1958	
***	CG (LMR)	3.2.1964	
ST ANN'S ROAD	OP	2.10.1882	
***	CP(All)	9.8.1942	
St Ann's Road SB	Opened	c.10.1882	
***	Closed	23.2.1957	
South Tottenham Jcn with the Great Eastern Railway	OG	1879	
***	OP	1.1.1880	
***	CP	7.1.1963	
***	CG	....	
SOUTH TOTTENHAM & STAMFORD HILL	OP	1.5.1871	
Altered to SOUTH TOTTENHAM	... ...	1.7.1903	*
South Tottenham Station Junction SB	Opened	1.7.1894	
Lever frame replaced by switch panel	... ...	23.5.1977	
South Tottenham and stations east thereof to Woodgrange Park transferred to the Eastern Region	... ...	20.2.1949	

Tottenham Depot

Powers: Midland Railway Act 1891, and Midland Deed No. 14917

PAGE GREEN (<u>OR</u> SOUTH TOTTENHAM) GOODS & COAL DEPOT, and branch	Opened	1881	?
***	Closed	4.7.1966	

Tottenham South Curve

Powers: Great Eastern Railway Act 1864 (Railway No. 5)

Tottenham West Jcn to Tottenham South Jcn	OG (MR)	3.1.1870
***	OG (GER)	1879
***	OP (GER)	1.1.1880
***	CP	7.1.1963
Tottenham West Jcn to Tottenham South Jcn transferred to the Great Eastern Railway	... ...	1.7.1883

Tottenham West Jcn to Tottenham North Jcn	RO(P) (GER)	1.7.1870
***	OG	1886
***	CP	1.11.1925
***	CG	11.6.1961

Between Tottenham West Junction and Fenchurch Street, Liverpool Street, Mint Street, Poplar, Thames Wharf, and Victoria Docks the Midland Railway possessed running powers over the Great Eastern line.

TOTTENHAM & FOREST GATE RAILWAY (Midland and London, Tilbury & Southend Joint)

Powers: The Tottenham & Forest Gate Railway was incorporated by the Tottenham and Forest Gate Railway Act 1890 as a joint Midland and London, Tilbury & Southend line after an agreement made between those two companies on 12 December 1889.

Tottenham West Jcn to Woodgrange Park Jcn	OG	2.7.1894
Passenger trains to and from East Ham	Commenced	9.7.1894
Goods depots	Opened	1.9.1894

The line was worked by the block telegraph system from its opening.

Tottenham East Sidings SB	Opened	1.7.1894
***	Raised	23.9.1894
Tottenham East Sidings SB closed and ground frame provided in lieu	... ...	29.9.1918
Tottenham East Sidings GF	t.o.u.	....
Black Horse Road SB	Opened	1.7.1894
***	Closed	23.3.1969
BLACK HORSE ROAD	OP	9.7.1894
***	OG	1.9.1894
***	CG	7.12.1964
BLACK HORSE ROAD: new platforms 200 yards west of old ones	Into use	14.12.1981
A new entrance hall and ticket office were provided by London Transport.		
Walthamstow SB	Opened	1.7.1894
***	Closed	9.8.1903
WALTHAMSTOW	OP	9.7.1894
Altered to WALTHAMSTOW QUEEN'S ROAD	... ...	6.5.1968
Boundary Road SB	Opened	1.7.1894
Boundary Road SB re-named Queen's Road SB	On/by	23.1.1895
Queen's Road SB	Closed	5.1982
WALTHAMSTOW QUEEN'S ROAD GOODS DEPOT	Opened	1.9.1894
***	Closed	6.5.1968
LEYTON	OP	9.7.1894
***	OG	1.9.1894
Altered to LEYTON MIDLAND ROAD	... ...	1.5.1949
***	CG	6.5.1968
Leyton SB	Opened	1.7.1894
Leyton SB: replacement box	Opened	19.12.1926
***	Closed	10.2.1969
Leyton to Leytonstone: temporary single-line working	Commenced by	5.10.1940
Double-line working	Restored by	9.11.1940
Leytonstone SB	Opened	1.7.1894
LEYTONSTONE	OP	9.7.1894
***	OG	1.9.1894
Altered to LEYTONSTONE HIGH ROAD	... ...	1.5.1949
***	CG	6.5.1968
Leytonstone to Wanstead Park: single-line working	Commenced by	5.4.1941
Double-line working	Restored	6.7.1941
Wanstead Park SB	Opened	1.7.1894
***	Closed	19.2.1965
WANSTEAD PARK	OP	9.7.1894
Woodgrange Park Junction SB	Opened	1.7.1894

WHITECHAPEL & BOW RAILWAY (LT&SR & Metropolitan District Railway Joint)

Powers: Whitechapel and Bow Railway Act 1897

Railway leased by Whitechapel & Bow Railway Joint Committee	... ...	12.8.1898
Vallance Road Jcn to Campbell Road Jcn	OP	2.6.1902
DC electric working	Commenced	20.8.1905
WHITECHAPEL (MILE END) -- Metropolitan District Railway	OP	6.10.1884
Altered to WHITECHAPEL	... ...	13.11.1901
Closed for reconstruction for the Whitechapel & Bow	... ...	2.2.1902
***	OP	2.6.1902
STEPNEY GREEN	OP	23.6.1902
MILE END	OP	2.6.1902
Rebuilt station for extension of the London Transport Central Line	Completed	4.12.1946
BOW ROAD	OP	11.6.1902

MIDLAND CITY DEPOTS, ETC

Bow Depot

Powers: Midland Railway Act 1889

Bow branches	Opened	1.9.1892
***	Closed	....
BOW GOODS SHED	Opened	1.12.1892
***	Closed	....

Mint Street Depot

Powers: Midland Railway (New Works Etc) Act 1876,
Midland Railway (Additional Powers) Act 1880,
Midland Railway (Additional Powers) Act 1883,
also: Midland Railway Act 1898 (stopping up part of Swallow's Gardens)

MINT STREET DEPOT (City), and branch	OM	1.10.1862
***	OG	1876
***	Closed	4.11.1969

West India Dock Depot

Powers: Midland Railway (Additional Powers) Act 1880,
Midland Railway (Additional Powers) Act 1881,
Midland Railway (Additional Powers) Act 1883

WEST INDIA DOCKS SIDINGS	Opened	1.12.1882
***	Closed	6.11.1967

Poplar Dock Depot

Powers: Midland Railway (New Works Etc) Act 1876,
Midland Railway (Additional Powers) Act 1881

Poplar goods and dock branch	O.Limited	1.12.1882
***	O.Fully	1.1.1883
***	Closed	4.5.1956
POPLAR DOCK altered to POPLAR DOCK RIVERSIDE	... ...	1.1951
Poplar Jcn to Poplar Dock Riverside	Closed	4.5.1956
Poplar Dock SB	Opened	....
***	Closed	2.1959
Poplar engine shed	Opened	Early 1890
***	Closed	....

Thames Wharf Depot

Powers: Midland Railway (Additional Powers) Act 1867

THAMES WHARF COAL DEPOT, and branch	Opened	....
***	Closed	4.10.1965

Victoria Docks Depot

Powers: Midland Railway (Additional Powers) Act 1867,
Midland Railway (New Works Etc) Act 1876

VICTORIA DOCKS DEPOT, and branch	Opened	1.6.1870 ?
***	Closed	3.4.1939

LONDON, TILBURY & SOUTHEND RAILWAY

The London, Tilbury & Southend Railway was constructed by the Eastern Counties and the London & Blackwall companies under an agreement of 17 June 1852 but was not incorporated as a separate company until 16 May 1862. It was leased for 21 years from 3 July 1854 to Messrs Brassey, Peto & Betts for payment of all debenture interest together with 6% on the share capital and half of any surplus profits. From 1 July 1875 the lease to Messrs Peto, Brassey & Betts was terminated and the London, Tilbury & Southend company took over the working of its own line. The company was vested in the Midland Railway by the Midland Railway Act 1912 under the title of the Midland Railway (London, Tilbury & Southend with effect from 1 January 1912 and it was fully merged into the Midland for all purposes with effect from 1 October 1920.

The London, Tilbury & Southend Railway possessed perpetual running powers between Fenchurch Street and Gas Factory Jcn and the use of Fenchurch Street station.

Between Fenchurch Street and Bow Junction, and between Stepney Junction and Limehouse Junction, the Midland Railway possessed running powers over the Great Eastern line. Between Forest Gate Junction and Barking and Little Ilford Sidings, and between Bow Junction and Bromley the Great Eastern Railway possessed running powers ove the Midland line.

Between Forest Gate Junction and Southend via Tilbury, between Bromley Junction and Barking, and over the Thames Haven branch the London & North Western Railway and the North London Railway possessed running powers over the London, Tilbury & Southend line.

Between Bromley Junction and Tilbury Docks via Barking and Purfleet the Great Northern Railway possessed running powers over the London, Tilbury & Southend line.

Between Campbell Road Junction and Barking the Metropolitan District Railway possessed running powers over the London, Tilbury & Southend line.

The London, Tilbury & Southend Railway had adopted the block telegraph throughout its system prior to its acquisition by the Midland Railway.

Commercial Road (OR Whitechapel) Branch

Powers: London, Tilbury, and Southend Railway Act 1882
London, Tilbury, and Southend Railway Act 1884 (Alteration of levels)

Christian Street Jcn to Commercial Road Goods Depot	O.Limited	17.4.1886
***	O.Fully	1.7.1886
***	Closed	3.7.1967
COMMERCIAL ROAD (OR WHITECHAPEL) GOODS DEPOT	O.Limited	17.4.1886
***	O.Fully	1.7.1886
***	Closed	3.7.1967

Bow to Barking

Powers: London, Tilbury, and Southend Railway (Extension and Branches) Act 1856 (Bow to Barking)
London Midland and Scottish Railway Act 1929 (deviation at Campbell Road Junction)
London, Tilbury, and Southend Railway Act 1898
(Alterations to bridges at West Ham and Barking)
London, Tilbury, and Southend Railway Act 1902 (Widenings at Bromley and West Ham)

Bow Common (now Gas Factory Jcn) to Barking West Jcn	Opened	31.3.1858
Gas Factory Jcn to Barking: electric working (6.25 kV AC)	Commenced	6.11.1961
Gas Factory Jcn to East Ham (west of): OLE converted to 25 kV AC	... ...	....
Campbell Road Jcn with the Whitechapel & Bow Railway	Opened	25.5.1902
Campbell Road Junction SB	Opened	25.2.1902
Campbell Road Junction SB: replacement box	Opened	26.2.1905
***	Closed	18.10.1959
Campbell Road Jcn: improvement of the junction	... ...	4.1923
Campbell Road Jcn: double junction	Removed	14.9.1959
Campbell Road Jcn to Plaistow: additional lines	Into use	1.8.1905
Campbell Road Jcn to East Ham: DC electric working	Commenced	20.8.1905
Campbell Road Jcn, Bromley Jcn, Abbey Mills Upper Jcn: semi-automatic two-aspect colour-light signalling for up and down local lines	Into use	18.7.1927
Bromley SB	Opened	c.1877
Bromley SB: replacement box	Opened	26.2.1905
***	Closed	1961
Bromley Jcn with the North London Railway	Opened	17.5.1869
***	Closed	14.9.1959
Bromley Jcn with the North London Railway	Re-located	1.10.1893
Bromley Jcn: main-line junction	Removed	10.4.1960
BROMLEY	Opened	31.3.1858
New station on new site	Opened	1.3.1894
Additional entrance from Devons Road	Opened	c.1895
Enlargement of the station	... ...	1904-5
Through-line platforms	t.o.u.	18.6.1962
On 26 April 1970 the following stations were transferred from British Railways to London Transport: Bromley, Upton Park, Becontree, Elm Park, West Ham, East Ham, Dagenham Heathway, Hornchurch, Plaistow, Upney, Dagenham East, Upminster Bridge.		
Abbey Mills Upper Junction SB	Opened	c.1877
Replacement box	Opened	1904
***	Closed	1961

Abbey Mills Curve (Worked by the Great Eastern Railway)
Powers: --

Upper Abbey Mills Jcn to Abbey Mills Lower Jcn with the Great Eastern Railway	OG	31.3.1858
***	OP	1.6.1858
***	CP	27.10.1940
***	CG	27.7.1958
***	Closed	7.8.1960
Abbey Mills Lower Jcn	Removed	27.7.1958

Abbey Mills Upper Jcn to Upton Park: semi-automatic two-aspect colour-light signalling for up and down local lines	Into use	19.7.1927
WEST HAM	OP	1.2.1901
Enlargement to two island platforms	... ...	1905
Altered to WEST HAM MANOR ROAD	... ...	11.2.1924
Altered to WEST HAM	... ...	1.1969
WEST HAM MANOR ROAD: through-line platforms	Into disuse	1913
***	Unusable	1940
West Ham SB	Opened	....
***	Closed	....
Plaistow Up Sidings SB	Opened	1904
***	Closed	13.9.1959
PLAISTOW SIDINGS	Into use	1877
***	Extended	1880
Plaistow works	Closed	1934
Plaistow running sheds	Closed	1960
Plaistow SB	Opened	1880
Plaistow SB: replacement box	Opened	11.10.1903
***	Closed	1961
PLAISTOW	OP&G	31.3.1858
Six platforms, including north and south bays	Completed	9.7.1905
Up-side bay (North London Bay) out of normal use	t.o.u.	1.1.1916
***	Removed	1956
Through-line platforms	t.o.u.	18.6.1962
***	CG	1.5.1953
Plaistow (probably east of station) to East Ham: additional tracks	Into use	15.5.1904
Plaistow East Down Through IBS	Into use	17.3.1935
Upton Park West Up Through IBS	Into use	17.3.1935
UPTON PARK	OP	17.9.1877
Four platforms	Completed	5.7.1903
Through-line platforms	t.o.u.	18.6.1962

UPTON PARK GOODS STATION (London & North Western Railway), and branch	Opened	1.4.1895
***	Closed	7.1984
Upton Park SB	Opened	c.1877
Replacement box	Opened	28.6.1903
Replacement box	Opened	15.12.1904
***	Closed	1961
Upton Park to Barking: semi-automatic two-aspect colour-light signalling for up and down local lines	Into use	27.2.1928 ?
East Ham (west of) to Barking: OLE converted to 25 kV AC	... ...	22.5.1988
East Ham SB	Opened	c.1881
***	Closed	c.1904
East Ham No. 1 SB	Opened	15.5.1904
***	Closed	13.9.1959
EAST HAM	OP&G	31.3.1858
***	CG	4.1962
***	Enlarged	1902-1904
Down-side bay	t.o.u.	15.9.1958
***	Removed	26.10.1958
Through-line platforms and lines re-siting	Completed	29.11.1959
Through-line platforms	t.o.u.	18.6.1962
East Ham No. 2 SB	Opened	15.5.1904
***	Closed	1961
East Ham to Barking: additional lines and DC electric working	Into use	1.4.1908
Little Ilford No. 1 SB	Opened	22.3.1908
***	Closed	30.11.1958
Little Ilford No. 2 SB	Opened	22.3.1908
***	Closed	1961
Little Ilford No. 3 SB	Opened	22.3.1908
***	Closed	1961
LITTLE ILFORD GOODS SIDINGS	O.Partly	31.5.1902
***	O.Fully	22.3.1908
***	Closed	1958-1961
Tanners Street Crossing SB	Opened	22.2.1903
***	Closed	23.2.1908

East Ham Curve

Powers: Tottenham and Forest Gate Railway Act 1890

East Ham to East Ham Loop North Jcn	OP	9.7.1894
***	OG	1.9.1894
***	CP	15.9.1958
***	CG	30.11.1958

Woodgrange Park to Tilbury

Powers: London, Tilbury, and Southend Extension Railway Act 1852
London, Tilbury, and Southend Railway Act 1904 (Little Ilford to Barking Widening)
London, Tilbury, and Southend Railway Act 1901 (Substitution of embankment for viaduct at Grays)
London, Tilbury, and Southend Railway Act 1898 (Alteration of levels at Tilbury station)

Forest Gate Jcn to Tilbury	O.Formal	11.4.1854
***	OP	13.4.1854
***	OG	....
Forest Gate Jcn to 8 m.p.: electric working (6.25 kV AC)	Commenced	6.11.1961
OLE converted to 25 kV AC	... ...	22.5.1988
Forest Gate Jcn to Woodgrange Park	CP	1.5.1918
***	RO(P)	6.1.1969
Woodgrange Park Junction SB	Opened	1.7.1894
WOODGRANGE PARK	OP	9.7.1894
***	OG	1.9.1894
***	CG	7.12.1964
East Ham Loop North Junction SB: replacement box	Opened	27.7.1908
***	Closed	1961
Woodgrange Park to Barking: down line	Diverted	15.12.1957
Barking West Junction SB	Opened	1876
Barking West Junction SB: replacement box	Opened	c.1894
***	Closed	21.2.1903
Barking West Junction SB: replacement box	Opened	23.2.1908
***	Closed	27.3.1961
Barking SB	Opened	1961
Barking Station Sidings SB	Opened	c.1907
***	Closed	15.6.1958
Barking GF	Abolished	1.12.1935
Barking, west of station: up line on flyover	Into use	5.1.1959
Flyover brought fully into use	... ...	11.5.1959
River Roding to Barking Queen's Road: new alignment of up and down through lines	Into use	14.4.1958
BARKING	OP&G	13.4.1854
***	CG	1.4.1957
Alterations in the station	Completed	6.12.1959
***	CG	1956-1962 ?
(Barking) Eastbury Road SB (precise location not known)	Closed	7.2.1921

Barking, east of station: up local line dive-under	Into use	9.11.1959
Barking East SB	Opened by	1881
Replacement box	Opened	c.1889
Replacement box	Opened	23.2.1908
***	Repaired	1919
***	Closed	27.3.1961

Barking & Pitsea line

See page 37

Barking East to Dagenham Dock: additional goods line	Into use	6.1961
8 m.p. to Tilbury: electric working (25 kV AC)	Commenced	6.11.1961
Rippleside SB	Opened	....
Replacement box	Opened	1961
Rippleside East Down IBS	Into use	17.11.1935
Ripple Lane Yard SB	Closed	24.10.1971
Ripple Lane Container Terminal SB	Opened	1961
RIPPLE LANE FREIGHTLINER TERMINAL	Opened	....
Ripple Lane No. 1 SB	Opened	2.5.1937
***	Closed	1961
Ripple Lane No. 1: reception lines Nos. 1 and 2	Into use	7.4.1940
RIPPLE LANE YARD	OG	....
***	C.Coal	6.8.1984
Ripple Lane SB	Opened	28.1.1923
Ripple Lane Crossing SB	Opened	....
Re-named Ripple Lane SB	... ...	1917
Re-named Ripple Lane No. 2 SB	... ...	2.5.1937
Replacement box on deviation line	Opened	21.7.1957
Ripple Lane No. 2: arrival line	Into use	27.5.1940
Ripple Lane to Dagenham Dock: deviation line	Into use	21.7.1957
DAGENHAM DOCK	OP&G	1.7.1908
***	CG	2.11.1964
Dagenham Dock SB	Opened	16.12.1901
RAINHAM	OP&G	13.4.1854
***	CG	4.10.1965
Rainham SB	Opened	1881
Rainham SB: replacement box	Opened	1924
***	Re-framed	1961
Rainham GF	Opened	11.6.1939
Wennington Agricultural Siding GF	Removed	3.12.1940
PURFLEET RIFLE RANGE HALT	OP(NA)	1911
***	OP	1921
***	CP(All)	31.5.1948
Ordnance Crossing SB	Opened	....
Replacement box	Opened	10.5.1909
Replacement box named Purfleet Rifle Range SB	Opened	5.12.1910
***	Closed	31.8.1980
Purfleet Station SB	Opened	1880
Replacement box	Opened	26.10.1924
PURFLEET	OP&G	13.4.1854
***	CG	2.11.1964
Anglo GF	Into use	21.1.1940
West Thurrock Sidings SB	Opened	20.5.1910
***	Closed	1961
Manor Road Crossing GF	Into use	23.1.1938
Grays Junction SB	Opened	c.1892
Re-named West Thurrock Junction SB	By	1895

Ockendon branch

See page 39

Grays West SB	Opened	5.11.1900
***	Closed	1961
Grays SB	Opened	1880
***	Closed	5.11.1900
GRAYS	OP&G	13.4.1854
Down-side bay (normally used for Ockendon trains)	Into use	5.11.1900
***	CG	6.1984
Grays East SB	Opened	5.11.1900
Tilbury North Junction SB	Opened	1886
Replacement box	Opened	c.6.1918
Re-named Tilbury Dock Junction SB	... ...	....

Tilbury Marine Spur

Powers: --

New line to Port of London Authority Berth No. 29	Opened	15.5.1927
TILBURY MARINE	OP&G	15.5.1927
***	CP&G	1.5.1932

Tilbury Dock Station SB	Opened	1885	
Replacement box	Opened	11.6.1922	
Re-named Tilbury Town SB	... ...	....	
***	Closed	1961	
TILBURY DOCKS	OP&G	15.6.1885	
Altered to TILBURY TOWN (FOR TILBURY DOCKS)	Officially	3.8.1934	
***	By notice	1.10.1934	
Tilbury West Junction SB	Opened	16.12.1906	
***	Closed	1961	
Tilbury Riverside SB	Opened	1961	
TILBURY	OP&G	13.4.1854	
Passenger station	Rebuilt	1906	
***	Rebuilt	1912	
Altered to TILBURY RIVERSIDE	... ...	1935	
Tilbury Dock	Opened	17.4.1886	

Gravesend Pier

Powers: Gravesend Town Quay and Pier Act 1833
London, Tilbury, and Southend Railway (Further Powers) Act 1880 (Enlargement of Pier)

GRAVESEND PIER	Opened	....	
GRAVESEND WEST STREET PIER altered to GRAVESEND CAR FERRY PIER	... ...	26.9.1949	

Tilbury North Curve

Powers: London, Tilbury, and Southend Extension Railway Act 1852

Tilbury West Jcn to Tilbury East Jcn	OG	c.1855	
***	OP by	1.7.1855	*
Electric working (25kV AC)	Commenced	6.11.1961	

Tilbury to Shoeburyness

Powers: London, Tilbury, and Southend Extension Railway Act 1852
London, Tilbury, and Southend Railway (Deviation and Amendment) Act 1854 (At Leigh)
London, Tilbury, and Southend Railway (Deviation and Amendment) Act 1854 (Westcliff to Southend)
London, Tilbury, and Southend Railway Act 1882 (Extension to Shoeburyness)

Tilbury South Jcn to Stanford-le-Hope	Opened	14.8.1854	
Tilbury South Jcn to Leigh-on-Sea (west of): electric working (25 kV AC)	Commenced	6.11.1961	
Tilbury South Junction SB	Opened by	1881	
Replacement box	Opened	29.7.1906	
***	Closed	1961	
Tilbury East Junction SB	Opened	....	
Replacement box	Opened	16.12.1906	
***	Closed	1961	
Low Street SB	Opened	1881	
Replacement box	Opened	4.1.1925	
LOW STREET	OP&G	1861	
***	CG	28.9.1964	
***	CP	5.6.1967	
Muckingford Crossing GF	Into use	10.12.1939	
EAST TILBURY HALT	OP	7.9.1936	
Altered to EAST TILBURY	... ...	2.1949	
Thames Haven Junction SB	Opened	1875	
Replacement box	Opened	1880	
Replacement box	Opened	30.1.1927	
Box closed and junction worked from Low Street	... ...	19.8.1973	
STANFORD-LE-HOPE	OP	14.8.1854	
***	OG	....	
New down platform opposite the up platform	Into use	23.6.1935	
Stanford-le-Hope SB	Opened	1881	
Replacement box	Opened	14.5.1922	
***	Closed	19.5.1985	
Thorndon Estate GF	Into use	1.12.1940	

Thames Haven branch
See page 39

Horndon to Leigh	Opened	1.7.1855	
***	Doubled	1856	
PITSEA	OP&G	1.7.1855	
New station (on opening of the line from East Horndon)	Opened	1.6.1888	
Altered to PITSEA FOR VANGE	... ...	18.7.1932	*
Altered to PITSEA	...	9.1952-1.1953	
Up bay-line	Removed	5.1956	
***	CG	5.6.1967	

Barking & Pitsea line
See page 37

Pitsea Junction SB	Opened	1881
Replacement box	Opened	c.1888
Replacement box	Opened	21.10.1934
Replacement box	Opened	1961
Benfleet West Up IBS and Benfleet West Down IBS	Into use	16.12.1934
BENFLEET	OP&G	1.7.1855
Altered to BENFLEET FOR CANVEY ISLAND	... ...	11.7.1927
Altered to BENFLEET	... ...	14.5.1984 *
***	CG	5.6.1967
Replacement passenger station	Opened	....
Benfleet SB	Opened	1881
Box made a ground frame/gate box	Before	1964
***	Closed	24.4.1977
Hadleigh SB	Opened	3.8.1901
Hadleigh SB: replacement box	Opened	30.8.1916
***	Closed	1961
Leigh-on-Sea (west of) to Shoeburyness: electric working (6.25 kV AC)	Commenced	6.11.1961
OLE converted to 25 kV AC	... ...	....
Leigh-on-Sea Station SB (new box with the new station)	Opened	1.1.1934
LEIGH-ON-SEA: replacement station 46 chains west of the old one	OP&G	1.1.1934
Passing loop with platform	Into use	18.9.1955
***	CG	4.12.1970
LEIGH (first station)	OP&G	1.7.1855
Altered to LEIGH-ON-SEA	... ...	1.10.1904 *
***	CP&G	1.1.1934
Leigh-on-Sea Station SB	Opened	1881
Replacement box	Opened	1885 ?
Re-named Leigh-on-Sea Crossing SB	... ...	1.1.1934
***	Closed	1961
Leigh to Southend	Opened	1.3.1856
***	Doubled	1856
CHALKWELL	OP	11.9.1933
New platform and reversing line	Into use	18.9.1955
Chalkwell East Up IBS	Into use	6.5.1934
Westcliff-on-Sea SB	Opened	1895
***	Closed	1961
WESTCLIFF-ON-SEA	OP	1.7.1895
Altered to WESTCLIFF	... ...	20.2.1969
Southend Station SB	Opened	c.1856
Replacement box	Opened	1881
Replacement box	Opened	1961
SOUTHEND	OP&G	1.3.1856
Altered to SOUTHEND-ON-SEA	... ...	1.6.1876
Additional bay platform lines	Into use	1889
Altered to SOUTHEND-ON-SEA CENTRAL	... ...	1.5.1949
Altered to SOUTHEND CENTRAL	... ...	20.2.1969
Southend to Shoeburyness	Opened	1.2.1884
Southend High Street Down IBS	Into use	24.3.1935
Southend Milton Road Up IBS	Into use	31.3.1935
Southend Bankside Up IBS	Into use	24.3.1935
Southend East SB	Opened	....
Re-named Southend Sidings SB	... ...	18.7.1932
***	Closed	1961
SOUTHEND EAST	OG	1.1.1908
***	OP	18.7.1932
Additional passenger platform	Into use	1.7.1933
Altered to SOUTHEND-ON-SEA EAST	... ...	1.5.1949
Altered to SOUTHEND EAST	... ...	20.2.1969
***	CG	5.6.1967
Platforms 1 and 2	t.o.u.	10.1.1982
SOUTHCHURCH-ON-SEA	OP&G	1.7.1910
Altered to THORPE BAY	... ...	18.7.1910
***	CG	19.6.1967
Thorpe Bay West Up IBS and Thorpe Bay West Down IBS	Into use	10.2.1935
Thorpe Bay SB	Opened	....
***	Closed	1961
Shoeburyness SB	Opened	1884
Replacement box	Opened	24.4.1921
Replacement box	Opened	c.1934
SHOEBURYNESS	OP&G	1.2.1884
***	CG	5.6.1967

Barking to Pitsea Direct Line

Powers: London, Tilbury, and Southend Railway Act 1882

Barking to Upminster	Opened	1.5.1885
Additional pair of (DC electrified) tracks	Into use	12.9.1932
Barking to Upminster: conductor rails energised at midnight	... ...	21.8.1932
DC electric working of District Line trains	Commenced	12.9.1932

Barking to Upney: new local line alignment	Into use	9.3.1958
Barking to Upney (east of): electric working (6.25 kV AC)	Commenced	6.11.1961
OLE converted to 25 kV AC	... ...	22.5.1988
UPNEY (served by LT District Line trains only)	OP	12.9.1932
Upney SB	Opened	24.2.1903
Replacement box	Opened	c.1932
***	Closed	1961
Upney (east of) to Pitsea: electric working (25 kV AC)	Commenced	6.11.1961
GALE STREET	OP	28.6.1926
Four platforms	Completed	1932
Altered to BECONTREE HALT	... ...	18.7.1932
Made a station as BECONTREE	... ...	12.9.1932
Closed to British Railways passenger trains	... ...	12.6.1961
Through-line platforms	t.o.u.	18.6.1962
Gale Street SB	Opened	4.8.1906
Replacement box named Becontree SB	Opened	18.7.1932 ?
***	Closed	1961
Heathway Up Through IBS	Into use	27.3.1935
HEATHWAY (served by LT District Line trains only)	OP	12.9.1932
Altered to DAGENHAM HEATHWAY	... ...	1.5.1949
DAGENHAM	OP&G	1.5.1885
New connection at the east end with the up main line	Into use	6.6.1920
New down-side bay	Into use	24.11.1935
Altered to DAGENHAM EAST	... ...	1.5.1949
Closed to British Railways passenger trains	... ...	12.6.1961
***	CG	6.5.1968
Through-line platforms	t.o.u.	18.6.1962
Dagenham SB	Opened	1885
Replacement box	Opened	....
***	Re-framed	6.6.1920
***	Closed	1961
Dagenham: double junction	Removed	1.11.1959
ELM PARK	OP/Pcls	13.5.1935
Hornchurch West Up Through IBS	Into use	31.3.1935
Hornchurch SB	Opened	1885
Replacement box	Opened	7.12.1930
***	Closed	1961
HORNCHURCH	Opened	1.5.1885
Closed to British Railways passenger trains	... ...	12.6.1961
***	Actual CG	5.8.1981
***	Off. CG	8.2.1982
UPMINSTER BRIDGE (served by LT District Line trains only)	OP	17.12.1934
Upminster West Junction SB: replacement box	Opened	c.1893
***	Closed	1961
Upminster SB	Opened	1961
Upminster: last connection (at the west end) from Romford line	t.o.u.	4.5.1958

Romford branch
See page 39

Upminster: double junction	Removed	11.5.1958
Upminster: local trains to and from London Transport sidings only	... ...	11.5.1958
UPMINSTER	OP&G	1.5.1885
Enlargement and rebuilding of station	Completed	1932
Separate dead-end platform for the Romford trains	Into use	19.5.1957
Through-line platforms	t.o.u.	18.6.1962
***	CG	7.12.1964
Upminster: sidings for District Line trains	Into use	1932
Upminster: construction of the London Transport depot	Commenced	1.12.1958
***	Completed	12.6.1959

Ockendon branch
See page 39

Upminster to East Horndon	Opened	1.5.1886
Upminster East Junction SB	Opened	1885
Replacement box	Opened	c.1934
***	Closed	1961
Upminster Depot Control Tower	Opened	1961
Cranham SB	Opened	30.7.1906
***	Closed	1961
Warley SB	Opened	28.6.1925
***	Closed	1961
East Horndon Down IBS	Into use	6.3.1935
EAST HORNDON	OP&G	1.5.1886
Altered to WEST HORNDON	... ...	1.5.1949
***	CG	7.9.1964
East Horndon SB	Opened	1886
***	Closed	1961

East Horndon to Pitsea Jcn	Opened	1.6.1888
Dunton West SB	Opened	28.6.1925
***	Closed	1961
Dunton SB	Opened	10.6.1905
Re-named Dunton East SB	... ...	28.6.1925
***	Closed	1961
LAINDON	OP&G	1.6.1888
Passing loop with platform	Into use	1933
Rebuilding of station	Completed	1934
Locations of down main line and down loop reversed	... ...	3.11.1957
***	CG	5.6.1967
Laindon SB	Opened	1888
Replacement box	Opened	c.1934
Basildon Hall Up IBS	Into use	3.2.1935
Basildon SB re-named Basildon West SB	... ...	1.5.1923 ?
Replacement box 39 chains to the west	Opened	3.2.1935
***	Closed	1961
BASILDON	OP	25.11.1974
Basildon East SB	Opened	1.5.1923
***	Closed	1961

Romford Branch

Powers: London, Tilbury, and Southend Railway Act 1883

Upminster West Jcn to Romford Jcn	Opened	7.6.1893
Electric working (25 kV AC)	Commenced	12.5.1986
Upminster West Jcn to Romford: one engine in steam working	Commenced	16.9.1973
UPMINSTER: new No. 6 platform for the Romford branch	Into use	19.5.1957
Upminster West Junction SB: key token delivery apparatus	Into use	20.4.1937
EMERSON PARK & GREAT NELMES HALT	OP	1.10.1909
The double name appeared only on one board on the platform. In all other contexts only the name Emerson Park was used.		
Emerson Park: engine run-round loop	Into use	14.10.1909
***	t.o.u.	1.8.1934
***	Removed	1936
Romford Station SB closed; no signalman key token instrument in lieu	Into use	1.3.1936
Romford Jcn with the former Great Eastern line severed	... ...	c.1931
Junction restored with a new ground frame to work the connections	... ...	4.8.1940
ROMFORD	OG	1896
***	OP	7.6.1893
Entrance to former LMS station	Closed	1.4.1934
ROMFORD GOODS STATION altered to ROMFORD VICTORIA ROAD	... ...	1.5.1949
***	CG	4.5.1970

Ockendon Branch

Powers: London, Tilbury, and Southend Railway Act 1883

Upminster East Jcn to Grays Jcn	Opened	1.7.1892
Upminster East Jcn to Grays Jcn: electric train staff working in place of working by train staff & ticket	Commenced	c.1895
Upminster East Jcn to West Thurrock Jcn: tokenless block working in place of electric train staff working	Commenced	11.1978
Upminster East Jcn to West Thurrock Jcn: electric working (25 kV AC)	Commenced	6.11.1961
OCKENDON	OP&G	1.7.1892
***	CG	6.5.1968
Ockendon SB	Opened	1892
***	Closed	24.12.1977
West Thurrock Jcn to Grays West: independent extension of the Ockendon branch line	Into use	8.6.1959

Thames Haven Branch

Powers: Thames Haven Dock and Railway Act 1836
The London, Tilbury & Southend Railway Company bought the line, wharf, and 20 acres of land on 8 September 1855, for £49,500.
London, Tilbury, and Southend Railway Act 1886 (Thames Haven Wharf)

Thames Haven Jcn to Thames Haven	Opened	7.6.1855
***	CP	1.10.1880 *
Thames Haven Branch Jcn to Thames Haven Oil Company's Siding: electric train tablet working in place of train staff working	Commenced	8.12.1922
Miners Safety Explosive Company GF	Removed	14.6.1939
Thames Haven SB	Opened	....
Box closed and Terminus GF provided in lieu	... ...	19.8.1973
THAMES HAVEN	OP	7.6.1855
***	CP	8.1880
Thames Haven pier and wharf	Removed	1912

Occasional passenger trains to meet steamers continued until 1909, and a workmen's service ran from 1 January 1923 until about 1955 with halts at Stanford Road level crossing, Miners Safety, 29m 74ch, and 30m 21ch.

ACTON BRANCH (Midland & South Western Junction Railway)

Powers: The Midland & South Western Junction Railway was incorporated by the Midland and South Western Junction Railway Act 1864. It was vested in the Midland under the Midland Railway (Additional Powers) Act 1867 and absorbed under the Midland Railway (Additional Powers) Act 1874 with effect from 1 January 1875. The line was worked by the Midland from its opening.

Brent Jcn to Acton Wells Jcn	OG	1.10.1868
Between Brent Sidings and Acton Wells Junction the London & South Western Railway possessed running powers over the Midland line.		
Brent Jcn to Dudding Hill Jcn	OP	1.7.1905
***	CP	1.10.1908
Brent Junction No. 2 to Dudding Hill Jcn: block telegraph working	Resumed	6.7.1905
Brent Junction No. 2 to Dudding Hill Jcn: up main line bell-worked	... ...	22.2.1926
The down main line remained worked by block telegraph.		
Brent Junction No. 2 to Dudding Hill: up and down goods lines designated Brent Curve lines	... ...	6.5.1979

Cricklewood Curve

Powers: Midland Railway (Additional Powers) Act 1871

Child's Hill Passenger Jcn to Dudding Hill Jcn	Opened	3.8.1875
***	CP	2.7.1888
***	RO(P)	1.3.1893
***	CP	1.10.1902
Cricklewood Jcn to Dudding Hill Jcn: down line out of use after a derailment	... 11.1976 --	14.9.1977

Dudding Hill Junction SB	Opened	c.8.1875
Replacement box	Opened	2.3.1902
Dudding Hill Jcn to Acton Wells Jcn	OP	3.8.1875
Dudding Hill Jcn to Stonebridge Park	CP	2.7.1888
Dudding Hill Jcn to Acton Wells Jcn	RO(P)	1.3.1893
***	CP	1.10.1902
***	RO(P)	1.7.1905
***	CP	10.1908
Dudding Hill Jcn to Acton Wells Jcn designated goods lines	... ...	20.12.1942
The section continued to be worked by absolute block.		
DUDDING HILL	OG	1.1.1872
***	OP	3.8.1875
Altered to DUDDING HILL (FOR CHURCH END WILLESDEN)	... ...	1.2.1876 *
Altered to DUDDING HILL	... ...	1.5.1878 *
Altered to DUDDING HILL (FOR WILLESDEN AND NEASDEN)	... ...	1.6.1880 *
***	CP	2.7.1888
***	RO(P)	1.3.1893
***	CP	1.10.1902
***	CG	6.7.1964
Although Railway Clearing House evidence indicates that this station was called Willesden & Dudden Hill prior to November 1875, all Midland evidence agrees on the name Dudding Hill from the start.		
Dudding Hill Station SB	Open before	1.11.1875
Box closed and ground frame provided in lieu	... ...	10.5.1887
Dudding Hill Station SB (second box)	Opened	23.3.1923
Neasden Jcn with the Great Central Railway	OG	1.8.1899
Neasden Junction SB	Opened	30.7.1899
HARROW ROAD FOR STONEBRIDGE PARK & WEST WILLESDEN	OP&G	3.8.1875
Altered to HARROW ROAD (FOR STONEBRIDGE PARK AND HARLESDEN)	... ...	1.2.1876 *
Altered to HARROW ROAD	... ...	1.5.1878 *
Altered to HARROW ROAD FOR STONEBRIDGE & HARLESDEN	... ...	1.10.1879 *
Altered to HARROW ROAD FOR STONEBRIDGE PARK & HARLESDEN	... ...	1.11.1880 *
Altered to STONEBRIDGE PARK FOR WEST WILLESDEN & HARLESDEN	... ...	1.7.1884
***	CP	2.7.1888
***	OG	25.8.1890
***	RO(P)	1.3.1893
Altered to HARLESDEN FOR WEST WILLESDEN & STONEBRIDGE PARK	... ...	1.2.1901
***	CP	1.10.1902
***	CG	6.7.1964
Harrow Road SB	Open before	1.11.1875
Re-named Stonebridge Park SB	... ...	....
Replacement box	Opened	19.8.1890
Re-named Harlesden SB	... ...	....
***	Closed	31.10.1965
Harrow Road to Acton Wells Jcn	CP	1.2.1876
***	RO(P)	1.5.1878
***	CP	1.10.1880
***	RO(P)	1.3.1893
Harlesden: North Metropolitan Electric Power Supply Siding GF	Removed	24.5.1942
Harlesden: Taylor's Lane Sidings GF	Into use	14.6.1942

Harlesden to Acton Canal Wharf: up line taken out of use as running line (and down line worked by electric train tablet block)	... ...	30.12.1928
Up line restored and down line taken out of use	... ...	3.3.1929
Down line restored and up line taken out of use	... ...	2.6.1929
Up line restored	... ...	14.7.1929
Acton Canal Wharf SB	Open before	1.11.1875
Replacement box	Opened	17.11.1895
***	Re-framed	c.1965

Acton Canal Wharf Branch

Powers: --

Acton Canal Wharf branch	Opened	9.1873
***	Closed	1886

One source offers the above dates, whilst another suggests that the branch was not opened until about 1886.

Acton Canal Curve

Powers: --

Acton Canal Wharf SB to Willesden No. 7 SB	OG	21.7.1963

NORTH & SOUTH WESTERN JUNCTION RAILWAY

Powers: North and South Western Junction Railway Act 1851 (Willesden to Kew)
North and South Western Junction Railway Act 1868 (Deviation at Acton)

The North and South Western Junction Railway Act 1871 formed a joint committee of the London & North Western, Midland, and North London Railways to work the line with effect from 1 January 1871.

Willesden Jcn to Old Kew Jcn	OG	15.2.1853
***	OP	1.8.1853
Willesden Jcn to Acton Wells Jcn	CP	2.1.1860
Broad Street and Richmond: electric working	Commenced	1.10.1916
Old Oak Junction SB	Opened	1865
***	Closed	6.11.1977
Old Oak Jcn: original junction replaced by a junction with the new line from Willesden High Level	... ...	1.5.1892
Old Oak Jcn to Kew Bridge: electric working	Commenced	1.10.1916
Old Oak Jcn to Acton Wells Jcn: up and down goods lines made arrival and departure lines	... ...	6.11.1977
OLD OAK EXCHANGE SIDINGS	Into use	15.2.1853
***	t.o.u.	....
At Acton Wells Junction the Great Western Railway possessed running powers for coaching traffic over five chains of the North & South Western Junction line between the junction with the London & North Western curve from Willesden High Level Junction and the junction with its own Acton Wells Curve.		
Acton Wells Junction SB	Opened	9.1868
***	Re-located	8.1876
Acton Wells Jcn with the Midland Railway	OG	1.10.1868
***	OP	3.8.1875
Acton Wells Jcn moved 3 chains nearer to Hendon	... ...	20.7.1885
Acton Wells Jcn with the Great Western Railway	OG	1.1.1877
***	OP	2.1.1888
***	CP	10.3.1912
Friar's Place SB	Opened	1893
Box closed and intermediate block signals provided in lieu	... ...	10.2.1935
IBS semaphores replaced by colour-light signals	... ...	1971
Acton SB	Opened	1865
Re-named Acton Central SB	... ...	1.1.1925
***	Closed	16.5.1983
ACTON	OP	1.8.1853
***	OM	1856
***	OG	1867
Station rebuilt with subway	During	1876
Altered to ACTON CENTRAL	... ...	1.1.1925
***	CG	1.3.1965
New ticket-office	Opened	12.9.1976
Between Acton Town and South Acton Junction the Metropolitan District Railway possessed running powers over the Midland line.		
Acton Central to Kew Bridge: passenger service	Withdrawn	12.9.1940
Acton Lane level crossing	Closed	20.8.1874
Hammersmith Junction SB	Opened	1865
***	Closed	13.10.1909
Hammersmith Jcn to South Acton: extension of Hammersmith branch	Into use	1.1.1880
District Junction SB	Opened	5.1899
***	Closed	1915
South Acton Jcn with the Metropolitan District Railway	Opened	15.5.1899
***	t.o.u.	1915
***	Removed	c.1920

South Acton Jcn with the Hammersmith branch	Opened	1909
SOUTH ACTON	OP	1.1.1880
Covered connection with Metropolitan District station	Into use	13.6.1905
Original buildings	Removed	1968-1969
Renovation	Completed	2.1970
Richmond Junction SB	Opened	....
Re-named Acton Junction SB	... ...	11.1868
Re-named South Acton Junction SB	... ...	....
***	Closed	24.8.1970
South Acton Jcn: trains to and from Richmond	Commenced	1.1.1869
Between Acton Junction and Studland Road Junction, and between Acton Junction and Gunnersbury, the Midland Railway possessed running powers over the London & South Western line. Between Studland Road Junction and Kensington High Street Junction and West Kensington Junction the Midland possessed running powers over the Metropolitan District line.		
South Acton Jcn to Kew Bridge: electric working	Ceased	12.9.1940
Bollo Lane Crossing Gate Cabin	Opened	....
***	Made BP	1868
***	Closed	24.8.1970
Kew Curve Junction SB	Opened	1865
Re-named Kew East Junction SB	... ...	c.1915

Kew Curve (London & South Western Railway)

Powers: --

Kew Curve Jcn to New Kew Jcn	OP&G	1.2.1862
***	CP	12.9.1940
New Kew Junction SB	Opened	1.1862
***	Closed	28.7.1974

Kew Curve Jcn to Old Kew Jcn	CP	10.1866
Kew Curve Jcn to Old Kew Jcn made a goods line	... ...	1891
KEW	OP	1.8.1853
***	OM	7.1856
Closed to passengers except for one train per week	... ...	1.2.1862
***	OG	1863
Remaining passenger service	Withdrawn	10.1866
Altered to KEW BRIDGE NORTH	... ...	26.9.1949
***	Closed	2.8.1982
KEW: second station	OP	1.2.1862
Altered to KEW BRIDGE	... ...	1868
***	CP(All)	12.9.1940
Old Kew Junction SB	Opened	....
Replacement box	Opened	18.10.1942
Replacement PSB	Opened	28.7.1974
***	Closed	8.9.1974

Hammersmith branch

Powers: North and South Western Junction Railway Act 1853

Acton Gate House Jcn to Hammersmith	OG	1.5.1857
***	OP	8.4.1858
***	CP	1.1.1917
***	CG	3.5.1965
***	Abandoned	1.1.1966
Hammersmith branch: working by electric train staff	Commenced	10.1910
One engine in steam working	By w/e	21.3.1917
Working by staff alone	Commenced	27.11.1928
ACTON COAL STATION	O.Coal	1867
***	C.Coal(All)	4.1.1965
RUGBY ROAD HALT	OP	8.4.1909
***	CP(All)	1.1.1917
WOODSTOCK ROAD HALT	OP	8.4.1909
***	CP(All)	1.1.1917
BATH ROAD HALT	OP	8.4.1909
***	CP(All)	1.1.1917
Hammersmith Passenger Station SB	Opened	8.1892
***	Closed	....
HAMMERSMITH	OG	1.5.1857
***	OP	8.4.1858
Altered to HAMMERSMITH & CHISWICK	... ...	1.7.1880
***	CP	1.1.1917
***	CG	3.5.1965

KENSINGTON COAL STATIONS

West Kensington Coal Depot:

Powers: Midland Railway (New Works Etc) Act 1877,
Midland Railway (Additional Powers) Act 1880

West Kensington to West Kensington Coal Depot	Into use	25.3.1878
***	Last train	29.7.1965
***	Closed	14.7.1965
WEST KENSINGTON COAL BAYS	Opened	1.8.1878 *
***	Closed	14.7.1965

High Street Kensington Coal Depot:

Powers: Midland Railway (Additional Powers) Act 1878

Kensington High Street to Midland Coal Depot	Opened	1.3.1878
***	Closed	25.11.1963
HIGH STREET, KENSINGTON, COAL BAYS	Opened	4.3.1878
***	Closed	25.11.1963

HEMEL HEMPSTEAD AND LONDON & NORTH WESTERN JUNCTION RAILWAY

The Hemel Hempstead and London & North Western Junction Railway was worked by the Midland under an agreement of 1 December 1876 ratified by the Midland Railway (Further Powers) Act 1877. The rent was commuted for Midland stock on 4 February 1880. The company was dissolved and vested in the Midland under the Midland Railway Act 1886 from the passing of the Act on 25 June 1886.

Powers: Hemel Hempstead and London and North Western Railway Act 1866
Hemel Hempstead and London and North Western Railway Act 1872 (alteration of levels between Harpenden and Goodwin's Halt and at Hemel Hempstead; deviation at Goodwin's Halt)
Hemel Hempstead and London and North Western Railway Act 1863 (at Heath Park Halt)

Harpenden Jcn to Hemel Hempstead	OP&G	16.7.1877
Harpenden Jcn to Hemel Hempsted: working by train staff only in place of working by block telegraph and train staff	Introduced	6.4.1887
Harpenden Jcn (old junction) to junction with the new south curve	CP&G	1.7.1888

Harpenden South Curve
Powers: Midland Railway Act 1888

Harpenden Jcn (new junction) to junction with old line	OP&G	2.7.1888

Harpenden Jcn (new junction) to Heath Park Halt	CP	16.6.1947
Harpenden Jcn to Claydale closed by British Railways: line purchased by Hemel Hempstead Lightweight Concrete Co. Ltd as private siding	... ...	29.4.1968
Harpenden Jcn to Claydale private siding	t.o.u.	1.7.1979
ROUNDWOOD HALT	OP	8.8.1927
***	CP(All)	16.6.1947
REDBOURN	OP&G	16.7.1877
***	CP	16.6.1947
***	CG	6.7.1964
Redbourn SB	Opened	16.7.1877
***	Closed	4.1883-11.1885
Redbourn and Godwin's Sidings are named in a list of "signal posts" returned to the Board of Trade in November 1880, but they may not have been actual signalbox structures.		
Redbourn: west GF	Removed	5.12.1904
BEAUMONT'S HALT	OP	9.8.1905
***	CP(All)	16.6.1947
Owen's Sidings GF	Removed	23.9.1935
Line severed 220 yards west of Claydale Sidings	... ...	28.7.1964
GODWIN'S HALT	OP	9.8.1905
***	CP(All)	16.6.1947
Godwin's Sidings SB	Opened	16.7.1877
***	Closed	4.1883-11.1885
GODWIN'S DEPOT	Opened	1900-1904
***	Closed	2.3.1964
Godwin's Depot to Hemel Hempsted	Closed	1.7.1963
Hemel Hempsted SB	Opened	16.7.1877
***	Closed	6.4.1887
HEMEL HEMPSTEAD	OP&G	16.6.1877
Altered to HEMEL HEMPSTED	... ...	1.6.1880 *
***	CP	16.6.1947
***	CG	1.7.1963
Hemel Hempstead engine shed	Opened	c.7.1877
***	Closed by	1911
Hemel Hempsted to Boxmoor	OG	....
Hemel Hempsted to Heath Park Halt	OP	9.8.1905

Hemel Hempsted (12 chains west of) to Boxmoor gas works	Closed	31.8.1959
HEATH PARK HALT	OP	9.8.1905
***	CP(All)	16.6.1947
HEATH PARK GOODS DEPOT	Opened	1891
***	Closed	31.8.1959
(BOXMOOR) GAS WORKS SIDINGS	Into use	....
***	t.o.u.	1.4.1960
Connection from Boxmoor Gas Works to Boxmoor goods yard	Into use	31.8.1959
***	t.o.u.	1.4.1960

II. BETWEEN BEDFORD AND WIGSTON JUNCTION

LEICESTER & HITCHIN LINE

Powers: Midland Railway (Leicester and Hitchin) Act 1853
Midland Railway (Additional Powers) Act 1873 (Rushton & Bedford Widening)
Midland Railway (New Works Etc) Act 1876 (Rushton & Bedford Widening: Wymington Deviation)
London and North Western and Midland Railway Companies (Market Harborough New Line) Act 1882 (Market Harborough Loop Line)
London Midland and Scottish Railway Act 1924 (Kibworth to Wistow Widening)
Midland Railway Act 1898 (Kilby Bridge to Wigston Widening)
Midland Railway (Additional Powers) Act 1869 (Wigston Engine Shed and Sidings)

Hitchin to Leicester	OM	15.4.1857	
***	OG	4.5.1857	
***	O.Formal	7.5.1857	
***	OP	8.5.1857	
Between Hitchin station and Hitchin Junction the Midland Railway possessed running powers for all traffic over the Great Northern line.			
Hitchin to Bedford	CP	1.1.1962	
Cambridge Junction SB (Great Northern Railway) to Midland Goods Yard SB: block telegraph working	Commenced	29.12.1890	
Cambridge Jcn to Midland Goods Yard SB	Tfc ceased	2.12.1963	
***	Closed	6.1.1964	
HITCHIN MIDLAND GOODS DEPOT	Opened	4.5.1857	
***	Closed	1.8.1917	
***	Re-opened	16.8.1921	
***	Closed	1.1.1964	
Hitchin engine shed	Opened	....	
***	Replaced	1860	
***	Replaced	1892	
***	Closed	....	
Hitchin Midland Goods Yard to Midland Goods Yard SB	Tfc ceased	2.12.1963	
***	Closed	6.1.1964	
Hitchin SB	Open before	16.8.1877	
Re-named Midland Goods Yard SB	... ...	1880-1881	
Replacement box named Hitchin Goods Yard SB	Opened	30.7.1911	
***	Closed	1964-1972	
Midland Goods Yard SB to Southill Station SB: block telegraph working	Commenced	3.6.1890	
Hitchin Goods Yard SB to Shefford SB	Singled	30.7.1911	
Hitchin Goods Yard to Shefford	Closed	30.12.1963	
HENLOW	OP	8.5.1857	
***	OG	1.11.1857	*
Altered to HENLOW CAMP	... ...	1.3.1933	
Disused up platform lengthened and brought back into use by sluing the single line	... ...	17.12.1939	
***	CP	1.1.1962	
***	CG	2.12.1963	
Henlow: goods loop line	Into use	30.9.1917	
***	t.o.u.	24.2.1924	
Henlow SB	Opened	3.6.1890	
Made an intermediate tablet station	... ...	19.8.1917	
***	Re-framed	30.9.1917	
Made a gate box only	... ...	24.2.1924	
Re-named Henlow Camp SB	... ...	1.3.1933	?
***	Closed	29.12.1963	
Shefford SB	Opened	3.6.1890	
Made a ground frame	... ...	12.1.1964	
***	t.o.u.	28.12.1964	
Shefford: line severed opposite the signalbox	... ...	29.12.1963	
Shefford to Southill: up line	t.o.u.	12.1.1964	
Shefford to Bedford No. 1: line made a goods line with one engine in steam working	... ...	12.1.1964	
SHEFFORD	OM	15.4.1857	
***	OG	4.5.1857	
***	OP	8.5.1857	
***	CP	1.1.1962	
***	CG	28.12.1964	
Shefford to Cardington Air Ministry Siding	Closed	28.12.1964	
Southill SB	Opened	3.6.1890	
***	Closed	12.1.1964	
SOUTHILL	OP	8.5.1857	
***	OG	1.5.1858	*
***	CP&G	1.1.1962	
Southill to Cardington: block telegraph working on the up line	Intro. by	1873	
Block telegraph working on the down line	Introduced	1876	
Southill SB to Bedford L. & N. W. Crossing	Singled	19.11.1911	
CARDINGTON	OP	8.5.1857	
***	OG	1.5.1858	*
***	CP&G	1.1.1962	
***	C.Sidings	28.12.1964	

Cardington SB (first box)	Open before	16.8.1877
Replacement box	Opened	21.1.1896
***	Closed	20.11.1911
Cardington SB (second box)	Opened	27.8.1916
***	Closed	15.4.1923
Cardington: made intermediate tablet station (not crossing-place)	... ...	27.8.1916
Cardington to Bedford L. & N. W. Junction: block telegraph working	Introduced	1877
Cardington: 2 loop sidings	Into use	7.8.1916
CARDINGTON WORKMEN'S PLATFORM	OP(NA)	c.9.1917
***	CP(All)	3.10.1921 *
Cardington Aircraft Factory Sidings to Bedford	Last train	4.2.1969
***	Closed	28.4.1969
Bedford L. & N. W. Crossing SB	Open before	16.8.1877
This signalbox was the London & North Western's Bedford No. 1 SB.		
Bedford L. &. N. W. Crossing SB alias Bedford No. 1 SB re-named Bedford St John's No. 1 SB	... ...	2.6.1924 ?
Re-named Bedford St John's SB	... ...	25.1.1970
Bedford L. & N. W. Crossing to L. & N. W. Junction	Singled	6.6.1966
Bedford L. & N. W. Junction to Bedford Jcn: block telegraph working	Introduced	25.1.1892
KING'S PLACE SIDINGS	Into use	1904-1910
***	t.o.u.	7.7.1969
Bedford St John's No. 1 SB (London & North Western Railway) to Bedford Jcn: line designated a through siding	... ...	16.7.1966
Through siding designated up & down Bletchley line	... ...	13.5.1984
L. & N. W. Junction SB	Open before	16.8.1877
Replacement box	Opened	1.6.1902
***	Closed	16.7.1966
At L. & N. W. Junction the London & North Western Railway possessed powers to cross the Midland line to obtain access to Howards' works.		
Ouse Bridge SB	Open before	16.8.1877
Replacement box	Opened	12.1.1930
***	Closed	16.7.1966
BEDFORD COAL YARD	Opened	15.4.1857
***	Closed	7.7.1969
Kempston Road Jcn to Bedford North SB: down slow line designated up & down slow line	w.e.f	26.11.1978
Bedford Junction SB	Open before	16.8.1877
***	Raised	24.6.1906
Replacement box	Opened	7.3.1920
***	Closed	2.11.1980
Bedford Jcn to Desborough North: block telegraph working	Introduced	1869-1872
At the opening of the Leicester & Hitchin line there was no station in Bedford; a junction with the London & North Western line was brought into use to allow Midland trains to use that company's station.		
BEDFORD	OP&G	1.2.1859
Replacement through platforms brought into use and existing platforms converted into bays	... ...	1870
Hitchin departure bay made arrival and departure bay	... ...	13.8.1922
Former Hitchin arrival bay made a siding	... ...	20.8.1922
Altered to BEDFORD MIDLAND ROAD	... ...	2.6.1924
Additional footbridge near the north end of the station	... ...	c.1942
Hitchin bay line made a siding and adjacent siding made the Hitchin bay line	... ...	....
***	CG	30.8.1971
Altered to BEDFORD MIDLAND	... ...	8.5.1978
Down slow line diverted to outer face of new island platform and old down slow line made up & down No. 1 goods line between Bedford Junction and Bedford North	... ...	24.9.1978
New station buildings on changed site, with new footbridge	Into use	1.10.1978
Official opening of new station	... ...	9.10.1978
Down slow line made up & down slow line and part of inner face of new island platform brought into use as a turnback platform	... ...	26.11.1978
Up slow line diverted to inner face of island platform and old up slow line made up & down No. 2 goods line between Bedford Junction and Bedford North; last part of old station closed	... ...	10.12.1978
Nos. 1 and 2 up & down goods lines	t.o.u.	....
St John's line diverted over former Engineer's siding to join up slow line at south end of the station	... ...	....
Up slow line slued into new platform No. 1 and platform No. 2 taken temporarily out of use	... ...	8.6.1980
Platform No. 1	Into use	9.6.1980
Platform No. 2 returned to use as down slow line after extension northwards and platform No. 3 taken temporarily out of use	... ...	3.11.1980
Platform No. 3 returned into use after extension northwards	... ...	2.2.1981
St John's line doubled for about 350 yards at northern end and carriage washer siding with facing connection in the up slow line brought into use	... ...	1.11.1981
New bay platform line brought into use and connection to carriage washer siding removed from up slow line and made with this line	... ...	24.4.1988
Altered to BEDFORD	... ...	16.5.1988 *

Bedford North SB	Open before	16.8.1877
Replacement box	Opened	7.9.1890
Replacement box	Opened	7.10.1894
Replacement box	Opened	25.11.1978
***	Closed	2.11.1980
Bedford North Jcn: double junction (DSL-DPL, UPL-USL)	Into use	7.10.1894
Up fast line to up slow line crossover	Removed	26.11.1978
Down slow line to down fast line crossover	Removed	1.11.1980
Bedford North Jcn (new layout between Bedford North and Bromham): up fast line to up slow line ladder	Into use	26.11.1978
Remaining connections to create a double ladder junction allowing parallel movements DSL-DFL and UFL-USL	Into use	1.11.1980
Trailing crossover between the slow lines to allow fully reversible use of all platforms at Bedford	Into use	29.11.1981
Bedford North Jcn to Oakley Jcn: up goods line	Into use	9.11.1890
Bedford North Jcn to Oakley Station Jcn: down goods line	Into use	c.12.11.1890

Between Bedford and Glendon North Junction the goods/slow lines were built on the up side of the railway except through Kettering station, where the new pair of lines was on the down side and a re-arrangement of tracks took place. The ruling gradient of the new lines was kept down to 1:200 against the load, resulting in significant differences in levels between Oakley and Wellingborough and between Kettering and Glendon North Junction, as well as the choice of a separate alignment between Souldrop and Irchester South.

Bedford North to Oakley Jcn: passenger lines closed to allow rebuilding of Bromham viaduct	... ...	10.5.1891
Four-track working on completion of new Bromham viaduct	Restored	14.2.1892
Bedford North Jcn to Sharnbrook: goods lines made slow lines	... ...	17.5.1981
Bromham SB (first box)	Opened	10.5.1891
***	Closed	14.2.1892
Bromham SB (second box)	Opened	20.7.1902
***	Closed	19.2.1967
Bromham: double junction (DPL-DGL, UGL-UPL)	Into use	20.7.1902
***	t.o.u.	....
Oakley Junction SB	Open before	16.8.1877
Replacement box	Opened	9.11.1890
***	Re-framed	10.5.1891
***	Re-framed	14.2.1892
Replacement box	Opened	12.12.1937
***	Closed	10.5.1970
Oakley Jcn: double junction (DGL-DPL, UPL-UGL)	Into use	11.9.1892
***	t.o.u.	....

Bedford & Northampton Railway

See page 54

Oakley Jcn to Oakley Station Jcn: up goods line	Into use	21.9.1890
Oakley Jcn to Oakley Station Jcn: passenger lines closed to allow rebuilding of Clapham viaduct	... ...	21.2.1892
Four-track working restored on completion of new Clapham viaduct, double junction at Oakley Junction removed and replaced by another one in the reverse direction	... ...	11.9.1892
Oakley Station SB	Open before	16.8.1877
Replacement box named Oakley Station Junction SB	Opened	21.9.1890
Re-named Oakley Station SB	... ...	9.7.1893
***	Closed	9.6.1965
Oakley Station Jcn to Milton Goods Jcn: up and down goods lines	Into use	9.7.1893
Oakley Station Jcn: junction between the passenger and goods lines	Removed	9.7.1893
OAKLEY	OP	8.5.1857
***	OG	1.9.1857 *
***	CP	15.9.1958
***	CG	1.8.1963
Oakley troughs	Into use	5.2.1904
***	t.o.u.	5.10.1964
Milton SB	Opened	1871
Replacement box named Milton Goods Junction SB	Opened	25.9.1892
***	Closed	9.7.1893
Milton Goods Jcn: junction between the passenger and goods lines	Removed	9.7.1893
Milton Goods Jcn to Sharnbrook Station Jcn: up and down goods lines	Into use	25.9.1892
Sharnbrook: new viaduct	Inspected	19.3.1880

The main lines were diverted to a new viaaduct and the old one, of which one pier had sunk, was closed. It was brought back into use after rebuilding.

Sharnbrook: reception line, run-round line, and 4 sidings	Into use	14.11.1943
***	t.o.u. after	1962
Sharnbrook Station SB	Opened	1869
Replacement box named Sharnbrook Station Junction SB	Opened	c.5.1884
Replacement box	Opened	25.9.1892
***	Alt.levers	17.8.1913
***	Closed	17.5.1981

Sharnbrook Station Junction to Irchester South SB:		
up and down goods lines	Into use	4.5.1884
Sharnbrook Station Jcn: down main line to down goods line connection	Removed	25.9.1892
Down passenger line to down goods line crossover	Into use	17.8.1913
Double junction (DPL-DGL, UGL-UPL)	t.o.u.	16.9.1973 ?
The UGL-UPL crossover here had been retained when the goods lines were extended south on 25 September 1892.		
SHARNBROOK	OM	15.4.1857
***	OG	4.5.1857
***	OP	8.5.1857
***	CP	2.5.1960
***	CG	4.5.1964
Sharnbrook: ladder junction with south end in the down main line	Into use	16.9.1973
Ladder junction with south end in the up goods line	Into use	17.5.1981
Sharnbrook SB (temporary box)	Opened	25.10.1987
***	Closed	5.12.1987
Sharnbrook Jcn to the new Wellingborough Station Jcn:		
down goods line	t.o.u.	18.10.1987
Sharnbrook Jcn to Harrowden Jcn: up & down slow line	Into use	6.12.1987
Souldrop SB	Open before	1.11.1875
***	Alt.levers	23.2.1914
Replacement box	Opened	13.7.1920
***	Closed	20.12.1966
Sharnbrook Summit SB	Open before	16.8.1877
***	Closed	c.10.1884
Puddington SB	Opened	2.1881
***	Closed	c.10.1884
Wymington Goods Line SB	Opened	26.10.1891
***	Closed	4.3.1963
Wymington SB	Open before	1.11.1875
Re-named Wymington Passenger Line SB	... ...	26.10.1891
***	Closed	22.10.1892
Irchester South SB	Opened	c.10.1881
Replacement box	Opened	27.6.1897
***	Re-framed	27.7.1913
***	Closed	5.12.1987
Irchester South SB: double junction (DGL-DPL, UPL-UGL)	Into use	7.9.1913
***	t.o.u.	12.10.1969
Irchester South SB to Wellingborough South SB:		
up and down goods lines	Into use	3.12.1883
IRCHESTER	OM	15.4.1857
***	OG	4.5.1857
***	OP	8.5.1857
Altered to IRCHESTER FOR HIGHAM FERRERS	... ...	1.11.1881
New goods yard and shed	Into use	24.6.1883
Altered to IRCHESTER FOR RUSHDEN & HIGHAM FERRERS	... ...	1.10.1888
Altered to IRCHESTER	... ...	1.5.1894
***	CP	7.3.1960
***	CG	4.1.1965
Irchester Station SB	Open before	16.8.1877
Re-named Irchester North SB	... ...	5.1899-6.1904
Replacement box	Opened	10.12.1905
***	Closed	29.11.1964
Irchester Junction SB (no signals for the fast lines)	Opened	3.7.1893
***	Closed	21.12.1969

Irchester & Raunds line

See page 56

Irchester Jcn to Wellingborough Station SB:		
up and down goods lines made up and down slow lines	... ...	22.4.1894
Up and down slow lines made up and down goods lines	... ...	15.6.1959
Wellingborough South SB	Open before	16.8.1877
Replacement box	Opened	26.11.1905
***	Closed	27.6.1943
Wellingborough South SB to Finedon Road SB: down goods line	Into use	12.3.1882
Wellingborough South SB to Wellingborough North SB: up goods line	Into use	19.3.1882
Wellingborough South SB to Wellingborough Jcn:		
passenger lines closed to allow re-building of the Ise viaduct	... ...	14.3.1886
Four-track operation on completion of new Ise viaduct	Restored	7.11.1886
Wellingborough South Sidings GF	Into use	....
***	t.o.u.	6.6.1982

Wellingborough Curve

Powers: Midland Railway (Leicester and Hitchin) Act 1853

Midland Jcn (London & North Western) to Wellingborough Jcn	Opened by	1.1.1859 *
***	OP	1.10.1866
***	CP	4.5.1964
Line singled and made a through siding	... ...	9.11.1969
Single-line through siding (to Whitworth's Siding only)	C.Tfc	30.11.1981
***	Off. closed	13.6.1982

Wellingborough Junction SB	Open before	16.8.1877	
***	Alt.levers	4.2.1894	
Replacement box adjacent to the south	Opened	27.6.1943	
***	Closed	13.11.1983	
Between Wellingborough Junction and Wellingborough station the London & North Western Railway had running powers over the Midland line for coaching and coal traffic.			
Wellingborough Jcn to Wellingborough North SB: up goods line	Into use	4.1874-11.1874	
This line may have come into use at the end of 1873.			
WELLINGBOROUGH	OM	15.4.1857	
***	OG	4.5.1857	
***	OP	8.5.1857	
Platforms on the slow lines	Into use	1.5.1894	
Slow-line platforms taken out of regular use	... ...	15.6.1959	
Altered to WELLINGBOROUGH MIDLAND ROAD	... ...	2.6.1924	
Altered to WELLINGBOROUGH	... ...	14.6.1965	*
***	C.Coal	6.8.1979	
***	CG	1.11.1980	
Wellingborough Station SB	Opened	c.1866	
Replacement box	Opened	1872	?
Replacement box	Opened	6.8.1893	
***	Re-framed	4.7.1915	
***	Closed	5.12.1987	
Wellingborough: down goods line to down passenger line crossover	Into use	4.7.1915	
Down passenger line to reception line connection	Into use	1.8.1915	
Down goods line to down passenger line crossover	t.o.u.	18.10.1987	
Wellingborough: down reception line made down goods line	... ...	6.12.1987	
Butlin's Sidings SB	Open before	1869	
***	Closed by	16.8.1877	
Wellingborough North SB to Finedon Road Jcn: up goods line	Into use	21.7.1879	
Wellingborough North SB	Opened	....	
Replacement SB	Opened	20.8.1893	
***	Closed	9.12.1962	
Wellingborough engine shed	Opened	....	
***	Replaced	1868	
***	Demolished	7.1964	
Wellingborough No. 2 engine shed	Opened	1872	
***	C.Steam	13.6.1966	
Shed closed as a maintenance centre	... ...	29.3.1969	
Wellingborough diesel fuelling point	Into use	10.5.1965	
***	t.o.u.	....	
Wellingborough Engine Sidings SB (not a block post)	Opened	....	
Replacement box	Opened	22.10.1888	
Replacement box	Opened	20.1.1924	
***	Closed	2.6.1931	
Wellingborough Engine Shed to Finedon Road Bridge: up and down passenger lines replaced by new lines a little further from the goods lines (to ease curves)	... ...	20.8.1893	
Wellingborough Engine Shed (site) to Finedon Road Bridge: down goods line re-aligned to lie alongside passenger lines	... ...	12.10.1986	
Finedon Road SB	Opened	....	
Replacement box	Opened	16.7.1893	
***	Re-framed	....	
***	Closed	5.12.1987	
Wellingborough, Stanton Iron Company's branch: working by brass tablet instead of by train staff	Commenced	13.6.1887	
Branch closed	... ...	2.7.1977	?
Rushton & Bedford Widening (Finedon Road Jcn to Glendon North Jcn)	Approved	13.12.1879	
Finedon Road Jcn to Finedon Station: up goods line	Into use	18.5.1879	
Finedon Road Jcn to Isham: down goods line	Into use	18.5.1879	
Finedon Road to Neilson's Sidings: down goods line	t.o.u.	15.11.1987	
Finedon Road Jcn: up goods line to up passenger line crossover	Into use	21.9.1913	
***	t.o.u.	....	
Wellingborough South Sidings SB (not a block post)	Opened	26.11.1893	
***	Raised	29.9.1895	
Box closed and ground frame provided in lieu	... ...	26.7.1909	
***	t.o.u.	....	
WELLINGBOROUGH SIDINGS	Opened	....	
***	t.o.u.	....	
Wellingborough North Sidings SB (not a block post)	Opened	26.11.1893	
Box closed and ground frame provided in lieu	... ...	10.8.1909	
***	t.o.u.	....	
Charlton Iron Company's Sidings SB	Open before	1.11.1875	
***	Closed	1879	
Neilson Sidings SB (not a block post -- point box only)	Opened	1962-1969	
***	Closed	c.1986	
Neilson's Sidings SB	Opened	1879	
Replacement box	Opened	16.7.1893	
***	Re-framed	....	
***	Closed	5.12.1987	
Neilson's Sidings: up passenger line to up goods line crossover	Into use	2.7.1911	
***	t.o.u.	5.12.1987	

Neilson's Sidings: down passenger line to down goods line crossover	Into use	....
***	t.o.u.	15.11.1987
These two facing crossovers did not form a pair.		
Neilson's Sidings to Kettering Jcn: up and down goods lines	t.o.u.	15.11.1987
FINEDON SIDINGS	Opened	24.8.1891
***	Closed	....
Finedon Sidings SB	Open before	1.11.1875
Box closed and ground frame provided in lieu	... ...	13.8.1895
***	t.o.u.	14.5.1979
Harrowden Jcn: down fast line to up fast line crossover	Into use	6.12.1987
Up main line to down main line crossover	Into use	6.12.1987
FINEDON	OP	1.7.1857 *
***	OG	1.9.1857 *
***	CP	2.12.1940
***	CG	6.7.1964
Finedon Station SB	Open before	16.8.1877
Replacement box	Opened	1879
***	Alt.levers	23.10.1892
Replacement box	Opened	23.2.1902
***	Closed	11.5.1980
Finedon Station (north end) to Isham: up goods line	Into use	8.12.1878
Finedon: up goods line to up passenger line crossover	Into use	24.11.1912
***	t.o.u.	....
ISHAM	OP	8.5.1857
***	OG	1.5.1858 *
Altered to ISHAM & BURTON LATIMER	... ...	11.1858-3.1859 *
Altered to BURTON LATIMER (FOR ISHAM)	... ...	1.10.1923 *
***	CP	20.11.1950
***	CG	4.5.1964
Isham Station SB	Opened	1860
Replacement box	Opened	....
***	Re-framed	1.12.1895
Replacement box	Opened	27.3.1904
Re-named Burton Latimer Station SB	... ...	1.10.1923
Box ceased to signal the passenger lines	... ...	13.2.1966
***	Closed	23.4.1967
Burton Latimer Up GF	t.o.u.	3.9.1972
Isham to Kettering Jcn: up goods line	Into use	10.8.1879
Isham to Kettering: down goods line	Into use	10.8.1879
Pytchley SB (no signals for the fast lines)	Opened	18.2.1906
***	Closed	28.4.1935
Pytchley to Kettering Jcn: down goods line made down slow line; branch line made up slow line for use by branch-line trains only	... ...	18.2.1906
Down slow line made down goods line; up slow line made up and down branch line	... ...	28.2.1935
Kettering Junction SB	Opened	....
Replacement box (with re-located junction)	Opened	1.11.1874
Replacement box	Opened	24.4.1887
***	Re-framed	18.2.1906
Replacement box	Opened	28.4.1935
***	Closed	5.12.1987

Kettering, Thrapstone & Huntingdon Railway
See page 56

Kettering Jcn: double junction (DPL-DSL, USL-UPL)	Into use	2.1879-2.1880
Replaced by ladder junction with south end in down passenger line	... ...	11.12.1977
Kettering Jcn to Kettering: up goods line	Into use	....
Kettering South SB	Opened	1875
Replacement box	Opened	12.8.1917
Box closed and ground frame provided in lieu	... ...	19.11.1967
***	t.o.u. by	6.11.1987
Kettering South: double junction (DSL-DFL, UFL-USL)	Into use	2.1879-2.1880
***	t.o.u.	19.11.1967
Kettering Station SB	Opened	....
Replacement box	Opened	11.1870
***	Re-framed	22.11.1896
Replacement box	Opened	8.6.1913
***	Closed	5.12.1987

Kettering Ironstone Branches
See page 58

KETTERING	OM	15.4.1857
***	OG	4.5.1857
***	OP	8.5.1857
New platforms (for the fast lines)	Into use	10.8.1879
New main buildings	Approved	3.10.1898
Altered to KETTERING FOR CORBY	... ...	4.5.1970 *
Altered to KETTERING & CORBY	... ...	5.5.1975 *

KETTERING (continued)			
Altered to KETTERING FOR CORBY	... ...	2.5.1977	*
***	CG	1.11.1980	
Altered to KETTERING	... ...	16.5.1988	*
Between Kettering station and Market Harborough Junction, and between Glendon Junction and Lloyd's Sidings at Weldon & Corby the London & North Western Railway possessed running powers for merchandise traffic over the Midland line.			
Kettering to Glendon North Jcn: up and down goods lines	Into use	19.10.1879	
Up and down goods lines re-named up and down slow lines	... ...	1.3.1880	?
Up and down slow lines	t.o.u.	28.11.1987	
Kettering to Corby North: single running line	Into use	29.11.1987	
Kettering engine shed	Opened	1865	
***	Replaced	1876	
***	Closed	14.6.1965	
Kettering North SB	Opened	1879	
***	Re-framed	17.11.1895	
Replacement box	Opened	20.2.1898	
***	Closed	19.11.1967	
Kettering North: double junction (DFL-DSL, USL-UFL)	Into use	17.4.1898	
***	t.o.u.	19.11.1967	
Wallis Sidings SB	Open before	1.11.1875	
Re-named Kettering Iron & Coal Company's Sidings SB	... ...	4.1878-2.1879	
Replacement box	Opened	4.5.1913	
***	Closed	10.9.1967	
Kettering North Jcn	Into use	6.12.1987	
Glendon Sidings SB	Open before	1.11.1875	
***	Closed	1879	
Glendon South Junction SB (no signals for the fast lines)	Opened	1879	
Replacement box	Opened	18.3.1906	
***	Closed	3.6.1973	

Kettering & Manton line

See page ...

Glendon North Junction SB	Opened	1879	
Replacement box	Opened	8.5.1904	
***	Re-framed	....	
***	Closed	5.12.1987	
RUSHTON	OM	15.4.1857	
***	OG	4.5.1857	
***	OP	8.5.1857	
Altered to GLENDON & RUSHTON	... ...	1.3.1896	
***	CP	4.1.1960	
***	CG	4.5.1964	
Rushton Station SB	Opened	1868	
Re-named Glendon & Rushton Station SB	... ...	....	
Replacement box	Opened	30.7.1899	
***	Closed	11.2.1973	
Gaultney Wood SB	Open before	1.11.1875	
Gaultney Wood SB: replacement box	Opened	15.11.1887	
***	Raised	19.1.1909	
Replacement box	Opened	8.5.1923	
Box closed and up and down IBS provided in lieu	... ...	25.1.1942	
Up IBS	Removed	1960-1969	
Down IBS	Removed	29.6.1986	
Desborough Station SB	Open before	1871	
Replacement box	Opened	....	
Replacement box	Opened	2.2.1902	
***	Closed	26.5.1968	
DESBOROUGH	OM	15.4.1857	
***	OG	4.5.1857	
***	OP	8.5.1857	
Altered to DESBOROUGH FOR ROTHWELL	... ...	1.10.1857	*
Altered to DESBOROUGH & ROTHWELL	... ...	1.11.1899	
***	CP&G	1.1.1968	
Desborough North SB	Opened	....	
***	Re-framed	16.2.1896	
Replacement box	Opened	19.12.1897	
***	Re-framed	11.5.1924	
***	Closed	14.3.1981	
Desborough North to Little Bowden Crossing: block telegraph system on the down line	Installed	1869-1872	
Block telegraph system on the up line	Installed	1872-1873	
Desborough North SB to Little Bowden Jcn: up goods line	Into use	10.10.1875	
***	t.o.u.	14.3.1981	
Desborough North SB to Braybrook SB: down goods line	Into use	25.5.1924	
Desborough North SB: down goods line cut short to form loop	... ...	18.9.1966	
Down goods loop	t.o.u.	....	
Braybrook SB	Open before	1873	
Replacement box	Opened	3.1.1892	
***	Closed	18.9.1966	

Braybrook: up goods line to up passenger line crossover	Into use	12.1891
***	t.o.u.	....
Little Bowden Junction SB	Opened	10.10.1875 ?
Replacement box	Opened	c.6.1897
***	Closed	29.6.1986
Little Bowden Crossing to Market Harborough Jcn: block telegraph system	Installed	1872–1873
Market Harborough South Jcn: facing and trailing crossovers	Into use	30.6.1986
Market Harborough South SB	Opened	c.3.1885
***	Raised	28.10.1906
Replacement box	Opened	15.2.1920
***	Closed	4.1.1931
Market Harborough Jcn to Great Bowden Jcn (London & North Western line): block telegraph system	Installed	....
Market Harborough: new Midland line	Opened	28.6.1885
MARKET HARBOROUGH: old London & North Western station closed at noon and new joint London & North Western and Midland station opened	... ...	14.9.1884
The work at the new station was not completed until 15 February 1886. The London & North Western Railway had powers to use the Midland portion of the Market Harborough Joint Passenger Station for coaching traffic. Between Market Harborough Junction and Wigston North Junction the London & North Western Railway had running powers for merchandise traffic over the Midland line.		
MARKET HARBOROUGH MIDLAND GOODS SHED	Opened	24.12.1884
***	CG	6.8.1979 ?
	or	3.9.1979 ?
Market Harborough North SB	Opened	7.1885
Replacement box	Opened	14.9.1919
***	Closed	4.1.1931
Market Harborough No. 2 SB: replacement Western Division box	Opened	4.1.1931
***	Closed	20.10.1968
MARKET HARBOROUGH EXCHANGE SIDINGS	Opened	....
Last two sidings	t.o.u.	27.1.1985
Market Harborough Jcn to Great Bowden Jcn: Midland user of the London & North Western line	Commenced	15.4.1857
***	Ceased	28.6.1885
Market Harborough Junction SB (London & North Western box)	Opened	....
***	Closed	....
MARKET HARBOROUGH (original station)	Opened	29.4.1850
***	Closed	14.9.1884
Market Harborough to Great Bowden Jcn	Opened	9.6.1851
Market Harborough No. 3 SB (London & North Western box)	Re-framed	1924
Re-named Market Harborough SB	... ...	20.10.1968
***	t.o.u.	27.4.1986
***	Closed	29.6.1986
Market Harborough No. 3 SB: double junction with the Northampton line	Into use	27.7.1924
Up main line to up Northampton line crossover	t.o.u.	13.6.1982
Down Northampton line to down main line crossover and remains of Northampton line and sidings	t.o.u.	27.1.1985
Great Bowden Junction SB (London & North Western box)	Open before	3.11.1871
***	Closed	....
Great Bowden Jcn with the London & North Western Railway	Closed	18.11.1885
Great Bowden Jcn to Wigston North Jcn: block telegraph system	Installed	1869–1872
Great Bowden Sidings SB	Open before	3.11.1871
Replacement box	Opened	7.1885
Replacement box	Opened	1.12.1929
***	Closed	15.10.1972
Gallow SB	Open before	1.11.1875
***	Closed	1885
LANGTON	OP	2.10.1876
***	OG	12.1882
Altered to EAST LANGTON	... ...	1.5.1891
***	CG	2.3.1964
***	CP	1.1.1968
Langton SB	Open before	2.1874
Re-named East Langton SB	... ...	1.5.1891
Replacement box	Opened	14.7.1895
***	Closed	29.7.1984
This box was switched out permanently in August 1981, but brought back into use briefly whilst Kibworth SB was being restored in 1984.		
Gumley SB	Open before	16.8.1877
Replacement box	Opened	16.5.1897
Box closed and up and down IBS provided in lieu	... ...	29.9.1946
***	Removed	28.6.1986
Kibworth Station SB	Open before	2.1874
Replacement box	Opened	4.3.1889
***	Re-framed	20.9.1914
Replacement box	Opened	17.10.1926
***	Burnt out	8.1.1984
***	Restored	1.1984
***	Closed	29.6.1986

KIBWORTH	OM	15.4.1857
***	OG	4.5.1857
***	OP	8.5.1857
***	CG	4.7.1966
***	CP	1.1.1968
Kibworth Station to Kibworth North: down goods line	Into use	7.12.1926
Down goods line made down slow line	... ...	17.11.1929
Kibworth Station to Wistow: down slow/goods line made down goods loop	... ...	28.4.1968
***	t.o.u.	2.4.1986
Kibworth North SB	Opened	1868
Replacement box	Opened	....
Replacement box	Opened	25.1.1903
Replacement box	Opened	3.1.1926
***	Closed	28.4.1968
Kibworth North: down slow line to down passenger line crossover	Into use	17.11.1929
***	t.o.u.	28.4.1968
Kibworth North to Wistow: up goods line	Into use	16.1.1927
Down goods line	Into use	17.11.1929
Up goods line made up goods loop	... ...	28.4.1968
Up goods loop	t.o.u.	16.3.1985
Wistow SB (signalling the up line only)	Open before	1.11.1875
Replacement box	Opened	11.3.1894
Replacement box signalling both main lines	Opened	17.11.1926
***	t.o.u.	2.4.1986
***	Closed	29.6.1986
Great Glen SB	Open before	2.1874
Replacement box	Opened	23.11.1902
***	Closed	3.9.1967
GLEN	OM	15.4.1857
***	OG	4.5.1857
***	OP	8.5.1857
Altered to GREAT GLEN	... ...	18.1.1897
***	CP	18.6.1951
***	CG	6.7.1964
Newton SB	Opened	1875
Replacement box	Opened	20.3.1893
Box closed and up and down IBS provided in lieu	... ...	29.3.1942
***	Removed	....
Kilby Bridge Jcn: facing and trailing crossovers, and junction to up & down slow line	Into use	30.6.1986
Kilby Bridge SB	Open before	2.1874
Replacement box	Opened	16.12.1900
***	Closed	29.6.1986
Kilby Bridge SB to Wigston South Sidings: down goods line	Into use	27.1.1901
Up goods line	Into use	3.2.1901
Kilby Bridge SB to Wigston North Jcn: down goods line	t.o.u.	27.4.1986
Former down goods line restored to use as up & down slow line	... ...	30.6.1986
Kilby Bridge SB to Wigston South Jcn: up goods line	t.o.u.	27.4.1986
Wigston South Sidings SB	Open before	1.11.1875
Replacement box	Opened	25.11.1900
***	Closed	22.5.1966
Wigston South Sidings: up goods line to up passenger line crossover	Removed	3.2.1901
Down goods line to down passenger line crossover	Into use	31.3.1901
Up passenger line to up goods line crossover	Into use	10.2.1901
First up goods line to up passenger line crossover	Into use	22.11.1908
Crossovers	t.o.u.	....
Wigston South Sidings to Wigston South Jcn: up goods line	Into use	2.12.1900
Down goods line	Into use	31.3.1901
Wigston South Sidings to Wigston South Jcn: second up goods line	Into use	22.11.1908
WIGSTON	OP	8.5.1857
***	OG	1.1.1872 *
New station	Opened	1901
***	Approved	26.9.1902
***	CG	1.1.1902
Altered to WIGSTON MAGNA	... ...	2.6.1924
***	CP	1.1.1968
Wigston South Junction: ladder junction with Birmingham Curve	Into use	....
Wigston South Junction: all connections except up & down slow line to Birmingham Curve and up fast line to Engineer's siding	t.o.u.	28.6.1986
Wigston South Junction SB	Opened	12.1870
Replacement box	Opened	8.9.1889
Replacement box	Opened	25.11.1900
***	Re-framed	....
***	Closed	29.6.1986

Wigston South Curve (Birmingham Curve)

Powers: Midland Railway (Additional Powers) Act 1869

Wigston South Jcn to Blaby Jcn	OG	1.1.1871
***	OP	2.12.1872

Between Wigston South Junction and Glen Parva Junction the London & North Western Railway had running powers for merchandise traffic over the Midland line.

Wigston South Jcn to Wigston Central Jcn West	CP	1.7.1902 *
Wigston Central Jcn West to Glen Parva Jcn	CP	....
Wigston South Jcn to Glen Parva Jcn	RO(P)	5.11.1962
***	CP	18.4.1966
Blaby Jcn re-named Glen Parva Jcn	... ...	....
SOUTH CURVE SIDINGS	Into use	....
***	t.o.u.	31.10.1984

Wigston Central Curve (Leicester Curve)

Powers: Midland Counties Railway Act 1836 (Land Powers only), Midland Railway (Additional Powers) Act 1869

Wigston Central Jcn North to Wigston Central Jcn West	Approved	26.7.1871
	... ...	1.9.1871
Central curve: use by all Midland passenger services	CP	1.1.1962 ?
Wigston Central Curve	Closed	3.7.1967 ?
***	**or**	26.11.1967 ?

WIGSTON CARRIAGE & WAGON DEPOT SIDINGS	Into use	....
***	t.o.u.	18.3.1984
Wigston South Jcn: up through goods line to up local goods line crossover	Into use	....
***	t.o.u.	....
Wigston South Jcn: up goods line to up passenger line crossover	Into use	2.12.1900
	and/or	16.12.1900
***	t.o.u.	....
Wigston South Jcn: down goods line to Central Curve connection	Into use	31.3.1901
Wigston South Jcn to Knighton South Jcn: up (through) goods line	Into use	14.6.1874
Up local goods line	In use by	8.2.1875
Wigston South Jcn to Wigston North Jcn: down goods line	Into use	4.1874-11.1874
Up goods line	t.o.u.	20.5.1973
Re-alignment of the main lines	Completed	22.7.1973
Wigston Up Sidings SB (not a block post)	Opened	12.1888-8.1893
Replacement box	Opened	22.8.1898
Replacement box	Opened	1.3.1914
***	Closed	28.2.1965
Wigston Down Sidings SB (not a block post)	Opened	12.1888-8.1893
Replacement box	Opened	16.4.1893
***	Closed	14.3.1938
***	Re-opened	....
***	Closed	30.8.1953
WIGSTON DOWN SIDINGS	Into use	....
***	t.o.u.	17.3.1974
Wigston Engine Shed Sidings SB (not a block post)	Opened	12.1888-8.1893
Replacement box	Opened	3.5.1903
***	Closed	14.8.1910
Wigston engine shed	Opened	1873
***	Closed	5.11.1934
***	Re-opened	Late war
***	Closed	4.1955

BEDFORD & NORTHAMPTON RAILWAY

The Bedford & Northampton Railway was worked by the Midland from its opening and amalgamated with the Midland under the Midland Railway (Additional Powers) Act 1885 with effect from 1 January 1886.

Powers: Bedford and Northampton Railway Act 1865
Bedford and Northampton Railway Act 1867 (Deviation at Olney)

Oakley Jcn to Northampton	OP&G	10.6.1872
***	CP	5.3.1962

The line was worked by the block telegraph system from its opening. Between points on the Bedford & Northampton line and Hardingstone Junction the London & North Western Railway had running powers, with use of stations, over the Midland line. These powers were not exercised.

Oakley Jcn to Piddington (Yardley Chase OESD Siding)	Closed	20.1.1964
TURVEY	OP&G	10.6.1872
***	CP	5.3.1962
***	C.Tfc	20.1.1964
Turvey SB	Opened	10.6.1872
Replacement box	Opened	13.4.1902
***	Closed after	20.1.1964
Turvey to Olney: single-line working over the up line by pilotman	Intro. by	6.1913
Electric train tablet working	Introduced	5.6.1913
Double-line working	Resumed	8.9.1913
Single-line working by tablet on up line	Introduced	14.2.1915
Turvey: facing crossover brought into use; down line officially designated a siding	... ...	27.8.1940

Olney SB	Opened	10.6.1872
***	Alt.levers	18.3.1890
Replacement box	Opened	3.5.1942
***	Closed after	20.1.1964
OLNEY	OP&G	10.6.1872
***	CP	5.3.1962
***	CG	6.1.1964
Olney engine shed	Opened	Early 1890s
***	Closed	1928
Ravenstone Wood Junction SB	Opened	29.6.1891
***	Closed	27.7.1964

Between Ravenstone Wood Junction and Broom Junction, and between Cockley Brake Junction and Blisworth, the Midland Railway possessed running powers over the Stratford-on-Avon & Midland Junction line. Between Ravenstone Wood Junction and Olney the Stratford-on-Avon & Midland Junction Railway possessed running powers over the Midland line.

Ravenstone Wood Jcn	Closed	27.7.1964
Ravenstone Wood Jcn to Piddington: single-line working over up main line by electric train tablet	Introduced	28.2.1915
Double-line working by block telegraph	Resumed	20.8.1917
Piddington: line severed at this point	... ...	5.1967
Yardley Chase OESD Siding to Hardingstone Jcn	Singled	17.12.1967
This section transferred to the Ministry of Defence	... ...	5.2.1968
	<u>or</u>	1.3.1968
***	Closed	....
Piddington & Horton SB	Opened	10.6.1872
Replacement box	Opened	2.7.1899
***	Closed	17.12.1967
HORTON	OP&G	10.6.1872
Altered to PIDDINGTON & HORTON	... ...	1.5.1876
Altered to PIDDINGTON	... ...	1.4.1904
***	CP	5.3.1962
***	CG	7.9.1964

<u>Northampton Station Lines</u>

The Midland Railway first reached Northampton by running over the London & North Western line from Wellingborough to Hardingstone Junction, from which point it built its own line to a separate station in Northampton under the powers of the 1863 Act. Arrangements in the town were modified under the Bedford & Northampton Acts of 1866 and 1867. The Midland also had running powers by arrangement for coal and coke traffic over the London & North Western line to the Islip Iron Company's Siding at Thrapston.

Between Hardingstone Junction and Northampton Goods Station the London & North Western Railway had running powers for merchandise traffic.

Powers: Bedford and Northampton Railway Act 1866 (Northampton)
Midland Railway (New Lines and Additional Powers) Act 1863 (Northampton)
Bedford and Northampton Railway Act 1867 (Northampton)

Hardingstone Jcn (London & North Western Railway) to Northampton	OP&G	1.10.1866
NORTHAMPTON (Far Cotton station)	OP&G	1.10.1866
***	CP	10.6.1872
Name of goods station altered to FAR COTTON	... ...	2.6.1924 ?
***	CG	6.1983
Northampton Goods Junction SB	Opened	1.1.1873
Re-named Northampton Junction SB	... ...	1896
Midland box took over control of the London & North Western line points and signals and was re-named Hardingstone Junction SB	... ...	26.5.1907
Replacement box	Opened	10.7.1938
***	Closed	31.5.1970
Hardingstone Jcn with the London & North Western Railway: Midland points moved 16 chains nearer to Wellingborough	... ...	1.1.1873 ?
Hardingstone Jcn to Northampton St John's: up and down main lines designated sidings	... ...	2.7.1939
***	Removed	5.1969
NORTHAMPTON: Far Cotton temporary station for Wellingborough trains and new Northampton station opened	... ...	10.6.1872
Altered to NORTHAMPTON (ST JOHN'S STREET)	... ...	2.6.1924
***	CP(All)	3.7.1939
Northampton Station SB	Opened	1.1.1873
Replacement box	Opened	12.8.1891
***	Closed	2.7.1939
Northampton engine shed	Opened	1864-1865
***	Replaced	1873
***	Closed	1.10.1924
Northampton Far Cotton to Brackmills Hammer Steel Siding	Closed	19.9.1988

IRCHESTER & RAUNDS LINE

Powers: Midland Railway (Additional Powers) Act 1890 (Irchester Junction to Raunds)
The section between Higham Ferrers and Raunds was not constructed.

Portion of branch between junction with up goods line and first overbridge brought into use (for ironstone traffic)	OG	3.7.1893
Higham Ferrers to Irchester Jcn	OG	1.9.1893
***	OP	1.5.1894
***	CP	15.6.1959
***	C.Tfc	3.11.1969
***	t.o.u.	21.12.1969
Higham Ferrers branch: working by electric train tablet	Commenced	25.2.1894
Working by token in place of working by electric train tablet	Commenced	28.2.1932
Tablet working withdrawn, Higham Ferrers to Rushden made a siding and Rushden to Irchester Jcn working one engine in steam	Commenced	11.6.1966
HIGHAM FERRERS	OG	1.9.1893
***	OP	1.5.1894
Altered to HIGHAM FERRERS & IRTHLINGBOROUGH	... ...	1.7.1902
Altered to HIGHAM FERRERS	... ...	1.10.1910
***	CP	15.6.1959
***	CG	3.2.1969
Higham Ferrers SB	Opened	25.2.1894
Replacement box	Opened by	22.8.1914
Box closed and ground frame provided in lieu	... ...	28.2.1932
***	t.o.u.	....
Rushden SB	Opened w/e	22.8.1914
***	Closed	18.7.1915
RUSHDEN	OG	1.9.1893
***	OP	1.5.1894
***	CP	15.6.1959
***	CG	1.9.1969
Stanton Company's Siding alongside branch made running line, and this section of running line made into the private siding	... ...	22.1.1899

KETTERING, THRAPSTONE & HUNTINGDON RAILWAY

The Kettering & Thrapstone Railway changed its name to the Kettering, Thrapstone & Huntingdon Railway on 28 July 1863. It was worked by the Midland under an agreement of 1 May 1866 and was vested in the Midland under the Midland Railway (Additional Powers) Act 1897 with effect from 1 July 1897.

Powers: Kettering and Thrapstone Railway Act 1862
Kettering, Thrapstone, and Huntingdon Railway Act 1863 (Thrapstone to Huntingdon)

The direction of the line was DOWN from Huntingdon to Kettering Junction.

Kettering Jcn to Huntingdon East Jcn with the Great Eastern Railway	OG	21.2.1866
***	OP	1.3.1866
Train staff working was introduced on the opening for passenger traffic.		
Kettering to Huntingdon (and on to St Ives)	CP	15.6.1959
Kettering Jcn to Twywell: train staff with block telegraph working	Introduced	1877
Kettering Junction re-located 30 chains to the north	... ...	1.3.1887
Pytchley SB opened, and line to Thrapston worked by electric tablet	... ...	18.2.1906
Kettering Jcn to Butlin's Sidings: working by train tablet	Commenced	23.6.1964
Kettering Jcn to Twywell: one engine in steam working	Commenced	24.4.1966
Kettering Jcn to Twywell	Last train	20.1.1978
***	C.Tfc	20.3.1978
***	t.o.u.	13.6.1978
Butlin's Sidings West SB	Opened	6.1881-4.1883
***	Closed	10.1886
Butlin's Sidings East SB	Opened	6.1881-4.1883
***	Closed	....
Butlin's Sidings SB (the former Butlin's Sidings East SB)	Re-opened	11.11.1891
Replacement box (with new loop)	Opened	26.7.1903
***	Closed	24.4.1966
Butlin's Sidings to Islip Sidings: one engine in steam working	Commenced	23.6.1964
Cranford Iron Ore Company's Sidings SB	Opened	c.9.1876
Replacement box	Opened	9.9.1893
Re-named Cranford Sidings West SB	... ...	14.8.1898
Loop removed and box closed as block post	... ...	26.7.1903
***	Closed	18.2.1906
Cranford Station SB (not a block post)	Opened	11.2.1892
***	Closed	18.2.1906
CRANFORD	OG	21.2.1866
***	OP	1.3.1866
***	CP	2.4.1956
***	CG	6.11.1961
Cranford Sidings East SB	Opened	14.8.1898
***	Closed	18.2.1906

Cranford Sidings East to Kimbolton	Closed	28.10.1963	
Cranford Sidings East to Islip Sidings	Re-opened	....	
Line cut 200 yards east of Bridge 14 (near Twywell), and section of line thence to Islip Sidings closed	... ...	27.7.1971	
Marshalls Sidings SB (not a block post)	Opened	....	
***	Closed	11.1885-12.1888	
TWYWELL	OG	21.2.1866	
***	OP	1.3.1866	
***	CP&G	30.7.1951	
Twywell SB	Open before	1.10.1876	
Replacement box	Opened	3.2.1892	
***	Closed	30.8.1953	
Twywell to Thrapstone: train staff with block telegraph working	Introduced	1875	
Islip Sidings East SB (not a block post)	Opened	1885	
***	Closed	18.2.1906	
Islip Sidings West SB (not a block post)	Opened	1885	
***	Closed	18.2.1906	
Line severed 400 yards east of Islip Sidings GF	... ...	23.6.1964	
Thrapston: diversion to new Nene viaducts 21 and 22 and bridge 23 and new loop-line facing point connection with main line	Into use	6.6.1920	
THRAPSTONE	OG	21.2.1866	
***	OP	1.3.1866	
Altered to THRAPSTON	... ...	1.10.1885	*
Altered to THRAPSTON MIDLAND ROAD	... ...	2.6.1924	
***	CP	15.6.1959	
***	CG	28.10.1963	
Thrapston: loop extended about 80 yards at the Huntingdon end	... ...	2.2.1921	
Thrapstone SB	Open before	1.10.1876	
Re-named Thrapston SB	... ...	....	
Replacement box	Opened	3.2.1892	
***	Closed	28.6.1964	?
Thrapstone to Huntingdon: train staff with block telegraph working	Introduced	1878	
Thrapston to Kimbolton: train staff and ticket working	Introduced	18.7.1959	
RAUNDS	OG	21.2.1866	
***	OP	1.3.1866	
***	CP	15.6.1959	
***	CG	28.10.1963	
Raunds SB	Open before	16.8.1877	
Replacement box	Opened	29.7.1891	
***	Closed	28.6.1964	
Kimbolton SB	Open before	1.10.1876	
Kimbolton SB: replacement box	Opened	29.11.1891	
***	Closed	28.6.1964	?
KIMBOLTON	OG	21.2.1866	
***	OP	1.3.1866	
***	CP	15.6.1959	
***	CG	28.10.1963	
Kimbolton to Huntingdon East Jcn	Closed	15.6.1959	
Long Stow Goods SB	Opened	4.1883-11.1885	
Replacement box	Opened	11.8.1891	
Box ceased to be a block post	... ...	13.3.1955	
LONG STOW GOODS DEPOT	Opened	21.2.1866	
***	Closed	1.6.1953	
Grafham SB	Opened	9.6.1891	
***	Closed	1955	?
GRAFFHAM	OG	21.2.1866	
***	OP	1.3.1866	
Altered to GRAFHAM	... ...	1.2.1877	
***	CP&G	15.6.1959	
BRAMPTON	OG	21.2.1866	
***	OP	1.3.1866	
Altered to BUCKDEN	... ...	1.2.1868	
***	CP&G	15.6.1959	
Buckden Station SB	Open before	1884	
***	Closed	1955	?
HUNTINGDON: new Great Eastern station	OP	1.5.1883	
HUNTINGDON altered to HUNTINGDON EAST	... ...	1.7.1923	
HUNTINGDON EAST	CP(All)	18.9.1959	
Huntingdon East Junction SB	Opened	....	
	Closed	....	

Between Huntingdon Junction and St Ives the Midland Railway possessed running powers over the Great Northern & Great Eastern Joint line and between St Ives and Cambridge the Midland Railway possessed running powers over the Great Eastern line.

Cambridge Midland Goods Depot

Powers: Midland Railway (Additional Powers) Act 1884,
Midland Railway Act 1909

CAMBRIDGE MILL ROAD GOODS (Midland)	Opened	6.1883
***	Closed	W.War I
***	Re-opened	16.8.1921
***	Closed	1.7.1971
Cambridge Midland engine shed	Opened	....
***	Closed	....

KETTERING IRONSTONE BRANCHES

Powers: Midland Railway (New Works Etc) Act 1877 (Acquisition of Cransley Branch)
Midland Railway Act 1895 (Acquisition of Cransley Branch Extension Line)

Cransley branch	OG	19.2.1877
This branch was worked by train staff without tickets.		
Cransley Sidings SB	Opened	19.2.1877 ?
***	Closed	9.9.1893
Loddington branch (from the Cransley branch)	OG	28.1.1893
This branch - worked by pilot guard - had been a tramway before it was taken over by the Midland Railway.		
Kettering to Loddington became one section worked by train staff without tickets	... ...	11.9.1893
Kettering to Loddington branch made a through siding	... ...	6.5.1963
Cransley Jcn to Loddington	Tfc ceased	6.1963
***	t.o.u.	22.6.1970
Branch severed at 1m 593yds and Cransley Ironworks Sidings GF t.o.u.	... ...	23.6.1970
Branch severed at 1m 475yds	... ...	26.5.1971
Remainder of branch altered from through siding to one train working	... ...	3.9.1972
Remainder of the line (G. Cohen & Sons Ltd's Siding)	t.o.u.	1.10.1980

KETTERING & MANTON LINE

Powers: Midland Railway (Additional Powers) Act 1874

Glendon South Jcn to Manton Jcn	O through M	1.12.1879
***	OG	1.1.1880
***	OP	1.3.1880
***	Fast trains	1.6.1880
***	CP	1.5.1967
The line was worked by the block telegraph system from its opening.		
Glendon South Jcn: improvement of curve when junction was re-laid	... ...	14.10.1894
Kettering (to former Glendon South Jcn) to Corby North	Singled	29.11.1987
Glendon Sidings SB	Opened	1.12.1879
Replacement box	Opened	28.5.1899
Replacement box	Opened	20.9.1908
***	Closed	27.11.1983
Storefield SB	Opened	28.3.1898
***	Closed	26.7.1973
GEDDINGTON	OG	1.1.1880
***	OP	1.3.1880
***	CP&G	1.11.1948
Geddington SB	Opened	1.12.1879
***	Re-framed	13.10.1895
Replacement box	Opened	15.7.1900
***	Closed	4.10.1965
Weldon South SB	Opened	12.8.1923
Replacement box	Opened	7.3.1937
Re-named Corby South SB	... ...	....
***	Closed	7.7.1968
Weldon South to Weldon North: up and down goods lines	Into use	12.8.1923
***	t.o.u.	....
Weldon: 5 new reception sidings	Into use	8.8.1937
***	t.o.u.	....
Weldon & Corby Station SB	Opened	1.12.1879
***	Re-framed	20.10.1895
Replacement box	Opened	30.7.1905
Re-named Weldon North SB	... ...	12.8.1923
Replacement box	Opened	7.3.1937
Re-named Corby North SB	... ...	....

CORBY & COTTINGHAM	OG	1.1.1880
***	OP	1.3.1880
Altered to WELDON	... ...	1.11.1880
Altered to WELDON & CORBY	... ...	1.11.1881
Altered to CORBY & WELDON	... ...	1.5.1937
Altered to CORBY	... ...	4.3.1957
***	CP	18.4.1966
***	RO(P)	13.4.1987
Platform line made single dead-end spur	... ...	29.11.1987
***	C.Coal	3.1984
***	CG	3.4.1989
Lloyd's Sidings South SB	Opened	27.2.1910
***	Closed	26.11.1972
Lloyd's Sidings SB	Opened	1883
***	Re-framed	27.10.1895
Re-named Lloyd's Sidings North SB	... ...	1897
Replacement box	Opened	29.11.1903
Replacement box	Opened	13.1.1935
***	Closed	27.6.1981
Corby BSC Works branch taken over by British Railways	... ...	26.7.1981
Gretton up-line IBS	Into use	18.11.1923
***	t.o.u.	....
Gretton Station SB	Opened	1.12.1879
***	Re-framed	3.11.1895
Replacement box	Opened	13.1.1901
***	Closed	12.2.1967
GRETTON	OG	1.1.1880
***	OP	1.3.1880
***	CG	6.4.1964
***	CP	18.4.1966
HARRINGWORTH	OG	1.1.1880
***	OP	1.3.1880
***	CP&G	1.11.1948
Harringworth SB	Opened	1.12.1879
***	Re-framed	3.11.1895
Replacement box	Opened	1906
Replacement box	Opened	1928 ?
Harringworth to Manton: temporary single-line working	Commenced	8.1.1972
***	Ceased	5.2.1972
Glaston IBS	Into use	19.1.1941
Down-line IBS	t.o.u.	11.7.1988
Wing Sidings SB	Opened	1.12.1879
Replacement box	Opened	22.10.1905
Replacement box	Opened	11.11.1923
***	Closed	12.2.1967
Wing Sidings: up and down goods lines	Into use	11.11.1923
***	t.o.u. after	1960
Manton South SB	Opened	1.12.1879
Replacement box	Opened	4.4.1886
Replacement box	Opened	7.10.1924
Box closed and up-line IBS provided in lieu	... ...	22.1.1933
***	t.o.u.	....
Manton Jcn: Kettering line made the "straight" line	... ...	4.4.1886
Kettering line became the diverging line again	... ...	24.7.1988

III. THE MIDLAND COUNTIES

MIDLAND COUNTIES RAILWAY: RUGBY TO DERBY

The Midland Counties Railway was amalgamated with the North Midland Railway and the Birmingham & Derby Junction Railway as the Midland Railway on and from 10 May 1844.

Powers: Midland Counties Railway Act 1836
Midland Railway (Additional Powers) Act 1872
(Wigston & Knighton Widening - land powers only)
Midland Railway (Additional Powers) Act 1890 & Midland Railway Act 1892
(Knighton second tunnel - land powers only)
Midland Railway (New Lines and Additional Powers) Act 1865
(Widening at Leicester Cemetery - land powers only)
Midland Railway Act 1889 (Leicester New Walk to London Road Widening - land powers only)
Midland Railway (Extension to Hitchin, Northampton, and Huntingdon) Act 1847
(enlargement of Leicester station)
Midland Railway Act 1899 (Leicester New Goods Branch, Nedham Street)
Midland Railway (New Lines and Additional Powers) Act 1865
(Humberstone Road Coal Depot - land powers only)
Midland Railway (Additional Powers) Act 1873 (Leicester & Trent Widening)

Rugby to Leicester	Opened	30.6.1840	
Leicester to Sawley Jcn and Long Eaton Jcn	O.Formal	4.5.1840	
***	Opened	5.5.1840	
Nottingham to Derby	O.Formal	30.5.1839	
***	Opened	4.6.1839	
The Nottingham to Derby line was single when opened. It was doubled before the opening southwards to Leicester took place.			
Rugby to Derby and Nottingham	O.Mails	17.8.1840	
***	OG	7.9.1840	
Rugby: junction between the Midland Counties and the London & Birmingham lines	Opened	17.8.1840	
Between Northampton Bridge Street station and Rugby the Midland Railway had running powers for merchandise traffic over the London & North Western line.			
At Rugby the London & North Western Railway had powers to use a portion of the station owned by the Midland company for all traffic.			
Between Rugby and Wigston Central Junction the London & North Western Railway had running powers for merchandise traffic over the Midland line.			
RUGBY: temporary Midland Counties station at north end of viaduct	Opened	30.6.1840	
***	Closed	....	
RUGBY (second station for Midland and London & North Western)	Opened	4.7.1840	
Enlargement of station	Authorized	14.8.1848	
***	Carried out	1848-1852	
Midland approach-lines	Altered	12.1882	
Old down platform	t.o.u.	5.7.1885	
RUGBY (third station): down platform	Into use	5.7.1885	
Remainder of the station	Completed	10.4.1886	
Midland trains began to use the passenger bays	... ...	6.6.1886	
***	Opened	7.6.1886	
Altered to RUGBY MIDLAND	Goods	1.7.1950	
***	Passenger	25.9.1950	
Altered to RUGBY	... ...	4.5.1970	*
RUGBY TICKET PLATFORM	Closed	8.1886	
Rugby to Ullesthorpe: block telegraph working	Introduced	1874	
Rugby to Wigston North Jcn	CP	1.1.1962	
Rugby No. 5 (AEI Sidings) to Newbold Wharf	CG(All)	3.5.1965	
Rugby engine shed	Opened	....	
***	Closed	2.4.1909	
Between about 1860 and about 1880 there were two sheds at Rugby.			
RUGBY SORTING SIDINGS	Completed by	2.1856	
***	t.o.u.	....	
Rugby SB	Open before	16.8.1877	
Re-named Midland Goods Yard SB	... ...	8.1877-4.1878	
Replacement box named Rugby Midland SB	Opened	6.6.1886	
Replacement box	Opened	29.3.1925	
***	Closed	19.4.1935	
Rugby Wharf SB	Opened	....	
Replacement box	Opened	10.12.1918	
***	Closed after	1960	

Canal Wharf Branch

Branch to the Rugby Canal Wharf at Newbold	Opened	....	
***	Closed	3.5.1965	
RUGBY WHARF altered to NEWBOLD WHARF	... ...	1939	

Newbold Wharf to Wigston South	CP&G	1.1.1962	
Willey Crossing SB	Opened	....	
***	Made BP	8.7.1935	
***	Closed	1.1.1962	

Gill's Corner Tunnel South SB	Opened	7.2.1892	
***	Closed	18.9.1892	
Gill's Corner tunnel: single-line working (re-building of tunnel)	Commenced	7.2.1892	
Double-line working	Restored	18.9.1892	
Gill's Corner Tunnel North SB	Opened	7.2.1892	
***	Closed	18.9.1892	
Ullesthorpe SB	Open before	16.8.1877	
Replacement box	Opened	1892-1901	
***	Closed	1.1.1962	
ULLESTHORPE	Opened	30.6.1840	
Altered to ULLESTHORPE FOR LUTTERWORTH		1.5.1879	*
Altered to ULLESTHORPE & LUTTERWORTH	... ...	1.8.1897	
Altered to ULLESTHORPE	... ...	1.2.1930	
***	CP&G	1.1.1962	
Ullesthorpe to Wigston South station: block telegraph working	Introduced	1875	
LEIRE HALT	OP	2.3.1925	
***	CP(All)	1.1.1962	
Broughton SB	Open before	1.11.1875	
Re-named Broughton Astley SB	... ...	1.10.1879	
Replacement box	Opened	24.6.1900	
***	Closed	1.1.1962	
Broughton Astley to Countesthorpe: single-line working	Commenced by	4.6.1913	
Double-line working	Restored by	6.8.1913	
BROUGHTON(-ASTLEY)	Opened	30.6.1840	
Altered to BROUGHTON ASTLEY	... ...	1.7.1845	
Altered to BROUGHTON	... ...	1.10.1870	*
Altered to BROUGHTON ASTLEY	... ...	15.9.1879	
***	CP&G	1.1.1962	
COUNTESTHORPE	Opened by	6.1842	
***	CP&G	1.1.1962	
Countesthorpe SB	Open before	16.8.1877	
Replacement box	Opened	1892-1901	
***	Closed	1.1.1962	
Wigston South Station SB	Open before	16.8.1877	
Replacement box	Opened	17.8.1890	
***	Closed	10.1.1965	
WIGSTON	Opened	30.6.1840	
Altered to WIGSTON SOUTH	... ...	1.10.1868	*
Replacement up platform south of the level crossing	Into use	20.7.1890	
***	CP	1.1.1962	
***	CG	2.5.1966	
Wigston South to Wigston North Jcn: block telegraph working	Intro. by	1873	
Wigston South SB to Wigston Central SB: siding (old up main line)	t.o.u.	3.7.1967	
Wigston Central Junction SB	Open before	16.8.1877	
Replacement box	Opened	18.2.1889	
***	Closed	26.11.1967	
Wigston Central Jcn to Wigston North Jcn	Closed	26.11.1967	

Between Wigston Central Junction and Wigston North Junction the London & North Western Railway had running powers for merchandise traffic over the Midland line.

Wigston (South Jcn) to Knighton South Jcn: up (through) goods line	Into use	14.6.1874
Up (local) goods line	In use by	8.2.1875
Wigston Junction SB	Opened	1857
Replacement box	Opened	1865
Replacement box	Opened	....
Re-named Wigston North Junction SB	... ...	1872
Replacement box	Opened	13.7.1890
***	Re-framed	....
***	Closed	29.6.1986

Between Wigston North Junction and the north end of the Midland stations in Leicester the London & North Western Railway had running powers for all traffic.

Leicester & Hitchin line

See page 45

Wigston North Jcn: trailing crossover between main lines to allow reversible working of both main lines	Into use	30.6.1986

The facing crossover at Wigston North Junction was provided in 1973 when the junction was remodelled.

Wigston North Jcn to London Road Jcn: block telegraph working	Introduced	1869-1870
Wigston North Jcn to Knighton South Jcn:		
up through goods line made down goods line	... ...	20.7.1890
Up local goods line designated up goods line	... ...	20.7.1890
Down goods line	t.o.u.	29.6.1986
Up goods line made up & down goods line	... ...	30.6.1986
Aylestone down-line IBS	Into use	1973
***	t.o.u. after	1975
Aylestone SB	Open before	1.11.1875
Replacement box	Opened	13.7.1890
Re-named Aylestone Junction SB	... ...	20.7.1890
***	Closed	22.7.1973

Aylestone Jcn: double junction (DPL-DGL, UGL-UPL)	Into use	20.7.1890
***	t.o.u.	22.7.1973 ?
Knighton South Junction SB	Opened	....
Replacement box	Opened	9.1874
Replacement box	Opened	20.7.1890
Box moved further away from the lines	... ...	16.4.1893
Replacement box	Opened	26.4.1936
***	Closed	29.6.1986
Knighton South Junction re-named Knighton Junction	... ...	30.6.1986
Knighton South Jcn: double junction (DGL-DPL, UPL-UGL)	Into use	....
***	t.o.u.	....
Ladder junction	Into use	....

Leicester & Burton line

See page 72

Knighton South Jcn to south end of tunnel: up and down goods lines	Opened	13.8.1893
Knighton South Jcn to Bell Lane: up and down goods lines	t.o.u.	1.6.1986
KNIGHTON SOUTH JUNCTION SIDINGS	Opened	....
***	t.o.u.	....
AYLESTONE WHARF	Opened	....
***	Closed	4.7.1966

Knighton North Curve

See page 72

Knighton North Junction SB	Open before	16.8.1877
Replacement box	Opened	28.2.1892
***	Closed	5.5.1968
Knighton second tunnel	Opened	13.8.1893
Knighton: up and down goods lines	Into use	22.10.1893
WELFORD ROAD	OP	4.11.1874
Local trains from Nuneaton (last to call)	Ceased	6.2.1918
Early morning trains had called on Wednesdays and Saturdays only at a platform serving the down line.		
Welford Road down-line IBS	Into use	1969-1972
***	t.o.u. after	1975
Welford Road Platform (north of) to Cattle Market Sidings (north of): position of the down main line	Altered	15.10.1893
Cattle Market Sidings SB	Open before	16.8.1877
Replacement box (on girders above the line)	Opened	15.10.1893
Replacement box (on up side of the line)	Opened	7.11.1915
***	Closed	27.4.1969
LEICESTER CATTLE MARKET SIDINGS	Dispensed	28.3.1872
Cattle Market Sidings to London Road Jcn: up goods line	Into use	28.5.1893
Leicester South Jcn to Bell Lane: up & down slow line	Into use	30.6.1986
Lancaster Road Bridge: main lines re-located to pass over new portion of the bridge	... ...	12.2.1893
London Road Jcn: up goods line to up passenger line crossover	Into use	28.5.1893
Down passenger line to down goods line crossover	Into use	22.10.1893
Double junction	t.o.u.	1.6.1986
London Road Junction SB (second location)	Opened	9.10.1892
Replacement box	Opened	20.12.1935
***	Closed	29.6.1986
London Road Junction SB (original box)	Open before	16.8.1877
Re-named Leicester Passenger Station South SB	... ...	9.10.1892
***	Closed	23.9.1894
The section of line between London Road Junction SB and Leicester North SB was worked as a station yard.		
London Road Jcn (old) to Leicester Goods Jcn: up and down goods lines	In use by	1.6.1858 *
LEICESTER TICKET PLATFORM	Into use	1846
***	Closed	25.5.1891
LEICESTER	Opened	5.5.1840
Second platform	Into use	1857
Suffix CAMPBELL STREET first appears in Bradshaw	... ...	1.6.1867 *
Excursion platform	In use by	1.10.1868 *
New booking and parcels offices opened and name altered to LEICESTER LONDON ROAD	... ...	12.6.1892
Replacement goods lines past the station	Into use	9.10.1892
Suffix LONDON ROAD first appears in Bradshaw	... ...	1.12.1893 *
Rebuilding seems to have been completed about the end of 1895.		
Station made "closed" for tickets	... ...	1.2.1918
New parcels office	Opened	1925
Swain Street bridge entrance	Closed	c.1933
Altered to LEICESTER	... ...	4.5.1970
Demolition of overall roof	During	1975
Rebuilding works	Commenced	24.10.1977
New buildings on up island platform	Opened	6.11.1979
New buildings on down island platform	Opened	....
Old booking office	Closed	13.5.1985
New booking office and travel centre	Into use	11.5.1986
***	Off. opened	30.5.1986

Leicester Passenger Station West SB	Opened	2.10.1892
Replacement box	Opened	13.8.1893
***	Closed	28.6.1970
Leicester Passenger Station SB	Open before	16.8.1877
Re-named Leicester Passenger Station East SB	... ...	2.10.1892
Replacement box	Opened	13.8.1893
Box moved a little to the north	... ...	6.5.1894
Replacement box	Opened	23.9.1894
***	Closed	28.6.1970
Leicester station ceased to be signalled as a terminal station	... ...	28.6.1970
Leicester North: up passenger line to up goods line crossover	In use before	1890
***	t.o.u.	1.6.1986
Leicester Goods Junction SB	Opened	....
Re-named Leicester North SB	Before	16.8.1877
Replacement box	Opened	14.5.1911
***	Re-framed	....
***	Closed	29.6.1986
LEICESTER N.C.L. SIDING	Closed by	18.4.1985
Leicester North Jcn: new crossovers	Into use	30.6.1986
Leicester North to Humberstone Road: block telegraph working	Introduced	1875
Leicester North to Bell Lane: goods lines made absolute block	... ...	4.2.1984
Up & down goods line (down side)	Into use	30.6.1986
Leicester Goods Jcn to Syston North Jcn: up goods line	Into use	12.7.1874
Leicester Goods Jcn to Humberstone Road: down goods line	Into use	21.2.1875
LEICESTER COAL WHARF	Opened	3.1841
***	Closed	....
LEICESTER LONDON & NORTH WESTERN RAILWAY GOODS DEPOT, and branch	Opened	18.11.1872
LEICESTER: Sussex Street (London & North Western) Goods Shed	Opened	8.1897
Between the junction of the London & North Western goods branch in Leicester and Trent Station South Junction the London & North Western Railway had running powers for merchandise traffic over the Midland line.		
Leicester: connection from the reception line to the LNWR yard and Queen Street goods yard	Recovered	16.11.1986
There was no rail access to Queen Street depot from December 1984.		
Leicester PSB:		
1. Glendon North Jcn (exclusive) to Syston South Jcn (exclusive)	Into use	27-30.6.1986
2. Syston South Jcn to Loughborough	Into use	11-13.4.1987
3. Irchester South SB to Glendon North Junction SB / Corby	Into use	5-7.12.1987
Leicester engine shed	Opened	1840
Leicester No. 2 engine shed	Opened	Mid-1850s
Leicester No. 3 engine shed	Opened	1893
Leicester sheds replaced by a single large roundhouse	... ...	1945
***	Closed	13.6.1966
Engine Shed SB	Opened	1875
Re-named Engine Shed Sidings SB	... ...	8.1877-4.1878
***	Alt.levers	12.6.1887
Replacement box	Opened	18.9.1898
***	Closed	29.12.1968
Engine Shed Sidings to Bell Lane: position of goods lines altered	... ...	7.7.1918
Engine Shed Sidings to Humberstone Road Sidings: second down goods line	Into use	30.12.1888
Engine Shed Sidings to Bell Lane: second down goods line made a siding	... ...	3.7.1943
Bell Lane: down goods line to down passenger line crossover	Into use	1874-1875
***	t.o.u.	....
Bell Lane SB	Open before	16.8.1877
Replacement box	Opened	27.9.1891
***	Re-framed	1959
***	Closed	29.6.1986
BELL LANE SIDINGS	Opened	....
***	t.o.u.	....
Bell Lane to Humberstone Road Jcn: goods lines worked telegraph bell	... ...	22.10.1893
Bell Lane to Humberstone Road Sidings: second down goods line and No. 3 siding made reception lines	... ...	3.7.1943
Nos. 1 and 2 reception lines	t.o.u.	....
Bell Lane to Syston South Jcn: down goods line taken out of use and up goods line made up & down slow line	... ...	....
LEICESTER NEDHAM STREET DEPOT	Opened	....
Closed for siding-to-siding traffic	... ...	28.3.1983
Sidings 5, 6, and 7	t.o.u. by	30.10.1987
LEICESTER SYSTON STREET GOODS DEPOT	Opened	....
***	CG	6.2.1967
***	RO(G)	....
***	CG	30.6.1980
HUMBERSTONE ROAD	OP	1.7.1875
***	OG before	1890
***	CG before	1925
***	CP	4.3.1968
Humberstone Road Sidings SB (second box) (not a block post)	Opened	30.12.1888
***	Closed	2.10.1949

HUMBERSTONE ROAD SIDINGS	Opened	....
Remodelled in stages	... 27.11.1984-27.1.1985	
Sidings 15, 16, and 17	t.o.u. by	4.11.1987
Remaining sidings	t.o.u.	....
Humberstone Road Sidings: reception line	Into use	3.7.1943
***	t.o.u.	....
Humberstone Road New Wharf SB (not a block post)	Opened	....
***	Re-framed	7.2.1913
***	Closed	....
Humberstone Road New Wharf GF	Into use	7.2.1913
***	t.o.u.	10.9.1967
Humberstone Road to Trent: block telegraph working	Introduced	1870
Humberstone Road to Sileby: down goods line	Into use	4.10.1874
Humberstone Road Sidings SB (first box)	Open before	16.8.1877
Replacement box named Humberstone Road Junction SB	Opened	30.12.1888
***	Re-framed	26.1.1902
***	Raised	22.2.1903
***	Closed	29.9.1979
Humberstone Road Jcn with the Great Northern Railway	Approved	7.8.1883
***	Abandoned	8.6.1908
***	Removed	12.7.1908
***	Restored	31.5.1964
***	Closed	1.1.1969
The junction between the goods lines and the Great Northern line was never opened to traffic.		
Thurmaston SB	Opened	1870
Replacement box	Opened	31.12.1881
Replacement box	Opened	9.1.1898
Box closed and up and down IBS provided in lieu	... ...	2.9.1973
***	t.o.u.	....
Thurmaston to Syston South Jcn: down goods line working by telegraph bell instead of by block telegraph	Commenced	28.2.1909
Wilcox Siding SB	Opened	1875
Replacement box	Opened	30.1.1898
***	Closed	23.10.1966
SYSTON	Opened	5.5.1840
New passenger station	Opened	....
***	CP&G	4.3.1968
Syston Junction SB	Opened	1846
Replacement box named Syston South Junction SB	Open before	12.1873
Replacement box	Opened	6.3.1887
***	Raised	9.9.1894
Replacement box	Opened	26.11.1911
***	Closed	11. 4.1987
Syston South Jcn: re-modelled layout	Into use	7.7.1974

Syston & Peterborough line

See page 79

Syston North Junction SB	Open before	12.1873
Replacement box	Opened	c.10.1891
***	Re-framed	24.7.1910
***	Closed	11.4.1987

Syston North Curve

See page 79

Syston North Jcn to Cossington Gate: up goods line	Into use	8.3.1874
Syston North Jcn to Sileby: replacement up goods line	Into use	2.8.1874
Syston North Jcn: double junction (DGL-DPL, UPL-UGL)	Into use	24.7.1910
***	t.o.u.	11.4.1987
COSSINGTON GATE	Opened	1.12.1845
***	CP(All)	29.9.1873
Cossington Gate to Barrow Jcn: up goods line	Into use	16.11.1873
SILEBY	Opened	5.5.1840
***	CG	6.4.1964
***	CP	4.3.1968
Sileby SB	Open before	16.8.1877
Replacement box	Opened	18.12.1898
***	Re-framed	11.2.1906
***	Closed	11.4.1987
Sileby to Ratcliffe Jcn: down goods line	Into use	....
Sileby: up goods line to up passenger line crossover	Into use	11.2.1906
***	t.o.u.	....
Sileby: ladder junction (south end in up slow line)	Into use	....
Barrow Lime Works SB	Opened	1860
Replacement box	Opened	....
Replacement box	Opened	13.9.1891
***	Closed	6.12.1908

Mount Sorrel Junction SB	Opened	1861
Box ceased to signal the goods lines	... ...	6.12.1908
Replacement box	Opened	9.5.1909
Box closed and ground frame provided in lieu	... ...	22.11.1964
***	t.o.u.	15.2.1987
Mountsorrel Jcn with Mount Sorrel Company's line	Opened	1861
***	Closed	1977
MOUNT SORREL	OG before	1872
***	Closed	....
BARROW	Opened	5.5.1840
Altered to BARROW-ON-SOAR	... ...	1.5.1871 *
Altered to BARROW-ON-SOAR & QUORN	... ...	1.7.1899 *
***	CG	6.4.1964
***	CP	4.3.1968
Barrow-on-Soar SB	Open before	16.8.1877
Replacement box	Opened	9.11.1919
Box closed and up and down IBS provided in lieu	... ...	14.10.1973
***	t.o.u.	....
Barrow Jcn to Hathern: up goods line	Into use	9.8.1874
Soar Bridge SB (at bridge No. 64)	Opened	18.4.1926
***	Closed	18.7.1926

Loughborough Chord

Powers: British Railways Act 1971

Spur to the former Great Central line	OG	8.4.1974

Loughborough Goods Lines SB	Opened	17.2.1895
***	Closed	13.11.1896
Loughborough South SB	Open before	16.8.1877
***	Closed	31.3.1879
LOUGHBOROUGH	Opened	5.5.1840
Old goods yard (south of the station)	Closed	31.3.1879
Replacement station on north side of road bridge	Opened	13.5.1872
New goods depot	Opened	1875
Altered to LOUGHBOROUGH TOWN	... ...	1923
Altered to LOUGHBOROUGH MIDLAND	... ...	9.7.1923
Altered to LOUGHBOROUGH	... ...	4.5.1970
***	CG	1.5.1972
Loughborough North SB	Open before	16.8.1877
Re-named Loughborough SB	... ...	31.3.1879
Replacement box	Opened	19.6.1892
***	Re-framed	7.11.1920
***	Closed	11.4.1987
Loughborough: ladder junction (south end in down fast line)	Into use	....
Loughborough (exc) to Ratcliffe Jcn: track circuits altered in order to re-classify the goods lines as slow lines	... ...	12.4.1987
Loughborough (Hathern) troughs	Into use	18.4.1904
Indicators to mark the start	Into use	27.5.1907
Troughs taken out of use	... ...	....
These indicators were the first: on 23 August 1915 similar ones were brought into use for the troughs at Oakley, Melton, Tamworth, and Hawes Junction.		
Soar Bridge SB (at bridge No. 81)	Opened	25.2.1923
***	Closed	27.5.1923
Hathern South: double junction (DGL-DPL, UPL-UGL)	Into use	25.6.1911
***	t.o.u.	....
Hathern South SB	Open before	16.8.1877
Replacement box	Opened	8.5.1892
***	Alt.levers	25.6.1911
Re-named Hathern SB	... ...	7.7.1958
***	Closed	28.9.1969
HATHERN	Opened	17.2.1868
***	CP	1.1.1960
***	CG	4.1.1960
Hathern North SB	Open before	1.11.1875
***	Closed by	16.8.1877
Hathern Brick Company's SB	Open before	1.10.1876
***	Closed	10.7.1898
It is possible that Hathern North SB and Hathern Brick Company's SB were the same location.		
Hathern Brick & Tile Company's Siding GF	t.o.u.	19.8.1928
Hathern to Kegworth: up goods line	Into use	31.8.1873
KEGWORTH	Opened	5.5.1840
***	CG	5.7.1965
***	CP	4.3.1968
Kegworth SB	Opened	1868
Replacement box	Opened	1873
Replacement box	Opened	19.6.1892
***	Closed	28.9.1969
Kegworth: Lord Belper's Branch Junction	Opened	1883-1890
***	Closed	8.1.1972
Kegworth: new up goods line	Into use	31.10.1873

Kegworth to Ratcliffe Jcn: up goods line	Into use	12.1.1873
Ratcliffe (South) Jcn: new connection (for the up goods line)	Dispensed	9.1.1873
Junction with up and down goods lines	Dispensed	3.12.1874
Old junction removed and new ones laid in	... ...	23.7.1893
Double junction (DGL-DPL, UPL-UGL)	Into use	13.8.1893
Ratcliffe Sidings SB	Open before	3.1872
Re-named Ratcliffe Junction SB	... ...	1873
Replacement box	Opened	23.7.1893
***	Closed	28.9.1969
Ratcliffe (North) Jcn: up goods line to up passenger line crossover	Into use	13.8.1893
Down passenger line to down goods line crossover	Into use	3.2.1901
Double junction	t.o.u.	2.7.1989
Ratcliffe (North) Jcn: power station connections	Into use	8.10.1967
South ground frame (completing the circle)	Into use	24.12.1967
Ratcliffe Jcn to Trent Jcn: up and down goods lines	Opened	13.8.1893
This widening included the second Red Hill tunnel.		
Trent Temporary Junction SB (in place of Trent Junction SB)	Opened	28.9.1902
***	Closed	11.1.1903
Trent Junction SB	Open before	1861
Replacement box	Opened	....
Replacement box	Opened	13.8.1893
***	Re-framed	3.3.1901
***	Closed	28.9.1969
Trent to Spondon Jcn: block telegraph working	Introduced	1869
Trent Jcn to Sheet Stores Jcn	CP	1.5.1862 *
***	RO(P)	1.5.1876 *
Trent Jcn to Sheet Stores Jcn: down goods line	Into use	5.11.1893
Sheet Stores Junction SB	Open before	1868
Replacement box	Opened	....
Replacement box	Opened	1.6.1890
***	Raised	5.6.1904
***	Re-framed	16.3.1919
***	Closed	28.9.1969

Sheet Stores or Gas Works Curve

See page 69

Sawley & Weston line

See page 218

SHEET STORES (TRENT) GOODS DEPOT	Opened	1879
***	Closed	5.1927
Sawley Junction SB	Opened	1846
Replacement box	Opened	1859
Replacement box	Opened	....
Replacement box	Opened	19.7.1891
***	Closed	28.9.1969

Trent North Curve

See page 69

SAWLEY JUNCTION	OP	3.12.1888
Altered to SAWLEY JUNCTION FOR LONG EATON	... ...	1.3.1933
Altered to LONG EATON	... ...	6.5.1968
Sawley Station SB	Open before	16.8.1877
Replacement box	Opened	19.7.1896
Box closed and AHBs provided in lieu	... ...	29.1.1967
BREASTON	Opened	4.6.1839
Altered to SAWLEY	By	30.6.1840
***	CP	1.12.1930
Excursion trains continued to call at least until 1936.		
Draycott SB	Opened	1873
Replacement box	Opened	9.2.1891
***	Closed	28.9.1969
DRAYCOTT	Opened	1.4.1852 *
Altered to DRAYCOTT & BREASTON	... ...	7.8.1939
***	CG	5.7.1965
***	CP	14.2.1966
BORROWASH	Opened	4.6.1839
Replacement station on the west side of the road bridge	Opened	1.5.1871
Altered to BORROWASH FOR OCKBROOK	... ...	1.5.1898 *
Altered to BORROWASH	... ...	1.4.1904 *
***	CG	4.1.1965
***	CP	14.2.1966
Borrowash SB	Open before	1.11.1875
Replacement box	Opened	15.5.1892
***	Closed	6.6.1965
SPONDON	Opened	11.11.1839
Bay platform	Into use	23.6.1918
***	CG	4.1.1965
Bay-line connection	Removed	23.3.1969 ?

Spondon Station SB	Open before	16.8.1877
Replacement box	Opened	15.7.1889
Replacement box	Opened	26.5.1918
Box made a shunting frame and gate box	... ...	13.7.1969
***	t.o.u.	19.12.1988
Spondon Station to Spondon Jcn: down goods line	Into use	1.12.1918
Spondon Junction SB	Opened	1869
Replacement box	Opened	18.12.1887
Box slightly moved	... ...	18.6.1893
Replacement box	Opened	23.6.1918
***	Closed	18.5.1969
Spondon (Loom's Sidings) to Chaddesden	Closed	5.5.1969

Litchurch Loop
See page 68

Spondon Jcn to Chaddesden South Jcn: block telegraph working	Intro. by	1873
Spondon Jcn to Derby Jcn	CP	1.12.1867 *
***	RO(P)	1.2.1870 *
***	CP	7.10.1968
Spondon Jcn to Chaddesden South Jcn: main-line curves	Altered	12.6.1904
Chaddesden Coal Stage SB	Open before	1.11.1875
***	Closed by	16.8.1877
Engine Turntable Sidings SB	Open before	16.8.1877
Replacement box	Opened	3.7.1892
Replacement box	Opened	22.2.1925
***	Closed	9.10.1968
These two signalboxes may have been one and the same location.		
Chaddesden South Junction SB	Open before	16.8.1877
Replacement box	Opened	24.3.1907
Box made a shunting frame	... ...	4.5.1969
***	t.o.u.	17.7.1977
Chaddesden South Jcn to Chaddesden Centre: block telegraph working	Introduced	1873
Chaddesden South Jcn to Derby Jcn: down goods line (up side)	In use by	1.10.1876
Chaddesden South Jcn to Derby Jcn: section of line made a siding	... ...	13.7.1969
CHADDESDEN SIDINGS:		
Original sidings	Opened	....
(Additional ?) goods sidings	Opened	2.12.1872
New sidings (Chaddesden down marshalling sidings)	Opened	1.2.1901
Sidings ceased to be a marshalling yard	... ...	4.5.1969
Chaddesden Bank arrival lines	t.o.u.	6.3.1972
Down marshalling sidings	t.o.u.	1977
Storage sidings designated Engineer's tip sidings	... ...	29.5.1982
Engineer's tip sidings	t.o.u. by	3.6.1988
Chaddesden Sidings Centre SB	Open before	16.8.1877
Replacement box	Opened	13.11.1892
***	Slued	16.6.1901
***	Re-framed	6.10.1901
***	Closed	2.10.1904
Chaddesden Centre to Derby Jcn: block telegraph working	Introduced	1874
Chaddesden Sidings No. 2 SB	Opened	....
Replacement box	Opened	2.10.1904
***	Closed	6.11.1955
Chaddesden Sidings No. 1 SB	Opened	12.1888-8.1893
***	Re-framed	3.5.1896
Replacement box	Opened	8.5.1905
Box closed and ground frame provided in lieu	... ...	21.11.1909
***	t.o.u.	....
Chaddesden: goods lines	Extended	20.4.1873

By October 1876 there was a down goods line on the up side between Chaddesden South Junction and Derby South Junction and an up goods line between Chaddesden No. 1 and Derby South Junction. It has not been possible to trace exactly the development of the goods lines through the Chaddesden area, but it appears that an additional line of some sort was already in use by February 1866 and that this was gradually extended. The work in April 1873 seems to have involved the extension of the goods lines to St Mary's Junction.

Derby South Junction SB	Opened	1865
Replacement box	Opened	....
Replacement box	Opened	22.5.1892
***	Lifted	22.10.1922
Box made a shunting frame	... ...	4.5.1969
***	t.o.u. by	7.1969
Derby South Jcn to Derby Jcn: down goods line	In use by	1.5.1868 *
Working of the down goods line by bell	Commenced	28.7.1895
***	Singled	4.5.1969
DERBY (temporary Midland Counties Railway station)	Opened	4.6.1839
***	Closed	11.5.1840

DERBY - see SECTION V (North Midland Railway)

Derby North Curve or Avoiding Line

Powers: North Midland Railway Act 1836 (Land Powers only)

Derby South Jcn to Derby North Jcn	OG	....
***	OP	1.10.1846
***	CP	....
***	RO(P)	1.6.1855 *
Through goods line (up side)	In use by	1.9.1866 *
***	CP	....
***	RO(P)	1.7.1884 *
***	CP	1.4.1904 *
***	RO(P)	1.7.1904 *
***	CP	1.1.1917 *
***	RO(P)	4.7.1960
***	CP	18.4.1966
Up and down passenger lines	t.o.u.	17.11.1968
Up and down goods lines	t.o.u.	4.5.1969
***	CG(All)	5.5.1969
Derby South Jcn to St Mary's Jcn: up goods line	In use by	1.1.1869 *
Down goods line (up side)	In use by	1.9.1873 *
The original up through goods line most probably became the new down goods line round the curve from Derby South Junction.		

Litchurch & Spondon curve

This section of line was also known as the **Litchurch Loop** or the **Derby Curve** or the **Spondon Curve**.

Powers: Midland Railway (New Lines and Additional Powers) Act 1865 (Spondon end)
Midland Railway (Branches Etc) Act 1866 (Derby end)

Spondon Jcn to Derby London Road Jcn	Opened	27.6.1867
Deadman's Lane end of new engine shed to Engine Sidings No. 2 SB: locomotive lines	Into use	13.4.1890
Deadman's Lane to Engine Sidings No. 2 SF: up locomotive line recovered and down locomotive line re-named pilot line	By	13.2.1987
Gas Works Crossing SB	Open before	16.8.1877
***	Closed	4.1878-2.1879
Way & Works SB	Opened	4.1878-2.1879
Replacement box	Opened	15.6.1890
Replacement box	Opened	2.4.1905
***	Re-framed	c.1932
***	Closed	13.7.1969
It is possible that Gas Works Crossing SB and Way & Works SB were the same location.		
Way & Works SB to London Road Jcn: up and down intermediate lines	Into use	13.4.1890
Derby PSB:		
1. Clay Mills to Tamworth (exc) / Alrewas (exc) / Moira West Jcn (exc)	Into use	14-16.6.1969
2. London Road Jcn (exc) to Repton / Egginton Jcn (exc) / Back Lane Level Crossing (exc)	Into use	28-30.6.1969
3. Draycott (exc) to London Road Jcn to Stretton (exc)	Into use	12-14.7.1969
DERBY LONDON ROAD TICKET PLATFORM	Closed	1.12.1900
DERBY - see SECTION V (North Midland Railway)		

MIDLAND COUNTIES RAILWAY: TRENT JCN/SAWLEY JCN TO NOTTINGHAM

Powers: Midland Counties Railway Act 1836
Midland Railway Act 1899 (Trent & Toton Lines)
Midland Railway Act 1892 (Widening at Trent)
Midland Railway (Rowsley and Buxton) Act 1860 (Trent Station - Land Powers only)
Midland Railway Act 1891 (Widening at Lenton)
Midland Railway (New Lines and Additional Powers) Act 1865 (Alteration of levels at Nottingham)
Midland Railway Act 1897 (Widening at Nottingham)
Midland Railway (Nottingham and Saxby Lines) Act 1872 (Nottingham Goods Lines - Land Powers only)
Midland Railway (Additional Powers) Act 1879 (Nottingham: widening canal bridge)

(Derby to) Sawley Junction to Nottingham	Opened	4.6.1839
The Derby to Nottingham line was single when first opened.		
Trent Jcn to Long Eaton Jcn	O.Formal	4.5.1840
***	Opened	5.5.1840
Trent Jcn: down goods line to second down goods line crossover	Into use	2.6.1901
Down goods line to down passenger line crossover	Into use	13.8.1893
Up passenger line to up goods line crossover	Into use	....

Trent Jcn to Trent Station South Jcn: block telegraph working	Introduced	1868–1869
Down goods line (down side)	Into use	13.8.1893
Down-side down goods line designated second down goods line and first down goods line on the up side brought into use	... ...	2.6.1901
Second down goods line	t.o.u.	26.5.1968
Trent High Level Goods Lines (SEE SECTION IV)	Into use	2.6.1901
High level goods lines designated passenger lines	... ...	19.2.1984
Trent Jcn to Trent Station North Jcn: up goods line	In use by	1.9.1870 *
Trent Station South Junction SB	Opened	1862
Replacement box	Opened	....
***	New top	4.10.1891
***	Alt.levers	27.12.1891
***	Re-framed	10.12.1893
Box ceased to signal the high level goods lines	... ...	3.6.1917
***	Closed	26.5.1968

Sheet Stores Curve or Gas Works Curve

Powers: Midland Railway (Rowsley and Buxton) Act 1860

Trent Station South Jcn to Sheet Stores Jcn	Opened	1.5.1862
Trent Station South Jcn: connection from line from Sheet Stores Jcn to No. 1 down passenger line	t.o.u.	9.5.1968

The London & North Western Railway had running powers for merchandise traffic over the Sheet Stores Curve as part of a running powers route between Stenson Junction and Nottingham.

The North Staffordshire Railway had running powers over the Sheet Stores Curve as part of a running powers route between Stenson Junction and Nottingham.

Trent Station South Jcn: connection from up main line from Sheet Stores Junction to down outside line to allow direct running	Into use	3.6.1917
Connection from up goods line from Long Eaton Junction to up goods line from Meadow Lane Junction	t.o.u.	30.3.1903
Crossover between up and down goods lines	t.o.u.	30.3.1903
Trent Stations South Jcn to Trent Station North Jcn: permissive working on first up and down passenger lines and absolute block working on the second and third passenger lines	Commenced	28.4.1940
Revised layout after removal of station	Into use	1969
Further revision of layout	Into use	21.4.1984

Between Trent Station South Junction and Sneinton Junction the London & North Western Railway possessed running powers for merchandise traffic over the Midland line.

Between Trent Station South Junction and Sneinton Junction the North Staffordshire Railway possessed running powers over the Midland line as part of a running powers route between Stenson Junction and Nottingham.

TRENT	OP	1.5.1862
Permissive block working on first up and down lines	Commenced	28.4.1940
Absolute block working on second and third up and down lines	Commenced	28.4.1940
Trent station was worked as a station yard prior to 28 April 1940.		
Second up passenger line	t.o.u.	18.11.1962
Second down passenger line	t.o.u.	27.10.1963
***	CP(All)	1.1.1968
First up passenger line	t.o.u.	26.5.1968
Trent Station North Junction SB	Opened	1862
Replacement box	Opened	....
Replacement box	Opened	1884–1886
***	Alt.levers	27.12.1891
***	Alt.levers	22.10.1893
***	Closed	28.9.1969

Trent North Curve

Powers: Midland Railway (Rowsley and Buxton) Act 1860 (Land Powers only)

Trent Station North Jcn to Sawley Jcn	Opened	1.5.1862
***	CP(All)	6.3.1967
***	t.o.u.	30.4.1967
***	Off. closed	6.11.1967
TRENT GIRDER YARD	Opened	....
Last siding	t.o.u.	17.7.1971

The Trent North Curve used most of the original main line between Sawley Junction and Long Eaton Junction. The section between Platt's Crossing and Long Eaton Junction was abandoned as a running line.

Trent Station North Jcn to Nottingham: block telegraph working	Introduced	1870
Trent Station North Jcn to Long Eaton Jcn: up and down goods lines	Into use	22.10.1893
Up goods line made up slow line	... ...	21.7.1968

Trent PSB:

1. Loughborough (exc) to Draycott / Meadow Lane Jcn / Attenborough Jcn / Lock Lane Level Crossing	Into use	27-29.9.1969
2a. Trowell Jcn (exc) to Tapton Jcn (exc) / Stretton / Sleights Sidings East / Blackwell East Jcn / Tibshelf East Jcn	Into use	11-13.10.1969
2b. Long Eaton Town Crossing / Toton East Jcn to Trowell Jcn, including Radford (exc) to Trowell Jcn	Into use	18-20.10.1969
3. Attenborough to Netherfield Jcn / Lincoln Street Crossing	Into use	6-8.12.1969
Long Eaton Junction SB	Opened	1864
Replacement box	Opened	....
Replacement box	Opened	22.10.1893
Box made a shunting frame named Meadow Lane Crossing SF	... ...	28.9.1969
***	Closed	16.7.1978
Crossing controlled by CCTV from Trent PSB	... ...	3.12.1978
LONG EATON	Opened	4.6.1839
Altered to LONG EATON JUNCTION	... ...	6.9.1847 ?
***	CP(All)	1.5.1862
Attenborough Junction SB	Opened	30.9.1900
***	Closed	28.9.1969
CHILWELL SIDINGS: workmen's service	Introduced	....
***	Withdrawn	4.11.1963
Attenborough Station SB	Opened	c.1871
Replacement box	Opened	4.2.1894
Box made a shunting frame for the level crossing only	... ...	7.12.1969
Shunting frame closed and crossing controlled from Trent PSB	... ...	27.6.1982
ATTENBOROUGH GATE	OP	1.12.1856 *
***	CP(All)	1.11.1858 *
ATTENBOROUGH (on the same site)	OP	1.9.1864 ?
***	OG	1.2.1916
Altered to CHILWELL	... ...	19.4.1937
Altered to ATTENBOROUGH	... ...	27.9.1937
***	CG	....
BEESTON	Opened	4.6.1839
***	CG	29.12.1969
Beeston Station SB	Opened	c.1871
Replacement box	Opened	20.9.1891
***	Closed	7.12.1969
Beeston Station to south end of Beeston Sidings: up goods line	Into use	28.9.1884
Up goods line cut and made a siding	... ...	5.3.1967
Beeston Sidings South Junction SB	Opened	1875
Replacement box	Opened	10.11.1895
Replacement box named Beeston South Junction SB	Opened	21.9.1930
***	Closed	7.12.1969
Beeston South Jcn: up goods line to up passenger line crossover	Into use	....
***	t.o.u.	....
BEESTON SIDINGS	Opened	15.4.1875
***	Closed	....
Beeston Sidings south end to north end: up and down goods lines	Into use	11.1874-11.1875
Beeston Sidings: goods line from north end to south end (i.e. up?)	Into use	21.2.1875
7 new sidings	Into use	12.4.1875
Second up goods line	Into use	12.6.1876
New sidings	Into use	2.10.1876
Beeston Sidings No. 1 SB	Opened	....
***	Closed by	1937
Beeston Sidings No. 2 SB	Opened	....
Replacement box	Opened	2.5.1893
Replacement box	Opened	2.9.1924
***	Closed	29.8.1965
Beeston Sidings No. 3 SB	Opened	....
Replacement box	Opened	30.10.1921
***	Closed	21.9.1930 ?
***	C. temp.	24.5.1931 ?
Beeston Sidings No. 4 SB	Opened	....
Replacement box	Opened	22.11.1909
Replacement box	Opened	28.10.1923
***	Closed by	1937
Beeston Sidings No. 5 SB	Opened	....
Replacement box	Opened	23.9.1895
***	Closed	30.10.1921
Beeston Sidings No. 6 SB	Opened	....
***	Closed	28.10.1923
Beeston Sidings No. 7 SB	Opened	....
Replacement box	Opened	22.11.1909
***	Closed by	1937
Beeston Sidings No. 8 SB	Opened	....
Replacement box	Opened	22.11.1909
***	Closed by	1937
BEESTON FREIGHTLINER TERMINAL and controlling ground frame	Opened	29.6.1969
Control taken over by Trent PSB	... ...	4.10.1970
***	Closed	6.4.1987

Beeston Sidings North Junction SB	Opened	1875
Replacement box	Opened	22.2.1891
Replacement box	Opened	17.6.1894
Replacement box named Beeston North Junction SB	Opened	21.9.1930
***	Closed	7.12.1969
Beeston Sidings North Jcn:		
up goods line to up passenger line crossover	Into use	17.6.1894
Second down goods line to down passenger line to down goods line crossover	Into use	17.6.1894
Down goods line to down goods line connection	Into use	17.6.1894
Down goods line to down passenger line crossover	Into use	17.6.1894
Down goods line to second down goods line crossover	Into use	17.6.1894
Second down goods line to Lenton Curve connection	Into use	....
Beeston Sidings North Jcn to Lenton South Jcn: up and down goods lines	Into use	17.6.1894
Beeston Sidings North to Lenton: extension of existing down goods line from Beeston South as a second down goods line	Into use	17.6.1894
Beeston North Jcn to Mansfield Jcn:		
up main line made up & down main line	... ...	30.9.1984
Lenton South Junction SB	Opened	1.1870
Replacement box	Opened	1880
Replacement box	Opened	17.6.1894
***	Re-framed	6.5.1923
***	Closed	7.12.1969

Lenton Curve

See page 104

Lenton South Jcn: up passenger line to up goods line crossover	Into use	17.6.1894
Lenton South Junction: connection with the Clifton Colliery line	Opened	....
***	t.o.u.	17.5.1981
Lenton South Jcn to Mansfield Jcn: up and down goods lines	Into use	1880
Mansfield Junction SB	Open before	1866
Replacement box	Opened	28.9.1879
Replacement box	Opened	23.11.1902
Box enlarged and new frame fitted	... ...	1933
***	Closed	7.12.1969

Nottingham & Mansfield line

See page 104

Mansfield Jcn: up goods line to up passenger line crossover	Into use	....
Down passenger line to down goods line crossover	Into use	17.6.1894
Double junction (DPL-DGL, UGL-UPL)	Into use	....
Layout altered on commissioning of Trent PSB	... ...	....
Mansfield Jcn to Queen's Road Jcn: up and down goods lines (down side)	In use by	1.6.1868 *
Goods lines moved from down side of the line to the up side	... ...	28.9.1879
Mansfield Jcn to Nottingham: up goods line made up & down goods line	... ...	30.9.1984
Nottingham Goods Yard North SB	Opened	2.12.1900
Replacement box	Opened	1950-1969
***	Closed	1985
Nottingham Goods Yard West SB	Opened	7.11.1897
***	Closed	26.6.1910
Nottingham Goods Yard West SB (second box)	Opened	1950-1969
Box made Nottingham West GF	... ...	....
***	t.o.u.	23.6.1985
Lenton Permanent Way Depot GF, and all connections	t.o.u. by	24.6.1988
NOTTINGHAM NEW COAL DEPOT (at Goods Yard West)	Opened	1897
***	Closed	....
Nottingham engine shed	Opened	1839
***	Replaced	1850
Replacement shed on "The Meadows"	Opened	1868
No. 2 engine shed	Opened	1877
No. 3 engine shed	Opened	7.11.1892
All the sheds	Closed	4.1965
Nottingham Goods Yard SB	Open before	16.8.1877
***	Closed	28.9.1879
NOTTINGHAM NEW CATTLE DOCKS (at Goods Yard East)	Opened	1897
***	Closed	....
Nottingham Goods Yard East SB (not a block post)	Opened	9.5.1897
***	Closed	26.6.1910
Nottingham Goods Yard East SB (second box)	Opened	1950-1969
Box made Nottingham East GF	... ...	....
***	t.o.u.	23.6.1985
Wilford Road No. 2 SB	Opened	25.11.1894
***	Closed	24.11.1935
Wilford Road SB	Opened	24.11.1935
***	Closed	7.12.1969
Wilford Road Bridge SB	Opened	28.9.1879
Replacement box	Opened	19.6.1892
Re-named Wilford Road No. 1 SB	... ...	25.11.1894
***	Closed	24.11.1935

NOTTINGHAM NEW GOODS WAREHOUSE	Opened	13.4.1896
***	Closed	....
QUEEN'S ROAD GOODS DEPOT	Opened	1904-1910
***	Closed	3.1.1966
Queen's Road Junction SB	Open before	12.1868
***	Closed	28.9.1879
Queen's Road Jcn to London Road Jcn: up and down goods lines (up side)	In use	1.1.1866 *
Nottingham West SB	Opened	28.9.1879
***	Re-located	1897
Replacement box	Opened	26.10.1902
***	Re-framed	16.8.1903
***	Closed	7.12.1969
Nottingham West Temporary SB	Opened	12.10.1902
***	Re-framed	26.10.1902
Replacement box	Opened	10.1.1904
***	Closed	24.4.1904
NOTTINGHAM WEST TICKET PLATFORM	Closed	....
Carrington Street bridge to London Road Jcn: replacement goods lines	Into use	14.9.1902
NOTTINGHAM	Opened	4.6.1839
Original terminal station west of the road closed and new through station opened	... ...	22.5.1848
Replacement goods lines through the station	Into use	14.9.1902
Carrington Street bridge buildings	Opened	17.1.1904
All track-work in new station	Completed	25.9.1904
Station made "closed" for tickets	... ...	12.2.1917
Altered to NOTTINGHAM CITY	... ...	25.9.1950
Altered to NOTTINGHAM MIDLAND	... ...	18.6.1951
Second up middle line	t.o.u.	4.9.1967
Scissors crossings	t.o.u.	12.5.1968
Nottingham Station "A" SB	Opened	28.2.1904
***	Closed	7.12.1969
Nottingham Passenger Station SB	Opened	1879
Replacement box	Opened	21.6.1903
Replacement box named Nottingham Passenger Station East SB	Opened	30.8.1903
Re-named Nottingham Passenger Station "B" SB	... ...	28.2.1904
***	Closed	7.12.1969

LEICESTER & BURTON LINE

Knighton & Desford section

Powers: Midland Railway (Leicester and Swannington Amendment) Act 1847

Knighton South Jcn to Saffron Lane Jcn	OG	15.2.1850
Block telegraph working	Commenced	11.8.1890
Reception line	Into use	1.7.1906
Knighton South Jcn to Moira West Jcn: line designated a goods line	... ...	23.11.1969
Knighton South Jcn to Desford Colliery Sidings	Singled	12-14.12.1970

The London & North Western Railway possessed running powers to all collieries on the Leicester & Burton line and its branches for traffic passing over the Ashby & Nuneaton Joint Line, and it ran to the brick and tile works at Ibstock, Ellistown, and Whitwick. It also possessed running powers for all traffic, toll free, between Leicester and Burton, and for all traffic, on terms laid down, between Ashby-de-la-Zouch and Burton inclusive and over the branches between Moira and the Leicester Junctions at Burton inclusive, together with the use of stations except for the Midland goods station at Burton.

Knighton North Curve

Powers: Midland Railway (Leicester and Swannington Amendment) Act 1847

Knighton North Jcn to Saffron Lane Jcn	OG	6-7.1849
***	OP	1.8.1849
Block telegraph working	Intro. by	1873
***	CP	7.9.1964
***	Closed	2.8.1967
***	t.o.u.	6.8.1967

Saffron Lane Jcn to Desford Jcn	OG	6-7.1849
***	OP	1.8.1849
Block telegraph working	Introduced	1875
Saffron Lane Jcn to Leicester Jcn (Burton-on-Trent)	CP	7.9.1964
Saffron Lane Junction SB	Opened	1859
Replacement box	Opened	....
Replacement box	Opened	7.2.1892
Replacement box	Opened	6.10.1929
Replacement box	Opened	17.1.1960
***	Closed	6.8.1967
Saffron Lane Crossing SB	Opened	8.1877-4.1878
Replacement box	Opened	1892-1901
Box closed and ground frame provided in lieu	... ...	13.12.1970

Saffron Lane Crossing: curve to Leicester Central Goods North	OG	14.6.1965
Aylestone Viaduct SB	Opened	3.3.1901
***	Closed	8.6.1902
NARBOROUGH ROAD WHARF (BIRKINSHAW, BROWN & CO.)	Opened	1910-1912
***	Closed	7.3.1966
BRAUNSTON	Opened	1.6.1850 *
***	Closed	1.7.1859 *
KIRBY MUXLOE	OP&G	1.7.1859 *
***	CG	13.1.1964
***	CP	7.9.1964
Kirby Muxloe SB	Open before	16.8.1877
Replacement box	Opened	7.3.1897
***	Closed	18.2.1968

Leicester & Swannington Railway

The Leicester & Swannington Railway was dissolved and vested in the Midland Railway under the Midland Railway (Leicester and Swannington No. 2) Act 1846 with effect from 27 July 1846.

Powers: Leicester and Swannington Railway Act 1830
Midland Railway (Leicester and Swannington Amendment) Act 1847 (Enlargement of West Bridge station)
Leicester and Swannington Railway Act 1833 (Leicester: Soar Lane Branch)
Midland Railway (Leicester and Swannington Amendment) Act 1847 (Re-alignment west of Desford)

West Bridge to Bagworth, Staunton Road	O.Formal	17.7.1832
***	Opened	18.7.1832
It is reported that two wagons of coal were brought to Leicester from Bagworth Colliery on 30 May 1832.		
Staunton Road to Ashby Road	OG on/by	1.2.1833
***	OP	22.2.1833
Ashby Road to Long Lane (Coalville)	O.Coal	22.4.1833
***	OP	27.4.1833
Long Lane to Swannington (with rope-worked incline)	O.Coal	25.11.1833
Leicester to Long Lane	CP after	12.1847 *
***	RO(P)	1.5.1848 *
The branch was worked by one engine in steam, and train staff working was introduced in 1877.		
LEICESTER	O.Formal	17.7.1832
***	OP&M	18.7.1832
***	OG	....
Altered to WEST BRIDGE	By	26.4.1833
Replacement passenger station	Opened	13.3.1893
***	CP	24.9.1928
***	CG	4.4.1966
WEST BRIDGE WHARF	Opened	1900-1904
***	Closed	....
PINGLE COAL WHARF purchased by the Midland Railway	... ...	1891
***	Closed	....
West Bridge engine shed	Opened	1832
***	Closed	26.6.1926
West Bridge to Desford: working with two staffs instead of one	... ...	24.2.1895
West Bridge branch	CP	24.9.1928
***	CG	4.4.1966
West Bridge, Glenfield, and Ratby are named on a list of "signal posts" returned to the Board of Trade in November 1880, but there may not have been any signalbox structure in these locations.		
West Bridge to Groby Quarry Sidings	C.Tfc	2.5.1966
Leicester Soar Lane branch, with lifting bridge over canal	OG	4.10.1834
SOAR LANE COAL WHARF	Opened	1900-1904
***	Closed	....
FOSSE ROAD WHARF	Opened	....
Replacement depot	Opened	1900-1901
***	Closed	4.4.1966
Fosse Road Crossing SB	Opened	9.12.1901
Box closed and ground frame provided in lieu	... ...	28.4.1929
***	t.o.u.	1922-1937
GLENFIELD	OP&M	18.7.1832
***	OG	....
Replacement station east of the level crossing	Opened	1875
***	CP	24.9.1928
***	CG	6.12.1965
Groby Quarry Sidings to Desford Jcn	CG(All)	3.9.1967

RATBY LANE	OP&M	18.7.1832
***	OG	....
Altered to RATBY	By	26.4.1833
Replacement station west of the level crossing	Opened	1873
***	CP	24.9.1928
***	CG	4.10.1954
Desford East Junction SB	Opened	29.5.1876
***	Closed	1882
Desford Junction SB	Opened	....
***	Closed	29.5.1876
Desford Junction SB (second box)	Opened	1882
Replacement box	Opened	1.7.1917
Box closed and ground frame provided in lieu	... ...	13.12.1970
***	t.o.u.	15.3.1972
Desford West Junction SB	Opened	29.5.1876
***	Closed	1882
Desford Junction SB and Desford West Junction SB were probably the same location.		
Desford Jcn to Desford: block telegraph working	Introduced	1876
Desford Jcn to Desford Colliery Sidings	Singled	12-14.12.1970
Desford Station SB	Opened	1869
Replacement box	Opened	4.4.1897
***	Closed	14.5.1967
DESFORD LANE	OP&M	18.7.1832
***	OG	....
Altered to DESFORD	By	26.4.1833
Replacement station about 150 yards west	Opened	27.3.1848
***	CG	2.3.1964
***	CP	7.9.1964
Desford to Bagworth: block telegraph working	Intro. by	1872
Desford Colliery Sidings SB	Opened	7.7.1901
***	Closed	29.6.1986
Desford Colliery Sidings to Bardon Hill	Singled	30.6.1986
MERRY LEES	OP&M	18.7.1832
***	OG	....
Replacement passenger station 150 yards west of the bridge	Opened	27.3.1848
Altered to MERRYLEES	... ...	....
***	CP(All)	1.3.1871
MERRYLEES SIDING	Opened	19.7.1875
***	Removed	20.4.1941
STAG & CASTLE INN	Opened	18.7.1832
Altered to THORNTON	... ...	1841
***	CP(All)	1.1.1842
THORNTON LANE	OP	1850
***	CP(All)	1.10.1865
Bagworth Incline (rope-worked) replaced by deviation line	... ...	27.3.1848

Bagworth Branch

Powers: Midland Railway (Leicester and Swannington Amendment) Act 1847 (Land Powers only), Midland Railway (Additional Powers) Act 1868

Bagworth station to Bagworth Colliery	Opened	17.7.1832
***	Closed	....
Branch taken over by the Midland Railway	... ...	....
This branch had to be re-aligned when the deviation line avoiding the Bagworth incline was brought into use.		

Tarmac Ltd Stud Farm Quarry Branch

Powers: No powers

Bagworth Colliery Jcn to Stud Farm Quarry	Into use	3.7.1988

Bagworth SB	Opened	c.6.1873
Re-named Bagworth & Ellistown SB	... ...	1.10.1894
Replacement box	Opened	3.9.1899
***	Closed	26.8.1979
BAGWORTH	OP&M	18.7.1832
***	OG	....
Replacement station on the deviation line	Opened	27.3.1848
Altered to BAGWORTH & ELLISTOWN	... ...	1.10.1894
***	CG	2.3.1964
***	CP	7.9.1964
Bagworth to Coalville: block telegraph working	Introduced	1874
Ibstock Sidings SB	Open before	1.11.1875
Replacement box	Opened	14.7.1901
***	Closed	7.1.1953
Ellistown Colliery Sidings SB	Open before	1.11.1875
Replacement box	Opened	7.5.1899
***	Closed	22.3.1972
Cliff Hill SB	Open before	1.11.1875
Replacement box	Opened	11.4.1892
Box closed and 2 ground frames provided in lieu	... ...	17.12.1972

ASHBY ROAD	Opened	27.4.1833
Altered to BARDON HILL	... ...	1.1.1847
***	CP	1.3.1849 ?
***	RO(P)	1.9.1849 ?*
***	CP&G	12.5.1952
Bardon Hill Station SB	Opened	c.9.1874
Replacement box	Opened	27.8.1899
***	Closed	....
Bardon Hill Sidings SB	Opened	c.9.1876
Replacement box	Opened	16.4.1899
Re-named Bardon Hill West SB	... ...	....
***	Raised	13.11.1910
***	Closed	27.9.1925

Coalfields Farm Branch

Powers: --

Former Coalville East branch	Closed	16.4.1967
Coalville Jcn to Coalfields Farm Opencast Site	OG	14.6.1976
***	Closed	....

The branch is on the site of the Ashby & Nuneaton Joint line to Charnwood Forest.

Coalville Junction SB	Opened	1872
Replacement box	Opened	22.7.1894
Replacement box	Opened	7.1.1912
***	Closed	16.4.1967

Between Coalville Junction and Coalville station the London & North Western Railway possessed running powers for coaching traffic over the Midland line.

Coalville No. 1 SB	Open before	1.11.1875
Replacement box	Opened	30.1.1898
Box closed and ground frame provided in lieu	... ...	16.4.1967
***	t.o.u.	....

Whitwick Colliery Branch

Powers: --

Coalville to Whitwick Colliery	Opened	....
***	Closed	27.3.1972

Coalville Station Crossing SB	Opened	1860
***	Re-framed	12.6.1898
Replacement box	Opened	16.2.1908
Re-named Coalville Crossing SB	... ...	4.5.1969 ?
Coalville Station [sic] SB	Closed	1.12.1985
LONG LANE	Opened	27.4.1833
Altered to COALVILLE	... ...	27.3.1848 ?
Passenger station	Enlarged	1898
Altered to COALVILLE TOWN	... ...	2.6.1924
***	CP	7.9.1964

Evidence for the change of name to Coalville is conflicting, but it is certain that the alteration was before October 1848.

Coalville to Swannington Colliery No. 3: block telegraph working	Introduced	1877
Coalville Crossing to Mantle Lane: second down goods line	Into use	14.6.1976
Second down goods line designated down goods loop	... ...	1.12.1985
Coalville engine shed	Opened	....
***	Replaced	1890
***	Closed	10.1965
Mantle Lane Crossing SB	Opened	1884
Replacement box named Mantle Lane East SB	Opened	27.2.1910
Re-named Mantle Lane SB	... ...	4.5.1969
Mantle Lane East to the foot of the Swannington incline	Tfc ceased	14.11.1947
Swannington Incline	Closed	6.1881-4.1883
***	Re-opened by	1892
***	Closed	2.1948
Section from 113m 48ch to foot of incline	Recovered	19.11.1951
Remaining siding shortened by 400 yards	... ...	7.8.1972

Extension to Burton-on-Trent

Powers: Midland Railway (Leicester and Swannington Amendment) Act 1847 (Desford to Gresley)
Midland Railway (Leicester and Swannington Alteration) Act 1846 (Gresley to Burton-on-Trent)

Mantle Lane Jcn to Leicester Jcn	OG	2.10.1848
***	OP	1.3.1849
Mantle Lane (East) to Lounge Jcn (116m 70ch)	Singled	14.12.1986

Coalville Goods Branch

Powers: --

COALVILLE NEW GOODS DEPOT	Opened	1897
***	Closed	4.10.1971

MANTLE LANE SIDINGS	Opened	....
***	t.o.u.	....
Mantle Lane East to Mantle Lane West: reception line (up side)	Into use	27.2.1910
Swannington Colliery Sidings No. 3 SB	Open before	1.10.1876
Replacement box	Opened	19.3.1899
***	Re-framed	23.1.1910
Re-named Mantle Lane West SB	... ...	27.2.1910
Box closed and ground frame provided in lieu	... ...	18.8.1968
***	t.o.u.	16.12.1979
Swannington Colliery No. 3 to Swannington Colliery No. 2: block telegraph working	Introduced	1875
Swannington Station SB	Open before	1.10.1876
Replacement box	Opened	23.3.1902
Box closed and AHBs provided in lieu	... ...	18.6.1967
SWANNINGTON	OP	1.9.1849
***	CP(All)	18.6.1951
Swannington No. 2 SB	Open before	1.11.1875
***	Closed by	1.10.1876
Swannington Colliery Sidings No. 2 SB	Opened	26.7.1891
***	Closed	27.10.1902
Swannington Colliery Sidings No. 2 to Swadlincote Jcn: block telegraph working	Introduced	1873
Coleorton Colliery Sidings SB	Opened	3.1877
Replacement box	Opened	10.1.1897
***	Closed	2.6.1935
ASHBY	Opened	1.3.1849
Altered to ASHBY-DE-LA-ZOUCH	... ...	13.7.1925 *
***	CG	4.11.1963
***	CP	7.9.1964
Ashby Station SB	Open before	1.11.1875
Replacement box	Opened	20.8.1899
***	Closed	27.7.1964

Ashby & Breedon line
See page 217

MOIRA	Opened	1.3.1849
***	CG	4.11.1963
***	CP	7.9.1964
Moira Station SB	Open before	1.11.1875
Replacement box	Opened	28.5.1899
***	Closed	7.6.1925
Moira East Junction SB	Opened	1872
Replacement box	Opened	13.9.1896
Replacement box	Opened	7.6.1925
***	Closed	21.7.1968

Ashby & Nuneaton Joint Line
See page 222

Moira West Junction SB	Opened	1872
Replacement box	Opened	14.6.1896
***	Re-framed	c.12.1986

Rawdon Branch
Powers: --

Rawdon Branch	Opened	....
***	Closed	....
Branch reduced to the status of a siding	... ...	8.8.1939
WOODVILLE JUNCTION SIDINGS	Opened	....
***	t.o.u.	....
Woodville Sidings SB	Open before	16.8.1877
Re-named Woodville Junction SB	... ...	....
Replacement box	Opened	5.1.1902
***	Re-framed	13.12.1903
***	Slued	28.1.1923
***	Re-framed	13.5.1923
Box and down-side ground frame	Closed	26.11.1967

Woodville branch
See page 78

GRESLEY	Opened	1.3.1849
Replacement station east of the road bridge	Opened	c.1869
***	CG	4.11.1963
***	CP	7.9.1964
Gresley SB	Opened	1.1869
***	Re-located	1889-1893
Replacement box	Opened	19.3.1911
***	Closed	15.6.1969
Gresley: down sidings and ground frame	t.o.u.	18.9.1966

Coton Park (OR Netherseal) Branch

Powers: Midland Railway (Additional Powers) Act 1870

Coton Park (OR Netherseal Colliery) branch	OG	1.7.1872
***	OP(NA)	6.1877 ?
***	CP	....
***	Closed	1.6.1963
Branch severed at bridge No. 5	... ...	23.2.1964
Remainder of branch	Closed	18.9.1966
***	t.o.u.	10.4.1968

Linton Sidings SB	Open before	1.11.1875
***	Closed by	1.10.1876
Coton Park Colliery SB	Opened	1.1872
Box closed and ground frame provided in lieu	... ...	19.11.1899
***	t.o.u.	11.9.1905
Coton Park SB: new box near 123 1/4 miles	Opened	22.7.1923
***	Closed	14.5.1939
Coton Park SB: new box 631 yards nearer to Burton	Opened	10.9.1944
***	Closed	23.8.1964
COTON PARK SIDINGS	Into use	10.9.1944
***	t.o.u.	....
Swadlincote Junction SB	Open before	1.11.1875
Replacement box	Opened	1883
Replacement box	Opened	27.1.1924
Box closed and ground frame provided in lieu	... ...	15.6.1969
***	t.o.u.	14.7.1988

Swadlincote branch

See page 78

Swadlincote Jcn to Leicester Jcn: block telegraph working	Introduced	1874
Bretby Junction SB	Opened	12.1868
Replacement box	Opened	15.7.1894
Replacement box	Opened	22.1.1928
Box closed and ground frame provided in lieu	... ...	20.4.1952
***	t.o.u.	25.8.1968

Bretby Branch

Powers: Midland Railway (Additional Powers) Act 1866

Swadlincote Jcn to Bretby Colliery	Opened	1.10.1868
***	Closed	1.6.1963
Branch curtailed by 1m 1190yds	... ...	6.7.1963
Remainder of the branch	Closed	25.8.1968

Drakelow SB	Opened	26.4.1954
***	Closed	15.6.1969
Birmingham Curve Junction SB	Opened	3.1873
Replacement box	Opened	25.7.1887
Replacement box	Opened	23.9.1906
***	Closed	15.6.1969
Leicester Junction Sidings SB	Opened	....
***	Raised	6.10.1895
Replacement box	Opened	20.6.1909
***	Closed	....

Birmingham Curve at Burton

Powers: Midland Railway (Burton Branches) Act 1860

Birmingham Curve Jcn to Branston Jcn	OG	2.2.1863 *
BRANSTON SIDINGS	Opened	....
***	t.o.u.	....
Centre of Branston Sidings SB	Open before	16.8.1877
Replacement box	Opened	14.1.1889
Re-named Branston Sidings No. 2 SB	... ...	1889–1893
Replacement box	Opened	18.7.1927
***	Closed	8.1.1939
Elevated Box (SB)	Open before	16.8.1877
Re-named Branston Sidings No. 1 SB	... ...	1889–1893
Replacement box	Opened	6.4.1908
Re-named Branston Sidings SB	... ...	8.1.1939
Box closed and ground frame provided in lieu	... ...	13.10.1963
***	t.o.u.	....
Branston Jcn: 27-chain branch to National Machine Gun Factory	Into use	24.3.1918
Branch re-named the Crosse & Blackwell Siding	... ...	1921

Woodville Loop

Powers: Midland Railway (Burton-upon-Trent to Nuneaton) Act 1846
(Wooden Box Junction to Wooden Box)
Midland Railway (Additional Powers) Act 1878 (Woodville Goods Junction to Woodville)
Midland Railway (Additional Powers) Act 1875 (Woodville to Swadlincote)
Midland Railway (Leicester and Swannington Alteration) Act 1846
(Swadlincote to Swadlincote Junction)

Wooden Box Branch:

Wooden Box Jcn to Wooden Box	OG	1850
***	CG by	1.10.1856 *
***	RO(G)	1.4.1859
This line was worked by train staff.		
Woodville Jcn to Woodville Goods Jcn	OP	1.9.1884
Woodville Jcn to Swadlincote Station: working by electric train tablet block	Commenced	16.8.1896
Woodville & Swadlincote Loop Line	CP	6.10.1947
***	CG	2.3.1964
Woodville Jcn to Gresley Colliery Sidings	Closed	24.5.1964
***	Abandoned	26.9.1964
***	Closed	2.11.1964
Swains Park Crossing SB	Opened	19.2.1899
***	Closed	2.3.1964
Swains Park Crossing to Woodville Goods Depot	Closed	2.3.1964
Church Gresley Colliery Sidings East SB (not a block post)	Opened	1883
***	Closed	16.8.1896
Church Gresley Colliery Sidings West SB (not a block post)	Opened	1883
***	Closed	16.8.1896
Weighing Machine Sidings SB (not a block post)	Opened	1883
***	Closed	16.8.1896
Woodville Goods Junction SB	Opened	1883
Replacement box	Opened	18.9.1923
***	Made NBP	1922-1931
Box closed and ground frame provided in lieu	... ...	24.6.1934
***	t.o.u.	....
WOODEN BOX	OG	1850
***	CG by	1.10.1856 *
***	RO(G)	1.4.1859
Altered to WOODVILLE	... ...	1.10.1868
***	CG	2.3.1964

Swadlincote Branch:

Swadlincote Jcn to Swadlincote	OG	2.10.1848 ?
***	OP	1.3.1849 ?
***	CP	10.1853-1.1855
***	RO(P)	1.6.1864
This branch was worked by one engine in steam and train staff until 1883, and then by block telegraph and train staff between Swadlincote Junction and Swadlincote West.		
Swadlincote Jcn to Swadlincote West: train tablet working	Commenced	15.9.1895
Swadlincote Jcn to Cadley Hill Colliery Empty Wagon Sidings GF: one engine in steam working	Commenced	2.3.1964
Section of line designated a siding	... ...	25.8.1968
***	t.o.u.	14.7.1988
This line was latterly known as the Cadley Hill Colliery Branch.		
Cadley Hill Colliery SB (not a block post)	Opened	1883
***	Closed	27.10.1895
Cadley Hill Colliery to Swadlincote	Closed	2.3.1964
Stanton Colliery Sidings SB (not a block post)	Opened	1883
***	Closed	15.9.1895
Hall & Boardman's Sidings SB (not a block post)	Opened	1883
***	Closed	27.10.1895
Swadlincote SB	Opened	1864
***	Closed	1883 ?
Swadlincote West to Swadlincote East: block telegraph working	Introduced	1883
SWADLINCOTE	OG	2.10.1848 ?
***	OP	1.3.1849 ?
***	CP	10.1853-1.1855
***	RO(P)	1.6.1864
***	CP	1.5.1883
***	CG	2.3.1964

Swadlincote & Woodville Extension Line:

Swadlincote to Woodville new passenger station	OG	....
***	OP	1.5.1883
Swadlincote to Wragg's Sidings	Closed	2.3.1964

Swadlincote West SB	Opened	1883
Replacement box	Opened	15.6.1919
***	Closed	2.3.1964
SWADLINCOTE	OP	1.5.1883
***	CP(All)	6.10.1947
Excursion trains continued to call at this station.		
Swadlincote East SB	Opened	1883
Replacement box	Opened	10.7.1905
***	Closed	23.1.1955
Swadlincote (Wragg's Sidings) to Woodville Goods Jcn	Closed	9.9.1963
Woodville Passenger Station SB	Opened	1883
Replacement box	Opened	9.9.1923
***	Closed	2.3.1964
WOODVILLE	OP	1.5.1883
***	CP(All)	6.10.1947
Excursion trains continued to call at this station.		
Woodville new passenger station to Tugby's Works	OG	....
Woodville new passenger station to Woodville Goods Jcn	OP	1.9.1884
Tugby's Works to Woodville Goods Jcn	OG	12.4.1880
Boothorpe SB (not a block post)	Opened	1883
Replacement box	Opened	20.3.1922
***	Closed	24.6.1934

BURTON & ASHBY LIGHT RAILWAY

Powers: Burton & Ashby Light Railway Order 1903 (Burton to Swadlincote)
Burton & Ashby Light Railway (Amendment) Order 1906 (Swadlincote)
Burton & Ashby Light Railway Order 1903 (Swadlincote and Gresley to Ashby)

Burton to Swadlincote	Opened	13.6.1906
Swadlincote to Ashby	Opened	2.7.1906
Swadlincote to Gresley	Opened	24.9.1906
Woodville to Gresley	Opened	15.10.1906
Woodville to Gresley	Closed	pr.11.1912
Closure: last car ran	... ...	19.2.1927

SYSTON & PETERBOROUGH RAILWAY

Powers: Midland Railway (Syston and Peterborough Railway) Act 1845
Midland Railway (Syston and Peterborough Alterations) Act 1846 (Brooksby to Frisby)
Midland Railway (Syston and Peterborough Deviations and Manton Approach) Act 1847 (Melton to Saxby)
Midland Railway Act 1903 (Melton to Brentingby Widening)
Midland Railway Act 1889 (Saxby Curve)
Midland Railway (Syston and Peterborough Deviations and Manton Approach) Act 1847 (Whissendine to Ashwell)
Midland Railway (Syston and Peterborough Alterations) Act 1846 (Stamford to Uffington)

Syston to Melton Mowbray temporary station	OP&G	1.9.1846
Melton temporary station to Stamford	OG	20.3.1848
***	OP	1.5.1848
Stamford (temporary station) to Peterborough (Nene Jcn with the London & North Western Railway)	OP&G	2.10.1846
The temporary station was at the east end of the tunnel. The line was worked by the London & North Western Railway for a few months until the Eastern Counties Railway was completed to Peterborough, when that company took over.		
Syston South Jcn to Syston East Jcn: block telegraph working	Introduced	1874
Syston Jcns to Melton Jcn: direction changed from DOWN to UP	... ...	1960-1969
Syston South Jcn to Syston East Jcn	Singled	....
Syston East Junction SB	Open before	16.8.1877
Replacement box	Opened	10.10.1887
Replacement box	Opened	27.11.1927
Box closed, ground frame provided in lieu, and main-line points worked by Syston South Junction SB	... ...	2.9.1973

Syston North Curve

Powers: Midland Railway (Syston and Peterborough Alterations) Act 1846

Syston North Jcn to Syston East Jcn	Opened	1854
The curve has never carried a regular passenger service.		

Syston East Jcn to Melton: block telegraph working	Introduced	1875
QUENIBOROUGH	OP(NA)	10.11.1941
***	CP(All)	....
Platform lines and run-rounds	t.o.u.	8.2.1970
Queniborough SB	Opened	9.11.1941
Box closed and up and down IBS provided in lieu	... ...	19.12.1976
***	t.o.u.	....
Broom Lane: up and down IBS	Into use	16.2.1941
***	t.o.u.	....

REARSBY	OP	1.9.1846	
***	CP(All)	2.4.1951	
Rearsby SB	Open before	16.8.1877	
Replacement box	Opened	1899	
***	Closed	22.1.1967	
Brooksby SB	Open before	16.8.1877	
Replacement box	Opened	14.1.1890	
***	Closed	22.1.1967	
BROOKSBY	Opened	1.9.1846	
***	CP	3.7.1961	
***	CG	4.5.1964	
FRISBY	OP	1.1.1847	
***	CP(All)	3.7.1961	
Frisby SB	Opened	23.2.1941	
KIRBY	Opened	1.9.1846	
Altered to ASFORDBY (LATE KIRBY)	... ...	1.12.1857	*
Altered to ASFORDBY	... ...	1.5.1903	*
***	CP	2.4.1951	
***	CG	4.5.1964	
Asfordby SB	Open before	16.8.1877	
Replacement box	Opened	29.1.1899	
***	Closed	18.12.1966	
Melton Jcn to Manton Jcn: direction changed from DOWN to UP	... ...	1880	
Melton Junction SB	Open before	1.11.1875	
Replacement box	Opened	10.12.1905	
***	Re-framed	28.4.1907	
Box closed and ground frame provided in lieu	... ...	6.5.1973	

Nottingham & Melton line

See page 84

Melton: London & North Western and Great Northern joint line junction	Opened	End 1879	?
***	Severed	31.10.1882	
***	Re-opened	16.4.1883	
***	Closed	18.4.1887	
***	Severed	5.7.1887	
Melton West SB	Opened	....	
***	Closed	28.4.1907	
Melton Sidings SB	Open before	16.8.1877	
Replacement box	Opened	3.7.1892	
***	Closed	9.8.1942	
Melton Station SB (new site)	Opened	9.8.1942	
MELTON temporary station	Opened	1.9.1846	
Permanent station	OG	20.3.1848	?
***	OP	1.5.1848	?
Altered to MELTON MOWBRAY	... ...	1.11.1876	*
Altered to MELTON MOWBRAY SOUTH	... ...	1923	
Altered to MELTON MOWBRAY MID.	... ...	25.9.1950	?*
Altered to MELTON MOWBRAY TOWN	Before	13.9.1957	*
Altered to MELTON MOWBRAY	... ...	14.6.1965	*
***	C.Coal	6.8.1979	
***	CG	3.4.1989	
Melton Crossing SB	Open before	16.8.1877	
Replacement box	Opened	3.7.1892	
Re-named Melton Station SB	... ...	1896	
Replacement box	Opened	10.10.1904	
***	Closed	9.8.1942	
Melton to Oakham Sidings: block telegraph working	Introduced	1877	
Melton Mowbray to Brentingby Jcn: replacement main lines	Into use	14.8.1904	
Up main line placed in its permanent position	... ...	30.10.1904	
Position of up main line altered	... ...	20.11.1904	
Up and down goods lines	Into use	4.12.1904	
Up and down goods lines	Closed	14.5.1978	
Goods lines restored as short loops controlled from Melton	... ...	25.6.1978	
Up goods loop converted to a private siding	... ...	2.2.1986	
Melton troughs	Into use	3.5.1905	
Goods lines troughs	Removed	1926	
Indicating lamps	Removed	14.5.1940	
Troughs	t.o.u.	....	
Brentingby Junction SB	Opened	14.8.1904	
***	Closed	25.6.1978	
Brentingby SB	Opened	1879	
***	Made NBP	14.8.1904	
Re-named Brentingby Crossing SB as gate box only	... ...	4.12.1904	
Box closed and covered gate frame provided in lieu	... ...	3.11.1918	
***	t.o.u.	....	
Brentingby Crossing made an occupation crossing	... ...	31.10.1964	
Wyfordby: up-line IBS	Into use	9.4.1933	
Down-line IBS	Into use	....	
Down-line IBS	t.o.u.	31.1.1971	
Up-line IBS	t.o.u.	....	

Saxby West Junction SB	Opened	28.8.1892	
***	Raised	24.5.1908	
***	Re-framed	....	
Re-named Saxby Junction SB	... ...	1.10.1962	
***	Closed	....	
Saxby West Jcn to Wymondham Goods Jcn (Saxby Curve)	Opened	28.8.1892	
There were four tracks between the Melton end of Saxby Goods Yard and Wymondham Junction. As far as the Manton end of Saxby station the additional tracks were slow lines on the north side, and thence they were goods lines, one on either side.			
Saxby West Jcn to Saxby Station Jcn: down (westbound) slow line as a down goods line	Into use	4.6.1893	
Up and down slow lines	Into use	1.5.1894	
Down slow line taken out of use, leaving the Bourne line connecting into up slow line only	... ...	2.9.1962	
Saxby Jcn: former down slow line re-opened as the up goods line	... ...	1.10.1962	
Up slow line & South Witham (Bourne) branch line made single goods line worked one engine in steam	... ...	1.10.1962	
Saxby Jcn to Wymondham Goods Jcn: up and down goods lines	t.o.u.	27.11.1966	
Saxby Station SB (first station site)	Open before	16.8.1877	
***	Closed	28.8.1892	
Saxby Station SB to Wymondham Goods Jcn: down goods line	Into use	23.8.1891	
SAXBY (first station)	Opened	1.2.1849	*
***	Closed	28.8.1892	
Saxby Crossing SB	Open before	16.8.1877	
***	Closed	28.8.1892	
SAXBY (second station)	Opened	28.8.1892	
***	CP	6.2.1961	
***	CG	6.2.1961	
Saxby Station Junction SB	Opened	28.8.1892	
***	Raised	5.11.1911	
***	Closed	1.10.1962	

Saxby & Bourne line

See page 84

Saxby Station Jcn: up slow line to up main line connection	t.o.u.	22.4.1962	
Wymondham SB	Opened	1881	
Replacement box named Wymondham Junction SB	Opened	11.8.1891	
***	Closed	27.11.1966	
WYMONDHAM	OG	20.3.1848	?
***	OP	1.5.1848	
Altered to WHISENDINE LATE WYMONDHAM	... ...	1.9.1848	*
Altered to WHISSENDINE LATE WYMONDHAM	... ...	1.10.1878	*
Altered to WHISSENDINE	... ...	1.5.1891	*
***	CP&G	3.10.1955	
Whisendine SB	Open before	16.8.1877	
Replacement box	Opened	6.3.1898	
Replacement box	Opened	10.11.1940	
***	Closed	....	
Teigh Crossing: up-line IBS	Into use	10.11.1940	
Down-line IBS	Into use	8.12.1940	
***	t.o.u. after	1975	
Ashwell Branch Junction SB	Opened	6.1881-4.1883	
***	Closed	6.6.1909	
Ashwell Branch Junction GF	t.o.u.	31.12.1973	

Ashwell (or Cottesmore) Branch

Powers: Midland Railway (Additional Powers) Act 1875, Midland Railway Act 1881 (Revival of Powers)

Ashwell Jcn to Cottesmore	OG	27.11.1882	
***	t.o.u.	13.3.1972	
***	Severed	1.12.1972	
***	Closed	2.12.1973	
Ashwell Branch Sidings SB (this box was never opened)	Erected	1919	
***	Demolished	1937	
ASHWELL	OG	20.3.1848	?
***	OP	1.5.1848	
***	CG	4.5.1964	
***	CP	6.6.1966	
Ashwell Station SB	Open before	16.8.1877	
***	Re-framed	6.6.1909	
Replacement box	Opened	30.6.1912	
***	Re-framed by	1950	
***	Closed	....	
Ashwell GF, and up and down sidings	t.o.u. by	17.6.1988	
Langham SB	Opened	1881	
***	Closed	15.3.1891	
Langham Crossing SB	Opened	27.10.1890	
Re-named Langham Junction SB	... ...	15.3.1891	
***	Closed	....	

Langham Jcn to Oakham Jcn: up and down goods lines	Into use	15.3.1891	
Up goods line made through siding	... ...	7.1.1973	
Down goods line worked no block	... ...	1.4.1973	
Oakham Sidings SB	Open before	16.8.1877	
Replacement box named Oakham Junction SB	Opened	15.3.1891	
***	Closed	1.4.1973	
Oakham Sidings to Oakham Crossing: block telegraph working	Introduced	1874	
OAKHAM	OG	20.3.1848	?
***	OP	1.5.1848	
***	CG	3.5.1971	
Oakham Crossing SB	Opened	1875	
Replacement box	Opened	8.10.1899	
***	Closed	....	
Oakham Crossing to Manton: block telegraph working	Intro. by	1870	
Egleton SB	Open before	16.8.1877	
***	Alt.levers	6.10.1890	
***	Closed	2.6.1968	
Manton North down-line IBS	Into use	24.11.1940	
***	t.o.u. after	1975	
Manton Junction SB	Opened	1.12.1879	
Replacement box	Opened	4.4.1886	
Replacement box	Opened	9.11.1913	
Replacement box	Opened	24.7.1988	
Manton Junction re-aligned making the Kettering line the through line	... ...	14.3.1888	
Re-aligned making the Peterborough line the through line	... ...	24.7.1988	

Kettering & Manton line

See page 58

MANTON FOR UPPINGHAM	OG	20.3.1848	?
***	OP	1.5.1848	
Altered to MANTON	... ...	1.10.1934	*
***	CG	4.5.1964	
***	CP	6.6.1966	
Manton to Peterborough: direction changed from DOWN to UP	... ...	4.6.1961	
Manton SB	Open before	16.8.1877	
***	Closed	1879	
Manton to Stamford: block telegraph working	Introduced	1874	
Manton East SB	Opened	1879	
Replacement box	Opened	12.5.1931	
***	Closed	23.11.1958	
Lyndon down-line IBS	Into use	23.12.1940	
***	t.o.u. after	1975	
Pilton SB	Opened	11.7.1920	
Box closed and ground frame provided in lieu	... ...	26.5.1957	
***	t.o.u.	19.7.1970	
Lord Aveland's Siding SB	Open before	16.8.1877	
Replacement box	Opened	10.6.1890	
***	Made NBP	28.9.1908	
***	Closed	11.7.1920	
Luffenham Junction SB	Open before	1.11.1875	
Replacement box	Opened	20.10.1889	
Replacement box	Opened	14.9.1924	
Luffenham Junction with the London & North Western Railway's Rugby & Stamford line	Opened	2.6.1851	
***	Closed	6.6.1966	
Between Luffenham Junction and Stamford the London & North Western Railway possessed running powers for all traffic.			
Luffenham Jcn to Luffenham Sidings: down platform line	In use before	10.1872	
***	t.o.u.	1966	?
LUFFENHAM	OG	20.3.1848	?
***	OP	1.5.1848	
***	CG	4.5.1964	
***	CP	6.6.1966	
Luffenham Sidings SB	Open before	1.11.1875	
Replacement box	Opened	11.12.1898	
***	Closed	20.11.1932	
Foster's Bridge SB	Made ready	30.3.1919	
***	Into use	15.12.1919	
***	Closed	19.12.1943	
Ketton SB	Open before	16.8.1877	
Replacement box	Opened	14.1.1900	
***	Closed	....	
KETTON	OG	20.3.1848	?
***	OP	1.5.1848	
Altered to KETTON & COLLYWESTON	... ...	8.7.1935	
***	CG	26.4.1965	
***	CP	6.6.1966	
Ward's Sidings GF	Into use	25.8.1928	
Ground frame taken out of use and signalbox provided in lieu	... ...	24.6.1930	
Box closed and ground frame provided in lieu	... ...	8.12.1963	
***	t.o.u.	....	

Welland Bridge SB	Opened	18.6.1899	
***	Closed	4.2.1900	
Tinwell Crossing SB	Open before	1.11.1875	
Replacement box	Opened	19.12.1905	
***	Made NBP	24.6.1930	
Stamford L. & N. W. R. engine shed	Opened	1881	
***	Closed	20.9.1926	
Stamford engine shed	Opened	....	
***	Closed	....	
Stamford Station SB	Open before	16.8.1877	
Replacement box	Opened	19.11.1893	
***	Closed	15.5.1984	
Stamford to Stamford Jcn: block telegraph working	Intro. by	1873	
STAMFORD	OG	20.3.1848	?
***	OP	1.5.1848	?
Altered to STAMFORD TOWN	... ...	25.9.1950	
Altered to STAMFORD	... ...	18.4.1966	
***	CG	16.5.1983	
Between Stamford station and Stamford Junction the Great Northern Railway possessed running powers over the Midland line.			
STAMFORD (temporary station east of the tunnel)	Opened	2.10.1846	
***	CG	20.3.1848	
***	CP	19.6.1848	
Stamford Junction SB	Open before	16.8.1877	
Replacement box	Opened	19.3.1882	
Replacement box	Opened	13.4.1913	
Box closed and Stamford East SB (Great Northern line) brought into use instead of it	... ...	9.3.1957	
***	Closed	26.5.1968	
Between Stamford Junction and Bourne Junction the Midland Railway possessed running powers over the Great Northern line.			
Stamford Jcn to Wisbech Jcn: block telegraph working	Introduced	1876	
Stamford: junction with the Great Northern Railway	Opened	1.7.1867	
***	Closed	4.3.1963	
Uffington & Barnack Station SB	Open before	16.8.1877	
Replacement box	Opened	29.6.1909	
UFFINGTON	Opened	2.10.1846	
Altered to UFFINGTON & BARNACK	... ...	1.2.1858	*
***	CP	1.9.1952	
***	CG	17.8.1964	
BAINTON GATE	OP	1.11.1854	
***	CP(All)	1.8.1856	*
Helpston Ballast Sidings SB	Open before	16.8.1877	
Altered to Uffington Ballast Sidings	By	1.2.1880	
Replacement box	Opened	14.5.1899	
Replacement box	Opened	1918-1930	
***	Closed	20.9.1970	
Maxey Crossing SB (not a block post)	Opened	24.7.1900	
***	Closed	14.11.1971	
Helpston West SB	Open before	16.8.1877	
Replacement box	Opened	5.8.1894	
Re-named Helpston Station SB	... ...	10.4.1906	
***	Closed	28.3.1971	
Helpston to Spital Jcn: TCB working introduced	... ...	26.6.1972	
HELPSTONE	Opened	2.10.1846	
Altered to HELPSTONE FOR MARKET DEEPING	... ...	1.7.1858	*
Altered to HELPSTON FOR MARKET DEEPING	... ...	1.5.1877	*
Altered to HELPSTON	... ...	1.5.1912	*
***	CG	3.5.1965	
***	CP	6.6.1966	
Helpston East SB	Open before	16.8.1877	
***	Closed	10.4.1906	
Helpston: connection from the northbound Midland line to the former Great Northern down slow line	Into use	28.3.1971	?
Helpston Jcn to Walton (south of): OLE on the northbound line only	Energised	7.3.1988	
Walton Station SB	Open before	16.8.1877	
Replacement box	Opened	26.7.1904	
New box in place of the former Midland and Great Northern boxes	Opened	21.3.1971	
Box made a gate box only	... ...	28.3.1971	
***	Closed	20.12.1976	
WALTON	OP	2.10.1846	
***	CP(All)	7.12.1953	
Walton (south of) to Peterborough: OLE on the northbound line only	Energised	16.3.1987	
Wisbech Sidings West SB	Open before	1.11.1875	
Replacement box	Opened	20.12.1891	
Re-named Wisbech West Junction SB	... ...	6.3.1892	
***	Closed	26.8.1964	
Wisbech Sidings West to Wisbech Jcn: down goods line	Into use	6.3.1892	
New England North: ladder junction with Great Northern lines	Into use	21.3.1971	?
WISBECH JUNCTION SIDINGS	Opened	....	
***	t.o.u.	....	

Wisbech Junction SB	Open before	16.8.1877
Replacement box	Opened	4.3.1906
***	Closed	21.3.1971
Junction with Peterborough, Wisbeach, & Sutton Bridge Railway	Opened	1.6.1866
***	Closed	....
Between Wisbech Junction and Westwood Junction the Midland & Great Northern Joint Railway possessed running powers over the Midland line.		
Wisbech Junction with the Great Northern Railway	Opened	1.8.1866
Wisbech Jcn to Crescent Crossing: block telegraph system	Installed	1892-1893
Spital Bridge SB	Open before	16.8.1877
Replacement box	Opened	24.1.1892
***	Closed	25.6.1972
Peterborough engine shed	Opened	1872
***	Closed	1.2.1960
Crescent Crossing SB	Open before	16.8.1877
Replacement box	Opened	6.6.1915
Re-named Crescent Sidings SB	... ...	....
***	Closed	7.12.1964
Crescent Crossing to Nene Jcn: block telegraph system	Installed	1876
PETERBOROUGH CRESCENT	OP	1.2.1858 *
Station closed and Midland trains began to use the Great Northern station	... ...	1.8.1866
Crescent Junction with the Great Northern Railway	Opened	1.8.1866
PETERBOROUGH NEW GOODS SIDINGS	Opened	6.1.1873
Crescent Sidings	Opened	12.11.1879
Nene Junction SB	Open before	16.8.1877
Replacement box	Opened	22.1.1888
***	Raised	15.11.1908
Replacement box	Opened	24.5.1921
***	Closed	25.6.1972
Nene Jcn to Great Northern Jcn: block telegraph system	Installed	1875
Nene Jcn to Great Eastern Jcn: block telegraph system	Installed	1876
Between the junction of the Midland and Great Northern lines and the junction of the Midland and Great Eastern lines in Peterborough the London & North Western Railway possessed running powers for all classes of traffic.		
Between Peterborough Junction and Peterborough station the Midland Railway possessed running powers over the Great Eastern line.		
PETERBOROUGH altered to PETERBOROUGH NORTH	... ...	1.7.1923
Station made "closed" for tickets	... ...	9.1938
Altered to PETERBOROUGH	... ...	....
New platform for the Midland lines (available to all traffic)	Into use	25.6.1972
Old Great Northern station rebuilt	... ...	....
Bridge No. 78: single-line over the up line working	Commenced	1.5.1932
Down line became single line	... ...	2.10.1932
Double-line working	Restored	1.1.1933
Fletton Road SB: replacement box at west end of the platforms of Peterborough East station	Opened	17.4.1932
***	Closed	....
Peterborough: Midland Railway Company worked into the station	From	21.2.1866
PETERBOROUGH altered to PETERBOROUGH EAST	... ...	1.7.1923
Station made "closed" for tickets	... ...	9.1938
***	CG	17.4.1966
***	CP	6.6.1966
***	C.Parcels	29.6.1970
***	RO(Parcels)	21.9.1970
***	C.Parcels	24.12.1970
Peterborough (Great Eastern station): Midland & Great Northern Joint Line trains ceased to run to and from this station	... ...	1.10.1904

NOTTINGHAM & MELTON LINE

Powers: Midland Railway (Additional Powers) Act 1873 (Melton Jcn to Upper Broughton)
Midland Railway (Nottingham and Saxby Lines) Act 1872, and
Midland Railway (Additional Powers) Act 1878 (Upper Broughton to Nottingham)

Melton Jcn to Nottingham London Road Jcn	OG	1.11.1879
***	OP	2.2.1880
The line was worked by the block telegraph system from its opening.		
Melton Jcn to Nottingham London Road Jcn	CP	1.5.1967
Line closed as a through route	... ...	4.11.1968
Melton Jcn: re-aligned curve	Into use	15.11.1886
Melton Jcn to Edwalton: down line "out of use for traffic purposes"; one engine in steam working Melton Junction to Old Dalby on up line and remainder of up line to Edwalton closed completely	... ...	18.12.1968
Melton Jcn to Melton GF (106 3/4 mls): down line closed and up line re-designated up and down through siding	... ...	30.8.1970
106 3/4 miles to Edwalton: former down line made up & down single line for Research Department use	... ...	30.8.1970

106 3/4 miles to Holwell Sidings GF:		
former up line made single line to and from Holwell Sidings	... ...	30.8.1970
***	Closed	1.9.1980
HOLWELL JUNCTION GOODS DEPOT	Opened	1.7.1887
***	Closed	6.7.1965
Holwell Sidings SB	Opened	1.11.1879
Replacement box	Opened	4.5.1902
Box closed and ground frame provided in lieu	... ...	15.12.1968
***	t.o.u.	....
Holwell Sidings to Old Dalby army depot	Closed	6.10.1969
HOLWELL SIDINGS	Opened	1.11.1879
***	C.Tfc	1.9.1980
***	t.o.u.	17.5.1983

Holwell branch
See page 85

SAXILBY	OG	1.11.1879
Altered to GRIMSTON	... ...	10.1.1880
***	OP	2.2.1880
***	CP&G	4.2.1957
Saxilby SB	Opened	1.11.1879
Re-named Grimston SB	... ...	2.2.1880
Replacement box	Opened	2.4.1895
***	Closed	23.12.1962
Old Dalby SB	Opened	1.11.1879
***	Re-framed	3.5.1896
***	Raised	12.6.1898
Replacement box	Opened	31.3.1901
Replacement box	Opened	12.10.1941
***	Closed	18.12.1968
Old Dalby: loops and sidings	Into use	12.10.1941
***	t.o.u.	18.12.1968
Old Dalby army depot to Nottingham London Road Jcn	Closed	4.11.1968
OLD DALBY	OG	1.11.1879
***	OP	2.2.1880
***	CP&G	18.4.1966
UPPER BROUGHTON	OP	2.2.1880
***	CP(All)	31.5.1948
Upper Broughton: up-line distant and home IBS	Into use	21.9.1941
Down-line distant and home IBS	Into use	12.10.1941
Upper Broughton up and down IBS	t.o.u.	1.8.1965
Upper Broughton SB	Opened	1.11.1879
***	Closed	1881-1885
Widmerpool SB	Opened	1.11.1879
***	Re-framed	26.4.1896
Replacement box	Opened	17.3.1901
***	Closed	1.8.1965
WIDMERPOOL	OG	1.11.1879
***	OP	2.2.1880
***	CP	28.2.1949
***	C.Parcels by	15.8.1958
***	CG	1.3.1965
PLUMTREE & KEYWORTH	OG	1.11.1879
***	OP	2.2.1880
Altered to PLUMTREE	... ...	1.5.1893 *
***	CP	28.2.1949
***	CG	1.11.1965
Plumtree SB	Opened	1.11.1879
***	Re-framed	19.4.1896
Replacement box	Opened	27.4.1902
***	Closed	15.11.1966
Research Department single line severed at 118 1/4 mls	... ...	16.12.1980
"9 1/2 mls north of Old Dalby" to Nottingham London Road Jcn	t.o.u.	3.11.1968
Edwalton SB	Opened	1.11.1879
Replacement box	Opened	27.10.1901
***	Closed	3.4.1966
EDWALTON	OG	1.11.1879
***	OP	2.2.1880
***	CP	28.7.1941
***	CG	1.11.1965

HOLWELL BRANCH

Powers: Midland Railway (Additional Powers) Act 1883
Midland Railway Act 1884 (Holwell Branch Extension)

Holwell Sidings to Holwell Mines	OG	1.1.1887

A line was in use by the beginning of 1877. This Midland opening must have been to the Holwell Iron Company's Siding. The branch was worked by train staff without tickets.

Holwell Jcn and Holwell Iron Company's gas works: new running line	Into use	9.5.1898
Holwell Jcn to Welby Sidings East GF	Closed	1.9.1980
Welby Sidings: Engineer's connection with Holwell branch about 200 yards on the Wycombe Junction side of the 3/4 milepost became the traffic connection, and the existing connection between the Wycombe Junction end of Welby Sidings and the main line of the Holwell branch was taken out	... ...	4.4.1904
WELBY SIDINGS	Closed	24.2.1972
	or	1.9.1980
Welby Sidings East GF to Wycombe Jcn	Last train	24.10.1962
***	Off. closed	27.7.1963
HOLWELL WHARF	Opened by	28.11.1887
***	Closed	2.6.1958
Extension line, and Wycombe Jcn with the Great Northern Railway	OG	18.4.1887

Between Wycombe Junction and Waltham-on-the-Wolds, and over the branches from the line, the Midland Railway possessed running powers over the Great Northern line.

SAXBY & BOURNE LINE

Powers: Midland Railway Act 1889
Midland Railway (Additional Powers) Act 1890 (Witham Deviation)
Eastern and Midlands Railway (Extensions) Act 1888 (At Bourne)

Saxby to Bourn	OG	5.6.1893
Passenger excursion trains began to run	... ...	7.1893
***	OP	1.5.1894
***	CP	2.3.1959
***	CG	6.4.1964
The Saxby & Bourn line was Midland property between Saxby Junction and the end-on junction with the Great Northern Railway at Little Bytham Junction, just east of the bridge over the Great Northern main line. The remainder of the line was Midland & Great Northern Joint Railway property.		
Saxby to Bourn: automatic tablet-exchange apparatus	Into use	10.2.1908
Saxby Jcn to South Witham: one engine in steam working	Commenced	29.4.1962
Line closed	... ...	3.1966
Saxby Jcn to Buckminster	Closed	10.9.1967
Edmondthorpe & Wymondham SB	Opened	5.6.1893
***	Closed	29.4.1962
EDMONDTHORPE & WYMONDHAM	OG	5.6.1893
***	OP	1.5.1894
***	CP	2.3.1959
***	CG	3.10.1960
Edmondthorpe loop	Extended	13.4.1941
Pain's Siding to Buckminster Siding	Closed	6.4.1964
***	Re-opened	3.1966
***	Closed	9.1966
***	Re-opened	2.10.1967
***	Closed	3.1.1972
The first closure may have been on 11 April 1964. From the re-opening in March 1966 the line was worked by Stewarts & Lloyds, not by British Railways.		
Buckminster Siding to South Witham	Closed	6.4.1964
South Witham SB	Opened	5.6.1893
***	Closed	29.4.1962
SOUTH WITHAM	OG	5.6.1893
***	OP	1.5.1894
***	CP	2.3.1959
***	CG	6.4.1964
Line severed at South Witham	... ...	29.4.1962
South Witham to Bourne	Closed	2.3.1959
CASTLE BYTHAM	OG	1.1.1898
***	OP	4.4.1898
***	CP&G	2.3.1959
Little Bytham Junction SB	Opened	5.6.1893
***	Closed	29.4.1962
Kingsland Sidings SB: replacement box on up side	Opened	24.10.1899
***	Closed	24.10.1920
BOURN (Great Northern station) altered to BOURNE	... ...	23.6.1893
***	CP	2.3.1959
***	CG	5.4.1965
Bourne engine shed transferred to the Midland & Great Northern Joint Committee	... ...	1897
Shed ceased to be used by LMS engines	... ...	31.12.1932

IV. THE EREWASH VALLEY AND NOTTINGHAMSHIRE

TRENT HIGH LEVEL GOODS LINES (TRENT & TOTON LINES)

Powers: Midland Railway Act 1899

Trent Jcn to Toton East Jcn: down goods line	Into use	2.6.1901
Trent Station South Jcn to Toton Sidings south end: up goods line	Into use	2.6.1901
Toton East Jcn to Toton Jcn: down goods line	Into use	25.5.1902
Toton East Jcn to Toton Down Sidings: east and west arrival lines	Into use	2.6.1901
Attenborough Jcn to Meadow Lane Jcn Curve	OG	2.6.1901
***	OP	12.5.1986
Meadow Lane Junction SB	Opened	2.6.1901
***	Closed	28.9.1969 ?
	or	12.10.1969 ?
Meadow Lane Jcn to Toton Jcn	OP	12.5.1986
Toton East Junction SB	Opened	2.6.1901
Replacement box	Opened	29.5.1949
Box made a shunting frame	... ...	19.10.1969
***	Closed	27.4.1986

EREWASH VALLEY RAILWAY

The Erewash Valley Railway Act 1845 included powers for the company to be sold to the Midland. The date of the effective take-over by the Midland was, in fact, February 1845, and it was the Midland that built the line.

Powers: Erewash Valley Railway Act 1845
Midland Railway Act 1891 (Ilkeston to Langley Mill Widening)
Midland Railway (Additional Powers) Act 1884 (Langley Mill to Pye Bridge Widening)
Midland Railway Act 1891 (Codnor Park to Coates Park Widening)

Long Eaton Jcn to Codnor Park Iron Works	OM	1.7.1847
***	OP	6.9.1847
***	OG	....

North Erewash Curve

Powers: Erewash Valley Railway Act 1845

South Erewash Jcn to North Erewash Jcn	OM	1.7.1847 ?
***	OG	....
***	OP	1.5.1862 *

Trent to Pye Bridge Jcn: block telegraph working	Introduced	1870-1871
South Erewash Junction re-named Trent Station North Junction	... ...	1.5.1862
Long Eaton Jcn to North Erewash Jcn	CP	1.5.1862 *
***	RO(P)	6.6.1863 *
***	CP	2.1.1967
***	Closed	29.7.1968
Trent Station North Jcn to North Erewash Jcn: up goods line	Into use	7.6.1896
Down goods line	Into use	14.6.1896
Trent Station North Jcn to Trowell Jcn	CP	6.11.1967
***	RO(P)	4.10.1971
***	CP	14.5.1984
North Erewash Junction SB	Opened	1860
***	Re-located	1886
Replacement box	Opened	16.5.1886
***	Re-framed	7.9.1896
Box made a shunting frame for level crossing only	... ...	28.9.1969
Crossing CCTV-controlled from Long Eaton Town SB	... ...	30.1.1977
Crossing brought under the control of Trent PSB	... ...	23.10.1988
Long Eaton Station SB	Open before	16.8.1877
Replacement box	Opened	24.7.1904
Replacement box	Opened	c.4.1941
Box made a shunting frame for level crossing only	... ...	19.9.1969
Box closed and crossing brought under the control of Trent PSB	... ...	23.10.1988
LONG EATON	Opened	6.9.1847
Altered to TOTON FOR LONG EATON	... ...	1.10.1851 *
Altered to LONG EATON	... ...	1.5.1862 *
Replacement station about 1/4 mile south	Opened	7.1863
***	CP	2.1.1967
TOTON GOODS DEPOT altered to LONG EATON GOODS DEPOT	... ...	1.5.1881
***	CG	7.1979
Long Eaton to Toton South Jcn: up and down goods lines	Into use	27.4.1941
Toton South Junction SB	Open before	16.8.1877
Replacement box	Opened	29.1.1905
Replacement box	Opened	2.10.1938
***	Closed	27.4.1941
Toton South Jcn to Sandiacre: up and down goods lines	In use by	1.9.1870 *

Toton South Jcn to Toton Jcn: second up goods line	Into use	2.6.1901
***	t.o.u.	7.8.1966
Toton Junction SB	Opened	2.6.1901
Replacement box	Opened	2.4.1950
***	Closed	19.10.1969
Toton Jcn: down goods line to down passenger line crossover	Into use	25.5.1902
Up passenger line to up goods line crossover	Into use	....
Up passenger line to second up goods line crossover	Into use	2.6.1901
First up goods line to second up goods line crossover	Into use	2.6.1901
Toton Jcn: No. 1 and No. 2 departure lines	Opened	20.7.1902
Toton Jcn to Trowell Jcn	RO(P)	12.5.1986
Toton Jcn to Stanton Gate North: down goods line (up side)	Into use	31.8.1902
TOTON SORTING SIDINGS	Opened	1.5.1856 *
New Empty Wagon Sidings	Into use	7.10.1900
TOTON YARD: down side mechanisation	Introduced	30.5.1939
***	t.o.u.	18.12.1983
TOTON YARD: up side mechanisation	Introduced	1949–1950
***	t.o.u.	5.8.1984
TOTON YARD: down yard -- Meadow Storage Sidings, Meadow Sidings 1–10, and Meadow Departure line	t.o.u.	8.1.1984
Up Sidings Control Tower and Down Sidings Control Tower closed and many sidings taken out of use	... ...	21.4.1985
Toton Down Sidings South SB	Opened	2.6.1901
***	Closed	16.5.1932
Toton Up Sidings South SB	Opened	3.8.1902
Box closed and ground frame provided in lieu	... ...	12.7.1909
***	t.o.u.	....
South End of Toton Sidings SB	Opened	....
Replacement box	Opened	30.9.1894
***	Closed	....
Toton Centre SB	Opened	....
***	Closed	10.11.1891
Toton Centre No. 1 SB	Opened	31.8.1902
Re-named Toton Centre SB	... ...	....
Replacement box	Opened	2.7.1950
***	Closed	19.10.1969
Toton Centre No. 2 SB	Opened	31.8.1902
Box closed and ground frame provided in lieu	... ...	15.11.1908
Toton Centre No. 2 SB (second box)	Opened	....
***	Closed	2.7.1950
Toton Centre No. 2 Down Sidings GF	t.o.u.	22.9.1968
Toton Down Sidings Centre SB	Opened	....
***	Closed	....
Toton Up Sidings Centre SB	Opened	....
***	Closed	....
Toton Down Sidings South SB	Opened	....
***	... ...	16.5.1932
Toton Down Sidings No. 1 SB:	Opened	....
Replacement box	Opened	16.9.1893
Replacement box	Opened	16.5.1932
Box made a pointsman's box	... ...	30.4.1939
***	Closed	30.5.1939
Toton Down Sidings No. 2 SB	Opened	....
Box made a pointsman's box	... ...	....
***	Closed	30.5.1939
Toton Down Sidings No. 3 SB	Opened	....
Replacement box	Opened	10.4.1932
Box made a pointsman's box	... ...	....
***	Closed	30.5.1939
Toton Down Sidings No. 4 SB	Opened	....
Box made a pointsman's box	... ...	....
***	Closed	30.5.1939
Toton No. 5 SB	Opened	....
***	Closed	31.8.1902
Toton Down Sidings No. 5 SB: replacement box	Opened	....
***	Closed	10.4.1932
Toton No. 6 SB	Opened	....
***	Closed	1949–1950
Toton No. 7 SB	Opened	....
***	Closed	1949–1950
Toton No. 8 SB	Opened	....
***	Closed	31.8.1902
Toton No. 9 SB	Opened	12.7.1886
***	Closed	31.8.1902
Toton Sidings SB	Opened	....
Replacement box named Toton Down Sidings North SB	Opened	31.8.1902
***	Closed	19.10.1969
Toton Up Sidings North SB	Opened	....
***	Closed	5.2.1950
Toton North SB: replacement box	Opened	21.9.1890
***	Closed	....

North End of Toton Sidings SB	Opened	....
***	Slued	3.2.1901
***	Closed	....
Toton engine shed (situated at Sandiacre)	Opened	c.1857
Toton No. 1 engine shed (situated at Toton)	Opened	1870
Toton No. 2 engine shed	Opened	1873
Toton No. 3 engine shed	Opened	1901
Sheds closed to steam traction	... ...	12.1965
Toton diesel depot	Opened	9.1963
Stapleford & Sandiacre: new fan of sidings alongside up goods line	Into use	28.10.1900
Ten new reception lines	Into use	24.3.1901
Sandiacre & Stapleford Station SB	Open before	16.8.1877
Re-named Stapleford & Sandiacre SB	... ...	10.1884
Replacement box	Opened	28.10.1900
Replacement box	Opened	4.9.1949
Box made a shunting frame	... ...	19.10.1969
SANDIACRE & STAPLEFORD	Opened	6.9.1847
New station	Opened	1.5.1872
Altered to STAPLEFORD & SANDIACRE	... ...	10.1884
Up back platform line	Into use	5.5.1901
***	CG	5.10.1964
***	CP	2.1.1967
Sandiacre to Stanton Gate Jcn: up and down goods lines	Into use	24.11.1872
Sandiacre: up goods line through Stapleford & Sandiacre station placed in its permanent position; siding alongside up goods line superseded by new siding alongside new up goods line	... ...	17.3.1901
Stapleford & Sandiacre: down goods line altered so as to lead only to the West Hallam branch	... ...	12.1.1985
Stanton Gate South Sidings SB	Open before	1.11.1875
Replacement box	Opened	1881
Re-named Stanton Gate South Junction SB	... ...	25.11.1889
***	Closed	.... ?
Stanton Gate South Sidings SB (second box)	Opened	.... ?
Replacement box	Opened	29.9.1901
***	Raised	8.1.1911
***	Closed	19.10.1969
Stanton Gate South:		
second down goods line to down goods line crossover	Into use	20.10.1901
Up goods line to up passenger line crossover	Into use	....
Stanton Gate South to Stanton Gate North: replacement up goods line	Into use	29.9.1901
Stanton Gate South to Stanton Gate North: second down goods line	Slued	17.10.1921
Made a reception line	... ...	17.3.1968
Stanton Gate South to Bennerley Jcn: down goods line (up side)	Into use	20.10.1901
STANTON GATE SIDINGS	Opened	....
***	t.o.u.	....
Stanton Gate SB	Open before	16.8.1877
Replacement box	Opened	28.6.1891
***	Closed	....
Stanton Gate North SB	Opened	12.1888-8.1893
Replacement box	Opened	29.9.1901
Box closed and shunting frame provided in lieu	... ...	19.10.1969
Stanton Gate North:		
down goods line to second down goods line crossover	Into use	....
Up passenger line to up goods line crossover	Into use	29.9.1901

Stanton Gate branches

See page 94

Stanton Gate to Ilkeston (later South Junction): up goods line	Into use	14.11.1875
Down goods line (down side)	Into use	7.8.1876
Down-side down goods line named second down goods line	... ...	....
Second down goods line made down through siding	... ...	6.11.1950
Down through siding severed 1/2 mile north of Trowell	... ...	10.11.1968
STANTON GATE	Opened	1.7.1851 *
New station	Opened	1873
***	CG	2.11.1964
***	CP	2.1.1967
Stanton Gate to Trowell Jcn: passenger lines	Slued	30.10.1910
Trowell Junction SB	Opened	1875
Replacement box	Opened	21.7.1901
***	Closed	19.10.1969

Radford & Trowell line

See page 109

TROWELL	OP&G	2.6.1884
***	CG	2.11.1964
***	CP	2.1.1967

Babbington Branch
Powers: Midland Railway (Erewash Valley Branches) Act 1846

Babbington branch	Opened	5.1849	
***	Closed	....	
Erewash Valley Iron Company's Sidings SB	Open before	1.11.1875	
***	Closed by	16.8.1877	
Granby Sidings SB	Open before	1.11.1875	
***	Closed by	16.8.1877	
Ilkeston Junction SB	Open before	16.8.1877	
***	Closed	1882	
Ilkeston South Junction SB	Opened	1882	
Replacement box	Opened	31.3.1901	
***	Closed	12.10.1969	

Ilkeston branch
See page 95

Ilkeston South Jcn to Bennerley Jcn: up goods line	Into use	16.12.1900	

Cossall Colliery Branch
Powers: --

Cossall Colliery Branch	Opened	1849	
***	Closed	....	
Ilkeston Junction up sidings (former Cossall Colliery branch)	t.o.u.	12.3.1967	
ILKESTON JUNCTION (exchange station)	OP(NA)	6.9.1847	
***	OP	1.8.1858	*
New station	Erected	1861	
Replacement station named Ilkeston, 13 chains to the north	Opened	2.5.1870	?
Altered to ILKESTON JUNCTION	... ...	1.7.1879	*
Altered to ILKESTON JUNCTION & COSSALL	... ...	1.12.1890	
***	CP(All)	2.1.1967	
Ilkeston Common Crossing SB	Open before	16.8.1877	
***	Closed	1882	
Ilkeston Common Crossing to Bennerley Jcn: up goods line	Into use	2.1879–2.1880	
Ilkeston North Junction SB	Opened	1882	
***	Closed	6.1.1901	
Ilkeston North Jcn: connection between the line from Kimberley and the up main line from Shipley Gate	Removed	14.10.1900	
Ilkeston North Jcn (v. Ilkeston branch entry)	Removed	6.1.1901	

Ilkeston North Curve
See page 96

Bennerley NCB Sidings: rapid loading bunker. The existing ground frame was abolished and control of the points was taken over by Trent PSB.	Into use	19.2.1984	
Bennerley Junction SB	Opened	1879	
Replacement box	Opened	2.9.1900	
***	Closed	12.10.1969	
Bennerley Junction: up goods line to up passenger line crossover	Into use	....	
Down passenger line to down goods line crossover	Into use	14.10.1900	
Facing connection to the branch	t.o.u.	3.12.1967	

Bennerley & Bulwell line
See page 109

Bennerley Jcn to Heanor Jcn: down goods line (up side)	Into use	14.10.1900	
Bennerley Jcn to Shipley Gate: up goods line	Into use	14.10.1900	
SHIPLEY GATE	Opened	1.7.1851	*
Station enlarged	... ...	1902	
***	CP&G	27.8.1948	
Shipley Gate SB	Open before	16.8.1877	
Replacement box	Opened	20.1.1895	
***	Re-framed	3.4.1898	
Box made a shunting frame for level crossing only	... ...	12.10.1969	

Eastwood Branch
Powers: Erewash Valley Railway Act 1845, Midland Railway (Erewash Valley Branches) Act 1846

Eastwood branch	Opened	1849	?
***	Closed	....	
Shipley Gate to Heanor Jcn: up goods line	Into use	18.9.1898	
Heanor Junction: double junction (DGL-DPL, UPL-UGL)	Into use	28.9.1902	?
Heanor Junction SB	Open before	1.11.1875	
Replacement box	Opened	31.5.1896	
Replacement box	Opened	3.2.1901	
***	Closed	12.10.1969	

Ripley branch
See page 144

HEANOR JUNCTION SIDINGS	Opened	....	
***	t.o.u.	....	
Heanor Jcn to south end of Langley Mill Sidings: up goods line	Into use	10.3.1901	
Heanor Jcn to Beggarlee Jcn: down goods line (up side)	Into use	28.9.1902	
LANGLEY MILL FOR HEANOR	Opened	6.9.1847	
Altered to LANGLEY MILL & EASTWOOD	... ...	1.11.1876	*
Altered to LANGLEY MILL & EASTWOOD FOR HEANOR	... ...	11.9.1933	*
***	CG	2.11.1964	
***	CP	2.1.1967	
New station named LANGLEY MILL opened on site of old one	... ...	12.5.1986	
Langley Mill SB	Open before	16.8.1877	
Replacement box	Opened	23.3.1902	
***	Closed	12.10.1969	
Langley Mill Sidings (south end) to Beggarlee Jcn: up goods line	Into use	1.6.1902	
Langley Mill Up Sidings (north end):			
Messrs Barber, Walker & Co.'s SB superseded by new box	... ...	4.9.1916	
LANGLEY MILL UP SIDINGS	Opened	....	
***	Closed	....	
LANGLEY MILL DOWN SIDINGS	Opened	....	
***	Closed	27.11.1966	

Beggarlee Branch
Powers: Midland Railway (Erewash Valley Branches) Act 1846

Beggarlee branch	Opened	1849	?
***	Closed	....	

Moor Green Colliery Branch
Powers: --

Beggarlee Branch to Moor Green Colliery	Opened	....
***	Closed	22.6.1985

Beggarlee Sidings SB	Open before	1.11.1875
Re-named Beggarlee Junction SB	... ...	....
Replacement box	Opened	25.5.1902
***	Raised	9.6.1895
***	Slued	13.7.1902
***	Closed	22.4.1928
Beggarlee Sidings to Codnor Park Station Jcn: down goods line	Into use	1.12.1889
Up goods line	Into use	30.3.1890
Beggarlee Sidings to Codnor Park Station Jcn: pairing by use	Introduced	28.9.1902

Brinsley Branch
Powers: Midland Railway (Erewash Valley Branches) Act 1846

Brinsley branch	Opened	1849	?
Junction and sidings	Removed	1922	

STONEYFORD	OG before	1877
***	CG(All) by	8.1894
Stoneyford Sidings SB	Open before	1.11.1875
Re-named Stoneyford Junction SB	... ...	1890
Re-named Stoneyford Sidings SB	... ...	28.9.1902
***	Closed	21.11.1921
Stoneyford Jcn: connection from up goods line to up passenger line	Removed	27.9.1902
Connection from down passenger line to down goods line	Removed	27.9.1902
Stoneyford North SB	Opened	22.6.1902
Re-named Stoneyford Junction SB	... ...	28.9.1902
***	Closed	16.2.1969
Stoneyford Jcn to Codnor Park Station Jcn:		
second down goods line on the down side of the line	Into use	28.9.1902
***	t.o.u.	17.4.1966
Great Northern Junction SB	Opened	29.10.1899
***	Re-framed	28.9.1902
***	Closed	3.2.1957
Great Northern Jcn (Codnor Park): junction laid in and commissioned	... ...	29-31.10.1899
Revenue-earning traffic	Commenced	1.11.1899
New RCH distances into effect	... ...	19.2.1900
***	Singled	24.6.1928
***	Removed	4.7.1954
Codnor Park Station Junction SB	Open before	1869
Replacement box	Opened	2.3.1890
Replacement box	Opened	28.9.1902
***	Closed	12.10.1969
Codnor Park Station Junction: double junction (DFL-DSL, USL-UFL)	Into use	28.9.1902
***	t.o.u.	....
Codnor Park Station Jcn to Codnor Park Jcn:		
up and down slow lines (up side)	Into use	28.9.1902

CODNOR PARK	Opened	6.9.1847
***	Closed	1.12.1851 ?
***	Re-opened	1.1.1852 ?
Altered to CODNOR PARK & IRONVILLE	... ...	17.11.1898
New platforms	Into use	9.1902/4.1903
***	CG	2.11.1964
***	CP	2.1.1967

Extension from Codnor Park to Pye Bridge

Codnor Park to Pye Bridge	OG	1850
***	OP	6.11.1851
Codnor Park Junction SB	Open before	16.8.1877
Replacement box	Opened	2.2.1890
***	Re-framed	19.5.1901
Replacement box	Opened	28.11.1954
Box closed and ground frame provided in lieu	... ...	12.10.1969 ?
***	t.o.u. by	27.11.1987

Codnor Park Curve

See page 97

Codnor Park Junction: double junction (DGL-DPL, UPL-UGL)	Into use	....
***	t.o.u.	....
Codnor Park Jcn: connection to Ironville Jcn curve moved 130 yards further south	... ...	12/18.5.1901
Codnor Park Jcn to Pye Bridge Jcn: new main lines (down side)	Opened	16.9.1900
Codnor Park Jcn to Riddings Jcn: up and down slow lines	Into use	19.5.1901
Codnor Park Jcn to Blackwell South Jcn: pairing by use	Introduced	8.6.1902
Codnor Park Jcn to Pye Bridge Jcn: slow lines made goods lines	... ...	6.8.1967
Riddings Junction SB	Open before	16.8.1877
***	Raised	12.6.1892
Replacement box	Opened	15.9.1900
Box closed and ground frame provided in lieu	... ...	12.10.1969 ?
***	t.o.u. by	27.11.1987

Duffield & Selston line

See page 96

Riddings Jcn to Pye Bridge Jcn: up and down slow lines (up side)	Into use	16.9.1900
PYE BRIDGE FOR ALFRETON	Opened	1.12.1851
Altered to PYE BRIDGE	... ...	1.5.1862 *
New station	Into use	1900-1901
***	CG	2.11.1964
***	CP	2.1.1967
Canal Junction SB	Opened	18.12.1876
***	Closed	1878
Pye Bridge: Canal Jcn with the Great Northern Railway	Completed	18.12.1876
RCH distances	Cancelled	20.11.1891
Pye Bridge Junction SB	Open before	1869
Replacement box	Opened	8.5.1892
***	Re-framed	8.3.1896
***	Re-framed	16.9.1900
***	Raised	31.5.1908
***	Closed	12.10.1969
Pye Bridge Jcn: up goods line to up fast line crossover	Into use	8.6.1902 ?
Down fast line to down goods line crossover	Into use	21.4.1901

Mansfield & Pinxton line

See page 97

EREWASH VALLEY EXTENSION RAILWAY

Powers: Midland Railway (Erewash Valley Extension) Act 1846 (Codnor Park to Clay Cross Junction)
Midland Railway Act 1891 (Codnor Park to Coates Park Widening)
Midland Railway (Erewash Valley) Act 1859 (Pye Bridge to Clay Cross, alteration of levels etc)
Midland Railway Act 1899 (Alfreton second tunnel & Alfreton to Clay Cross Widening)

Pye Bridge Jcn to Coates Park Colliery	OM before	10.1853
Pye Bridge to Clay Cross Jcn	OG	1.11.1861
***	OP	1.5.1862
Block telegraph working	Introduced	1870-1871
Some coal traffic may have run during October 1861.		
Pye Bridge Jcn to Coates Park South: up goods line	Into use	16.2.1896
Down goods line	Into use	8.3.1896
Pye Bridge Jcn to Coney Green: up and down goods lines	t.o.u.	....
Coates Park South SB	Open before	1.11.1875
Replacement box	Opened	16.2.1896
Replacement box	Opened	8.6.1902
***	Closed	12.10.1969

Coates Park South to Blackwell South Jcn: down goods line	Into use	8.6.1902
Coates Park South to Alfreton: up goods line	Into use	8.6.1902
COATES PARK	OG	....
***	CG(All) by	8.1894
Coates Park North SB	Open before	1.11.1875
Replacement box	Opened	8.6.1902
***	Closed	12.10.1969
Alfreton Tunnel SB	Opened	7.8.1900
***	Closed	9.2.1902
Alfreton second tunnel (passenger lines)	Opened	8.6.1902
Old tunnel	t.o.u.	....
ALFRETON	Opened	1.5.1862
Altered to ALFRETON & SOUTH NORMANTON	... ...	7.11.1891
***	CP	2.1.1967
***	CG	2.10.1967
New station named ALFRETON & MANSFIELD PARKWAY (the same site)	Opened	7.5.1973
Alfreton Station SB	Open before	16.8.1877
Replacement box	Opened	21.7.1901
***	Closed	12.10.1969

Alfreton Colliery Branch

Sanctioning: Midland Railway Act 1888

Alfreton Colliery branch	Opened	7.6.1886
***	Closed	4.1.1969 ?

Alfreton (north end of station) to Blackwell South Jcn: up goods line	Into use	21.7.1901
Blackwell South Junction: double junction (DPL-DGL, UGL-UPL)	Into use	4.5.1902
***	t.o.u.	....
Blackwell South Junction SB	Opened	1881
Replacement box	Opened	13.1.1895
Replacement box	Opened	4.5.1902 ?
***	Raised	27.6.1909
***	Closed	12.10.1969

Blackwell South Curve

See page 98

Blackwell South Jcn to Morton: bi-directional goods line	Into use	....
***	t.o.u.	....
Blackwell South Jcn to Westhouses & Blackwell station: up goods line	Into use	11.1885-12.1888
Down goods line	Into use	11.5.1902
Blackwell South Jcn re-located a little to the south	... ...	4.5.1902
Blackwell South Jcn to Clay Cross North Jcn: down goods line	t.o.u.	8.10.1969

Blackwell branch

See page 98

WEST HOUSE	OP	1.5.1862 *
***	CP(All)	1.8.1865
TIBSHELF JUNCTION (the site of West House)	OM	6.1876
Altered to WESTHOUSES & BLACKWELL and opened for passengers	... ...	17.10.1881
***	OG	5.1886
***	CG	2.11.1964
***	CP	2.1.1967
Westhouses & Blackwell Station SB	Opened	1881
Replacement box	Opened	27.4.1902
***	Closed	12.10.1969
Westhouses & Blackwell: down goods loop	Into use	1909
***	t.o.u.	....
Westhouses & Blackwell to Tibshelf Sidings SB: down goods line (up side) and bi-directional up goods line	Into use	22.9.1901
Westhouses & Blackwell to Weighing Machine Sidings: second down goods line made bi-directional	... ...	9.8.1908
Westhouses engine shed	Opened	1890
***	C.Steam	3.10.1966
This shed continued to look after NCB tank-engines till 7 October 1967.		
Blackwell Sidings SB	Open before	1.11.1875
***	Closed	6.1881-4.1883
Blackwell Sidings SB (second box)	Opened	28.3.1887
***	Closed	....
Tibshelf Sidings SB (not a block post)	Opened	....
Replacement box	Opened	22.9.1901
***	Closed	....

Tibshelf & Teversall line

See page 97

Tibshelf Sidings to Tibshelf South Jcn: up and down goods lines (up side)	Into use	11.1885-12.1888
TIBSHELF SIDINGS	Opened	....
***	Closed	....

Tibshelf Sidings: departure line	Into use	27.4.1902
New sidings	Into use	28.4.1902
Tibshelf Junction SB	Open before	12.1872
Replacement box named Tibshelf South Junction SB	Opened	1885
Replacement box	Opened	21.7.1901
***	Re-framed	11.5.1902
***	Raised	18.7.1915
***	Closed	20.11.1966
Tibshelf South Jcn: down reception line	Into use	6.6.1909
***	t.o.u.	....
Tibshelf South Jcn: double junction (DPL-DGL, UGL-UPL)	Into use	....
***	t.o.u.	....
Tibshelf South Jcn	Altered	21.7.1901
Up and down goods lines south of the junction joined to the up and down goods lines north of the junction	... ...	11.5.1902
Position of lines slightly altered	... ...	5.4.1908
Tibshelf South Jcn to Doe Hill: up goods line	Into use	4.2.1900
Tibshelf South Jcn to Morton Sidings: down goods line (up side)	Into use	11.8.1901
Doe Hill Station SB	Open before	12.1872
Replacement box	Opened	20.1.1895
***	Re-framed	4.2.1900
Replacement box	Opened	11.8.1901
***	Raised	27.4.1913
***	Closed	28.3.1965
Doe Hill to Morton Sidings: up goods line	Into use	11.8.1901
DOE HILL	Opened	1.5.1862
Station enlarged	... ...	1902
***	CP&G	12.9.1960
Morton Sidings SB	Opened	1873-1876
Replacement box	Opened	6.1.1895
Replacement box	Opened	28.7.1901
***	Closed	12.10.1969
MORTON SIDINGS	Opened	....
***	t.o.u.	....

Pilsley branch

Powers: Midland Railway (New Lines and Additional Powers) Act 1865
Midland Railway (Additional Powers) Act 1870 (Pilsley Branch Extension)

Pilsley Colliery to Morton Sidings (Pilsley Branch Jcn)	OM	5.7.1869
Branch made a siding	... ...	29.5.1962
Pilsley Crossing SB	Opened	....
***	Closed	....

Morton Branch

Powers: Midland Railway (New Lines and Additional Powers) Act 1865

Morton branch	Opened	1876
***	Closed	....

Morton Sidings to Coney Green: up and down goods lines (up side)	Into use	6.4.1902
Morton Sidings to Clay Cross North Jcn: up goods line	t.o.u.	8.10.1969
Pilsley Junction SB	Open before	12.1872
Replacement box	Opened	22.1.1893
***	Closed	2.3.1902
Danesmoor Sidings SB	Open before	1.11.1875
Replacement box	Opened	10.11.1901
***	Raised	2.12.1917
***	Raised	16.2.1919
***	Closed	23.1.1966
Coney Green Sidings SB	Open before	1870
Replacement box	Opened	15.5.1898
Replacement box	Opened	16.2.1902
***	Closed	22.3.1964
Coney Green: up passenger line to up goods line crossover	Into use	6.4.1902
***	t.o.u.	....
Coney Green Sidings: down passenger line to down goods line crossover	Into use	4.7.1909
***	t.o.u.	....
Coney Green to Clay Cross South: up goods line	Into use	16.2.1902
Replacement up goods line	Into use	1.6.1902
Coney Green to Clay Cross North Jcn: up and down goods lines (up side)	Into use	15.6.1902
Clay Cross South Jcn: new high-speed junction	Installed	21.11.1976

STANTON GATE BRANCHES

Stanton Old Iron Works Branch

Powers: Midland Railway (Erewash Valley Branches) Act 1846

Stanton Old Iron Works branch	Opened	8.12.1872
New connection north of underbridge No. 2	Into use	17.8.1941
Foundry Frame No. 2, and new connection	Into use	5.2.1941

Stanton Old Iron Works Branch designated a siding	... ...	7.2.1965
One train working	Commenced	15.9.1974
***	Closed	24.1.1984
Stanton Gate: connection between Old Works line and New Works line	Into use	17.8.1941

Stanton & Shipley Branch

Powers: Midland Railway (Additional Powers) Act 1867 (Stanton end)
Midland Railway (Branches Etc) Act 1866 (Shipley end)

Stanton Gate & Nutbrook branch (= Stanton & Shipley line) This line was worked as far as New Works Sidings by the electric train tablet block system.	Opened	1.11.1870
Branch cut at junction for West Hallam Colliery, and New Works Sidings to West Hallam made one engine in steam	... ...	27.6.1967
Stanton Gate SF to West Hallam: one train working	Commenced	10.4.1976
Stanton Gate New Works Sidings SB	Opened	30.4.1906
***	Closed	10.4.1976
Stanton Gate: connection to former Great Northern Railway	Into use	27.5.1968
Stanton New Works to Quarry Hill Road (formerly Great Northern)	Closed	10.4.1976
Remainder of the branch	Closed	....
Mapperley Junction SB	Open before	1.10.1876
***	Closed	1878–1879

West Hallam Branch

Powers: No construction powers

West Hallam Colliery branch	Opened	....
West Hallam Loaded Wagon Sidings GF to Shipley Colliery	Closed	26.8.1966
	or	27.6.1967

Mapperley Branch

Powers: Midland Railway (Additional Powers) Act 1867

Mapperley branch	Opened	1872
***	Closed	27.6.1967
Mapperley Jcn to Mapperley Colliery	Closed	12.5.1966
Mapperley branch: pilot guard replaced by staff without tickets	... ...	1.3.1909
Mapperley Jcn to Stanton New Iron Works Sidings: electric train tablet working	Introduced	14.11.1910
Stanton New Iron Works Sidings: connection between main line of Stanton & Mapperley branch and Stanton Gate end of new sidings	Into use	3.9.1911

Manners Colliery Branch

Powers: --

Manners Colliery branch	Opened	1897
*** This was the date on which the previously private branch was laid with Midland rails.	Closed	....
Branch made a siding	... ...	23.11.1959
Manners Colliery: connection between the Midland and Great Northern running lines to the empty wagon sidings and colliery sidings	Into use	19.9.1904

ILKESTON BRANCH

Powers: Erewash Valley Railway Act 1845

Ilkeston Jcn to Ilkeston	Opened	6.9.1847
***	CP	2.5.1870
***	RO(P)	1.7.1879
***	CP (temp.)	16.6.1947
***	CP	10.7.1950
***	CG	15.6.1959
Ilkeston Town branch, goods yard, etc worked by engines instead of by horses The line was worked by block telegraph and train staff from its re-opening in 1879.	... ...	22.6.1879
Ilkeston South Jcn: facing junction	Removed	21.9.1952
Ilkeston South Jcn, curve, and remainder of branch	Closed	24.8.1964
Ilkeston West Junction SB	Opened	1882
Replacement box	Opened	30.8.1903
***	Closed	7.9.1941
***	Re-opened	5.5.1946
***	Closed	10.4.1949
Ilkeston Town SB	Opened	1879
Replacement box	Opened	28.1.1900
***	Closed	....

Ilkeston Gas Works Sidings: new connection with the main line of the branch	Into use	1.5.1910

Ilkeston North Curve

Powers: Midland Railway (Additional Powers) Act 1880,
Midland Railway (Additional Powers) Act 1875
(Ilkeston North Curve Continuation: widening - land powers only)

Ilkeston West Jcn to Ilkeston North Jcn	Opened	1.9.1882
Curve extension (by 19 chains) north to Bennerley Jcn	Into use	6.1.1901
Ilkeston North Curve	CP	1.1.1917 *
Curve cut at Ilkeston West Jcn end and remainder made a siding	... ...	7.9.1941
Ilkeston West Jcn to Ilkeston North Jcn	Re-opened	5.5.1946
Curve cut at Ilkeston West Jcn, lines left as sidings from Bennerley Jcn	... ...	10.4.1949
Remaining sidings from Bennerley Jcn	t.o.u.	22.1.1967

Ilkeston Colliery	Closed	1915
ILKESTON	Opened	6.9.1847
***	CP	2.5.1870
ILKESTON TOWN	Opened	1.7.1879
***	CP (temp.)	16.6.1947
***	CP	10.7.1950
***	CG	15.6.1959

DUFFIELD & SELSTON LINE

Powers: Midland Railway (New Lines and Additional Powers) Act 1865
(Ambergate to Pye Bridge)
Midland Railway (Additional Powers) Act 1868 (Pye Bridge Deviation)

Swanwick Jcn to Ironville Jcn (to Codnor Park Jcn)	OM	1.6.1874
Crich Jcn to Pentrich Colliery Sidings	OM	29.7.1874
Pentrich Colliery Sidings to Swanwick Jcn	OM	1.2.1875
Crich Jcn to Riddings Jcn	OP	1.5.1875
***	CP	16.6.1947
Crich Jcn to Ironville Jcn (to Codnor Park Jcn)	OG	1.1.1885 ?
Ironville Jcn to Riddings Jcn	OG	1.5.1885 ?
Hammersmith to Swanwick Sidings (Midland Railway Trust)	RO(P)	22.8.1981

The line was worked by the block telegraph system from its opening.
A summer-Saturdays-only passenger service ran over the line between 14 June 1958 and 11 September 1961.

Crich Jcn to point of cut near Buckland Hollow	Singled	22.12.1968
Crich Jcn (General Refractories GF) to Swanwick Sidings	Closed	23.12.1968
Ambergate Colliery Sidings SB	Open before	1.11.1875
***	Closed	4.1883-11.1885
Buckland Hollow SB	Opened	c.9.1876
Replacement box	Opened	27.4.1902
***	Closed	1.9.1963
Line severed Buckland Hollow	... ...	22.12.1968

Buckland Hollow Branch

Powers: Midland Railway (Additional Powers) Act 1875

Buckland Hollow to Hartshay Colliery	Opened	....
***	Re-opened	1908
***	Closed	....

Pentrich Colliery Sidings SB	Open before	1.10.1876
Replacement box	Opened	11.2.1895
***	Raised	4.6.1907
***	t.o.u. by	18.11.1944
***	Off. closed	20.2.1949
Butterley Junction SB	Opened	1.6.1890
***	Closed by	10.2.1934
***	Removed	20.3.1938
Butterley Jcn to Butterley: single-line working on down line	Introduced	17.10.1926
Single-line working on up line	Introduced	25.11.1928
Double-line working	Restored	15.12.1929
BUTTERLEY	OP&G	1.5.1875
Altered to BUTTERLEY FOR RIPLEY & SWANWICK	... ...	29.7.1935
***	CP	16.6.1947
***	CG	2.11.1964
Excursion trains continued to serve Butterley until after 1964.		
Butterley Station SB	Open before	1.10.1876
Replacement box	Opened	21.12.1902
***	Closed	7.3.1965
Swanwick West SB	Open before	1.10.1876
***	Closed	5.2.1894
Swanwick Sidings: line severed 200 yards west of the signalbox	... ...	22.12.1968
Swanwick Sidings (termination of line) to Riddings Jcn	Singled	22.12.1968

Swanwick Sidings to Codnor Park Jcn: one engine in steam working	Commenced	4.10.1969	
Line reverted to siding status	... ...	13.10.1971	
Swanwick Sidings (Adamson-Butterley Siding) to Ironville Jcn	Closed (BR)	4.10.1971	
***	CG(All)	30.4.1979	
This section of line was worked exclusively by Adamson-Butterley Ltd.			
Swanwick Sidings to Codnor Park Jcn	t.o.u.	11.6.1979	
Swanwick Sidings to Codnor Park Jcn: line re-instated and worked by the Midland Railway Trust by electric token from Ironville No. 1 GF	... ...	29.5.1982	
Swanwick Sidings SB	Opened	5.2.1894	
***	Closed	22.12.1968	
Swanwick East SB	Open before	1.10.1876	
***	Closed	5.2.1894	

Shirland Branch

Powers: Midland Railway (Branches Etc.) Act 1866

Swanwick Jcn to Swanwick Colliery	OM	1.6.1874	
***	t.o.u.	22.12.1968	
Ironville Junction SB	Open before	16.8.1877	
Replacement box	Opened	21.9.1902	
***	Closed	22.1.1967	
Ironville Jcn to Riddings Jcn	Closed	23.12.1968	

Codnor Park Curve

Powers: Midland Railway (Additional Powers) Act 1868

Ironville Jcn to Codnor Park Jcn	OM	1.6.1874	
***	OP	7.8.1875	*
***	OG	1.1.1885	?*
***	Closed	3.10.1966	
***	t.o.u.	22.1.1967	
Single-line siding	Re-instated	22.12.1968	
***	RO(G)	23.12.1968	
***	CG(All)	30.4.1979	

MANSFIELD & PINXTON LINE

Pye Bridge to Pinxton

Powers: Midland Railway (Erewash Valley Branches) Act 1846

Pye Bridge Jcn to Pinxton	OM	1850	
***	OP&G	6.11.1851	*
Pye Bridge Jcn to Kirkby Jcn: block telegraph working	Introduced	1874	
Pye Bridge Jcn to Kirkby Station Jcn	CP	16.6.1947	
***	CP(Off.)	10.9.1951	
Workmen's trains	Ceased	6.9.1965	
Pye Bridge Jcn to Shirebrook West designated a goods line	... ...	2.4.1972	
Sleights Sidings North SB	Open before	1.11.1875	
Re-named Sleights Sidings West SB	... ...	1876	
Replacement box	Opened	1.5.1904	
***	Closed	8.12.1968	
Sleights Sidings South SB	Open before	1.11.1875	
Re-named Sleights Sidings East SB	... ...	1876	
Replacement box	Opened	3.4.1892	
Box fitted with one-function switches	... ...	1969	
Langton Colliery Sidings SB	Open before	1.11.1875	
***	Closed	9.1886	
Langton Junction SB	Open before	16.8.1877	
***	Closed	4.1878-2.1879	
Langton Jcn with the Great Northern Railway	Completed	18.12.1876	
RCH distances	Cancelled	20.11.1891	

Mansfield & Pinxton Railway

The Mansfield & Pinxton Railway was purchased with effect from 15 February 1848 under the Midland Railway (Mansfield and Pinxton Branch) Act 1847.

Powers: Mansfield and Pinxton Railway Act 1817,
Midland Railway (Mansfield and Pinxton Railway) Act 1847

Pinxton Wharf to Mansfield (Portland Wharf)	OG	13.4.1819	
***	OP	1832	
Pinxton to Kirkby Jcn section, with deviations	Re-opened	6.11.1851	
PINXTON & SELSTON	Opened	6.11.1851	?
***	CP	16.6.1947	
Altered to PINXTON NORTH	Goods	1.7.1950	
***	CG	2.11.1964	
Excursion trains continued to run until the 1960s.			

Pinxton Station SB (not a block post)	Open before	1.11.1875
Replacement box opened as a block post	... ...	24.1.1897
Langton Branch Sidings SB	Opened	1885
Re-named Langton Branch Junction SB	... ...	12.1888-8.1893
***	Closed	27.6.1897 ?

Langton Branch

Powers: Midland Railway (Additional Powers) Act 1884

Langton Colliery Sidings to Langton Colliery Empty Wagon Sidings	Opened	29.12.1885
Langton branch extension	Opened	27.6.1897
Branch as far as Pinxton Co.'s No. 2 Pit Loaded Wagon Sidings line: working taken over by the Midland Railway	... ...	18.9.1905
Langton Colliery Sidings SB	Open before	16.8.1877
Box made made a gate box only	... ...	9.1886
Ground frame	t.o.u.	8.11.1970
Bentinck Colliery Loaded Wagon Sidings Branch Jcn to Langton Colliery Empty Wagon Sidings	t.o.u.	8.11.1970

Bentinck Loaded Wagon Sidings Branch

Powers: No construction powers

Langton Colliery Sidings to Bentinck Colliery Loaded Wagon Sidings	Opened by	21.12.1898
Langton Colliery Sidings GF to Bentinck Colliery Empty Wagon Sidings	Closed	8.11.1970

Lower Portland SB	Open before	1.11.1875
***	Closed	2.1880-6.1881
Upper Portland SB	Open before	1.11.1875
Replacement box	Opened	19.3.1905
Box closed and AHBs provided in lieu	... ...	3.2.1988
Upper Portland SB to Bentinck Colliery Sidings SB made an interlaced single line with key token working on account of a slip	... ...	10.5.1959
Double-line working	Restored	13.12.1959
Bentinck Colliery Sidings SB	Opened	30.11.1897
***	Closed	26.8.1977

Bentinck Empty Wagon Sidings Branch

Powers: --

Bentinck Colliery Sidings to Bentinck Colliery Empty Wagon Sidings	Opened	4.1894 ?
	<u>or</u>	30.11.1897 ?
***	Closed	29.8.1977

Kirkby Lane Crossing SB	Open before	16.8.1877
Replacement box	Opened	13.5.1889
***	Closed	14.8.1892

Kirkby Curve

Powers: Midland Railway (Additional Powers) Act 1890

Kirkby Deviation (also called the Kirkby Curve)	Opened	14.8.1892

Kirkby Deviation

Powers: British Railways Act 1971

Kirkby to Summit Colliery: deviation over the former Great Northern line	Into use	2.4.1972
***	Opened	4.4.1972
Kirkby Summit SB	Opened	2.4.1972

BLACKWELL BRANCH

Blackwell South Curve

Powers: Midland Railway (Additional Powers) Act 1880 (land powers only)

Blackwell South Jcn to Blackwell East Jcn	Opened	24.7.1882
***	Closed	23.9.1984
No block working in place of working by telegraph bell	Commenced	22.12.1968

Blackwell Branch

Powers: Midland Railway (Additional Powers) Act 1875 (Tibshelf & Blackwell Branch)
Midland Railway (Additional Powers) Act 1875 (Tibshelf & Blackwell Branch - land powers only)
Midland Railway (New Works Etc) Act 1877 (Acquisition of Blackwell Branch)
Midland Railway Act 1889 (Blackwell Branch Extension)

Tibshelf & Blackwell Branch Jcn to end of branch	Opened	c.1871
Working by the Midland Railway	Commenced	1.7.1877
Agreement with the Blackwell Colliery Company	... ...	20.1.1879
Blackwell to New Hucknall Colliery Sidings: pilot guard working discontinued, train tablet working established from Blackwell East Junction to "B" Winning Colliery, and staff without tickets working thence to New Hucknall Colliery Sidings	... ...	30.5.1893 ?
Blackwell East Jcn to Tibshelf & Blackwell Branch Jcn	Closed	23.9.1984
Blackwell East Junction SB	Opened	....
Replacement box	Opened	30.5.1893
***	Re-framed	....
***	Closed	23.9.1984
Blackwell East Jcn to New Hucknall Colliery: working by key token	Commenced	4.12.1966
Section made one engine in steam	... ...	3.10.1971
Blackwell East Jcn to New Hucknall Tip	Closed	30.6.1984
Line severed 268 yards beyond Blackwell East Jcn	... ...	15.8.1982
BLACKWELL SIDINGS	Opened	24.7.1882
***	Closed	....
Blackwell Colliery "A" Winning Sidings	Closed	22.8.1969
Blackwell Colliery "A" Winning Sidings and ground frame	t.o.u.	5.1.1974
"B" Winning Colliery SB	Opened	30.5.1893
***	Closed	4.12.1966

New Hucknall Colliery Branch

Powers: --

New Hucknall Colliery branch	Opened	1.9.1879
Midland Railway took possession under its Act of 1889	... ...	25.12.1889
Branch worked by train staff without tickets	By	1.1890
New Hucknall Colliery Sidings SB	Opened	18.4.1893
Replacement box	Opened	....
Box made a ground frame	... ...	3.10.1971
Box demolished in an accident	... ...	5.11.1980
Box officially closed and ground frame provided in lieu	... ...	20.12.1980
New Hucknall Colliery Sidings closed, leaving the line to the tip (reached by reversal)	... ...	28.2.1981

TIBSHELF TO PLEASLEY JUNCTION

Tibshelf & Teversall Line

Powers: Midland Railway (New Lines) Act 1861,
Midland Railway (Additional Powers) Act 1883 (Tibshelf Curve - not made)

Tibshelf & Blackwell Branch Jcn to Teversall	OG	1.5.1866
***	OP	1.5.1886
***	CP	28.7.1930
Tibshelf to Seeley's Sidings	Doubled	3.11.1873
Tibshelf to former Tibshelf East Jcn	Singled	....
Tibshelf South Jcn to Tibshelf East Jcn: passenger lines	Into use	18.4.1886
***	OP	1.5.1886
***	CP	28.7.1930
***	Closed	6.12.1966
Tibshelf South Jcn to Tibshelf Sidings: up goods line	Into use	25.5.1902
Westhouses Station SB to Tibshelf East Jcn made no block	... ...	2.3.1969
Tibshelf Sidings to Tibshelf East Jcn: up and down goods lines	Into use	11.1885-12.1888
Weighing Machine Sidings SB	Opened	18.4.1886
***	Raised	3.2.1901
Replacement box	Opened	25.5.1902
***	Closed	2.3.1969
Tibshelf East Junction SB	Opened	4.1883-11.1885
Replacement box	Opened	18.4.1886
***	Re-framed	11.5.1902
Replacement box	Opened	20.5.1917
Replacement box	Opened	2.3.1969
Box closed and key token instrument placed in shunters' cabin	... ...	28.1.1984
Tibshelf East Jcn to Sutton Colliery (on Skegby branch)	Singled	18.10.1970
From Tibshelf East Junction to Butcherwood GF went over to key token working, whilst Butcherwood GF to Pleasley East GF became one engine in steam.		
NEWTON ROAD	OG	1.5.1866
Altered to TIBSHELF & NEWTON	... ...	1.5.1886
***	OP	1.5.1886
***	CP	28.7.1930
***	CG	6.5.1957
Newton Road SB	Open before	1.10.1876
Re-named Tibshelf & Newton Station SB	... ...	1.5.1886
***	Raised	4.6.1905
Replacement box	Opened	1918-1928
***	Closed	1.11.1964

Seeley's Sidings SB	Open before	16.8.1877	
***	Closed	4.1883-11.1885	
Seeley's Sidings No. 1 SB	Opened	....	
Replacement box	Opened	1.12.1895	
***	Closed	7.3.1938	

Tibshelf Extension

Powers: Midland Railway Act 1892 (Tibshelf Colliery Branch)

The last 36 chains of the line were Great Central & Midland Joint.

Tibshelf & Newton to Tibshelf Colliery (74 chains)	OG	1894	
***	CG	28.1.1965	
Tibshelf & Newton to Seeley's Colliery	Closed	4.5.1964	
Seeley's Sidings No. 2 SB	Opened	2.1.1905	
***	Closed	7.3.1938	
Seeley's Sidings East Curve (No. 1 SB to No. 2 SB)	Opened	....	
***	Closed	7.3.1938	
Seeley's Sidings No. 3 SB	Opened	2.1.1905	
Box closed and ground frame provided in lieu	... ...	4.7.1937	
***	t.o.u.	....	

CHAMBERS' DIMSDALE SIDING	Opened	1.11.1868	*
***	CG by	1890	
WOODEND	OP&G	1.5.1886	
Altered to WOODEND FOR HUCKNALL HUWTHWAITE	... ...	1.10.1886	*
Altered to WHITEBOROUGH FOR HUCKNALL HUWTHWAITE	... ...	20.1.1893	
Altered to WHITEBOROUGH	... ...	1.1.1908	
***	CP&G	4.10.1926	
Skegby Junction SB	Open before	1.10.1876	
Replacement box	Opened	28.3.1926	
Re-named Sutton Colliery Junction SB	... ...	27.4.1963	
Box closed and ground frame provided in lieu	... ...	18.10.1970	
Skegby Jcn: colliery connection	Removed	3.6.1945	

Skegby Branch

Powers: Midland Railway (New Lines and Additional Powers) Act 1864

Midland Railway (Additional Powers) Act 1873 (Skegby Branch Extension)

Skegby branch: 17-chain section	OM	1866	
Skegby branch extension	Opened	1876	
***	OG	2.4.1877	
***	t.o.u.	3.6.1945	?
STONEYFORD LANE SIDING	Opened	2.7.1877	*
***	Closed	6.11.1961	

Skegby Jcn to Pleasley Jcn: train staff and ticket working	Introduced	29.4.1886	
Skegby Jcn to Butcherwood Sidings: train tablet working	Commenced	8.12.1889	
TEVERSALL	OG	1.5.1866	
***	OP	1.5.1886	
***	CP	28.7.1930	
Altered to TEVERSALL MANOR	... ...	1.7.1950	
***	CG	7.10.1963	
Excursion trains continued to serve Teversall until 7 October 1963.			
Teversall SB	Open before	16.8.1877	
Replacement box named Teversall Junction SB	Opened	29.4.1886	?
***	Closed	8.12.1889	?

Butcherwood Branch

Powers: Midland Railway (Additional Powers) Act 1867

This Act authorised the Teversall Branch Extension (Butcherwood Branch) line from the termination of the Tibshelf & Teversall branch at the east end of Teversall station.

Teversall to Butcherwood (OR Teversall) Colliery	OG	1.11.1869	*
***	Closed	25.7.1980	
Teversall to Butcherwood Colliery Sidings	OP	1.5.1886	
***	CP	28.7.1930	
Butcherwood Colliery Sidings SB	Opened	29.4.1886	
***	Raised	28.7.1907	
Box closed and ground frame provided in lieu	... ...	8.5.1934	
Butcherwood Colliery Sidings to Pleasley Colliery West was worked by train staff.			
Butcherwood Colliery Sidings to Pleasley Colliery West: electric train tablet block working in place of working by staff	Introduced	1890-1891	

Teversall & Pleasley Extension Line

Powers: Midland Railway (Additional Powers) Act 1873

Butcherwood Colliery Sidings to Pleasley Colliery Sidings	OG	2.4.1877
***	OP	1.5.1886
***	CP	28.7.1930
***	Closed	7.1.1981

Pleasley Extension Line

Powers: Midland Railway (Additional Powers) Act 1874

Pleasley Colliery Sidings to Pleasley Jcn	OG by	8.1882
***	OP	1.5.1886
***	CP	28.7.1930
Pleasley Colliery Sidings to Pleasley Colliery East	Closed	....
Pleasley Colliery West Junction SB	Opened	27.7.1890
***	Closed	22.10.1939

Doe Lea & Teversall Junction line
See page 118

Pleasley Colliery West Jcn to Pleasley Colliery East Jcn	Doubled	27.7.1890
***	Singled	22.10.1939
Pleasley West No. 2 GF	t.o.u.	15.6.1974
Pleasley Colliery Sidings SB	Opened	....
***	Closed	27.7.1890
Pleasley Colliery East Junction SB	Opened	27.7.1890
***	Closed	22.10.1939
Pleasley East GF	t.o.u.	24.8.1980
Pleasley Colliery East to Pleasley Jcn: electric train tablet block working in place of working by train staff	Introduced	1890–1891
Line severed 175 yards east of Pleasley Colliery East GF	... ...	2.3.1964
Pleasley Colliery East to Hollins Sidings	Closed	4.1.1965
Pleasley Station SB	Opened	29.4.1886
***	Closed	13.12.1925
PLEASLEY	OP&M	1.5.1886
***	OG	1.12.1891
***	CP	28.7.1930
***	CG	1.9.1952
Hollins Siding to Pleasley Jcn	Closed	3.3.1964

NOTTINGHAM & LINCOLN LINE

Powers: Midland Railway (Nottingham and Lincoln Railway) Act 1845
Midland Railway Act 1902 (Nottingham Sneinton Jcn – land powers only)
Midland Railway Act 1895 (Widening at Lincoln)

Nottingham (junction with line to old terminus) to Lincoln	O.Formal	3.8.1846
***	OP	4.8.1846
***	OG	....

From Nottingham to Sneinton Junction was worked as a station yard. Between Nottingham station and Sneinton Junction the Great Northern Railway possessed running powers over the Midland line.

Nottingham East SB	Opened	c.1880
Replacement box	Opened	14.12.1902
Replacement box	Opened	9.8.1903
Replacement box	Opened	30.8.1903
***	Closed	7.12.1969
London Road Junction SB	Open before	16.8.1877
Replacement box	Opened	1879
Replacement box	Opened	21.4.1901
***	Re-framed	11.10.1903
***	Closed	7.12.1969

Nottingham & Melton line
See page 84

London Road Jcn to Sneinton Jcn: second up and down passenger lines	Into use	10. 8.1879
Additional lines made goods lines	... ...	2.1880–6.1881
Replacement goods lines	Into use	21.4.1901
NOTTINGHAM EAST TICKET PLATFORM	Closed	....
SNEINTON JUNCTION EXCHANGE SIDINGS	Opened	1.5.1866
***	Closed	11.7.1988
Great Northern Junction SB	Open before	1.11.1875
***	Closed by	16.8.1877

Sneinton Junction SB	Open before	1869	
***	Re-framed	10.11.1895	
Replacement box	Opened	26.7.1914	
Box made a shunting frame named Sneinton Crossing SF	... ...	7.12.1969	
Sneinton Jcn to Carlton & Netherfield: block telegraph working	Introduced	1876	
Sneinton Jcn with the Great Northern Railway	OG	3.10.1857	?
***	Closed	1.5.1866	*
Colwick Crossing SB	Opened	29.5.1893	
Box made a shunting frame for level crossing only	... ...	7.12.1969	
Crossing made CCTV worked from Sneinton Crossing	... ...	14.12.1975	
Carlton Jcn with the Ambergate Company	OP	15.7.1850	
***	OG	22.7.1850	
***	Removed	1866	?
***	Rest'd & OG	13.12.1964	
***	OP(Sundays)	10.1.1965	
***	OP daily	3.7.1967	
CARLTON	Opened	4.8.1846	
Altered to CARLTON & GEDLING	... ...	1.11.1871	
Altered to CARLTON & NETHERFIELD FOR GEDLING & COLWICK	... ...	1.11.1896	
***	CG	2.8.1965	
Altered to CARLTON & NETHERFIELD	... ...	7.5.1973	*
Altered to CARLTON	... ...	6.5.1974	*
Carlton & Netherfield Station Crossing SB	Open before	1.11.1875	
Replacement box	Opened	....	
***	Alt.levers	10.4.1904	
Box closed and CCTV from Netherfield Junction provided	... ...	28.9.1980	
Carlton & Netherfield to Newark North: block telegraph working	Introduced	1877	
Carlton Goods Yard SB	Opened	10.4.1904	
***	Closed	28.4.1957	
BURTON JOYCE	OP	4.8.1846	
***	OG	1.5.1889	
***	CG	27.4.1964	
Burton Joyce Station SB	Open before	1.10.1876	
Replacement box	Opened	26.6.1910	
Box made a gate box	... ...	11.10.1970	
Box closed and crossing made open	... ...	8.4.1984	
Lowdham Station SB	Open before	11.1873	
Replacement box	Opened	14.6.1896	
***	Closed	....	
LOWDHAM	Opened	4.8.1846	
***	CG	15.6.1964	
Thurgarton Station SB	Open before	1.10.1876	
***	Re-framed	15.3.1896	
Replacement box	Opened	22.6.1902	
Box made a gate box	... ...	4.10.1970	
	<u>or</u>	11.10.1970	
Box closed and crossing made open	... ...	8.3.1982	
THURGARTON	Opened	4.8.1846	
***	CG	7.12.1964	
Bleasby SB	Open before	1.10.1876	
***	Closed	....	
This location is named in a list of "signal posts" returned to the Board of Trade in November 1880, but its may not have been a signalbox structure.			
BLEASBY GATE	OP	1.10.1850	*
Altered to BLEASBY	... ...	Early 1889	
New up platform on west side of level crossing	Opened	12.12.1973	
Stops at Bleasby are indicated in the December 1848 Public Time Table.			
FISKERTON	Opened	4.8.1846	
Altered to FISKERTON FOR SOUTHWELL	... ...	1.1.1850	*
Altered to FISKERTON	... ...	1.5.1860	*
***	CG	15.6.1964	
Fiskerton Junction SB (at Morton Crossing)	Opened	7.4.1929	
Fiskerton SB	Open before	16.8.1877	
Replacement box	Opened	6.7.1902	
Box made a gate box only	... ...	2.12.1934	

<u>Rolleston West Curve</u>

See page 108

SOUTHWELL JUNCTION	OP(NA)	1.7.1847	
***	CP	1.8.1849	
***	RO(P)	12.4.1852	
***	CP&G	14.3.1853	
***	Re-opened	1.9.1860	
Altered to ROLLESTON JUNCTION	... ...	1.11.1860	
***	OM before	1872	
***	CM	....	
Altered to ROLLESTON	... ...	7.5.1973	*
Rolleston Junction SB	Open before	11.1873	
***	Re-framed	15.6.1902	
***	Closed	2.10.1966	

Southwell branch

See page 108

Staythorpe Crossing SB	Opened	8.10.1950
***	Re-framed	1957
Averham Viaduct (bridge No. 50 repairs)	Singled	15.6.1902
***	Doubled	13.7.1902
***	Singled	21.9.1902
***	Doubled	30.9.1902
***	Singled	19.10.1902
***	Doubled	26.10.1902
Thorpe's Sidings SB	Open before	16.8.1877
Re-named Parnham's Mill SB	... ...	10.1886
***	Closed	17.4.1888

Parnham's Mill Branch

Powers: --

Parnham's Flour Mill branch	Opened	1852
Ground frame and connection	Removed	20.12.1942
Newark Station SB	Open before	16.8.1877
Replacement box	Opened	3.7.1887
Replacement box	Opened	15.9.1912
NEWARK	Opened	4.8.1846
Altered to NEWARK CASTLE	... ...	25.9.1950
Closed to full-load traffic and coal	... ...	4.4.1983
Newark North SB	Open before	16.8.1877
Replacement box	Opened	1.3.1891
***	Closed	21.3.1965
Newark North to Collingham: block telegraph working	Introduced	1876

Newark Curve (Midland & Great Northern Joint)

Powers: Midland Railway (New Lines and Additional Powers) Act 1865

Newark Curve	OG	1.1869
Newark Castle to Newark Northgate Exchange Siding	t.o.u.	14.10.1973

Newark Spur Line (Midland & Great Northern Joint)

Powers: No Construction Powers

Cow Lane Wharf spur	Opened	1.12.1869
***	Closed	....
Great Northern Crossing SB (Great Northern box)	Opened	12.1869
***	Re-framed	1885
***	Re-framed	1897 ?
***	Closed	17.5.1981

Newark South-to-East Curve

Powers: --

Curve from the East Coast Main Line to the Lincoln Line	OG	28.2.1965
***	OP(Suns.)	20.6.1965
***	OP	1.11.1965
Winthorpe SB	Opened	31.7.1892
***	Closed	4.10.1914
WINTHORPE	Opened	....
***	Closed	....
Cottage Lane Crossing SB	Opened	8.1877-4.1878
Replacement box	Opened	20.10.1895
***	Re-framed	4.10.1914
Replacement box	Opened	6.3.1927
Box closed and AHBs provided in lieu	... ...	22.11.1967
Collingham Station SB	Open before	1.11.1875
Replacement box	Opened	28.4.1901
***	Closed	17.12.1967
COLLINGHAM	Opened	4.8.1846
***	CG	27.4.1964
Collingham to Lincoln: block telegraph working	Introduced	1877
SWINDERBY	Opened	1.5.1847
***	CG	15.6.1964
Swinderby SB	Open before	1.11.1875
***	Re-framed	13.10.1895
Replacement box	Opened	6.1.1901
Thorpe-on-the-Hill SB	Open before	1.11.1875
Replacement box	Opened	12.5.1907
Box closed and AHBs provided in lieu	... ...	19.3.1988
Thorpe to Lincoln West: single-line working	Intro. w/e	7.2.1917
Double-line working	Restored	6.3.1921
THORPE	Opened	4.8.1846
Altered to THORPE-ON-THE-HILL	... ...	1.10.1890
***	CP	7.2.1955
***	CG	15.6.1964

Hykeham SB	Open before	1.10.1876
Box closed and 2 ground frames provided in lieu	... ...	9.11.1886
HYKEHAM	Opened	1.1.1849 *
***	CG	15.6.1964
Doddington Ballast Siding SB	Open before	16.8.1877
Replacement box	Opened	15.5.1898
Doddington Ballast Siding SB closed and AHBs provided in lieu	... ...	23.3.1980
Boultham Crossing SB (not a block post)	Open before	16.8.1877
Replacement box as a block post	Opened	19.4.1925
***	Made NBP	....
***	Made BP	23.11.1941
***	Re-framed	1943
***	Closed	19.3.1988
Boultham Crossing: new down-side sidings on the Lincoln side of the signalbox, with a new connection	Into use	26.9.1943
Boultham Crossing to Durham Ox Jcn (former Great Central Railway)	CP&G	13.5.1985

Lincoln New Junctions

Powers: --

Boultham Crossing to West Holmes	Into use	12.5.1985
***	OP&G	13.5.1985
Boultham Jcn to Pyewipe Jcn	Into use	12.5.1985
***	OG	13.5.1985

Manvers Street Goods Yard SB closed and hand-points provided	... ...	10.11.1934
LINCOLN TICKET PLATFORM	Closed	1.8.1904
The ticket platform may possibly have re-opened on 1 April 1906.		
Lincoln West SB	Open before	16.8.1877
Replacement box	Opened	3.12.1893
***	Re-located	22.9.1912
***	Closed	12.5.1985
Lincoln Station SB	Open before	16.8.1877
Replacement box	Opened	15.11.1903
***	Closed	12.5.1985
LINCOLN	Opened	4.8.1846
Altered to LINCOLN ST MARK'S	... ...	25.9.1950
***	CP&G	13.5.1985
Lincoln engine shed	Opened	8.1846
***	Replaced	1867
***	Closed	1.1959
High Street Crossing SB (former Great Central box) closed, and section made St Mark's station to East Yard	... ...	21.8.1960
Lincoln: end-on junction with the Manchester, Sheffield & Lincolnshire Railway	Opened	18.12.1848
Manchester, Sheffield & Lincolnshire user of the Midland station	Commenced	1854
***	Ceased	1.4.1906

The Manchester, Sheffield & Lincolnshire Railway possessed running powers into the Midland station, and the Midland possessed running powers over the Sheffield line between Lincoln Junction and Durham Ox Junction.

NOTTINGHAM & MANSFIELD LINE

Powers: Midland Railway (Nottingham and Mansfield Railway) Act 1846 (Mansfield Junction to Kirkby-in-Ashfield)
Midland Railway (Additional Powers) Act 1874 (Deviations at Radford)
Mansfield & Pinxton Railway Act 1817,
Midland Railway (Mansfield and Pinxton Railway) Act 1847 (Kirkby-in-Ashfield to Mansfield old station)
Mansfield & Pinxton Railway Act 1817,
Midland Railway (Mansfield and Pinxton Railway) Act 1847 (King's Mill Branch)
Midland Railway (Mansfield Etc. Lines) Act 1865 (Mansfield new station)

Nottingham to Kirkby

Mansfield Jcn to Kirkby	Opened	2.10.1848
Mansfield Jcn to Lenton North Jcn: block telegraph working	Introduced	1874
***	CG	....
***	CP(All)	....
Mansfield Jcn to Radford Jcn	CP(temp.)	2.9.1988 ?
Nottingham Goods Yard North SB	Opened	2.12.1900
Box replaced by hand-worked points and ground frame	... ...	6.10.1935
***	t.o.u.	1985
West end of Nottingham Goods Yard to Lenton North Jcn: departure line and two arrival lines	Into use	2.12.1900
***	t.o.u.	....

Lenton Curve

Powers: Midland Railway (New Lines and Additional Powers) Act 1865

Lenton South Jcn to Lenton North Jcn	OM	17.1.1870
***	OP(NA)	28.10.1940
***	CP	4.11.1963

Lenton: second down goods line	Into use	....
***	t.o.u.	19.11.1967
Lenton North Jcn: departure line	Into use	14.10.1928
***	t.o.u.	....
Lenton North Junction SB	Opened	c.1.1870
Replacement box	Opened	27.3.1887
Replacement box	Opened	2.12.1900
***	Closed	7.12.1969
Lenton North Jcn to Mansfield North: block telegraph working	Introduced	1875
Lenton North Jcn to Radford Jcn: up goods line	Into use	1953
***	t.o.u.	27.4.1969
Church Crossing SB (not a block post)	Open before	1.10.1876
***	Closed	11.1885-12.1888
Lenton Station South SB (signalling the down line only)	Opened	2.7.1888
***	Closed by	17.12.1888
LENTON	Opened	2.10.1848
***	CP	1.7.1911
***	CG	4.5.1953
Lenton Station SB	Open before	1.11.1875
***	Closed	20.12.1908
Marsh's Crossing SB	Open before	1.10.1876
***	Closed	11.1885-12.1888
RADFORD	Opened	2.10.1848
Replacement station on deviation line to the west	Opened	10.9.1876
***	CP	12.10.1964
***	CG	28.4.1969
Radford: replacement junction with the Radford & Trowell line	Into use	10.9.1876
Radford Junction SB	Open before	1.11.1875
Replacement box	Opened	29.1.1893
***	Re-framed	....
***	Closed	7.12.1969

Radford & Trowell line

See page 109

Radford Jcn to Worksop	CP	12.10.1964
Radford Jcn to Bobber's Mill: up and down goods lines	Into use	29.1.1893
Up goods line	t.o.u.	....
Radford Jcn to Radford North: down goods line	t.o.u.	5.9.1965

Radford Colliery Branch

Powers: --

Radford Colliery branch	Opened	1901
***	Closed	....

Radford North SB	Open before	16.8.1877
***	Alt.levers	21.4.1890
Replacement box	Opened	15.1.1893
***	Raised	15.8.1909
***	Raised	26.1.1919
***	Closed	6.2.1966
Radford North to Bobber's Mill: down goods line	t.o.u.	....
Bobber's Mill SB	Open before	1.10.1876
Replacement box	Opened	22.3.1886
Replacement box	Opened	1.1.1893
Replacement box	Opened	9.12.1928
***	Closed	14.1.1968
Basford South SB	Open before	16.8.1877
***	Raised	1.9.1895
Basford Station SB	Open before	1.11.1875
Re-named Basford Sidings SB	... ...	....
Replacement box	Opened	c.1936
***	Closed	7.12.1969
BASFORD	Opened by	1.12.1848 *
Altered to BASFORD VERNON	Goods	1.7.1950
***	Passenger	11.8.1952
***	CP	4.1.1960
***	CG	2.10.1967
Excursion trains continued to call at this station.		
Basford No. 2 Crossing SB (not a block post)	Open before	16.8.1877
Bulwell No. 2 Crossing SB re-named Lincoln Street Crossing SB	... ...	8.1877-4.1878
Replacement box	Opened	24.9.1916
***	Made BP	31.1.1927
Basford Junction SB	Open before	1.11.1875
***	Re-framed	21.1.1894
***	Raised	8.3.1896
Replacement box	Opened	18.6.1899
***	Re-framed	18.3.1906
***	Closed	7.12.1969

Cinder Hill Branch

Powers: Midland Railway (Ripley Branches) Act 1848

Lincoln Street Jcn to Cinder Hill Colliery	Opened	1852
Midland Railway working of the branch	Commenced	19.3.1877
The line was worked by train staff.		
Suncole Siding and (southern) GF	Into use	9.8.1938
Suncole Siding and (northern) GF	Into use	7.3.1938
Great Northern Junction SB	Opened	4.1878-2.1879
Replacement box named Cinder Hill Junction SB	Opened	22.11.1896
Box made a ground frame	... ...	19.7.1964
Re-named Babbington Colliery GF	... ...	3.11.1974
Cinder Hill Colliery and branch re-named Babbington Colliery and branch	... ...	3.11.1974
Lincoln Street Jcn to Babbington Colliery	Closed	18.7.1983
***	t.o.u.	12.5.1985

Bennerley & Bulwell line

See page 107

Basford Jcn: new connection for up-side sidings	Into use	18.3.1906
Bulwell SB	Open before	1.11.1875
Re-named Bulwell Sidings SB	... ...	4.1883-11.1885
Re-named Bulwell South SB	... ...	4.1885-11.1888
Replacement box	Opened	23.1.1888
Re-named Bulwell Station SB	... ...	1.8.1888
Replacement box	Opened	25.11.1923
***	Closed	8.9.1968
BULWELL	Opened	2.10.1848
Altered to BULWELL MARKET	Goods	1.7.1950
***	Passenger	11.8.1952
***	CP	12.10.1964
***	CG	7.8.1967
Bulwell North SB	Opened	c.12.1883
***	Closed	1.8.1888
Bulwell Forest Crossing SB	Open before	1.10.1876
Replacement box	Opened	1.10.1888
***	Raised	25.6.1899
Replacement box	Opened	11.9.1927
Box closed and CCTV from Bestwood Park in lieu	... ...	9.8.1981
Bestwood Park Junction SB	Open before	1.10.1876
***	Re-framed	29.11.1896
Replacement box	Opened	9.12.1923
Replacement box	Opened	11.3.1951
Bestwood Park Jcn: layout re-modelled to provide single-leads connections to the up and down Linby lines	... ...	2.8.1987

Bestwood Park Branch

Powers: Midland Railway (Additional Powers) Act 1873

Bestwood Park branch	Opened	17.1.1876
***	t.o.u.	12.10.1971
The line was worked by train staff.		
Colliery branch siding	Re-opened	30.1.1972
Branch shortened to 133 yards	... ...	13.3.1982
Remainder of the branch	Closed	....
Great Northern (OR Bestwood) Junction SB (at the colliery)	Opened	2.5.1876
***	Re-framed	1.3.1896
Replacement box	Opened	28.10.1906
***	Closed	2.8.1936

Calverton Colliery Branch

Powers: London Midland and Scottish Railway Act 1947

Calverton Branch Jcn (Leen Valley line) to Papplewick Jcn	... ...	Never opened
Bestwood Park Jcn (Midland line) to Calverton Colliery	Into use	22.7.1952
***	O.Formal	24.9.1952
***	OG	....
***	Closed	....
Branch worked by key token instead of one engine in steam	... ...	31.1.1965
Reverted to one train working	... ...	12.12.1971
Calverton Colliery dead road shortened to 1114 yards	... ...	13.3.1982

Hucknall No. 1 SB	Open before	1.11.1875
Replacement box	Opened	19.4.1896
***	Closed	29.4.1951
Hucknall No. 2 SB	Open before	1.11.1875
Replacement box	Opened	11.2.1894
***	Re-framed	....
Re-named Hucknall Colliery Sidings SB	... ...	29.4.1951
***	Closed	15.1.1987
HUCKNALL COLLIERY SIDINGS	Into use	....
***	t.o.u. by	10.1.1987

Hucknall South SB	Opened	4.1883-11.1885
Replacement box	Opened	7.4.1895
Re-named Hucknall Station SB	... ...	29.10.1895
***	Closed	29.12.1957
HUCKNALL	Opened	2.10.1848
Replacement station 4 chains south	Opened	22.12.1895
Altered to HUCKNALL BYRON	Goods	1.7.1950
***	Passenger	11.8.1952
***	CG	5.5.1952
***	CP	12.10.1964
Hucknall Station SB	Open before	1.11.1875
Re-named Hucknall North SB	... ...	4.1883-11.1885
***	Closed	....
***	Re-opened	31.3.1895
***	Closed	29.10.1895
Linby Crossing SB	Open before	1.10.1876
Replacement box	Opened	11.3.1894
Re-named Linby Colliery Sidings SB	... ...	....
***	t.o.u. by	19.3.1988
LINBY	Opened	2.10.1848
***	CG	6.1.1964
***	CP	12.10.1964
Linby Station SB	Open before	1.11.1875
Replacement box	Opened	23.6.1895
***	t.o.u. by	19.3.1988
Linby to Newstead	CG(All)	8.8.1983
NEWSTEAD private station	Opened	1.4.1863 *
Station opened for public traffic	... ...	1.7.1883
***	CG	6.1.1964
***	CP	12.10.1964
Newstead Station SB	Opened	c.1872
Replacement box	Opened	1884
***	Closed	19.3.1967
Newstead: new fan of sidings alongside existing loaded wagon sidings	Into use	8.12.1907
Newstead level crossing to Annesley Colliery Sidings	C.Tfc	25.2.1980
***	Closed	7.1.1984
ANNESLEY COLLIERY SIDINGS PLATFORM	Opened	1.3.1882
***	Closed	....
Annesley Colliery Sidings to Kirkby Station Jcn	Closed	6.5.1968
The closure was on account of the deterioration of the tunnel.		
Line cut 750 yards north of Annesley and taken out thence to the junction points at Kirkby	... ...	11.10.1970
ANNESLEY	OP&G	1.7.1874
***	CP&G	6.4.1953
Annesley Station SB	Open before	1.11.1875
Replacement box	Opened	9.7.1905
Box made a shunting frame	... ...	30.12.1973
***	t.o.u.	25.2.1980 ?
Kirkby Station SB: replacement box at the level crossing	Opened	18.2.1889
Re-named Kirkby Station Junction SB	... ...	14.8.1892
Replacement box	Opened	17.9.1922
***	Closed	2.4.1972

Mansfield & Pinxton line

See page 97

KIRKBY	Opened	2.10.1848
Altered to KIRKBY-IN-ASHFIELD	... ...	1.1.1901
Altered to KIRKBY-IN-ASHFIELD EAST	Goods	1.7.1950
***	Passenger	15.6.1959
***	CG	6.1.1964
***	CP	12.10.1964
Workmen's trains	Ceased	6.9.1965
Kirkby Station SB	Open before	1.11.1875
***	Closed	18.2.1889

Kirkby to Mansfield

Kirkby Jcn to Mansfield	OP&G	9.10.1849
KIRKBY NEW SIDINGS	Opened	1.11.1899
***	Closed	....
Kirkby-in-Ashfield engine shed	Opened	24.8.1903
***	Closed	3.10.1966
Kirkby Station to Kirkby Colliery Sidings: down reception line	Into use	17.4.1910
***	t.o.u.	....
Kirkby Junction SB	Open before	1.11.1875
***	Alt.levers	18.5.1890
Re-named Kirkby Colliery Sidings SB	... ...	14.8.1892
Replacement box	Opened	2.7.1893
***	Slued	13.11.1898
***	Re-framed	15.10.1899
***	Closed	2.12.1958

Kirkby Colliery Sidings: connections to empty wagon sidings and loaded wagon sidings, working by train staff without tickets	Commenced	1.1.1894
Kirkby Colliery Sidings to Kirkby Colliery Sidings North: down goods line	Into use	7.1.1912
***	t.o.u.	....
Kirkby Colliery Sidings to Kirkby Sidings North: 2 up-side reception lines	Into use	15.10.1899
***	t.o.u.	....
Kirkby Sidings SB (replacing Kirkby Colliery Sidings SB)	Opened	2.12.1958
***	Closed	2.4.1972
Kirkby Sidings North SB	Opened	15.10.1899
***	Closed	15.5.1960
Sutton South SB	Open before	1.10.1876
Replacement box	Opened	1884
Replacement box named Sutton-in-Ashfield Junction SB	Opened	20.11.1892
Re-named Sutton Junction South SB	... ...	24.4.1893
***	Re-framed	13.7.1924
***	Closed	28.2.1960
SUTTON	Opened	....
***	CG	1893
***	RO(G)	....
Altered to SUTTON-IN-ASHFIELD	... ...	1.11.1883 *
Altered to SUTTON	... ...	1.7.1892 *
Altered to SUTTON JUNCTION	... ...	24.4.1893
Siding behind down platform made a bay platform	... ...	13.7.1902
***	CG	6.1.1964
***	CP	12.10.1964
Sutton-in-Ashfield Station SB	Open before	1.11.1875
Re-named Sutton-in-Ashfield Junction Station SB	... ...	....
Re-named Sutton Junction North SB	... ...	24.4.1893
Replacement box	Opened	18.9.1910
Re-named Sutton Station SB	... ...	28.2.1960

Sutton-in-Ashfield branch

See page 112

Sutton Forest Crossing SB	Open before	16.8.1877
***	Made BP	22.7.1894
Replacement box	Opened	7.2.1904
Box closed and AHBs provided in lieu	... ...	10.12.1967
Sutton Jcn to Mansfield Deviation: three-quarter mile diversion avoiding the King's Mill viaduct	Into use	25.2.1872
Hermitage Viaduct replaced by embankment	... ...	10.8.1924
Mansfield South Junction SB	Open before	1.11.1875
Replacement box	Opened	20.1.1895
***	Re-framed	28.1.1906
***	Closed	15.10.1983

Mansfield South Curve

See page 112

Mansfield South Jcn: King's Mill Siding	t.o.u.	28.11.1970
The King's Mill Siding was part of the original Mansfield & Pinxton line.		
Mansfield engine shed	Opened	....
***	Replaced	1882
***	Closed	11.4.1960
Mansfield North Junction SB	Open before	1.11.1875
Replacement box	Opened	28.2.1904
***	Closed	24.11.1968

Mansfield & Southwell line

See page 111

Mansfield Station SB	Open before	1.11.1875
Re-named Mansfield Station South SB	... ...	24.7.1892
Replacement box	Opened	4.9.1892
Replacement box	Opened	14.10.1923
***	Closed	5.6.1966
MANSFIELD TICKET PLATFORM	Closed	....
MANSFIELD (original station)	Opened	9.10.1849
MANSFIELD GOODS DEPOT	Opened	1875
This was the old passenger station.		
MANSFIELD: through station replacing the former terminus	Opened	1.3.1872
Additional back platform line and back platform siding	Into use	4.9.1892
Altered to MANSFIELD TOWN	Goods	1.7.1950
***	Passenger	11.8.1952
***	CP	12.10.1964
***	CG	2.6.1975
Mansfield Station North SB	Opened	24.7.1892
***	Closed	22.12.1963

RADFORD & TROWELL LINE

Powers: Midland Railway (Branches Etc.) Act 1866

Radford Jcn to Woolaton [sic] Colliery Siding	OM	6.1.1875
Radford Jcn to Trowell Jcn	OP	1.5.1875
***	OG	1.5.1881 *
***	CG	11.5.1985 *
***	CP(temp.)	2.9.1988
The line was worked by the block telegraph system from its opening.		
Radford and Trowell: new coal sidings	Into use	25.1.1876
Newcastle Colliery Sidings SB	Open before	1.10.1876
***	Closed by	16.8.1877
Babbington Crossing SB	Open before	1.11.1875
Replacement box	Opened	1.5.1904
***	Raised	10.6.1906
***	Raised	4.9.1910
***	Closed	12.8.1934
Wollaton Colliery Sidings East SB	Open before	1.11.1875
Replacement box	Opened	28.7.1901
Re-named Wollaton Colliery Sidings SB	... ...	12.9.1909
***	Closed	25.4.1965
WOLLATON COLLIERY PLATFORM	OP(NA)	31.3.1913
***	CP	6.7.1936 *
Wollaton Colliery Sidings West SB	Open before	1.11.1875
Replacement box	Opened	7.7.1901
***	Closed	12.9.1909
BRAMCOTE (private station)	OP(NA)	1875 ?
***	CP(All)	c.1892 ?
Trowell Moor Colliery Sidings SB	Opened	6.1881–4.1883
Replacement box	Opened	12.4.1908
***	Closed	9.4.1951
***	Abolished	11.1.1953

BENNERLEY & BULWELL LINE

Powers: Midland Railway (Additional Powers) Act 1873 (Bulwell end)
Midland Railway (Additional Powers) Act 1872 (Bennerley end)

Basford Jcn to Watnall Colliery Sidings	OM	3.12.1877
***	CG	1.2.1954
***	Off.closed	12.3.1956
The line was worked by the block telegraph system from its opening.		
Watnall Jcn to Kimberley station	OG	11.8.1879
Kimberley station to Bennerley Jcn	OG	13.10.1879
The first 55 chains of the line from Bennerley Junction may have been open by January 1877.		
Basford Jcn to Bennerley Jcn	OP	1.9.1882
***	CP	1.1.1917
Basford Jcn to Watnall Jcn	Singled	11.2.1923
Bulwell Colliery Sidings SB	Opened	1897
***	Closed	11.2.1923
Watnall Branch Junction SB	Opened	11.8.1879
Replacement box	Opened	14.9.1902
***	Closed	11.2.1923

Watnall Colliery Branch

Powers: Midland Railway (Additional Powers) Act 1872 (Land Powers only)
Midland Railway (Additional Powers) Act 1872 (Watnall New Colliery Branch)

Watnall Jcn to Watnall Colliery	OM	3.12.1877
***	C.Tfc	1.2.1954
***	Off. closed	12.3.1956

Watnall Jcn to Kimberley	CG	1.2.1954
WATNALL	OP&G	1.9.1882
***	CP	1.1.1917
***	CG	1.2.1954
Watnall Station SB	Opened	1.9.1882
***	Closed	4.1883–11.1885
Kimberley East SB	Opened	1.9.1882
***	Re-framed	22.9.1895
***	Closed	31.12.1916 ?
KIMBERLEY	OG	8.1880
***	OP	1.9.1882
***	CP	1.1.1917
Altered to KIMBERLEY WEST	... ...	1.7.1950
***	CG	1.1.1951
Kimberley West SB	Opened	1.9.1882
***	Re-framed	22.9.1895
Replacement box	Opened	8.5.1904
***	Closed	31.12.1916 ?

Kimberley West to Bennerley Sidings	C.Tfc	1.1.1917
***	Off. closed	1919

Digby Colliery Branch

Powers: --

Digby Colliery Branch Jcn to Digby Colliery	Opened	1879
***	Closed	5.11.1937

This branch was bought by the Midland in 1879.

Bennerley Sidings SB	Opened	13.10.1879
***	Closed	24.1.1886
***	Re-opened	30.1.1888
***	Re-framed	22.9.1895
Replacement box	Opened	17.3.1901
***	Closed	31.12.1916
Bennerley Park: facing junction	t.o.u.	3.12.1967
Line lifted	... ...	12.3.1956

SUTTON-IN-ASHFIELD BRANCH

Powers: Midland Railway (Additional Powers) Act 1890

Sutton-in-Ashfield Jcn to Sutton-in-Ashfield	OG	20.11.1892
***	OP	1.5.1893
***	CP	1.1.1917
***	RO(P)	9.7.1923
***	CP&G	4.5.1926
***	RO(P&G)	20.9.1926
***	CP	26.9.1949
***	CG	1.10.1951
Sutton-in-Ashfield branch: double-line working by block telegraph	Introduced	24.4.1893
Branch made a siding	... ...	17.5.1953
SUTTON (NEW STATION)	OG	20.11.1892
Altered to SUTTON-IN-ASHFIELD	... ...	1.5.1893
***	OG	20.11.1892
***	OP	1.5.1893
***	CP	1.1.1917
***	RO(P)	9.7.1923
***	CP&G	4.5.1926
***	RO(P&G)	20.9.1926
***	CP	26.9.1949
Altered to SUTTON-IN-ASHFIELD (FOR HUWTHWAITE)	... ...	1.1.1908
Altered to SUTTON-IN-ASHFIELD TOWN	... ...	1.7.1923
Altered to SUTTON-IN-ASHFIELD GENERAL	... ...	1.7.1950
***	CG	1.10.1951

Workmen's trains were withdrawn on and from the same date.

Sutton-in-Ashfield SB	Opened	24.4.1893
***	Closed	16.4.1917
***	Re-opened	7.7.1923
***	Closed	1.10.1951 ?

SOUTHWELL BRANCH

Powers: Midland Railway (Clay Cross and Newark) Railway Act 1846

Southwell Junction to Southwell	Opened	1.7.1847
***	CP	1.8.1849
***	RO(P)	12.4.1852
***	CP&G	14.3.1853
***	Re-opened	1.9.1860
***	CP	15.6.1959
***	CG	7.12.1964
Working by electric train tablet block	Introduced	27.10.1890
***	Closed	2.5.1966
***	t.o.u.	2.10.1966
Rolleston West Junction SB	Opened	7.4.1929
***	Closed	2.10.1966

Rolleston West Curve

Powers: London Midland and Scottish Railway Act 1927

Fiskerton Jcn to Rolleston West Jcn	OG	7.4.1929
***	C.Tfc	1.3.1965

Upton Crossing SB	Opened	1885
Replacement box on up side of line	Opened	29.10.1916
***	Closed	2.10.1966

SOUTHWELL	Opened	1.7.1847
***	CP	1.8.1849
***	RO(P)	12.4.1852
***	CP&G	14.3.1853
***	Re-opened	1.9.1860
***	CP	15.6.1959
***	CG	7.12.1964
Excursion trains continued to call at this station.		
Southwell SB	Open before	1.11.1875
Replacement box	Opened	1885
***	Re-framed	26.10.1902
***	Closed	....
Replacement box	Opened	19.10.1926
***	Closed	2.10.1966
Southwell engine shed	Opened	c.1847
***	Closed	10.1.1955

MANSFIELD & SOUTHWELL LINE

Powers: Midland Railway (Mansfield Etc. Lines) Act 1865

Southwell to Mansfield North Jcn	OP&G	3.4.1871
***	CP	12.8.1929
Working by electric train tablet block	Introduced	27.10.1890
Southwell to Blidworth Jcn	C.Tfc	1.3.1965
KIRKLINGTON	OP&G	3.4.1871
Altered to KIRKLINGTON & EDINGLEY		1.9.1871 *
Altered to KIRKLINGTON	... ...	1.4.1904
***	CP	12.8.1929
***	CG	25.5.1964
Kirklington: goods loop line	Into use	6.5.1928
Kirklington SB	Open before	1.11.1875
***	Closed	27.10.1890
Kirklington SB (second box)	Opened	6.5.1928
***	Closed	1.12.1965 ?
Farnsfield SB (second box)	Opened	20.10.1929
***	Closed	1.12.1965 ?

Mid-Nottinghamshire Joint Line

See page 113

Farnsfield to Blidworth Jcn: electric key token working in place of electric train tablet block	Commenced	20.10.1929
Farnsfield East SB	Opened	4.1883-11.1885
***	Closed	20.10.1929
Farnsfield SB	Open before	1.11.1875
***	Closed	4.1883-11.1885
FARNSFIELD	OP&G	3.4.1871
***	CP	12.8.1929
***	CG	27.4.1964
Excursion trains continued to serve Farnsfield until after 1949.		
Farnsfield West SB (not a block post)	Opened	4.1883-11.1885
Box closed and ground frame provided in lieu	... ...	5.7.1921
***	t.o.u.	....
Farnsfield to Blidworth Jcn made into a siding	... ...	1.12.1965
***	CG	18.2.1967
Blidworth Junction SB	Opened	9.11.1926
***	Closed	c.1967

Blidworth branch

Powers: --

Blidworth Jcn: permanent connection to colliery branch	Opened	21.12.1925
The branch was worked by train staff without tickets.		
Blidworth Colliery GF	Into use	26.8.1935
Blidworth Colliery branch	CG	2.10.1966

Blidworth Jcn to Mansfield Colliery Sidings: electric key token working in place of electric train tablet block	Commenced	7.4.1929
Blidworth Colliery GF	Into use	26.8.1935
***	t.o.u.	....
Blidworth Colliery GF to Blidworth Jcn to Rufford Jcn	Closed	2.10.1966
***	t.o.u.	24.6.1967
RAINWORTH	OP&G	3.4.1871
Altered to BLIDWORTH	... ...	1.5.1877
Altered to BLIDWORTH & RAINWORTH	... ...	27.4.1894
***	CP	12.8.1929
***	CG	1.2.1965

Rainworth SB	Open before	1.11.1875
Re-named Blidworth SB	... ...	1.5.1877
***	Re-framed	9.4.1911
***	Alt.levers	21.3.1915
***	Closed	....
Rufford Colliery Sidings SB	Opened	21.3.1915
Re-named Rufford Colliery Junction SB	... ...	1.1.1929
***	Re-framed	17.2.1929
Re-named Rufford Junction SB	... ...	7.4.1929
***	Closed	16.6.1968
Rufford Colliery Sidings SB became an intermediate tablet station but not a crossing-place	... ...	21.3.1915
Rufford Colliery Sidings: facing connection from main line to branch	Into use	21.3.1915
Down loop and additional siding	Into use	21.5.1916

Rufford branch

Powers: No Construction Powers

Rufford Colliery Sidings to Rufford Colliery	Opened	20.6.1912
***	Closed	7.2.1971
Rufford Colliery Sidings SB: facing connection to branch	Into use	21.3.1915
The single line to Rufford Colliery was worked as a siding.		
Rufford branch: electric train tablet block working	Introduced	1928
No Signalman Key Token working	Introduced	29.11.1981
Rufford Colliery SB	Opened	10.2.1918
Re-named Rufford Colliery Sidings SB	... ...	....
Replacement box	Opened	c.12.1928
Box closed and ground frame provided in lieu	... ...	29.11.1981
***	t.o.u.	11.12.1983
RUFFORD COLLIERY PLATFORM	OP(NA)	10.2.1918
***	CP(All)	....

Clipstone branch

Powers: London Midland and Scottish Railway Act 1925

Rufford Colliery to Clipstone Colliery	Into use	29.12.1928 ?
	or	1.2.1929 ?
***	Closed	19.2.1980

Rufford Colliery Sidings to Mansfield South Jcn	CG	15.10.1983 ?
	or	12.12.1983 ?
Barringers Sidings SB	Open before	16.8.1877
***	Closed	4.1878-2.1879
Mansfield Colliery Sidings SB	Opened	28.1.1906
***	Re-framed	9.4.1911
***	Re-framed	27.1.1929
Re-named Mansfield Colliery Junction SB	... ...	7.4.1929
***	Closed	15.10.1983

Mansfield Colliery branch

Powers: No Construction Powers

Crown Farm Colliery Sidings to Bolsover Co.'s New Colliery branch	Opened w/e	11.1.1905
Branch re-named Mansfield Colliery Branch, and electric train tablet working introduced	... ...	28.1.1906
Working as a siding instead of by electric train tablet	Commenced	25.1.1909
Method of working changed	... ...	....
Working as a siding	Commenced	17.2.1929
Mansfield Colliery Jcn to Mansfield Colliery Empty Wagon Sidings	t.o.u.	17.7.1967
***	Closed	18.7.1967

Mansfield East Junction SB	Opened	28.1.1906
***	Raised	30.11.1913
***	Closed	11.12.1966
Mansfield East Jcn to North Jcn designated a through siding	... ...	28.11.1965
Through siding severed	... ...	11.12.1966

Mansfield Curve

Powers: Midland Railway (Mansfield Etc. Lines) Act 1865

The south curve was originally considered the main line.

Mansfield East Jcn to South Jcn	Approved	12.3.1872
***	Closed	10.1872
***	Re-opened	28.1.1906
***	Closed	....

MID-NOTTINGHAMSHIRE JOINT LINE (LNER & LMS Joint Line)

Powers: Mid-Nottinghamshire Joint Railways Act 1926
London Midland and Scottish Railway Act 1928 (Farnsfield Curve)

Farnsfield station to New Ollerton (First 1m 27ch purely LMS)	OG	30.11.1931
The first 1m 27ch of the line belonged to the LMS and formed the Farnsfield Curve; the joint line south of the junction with this curve was never built.		
The line was worked by the electric train tablet block system.		
Farnsfield to Bilsthorpe	Tfc ceased	12.1963
***	Closed	2.5.1966
***	Off. closed	8.10.1966
The colliery was inaccessible from the Southwell end after 1 March 1965.		
Bilsthorpe to Bilsthorpe Colliery Sidings and to Bilsthorpe Colliery Empty Wagon Sidings	Opened	12.8.1940
Bilsthorpe: south end of Mid-Nottinghamshire Joint line loop to Bilsthorpe Colliery Empty Wagon Sidings	Closed	12.1975
Bilsthorpe SB	Opened	1931 ?
***	Closed	7.9.1962
BILSTHORPE GOODS DEPOT	Opened	....
***	Closed	10.9.1962
Bilsthorpe to Eakring Road Siding	Closed	19.1.1959
Line severed at Eakring Siding (access from Ollerton end only)	... ...	30.9.1961
EAKRING ROAD SIDINGS: two sidings, and Nos. 1 and 2 ground frames	Into use	12.8.1940
***	t.o.u.	1.8.1966
Eakring Road Siding to Ollerton Colliery Empty Wagon Sidings GF	Closed	1.8.1966
BOUGHTON GOODS YARD	Opened	2.1932
Altered to NEW OLLERTON GOODS YARD	By	13.2.1932
***	Closed	17.10.1938

MANSFIELD & WORKSOP LINE

Powers: Midland Railway (Mansfield Etc. Lines) Act 1865

Mansfield to Shire Oaks Colliery	OG	18.1.1875
Mansfield to Shireoaks East Jcn and Shireoaks West Jcn	OP	1.6.1875
***	CP	12.10.1964
This line was worked by the block telegraph system from its opening.		
From the opening of the New Goods Depot in Mansfield the Great Central Railway possessed running powwers for all except coaching traffic between that depot and Shirebrook Junction.		
Sherwood Colliery Sidings South SB	Opened	25.10.1903
Box closed and ground frame provided in lieu	... ...	24.1.1988
***	t.o.u.	....
SHERWOOD COLLIERY SIDINGS	Into use	1903
New down sidings	Into use	14.6.1938
Empty wagon sidings and down lie-by	t.o.u.	12.2.1987
The Great Central Railway possessed running powers through the connections into Sherwood Colliery for all except coaching traffic.		
Sherwood Colliery Sidings South to North: colliery running line and three running-round sidings	Into use	31.10.1904
Sherwood Colliery Sidings SB	Opened	....
Re-named Sherwood Sidings SB	... ...	12.10.1929
Sherwood Sidings No. 1 GF	Into use	14.6.1938
***	t.o.u.	....
Sherwood Colliery Sidings North SB	Opened	28.8.1904
Box closed and ground frame provided in lieu	... ...	17.11.1968
Sherwood Colliery Sidings North: new carriage sidings	Into use	28.1.1906
***	t.o.u.	....
MANSFIELD WOODHOUSE	OG	18.1.1875
***	OP	1.6.1875
***	CP	12.10.1964
***	CG	2.1.1967
Mansfield Woodhouse Station SB	Open before	1.11.1875
Replacement box	Opened	26.2.1895
***	Closed	4.6.1967
Pleasley Junction SB	Opened	1885
***	Closed	2.3.1964

Tibshelf & Teversall line

See page 99

Shirebrook Colliery Sidings SB	Opened	13.12.1897
Replacement box	Opened	9.6.1929
Re-named Shirebrook Sidings SB	Before	12.10.1929
Replacement box	Opened	8.1971
SHIREBROOK COLLIERY SIDINGS	Opened	....
Two new reception lines and fan of sidings	Into use	23.2.1930
***	t.o.u.	....

SHIREBROOK COLLIERY STATION	OP(NA)	1.7.1901 *
***	CP before	7.1954
Shirebrook Colliery Branch		
Powers: --		
Shirebrook Colliery branch	Opened	26.11.1895
***	Closed	....
Shirebrook Colliery: empty wagon line	Into use	18.5.1898
New down sidings and ground frame	Into use	14.6.1938
Warsop Colliery Branch		
Powers: --		
Warsop Colliery Branch Junction to Warsop Main Colliery	Opened	1.3.1897
***	Closed	1962
***	Restored	7.1976
The line was the property of the Staveley Company except for the first 18 chains.		
Warsop Main Colliery: replacement departure sidings (6)	Into use	1.1.1904
Shirebrook Station SB	Open before	1.11.1875
Replacement box	Opened	28.1.1890
***	Re-framed	1979
SHIREBROOK	OG	18.1.1875
***	OP	1.6.1875
Altered to SHIREBROOK WEST	... ...	18.6.1951
***	CG	1.5.1962
***	CP	12.10.1964
Welbeck Colliery Branch		
Powers: London Midland and Scottish Railway Act 1926		
Welbeck Colliery Branch	Opened	1.1.1929 ?
	or	3.1.1929 ?
***	Closed	
		2.11.1959 ?
Shirebrook Junction SB	Opened	1.1.1899
***	Re-framed	25.9.1904
Shirebrook Jcn with the Lancashire, Derbyshire & East Coast Railway	Into use	9.1.1899
***	OG	16.1.1899
***	OP	20.3.1899
Between Shirebrook Junction and Edwinstowe the Midland possessed running powers for coaching traffic over the Lancashire, Derbyshire & East Coast line.		
Langwith Junctions		
Powers: Midland Railway Act 1904		
Shirebrook Jcn with Lancashire, Derbyshire & East Coast Railway	Opened	1.10.1904
Between Shirebrook Junction and Langwith Junction the Great Central Railway possessed running powers for goods and mineral traffic over the Midland line.		
Between Langwith Junction and Beighton Junction the Midland possessed running powers for all traffic over the Lancashire, Derbyshire & East Coast line.		
Langwith Junction East SB	Opened	1904
***	Closed	1951
Langwith Station SB	Open before	1.11.1875
Replacement box	Opened	30.9.1900
***	Closed	27.9.1964
LANGWITH	OG	18.1.1875
***	OP	1.6.1875
***	CG	6.1.1964
***	CP	12.10.1964
LANGWITH COLLIERY PLATFORM	OP(NA)	4.11.1894
***	CP after	1945
Langwith Colliery Sidings South SB	Opened	2.1880-6.1881
Replacement box	Opened	16.12.1894
***	Closed	22.3.1942
Langwith Colliery Sidings SB	Open before	1.10.1876
Re-named Langwith Colliery Sidings North SB	... ...	c.1880
Replacement box	Opened	31.1.1897
Re-named Langwith Colliery Sidings SB	... ...	22.3.1942
***	Closed	16.5.1981
Norwood Sidings SB	Open before	1.10.1876
Box closed and ground frame provided in lieu	... ...	14.12.1886
***	t.o.u.	2.11.1964 ?
NORWOOD SIDINGS	Opened	....
***	Closed	2.11.1964
Elmton South IBS	Into use	28.4.1946
***	t.o.u.	....
Cresswell Colliery Sidings South SB	Opened	17.8.1896
***	Closed	14.3.1942

Cresswell Colliery Branch
Powers: --

Cresswell Colliery Sidings to Cresswell Colliery	Opened	4.1894 ?
***	Closed	....
Cresswell Colliery Sidings North SB	Opened	18.5.1896
***	Closed	28.4.1946
CRESSWELL	OG	18.1.1875
***	OP	1.6.1875
Altered to ELMTON & CRESSWELL	... ...	10.4.1886
Altered to ELMTON & CRESWELL	... ...	1.5.1887 *
***	CG	6.1.1964
***	CP	12.10.1964
Cresswell Station SB	Open before	1.11.1875
Re-named Elmton & Cresswell Station SB	... ...	1886
Replacement SB	Opened	6.11.1887
Replacement box named Cresswell Junction SB	Opened	28.4.1946

Clown branch
See page ...

Whitwell Station SB	Open before	1.11.1875
Replacement box	Opened	14.2.1893
***	Re-framed	1953
WHITWELL	OG	18.1.1875
***	OP	1.6.1875
***	CP	12.10.1964
***	CG	14.6.1965
Steetley Colliery Sidings SB	Open before	1.10.1876
Replacement box	Opened	7.6.1896
***	Closed	7.1985
Woodend Junction SB	Open before	1.11.1875
Replacement box	Opened	20.1.1901
***	Closed	9.12.1979

Between Shireoaks East Junction, Retford North Junction, and Retford Goods Station the Midland possessed running powers for all traffic over the Manchester, Sheffield & Lincolnshire line.
Between Retford North Junction and Retford station the Midland Railway possessed running powers over the Manchester, Sheffield & Lincolnshire line.

Shireoaks West Curve

Powers: Midland Railway (Mansfield Etc. Lines) Act 1865

Woodend Jcn to Shireoaks Colliery	OG	18.1.1875
Shireoaks Colliery to Shireoaks West Jcn	OG	....
Woodend Jcn to Shireoaks West Jcn	OP	1.6.1875
***	Singled	9.12.1979
***	CP	1.7.1905 *

Between Shireoaks West Junction and Shireoaks station the Midland possessed running powers for all traffic over the Manchester, Sheffield & Lincolnshire line.
Between Shireoaks West Junction and Brantcliffe Junction the Midland possessed running powers for all traffic over the Great Central line.

Shireoaks Colliery Sidings SB	Open before	1.11.1875
Replacement box	Opened	9.2.1904
***	Closed	25.9.1966
Shireoaks Colliery: connection between sidings and down main line	Into use	8.1.1893

STAVELEY RAILWAYS: SPEEDWELL BRANCH

Powers: Midland Railway (New Lines and Additional Powers) Act 1865
(acquisition of the Staveley Railways)
London Midland and Scottish Railway Act 1924
(Hall Lane and Seymour Junction Widening)
Midland Railway Act 1886 (improvement at Staveley)

Staveley (Goods) Jcn to Seymour Colliery: line acquired	... ...	1.5.1866
Midland working	Commenced	1.8.1866
***	OP(NA)	2.8.1875 *

Some evidence indicates that workmen's trains were running even before the acquisition of the line by the Midland, but none is shewn in the timetables before August 1875.

Staveley Goods Jcn re-named Barrow Hill Jcn	... ...	....
Barrow Hill Jcn - Summit - Hall Lane Jcn designated up line only	... ...	8.4.1973
Barrow Hill Jcn to Hall Lane Jcn: up Summit goods line made up & down Staveley single goods line	... ...	15.11.1981
BARROW HILL SUMMIT SIDINGS	Opened	....
***	t.o.u.	....
Summit Sidings SB	Opened	11.1885-12.1888
***	Closed	8.4.1973

Hartington Colliery to Lowgates Bridge: replacement line	Into use	20.11.1887
Hall Lane Crossing SB	Open before	16.8.1877
***	Closed	7.3.1887
Hall Lane Junction SB	Opened	26.8.1888
***	Re-framed	28.3.1920
Replacement box	Opened	23.11.1927
***	Closed	15.11.1981

Hartington Colliery Branch

Powers: --

Summit Sidings Jcn to Hartington Colliery	Opened	....
***	Closed	....
Hall Lane Jcn to Seymour Jcn	Doubled	28.5.1928
Eckington Lane Crossing SB	Open before	16.8.1877
***	Closed	11.1885-12.1888
Bell House Lane Crossing SB	Open before	16.8.1877
***	Closed	11.1885-12.1888
BELL HOUSE SIDING	Opened	1893-1895
***	Closed	1.3.1958
Lowgates Bridge to Seymour Jcn: replacement line	Into use	23.4.1888

Speedwell Colliery Branch

Powers: acquisition of the branch was authorized by the Midland Act of 1865 and further powers were taken by the Act of 1886.

Speedwell Colliery Branch Jcn to Speedwell Colliery	Opened	....
***	Closed	2.3.1977
Speedwell Colliery closed and Ireland Colliery opened	... ...	....
Running line at Staveley from Ireland Colliery to St John's Colliery: working by train staff without tickets	Commenced	27.3.1893

Arkwright Curve

Powers: British Railways (No. 2) Act 1981

Junction-curve to the former Great Central line for access to Arkwright Colliery (Arkwright Branch)	Into use	23.8.1982
***	Severed	24.7.1988
Staveley Town SB	Opened	28.5.1928
***	Closed	2.3.1977
NETHERTHORPE	OP	1.11.1888
Altered to NETHERTHORPE FOR STAVELEY TOWN	... ...	25.10.1893
Altered to STAVELEY TOWN	... ...	1.6.1900
***	CP(All)	5.8.1952
Seymour Lane Crossing SB	Open before	16.8.1877
	Closed	11.1885-12.1888
Clowne Branch Junction SB	Open before	16.8.1877
Replacement box	Opened	19.6.1888
Re-named Seymour Junction SB	... ...	....
***	Re-framed	14.3.1920
Replacement box	Opened	28.5.1928
Replacement box	Opened	1963
SEYMOUR JUNCTION	OP(NA) by	1915
***	CP	14.9.1931 *
SEYMOUR SIDINGS	Opened	....
Additional siding accommodation	Into use	30.5.1928
***	t.o.u.	....

BARROW HILL CURVES

Barrow Hill Passenger Line

Powers: Midland Railway (Additional Powers) Act 1883

Staveley Jcn to Hall Lane Jcn	Into use	26.8.1888
***	OP	1.11.1888
Electric key token working in place of electric train tablet block	Commenced	19.8.1928
***	t.o.u.	15.11.1981

Foxlow Curve (Staveley North Curve)

Powers: Midland Railway Act 1907

Hall Lane Jcn to Foxlow Jcn	Opened	25.11.1928
***	t.o.u.	6.1980
Singled running line	Into use	15.11.1981

DOE LEA BRANCH

Staveley & Doe Lea Valley Line

Powers: Midland Railway (New Lines and Additional Powers) Act 1863

Seymour Jcn to end of Doe Lea branch (1m 28ch)	OM by	8.1866	
***	OG	10.11.1884	
***	OP	1.9.1890	
***	CP	28.7.1930	
***	CP(NA)	14.9.1931	*
The Doe Lea branch was worked by electric train tablet block from 14 July 1890, and by train staff prior to that.			
Seymour Jcn to Markham Colliery Sidings: new goods line	Into use	9.7.1893	

Doe Lea Extension Line

Powers: Midland Railway (Additional Powers) Act 1865 (Doe Lea Extension Deviation)

End of Doe Lea branch to Glapwell	OG	10.11.1884	
End of Doe Lea branch to new junction at Glapwell	OP	1.9.1890	
***	CP	28.7.1930	
Seymour Jcn to Markham Colliery Sidings: new goods line	Into use	9.7.1893	
Markham Colliery Sidings SB	Opened	1890	
***	Raised	27.4.1919	
Replacement box	Opened	28.10.1928	
***	Closed	15.8.1982	
Markham Colliery Sidings SB to Glapwell Colliery Sidings SB: train tablet working in place of train staff working	Commenced	14.7.1890	

Markham Colliery Branch (Staveley Company)

Markham Colliery branch	Opened	....	
Working by staff without tickets	Commenced	11.7.1892	
***	Closed	19.7.1970	
Markham Collieries SB	Opened	1897	
***	Closed	....	

MARKHAM COLLIERY	OP(NA)	1.9.1886	*
***	CP	14.9.1931	*
Markham Colliery Sidings to Glapwell GF: one engine in steam working	Commenced	23.4.1978	
Bolsover Colliery Sidings: 2 down reception lines	Into use	1.6.1947	
BOLSOVER	OP	1.9.1890	
***	OG	19.9.1890	
***	CP	28.7.1930	
***	CP(NA)	14.9.1931	*
Altered to BOLSOVER CASTLE	... ...	25.9.1950	
***	CG	1.11.1962	
Excursion trains continued to call at least until 1939. Such traffic ran again between 1977 and 1981.			
Bolsover SB (new intermediate tablet station)	Opened	11.6.1893	
***	Closed	23.4.1978	
Bolsover: goods loop	Into use	18.6.1893	
Bolsover to Glapwell Colliery	Tfc ceased	Late 1976	
***	t.o.u. by	31.10.1978	
The line ceased to be used by any significant traffic after the closure of Glapwell Colliery in June 1974.			
Line cut at Bolsover	... ...	18.3.1979	
PALTERTON & SUTTON	OP	1.9.1890	
***	OG	19.9.1890	
***	CP	28.7.1930	
***	CP(NA)	14.9.1931	*
***	CG	12.1939	
Palterton & Sutton: new signalbox, as intermediate tablet station but not as crossing-place	Opened	11.8.1918	
Palterton & Sutton SB closed and ground frame for Ramcroft Colliery connection provided in lieu	... ...	31.7.1934	

Ramcroft Colliery Branch

Ramcroft Colliery branch: working by the Midland Railway	Commenced	16.9.1918	
RAMCROFT COLLIERY	OP(NA)	16.9.1918	
***	CP	3.10.1927	
Ramcroft Colliery	Closed	10.1966	

Glapwell Colliery Sidings SB	Opened	14.7.1890	
Replacement box	Opened	29.3.1925	
***	Closed	1969-1972	
Glapwell Colliery empty wagon running line	Into use	29.3.1925	
GLAPWELL COLLIERY SIDINGS	OP(NA)	1.9.1886	*
***	CP(All)	14.9.1931	*
Glapwell to Glapwell Colliery	Lifted	4.1959	
Glapwell Colliery	Closed	6.1974	
Glapwell Colliery: lines and sidings	t.o.u. by	End 1977	

GLAPWELL (first station)	OG	10.11.1884 ?
***	CG(All)	29.9.1890 ?

Doe Lea & Teversall Junction Line

Powers: Midland Railway (Additional Powers) Act 1883
Midland Railway (Additional Powers) Act 1873 (Glapwell - Doe Lea Extension)

Glapwell Jcn to Pleasley Colliery West Jcn	OP	1.9.1890
***	OG	29.9.1890
GLAPWELL (second station)	OP&M	22.8.1892
***	CP	28.7.1930
***	C.Parcels	23.9.1946
Glapwell to Pleasley Colliery West Jcn	C(All)	28.7.1930
***	Lifted	17.10.1932
ROWTHORN & HARDWICK	OP	1.9.1890
***	OG	19.9.1890
***	CP&G	28.7.1930
Pleasley Colliery Sidings West: connection from Doe Lea branch into sidings on the down side of the line	Into use	14.9.1896

CLOWN BRANCH

Powers: Midland Railway (Mansfield Etc Lines) Act 1865 (Staveley Branch Railway)

Staveley to Elmton & Cresswell	OG	1.6.1875
***	OP	1.11.1888
***	CP	5.7.1954
Creswell: see note on spelling of place-name under entry for Mansfield & Worksop line.		
Clown branch: new sidings	Into use	5.1.1881
Oxcroft Junction SB	Opened	21.6.1908
***	Closed	5.9.1915

Oxcroft Colliery Branch

Sanctioning: Midland Railway Act 1903

Oxcroft Colliery branch	Opened	1.9.1902
***	Closed	27.2.1976
The colliery branch was worked by train staff without tickets.		
Oxcroft Colliery branch: control by tablet for Seymour Junction to Barlborough Colliery Sidings section	Commenced	5.9.1915
Oxcroft Jcn to Oxcroft opencast disposal point	RO(G)	21.1.1980
This was the former Oxcroft Colliery branch.		
Workmen's trains to OXCROFT NO. 1	OP(NA)	25.2.1907
***	CP(All)	15.4.1918

Barlborough Colliery Sidings SB	Opened	2.2.1902
***	Raised	9.8.1914
Re-named Oxcroft Colliery Sidings No. 3 SB	... ...	9.1.1931
***	Closed	30.11.1969
CLOWN	OG	1.1878
***	OP	1.11.1888
Altered to CLOWNE	... ...	27.9.1937
Altered to CLOWN	... ...	Early 1938
Altered to CLOWN & BARLBOROUGH	... ...	4.7.1938
Altered to CLOWNE & BARLBOROUGH	Passenger	18.6.1951
Altered to CLOWNE NORTH	Goods	18.6.1951
***	CG	29.10.1951
***	CP	5.7.1954
Clown SB	Opened	6.1881-4.1883
***	Closed	11.1885-12.1888
Clown: points connecting the Lancashire, Derbyshire & East Coast Railway's sidings with the main line of the Clown branch	Into use	10.5.1896
Clown Jcn with the Lancashire, Derbyshire & East Coast Railway	Opened	16.11.1896
***	Closed	25.4.1937

SHIREOAKS & LAUGHTON BRANCH (Great Central & Midland)

The Shireoaks, Laughton & Maltby Railway was vested jointly in the Midland and Great Central companies from 31 July 1902 by the Great Central and Midland Railways Act 1902. The section between Dinnington Junction and Dinnington station was vested in the South Yorkshire Joint Line Committee from 14 August 1903 by the South Yorkshire Joint Railway Act 1903.

Powers: Shireoaks, Laughton and Maltby Railway Act 1902 (At Brantcliffe Junction)
Great Central and Midland Railways Act 1902 (Anston Deviation)
Shireoaks, Laughton and Maltby Railway Act 1901 (Anston to South Yorkshire Junction)

Brantcliffe (East) Jcn to Dinnington Jcn	OG	2.10.1905
***	OP	1.12.1910
***	CP	4.1926
***	RO(P)	25.7.1927
***	CP	2.12.1929
The line was opened for coal traffic as far as Dinnington Colliery on 20 February 1905.		
Brantcliffe Junction SB re-named Brantcliffe East Junction SB	... ...	15.6.1908
Brantcliffe North Junction SB	Opened	15.6.1908

Brantcliffe Curve

Powers: --

Brantcliffe West Jcn to Brantcliffe North Jcn	Completed by	1.1910
***	Into use	4.1914
***	Closed	1919 ?

Brantcliffe East, North, and West Junctions re-named Brancliffe East, West, and North Junctions	... ...	1917-1918
NORTH & SOUTH ANSTON	OG	13.8.1906
Altered to ANSTON	... ...	1906
Anston Junction SB	Opened	26.6.1907
***	Closed	....
ANSTON	OP	20.5.1912
***	CP	4.1926
***	RO(P)	25.7.1927
***	CP	2.12.1929
***	CG	4.12.1950
Dinnington Colliery Junction SB	Opened by	2.1.1907

ROTHERHAM, MALTBY & LAUGHTON LINE (Great Central & Midland Joint Lines)

The Rotherham, Maltby & Laughton Railway was was vested in the Great Central with effect from 20 July 1906 by the Hull and Barnsley and Great Central Railways Act 1906. It was vested in the Great Central & Midland Joint Committee from 9 August 1907 by the Midland Railway (Additional Powers) Act 1907.

Powers: Rotherham, Maltby and Laughton Railway Act 1905 (Anston Junction to Laughton Junction)
Hull and Barnsley Railway Act 1902 (Laughton Junction to Braithwell Junction)
Rotherham, Maltby and Laughton Railway Act 1905 (Braithwell Junction to Roundwood Junction)

Anston Jcn to Silverwood Jcn	OG	1.10.1909
Dalton Main Colliery to Roundwood Colliery Sidings	OG	1.10.1909
Don Bridge East Jcn to Thrybergh Jcn (Great Central Railway)	OG	1.10.1909

The section of the line between Laughton Junction and Braithwell Junction was made joint between the Midland, the Great Central, and the Hull & Barnsley Railways.

Between Thrybergh Junction and Dinnington Junction, and between Dinnington Junction and Dinnington Main Colliery, the Hull & Barnsley Railway possessed running powers over the Great Central & Midland Joint line.

Between Dinnington and all collieries and works on the Shireoaks Railway, and between Southern Junction and Thurcroft Colliery, the Lancashire & Yorkshire Railway possessed running powers over the Great Central & Midland Joint line.

Dinnington Colliery Jcn to Thurcroft: one engine in steam working	Commenced	29.5.1969
Anston Junction SB	Closed	10.4.1938
Anston Jcn to Laughton West Jcn: block telegraph working	Commenced	9.1.1911
Anston Jcn to Laughton West Jcn	Closed	10.4.1938
Laughton West Jucntion SB	Closed	10.4.1938
Thurcroft Sidings SB	Opened	....
***	Closed	29.5.1969

Thurcroft Colliery Branch

Powers: No Construction Powers

Thurcroft Sidings to Thurcroft Colliery	Opened	11.10.1913

THURCROFT COLLIERY SIDINGS	OP(NA)	1920 ?
***	CP(All)	....
Thurcroft Sidings to Silverwood Sidings	Closed	10.1966
***	Re-opened	23.12.1968
Line severed two miles north of Thurcroft	... ...	29.5.1969
Line severed just south of Hellaby	... ...	....
BRAMLEY & MALTBY GOODS altered to HELLABY	... ...	1.6.1920
HELLABY	CG(All)	31.10.1966
Line severed 400 yards north of Hellaby	... ...	2.1967
Braithwell Junction SB	Opened	1.5.1916
***	Closed	....

Between Braithwell Junction and Aire Junction the Midland possessed running powers for all traffic over the Hull & Barnsley and Great Central Joint line, and any intermediaate branches.

Braithwell Jcn to Silverwood Sidings	Singled	1.1.1944
Line severed 440 yards south of Silverwood Sidings	... ...	6.1961
Silverwood Sidings SB	Opened	1.11.1909
***	Closed	1969-1972
Silverwood Sidings to Silverwood Jcn: down goods loop	Into use	18.12.1927

Silverwood Colliery Branch

Powers: No Construction Powers

Silverwood Colliery Branch	Opened	....
***	Closed	....

Silverwood Junction SB	Opened	1.10.1909
Box closed and made a ground frame	... ...	23.3.1975
***	t.o.u.	4.7.1976
Silverwood to Thrybergh Jcn with the Great Central Railway	Singled	23.3.1975
Don Bridge East Junction SB	Opened	1.10.1909
***	Closed	5.12.1971
Don Bridge East Jcn to Roundwood: pilot guard working ceased and working by interlocked acceptance levers commenced	... ...	21.7.1957
Don Bridge East Jcn to Roundwood closed and Don Bridge East Jcn	t.o.u.	2.8.1966
Don Bridge West Jcn to Roundwood Jcn with the Great Central Railway	Closed	1.9.1913
Don Bridge West Jcn to Thrybergh Jcn with the Midland Railway	... ...	Not built

SOUTH YORKSHIRE JOINT LINE

(Owned jointly by the Great Central, the Great Northern, the Lancashire & Yorkshire, the Midland, and the North Eastern Railways.)

Powers: The South Yorkshire Joint Line Committee was incorporated on 14 August 1903.

Dinnington Jcn to Dinnington & Laughton	OG	2.10.1905
***	OP	1.12.1910
***	CP	4.1926
***	RO(P)	25.7.1927
***	CP	2.12.1929
Dinnington Colliery branch	Opened	20.2.1905
DINNINGTON & LAUGHTON	OG	2.10.1905
***	OP	1.12.1910
***	CP	4.1926
***	RO(P)	25.7.1927
***	CP	2.12.1929
***	CG	3.5.1965
Dinnington Station SB	Opened	....
***	Closed	20.5.1973
Dinnington to Dinnington North SB: station loop extension on up side to Rotherham Lane bridge	Into use	21.12.1913
Dinnington North SB	Opened	21.12.1913
***	Closed	15.4.1956
Dinnington & Laughton to Kirk Sandall Jcn; Low Ellers Jcn to Potteric Carr Jcn	OG	1.1.1909
***	OP	1.12.1910
***	CP	4.1926
***	RO(P)	25.7.1927
The South Yorkshire Joint Line was closed completely for four months during the 1921 coal strike.		
Dinnington & Laughton to Maltby	CP	2.12.1929

Laughton Curve

Powers: --

Laughton East Jcn to Laughton West Jcn	Opened	9.1.1911
***	Closed	12.9.1912
***	Re-opened by	10.4.1938

MALTBY	OG	1.3.1909
***	OP	1.12.1910
***	CP	4.1926
***	RO(P)	25.7.1927
***	CP	2.12.1929
***	CG	14.6.1965
Maltby to Potteric Carr Jcn	CP	8.7.1929
Maltby Station SB to Maltby Colliery Sidings SB	Doubled	12.6.1911
Maltby Colliery Sidings SB	Opened	12.6.1911

Maltby Colliery Branch

Powers: --

Maltby Colliery branch	OG	22.3.1911
***	Closed	....

Maltby Colliery North SB	Opened	7.12.1913

Firbeck Colliery Branch		
Powers: --		
Firbeck Colliery branch	Opened	1.10.1926
Firbeck Colliery SB closed and shunter's cabin provided in lieu	... ...	9.4.1929
Firbeck Colliery, and Firbeck Colliery branch	Closed	31.12.1968
Haworth Colliery Branch		
Harworth Colliery branch, with east curve at Harworth Jcn	Opened	22.4.1929
Harworth Jcn east curve	Closed	1.8.1930
Harworth Junction SB replaced by Harworth Junction GF Hut	... ...	c.8.1930
Harworth Junction SB	Closed	5.7.1931
Tickhill SB	Closed	31.5.1970
TICKHILL	OG	1.3.1909
***	OP	1.12.1910
Altered to TICKHILL & WADWORTH	... ...	1.7.1911
***	CP	4.1926
***	RO(P)	25.7.1927
***	CP	8.7.1929
***	CG	2.11.1964

V. THE NORTH MIDLAND LINE

NORTH MIDLAND RAILWAY

The North Midland Railway was amalgamated with the Midland Counties Railway and the Birmingham & Derby Junction Railway on 10 May 1844 as the Midland Railway.

Powers: North Midland Railway Act 1836
North Midland Railway Act 1839 (Derby to Nottingham Road - transfer of powers from the Birmingham & Derby Junction Railway Company)
Midland Railway Act 1891 (Derby to Derby North Junction Widening)
Midland Railway Act 1897 (Widening at Duffield - Land Powers only)
North Midland Railway Act 1837 (Duffield to south of Ambergate)
London Midland and Scottish Railway Act 1924 (Broadholme & Ambergate Widening)
Midland Railway (Additional Powers) Act 1873 (Ambergate Middle Curve - Land Powers only)
North Midland Railway Act 1837 (north of Ambergate to Wingfield)
Midland Railway (Additional Powers) Act 1873 (Clay Cross & Chesterfield Widening)
Midland Railway Act 1904 (Chesterfield Widening - land purchased - works not executed)
North Midland Railway Act 1837 (Chesterfield to Whittington)
North Midland Railway Act 1837 (Killamarsh to Woodhouse Mill)
Midland Railway Act 1898 (Beighton & Treeton Widening)
Midland Railway Act 1901 (Ickles Widening)
Midland Railway Act 1899 (Parkgate & Roundwood Widening, Kilnhurst & Swinton Widening, land powers only for the Wath Road Junction to Wath Widening)
Midland Railway Act 1898 (Wath & Darfield Widening, and Cudworth & Royston Widening)
London Midland and Scottish Railway Act 1923 (Chevet & Snydale Widening)
Midland Railway (Additional Powers) Act 1861 (Goose Hill Junction to Altofts Junction - Land Powers only)
Midland Railway Act 1898 (Waterloo & Stourton Widening)
North Midland Railway Act 1839 (Leeds Hunslet)

Derby to Masborough	Opened	11.5.1840	
Masborough to Leeds Hunslet	Opened	1.7.1840	
Derby to Tapton Jcn: block telegraph working	Intro. by	1873	
DERBY	Opened	11.5.1840	
Additional platforms	Into use	1867	
Several alterations to the station	Completed	15.10.1876	
Platforms Nos. 4, 5, and 6	Into use	7.1881	
Station made "closed" - Sunday 9 a.m. to midnight	... ...	6.5.1934	
Midnight Saturday to midnight Sunday	... ...	15.9.1934	
Midnight Saturday to 1 a.m. Monday	... ...	19.1.1935	
Weeknights 10 p.m. to 5 a.m., 10 p.m. Saturday to 5 a.m. Monday	... ...	28.3.1936	
Completely	... ...	27.6.1955	
Altered to DERBY MIDLAND	... ...	25.9.1950	
Platforms rebuilt	... ...	1952--1954	
Altered to DERBY	... ...	6.5.1968	
Station made "open"	... ...	1.10.1984	
New booking office and travel centre	Opened	....	
DERBY: scissors crossing	Into use	7.1881	
Scissors crossings between platforms Nos. 3 and 4	t.o.u.	14.4.1968	
Scissors crossings between platforms Nos. 1 and 2	t.o.u.	16.2.1969	
Derby: Midland Railway War Memorial	Dedicated	15.12.1921	
Derby: Cuff's Station Hotel	Opened	Mid-1842	?
Re-named Midland Hotel and re-opened under Midland Railway management	... ...	3.11.1860	
***	Sold	....	
Derby Station SB	Opened	....	
Replacement box (located on platform No. 6) named Derby "A" SB	Opened	7.1881	
Replacement box	Opened	1952	
***	Closed	13.7.1969	
Derby "B" SB	Opened	c.7.1881	
***	Closed	31.12.1922	
Derby: through goods lines and fish line	In use by	1.12.1861	*
Deadman's Lane end of new engine shed to Engine Sidings No. 2 SB: up and down locomotive lines	Into use	13.4.1890	
Up locomotive line recovered and down locomotive line re-named pilot line	By	13.2.1987	
Engine Sidings No. 2 SB	Opened	23.3.1890	
***	Into use	19.7.1891	
Position of the box slightly altered	... ...	1.4.1906	
Box made a shunting frame	... ...	13.7.1969	
***	t.o.u.	8.2.1987	

Derby engine shed	Opened	....
Second roundhouse	Opened	2.1847
Third roundhouse	Opened	1852
No. 4 engine shed	Opened	1890
All facilities for steam	Withdrawn	6.3.1967
Engine Sidings SB	Opened	2.1879-2.1880
Re-named Engine Sidings No. 1 SB	... ...	23.3.1890
Replacement box	Opened	18.12.1892
***	Closed	13.7.1969
Derby Goods Yard SB	Open before	16.8.1877
***	Closed	2.1879-2.1880
Bell Box Junction SB	Opened by	10.1868
***	Closed	28.10.1877
Passenger Station North Junction SB	Opened	28.10.1877
Replacement box	Opened	9.10.1892
***	Re-framed	14.10.1917
***	Closed	13.7.1969
Passenger Station North: down goods line to down passenger line crossover	Into use	3.12.1911
Passenger Station North Jcn to Derby North Jcn: up and down goods lines, and single goods line	Into use	9.10.1892
From 9 October 1892 to 18 December 1892 only the single goods line was in use as a goods line over the canal bridge, the up and down goods lines used temporarily as the up and down passenger lines.		
DERBY CATTLE DOCKS	Opened	....
***	Closed	1.1.1965
Derby Jcn: double junction (DGL-DPL, UPL-UGL)	Into use	....
Derby Junction SB	Open before	1870
Replacement box	Opened	9.10.1892
***	Closed	13.7.1969
DERWENT BRIDGE TICKET PLATFORM	Closed	19.9.1892
Derby North Junction SB	Open before	1870
Replacement box	Opened	25.9.1892
Replacement box	Opened	30.6.1957
***	Closed	13.7.1969

Derby North Curve

See page 68

Derby North Jcn: up and down goods lines through the junction	Into use	25.10.1903
Derby North Junction: double junction (DPL-DGL, UGL-UPL)	Into use	25.10.1903
***	t.o.u.	....
Derby North Jcn to St Mary's Jcn: up goods line	In use by	1.1.1869 *
Down goods line (up side)	Into use	20.4.1873
Down reception line	Into use	19.2.1939
NOTTINGHAM ROAD	OP	1.9.1856 *
Collection of tickets of main-line trains	Commenced	7.4.1873
***	CP(All)	6.3.1967

St Mary's Goods Depot and Branch

Powers: Midland Railway (Ripley Branches) Act 1848

ST MARY'S GOODS DEPOT	Opened	1855
***	C.Coal	3.1984
ST MARY'S SIDINGS	Opened	....
ST MARY'S NCL SIDINGS	Closed by	6.5.1988
St Mary's Wharf SB (not a block post)	Opened	....
Replacement box	Opened	21.3.1892
Re-named St Mary's Goods Yard SB	... ...	....
Replacement box	Opened	6.2.1898
Replacement box	Opened	4.1938 ?
Box made a shunting frame	... ...	13.7.1969
***	t.o.u.	20.4.1980
St Mary's Goods Depot: down reception line	Into use	19.2.1938
Middle siding and down reception line	Reversed	17.7.1984
CITY ROAD WHARF	Opened	....
***	Closed	....

Little Chester Junction SB	Opened	1868
Re-named St Mary's Junction SB	... ...	11.1875-8.1877
Replacement top installed	... ...	10.5.1891
Replacement box	Opened	30.5.1897
***	Closed	13.7.1969
St Mary's Jcn to Breadsall Crossing: up and down goods lines	Into use	26.7.1891
Breadsall Crossing SB	Open before	1.11.1875
Replacement box	Opened	c.8.1877
Replacement box	Opened	1.3.1891
***	Closed	13.7.1969
Breadsall Crossing: up goods line extended over the level crossing and up goods line to up passenger line connection removed	... ...	8.9.1901
Down goods line to down passenger line crossover	Into use	6.10.1901
Up passenger line to up goods line crossover	Into use	....
Breadsall Crossing to Peckwash Mill Sidings: down goods line	Into use	6.10.1901

Breadsall Crossing to Little Eaton Jcn: up goods line	Into use	1.3.1891
Second up goods line	Into use	26.7.1891
Second up goods line made a through siding	... ...	24.7.1950
Through siding	t.o.u.	....
Up goods line made "no block"	... ...	10.3.1969
Breadsall Crossing to Duffield Jcn: down goods line	t.o.u.	2.3.1969
Little Eaton Junction SB	Open before	1870
Replacement box	Opened	25.3.1900
***	Closed	13.7.1969

Ripley branch
See page 143

Little Eaton Jcn: up goods line to up passenger line crossover	Into use	5.1.1902
Little Eaton Jcn to Peckwash Mill Sidings: up goods line	Into use	5.1.1902
Little Eaton Jcn to Duffield Jcn: up goods line	t.o.u.	2.3.1969
Burleigh Bridge SB (first box)	Opened	21.9.1890
***	Closed	12.10.1890
Burleigh Bridge SB: temporary box for re-building bridge No. 15	Opened	2.12.1934
***	Closed	23.6.1935
Peckwash Mill Sidings SB	Opened	c.12.1877
Replacement box	Opened	14.3.1897
***	Closed	24.1.1965
PECKWASH MILL SIDINGS (Tempest's Peckwash Paper Mill Sidings)	Opened	15.12.1877
***	Closed by	1917
Peckwash Mill: up goods line to up passenger line crossover	Into use	23.5.1909
Down passenger line to down slow line crossover	Into use	....
Up goods line to up passenger line crossover	t.o.u.	....
Down passenger line to down slow line crossover	t.o.u.	24.1.1965
Peckwash Mill to Duffield Station SB: up goods line	Into use	4.10.1897
Down slow line	Into use	8.9.1901
Duffield Jcn: down through siding	t.o.u.	26.4.1987
Duffield Junction SB	Opened	1867
Replacement box	Opened	1875 ?
Replacement box	Opened	1897 ?
Box extended and re-framed	... ...	16.1.1910
***	Closed	13.7.1969

Wirksworth branch
See page 143

Duffield Jcn to Duffield Station: down slow/goods line	Into use	8.9.1901
Duffield Jcn to Milford Tunnel: down goods line	t.o.u.	3.6.1956
Up goods line	t.o.u.	....
DUFFIELD	Opened	6. 4.1841
Replacement station further south	Opened	1.10.1867
***	CG	4.1.1965
Duffield Station SB	Opened	28.2.1897
***	Alt.levers	8.9.1901
***	Closed	16.1.1910
Duffield: down slow line to down passenger line crossover	Into use	....
Duffield to Milford Tunnel: down goods line	Into use	16.5.1897
Up goods line	Into use	14.6.1897
Milford Tunnel SB	Opened	16.5.1897
***	Closed	3.6.1956
Belper Goods Yard (south end) to Belper Goods Yard Box: up goods loop	Into use	6.10.1912
***	t.o.u.	11.9.1968
BELPER	Opened	11.5.1840
Replacement passenger station at King Street	OP	10.3.1878
Old station goods depot	CG	2.7.1979
Belper SB	Open before	16.8.1877
Re-named Belper Goods SB	... ...	10.3.1878
Replacement box	Opened	15.9.1895
Replacement box at Belper end of yard	Opened	14.7.1912
***	Closed	13.7.1969
Belper Passenger Station SB	Opened	2.5.1897
***	Closed	19.7.1931
Belper North SB: temporary box for the re-building of bridge No. 36	Opened	7.5.1934
***	Closed by	22.10.1934
Broadholme SB	Open before	1.11.1875
Replacement box	Opened	1883
***	Re-framed	6.10.1895
Replacement box	Opened	24.9.1899
Replacement box 330 yards to the north	Opened	14.9.1930
***	Closed	13.7.1969
Broadholme to Ambergate South Jcn: up and down slow lines	Into use	13.12.1931
Up and down slow lines made up and down goods lines	... ...	13.7.1969
Broadholme to Ambergate South Jcn:		
down goods line made down passenger loop	... ...	12.6.1982
Up goods line made up passenger loop	... ...	4.7.1982
Ambergate: new viaduct carrying the lines into the station	Into use	29.11.1931

Ambergate South Junction SB	Opened	1863	?
Replacement box	Opened	25.6.1893	
Replacement box 300 yards to the south	Opened	29.11.1931	
Box closed and location re-named Ambergate Junction	... ...	13.7.1969	
Ambergate South Curve			
Ambergate South Jcn: curve to the Manchester, Buxton & Midland Junction line (Ambergate South Curve)	OP&G	1.6.1863	
See page 189 for the Manchester line.			
Ambergate Station Junction SB	Opened	c.12.1876	
Replacement box	Opened	25.6.1893	
***	Closed	12.5.1968	
Ambergate Station Jcn to Ambergate North Jcn (Ambergate Middle Curve)	Opened	10.12.1876	
***	Closed	12.5.1968	
AMBER GATE	Opened	11.5.1840	
Altered to AMBERGATE	... ...	1.11.1846	*
Replacement station at the south junction	Opened	1.6.1863	
Replacement triangular station	Opened	10.12.1876	
Second station building made a store for books and plans	... ...	1882	
***	CG	6.4.1964	
The original Ambergate station was north of Toadmoor tunnel, just south of the north-facing junction for the Rowsley line. The second station was opened at the same time as the south-to-west curve to the Rowsley line and it lay in the "V" of the junction. The only platform still in use is the former up Manchester platform.			
Ambergate North Junction SB	Open before	1876	
Replacement box	Opened	c.12.1876	
Replacement box	Opened	5.6.1904	
***	Closed	12.5.1968	
Matlock, Buxton, Manchester & Midland Junction line			
See page 189			
Ambergate North Jcn to Crich Jcn: reception line on the up side	Into use	6.3.1910	
Reception line on the down side	Into use	31.1.1915	
Up and down reception lines	t.o.u.	....	
Ambergate North Jcn to Way & Works Sidings (north): down goods line	Into use	....	
***	t.o.u.	....	
Crich Junction SB	Open before	16.8.1877	
Replacement box	Opened	24.4.1904	
***	Closed	13.7.1969	
Duffield & Selston line			
See page 96			
Crich Jcn: down goods line to down passenger line crossover	Into use	....	
***	t.o.u.	....	
Bull Bridge SB	Opened	c.1874	
Replacement box	Opened	18.11.1894	
***	Closed	17.7.1932	
BULL BRIDGE	OM before	1872	
***	OG	1896	
***	Closed	....	
Wingfield Colliery Sidings	Recovered	27.2.1965	
Oakerthorpe Colliery Branch			
Powers: --			
Wingfield Colliery Sidings to Oakerthorpe Colliery	Restored	1897	
Wingfield Station SB	Opened	1858	
Replacement box	Opened	....	
***	Alt.levers	8.5.1892	
Replacement box	Opened	5.7.1903	
***	Closed	13.7.1969	
WINGFIELD	Opened	11.5.1840	
Altered to WINGFIELD (ALFRETON)	Before	1.12.1848	*
WINGFIELD FOR ALFRETON altered to WINGFIELD	... ...	1.5.1862	*
***	CG	2.12.1963	
***	CP	2.1.1967	
Shirland Sidings SB	Open before	1.11.1875	
Replacement box	Opened	27.2.1898	
***	Closed	28.8.1966	
Shirland Branch			
Powers: --			
Shirland Sidings to Shirland Colliery	Opened	5.1866	
***	Closed	30.10.1965	

Stretton South SB	Open before	1.11.1875
Replacement box	Opened	21.2.1904
Box closed and up-line IBS provided in lieu	... ...	16.6.1935
Down-line IBS	Into use	....
Up-line and down-line IBS	t.o.u.	29.6.1968
Stretton South to Stretton: up and down goods lines	Into use	21.2.1904
Down-side sidings and up and down goods lines	t.o.u.	5.6.1968
SMITHY MOOR	Opened	6.4.1841
Altered to STRETTON	... ...	1841
Altered to STRETTON FOR ASHOVER	... ...	1.10.1872 *
***	CP	11.9.1961
***	CG	7.8.1967
Stretton North SB	Open before	16.8.1877
Replacement box	Opened	13.12.1887
Replacement box	Opened	22.3.1891
Replacement box	Opened	21.2.1904
Re-named Stretton Station SB	... ...	16.6.1935
***	Closed	12.10.1969
Clay Cross tunnel: warning telegraph wires	Installed	8.1904
Clay Cross Tunnel SB	Opened	16.3.1902
***	Closed	20.11.1932
Clay Cross Tunnel to Clay Cross North Jcn: down goods line	Into use	16.3.1902
Down goods line temporarily taken out of use and made a siding	... ...	13.4.1902
Down goods line re-opened on completion of Clay Cross widening	... ...	15.6.1902

Clay Cross Town Goods Branch

Powers: --

Clay Cross South Jcn to Clay Cross Town goods depot	Opened by	1.1895
Clay Cross Ironworks to Clay Cross Town goods depot	Closed	7.10.1963
Clay Cross South Jcn to Clay Cross Works Sidings	t.o.u.	23.9.1978

Clay Cross South Junction SB	Open before	1870
Replacement box named Clay Cross South SB	Opened	c.12.1877
***	Re-framed	4.10.1896
Re-named Clay Cross South Junction SB	... ...	....
Replacement box	Opened	13.4.1902
***	Closed	12.10.1969
Clay Cross South Jcn to Clay Cross North Jcn: Erewash Valley lines	Into use	23.12.1877

Erewash Valley line

See page 87

Clay Cross Station SB	Open before	16.8.1877
***	Closed	c.12.1877
CLAY CROSS	Opened	6.4.1841
***	CG	4.5.1964
***	CP	2.1.1967
CLAY CROSS SIDINGS	Opened	....
***	t.o.u.	....
Clay Cross North Junction SB	Open before	16.8.1877
Replacement box	Opened	c.12.1877
***	Alt.levers	30.3.1890
***	Raised	12.5.1895
Replacement box	Opened	16.3.1902
***	Closed	12.10.1969
Clay Cross North Junction: double junction (DGL-DPL, UPL-UGL)	Into use	23.12.1877 ?
Double junction (DPL-DGL, UGL-UPL)	Into use	23.12.1877 ?
Both double junctions	t.o.u.	....
Ladder junction (south end in DPL)	Into use	....
Clay Cross North Jcn to Horn's Bridge: up and down goods lines	Into use	5.11.1873
Avenue Crossing SB	Open before	1.11.1875
Replacement box	Opened	5.11.1899
***	Raised	9.5.1915
Replacement box named Avenue Sidings SB 100 yards to the south	Opened	20.11.1955
Box made a shunting frame	... ...	12.10.1969
Box closed and ground frame provided in lieu	... ...	29.10.1972
Avenue Sidings SB (original box)	Open before	1.11.1875
Points connecting Grassmoor Branch to new sidings connected up to be worked from the signalbox	... ...	25.2.1894
Replacement box	Opened	5.11.1899
***	Raised	7.5.1916
Box closed and ground frame provided in lieu	... ...	21.10.1934

Grassmoor branch

See page 146

AVENUE SIDINGS	Opened	....
***	t.o.u.	....
Avenue Sidings to Avenue Crossing: down reception line	Into use	27.8.1911
***	t.o.u.	....

Hasland Sidings SB	Opened	2.1880-6.1881
Replacement box	Opened	15.6.1902
***	Re-framed	....
***	Closed	12.10.1969
HASLAND	OM	7.1876
***	OG	1879
***	CG(All)	....
HASLAND NO. 9 PIT SIDINGS	OP(NA) by	5.3.1913
***	CP(All)	....
Hasland engine shed	Opened	29.3.1875
***	Closed	7.9.1964
Wingerworth South SB	Open before	1.11.1875
Re-named Broad Oaks South SB	... ...	26.4.1897
Replacement box	Opened	18.3.1900
***	Closed	1.11.1908
WINGERWORTH	OG before	1872
Altered to BROAD OAKS	... ...	....
***	Closed	....
Wingerworth North SB	Open before	1.11.1875
Re-named Broad Oaks North SB	... ...	26.4.1897
Replacement box	Opened	c.3.1900
Re-named Broad Oaks SB	... ...	....
Box closed and Glossop's ground frame provided in lieu	... ...	29.9.1936
Storforth Lane Colliery	Opened	24.10.1875
Horn's Bridge: up passenger line to up goods line crossover	Into use	12.4.1908
Down goods line to down passenger line crossover	Into use	10.11.1901
Double junction	t.o.u.	....
Horn's Bridge SB	Open before	16.8.1877
Replacement box	Opened	4.12.1892
***	Raised	15.6.1919
Replacement box	Opened	21.7.1963
***	Closed	12.10.1969
Horn's Bridge to Tapton Jcn: up and down goods lines	Into use	10.8.1874
Hollis Lane SB	Open before	16.8.1877
Replacement box	Opened	28.5.1899
***	Closed	12.4.1966

Chesterfield & Brampton Railway

Powers: Chesterfield and Brampton Railway Act 1870

The company was vested in Midland Railway by 34-5 Victoria cap. 86 with effect from 29 June 1871.

Chesterfield to Brampton Colliery	Opened	19.6.1873
***	Closed	20.6.1964
Chesterfield Tube Company's Sidings to Brampton	Closed	15.6.1964
Chesterfield Gas Company's branch (from Boythorpe Lane Jcn)	Opened	1880
BOYTHORPE ROAD WHARF	Opened	1900-1904
***	Closed	15.6.1964

Chesterfield Station South SB	Open before	16.8.1877
***	Re-framed	15.3.1896
Replacement box	Opened	1907-1915
***	Enlarged	12.9.1915
***	Closed	12.10.1969
LORDSMILL ROAD WHARF	Opened	....
***	Closed	1.8.1953
CHESTERFIELD	Opened	11.5.1840
Replacement station 100 yards to the north	Opened	2.5.1870
Station made "closed" for tickets	... ...	1.7.1903
Altered to CHESTERFIELD ST MARY'S	... ...	25.9.1950
Altered to CHESTERFIELD MIDLAND	... ...	18.6.1951
Altered to CHESTERFIELD	... ...	7.9.1964
Down bay platform	Closed	12.10.1969
Public delivery siding	CG	4.7.1983
Connection to up bay platform	Removed by	10.1988
Chesterfield Station North SB	Open before	16.8.1877
Replacement box	Opened	29.8.1915
***	Closed	7.6.1964
Tapton Junction SB	Opened	c.1874 ?
Replacement box	Opened	3.5.1891
***	Re-framed	20.4.1902
***	Closed	25.3.1973
Tapton Junction replaced Chesterfield Junction	... ...	12.1873-4.1874
Tapton Jcn: double junction (DPL-Beighton, Beighton-UPL)	Into use	10.8.1874 ?
Double junction (DGL-Sheffield, Sheffield-UGL)	Into use	20.4.1902
Replacement ladder junctions	Into use	....

Chesterfield & Sheffield line

See page 148

Tapton Jcn to Whittington: block telegraph working	Introduced	1874
Tapton Jcn to Masborough South Jcn	CP	5.7.1954

Tapton Jcn to Beighton Jcn	RO(P)	17.5.1982	
***	CP	11.5.1987	*
Chesterfield Junction SB	Opened	1870	
Box closed and Tapton Junction SB some 50 chains to the south opened as its replacement	... ...	12.1873-4.1874	
Dunston & Barlow South SB	Open before	1.11.1875	
Replacement box	Opened	15.1.1899	
***	Closed	13.1.1963	

Sheepbridge branch
See page 148

Dunston & Barlow SB	Opened	1865	
***	Closed by	1.11.1875	
Dunston & Barlow North SB	Open before	1.11.1875	
Replacement box	Opened	5.2.1899	
***	Re-framed	....	
***	Closed	15.11.1981	
WHITTINGTON	OP	1.10.1861	*
Replacement station about 220 yards to the north	OP	9.6.1873	
***	OM	1874	
New (third) station	OP	1.3.1876	
***	CM	....	
***	CP	4.2.1952	
Excursion trains continued to call, certainly until 1977.			
Whittington Station SB	Open before	16.8.1877	
Replacement box	Opened	12.9.1897	
***	Closed	15.11.1981	
Whittington to Masborough Jcn: block telegraph working	Introduced	1875	
Whittington to Staveley South: up goods line	Into use	31.10.1897	
Down goods line	Into use	20.2.1898	
Up and down goods lines	t.o.u.	....	
WHITTINGTON (north of): new sidings (up side)	Into use	19.8.1928	
New sidings (down side)	Into use	9.9.1928	
All sidings re-named STAVELEY SIDINGS	... ...	....	
***	t.o.u.	....	
Staveley Up Sidings SB (not a block post)	Opened	26.8.1928	
Re-named Barrow Hill Up Sidings SB	... ...	....	
***	Closed	17.10.1982	
Staveley Down Sidings SB (not a block post)	Opened	9.9.1928	
Re-named Barrow Hill Down Sidings SB	... ...	....	
***	Closed	5.1968	
STAVELEY UP DEPOT	Opened	23.9.1928	
***	Closed	....	
Staveley South: down goods line to down passenger line crossover	Into use	....	
Up passenger line to up goods line crossover	Into use	....	
Staveley South SB	Open before	16.8.1877	
Replacement box	Opened	24.10.1897	
Replacement box	Opened	1918-1928	
***	Closed	15.11.1981	

Springwell Branch (Staveley Railways)

Acquisition: Midland Railway (New Lines and Additional Powers) Act	1865		
Midland Railway (Additional Powers) Act 1870 (Springwell Curve)			
Staveley to Springwell Colliery: line acquired	... ...	1.5.1866	
Midland working	Commenced	1.8.1866	
***	Closed	....	
This line was worked by train staff without tickets.			
Engine Shed Sidings SB (not a block post)	Opened	....	
***	Alt.levers	20.1.1890	
Replacement box	Opened	11.1.1904	
***	Closed	2.1.1966	
Staveley engine shed	Opened	Late 1870	
***	C.Steam	4.10.1965	
Springwell New Curve, and sidings	Opened	22.3.1875	
***	Closed	....	

Staveley South to Staveley Jcn: up goods line	Into use	19.8.1928	
***	t.o.u.	....	
Staveley Station SB	Open before	16.8.1877	
BARROW HILL SOUTH SIDINGS	Opened	....	
***	t.o.u.	....	
Staveley Sidings SB: replacement box named Staveley Junction SB	Opened	15.7.1888	
***	Raised	10.8.1913	
***	Re-framed	5.11.1916	
Replacement box	Opened	19.8.1928	
Re-named Barrow Hill Junction SB	... ...	1951	?
***	Closed	15.11.1981	

Staveley branch
See page 115

Staveley Junction: curve into sidings alongside up main line	Into use	15.7.1888
***	t.o.u.	....
NEW WHITTINGTON SIDING	Opened	....
***	Closed	2.9.1968
STAVELEY	Opened	6.4.1841
Replacement station to the north, at the Clown branch junction	Opened	1.11.1888
Altered to BARROW HILL & STAVELEY WORKS	... ...	1.6.1900
Altered to BARROW HILL	... ...	18.6.1951
***	CP	5.7.1954
***	CG	12.7.1965
Excursion trains and trains for Open Days at the depot continued to call, probably until 1983.		

Barrow Hill Passenger line

See page 116

Foxlow SB	Opened	1875
Replacement box named Foxlow Goods Junction SB half a mile nearer to Staveley	Opened	22.8.1891
Replacement box 250 yards to the north	Opened	25.11.1928
***	Closed	15.11.1981

Foxlow Curve (Staveley North Curve)

See page 116

Foxlow Goods Jcn to Renishaw Park Goods Jcn: up goods line	Into use	20.9.1891
Down goods line	Into use	15.10.1891
Down goods line	t.o.u.	23.7.1978
Up goods line	t.o.u.	10.5.1981
Renishaw Park South SB	Opened	2.1880-6.1881
Replacement box named Renishaw Park Goods Junction SB	Opened	21.12.1890
Replacement box	Opened	2.4.1922
***	Closed	15.11.1981
Renishaw Park Sidings SB	Open before	16.8.1877
Re-named Renishaw Park Sidings North SB	... ...	2.1880-6.1881
***	Raised	14.3.1887
Replacement box	Opened	23.7.1905
***	Closed	13.6.1909
Eckington Sidings SB	Open before	16.8.1877
Replacement box	Opened	13.10.1901
Re-named Eckington South Sidings SB	... ...	....
***	Closed	3.10.1909
Eckington Station SB	Open before	16.8.1877
Re-named Eckington & Renishaw Station SB	... ...	....
Replacement box	Opened	20.4.1902
Replacement box	Opened	3.10.1909
***	Closed	1.5.1977
ECKINGTON	Opened	11.5.1840
Replacement station 14 chains to the north	Opened	13.9.1874
Altered to ECKINGTON & RENISHAW	... ...	10.4.1886
***	CP&G	1.10.1951
Excursion trains continued to call at this station.		
Plumbley Colliery Sidings SB	Open before	16.8.1877
***	Closed	22.7.1894
Holbrook Colliery Sidings SB	Opened	1879
Replacement box	Opened	14.9.1890
***	Re-framed	14.1.1917
***	Closed	26.2.1961
Killamarsh Station SB	Open before	1.11.1875
Replacement box	Opened	3.9.1899
***	Closed	4.10.1981
KILLAMARSH	Opened	6.4.1841
***	CP	2.1.1843 *
New station on the same site	Opened	21.7.1873
***	OG	1874
Altered to KILLAMARSH WEST	... ...	25.9.1950
***	CP&G	1.2.1954
Norwood Sidings SB	Open before	1.11.1875
Re-named Killamarsh Branch Sidings SB	... ...	10.1876-8.1877
Replacement box	Opened	14.9.1890
***	Closed	7.1959
These two boxes may well be one and the same location.		

Killamarsh Branch and Extension

Powers: Midland Railway (Branches Etc) Act 1866
Midland Railway (Additional Powers) Act 1874
(Killamarsh Branch Extension)

Killamarsh Branch Sidings to Norwood Colliery	Opened	1.10.1868 *
Killamarsh Branch Extension (to Kiveton Park Colliery)	Opened	19.8.1878
Branch severed at Yorkshire Tar Distillers' Siding (155m 41ch)	... ...	19.5.1961
Killamarsh Branch Sidings to Yorkshire Tar Distillers' Siding	Closed	15.11.1972

Beighton: junction with Lancashire, Derbyshire & East Coast Railway	Opened	16.12.1901
***	Closed	....
Beighton Junction SB	Opened	1864
Replacement box	Opened	....
Replacement box	Opened	3.8.1890
Replacement box	Opened	13.8.1899
***	Closed	16.5.1982
Beighton: junction with Manchester, Sheffield & Lincolnshire Railway	Opened	12.2.1849

North Staveley Curve to the Manchester, Sheffield & Lincolnshire Railway

Powers: Midland Railway (New Lines) Act 1861

Beighton Jcn to North Staveley Jcn	Opened	19.9.1866
Connection with the Midland running lines	Removed	30.7.1899
Midland ceased to use connection at the Great Central end	... ...	8.7.1906
Beighton Jcn to North Staveley Colliery Empty Wagon Sidings and running line from Beighton Jcn to Beighton Colliery Loaded Wagon Sidings: working by pilot guard without tickets	Commenced	27.1.1908
Line severed at 156m 6ch	... ...	10.5.1976
Beighton Jcn: section of line between junction with branch to coke ovens and Broomhouse Colliery	t.o.u.	10.5.1976

BEIGHTON	Opened	Mid-6.1840
***	Closed	2.1.1843 *
Beighton Jcn to Woodhouse Mill: up and down goods lines	Into use	7.1.1900
***	t.o.u.	....
Woodhouse Mill No. 1 SB	Opened	21.8.1938
***	Closed	31.3.1968
Woodhouse Mill South SB (signalling the down goods line only)	Opened	23.8.1903
***	Closed	27.9.1909
WOODHOUSE MILL SIDINGS	Into use	23.8.1903
***	Opened	31.8.1903
***	Closed	....
Woodhouse Mill South to Woodhouse Mill: second down goods line	Into use	23.8.1903
***	t.o.u.	27.9.1909
Woodhouse Mill Station SB	Open before	1.11.1875
Replacement box	Opened	12.9.1897
***	Re-framed	....
Re-named Woodhouse Mill No. 2 SB	... ...	21.8.1938
Re-named Woodhouse Mill Station SB	... ...	31.3.1968
Box closed and ground frame provided in lieu	... ...	29.4.1973
Woodhouse Mill: down goods line to down passenger line crossover	Into use	7.1.1900
Up goods line to up passenger line crossover	Into use	....
WOODHOUSE MILL	Opened	6.4.1841
***	CP	21.9.1953
***	CG	2.11.1964
Woodhouse Mill to Treeton South: up and down goods lines	Into use	1.10.1899
***	t.o.u.	....
Treeton South SB	Opened	1.10.1899
***	Raised	24.6.1917
***	Closed	3.10.1982
Treeton South: down goods line to down passenger line crossover	Into use	....
Up passenger line to up goods line crossover	Into use	....
Treeton South to Treeton Station: up goods line	Into use	1.4.1900
Existing line behind down platform made down goods line	... ...	8.4.1900
Up goods line	t.o.u.	2.10.1982
Down goods line	t.o.u.	....
TREETON	Opened	6.4.1841
***	CP	2.1.1843 *
New station on same site	OP&M	1.10.1884
***	CM	....
***	CP	29.10.1951
Excursion trains continued to call at this station.		
Orgreaves Sidings SB	Open before	16.8.1877
Re-named Treeton Station SB	... ...	....
Replacement box named Treeton Junction SB	Opened	1.4.1900
***	Re-framed	1965
***	Closed	3.10.1982
Treeton Jcn: down goods line to down passenger line crossover	Into use	....
Up passenger line to up goods line crossover	Into use	6.5.1900
Treeton Jcn with the Sheffield District Railway	Opened	6.5.1900

Treeton North Curve

Powers: British Transport Commission Act 1960

Treeton North Jcn to Treeton West Junction with the former Sheffield District line	Opened	12.7.1965

Treeton Colliery Sidings SB	Opened	1852
Replacement box	Opened	....
Replacement box	Opened	24.1.1892
***	Closed	17.6.1934
Canklow engine shed	Opened	19.11.1900
***	Closed	11.10.1965

Canklow Goods Junction SB	Opened	16.12.1891
***	Re-framed	28.4.1940
***	Closed	29.7.1979
Canklow Goods Jcn to Masborough Sorting Sdgs South Jcn: up goods line	Into use	6.11.1892
Down goods line	Into use	4.10.1896
Canklow Goods Jcn to Masborough Station South Jcn: up and down goods lines	t.o.u.	....
Masborough Sorting Sidings South (OR Ickles South): up passenger line to up goods line crossover	Into use	....
Down passenger line to down goods line crossover	Into use	4.10.1896 ?
Down goods line to down passenger line crossover	Into use	4.10.1896
Down goods line to down goods line crossover	Into use	4.10.1896
Masborough Sorting Sidings South Junction SB	Opened	c.8.1883
***	Alt.levers	27.7.1890
Replacement box	Opened	6.11.1892
***	Re-located	9.8.1896
***	Re-framed	4.10.1896
***	Re-framed	20.1.1924
***	Closed	29.7.1979
Masborough Sorting Sidings South to Centre: reception siding	Into use	24.2.1924
***	t.o.u.	....
Masborough Sorting Sidings South to North: up goods line	Into use	20.8.1883
Up and down goods lines	Inspected	8.8.1883
ICKLES DOCK	OG	1949-1956
***	Closed	1.10.1962
ICKLES	CG	1980
Coal Sorting Sidings to Masborough Sorting Sidings North: up coal line (on the west side of the up goods line)	Into use	9.8.1896
***	t.o.u.	....
Masborough Sorting Sidings South to North: machine line made into second down goods line	... ...	5.1.1908
Second down goods line	t.o.u.	....
MASBOROUGH SORTING SIDINGS	Opened	....
New sidings	Into use	1.3.1888
***	t.o.u.	....
Masborough Down Bank SB	Opened	11.1.1925
***	Closed	1964-1969
South Yorkshire Hoop Iron Company's SB	Open before	1.10.1876
***	Closed	c.8.1883
Masborough Sorting Sidings Centre SB (not a block post)	Opened	12.1888-8.1893
Replacement box	Opened	24.6.1923
***	Closed	1964-1969
Masborough Sorting Sidings Ground SB (not a block post)	Opened	12.1888-8.1893
***	Closed	1.12.1907
Masborough Down Bank SB	Opened	11.1.1925
***	Closed	....
MASBOROUGH FREIGHTLINER TERMINAL	Opened	....
***	Closed	....
Holmes Colliery Sidings SB	Open before	1.11.1875
***	Closed	c.8.1883
Masborough Sorting Sidings North SB	Opened	c.8.1883
***	Re-framed	3.5.1896
Replacement box	Opened	22.2.1903
***	Re-framed	12.7.1903
***	Closed	29.7.1979
Masborough Sorting Sidings North (OR Ickles North): down passenger line to down goods line crossover	Into use	....
Down goods line to down passenger line crossover	Into use	....
Up slow line to up fast line crossover	Into use	....
Up passenger line to up goods line crossover	Into use	....
Masborough Sorting Sdgs North to Masborough South Jcn: up goods line	Into use	12.7.1903
Down goods line (continuing round the curve to Holmes Jcn)	Into use	26.7.1903

Holmes Colliery Branch

Powers: --

Holmes Colliery Sidings to Holmes Colliery	Opened	1.4.1863 *
***	Closed	....
Masborough South Junction SB	Opened	c.11.1881
Replacement box	Opened	26.4.1903
***	Raised	20.8.1905
***	Closed	6.8.1978

Masborough South Curve

Powers: Midland Railway (New Works Etc) Act 1876

Masborough South Jcn to Holmes Jcn	OG	28.11.1881
***	OP	1.1.1890 *
***	CP	5.7.1954
***	RO(P)	25.4.1969
***	Closed	7.8.1978

Masborough South Jcn to Masborough Station South Jcn: down main line slued on to new portion of Rotherham branch bridge	... ...	1.3.1903
Up main line similarly slued	... ...	19.4.1903
Masborough South Jcn to Masborough Station North Jcn: up and down fast lines (down side)	Into use	20.3.1904
Masborough Junction SB	Open before	16.8.1877
Replacement box named Masborough Station South Junction SB	Opened	1883
Replacement box	Opened	29.3.1903
***	Closed	29.7.1979

Sheffield & Rotherham line

See page 150

Masborough Jcn to Goose Hill Jcn: block telegraph working	Introduced	1867-1868
Masborough Station South Junction: down goods line to down fast line connection	Into use	....
Up slow line to up goods line connection	Into use	....
Connections from North Midland lines to fast line platforms	Removed	....
Masborough: location of down goods line at south end	Altered	6.12.1903
MASBOROUGH (ROTHERHAM)	Opened	11.5.1840
Altered to MASBOROUGH FOR ROTHERHAM	... ...	12.1863-1.1865
Altered to MASBOROUGH & ROTHERHAM	... ...	1.5.1894 *
Altered to ROTHERHAM (MASBOROUGH STATION)	... ...	1.4.1908 *
***	CG	3.1.1966
Altered to ROTHERHAM	... ...	20.2.1969
Altered to ROTHERHAM MASBOROUGH	... ...	....
***	CP	3.10.1988
Masborough: down goods line	Into use	11.1875-10.1876
***	t.o.u.	....
Masborough Station North Junction SB	Opened	c.11.1883
Replacement box	Opened	17.1.1904
***	Closed	29.7.1979
Masborough Station North Junction: double junction (DFL-DSL, USL-UFL)	Into use	....
***	t.o.u.	....
Ladder junction (south end in the up Barrow Hill line)	Into use	....
Masborough Station North Jcn to Parkgate Jcn: pairing by use	Introduced	20.3.1904
Second down goods line (down side)	Into use	20.3.1904
Second down goods line made a through siding	... ...	17.10.1909
Through siding	t.o.u.	....
The new down goods line used a part of the Greasborough branch.		
Robin Hood's Bridge SB	Opened	1867
***	Closed	c.11.1883
Carr House Colliery Sidings SB	Opened	c.11.1883
Replacement box	Opened	10.8.1902
***	Closed	17.10.1909

Carr House Colliery Branch

Carr House Colliery Sidings to Carr House Colliery	Opened	....
***	Closed	1915
This branch was originally a part of the Greasborough branch of the Sheffield & Rotherham Railway.		

Carr House Colliery: up goods line to up passenger line crossover	Into use	27.9.1891
Parkgate Junction SB	Opened	c.11.1883
***	Raised	5.10.1895
***	Re-framed	13.12.1896
Replacement box	Opened	9.3.1902
***	Raised	15.5.1904
***	Closed	29.7.1979
Parkgate: double junction (DSL-DFL, UFL-USL)	Into use	13.10.1907
***	t.o.u.	....
Parkgate Jcn to Rawmarsh South: up and down goods lines	Into use	8.12.1901
Up and down passenger lines slued into permanent positions	... ...	15.12.1901
Fast and slow lines pairing by use	Introduced	23.3.1902
Rawmarsh South SB	Opened	13.10.1889
Replacement box	Opened	23.3.1902
Re-named Rawmarsh Station SB	... ...	24.3.1935
***	Closed	14.10.1973
Rawmarsh South to Rawmarsh North: up and down fast lines	Into use	23.3.1902
RAWMARSH	OP	1.5.1853
***	OG	1.1.1867 *
Altered to RAWMARSH & PARK GATE	... ...	1.11.1869 *
Altered to PARK GATE & RAWMARSH	... ...	1.12.1869 *
Altered to PARKGATE & RAWMARSH	... ...	5.1894 ?
***	CG	1.1.1966
***	CP	1.1.1968
Up fast line past the former station	Re-aligned	....
Down fast line past the former station	Re-aligned	....
Rawmarsh Station SB	Open before	16.8.1877
Re-named Rawmarsh North SB	... ...	28.10.1889
Replacement box	Opened	27.10.1901
***	Closed	24.3.1935

Rawmarsh North to High Thorn Jcn: up and down slow lines (up side)	Into use	27.10.1901
Aldwarke Jcn: ladder junction (south end in DFL)	Into use	7.10.1973
***	t.o.u.	....
Aldwarke Jcn to Cudworth Station South Jcn: up and down main lines	C.Tfc	11.5.1987 *
Aldwarke Jcn to Wath Road Jcn (site of): down main line slued into the down Pontefract line at Wath Road and restored to use and the down Pontefract line taken out of use pending recovery	... ...	4.6.1989
Up main line slued into the up Pontefract line at Wath Road and restored to use and the up Pontefract line retained as a siding between Aldwarke Jcn and the Croda Works only	... ...	11.6.1989
Aldwarke Junction PSB	Opened	7.3.1965
***	Closed	24.2.1980
Aldwarke Jcn: crossovers between the former Midland and the former Great Central lines	OG	7.3.1965
***	OP	5.4.1965
Both sets of crossovers	t.o.u.	....
Aldwarke Jcn: ladder junction (south end in USL)	Into use	7.10.1973
***	t.o.u.	....
Aldwarke Jcn: new junction between the up and down Tinsley lines and the up and down Midland main lines	Into use	....
Roundwood Colliery Sidings SB	Opened	1872
Replacement box	Opened	25.1.1891
Re-named Roundwood Goods Junction SB	... ...	....
***	Raised	20.2.1898
Re-named Roundwood Colliery Sidings SB	... ...	27.10.1901
***	Re-framed	25.11.1901
Replacement box named Roundwood SB	Opened	24.4.1938
Box closed and ground frame provided in lieu	... ...	5.2.1967
***	t.o.u.	23.11.1980
Roundwood Sidings No. 2 SB	Opened	1937–1945
***	Closed	1964–1969
Roundwood: junction for the Great Central & Midland Joint Silverwood branch	Opened	1.10.1909
***	Closed	....

Great Central & Midland Joint Lines

See page 119

Roundwood Goods Jcn to Kilnhurst Goods Jcn: up and down goods lines	Into use	5.4.1891
***	t.o.u.	27.10.1901
Down passenger line slued nearer to down goods line	... ...	25.8.1901
Kilnhurst Goods Junction SB	Opened	5.4.1891
Replacement box	Opened	19.5.1901
Re-named Kilnhurst South SB	... ...	27.10.1901
Replacement box	Opened	19.3.1939
***	Closed	23.11.1980
Kilnhurst (south) to Swinton South: up and down goods lines	Into use	....
Kilnhurst Station SB	Open before	16.8.1877
***	Closed	27.10.1901
KILNHURST	Opened	6.4.1841
Altered to KILNHURST WEST	... ...	25.9.1950
***	CG	1.1.1966
***	CP	1.1.1968
High Thorn Junction SB	Opened	30.6.1901
Re-named Kilnhurst North SB	... ...	27.10.1901
Box closed and ground frame provided in lieu	... ...	23.6.1957

Swinton Iron Works Branch

Powers: Midland Railway (New Lines and Additional Powers) Act 1864

Swinton Iron Works branch	Opened	....
Working of the branch as a siding	Commenced	31.8.1940
***	Closed	....

High Thorn Jcn to Swinton South: up and down fast lines (down side)	Into use	30.6.1901
Swinton Junction: ladder junction leading from the up Pontefract line to the down Leeds line	Into use	23.11.1980
Swinton Jcn to Cudworth Station South Jcn: up and down main lines	Closed	1.6.1987
Swinton South SB	Open before	1.11.1875
Replacement box	Opened	23.5.1897
***	Re-framed	30.6.1901
***	Closed	7.8.1910
Swinton South to Swinton Jcn: down goods line	Into use	29.10.1899
Swinton South to Swinton (north): up goods line	Into use	29.10.1899
Swinton South to Wath Road Jcn: pairing by use	Introduced	30.6.1901
Swinton Station SB	Open before	16.8.1877
Replacement box	Opened	29.10.1899
***	Re-framed	30.6.1901
Replacement box named Swinton SB some 10 chains to the south	Opened	7.8.1910
***	Closed	15.4.1973

SWINTON FOR DONCASTER	Opened	1.7.1840 ?
Altered to SWINTON	... ...	5.1852-10.1853 *
Replacement station about 200 yards to the north	Opened	2.7.1899
Altered to SWINTON TOWN	... ...	25.9.1950
Platform serving the up and down slow lines	t.o.u.	23.1.1951
***	CG	4.5.1964
***	CP	1.1.1968
Replacement SWINTON station for passenger traffic only	Opened	5.1990
Excursion trains served Swinton between its 1968 closure and the demolition of the platforms and buildings.		
Swinton Station: up goods line to up main line connection	Removed	29.10.1899
Swinton (north) to Swinton Jcn: up goods line	Into use	30.10.1898
Swinton Jcn: up goods line to up passenger line crossover	Into use	30.10.1898
Down passenger line to down goods line crossover	Into use	29.10.1899
Swinton Junction SB	Open before	16.8.1877
Replacement box	Opened	19.7.1891
***	Re-framed	19.11.1893
***	Raised	23.6.1901
***	Re-framed	30.6.1901
***	Lifted	29.5.1927
***	Closed	15.7.1973
Swinton Junction: double junction (DFL-DSL, USL-UFL)	Into use	30.6.1901
***	t.o.u.	....
Swinton: junction with the South Yorkshire Railway	OP	10.11.1849
***	OG	10.1853-1.1855 *
***	CG	....
***	t.o.u.	25.7.1965
***	CP(All)	26.7.1965
***	Restored	5.1990

Between Swinton Junction and Doncaster South Junction the Midland possessed running powers for all traffic over the South Yorkshire line. Between Doncaster South Junction and Doncaster station the Midland possessed running powers over the Great Northern line.

Swinton Curve

Powers: British Railways (No. 2) Act 1984

Swinton Jcn (site of) to Mexborough Jcn (site of)	OP	5.1990

Doncaster Goods Depot

Powers: --

DONCASTER CHERRY TREE LANE GOODS DEPOT: Midland user	Commenced	3.1857
***	Closed	5.6.1967

Swinton Jcn to Wath Road Jcn: up and down goods lines	Into use	11.2.1894
Swinton Jcn: South Yorkshire curve to Adwick Jcn	Approved	12.9.1854
***	Closed	....
***	Re-opened by	2.1875 ?
***	Closed by	1882
Knottingley Junction SB	Open before	16.8.1877
***	Closed	c.5.1879
Wath Road Junction SB	Opened	c.5.1879
Replacement box	Opened	25.6.1893
***	Raised	4.2.1894
Replacement box	Opened	30.6.1901
***	Closed	23.11.1980

Swinton & Knottingley line

See page 159

Wath Road Junction: double junction (DSL-DPL, UPL-USL)	Into use	7.7.1901
***	t.o.u.	23.11.1980
Wath Road Jcn to Goose Hill Jcn	CP	7.10.1968
***	RO(P)	1.5.1972
***	CP	4.10.1982
Wath Road Jcn to Darfield North Jcn: down goods line (up side)	Into use	9.9.1900
Wath Road Jcn to Manvers Main Colliery Sidings: up goods line	Into use	9.9.1900
Wath Road Jcn to Wath (North) North: goods lines made absolute block	... ...	20.3.1973
Wath Road Jcn to Dearne Valley Colliery Sidings: down goods line	t.o.u.	23.11.1980
Wath Road Jcn to Wath North: up goods line	t.o.u.	23.11.1980
The section of the up goods line between Wath North and Dearne Valley Colliery Sidings was retained as a headshunt.		
Manvers Main Colliery Sidings SB	Open before	1.10.1876
Replacement box	Opened	28.9.1890
Replacement box	Opened	15.7.1900
***	Closed	25.11.1962
Manvers Main Colliery Sidings to Wath North: up goods line	Into use	12.11.1899
WATH	OP	6.4.1841
Altered to WATH & BOLTON	... ...	1.5.1850
***	OM	1877
***	OG	9.1904
Altered to WATH-ON-DEARNE	... ...	4.1914

WATH-ON-DEARNE (continued)	CG	1.10.1941
Altered to WATH (NORTH)	... ...	25.9.1950
***	CP	1.1.1968
Wath Station SB	Open before	1.11.1875
Replacement box	Opened	28.2.1897
***	Raised	15.7.1900
***	Enlarged	1901
***	Closed	24.10.1976
Wath North SB	Opened	1880
***	Re-framed	30.4.1899
Replacement box	Opened	12.11.1899
***	Re-framed	....
***	Closed	29.3.1981
Wath North: up goods line to up passenger line crossover	Into use	12.11.1899
Up goods line to up passenger line crossover	Into use	15.12.1907
Down passenger line to down goods line crossover	Into use	....
Double junction	t.o.u.	....
The first crossover was between lines paired by direction, whilst the second was provided after pairing by use had been introduced.		
Wath North to Darfield South: up goods line	Into use	7.5.1899
Wath (North) North to Houghton Main Colliery Sidings: goods lines made absolute block	... ...	23.7.1973
Darfield: up passenger line to up goods line connection	Removed	9.9.1900
Darfield South to North: up goods line	Into use	9.9.1900
Darfield Station SB	Open before	16.8.1877
***	Re-framed	7.5.1899
Re-named Darfield SB	... ...	....
Replacement box at the south end of the station	Opened	30.6.1901
Box made a ground frame	... ...	27.8.1969
***	t.o.u.	16.8.1970
DARFIELD	Opened	1.7.1840
Replacement station about 45 chains to the north	Opened	30.6.1901
***	CP&G	17.6.1963
Darfield North SB	Opened	19.3.1899
Replacement box	Opened	18.3.1900
Re-named Darfield North Junction SB	... ...	29.4.1900
***	Closed	9.9.1900
Darfield North to Storr's Mill Jcn: up and down goods lines (up side)	Into use	29.4.1900
Dearne Valley Colliery Sidings SB (not a block post)	Opened	16.12.1901
***	Closed	6.3.1983
Dearne Valley Colliery Sidings to Dearne Valley North Jcn: up and down goods lines made sidings	... ...	29.3.1981
Houghton Colliery Sidings SB	Opened	1878
***	Alt.levers	23.3.1890
Replacement box	Opened	9.10.1898
***	Re-framed	25.3.1900
Box closed and ground frame provided in lieu	... ...	30.12.1976
***	t.o.u.	6.4.1980

Houghton Main Colliery Branch (Dearne Valley Railway)

Powers: --

Houghton Colliery Sidings to Houghton Main Colliery	Opened	....
***	Closed	3.11.1965
Houghton Colliery Sidings: down goods line to down passenger line crossover	Into use	22.12.1907
Up passenger line to up goods line crossover	Into use	23.5.1909
Double junction	t.o.u.	....
Houghton Colliery Sidings to Storr's Mill Jcn: down goods line	Into use	29.10.1899
***	t.o.u.	24.3.1900
Dearne Valley North Junction to the Dearne Valley line	OG	11.7.1966

Grimethorpe & Goldthorpe Colliery Branches: Revised Access

Powers: --

Dearne Valley North Jcn to Dearne Valley South Jcn	OG	11.7.1966
Access to the two collieries was provided from the Dearne Valley Railway direction.		
Dearne Valley South Jcn to Goldthorpe Colliery	Closed	7.5.1978
Replacement access was from the Swinton & Knottingley line.		
Dearne Valley North Jcn to Cudworth Station South: up and down goods lines	t.o.u.	....
Little Houghton SB	Open before	1.11.1875
***	Closed	1878
Storr's Mill SB	Opened	1882
Replacement box named Storr's Mill Junction SB	Opened	15.6.1890
***	Re-framed	11.9.1898
***	Closed	27.3.1966

Grimethorpe Colliery Branch

Sanctioning: Midland Railway Act 1895

Powers for the Grimethorpe branch:
Midland Railway Act 1895, and Manchester, Sheffield and Lincolnshire Railway Act 1894

Storr's Mill Jcn to Grimethorpe Colliery	OG	11.2.1895
Branch designated a siding	... ...	18.12.1949
Storr's Mill Jcn to the junction with the former Great Central line at Grimethorpe Sidings	Closed	3.10.1960
Grimethorpe branch	OP(NA)	21.2.1916
***	CP	10.9.1951
Grimethorpe Colliery: run-round siding alongside platform line	Into use	15.9.1915
***	t.o.u.	....
Grimethorpe Sidings SB	Opened	....
***	Closed	....
Grimethorpe Colliery: Rapid Loading Bunker No. 2	Into use	27.7.1985

Storr's Mill Jcn: down passenger line to down goods line crossover	Into use	29.10.1899
Down goods line to down passenger line crossover	Into use	29.10.1899
Up goods line to up passenger line crossover	Into use	23.5.1909
Storr's Mill Jcn to Cudworth Station South: up and down goods lines	Into use	14.9.1890
Pairing by use	Introduced	29.4.1900
Cudworth Station South: down Cudworth & Stairfoot line to down main line crossover	Into use	1.4.1900
Up main line to up Cudworth & Stairfoot line crossover	Into use	29.4.1900
Cudworth Station South to Royston Jcn: up main line	t.o.u.	8.4.1984
Down main line	t.o.u.	3.6.1984
Cudworth Station SB	Open before	16.8.1877
Re-named Cudworth Station South SB	... ...	4.1883-11.1885
Replacement box	Opened	17.8.1890
Replacement box	Opened	1.4.1900
***	Re-framed	30.5.1915
Re-named Cudworth Station SB	... ...	29.9.1957

Stairfoot & Cudworth line
See page 156

Cudworth Station South Jcn to Cudworth Station North Jcn: additional pair of tracks joining Stairfoot and Barnsley lines	Into use	26.11.1899
Cudworth Station South Jcn to Carlton Main Colliery Sidings: existing tracks re-arranged to give four tracks paired by use	... ...	20.5.1900
BARNSLEY	Opened	1.7.1840
Altered to CUDWORTH FOR BARNSLEY	... ...	1.8.1854 *
Replacement station slightly to the south	Opened	c.1854 ?
Altered to CUDWORTH	... ...	1.5.1870 *
Central (island) platform south of the footbridge	Into use	19.2.1900
Use by Hull & Barnsley trains of the east side of the up main-line platform	Commenced	22.4.1900
New station buildings	Completed	1901
Facing slip-points to allow trains to depart from platform No. 5 (Hull & Barnsley line) to the down slow line	Into use	22.2.1914
***	CG	4.5.1964
***	CP	1.1.1968

Between Cudworth Midland station and Cudworth Hull & Barnsley station the Midland possessed running powers over the Hull & Barnsley line.

Between Cudworth Junction and Sheffield the Hull & Barnsley Railway possessed running powers over the Midland line.

Cudworth Station North SB	Opened	4.1883-11.1885
Replacement box	Opened	7.5.1899
***	Re-framed	22.4.1900
***	Re-framed	18.4.1915
***	Closed	29.9.1957
Cudworth station to Royston Jcn: slow lines made goods lines	... ...	29.7.1973
Cudworth: junction with the Hull & Barnsley Railway	Opened	....
***	t.o.u.	1935
Cudworth Station North to Cudworth South Jcn: separate pair of lines for the Barnsley branch	Into use	4.6.1899
Cudworth South Junction SB	Open before	16.8.1877
Replacement box	Opened	19.12.1887
Replacement box	Opened	25.9.1898
***	Re-framed	24.1.1904
***	Closed	3.6.1984

Barnsley branch
See page 156

Cudworth South Jcn: double junction between slow lines and Hull & Barnsley lines	Into use	13.3.1904
Double junction (DML-DBa.L, UML-UBa.L)	Into use	4.6.1899
Both double junctions	t.o.u.	....

Cudworth South Jcn to Cudworth North Jcn: first and second down goods lines	Into use	25.9.1898
Down goods line nearest the down passenger line converted into an up goods line	... ...	26.11.1899
Cudworth North Junction SB	Open before	1.11.1875
***	Re-framed	1885
Replacement box	Opened	11.10.1896
***	Re-framed	26.11.1899
***	Re-framed	19.5.1900
***	Closed	3.6.1984

Cudworth North Curve

See page 156

Cudworth North Jcn to Carlton Main Colliery Siding: up goods line	Into use	18.10.1896
CARLTON EXCHANGE SIDINGS (with the Hull & Barnsley Railway)	Opened	27.7.1885
***	Closed	....
Carlton Main Colliery Sidings SB	Opened	1877
***	Re-framed	c.7.1885
Replacement box	Opened	12.11.1888
***	Raised	21.8.1892
***	Re-framed	18.10.1896
Replacement box	Opened	3.12.1899
***	Re-framed	....
Box ceased to signal the fast lines	... ...	19.3.1972
***	Closed	9.12.1973
CARLTON MAIN COLLIERY SIDING	Opened	10.12.1877
CARLTON OLD SIDINGS altered to CARLTON SOUTH SIDINGS	... ...	13.2.1928
Carlton Main Colliery Sidings to Royston Jcn: up and down fast lines	Into use	2.9.1900
Down goods line (up side)	Into use	17.7.1927
Down goods line	t.o.u.	6.3.1972
CARLTON NEW SIDINGS	Into use	17.7.1927
Altered to CARLTON NORTH SIDINGS	... ...	13.2.1928
Carlton Down Sidings SB	Opened	17.7.1927
Re-named Carlton North Sidings SB	By	7.1930
Replacement box	Opened	16.6.1957
***	Closed	19.3.1972
Carlton engine shed	Opened	....
Re-named Royston engine shed	... ...	27.7.1935
***	Closed	....
Royston Station SB	Opened	1.7.1900
***	Alt.levers	30.1.1916
***	Closed	6.3.1972
ROYSTON & NOTTON	OP	6.4.1841
***	OM before	1872
Replacement station 1 mile to the south	OP	1.7.1900
***	OG	1901
***	CG	31.7.1961
***	CP	1.1.1968
Location re-named ROYSTON (YORKS)	... ...	31.1.1980
Royston: connection with the Manchester, Sheffield & Lincolnshire	Into use	1.8.1882
***	Removed	27.2.1888
Lund Hill Lane SB	Opened	9.10.1898
***	Closed	1.7.1900
Hodroyd's & Monckton Main Colliery Sidings SB	Open before	1.11.1875
***	Re-framed	19.4.1896
Replacement box	Opened	30.9.1900
***	Re-framed	8.10.1905
***	Re-framed	....
***	Closed	4.6.1961
Hodroyd's & Monckton Main Colliery Sidings: Great Central and Midland laid in a branch and sidings on land owned by the colliery	... ...	1905
Hodroyd's & Monckton Main Colliery Sidings: 2 sidings alongside the down fast line south of the signalbox and 3 north of the box, entered by a facing connection from the down fast line	Into use	29.1.1911
Royston Junction SB (old site)	Open before	16.8.1877
Re-named Royston Station SB	... ...	27.2.1888
Re-named Royston Junction SB	By	22.3.1890
Replacement box	Opened	1891 ?
Replacement box	Opened	5.5.1901
***	Re-framed	1958
***	Closed	....
Royston Jcn: double junction (DSL-DFL, UFL-USL)	Into use	5.5.1901
Double junction (DFL-DGL, UGL-UFL)	Into use	2.9.1900
Double junctions	t.o.u.	....

Royston Drift-Mine Branch

Powers: --

Royston Jcn to new drift mine	Opened	18.9.1976

West Riding lines

See page 158

Royston Jcn to Chevet Jcn: up goods line	Into use	22.3.1891
Down goods line	Into use	26.7.1891
Pairing by use	Introduced	5.5.1901
Royston Jcn to Oakenshaw South Jcn: up and down passenger lines taken out of use and goods lines made passenger lines	... ...	29.11.1981
Chevet SB	Opened	1877
Replacement box named Chevet Goods Junction SB	Opened	15.3.1891
***	Raised	7.6.1896
***	Closed	11.7.1926
Chevet tunnel opened out	By	26.8.1925
Chevet Jcn to Sandal & Walton Station: up and down goods lines	Into use	11.7.1926
Chevet Cutting SB	Opened	31.1.1926
Re-named Chevet SB	... ...	11.7.1926
Box closed and IBS provided in lieu	... ...	28.8.1932
Sandal & Walton Station SB	Open before	1.11.1875
***	Re-framed	1885
***	Re-framed	14.1.1906
***	Re-framed	29.6.1926
***	Closed	29.4.1928
Sandal & Walton Station Jcn to West Riding Jcn: up goods line	Into use	1.4.1928
Down goods line	Into use	29.4.1928
SANDAL & WALTON	OP	1.6.1870
***	OG	1.10.1873 ?
***	OM	1887
Altered to WALTON	... ...	1.10.1951
***	CG	1.3.1957
***	CP	12.6.1961
West Riding Junction SB	Open before	1.11.1875
Replacement box	Opened	29.7.1887
Replacement box	Opened	15.4.1928
***	Closed	26.9.1965
West Riding Jcn with the West Riding & Grimsby Joint line	Opened	1.8.1868
***	CP	1.1.1917
***	Closed	c.1938
***	Severed by	3.11.1945

Midland services to Wakefield

On 1 August 1868 the Midland began to run passenger and goods trains into Wakefield, serving the Westgate Passenger Station (owned jointly with the Manchester, Sheffield & Lincolnshire and Great Northern companies) and the Westgate Goods Depot (owned jointly with the Manchester, Sheffield & Lincolnshire company).

West Riding Jcn to Snydale: up goods line	Into use	20.5.1928
Down slow/goods line	Into use	....
West Riding Jcn to Oakenshaw North Jcn: pairing by use	Introduced	26.9.1965
Oakenshaw Junction SB	Opened	1860
Replacement box	Opened	1862
Replacement box	Opened	....
***	Raised	22.2.1903
***	Raised	17.12.1911
Replacement box 110 yards closer to Normanton	Opened	12.12.1926
Re-named Oakenshaw South Junction SB	By	2.1927
***	Closed	26.9.1965
By 1918 there was a down loop between Oakenshaw (South) Junction and Oakenshaw Sidings SB (the site of the later Oakenshaw North Junction SB).		
Oakenshaw South Jcn with the Lancashire & Yorkshire Railway	Opened	15.7.1861
Junction re-modelled with single leads and curve singled	... ...	12.2.1989
Between Oakenshaw South Junction and Oakenshaw station the Lancashire & Yorkshire Railway possessed running powers over the Midland line.		
Oakenshaw South Jcn to Oakenshaw North Jcn: up and down goods lines became Crofton Curve lines	... ...	8.6.1967
Oakenshaw South Jcn to Goose Hill Jcn: up and down main lines	Closed	1.6.1987
WAKEFIELD	Opened	1.7.1840
Altered to OAKENSHAW FOR WAKEFIELD	... ...	1.3.1841
Altered to OAKENSHAW (WAKEFIELD)	Before	1.12.1848 *
Altered to OAKENSHAW	... ...	1.7.1861 ?
***	CP	1.6.1870
***	CG	9.3.1964
Oakenshaw Station SB	Open before	16.8.1877
Replacement box	Opened	15.2.1886
Re-named Oakenshaw Sidings SB	... ...	....
***	Re-framed	28.1.1906
Replacement box named Oakenshaw North Junction SB and situated 200 yards to the north	Opened	13.5.1928
***	Re-framed	c.1965
***	Closed	....

Description	Event	Date
Crofton Curve		
Powers: London Midland and Scottish Railway Act 1927		
Oakenshaw North Jcn to Crofton East Jcn	Opened	3.6.1928
Oakenshaw South Jcn to Oakenshaw North Jcn: former goods lines made Crofton Curve lines	... ...	8.7.1967
Oakenshaw North Jcn to Goose Hill Jcn: up and down goods lines	t.o.u.	8.7.1967
Snydale Branch Junction SB	Opened	1885
Replacement box named Snydale SB 250 yards to the north	Opened	20.5.1928
***	Closed	22.12.1968
Snydale Branches		
Powers: Midland Railway (Additional Powers) Act 1882		
Snydale Branch Jcn to Sharlestone Colliery (Ackton Hall Branch)	OG	8.6.1885
***	Closed	12.8.1968
Sharlestone Colliery to Don Pedro Colliery	OG	17.8.1885
***	Closed	1965
Featherstone Colliery branch	OG	17.8.1885
***	Closed	c.1931
Snydale to Goose Hill Jcn: up goods line	Into use	14.8.1892
Snydale to St John's Colliery Sidings: down goods line	Into use	2.10.1892
St John's Colliery Sidings SB	Open before	1.11.1875
Replacement box	Opened	22.5.1892
***	Raised	24.1.1909
***	Re-framed	....
***	Closed	17.2.1963
St John's Colliery Sidings: down goods line to down passenger line crossover	Into use	....
Down passenger line to down goods line crossover	Into use	....
Up goods line to up passenger line crossover	Into use	14.8.1892
Up passenger line to up goods line crossover	Into use	....
St John's Colliery Sidings to Goose Hill Jcn: down goods line	Into use	25.9.1892
Goose Hill Junction SB	Open before	16.8.1877
Replacement box	Opened	1882
Replacement box	Opened	11.10.1891
***	Re-framed	29.8.1915
***	Closed	2.10.1988
Goose Hill Jcn to Normanton North Jcn was worked as a station yard.		
Goose Hill Jcn with the Manchester & Leeds Railway	Opened	5.10.1840
Between Goose Hill Junction and St John's Colliery the Midland possessed running powers over the Lancashire & Yorkshire line. Between Goose Hill Junction and Leeds the Lancashire & Yorkshire Railway possessed running powers over the Midland line.		
Goose Hill Jcn: Lancashire & Yorkshire Railway main lines continued into the goods lines	... ...	11.10.1891
Down loop line	t.o.u.	....
Slow lines through the junction layout	t.o.u.	7.7.1985
Goose Hill Jcn to Normanton South Jcn: up and down goods lines	Into use	4.1883-11.1885
The goods running lines between Goose Hill Junction and Altofts Junction were located between the passenger lines and the goods sidings.		
Goose Hill Jcn to Altofts Jcn: up and down goods lines made up and down slow lines	... ...	....
***	t.o.u.	31.1.1988
Normanton South Junction SB	Open before	16.8.1877
***	Closed	1882
Normanton South Jcn to Normanton North Jcn: up goods line	In use by	1.9.1867 *
Down goods line	In use by	1.11.1867 *
Independent line	In use by	1.7.1870 *
Normanton Passenger Station South SB	Open before	16.8.1877
Replacement box	Opened	24.5.1891
***	Re-framed	....
Re-named Normanton SB	... ...	30.4.1972
***	t.o.u.	19.12.1973
***	Off. closed	8.9.1974
Normanton Station South: up through line extension southwards by about 90 yards and replacement connection with up passenger line near to signalbox	Into use	9.3.1919
Normanton Station South to Normanton Station North: up and down through lines	t.o.u.	9.1.1972
NORMANTON SIDINGS	Opened	....
***	t.o.u.	....
Normanton No. 1 Sidings SB (not a block post)	Opened	17.6.1893
***	Closed	10.1.1971
Normanton No. 2 Sidings SB (not a block post)	Opened	17.6.1893
***	Re-framed	18.10.1914
***	Closed	17.5.1971
NORMANTON	Opened	Late 1840
Second station (joint passenger station)	Opened	1844
Third station (single island-platform): up platform	Into use	5.1867
down platform	Into use	End 7.1867

NORMANTON (continued): third station station substantially completed	By	Mid-1868
Station made "closed" for tickets	... ...	1.5.1899
***	CG	30.9.1953
South-end bay No. 6	t.o.u.	14.12.1969
North-end bay No. 2	t.o.u.	23.8.1970
North-end bay No. 1	t.o.u.	9.1.1972
Up platform shortened by 85 yards at each end	... ...	10.1.1972
Between Normanton Joint Station and Altofts Junction the North Eastern Railway possessed running powers for all traffic over the Midland line.		
Under the terms of an agreement the Midland and North Eastern companies exchanged running powers: the North Eastern might run (i) between Milner Wood and Bradford via Guiseley, over the Guiseley to Shipley line, and between Burley Junction and Menston Junction, (ii) between Normanton and its junctions with the Midland in Leeds, and (iii) between Normanton and Sheffield, or over any portion of that line; the Midland might run (i) between Wortley Junction or Otley Junction and Harrogate, (ii) between Altofts Junction and York or Hull, (iii) between Methley Junction and York or Hull, (iv) between Ferrybridge Junction and York or Hull, including the Victoria Dock Branch at Hull.		
A general agreement between the Midland and the North Eastern companies made in 1903 provided for alternative routes in case of accidents. If the North Eastern lines between Altofts Junction and Whitwood Junction, Leeds Junction and Cross Gates East Junction, and Wortley Junction and Burley Junction were blocked, trains might run respectively via Methley Junction with reversal, via Woodlesford and Methley Junction, and via Menston and Apperley Junction. If the Midland lines between Methley Junction and Altofts Junction, Burley Junction and Wortley Junction, and Guiseley Junction and Esholt Junction were blocked, trains might run respectively via Whitwood Junction with reversal, and via Arthington, and North Eastern Bradford and Otley trains might run via Esholt and Apperley Junction.		
Normanton Station Hotel	Opened	....
***	Closed	....
Hotel re-opened after joint purchase by the Midland, the North Eastern, and the Lancashire & Yorkshire companies	... ...	1860
Normanton: luncheon-stop for the morning Scotch expresses	Withdrawn	1.7.1894 *
Normanton Passenger Station West SB	Opened	6.1881-4.1883
Replacement box	Opened	18.10.1891
***	Raised	17.9.1916
***	Closed	22.5.1932
Normanton Passenger Station East SB	Opened	6.1881-4.1883
Replacement box	Opened	18.10.1891
***	Closed	9.7.1922
Normanton Passenger Station North SB	Open before	16.8.1877
***	Raised	8.5.1887
Replacement box	Opened	18.10.1891
Replacement box	Opened	9.7.1922
***	Closed	30.4.1972
Normanton engine shed	Opened	1850
Additional roundhouse	Into use	1867
***	Closed	2.10.1967
Normanton No. 1 Sidings SB (first box) (not a block post)	Opened	24.7.1892
Re-named Normanton No. 3 Sidings SB	... ...	17.6.1893
***	Raised	19.2.1894
***	Closed	12.3.1916
Replacement box	Opened	6.2.1916
***	Closed	1961-1972
Normanton North Junction SB	Open before	16.8.1877
Replacement box	Opened	3.1.1892
***	Raised	6.6.1916
***	Re-framed	2.5.1926
***	Closed	26.9.1971
Normanton North Jcn: second up goods line to up goods line crossover	Into use	....
Normanton North Jcn to Altofts Jcn: block telegraph working on the up main line	Intro. by	1873
Block telegraph working on the down main line	Introduced	1874
Normanton North Jcn to Altofts Jcn: up and down goods lines on the down side and second up goods line on the up side	Into use	3.1.1892
Main lines re-aligned over former No. 1 goods lines	... ...	5.9.1971
Normanton No. 2 Sidings SB (first box) (not a block post)	Opened	24.7.1892
Re-named Normanton No. 4 SB	... ...	17.6.1893
***	Closed	6.2.1916
Normanton North Sidings SB	Opened	....
Replacement box	Opened	13.9.1891
***	Made NBP	3.1.1892
***	Closed	24.8.1931
Normanton North Sidings: second down goods line to down goods line crossover	Into use	....
***	t.o.u.	....
Normanton North Sidings to Altofts Jcn: down goods line	Into use	29.11.1891
Altofts Junction SB	Open before	16.8.1877

Altofts Junction SB: replacement box	Opened	29.11.1891
***	Raised	18.6.1916
***	Raised	11.1.1925
Replacement box	Opened	5.6.1927
***	Re-framed	26.9.1971
Altofts Jcn with the York & North Midland Railway	O.Formal	30.6.1840
***	Opened	1.7.1840
***	CP	5.1.1970
***	RO(P)	7.5.1973
***	CP	4.10.1982
***	RO(P)	....
Altofts Jcn to Water Lane Jcn: block telegraph working	Introduced	Late 1860s
Altofts Jcn to Methley Jcn	CP	....
Altofts Jcn: up passenger line to second up goods line connection	Into use	16.5.1915
Altofts Jcn	Re-modelled	....
ALTOFTS & WHITWOOD	OP&M	1.9.1870
***	CM	....
Altered to ALTOFTS	... ...	4.5.1970 *
Altofts Station SB	Open before	16.8.1877
Replacement box	Opened	21.1.1900
***	Raised	6.11.1921
Box closed and IBS provided in lieu	... ...	30.12.1956
Briggs Colliery Sidings SB	Open before	1.11.1875
Replacement box	Opened	8.12.1901
***	Closed	11.10.1903
Methley Junction SB	Opened	....
Replacement box	Opened	1868
Replacement box	Opened	19.4.1891
***	Raised	28.10.1906
Methley Jcn (exc) to Hunslet Goods Jcn (exc): brought under the control of Leeds PSB	... ...	5.7.1981
Methley Jcn with the York & North Midland Railway	Opened	27.7.1840
***	CP	1.4.1869
***	Severed	30.6.1929
***	RO(G)	31.7.1967
***	RO(P)	7.10.1968
Between Methley Junction and Castleford the Midland Railway possessed running powers for passenger traffic over the North Eastern line. The Midland company was also allowed to use the North Eastern line at Methley Junction for the purpose of shunting trains.		
Methley Jcn with the Lancashire & Yorkshire Railway	Opened	1.10.1849
***	CP	7.10.1968
Between Methley Junction and Prince of Wales Colliery the Midland possessed running powers over the Lancashire & Yorkshire line.		
Methley Jcn: remodelling with single leads for the Whitwood line	... ...	21.11.1982
METHLEY	OP	6.4.1841
***	OM	1874
***	OG	Early 1881
Altered to METHLEY NORTH	... ...	25.9.1950
***	CP	16.9.1957
***	CG	30.9.1963
Methley Station SB	Open before	1.11.1875
***	Closed	....
Methley Sidings SB	Open before	16.8.1877
Replacement box	Opened	1.6.1886
Replacement box	Opened	10.5.1903
***	Closed	5.7.1981
Woodlesford Station SB	Open before	16.8.1877
Replacement box	Opened	23.4.1899
***	Closed	25.1.1972
WOODLESFORD	Opened	1.7.1840
***	CG	27.4.1964
Waterloo Colliery Sidings SB	Open before	1.11.1875
Replacement box	Opened	1879
Replacement box	Opened	25.2.1900
***	Burnt out	5.1972
Temporary replacement box	Opened	14.5.1972
Replacement for burnt box	Opened	10.9.1972
***	Closed	28.6.1981
Waterloo Colliery Sidings: up main line to up goods line connection	t.o.u.	10.5.1981
Waterloo Colliery Sidings to Rothwell Haigh: up goods line	Into use	26.8.1900
Down goods line	Into use	23.9.1900
Waterloo Colliery Sidings to Stourton Jcn: down goods line	t.o.u.	11.11.1979
Up goods line	t.o.u.	10.5.1981
ROTHWELL HAIGH GOODS STATION	OG before	1.10.1853 *
***	CG(All) by	8.1894
Rothwell Haigh SB	Opened	1.1870
Replacement box	Opened	6.9.1896
***	Slued	12.8.1900
***	Re-framed	23.9.1900
***	Closed	21.5.1967

Rothwell Haigh: down goods line to down passenger line crossover	Into use	21.10.1900
Up goods line to up passenger line crossover	Into use	26.8.1900
Rothwell Haigh to Stourton Jcn: up goods line	Into use	6.9.1896
Down goods line	Into use	21.10.1900
Stourton Junction SB	Opened	24.11.1889
Replacement box	Opened	18.6.1893
***	Re-framed	9.8.1903
***	Re-framed	17.1.1954
Replacement box named Stourton SB on site of former Wakefield Road SB	Opened	5.7.1981
Stourton SB	Closed	....
Stourton Jcn: up passenger line to up goods line crossover	Into use	29.9.1907
Down passenger line to down goods line crossover	Into use	....
Up goods line to up passenger line crossover	Into use	6.9.1896
Stourton Jcn with East & West Yorkshire Union Railway	Prepared	22.11.1903
***	Opened	4.1.1904
Passenger lines junction	Removed	22.7.1906
The connection with the down goods line was retained.		
Stourton Jcn to Hunslet South Jcn: up goods line	Into use	24.11.1889
Down goods line	Into use	12.10.1890
Stourton Jcn to Wakefield Road: second up goods line	Into use	25.6.1893
Second up goods line made an up through siding	... ...	26.1.1969
First up goods line	t.o.u.	14.6.1981
Up through siding	t.o.u.	....
Stourton Jcn to Engine Shed Jcn: down goods line	t.o.u.	....
Stourton Jcn to Stourton Down Sidings: 2 down running lines	Into use	12.1888-8.1893
***	t.o.u.	....
STOURTON NEW SIDINGS	Opened	4.1897
***	Closed	....
Between Stourton Sidings and Leeds Junction and between Stourton Sidings and Wortley Junction the North Eastern Railway possessed running powers for goods, coal, coke, and cattle traffic over the Midland line. The two companies were to work traffic between Neville Hill and Stourton via Leeds Junction in alternate periods of five years.		
Stourton Up Sidings SB (not a block post)	Opened	....
***	Moved	26.4.1891
***	Re-located	3.1.1897
***	Closed	26.1.1969
Stourton Sidings engine shed	Opened	1.5.1894
***	Closed	1.1967
Stourton Down Sidings SB (not a block post)	Opened	12.10.1890
***	Moved	26.4.1891
***	Closed	19.4.1964
STOURTON FREIGHTLINER TERMINAL	Opened	....
STOURTON SIDINGS: all sidings except those for carriage & wagon shops	Recovered	30.11.1974
Carriage & wagon shops	Closed	12.12.1981
Wakefield Road: up passenger line to up goods line crossover	Into use	....
Down goods line to down passenger line crossover	Into use	....
Connections to the former Stourton MPD	t.o.u.	22.7.1974
Wakefield Road SB	Opened	29.1.1893
Replacement box	Opened	6.4.1924
***	Closed	5.7.1981
Wakefield Road to Engine Shed Jcn: up goods line	t.o.u.	....
Hunslet South Junction SB	Opened	1875
***	Re-framed	21.9.1890
Replacement box	Opened	25.10.1914
***	Closed	5.7.1981
Hunslet South Jcn (exc) to Engine Shed Jcn: signalled from Leeds PSB	... ...	1.1.1969
Hunslet South Jcn: up passenger line to up goods line crossover	Removed	28.12.1890
Up goods line to up passenger line crossover	Into use	....
Down goods line to down passenger line crossover	Into use	12.10.1890
Down goods line to down main line crossover	t.o.u. by	4.7.1981
Hunslet South Jcn to Hunslet Station Jcn: up and down goods lines	Into use	9.1873-12.1873
Up goods line made siding	... ...	18.12.1949
Down goods line made siding	... ...	9.12.1951
Hunslet South Jcn to Engine Shed Jcn: down goods line	t.o.u.	21.10.1979
Wagon Shop Sidings SB	Opened	21.9.1890
***	Closed	....

Hunslet Goods Depot Branch

Powers: --

HUNSLET GOODS DEPOT, and branch	Opened	c.1854
Altered to BALM LANE GOODS DEPOT	... ...	c.1904
***	CG	23.7.1984

Balm Road to signal L901: up Hunslet goods line	t.o.u.	25.11.1984
Hunslet Station Junction SB	Opened	1875
Replacement box	Opened	28.12.1890
***	Re-framed	....
***	Closed	1.6.1969

Hunslet Station Jcn: down goods line to down passenger line crossover	Into use	28.12.1890 ?
Up goods line to up passenger line crossover	Into use	....
Hunslet Station Jcn to Hunslet Goods Jcn: up goods line	Into use	28.12.1890
Down goods line on up side to Hunslet yard only	Into use	9.1873-12.1873
This line was probably opened at the same time as the new station.		
HUNSLET	OP	1.4.1850 *
Replacement station 28 chains to the north	OP	14.9.1873
***	CP(All)	13.6.1960
Hunslet Goods Jcn: down goods line to down passenger line crossover	Into use	28.12.1890 ?
Down passenger line to down goods line crossover	Into use	24.5.1903
Up goods line to up passenger line crossover	Into use	15.11.1903
Up passenger line to up goods line crossover	Into use	15.11.1903
Hunslet Goods Junction SB	Opened	1875
Replacement box	Opened	3.8.1890
Replacement box	Opened	24.5.1903
***	Closed	1.6.1969

Hunslet Connecting Line

See page 163

Hunslet Siding to Hunslet Lane widening	Into use	4.1874
Hunslet Goods Jcn to Hunslet Lane	CP	28.2.1851
Hunslet Goods Jcn to Hunslet Yard No. 2 SB: additional arrival line	Into use	21.12.1891
This gave two arrival and two departure lines, known as main and wallside arrival lines and main and wallside departure lines. It therefore seems likely that the widening between Hunslet Siding and Hunslet Lane in 1874 provided the additional departure line.		
Hunslet Goods Jcn to Hunslet Goods Yard Box: main departure line made bi-directional	... ...	20.12.1908
Hunslet Yard No. 1 SB (not a block post)	Opened	2.1879-2.1880
***	Closed	12.6.1892
Hunslet Yard No. 2 SB (not a block post)	Opened	2.1879-2.1880
***	Closed	12.6.1892
Hunslet Goods Yard SB (not a block post)	Opened	12.6.1892
***	Closed	1-3.12.1971
LEEDS	Opened	1.7.1840
Altered to HUNSLET LANE	... ...	1.1.1849 ?*
***	CP	1.3.1851
***	CG	3.1.1972
Between Hunslet Lane and Holbeck Junction the North Eastern Railway possessed running powers for goods, coke, and cattle traffic over the Midland line. These powers were extended to cover the section of line between Water Lane Junction and Leeds Junction.		
Hunslet Goods Yard lines	t.o.u.	5.7.1981
Remaining private sidings	t.o.u.	30.4.1983

RIPLEY BRANCH

Powers: Midland Railway (Ripley Branches) Act 1848

Little Eaton branch (450 yards long, to canal and quarries)	Opened by	8.1848
Little Eaton Jcn to Ripley	OM	9.1855
***	OG by	8.1856
***	OP	1.9.1856
Ripley branch: working by block telegraph and train staff in place of working by train porter	Introduced	8.1877-4.1878
Working by electric train tablet in place of working by train staff & tickets	Commenced	1.9.1889
Little Eaton Jcn to Ripley (new station)	CP	1.6.1930
Little Eaton Jcn to Little Eaton	Singled	2.3.1969
Little Eaton Jcn to Denby North: one engine in steam working	Commenced	2.3.1969
Little Eaton Station SB (not a block post)	Open before	16.8.1877
Replacement box	Opened	1918-1930
***	Closed	2.3.1969
LITTLE EATON	Opened	1.9.1856
***	CP	1.6.1930
***	CG	4.1.1965
Village Crossing SB (not a block post)	Open before	16.8.1877
Replacement box	Opened	9.11.1902
***	Closed	2.3.1969 ?
COXBENCH	Opened	1.9.1865
***	CP	1.6.1930
***	CG	5.8.1957
Coxbench Station SB	Open before	16.8.1877
***	Closed	19.7.1903
Holbrook Crossing SB	Open before	16.8.1877
***	Closed	2.3.1969 ?

KILBURN	OP	1.12.1856	
***	OM before	1872	
***	CM	1899	
***	CP	1.6.1930	
***	C.Parcels	30.1.1939	
Kilburn SB	Open before	16.8.1877	
Replacement box	Opened	10.5.1903	
Box made a shunting frame on the introduction of one train working	... ...	28.7.1968	
***	Closed	5.4.1972	
Kilburn to Denby South	Doubled	19.7.1903	
***	Singled	28.7.1968	
Denby SB	Open before	16.8.1877	
Replacement box named Denby South SB	Opened	1878	?
Replacement box	Opened	19.7.1903	
***	Closed	28.7.1968	
Denby South to Marehay Jcn: method of working altered to key token between Denby South and Denby North, tablet thence to Marehay Crossing, and key token thence to Marehay Junction	...	20.8.1945	
Denby North SB	Opened	1878	
Replacement box	Opened	10.8.1902	
Box made a shunting frame on the introduction of one train working	... ...	28.7.1968	
***	Closed	5.4.1972	
Denby Iron Company's Crossing SB	Open before	16.8.1877	
***	Closed	1878	
SMITHY HOUSES	Opened	1.9.1856	
Altered to DENBEY	... ...	1.11.1856	*
Altered to DENBY	... ...	1.2.1878	*
***	CP	1.6.1930	
***	CG	4.1.1965	
Excursion trains continued to call at least until 1961.			
Denby to Ripley (new station)	CG	1.4.1963	
Denby to Marehay Crossing included in one engine in steam section	... ...	27.4.1963	
Denby North to Marehay Crossing	Closed	29.7.1968	
DENBY GOODS WHARF SIDINGS	Opened	30.10.1904	
***	Closed	....	
Marehay Crossing: down reception siding	Into use	20.8.1945	
Marehay Crossing SB	Opened	1881	
Replacement box	Opened	16.10.1917	
***	Moved	29.7.1917	
***	Closed	27.4.1963	
Marehay Crossing to Ripley (new station)	Closed	1.4.1963	
Marehay Crossing: line severed at the crossing gates	... ...	27.4.1963	
Marehay Crossing to Ripley (new station): one engine in steam working	Commenced	12.5.1957	
Marehay Crossing to Ripley (new station)	Abandoned	27.4.1963	
Marehay Colliery Sidings SB	Opened	1879	
Replacement box named Marehay Junction SB	Opened	5.5.1889	
***	Closed	30.5.1954	

Ripley New Station Line

Powers: Midland Railway Act 1886

Marehay Jcn to Ripley new station	OP	2.9.1889	
On the opening of the new station, the original station was closed to passenger traffic and converted to a mineral depot.			
RIPLEY (second station)	OP	2.9.1889	
***	CP	1.6.1930	
***	CG	1.4.1963	
Excursion trains continued to call at least until 1961.			

Marehay Jcn to Ripley Old Yard: pilot guard without tickets working in place of electric train tablet block working	Commenced	10.7.1907	
Pilot guard working withdrawn and Old Yard worked as a siding	... ...	25.11.1945	
Marehay Jcn to Ripley Goods Station: working of the line as a siding	Commenced	24.8.1946	
Marehay Jcn to Ripley (old station)	Closed	31.5.1954	
RIPLEY	Opened	1.9.1856	
***	CP	2.9.1889	
***	CG	31.5.1954	
Ripley Station SB	Open before	16.8.1877	
Re-named Ripley Old Station SB	... ...	....	
Replacement box	Opened	16.3.1891	
Box closed and ground frame provided in lieu	... ...	10.7.1907	

HEANOR, RIPLEY & BUTTERLEY LINE

Heanor Branch

Powers: --

Heanor Jcn to Bailey Brook Colliery	OG by	1849	?
On the opening of the line to Ripley, this branch was named the Bailey Brook branch beyond the new Heanor Goods Junction.			
Heanor Jcn to end of remaining branch made a siding	... ...	12.7.1953	

Line severed 680 yards west of Heanor Branch Jcn home signals	... ...	12.7.1953
Heanor Goods Junction SB	Opened	17.11.1890
***	Re-framed	4.8.1895
***	Closed	23.8.1931
Heanor Goods Jcn to Bailey Brook Colliery: working by pilot guard without tickets	Commenced	13.1.1895
Heanor Goods Jcn to Bailey Brook Colliery	CG	23.8.1931

Ormonde Colliery Line

Powers: --

Ormonde Colliery line	Opened	....
***	Recovered	30.1.1971

Langley Mill New Curve (Heanor & Langley Mill Extension Line)

Powers: Midland Railway Act 1891

LANGLEY MILL BRANCH PLATFORM to Heanor Goods Jcn	OP	1.10.1895
***	CP(All)	1.1.1917
***	RO(P)	3.5.1920
***	CP	4.5.1926
***	Severed	3.9.1928

Working was by train staff without tickets.

Heanor Goods Jcn to Butterley Jcn

Powers: Midland Railway Act 1886 (Heanor Goods Jcn to Cross Hill & Codnor)
Midland Railway (Additional Powers) Act 1884 (Cross Hill & Codnor to Butterley Junction)

Heanor Goods Jcn to Heanor station	OG	17.11.1890
Working was by the electric train token block system, except that during the First World War passenger closure working was by train staff without tickets.		
Heanor Goods Jcn (Langley Mill Curve connection) to Ripley	CP	1.1.1917
***	RO(P)	3.5.1920
***	CP	4.5.1926
***	Severed	3.9.1928
Heanor Goods Jcn to Heanor: one engine in steam working	Commenced	3.9.1928
Heanor Goods Jcn to Heanor North	Closed	1.9.1951
Heanor to Ripley Jcn AND Ripley station to Butterley Jcn	OP&G	2.6.1890
The section between Ripley Junction and Ripley new station had already been opened for trains from Derby via Little Eaton.		
Heanor Station SB	Opened	1.6.1890
***	Closed	3.9.1928
Heanor: loop and two ground frames	t.o.u.	9.5.1932
HEANOR	OP	2.6.1890
***	OG	17.11.1890
***	CP	1.1.1917
***	RO(P)	3.5.1920
***	CP	4.5.1926
Altered to HEANOR NORTH	... ...	1.7.1950
***	CG	1.9.1951
Line severed west of Heanor	By	17.11.1926
Heanor to the cut at Crosshill	t.o.u.	3.9.1928
Rail removed 400 yards on the Heanor side of Crosshill station	... ...	2.4.1928
Crosshill & Codnor Station SB	Opened	1.6.1890
***	Closed	16.3.1896
CROSSHILL & CODNOR	OP	2.6.1890
***	CP	1.1.1917
***	RO(P)	3.5.1920
***	CP(All)	4.5.1926
Ripley Junction SB	Opened	1.9.1889
***	Closed	6.8.1928

Ripley branch

See page 143

Ripley to Butterley	CP	1.10.1917
***	RO(P)	3.5.1920
***	CP	4.5.1926
Ripley Station SB	Opened	1.6.1890
***	Closed	12.5.1957
RIPLEY	OP	2.9.1889
***	OG	....
***	CP	1.6.1930
***	CG	1.4.1963
Line severed just north of Ripley station	... ...	23.1.1938

WIRKSWORTH BRANCH

Powers: Midland Railway (New Lines and Additional Powers) Act 1863

Duffield Jcn to Wirksworth	OP	1.10.1867
***	OG	16.12.1867
***	CP	16.6.1947
Working was by the train staff and ticket system.		
Duffield Jcn to Hazelwood, and Hazelwood to Idridgehay - working by telegraph bells; Idridgehay to Wirksworth - working by block telegraph with Gorsey Bank as intermediate block post	Commenced	8.9.1890
Duffield Jcn to Idridgehay: electric train token block working in place of working by train staff	Commenced	1891
Duffield Jcn to Wirksworth: long-and-short section key token working	Commenced	8.7.1934
Duffield Jcn: new facing connection to branch	Into use	29.5.1977
Duffield Down Branch Sidings and ground frame	t.o.u.	7.4.1971
HAZLEWOOD	OP	1.10.1867
***	OG	16.12.1867
***	CP	16.6.1947
***	CG	5.1.1953
Hazlewood SB	Open before	16.8.1877
***	Closed	1890 ?
Hazlewood, Shottle, Idridgehay, and Wirksworth are named in a list of "signal posts" returned to the Board of Trade in November 1880, but these may not then have been signalbox structures.		
Shottle Siding and two ground frames	t.o.u.	2.3.1964
SHOTTLE	OP	1.10.1867
***	OG	16.12.1867
***	CP	16.6.1947
***	CG	2.3.1964
Shottle SB	Open before	16.8.1877
***	Closed	1890 ?
IDRIDGEHAY	OP	1.10.1867
***	OG	16.12.1867
***	CP	16.6.1947
***	CG	5.1.1953
Idridgehay SB	Open before	16.8.1877
***	Closed	1890 ?
Idridgehay SB	Opened	8.9.1890
***	Closed	8.7.1934
Idridgehay token station	Opened	9.7.1934
***	Closed	28.10.1956
Idrigehay GF taken out of use and level crossing made open	... ...	3.12.1978
Gorsey Bank Crossing SB (not a block post)	Opened	8.9.1890
***	Closed	3.6.1979 ?
Gorsey Bank: down loop siding	Into use	9.11.1970
***	t.o.u.	24.12.1977
Gorsey Bank level crossing made open	... ...	3.6.1979
Wirksworth SB	Open before	16.8.1877
***	Closed	8.9.1890 ?
Wirksworth Station SB	Opened	8.9.1890
***	Closed	8.7.1934
WIRKSWORTH	OP	1.10.1867
***	OG	16.12.1867
***	CP	16.6.1947
***	CG	1.4.1968
Excursion trains continued to call at this station.		
Wirksworth engine shed	Opened	....
***	Closed	....
Wirksworth Incline GF	Into use	29.9.1973
Incline beyond Wirksworth station up to siding alongside the Cromford & High Peak Railway	Lifted	1914
No connection was ever made and no winding engine was provided.		

GRASSMOOR LINES

Grassmoor branch

Powers: No construction powers (Avenue Sidings to Grassmoor)
Midland Railway (Additional Powers) Act 1870 (Pilsley Branch Extension)

The Midland appears to have used the name Grassmoor branch both for the Grassmoor branch proper and for the Pilsley Branch Extension.

Avenue Sidings to Grassmoor	Opened	1.7.1872
***	Closed	30.1.1971
Avenue Sidings: 4 existing dead-end sidings extended and formed into a connection to the Grassmoor branch	... ...	4.5.1944
Avenue Sidings to Grassmoor West: key token working	Commenced	2.9.1934

Avenue Sidings Inspector's Office to Alma Jcn: one engine in steam working	Commenced	8.10.1967
Avenue Sidings to Williamthorpe Colliery; Alma West Jcn to Alma South Jcn and Williamthorpe level crossing AND Alma East Jcn to Alma South Jcn	Closed	13.2.1971
Grassmoor Junction SB	Opened	9.6.1901
***	Closed	19.3.1911

Bond's Main Branch (Grassmoor New Railway)

Powers: Midland Railway Act 1897

Grassmoor Jcn to Bond's Main North Jcn	OM	9.6.1901
Bond's Main branch cut at 144m 740yds and remainder made a siding	... ...	31.7.1955
Bond's Main North Junction SB	Opened	9.6.1901 ?
***	Closed	15.11.1909

Calow branch (LD&EC, GC, and MR joint)

Powers: Lancashire, Derbyshire and East Coast Railway Act 1897
Lancashire, Derbyshire and East Coast Railway Act 1898 (Deviation)

Bond's Main North Jcn to Calow Colliery	OM	6.5.1901
***	Closed	17.11.1909

Grassmoor West SB	Open before	16.8.1877
Replacement box	Opened	27.6.1887
***	Closed	3.9.1934
GRASSMOOR COLLIERY PLATFORM	OP(NA)	1.1.1874 ?*
***	CP(All)	9.11.1927
Grassmoor East SB	Open before	16.8.1877
Replacement box	Opened	6.10.1903
***	Closed	8.10.1967
Grassmoor to Pewit	Opened by	31.8.1874 *
Grassmoor Sidings East to Holmwood Colliery: pilot guard working	Commenced	23.2.1903
Grassmoor East SB: new empty wagon sidings on Holmwood side of box	Into use	29.1.1894
Grassmoor East to Alma Jcn changed from one engine in steam to key token operation, and remainder of the lines to Williamthorpe Colliery and Holmwood Jcn worked as sidings	... ...	18.10.1959
Pilsley Branch Extension: Pewit to Holmwood Jcn	OM	1.3.1876
Extension line severed 500 yards south of Alma Jcn GF. The extension line had been severed near the south end in about 1926 because of a collapsed bridge.	... ...	27.6.1970
NORTH WINGFIELD COLLIERY PLATFORM	OP(NA) before	7.1915
***	CP	9.11.1927
Ling's Colliery Sidings SB	Open before	16.8.1877
***	Closed	1913-1914
LING'S COLLIERY PLATFORM	OP(NA) by	31.8.1874 ?*
***	CP(All)	9.11.1927
Williamthorpe Level Crossing SB	Open before	16.8.1877
***	Closed	1913-1914
WILLIAMTHORPE LANE SIDING	Opened	....
***	Closed	....
Holmwood Junction SB	Opened	1876
***	Closed	13.10.1896

Holmwood (OR Hardwick) Colliery Branch

Powers: Midland Railway (Additional Powers) Act 1871

Holmwood Colliery Branch Jcn to Holmwood Colliery	OM	c.1874
Working by pilot guard	Commenced	21.5.1894
British Railways ceased to work the Holmwood branch	... ...	7.12.1952

Holmwood Colliery Branch Jcn: additional loop siding. The National Coal Board then worked between this exchange siding and the colliery and British Railways ceased to work the branch.	Into use	7.12.1952
Holmwood Colliery Branch Jcn (quarter mile south of) to junction of Grassmoor branch with Pilsley branch	Closed by	1.5.1882 *
Buffer stop at end of branch near junction with Holmwood branch removed and Grassmoor branch extended for about one mile and connected to Pilsley branch at point near the Great Central's Pilsley station	... ...	19.9.1904
Pilsley Road SB	Opened	....
***	Closed	....

Williamthorpe branch

Powers: No Construction Powers (Williamthorpe Branch - Clay Cross end)
North Midland Railway Act 1837 (Williamthorpe Branch - Pilsley Branch end)
Midland Railway (Additional Powers) Act 1870 (Williamthorpe Incline: discontinuance, and Ling's Curves (Land Powers only)
No Construction Powers (Williamthorpe Colliery Branch)

Clay Cross Jcn to Williamthorpe Colliery	OM	....
Ling's Colliery Sidings: curves from West Jcn to East Jcn and from South Jcn to East Jcn to give access to Williamthorpe Colliery. These were the Ling's Colliery Branches OR Ling's Curves.	OM	1.3.1876 ?

LING'S ROW WHARF	Opened	1900-1904
***	Closed	Mid-1960
Williamthorpe New Colliery branch	Opened	1904
Ling's Colliery Sidings re-named Alma Junction	... ...	7.12.1952 ?
South Jcn: curve to give access to Alma Colliery and North Wingfield Colliery together with Ling's Row Wharf situated on Williamthorpe Incline line to the west of the Pilsley Extension Line	OM	1.3.1876 ?
Alma Colliery, and Alma South Jcn to Ling's Row Wharf	Closed	22.8.1969
Alma West Jcn to Williamthorpe Colliery	Closed	30.1.1971

SHEEPBRIDGE RAILWAYS

Acquisition: Midland Railway (Additional Powers) Act 1870

The direction of the line was DOWN from Monkwood and Nesfield Collieries to Dunston & Barlow North and South Junctions.

Dunston & Barlow South to Monkwood: working by the Midland Railway Working was by train staff without tickets.	Commenced	1.11.1870

Canal Branch

Powers: --

Canal branch	Opened	....
***	Closed	....
Dunston & Barlow South to 970 yards west of Cobnarwood GF made siding	... ...	30.8.1953

Dunston North Curve

Powers: --

Dunston & Barlow West Jcn to North Jcn	Open before	7.1873
Dunston & Barlow Sidings to Sheffield Road Crossing: second line	Into use	9.4.1905
Working of the second line as a siding instead of by train staff	Commenced	15.4.1929
Major alterations to Sheepbridge branch	... ...	2.7.1974
Sheepbridge branch severed at 148m 27ch	... ...	2.7.1979
Sheffield Road Crossing SB	Open before	1884
***	Closed	10.6.1973
SHEEPBRIDGE WHITTINGTON ROAD WHARF P.D.Ss.	CG	6.6.1983
Cobnarwood Jcn to Monkwood (end of Monkwood branch)	Disused by	1909
Cobnarwood GF to Monkwood	Closed	24.1.1964
Sheepbridge furnace bank to Nesfield	Closed	29.3.1965
Cobnarwood Jcn to Nesfield (end of Nesfield branch): Midland working	Commenced	1.11.1870 ?
Line made a siding	... ...	21.12.1942
One engine in steam working resumed	... ...	30.8.1953
***	Closed	11.1966

CHESTERFIELD & SHEFFIELD LINE

Powers: Midland Railway (Chesterfield and Sheffield) Act 1864
Midland Railway Act 1892 (Dore & Totley and Sheffield Widening)
Midland Railway Act 1898 (Sheffield Widening & Enlargement)
Midland Railway Act 1901 (Sheffield & Attercliffe Widening)

Chesterfield Jcn to Grimesthorpe Jcn Working was by the block telegraph system from the opening.	OP&G	1.2.1870
Tapton Jcn: down loop	Into use	26.4.1959
***	t.o.u. by	24.6.1988
SHEEPBRIDGE	OP	1.8.1870
Altered to SHEEPBRIDGE & WHITTINGTON MOOR	... ...	8.10.1897
Altered to SHEEPBRIDGE	... ...	18.6.1951
***	CP(All)	2.1.1967
This station continued to be used when for engineering reasons main-line trains were run over the goods lines at Chesterfield. The last such use was 1 June 1975. Excursion trains also ran at least until 31 August 1970.		
Sheepbridge Station SB	Open before	1.11.1875
Replacement box	Opened	16.2.1891
Box closed and intermediate block section semaphore signals provided in lieu	... ...	24.4.1932
***	t.o.u.	....
Broomhouse tunnel opened out	August - September	1969
Broomhouse Colliery Sidings SB	Open before	1.11.1875
***	Closed	21.7.1879

Unstone Colliery Sidings SB	Open before	16.8.1877
***	Re-framed	24.11.1895
Replacement box	Opened	8.10.1899
***	Closed	15.1.1972

Unstone goods loop
Powers: Midland Railway (Additional Powers) Act 1871 (Unstone Coal Branch)
Midland Railway (Additional Powers) Act 1874 (Unstone & Dronfield Branch)

Unstone to Crow Lane	Opened	1.2.1870
Crow Lane to Silkstone Colliery	Opened	1877
Silkstone Colliery to Dronfield Jcn	Open before	7.1873
Unston branch: Midland began to work the branch with engines between Unston Colliery Sidings and Summerley Colliery	... ...	19.5.1879
Closed between Two Oaks Dock Siding and the gate on the Unstone side of the sidings at Dronfield (75 chains)	... ...	1897
Closed section of the branch dismantled	... ...	1931
Boot's Siding to Dronfield	Closed	9.9.1969

UNSTON	OP&G	1.2.1870
Altered to UNSTONE	... ...	1.7.1908
***	CP	29.10.1951
***	CG	1.9.1961
Excursion trains continued to call at this station.		
Unstone Station SB	Open before	1.11.1875
Box closed and ground frame provided in lieu	... ...	19.4.1886
***	t.o.u.	....
CALLYWHITE SIDING	Opened	1910-1912
***	Closed	9.6.1969
Dronfield South SB	Open before	1.11.1875
***	Closed	4.1883-11.1885
Dronfield Station SB	Open before	16.8.1877
Replacement box	Opened	c.10.1884
Replacement box	Opened	21.12.1919
***	Closed	16.1.1972
DRONFIELD	OP&G	1.2.1870
***	CP	2.1.1967
***	CG	1.5.1967
***	RO(P)	5.1.1981
Excursion trains continued to call. A temporary re-opening from 15 to 19 February 1979 during a gritters' strike led to the permanent re-opening of the station in January 1981.		
Dronfield Colliery Sidings SB	Opened	4.1.1891
Replacement box	Opened	25.7.1920
***	Closed	2.1963
Andrews Sidings SB	Open before	16.8.1877
***	Closed	4.1883-11.1885
Bradway Tunnel SB	Opened	8.2.1904
***	Closed	17.5.1904
Bradway tunnel: alarm wires on the up and down sides	Into use	27.5.1940
Dore & Totley South Junction SB	Opened	29.10.1893
***	Closed	16.1.1972

Dore South Curve
See page 196

Dore & Totley Station SB	Open before	1.11.1875
Box closed and 2 ground frames provided in lieu	... ...	24.1.1887
Dore & Totley Station SB (new box)	Opened	6.1.1889
Replacement box named Dore & Totley Station Junction SB	Opened	29.10.1893
***	Closed	20.10.1901
Dore & Totley Station Jcn: position of junction altered	... ...	20.5.1894
Original junction	Removed	20.10.1901
Dore & Totley to Heeley Carriage Sidings: up and down slow lines	Into use	20.10.1901
The up and down slow lines (the Derby lines) were on the east side of the fast lines (the Manchester lines). The original junction between the Derby and Manchester lines at the south end of Dore & Totley station was removed.		
DORE & TOTLEY	OP	1.2.1872
Main-line platforms	Closed	21.1.1967
Altered to DORE	... ...	18.3.1971
Former west-bound Manchester line platform	t.o.u.	31.3.1985
Dore & Totley Station Junction SB (second box)	Opened	20.10.1901
Box re-framed and re-named Dore Station Junction SB	... ...	16.1.1972
***	Closed	25.3.1973

Dore & Chinley line
See page 196

Dore & Totley Station Jcn: double junction (DSL-DFL, UFL-USL) and double junction (DFL-DSL, USL-UFL)	Into use	20.10.1901
Double junctions	t.o.u.	....
Single leads junction for the Manchester line	Into use	....

Dore Station Jcn moved 55 yards to the north	... ...	8.4.1985
Dore & Totley Station Jcn to Sheffield: fast (Manchester) lines re-named slow lines and slow (Derby) lines re-named fast lines	... ...	14.6.1954
Dore & Totley Station Jcn to Heeley Carriage Sidings: up slow line	t.o.u.	3.5.1971
Dore & Totley Station Jcn to Millhouses: down slow line	t.o.u.	13.12.1971
Dore (north of): down main line	Re-aligned	1985
Up main line	Re-aligned	1985
ABBEY HOUSES	OP&G	1.2.1870
Altered to BEAUCHIEFF	... ...	1.4.1870
Altered to BEAUCHIEFF & ABBEY DALE	... ...	1.5.1874 *
Altered to BEAUCHIEF & ABBEY DALE	... ...	1.5.1888 *
Altered to BEAUCHIEF	... ...	19.3.1914
***	CP	2.1.1961
***	CG	15.6.1964
Beauchieff SB	Open before	1871
Replacement box	Opened	1881
***	Re-framed	29.3.1896
Replacement box	Opened	13.10.1901
***	Closed	18.7.1965
Beauchief to Millhouses & Ecclesall: up goods line	Into use	23.9.1900
***	t.o.u.	20.10.1901
ECCLESALL	OP&G	1.2.1870
Altered to ECCLESALL & MILL HOUSES	... ...	1.10.1871 *
Altered to MILL HOUSES & ECCLESALL	... ...	1.5.1884 *
Altered to MILLHOUSES & ECCLESALL	... ...	18.7.1932
***	CP	10.6.1968
***	CG	24.4.1972
Eccleshall SB	Open before	1.11.1875
Re-named Millhouses & Eccleshall SB	... ...	1885
Replacement box	Opened	23.9.1900
***	Slued	12.1.1902
***	Closed	21.1.1973
Millhouses to Sheffield South No. 2: down fast line	t.o.u.	25.6.1972
Up fast line taken out of use and former up slow line returned to use as the up main line	... ...	2.7.1972
Eccleshall engine shed	Opened	1901
Renamed Millhouses engine shed	... ...	1920
***	Closed	1.1.1962
Millhouses to Heeley: up goods loop	Into use	....
Heeley Carriage Sidings SB	Opened	2.10.1892
Replacement box	Opened	13.10.1901
***	Closed	21.1.1973
Heeley Carriage Sidings: shunting line and two fans	Into use	10.7.1893
No. 2 shunting line	Into use	15.1.1894
Heeley Carriage Sidings	Closed	12.12.1971
Heeley Carriage Sidings: double junction (DSL-DFL, UFL-USL)	Into use	8.3.1903
***	t.o.u.	....
Heeley Carriage Sidings to Heeley North Jcn: up and down slow lines	Into use	8.3.1903
Heeley Station SB	Open before	16.8.1877
Replacement box at the south end of the platforms	Opened	27.7.1902
Replacement box 226 yards north of the old box	Opened	18.10.1931
***	Closed	7.1.1973
HEELEY	OP&G	1.2.1870
Existing up main line and platform taken out of use and replaced by a new up main line and platform	... ...	27.7.1902
Existing down main line and platform taken out of use and replaced by a new down main line and platform	... ...	28.9.1902
***	CG	11.9.1967
***	CP	10.6.1968
Up main line re-aligned on site of former down fast line	... ...	....
Down main line re-aligned on site of former up slow line	... ...	....
Heeley North Junction SB	Opened	4.5.1902
***	Closed	18.10.1931
Heeley North Jcn: double junction (DFL-DSL, USL-UFL)	Opened	8.3.1903
***	t.o.u.	....
Heeley North Jcn to Sheffield South Jcn: down slow line on the up side with the underpass line at the south end of Sheffield station	Into use	4.5.1902
Up slow line	Into use	11.5.1902
Heeley North Jcn to Havelock Road Bridge: down goods line	Into use	28.9.1902
***	t.o.u.	....
Heeley East Bank SB	Open before	1.11.1875
***	Closed	18.9.1886
Heeley (north of) to Sheffield: down passenger loop	Into use	....
Down main line made passenger loop and down passenger loop made main line	... ...	25.11.1984
Havelock Road SB	Opened	12.1.1902
***	Closed	28.9.1902
Havelock Road Bridge to Queen's Road: down goods line	Into use	12.1.1902
***	t.o.u.	....
Queen's Road SB	Opened	18.10.1891
***	Slued	17.6.1900

Queen's Road SB (continued): replacement box	Opened	10.3.1901
***	Closed	21.1.1973
SHEFFIELD QUEEN'S ROAD GOODS DEPOT	Opened	6.6.1892
***	Closed	13.5.1963
SHEFFIELD TICKET PLATFORM	Closed	....
Sheffield South Junction SB	Opened	1870
Replacement box	Opened	10.9.1893
***	Closed	11.5.1902
Replacement box	Opened	4.5.1902
Re-named Sheffield South No. 1 SB	... ...	17.7.1904
***	Re-located	3.9.1904
***	Re-framed	c.1940
***	Closed	21.1.1973
Sheffield South Jcn to North Jcn: up and down goods lines (up side)	Into use	1.2.1870
***	t.o.u. by	1894
Sheffield Power Signal Box	Opened	21.1.1973
Sheffield PSB:		
1. Tapton Jcn (exc) to Dore Station Jcn (exc) / Dore West Jcn	Into use	15-16.1.1972
2. Nunnery Main Line Jcn taken over by Sheffield North	... ...	12.3.1972
3. Dore Station Jcn (exc) to Sheffield North Jcn	Into use	20-22.1.1973
4. Brightside Jcn	Into use	18.3.1973
5. Tapton Jcn, Dore Station Jcn	Into use	25.3.1973
6. Wincobank Station Jcn	Into use	14.1.1979
7. Holmes Jcn / Canklow Goods Jcn to Parkgate Jcn	Into use	29.7.1979
8. Aldwarke Jcn	Into use	24.2.1980
9. Kilnhurst South to Wath Road Jcn	Into use	23.11.1980
10. Dunston & Barlow North to Renishaw Park Goods Jcn	Into use	15.11.1981
11. Beighton Jcn	Into use	16.5.1982
12. Treeton South to Treeton North	Into use	3.10.1982
Sheffield South No. 2 SB	Opened	17.7.1904
***	Repaired	c.1940
***	Closed	21.1.1973
SHEFFIELD POND STREET GOODS DEPOT	Opened	1.2.1870
***	Closed	19.9.1960
SHEFFIELD NEW MIDLAND STATION	OP	1.2.1870
Altered to SHEFFIELD MIDLAND STATION	... ...	1.2.1876 *
Platforms numbered 1 to 7 after enlargement of the station	... ...	10.9.1893
New Nos. 1 and 2 platform lines (at first used from north only)	Into use	13.3.1904
Platforms re-numbered 1 to 9 for enlargement of station	... ...	19.6.1904
All new facilities	Into use	4.9.1904
Station made "closed" for tickets	... ...	1.1.1924
Altered to SHEFFIELD CITY	... ...	25.9.1950
Altered to SHEFFIELD MIDLAND	... ...	18.6.1951
New platform 2C	Into use	25.11.1984
Luggage bridge	Removed	1987
Between Sheffield passenger station and Grimesthorpe Junction the Lancashire, Derbyshire & East Coast Railway had running powers for coaching traffic over the Midland line.		
Between Sheffield passenger station and Brightside Junction the Great Eastern Railway had running powers over the Midland line.		
Sheffield Passenger Station SB	Opened	2.1880-6.1881
Replacement box	Opened	10.9.1893
***	Lowered	14.1.1894
Re-named Sheffield "B" SB	... ...	4.9.1904
***	Closed	21.1.1973
Sheffield "A" SB	Opened	4.9.1904
***	Re-located	5.3.1905
***	Closed	21.1.1973
Sheffield North Junction SB	Opened	1870
Replacement box	Opened	27.8.1893
Replacement box	Opened	13.3.1904
***	Raised	16.6.1912
***	Closed	21.1.1973
Nunnery Colliery Sidings SB	Opened	1.3.1886
Re-named Nunnery Main Line Junction SB	... ...	16.11.1924
Replacement box	Opened	11.5.1941
***	Closed	12.3.1972
Attercliffe Road SB	Open before	1.10.1876
***	Re-framed	20.9.1914
***	Closed	11.5.1941
ATTERCLIFFE ROAD	OP	1.2.1870
Mill Race Junction SB	Opened	17.10.1897
***	Closed	30.5.1965

Nunnery Curve to the Manchester, Sheffield & Lincolnshire Railway

Powers: Midland Railway (Chesterfield and Sheffield) Act 1864

Nunnery Main Line Jcn to the east junction with the Manchester, Sheffield & Lincolnshire Railway	Approved	27.7.1870 ?
***	Closed by	1898
***	Re-opened	4.10.1965

Between Beighton Junction or Sheffield Junction and Penistone Junction the Midland Railway possessed running powers for all traffic over the Manchester, Sheffield & Lincolnshire line. The Midland powers extended over the Lancashire & Yorkshire line from Penistone Junction to Springwood Junction, and over the joint Lancashire & Yorkshire and London & North Western line from Springwood Junction to Huddersfield station.

Nunnery Colliery branch	OG	3.8.1886
***	Closed	....
This branch was constructed under an agreement with the Duke of Norfolk.		
Working was by the block telegraph system.		
Nunnery Colliery Sidings SB: connection to the new carriage shed	Into use	4.1.1909
Nunnery Single Line Junction SB	Opened	16.11.1924
***	Closed	1964-1969

SHEFFIELD & ROTHERHAM RAILWAY

The Sheffield & Rotherham Railway was incorporated on 4 July 1836 and was taken over by Midland Railway (the locomotives being leased) with effect from 10 October 1844. It was vested in the Midland by by 8-9 Victoria cap. 90 of 21 July 1845.

Powers: Sheffield and Rotherham Railway Act 1836
Sheffield and Rotherham and Midland Railways Consolidation Act 1845
(Spital Hill Tunnel Line)
Midland Railway Act 1898 (Widening at Brightside)
Midland Railway Act 1893 (Widening at Wincobank)
Midland Railway (Additional Powers) Act 1874
(Wincobank & Holmes Widening - Land Powers only)

The direction of the line was DOWN from Grimesthorpe Junction to Wicker.

Sheffield to Rotherham Westgate	O.Formal	31.10.1838
***	Opened	1.11.1838
Commecting line to the (west) junction with the Sheffield, Ashton-under-Lyne, & Manchester Railway at Bridgehouses	Opened	11.1846
***	CP	Mid-March 1848
***	Closed	7.1948
SHEFFIELD	Opened	1.11.1838
Altered to SHEFFIELD WICKER	... ...	4.1852-10.1853 *
***	CP	1.2.1870
WICKER GOODS DEPOT	Opened	1.2.1870
Depot re-modelled and new goods shed opened	... ...	1894
***	Closed	12.7.1965
The line between Wicker station and Grimesthorpe Junction was worked by telegraph bells.		
Wicker to Grimesthorpe Junction No. 1	Closed	12.7.1965
Sheffield Bell Box SB	Open before	1865
***	Closed by	16.8.1877
Lockwood's Crossing SB	Open before	1.11.1875
Replacement box	Opened	21.10.1894
***	Closed	28.10.1956
Elevated Box SB (signalling the junction for the tunnel line)	Open before	1865
Replacement box	Opened	27.1.1896
***	Closed	18.7.1965
Firth's Sidings SB	Opened	....
Replacement box	Opened	26.6.1892
***	Closed	18.7.1965
Firth's Sidings SB to Grimesthorpe Jcn: second down main line alongside the existing down main line	Into use	1.10.1894
BRIGHTSIDE LANE WHARF	Opened	1882-1883
***	Closed	1.4.1963
GRIMESTHORPE BRIDGE	OP	1.11.1838
***	CP(All)	1.2.1843
Mill Race Jcn to Grimesthorpe Jcn: up and down goods lines (up side)	Into use	30.10.1898
Down goods line on the up side re-named the No. 2 down goods line and down goods line on the down side brought into use	... ...	15.1.1899
Mill Race Jcn to Brightside: up and second down goods lines designated up and down local lines	By	6.5.1900
Up and down local lines and down goods line	t.o.u.	....
Grimesthorpe Junction SB	Open before	16.8.1877
Replacement box	Opened	11.9.1887
***	Alt.levers	17.7.1892
Re-named Grimesthorpe Junction No. 1 SB	... ...	15.1.1899
Replacement box	Opened	23.4.1899
***	Slued	14.1.1900
***	Re-framed	10.9.1916
***	Closed	8.8.1965

Grimesthorpe Junction No. 1: shunting siding	Into use	14.1.1900
***	t.o.u.	....
Between Grimesthorpe Junction and Brightside Junction the Great Central had running powers for all traffic over the Midland line. Between Grimesthorpe Junction and Attercliffe station the Midland possessed running powers over the Sheffield District line.		
Grimesthorpe Junction No. 2 SB	Opened	15.1.1899
***	Re-framed	30.4.1899
***	Re-framed	3.9.1916
***	Closed	8.8.1965
Grimesthorpe Jcn to Holmes: block telegraph system	Installed	1870
Grimesthorpe Jcn to Brightside: down goods line	Into use	12.5.1873
Up goods line	Into use	14.5.1899
Second down goods line (up side)	Into use	4.6.1899
Grimesthorpe Jcn: additional shunting line on the down side of existing line leading to/from the old engine shed sidings	Into use	19.4.1896
***	t.o.u.	....
Grimesthorpe Jcn to Upwell Street Jcn: three up goods lines	Into use	24.4.1892
Up goods lines re-named up reception lines	... ...	....
Up reception lines	t.o.u.	....
Grimesthorpe engine shed	Opened	1861
Replacement shed	Opened	1877
***	Closed	11.9.1961
The Grimesthorpe shed replaced an earlier shed at Sheffield Wicker.		
GRIMESTHORPE SIDINGS	Opened	....
***	Closed	11.9.1961
SHEFFIELD FREIGHT TERMINAL: NCL SIDINGS	CG by	15.4.1988
Upwell Street Junction SB	Opened	20.4.1892
***	Re-framed	14.5.1899
***	Closed	8.8.1965
UPWELL STREET WHARF	Opened	8.1893-12.1895
***	Closed	1.4.1963
Cooke & Swinnerton's Sidings SB	Open before	1.11.1875
Replacement box	Opened	8.10.1888
***	Closed	20.4.1892

Jessop's Branch

Powers: --

Jessop's branch	Open before	7.1873
***	t.o.u.	23.1.1988
Brightside SB	Open before	16.8.1877
Replacement box	Opened	9.8.1896
Replacement box	Opened	13.11.1898
Re-named Brightside Station Junction SB	... ...	6.5.1900
Replacement box named Brightside Junction SB	Opened	25.4.1965
***	Closed	18.3.1973
Brightside: down goods line to down passenger line crossover	Into use	15.1.1899
Second down goods line to down passenger line crossover	Into use	4.6.1899
Down fast line to down goods line crossover	Into use	....
Up passenger line to up local line crossover	Into use	....
Up goods line to up fast line crossover	Into use	....
Various connections	t.o.u.	....
Brightside to Wincobank Station Jcn: up goods line	Into use	24.4.1898
***	t.o.u.	26.3.1972
Brightside to Wincobank Jcn: down goods line	Into use	4.7.1897
***	t.o.u.	....
BRIGHTSIDE	OP	1.11.1838
***	OM before	1872
***	CM	1880
Replacement station	OP	29.5.1898
Wincobank Station Jcn: up passenger line to up goods line crossover	Into use	5.8.1917
Wincobank Station Junction SB	Opened	4.4.1897
***	Closed	14.1.1979

Chapeltown branch

See page 155

Wincobank Station Jcn to Wincobank Station Box: up goods line	Into use	31.10.1897 ?
Wincobank Station Jcn to Wincobank Jcn: up goods line	Into use	4.4.1897 ?
***	t.o.u.	....
Wincobank Station SB	Open before	16.8.1877
***	Closed	4.4.1897 ?
WINCOBANK	OP&G	1.5.1868 *
***	CG by	1877
***	RO(G)	1.7.1897
New station	Opened	1897-1898
Altered to WINCOBANK & MEADOW HALL	... ...	1.7.1899 *
Altered to WINCOBANK	... ...	18.6.1951
***	CP	2.4.1956
***	CG	1.1.1966

Wincobank Junction SB	Open before	16.8.1877
Replacement box	Opened	26.10.1890
***	Closed	4.4.1897
Wincobank Jcn to Harrison & Camm's Sidings: down goods line	Into use	17.10.1875
Up goods line	Into use	21.12.1890
Up and down goods lines	t.o.u.	....
Blackburn Junction SB	Open before	1865
***	Closed by	16.8.1877
Brightside Jcn with the South Yorkshire Railway	Opened	4.9.1854
Re-named Blackburn Valley Junction	... ...	....
***	Closed	....
BLACKBURN FORGE	OP	1.11.1838
***	CP	25.3.1839
Wincobank North Junction SB	Opened	18.10.1896
***	Closed	21.3.1971

Wincobank North Curve

See page 155

Wincobank North Jcn: down passenger line to down goods line crossover	Into use	....
Up passenger line to up goods line crossover	Into use	....
Down goods line to down passenger line crossover	Into use	....
Up goods line to up passenger line crossover	Into use	....
Various connections	t.o.u.	....
WINCOBANK NORTH JUNCTION NEW UP SIDINGS	Into use	5.4.1897
***	Closed	....
WINCOBANK DOWN SIDINGS	Opened	1.1907 ?
***	Closed	....
Wincobank Sidings SB	Opened	2.1879-2.1880
Replacement box	Opened	6.6.1897
***	Raised	6.4.1902
***	Closed	11.4.1961
Harrison & Camm's Sidings SB	Opened	1871
Replacement box	Opened	21.12.1890
***	Closed	17.8.1975
THE HOLMES	Opened	1.11.1838 ?
Altered to HOLMES	... ...	1.1.1858 *
***	CG	1903
***	CM	....
***	CP	19.9.1955
HOLMES STATION SIDING	Opened	....
Altered to ROTHERHAM LANE	... ...	19.9.1968
***	Closed	....
Holmes Junction SB	Opened	1870
Replacement box	Opened	8.3.1903
Control of gates transferred from gate cabin to signalbox	... ...	7.2.1932
***	Closed	29.7.1979
Holmes Jcn to Rotherham Westgate	CP	5.10.1952
Booth's Sidings to Rotherham Westgate	CG(All)	6.10.1952

Holmes Chord

Powers: British Railways Act 1981

Holmes Jcn to Rotherham Central Jcn with the former Great Central line	Into use	12.4.1987
***	OP	11.5.1987

Greasborough Branch

Powers: Sheffield and Rotherham Railway Act 1836

Midland Railway Act 1899 (Holmes Curve)

Holmes Jcn to end of branch	OG	7.8.1839
Holmes Jcn to Masborough (Station South) Jcn section of branch	OP	11.5.1840
Block telegraph system installed	... ...	1878
Holmes Jcn to Masborough Station South Jcn: up and down fast lines	Into use	20.3.1904
Down goods line	In use by	1.1.1870 *
***	t.o.u.	2.3.1969 ?
Up and down slow lines	t.o.u.	5.6.1978
HOLMES LANE PUBLIC DELIVERY SIDINGS	CG	6.6.1983
Masborough Station South Jcn: down goods line to down passenger line crossover	Into use	....
Masborough Station North Jcn: down goods line to down passenger line crossover	Into use	....

Rotherham Station SB	Opened	1861
Replacement box	Opened	19.11.1893
***	Closed	8.10.1952
ROTHERHAM	Opened	1.11.1838
***	CG	1875
***	CM	1903 ?
Altered to ROTHERHAM WESTGATE	... ...	1.5.1896
***	CP	6.10.1952

CHAPELTOWN BRANCH & CHAPELTOWN BRANCH EXTENSION

Powers: Midland Railway (Additional Powers) Act 1890 (Wincobank to Chapeltown)
Midland Railway Act 1891 (Chapeltown)
Midland Railway Act 1892 (Chapeltown to Elsecar)
Midland Railway Act 1894 (Elsecar to Wombwell - Hemingfield Deviation)
Midland Railway Act 1892 (Wombwell to Barnsley West Junction)

Chapeltown Branch

Wincobank Station Jcn to Thorncliffe Ironworks	OM	1.9.1894
Chapeltown Branch & Chapeltown Branch Extension	OP&G	1.7.1897
Wincobank West Junction SB	Opened	23.8.1896
Box closed and connections controlled by Wincobank Station Jcn box	... ...	1.10.1933
Wincobank West Jcn to Chapeltown station	Doubled	23.8.1896

Wincobank North Curve

Powers: Midland Railway Act 1894

Wincobank North Jcn to Wincobank West Jcn	OM	7.12.1896
***	Closed	29.9.1969

Ecclesfield Station SB	Opened	23.8.1896
Re-named Ecclesfield West Station SB	... ...	25.9.1950
***	Re-framed	1979
***	Closed	....
ECCLESFIELD	OG&M	1.8.1894
***	OP	1.7.1897
Altered to ECCLESFIELD WEST	... ...	25.9.1950
***	CG	11.11.1963
***	CP	6.11.1967
Excursion trains continued to call at this station.		
Smithy Wood Colliery Sidings SB	Opened	11.4.1897
***	Raised	19.3.1905
***	Closed	3.1963

Smithy Wood Branch

Powers: --

Smithy Wood Colliery Sidings to Smithy Wood Colliery	Opened	1892–1893
***	Closed	9.1961

CHAPELTOWN	OG&M	1.8.1894
***	OP	1.7.1897
Altered to CHAPELTOWN SOUTH	... ...	18.6.1951
***	CG	12.7.1965
Altered to CHAPELTOWN	... ...	20.2.1969
Replacement station a little to the south	Opened	2.8.1982
Chapeltown Station SB	Opened	23.8.1896
Re-named Chapeltown South Station SB	... ...	25.9.1950
***	Closed	27.11.1973

Thorncliffe Iron Works Branch

Powers: No construction powers for the Thorncliffe High Level Branch

Thorncliffe Ironworks branches	OM	1.9.1894
***	Closed	17.4.1966

Chapeltown Branch Extensions

Chapeltown Jcn to Wombwell Colliery Jcn	OM	1.10.1896 ?
Wombwell Colliery Jcn to Wharncliffe Branch Sidings	OM	12.4.1897
Wharncliffe Branch Sidings to Barnsley West Jcn	OM	10.5.1897
Wentworth & Tankersley Station SB	Opened	12.4.1897 ?
Re-named Wentworth & Hoyland Common Station SB	... ...	1.7.1901
***	Raised	29.11.1914
***	Closed	18.12.1960
WENTWORTH & TANKERSLEY	OP&G	1.7.1897
Altered to WENTWORTH & HOYLAND COMMON		1.7.1901
Altered to WENTWORTH	... ...	18.6.1951
***	CP&G	2.11.1959
Skier's Spring SB	Opened	24.9.1944
***	Closed	....
Lidgett Colliery Sidings SB	Opened	12.4.1897 ?
Re-named Lidgett & Skier's Spring SB	... ...	30.5.1897
***	Closed	8.9.1935
Elsecar & Hoyland Station SB	Opened	12.4.1897 ?
***	Closed	11.1965
ELSECAR & HOYLAND	OP&G	1.7.1897
***	CG	2.11.1964
Altered to ELSECAR	... ...	17.3.1971
Hoyland Curve SB	Opened	12.4.1897 ?
***	Burnt out	1919–1931

Hoyland Curve

Powers: Midland Railway Act 1895

Hoyland Curve SB to junction with Manchester, Sheffield, & Lincolnshire line for access to Hoyland Silkstone Colliery	Opened	1896
***	Closed	....
WOMBWELL	OP&G	1.7.1897
Altered to WOMBWELL WEST	... ...	25.9.1950
***	CG	1.3.1965
Altered to WOMBWELL	... ...	20.2.1969
Wombwell Station SB	Opened	12.4.1897 ?
***	Closed	12.5.1970

Wombwell Colliery Branches

Powers: --

Wombwell Colliery Empty Wagon branch	Opened	....
***	Closed	....
Wombwell Colliery Loaded Wagon branch	Opened	....
***	Closed	....
Wharncliffe Branch Sidings SB	Opened	10.5.1897
***	Raised	29.9.1912
***	Closed	22.7.1962

Wharncliffe Branch

Powers: Midland Railway Act 1893

Wharncliffe Branch Sidings to end of branch	OG	1.9.1897
Working by pilot guard without tickets	Commenced	19.11.1906
Wharncliffe Branch Sidings to Rockingham Colliery	Closed	22.7.1962
Rockingham Colliery to Birdwell & Pilley Wharf	Closed	13.9.1954
BIRDWELL & PILLEY WHARF	Opened	....
***	Closed	13.9.1954
Monk Spring Junction SB	Opened	30.1.1899
***	Closed	1.8.1965
Doncaster Road Sidings SB	Opened	10.5.1897 ?
***	Closed	11.1.1953

Stairfoot & Cudworth Line

Powers: Midland Railway Act 1897
British Railways Act 1966 (new connection at Stairfoot)

Monk Spring Jcn to Cudworth Station South Jcn	OG	11.9.1899
***	OP	1.5.1900
***	CP&G	7.9.1964
Ardsley Sidings SB	Opened	2.10.1899
***	Closed	10.1962
ARDSLEY SIDINGS	Opened	18.2.1901
***	Closed	....
Stairfoot Jcn (north of Ardsley tunnel) to Cudworth Station South Jcn	RO(G)	3.7.1967
***	C.Tfc	14.7.1979 ?
***	Closed	4.6.1984

BARNSLEY & CUDWORTH BRANCH

Powers: Midland Railway (New Lines and Additional Powers) Act 1863
Midland Railway (New Lines and Additional Powers Act) 1864 (Barnsley)
Midland Railway (Additional Powers) Act 1868 (Darfield Junction Railway, Barnsley)

Cudworth South Jcn to Barnsley	OG	28.6.1869
Only local goods services were operated at first, as the junction with the Manchester, Sheffield & Lincolnshire line was not available for through traffic prior to its inspection.		
Cudworth Jcns to Barnsley: block telegraph system	Installed	c.1870

Cudworth North Curve

Powers: Midland Railway (New Lines and Additional Powers) Act 1863

Cudworth North Jcn to Cudworth West Jcn	OG	1.4.1870 *
***	OP	1.8.1870 *
***	CP	1.3.1872 *
***	RO(P)	1.8.1893 *
***	CP	1.10.1919 *
***	CG	....
CARLTON MAIN COLLIERY PLATFORM	OP(NA)	2.2.1885 *
***	Closed	1913
Cudworth South Jcn to Barnsley	OP	2.5.1870
***	CP	9.6.1958

Cudworth South Jcn to Cudworth West Jcn	Closed	9.6.1958
	or	18.4.1959
Cudworth West Junction SB	Open before	1.11.1875
Replacement box	Opened	1.2.1891
***	Closed	18.4.1959 ?
Monk Bretton Jcn with the Hull & Barnsley Railway	OM	1.6.1886
***	OG	20.7.1885 ?
***	Taken out	8.9.1935

Between Monk Bretton Junction and Monk Bretton Colliery the Hull & Barnsley Railway possessed running powers over the Midland line.

Monk Bretton Colliery Sidings SB	Open before	1.11.1875
***	Closed	4.5.1886
Monk Bretton Colliery Sidings to Oaks Colliery Sidings	Closed	9.6.1958 ?
Monk Bretton to Barnsley West Jcn	Closed	18.4.1959 ?
Monk Bretton Junction SB	Opened	4.5.1886
***	Closed	30.6.1963
MONK BRETTON	OG	....
***	OP (public)	1.1.1876
***	CG	1900-1904
***	CP	27.9.1937
Ryland Sidings SB (replacing the existing stage)	Opened	18.3.1893
Box closed and traffic dealt with through the connection at Oaks Colliery Sidings	... ...	18.9.1904
Oaks Colliery Sidings SB	Open before	1.11.1875
Replacement box	Opened	9.11.1886
Replacement box	Opened	19.1.1919
***	Closed	18.4.1959 ?

Between Normanton and the Monk Bretton and Oaks Collieries the North Eastern Railway possessed running powers for locomotive coal traffic over the Midland line. The arrangement lapsed in 1875.

Oaks Colliery Sidings to Barnsley West Jcn: main lines deviation	Into use	1.9.1895
Oaks Colliery Sidings to Barnsley West Junction	Closed	5.1.1959
Darfield East Junction SB	Opened	1869-1870
***	Closed by	16.8.1877

Darfield Junction Line

Powers: --

Darfield East (OR Oaks Colliery Sidings) Jcn to Darfield West (OR Quarry) Jcn with the Manchester, Sheffield & Lincolnshire Railway	Approved	6.4.1870

This spur was apparently used only for access to Oaks Colliery.

Quarry Jcn: new spur to divert traffic to the former Lancashire & Yorkshire Railway station	Into use	15-26.4.1960
Quarry Jcn to Court House station	Closed	19.4.1960

Mount Osborne Junction Line (Manchester, Sheffield & Lincolnshire Railway)

Powers: --

Mount Osborne East Jcn (Midland) to West Jcn	Opened	31.5.1870
***	Closed	19.4.1960
Mount Osborne West Junction SB	Opened	28.6.1869
Replacement box	Opened	26.7.1887
Replacement box named Barnsley West Junction SB	Opened	6.9.1895
***	Raised	25.6.1916
***	Closed	19.4.1960

Between Mount Osborne West Junction and Cockram Road Junction the Manchester, Sheffield & Lincolnshire Railway possessed running powers for all traffic over the Midland line.

Barnsley Station SB	Open before	16.8.1877
Replacement box	Opened	12.11.1905
***	Closed	19.4.1960
BARNSLEY	OP	2.5.1870
Altered to BARNSLEY COURT HOUSE	After	7.1912
***	CP	19.4.1960

The station buildings were jointly owned, but the two main running lines were the property of the Midland Railway.

BARNSLEY COURT HOUSE GOODS DEPOT	Opened	28.6.1869
***	Closed	31.1.1966
Barnsley to Cockram Road Jcn (Court House Jcn)	OG	1.4.1870
***	OP	1.8.1870
***	CP	7.12.1959

Between Barnsley and Manchester the Midland Railway possessed running powers over the Great Central line for all traffic, for traffic between stations in Yorkshire and on the North Eastern Railway and beyond and Lancashire and Cheshire.

Between Cockram Road Junction and Leeds, and on the Bradford, Ilkley, and Skipton branches the Manchester, Sheffield & Lincolnshire Railway possessed running powers for all traffic over the Midland line.

Barnsley engine shed	Opened	....
***	Closed	....
Barnsley Goods Yard SB	Open before	16.8.1877
Replacement box	Opened	29.11.1891
***	Closed	21.10.1962
Barnsley Goods Yard to Court House Junction: block telegraph working	Commenced	29.11.1891
Court House Goods Yard to Court House Jcn	Closed	31.1.1966
Court House Junction SB	Opened	....
***	Closed	24.9.1972
Cockram Road Junction with the Manchester, Sheffield & Lincolnshire	Opened	1.4.1870

WEST RIDING LINES

Powers: Midland Railway (West Riding Lines) Act 1898
Midland Railway Act 1903 (Dewsbury Goods Branch)

Royston Jcn to Crigglestone	OG	3.7.1905
Royston Jcn: normal double junction brought into use	... ...	28.4.1907
Royston Jcn to Dewsbury Goods Branch Jcn: up line temporarily taken out of use	By	16.10.1907
Double-line working restored	... ...	....
Royston Jcn to Thornhill (later Middlestown) Jcn	OP	1.7.1909
The Lancashire & Yorkshire company provided this passenger service with through trains. The intermediate stations were never opened for passenger traffic.		
Royston Jcn to Crigglestone East: permissive block working on up line	Commenced	30.12.1956
This section of the line	Closed	4.5.1968
Crigglestone Station SB	Opened	28.6.1909
***	Closed	4.5.1968 ?
CRIGGLESTONE	OG	1.3.1906
Altered to CRIGGLESTONE EAST	... ...	2.6.1924 ?
***	CG	10.2.1964
Crigglestone to Thornhill	OG	10.11.1905
Crigglestone to Middlestown Jcn: single-line working	Intro. by	25.4.1917
Double-line working	Restored	18.4.1921
Crigglestone East to Middlestown Jcn	Closed	1.8.1968
MIDDLESTOWN (FOR HORBURY)	OG	1.3.1906
***	CG	29.3.1937
The authority for the use of the suffix with this name is uncertain.		
Middlestown Station SB	Opened	28.6.1909
***	Closed	8.12.1938
Thornhill Junction SB	Opened	28.6.1909
Re-named Middlestown Junction SB	... ...	12.7.1909
***	Closed	4.5.1968 ?
Between Thornhill (Middlestown) Junction and Sheffield the Lancashire & Yorkshire Railway possessed running powers over the Midland line.		

Thornhill Junction Line to the Lancashire & Yorkshire Railway

Powers: Midland Railway Act 1899

Thornhill Jcn to Thornhill Midland Jcn	OP	1.7.1909
***	OG	6.3.1911
***	CP	1.1.1917
***	RO(P)	3.5.1920
***	CP	16.6.1947
***	RO(P)	4.1.1960
***	CP	13.6.1960
***	Closed	1.8.1968
Between Thornhill Junction and Mirfield Junction the Midland possessed running powers over the Lancashire & Yorkshire line.		

Thornhill to Dewsbury Goods Station Branch Jcn	OG	22.1.1906
Middlestown Jcn to Dewsbury Savile Town Goods Depot	Closed	18.12.1950
***	t.o.u.	14.10.1956
DEWSBURY (SAVILE TOWN)	OG	1.3.1906
***	CG	18.12.1950
The authority for the use of the suffix with this name is uncertain.		

Huddersfield Branch

Powers: Midland Railway Act 1899
Midland Railway Act 1906 (Huddersfield Railway Deviation)

Between Mirfield Junction and Huddersfield the Lancashire & Yorkshire Railway possessed running powers over the Midland line. Between Mirfield Junction and Halifax the Midland Railway possessed running powers over the Lancashire & Yorkshire line.

Mirfield No. 2 SB (Lancashire & Yorkshire Railway) to Huddersfield	OG	1.11.1910
Mirfield No. 2 SB to Red Doles Jcn	Closed	12.8.1937

Huddersfield: Red Doles Jcn with the former London & North Western line	OG	1.10.1923
Red Doles Jcn to Huddersfield New Town Goods Depot	Closed	5.8.1968
HUDDERSFIELD NEWTOWN GOODS DEPOT	Opened	1.11.1910
***	Closed	5.8.1968

TINSLEY PARK COLLIERY BRANCH (SHEFFIELD DISTRICT & MIDLAND)

Powers: Sheffield District Railway Act 1906

Tinsley Park Colliery branch	OM	20.11.1903
Tinsley Park Colliery branch made joint between the Midland and Great Central Railways	... ...	1906

Hadfield's Works Branch

Powers: --

Hadfield's Works branch	Opened	1903
***	Closed	....

SWINTON & KNOTTINGLEY JOINT RAILWAY (Midland & North Eastern)

Powers: Midland and North Eastern Railways Act 1874

The Manchester, Sheffield & Lincolnshire Railway possessed running powers for all traffic over the main line of the Swinton & Knottingley Joint Railway and over its branches.

Wath Road Jcn to Ferry Bridge Jcn	O thro' G&M	19.5.1879
***	OP	1.7.1879
***	OG	28.7.1879

Working was by the block telegraph system from the opening.

Wath East Curve from the Manchester, Sheffield & Lincolnshire Railway

Powers: Midland and North Eastern Railways Act 1875

Mexborough West Jcn to Dearne Jcn	OP	1.8.1879 *
***	OM	1.10.1879 *
***	CM	1.9.1882 *
***	RO(G)	13.3.1899 ?
***	t.o.u.	4.4.1965
***	CP(All)	5.4.1965

Wath West Curve

This was a Manchester, Sheffield & Lincolnshire Railway, Midland Railway, and North Eastern Railway Joint Line.

Powers: Manchester, Sheffield and Lincolnshire Railway Act 1875

Bolton-on-Dearne: junction with line to the Manchester, Sheffield & Lincolnshire Railway	Made ready	5.6.1882
***	Approved	8.7.1882
Wath Jcn to Dearne Jcn	OG	8.1882 ?
***	OP	1.4.1901 ?
***	CP	....
***	Singled	10.5.1981
Curve severed at the western end and made Manvers Colliery Branch	w/e	29.7.1988

Dearne Junction SB	Opened	19.5.1879
Replacement box	Opened	19.11.1905
***	Closed	3.5.1981
HICKLETON	OP	1.7.1879
***	OG	28.7.1879
Altered to BOLTON-ON-DEARNE	... ...	1.11.1879
Altered to BOLTON-ON-DEARNE FOR GOLDTHORPE	... ...	15.1.1924
Altered to BOLTON-ON-DEARNE	... ...	....
***	CG	5.9.1966
Hickleton Station SB	Opened	19.5.1879
Re-named Bolton-on-Dearne Station SB	... ...	1.7.1879
***	Re-framed	6.12.1896
Replacement box	Opened	10.7.1904
***	Closed	21.2.1967
GOLDTHORPE	OP	16.5.1988
Hickleton South Jcn with the Dearne Valley Railway	OG	13.3.1905
***	Closed	11.7.1966
New connection to the Dearne Valley line for access to Goldthorpe Colliery	Into use	14.5.1978
Hickleton Main South SB	Opened	19.5.1895
Replacement box on new site	Opened	29.11.1903
***	Closed	19.4.1931
Hickleton Main South to Hickleton Main Colliery Empty Wagon Sidings: replacement running line on the north side of the existing one	Into use	9.4.1906

Hickleton Main Colliery Sidings SB: new box 200 yards north of former South box	Opened	19.4.1931	
Re-named Hickleton SB	... ...	3.5.1981	
Hickleton SB	Closed	....	
Hickleton Main North SB	Opened	19.5.1895	
***	Closed	19.4.1931	
Between Hickleton South Junction and Frickley Colliery the Lancashire & Yorkshire Railway possessed running powers over the Midland line.			
THURNSCOE	OP	16.5.1988	
Lidgett Lane SB	Opened	19.5.1879	
***	Closed	1882	
CLAYTON	OP	1.7.1879	
***	OG	28.7.1879	
Altered to FRICKLEY	... ...	1.11.1882	
***	CP	8.6.1953	
***	CG	30.9.1963	
Clayton Station SB	Opened	19.5.1879	
Re-named Frickley Station SB	... ...	1.11.1882	
***	Re-framed	26.4.1896	
Replacement box	Opened	20.12.1903	
***	Closed	3.5.1964	
Frickley Colliery Sidings SB	Opened	8.7.1901	
***	Closed	27.2.1977	
Frickley Colliery Sidings to Moorthorpe South: 5 new sidings	Into use	15.11.1908	
***	t.o.u.	....	
Moorthorpe South SB	Opened	19.5.1879	
Replacement box	Opened	8.11.1908	
Re-named Moorthorpe SB	... ...	15.4.1984	
Moorthorpe South to Moorthorpe Station: alteration of the position of the up and down main lines	... ...	20.9.1908	
Up and down goods loops	Into use	8.11.1908	
MOORTHORPE	OP	1.7.1879	
***	OG	28.7.1879	
Altered to MOORTHORPE & SOUTH KIRKBY	... ...	1.7.1902	
Altered to MOORTHORPE	... ...	12.6.1961	
***	CG	10.2.1964	
Moorthorpe Station Junction SB	Opened	19.5.1979	
Replacement box	Opened	1.11.1908	
***	Closed	25.3.1979	

Moorthorpe West Curve to the West Riding & Grimsby Joint Line

Powers: Midland and North Eastern Railways Act 1875

Moorthorpe Jcn to South Kirkby Jcn	OP	1.8.1879	
***	OM	1.10.1879	*
***	CM	1.9.1882	
***	OG	1.6.1884	*
***	CP	1.5.1918	
***	RO(P)	1.5.1967	
***	CP	7.5.1973	
***	RO(P)	4.10.1982	
South Kirkby Colliery Sidings SB	Opened	....	
***	Closed	17.5.1931	

Moorthorpe East Curve from the West Riding & Grimsby Joint Line

South Elmsall Jcn to Moorthorpe North Jcn	OP	1.7.1879	
***	OG	1.5.1888	?
***	CP	1.1.1917	*
***	CG(All)	2.1928	
South Elmsall Junction re-named Moorthorpe North Junction	... ...	1.5.1882	*
Moorthorpe North Junction SB	Opened	....	
Replacement box	Opened	22.11.1914	
***	Closed	18.12.1961	
Moorthorpe North Jcn: Hull & Barnsley Railway east curve	Complete by	11.8.1884	
***	Lifted	c.1899	
The rails were laid, but the points and signals were never put in.			
Royd Moor SB	Re-opened	9.10.1907	
***	Closed	1926	
Brackenhill Junction SB	Opened	1.7.1914	
***	Closed	3.4.1966	

Brackenhill Light Railway (Independent company)

Powers: Light Railway Order of 19 March 1901

Brackenhill Jcn to Hemsworth Colliery, and branch to ACKWORTH MOOR TOP GOODS DEPOT	OG	1.7.1914	
Brackenhill Light Railway	Closed	1.1.1962	

ACKWORTH	OP	1.7.1879	
***	OG	28.7.1879	
***	CP	2.7.1951	
***	CG	1.8.1955	

Ackworth Station SB	Opened	1879
Replacement box	Opened	....
***	Closed	11.3.1956
Pontefract South SB: replacement box	Opened	....
***	Closed	14.1.1979
PONTEFRACT	OP	1.7.1879
***	OG	27.7.1879
Altered to PONTEFRACT BAGHILL	... ...	1.12.1936
***	CG	2.11.1964
Up bay	t.o.u.	28.7.1974

Between Pontefract station and Pontefract Junction the Lancashire & Yorkshire Railway possessed running powers over the Midland & North Eastern Joint line.

Pontefract Junction SB: replacement box	Opened	....
***	Closed	6.12.1959

Monk Hill Curve to the Lancashire & Yorkshire Railway

Powers: Midland and North Eastern Railways Act 1875

Pontefract Jcn to Pontefract (East) Jcn	OP	1.4.1880
***	OG	3.2.1890
***	CP	1.11.1926
***	t.o.u.	12.1.1957
***	Singled	....
***	Into use	6.12.1959
***	RO(P)	4.1.1960
***	CP(All)	2.11.1964

Ferrybridge West Curve

Powers: British Railways Act 1963

Pontefract (Monk Hill) East Jcn to Ferrybridge Jcn	Laid in	2.5.1965
***	OG	26.7.1965
***	Singled	8.11.1981

Ferry Bridge Junction SB	Opened	....
Replacement box 610 yards to the north	Opened	13.5.1956
***	Closed	....
FERRY BRIDGE	OP&G	1.5.1882
Altered to FERRYBRIDGE	... ...	1.7.1882 *
Altered to FERRYBRIDGE FOR KNOTTINGLEY	... ...	1.6.1901
***	CG	27.4.1964
***	CP	13.9.1965

W E S T & N O R T H O F L E E D S

LEEDS & BRADFORD RAILWAY

The Leeds & Bradford Railway was leased by the Midland Railway with effect from 1 July 1846 under powers contained in the Leeds and Bradford Railway (Shipley to Colne etc.) Act 1845. The company was acquired by the Midland and dissolved under the Midland Railway (Leeds and Bradford Railway) Act 1851 with effect from 4 October 1852.

Powers: Leeds and Bradford Railway Act 1844
Midland Railway Act 1891 (Widening at Leeds)
Midland Railway Act 1902 (Whitehall Junction & Holbeck Widening)
Midland Railway (Additional Powers) Act 1873 (Holbeck Connecting Line)
Midland Railway Act 1903 (Armley & Calverley Widening)
Midland Railway Act 1898 (Thackley Widening)
Midland Railway (Additional Powers) Act 1871
(Frizinghall & Manningham Widening - Land Powers only)
Midland Railway (Additional Powers) Acts 1863, 1873, 1874, and 1882
(Manningham to Bradford Widening - Land Powers only)
Midland Railway Act 1911 (Manningham to Low Moor: part of the land had been purchased under powers of the Midland Railway (West Riding Lines) Act 1898

Leeds (Wellington) to Bradford	O.Formal	30.6.1846
***	OP	1.7.1846
***	OG	7.9.1846 ?
LEEDS WELLINGTON: temporary station	Opened	1.7.1846
***	Closed	30.9.1850
Permanent station	Opened	1.10.1850
Midland Railway took over refreshment room	... ...	3.8.1863
Additional platform on south side	Into use	10.11.1872
Luncheon stops by Scotch expresses	Ceased	1.5.1896 *
Extension of platforms Nos. 1 and 2 apparently complete	By	15.1.1919
Combined with LEEDS NEW to form LEEDS CITY	... ...	2.5.1938
WELLINGTON section of LEEDS CITY	CP	13.6.1966
LEEDS WELLINGTON STREET GOODS STATION altered to LEEDS WELLINGTON STREET SOUTH GOODS STATION	By	6.4.1951
Leeds: Queen's Hotel	Opened	10.1.1863
New wing	Opened	28.3.1867
Replacement hotel	Opened	12.11.1937
***	Sold	....

Between Wellington station, Leeds Junction, and Holbeck Junction the North Eastern Railway possessed running powers for passenger traffic over the Midland line.
Between Leeds and Bradford and Colne Junction the Lancashire & Yorkshire Railway possessed running powers over the Midland line.
Between Leeds and Colne and Petteril Junction the North British Railway possessed running powers over the Midland line.

Leeds Bell Box	Open before	1868
***	Closed	1872
Leeds Passenger Station SB	Opened	1881
Replacement box	Opened	10.11.1918
***	Closed	11.9.1966
Leeds Power Signal Box	Opened	1.5.1967
Leeds No. 1 SB	Opened	1872
***	Closed	1881
Leeds No. 2 SB	Opened	1872
***	Closed	1881
LEEDS TICKET PLATFORM	Closed	....
Leeds to Manningham: block telegraph working	Introduced	Mid-1860s
Leeds to Leeds Jcn (east of): two additional passenger lines	Into use	6.1881-4.1883

Spur to the London & North Western and North Eastern Joint Line

Powers: --

Leeds Jcn to Canal Jcn	Opened	1.4.1869
Marsh Lane to Gelderd Road via Whitehall Jcn: OLE	Energised	4.7.1988
Leeds Junction SB	Open before	1857
Replacement box	Opened	....
Replacement box	Opened	30.8.1908
Replacement box	Opened	19.6.1927
***	Closed	29.4.1967

Between Leeds Junction and Wortley Junction the London & North Western possessed running powers over the Midland line for merchandise traffic.
Between Leeds Junction and Wortley Junction the North Eastern possessed running powers for all traffic over the Midland line.
Between Leeds Junction and Armley station and Armley Bridge Sidings the North Eastern possessed running powers for goods, coal, coke, and livestock traffic over the Midland line.

Between Leeds Junction and Aire Side Iron Works (later the Leeds Steel Works), and between Holbeck Junction and the iron works, the North Eastern possessed running powers over the Midland line for coal and coke traffic.
Between Leeds Junction and Bradford the North Eastern possessed running powers for coaching traffic over the Midland line.
Between Leeds Junction and Neville Hill Sidings the Midland possessed running powers for goods, coal, coke, and cattle traffic over the North Eastern line.

Hunslet to Leeds Wellington
Powers: Leeds and Bradford Railway Act 1844

Hunslet Goods Jcn to Leeds Jcn	OP by	3.1849
***	OG	7.9.1846
Hunslet Goods Jcn to Leeds Jcn: block telegraph working	Intro. by	1868
Hunslet Goods Jcn to Engine Shed Jcn: down goods line	Into use	24.5.1903
Up goods line	Into use	15.11.1903
Down goods line made down slow line	... ...	27.9.1903
Down slow line made down goods line	... ...	16.2.1908
Down goods line made down slow line	... ...	28.6.1908
Down slow line made down goods line	... ...	4.10.1908
Up goods line	t.o.u.	3.7.1983
Holbeck engine shed	Opened	1840
Additional shed	Into use	1848
Replacement shed	Into use	1866
***	Closed	30.9.1967
Holbeck MPD	Remodelled	30.10.1983
Engine Shed Junction SB	Open before	16.8.1877
Replacement box	Opened	20.8.1893
Replacement box	Opened	20.9.1903
***	Re-framed	....
***	Closed	1.6.1969
Engine Shed Jcn replaced Water Lane Jcn as the point of divergence for the Whitehall curve	... ...	17.9.1893
Engine Shed Jcn: remodelled with single leads	... ...	24.10.1983
Water Lane Junction SB	Opened	1868
Replacement box	Opened	....
Replacement box named Water Lane SB	Opened	17.9.1893
***	Closed	10.8.1930

Whitehall Curve
Powers: Leeds and Bradford Railway Act 1844

Water Lane Jcn to Whitehall Jcn	OG	7.9.1846
***	OP (GNR)	1.10.1849
***	CP (GNR)	1.11.1857
***	OP	....
***	CP	1.7.1903 *
Water Lane Jcn to Whitehall Jcn: block telegraph working	Intro. by	1868
Engine Shed Jcn to Whitehall Jcn	Singled	14.6.1987

(The former down line was made into a new connection to the Whitehall Goods Yard.)
The Whitehall Curve was used on summer Saturdays by passenger trains in many later years.

Monk Bridge Ironworks Branch
Powers: --

Branch to Monk Bridge Ironworks	Opened	....
***	Closed	....

Leeds Jcn: up and down fast lines through the junction	Into use	19.6.1927

From Leeds to just south of Armley Canal Junction the fast lines were on the up side, crossing at that point above the slow lines to continue on the down side to Shipley.

Leeds Jcn to Whitehall Jcn: up and down slow lines (down side)	Into use	27.9.1908
Whitehall Jcn: double junction (DSL-DFL, UFL-USL)	Into use	27.9.1908
Whitehall Junction SB	Open before	1857
Replacement box	Opened	....
Replacement box	Opened	1878
Replacement box	Opened	27.8.1893
Replacement box	Opened	27.9.1908
***	Closed	29.4.1967
Whitehall Jcn: crossovers and signalling	Altered	20.9.1903
Position of main lines	Altered	5.7.1908
Whitehall Jcn: junction with the London & North Western Railway	Opened	1.10.1850
Layout of the London & North Western junction altered	... ...	26.4.1908
Junction with the former London & North Western line restored	... ...	....

The junction with the line to Farnley was considerably altered in the course of the concentration of all passenger traffic on Leeds City station. The powers for the various works were taken under the British Transport Commission Act 1960.
Between Whitehall Junction and Three Signal Bridge Junction the Midland possessed running powers over the London & North Western line.

Between Three Signal Bridge Junction and Wellington Street Goods Depot the Midland Railway possessed running powers over the joint London & North Western and Lancashire & Yorkshire line.
The Midland also possessed running powers over the London & North Western line between Copley Hill Junction and Copley Hill station for merchandise traffic, and between that station and the cattle market for livestock traffic.
Between Whitehall Junction and Wortley Junction the North Eastern possessed running powers for goods trains between Copley Hill and Geldard Junction to be exercised only in the case of necessity.

Whitehall Jcn: double junction (DFL-DSL, USL-UFL)	Into use	4.10.1908
Layout remodelled with single leads	... ...	13-14.6.1987
Whitehall Jcn to Wortley Jcn: two additional passenger lines	Into use	19.5.1878
Pairing by use	Introduced	27.9.1908
Holbeck Jcn with the Leeds & Thirsk Railway	O.Formal	9.7.1849
***	OP	10.7.1849
***	OG	....
HOLBECK (Midland & North Eastern joint station)	OP	2.6.1862
Joint staff appointed	... ...	1.11.1898
Altered to HOLBECK LOW LEVEL	... ...	2.3.1951
***	CP	7.7.1958
Gelderd Jcn re-named Leeds Holbeck Jcn	... ...	1875

Spur to the North Eastern Railway

Powers: --

Gelderd Jcn to New Wortley Jcn	Opened by	1.1877
Leeds Northern SB	Opened	1877
***	Closed	1878
Wortley Junction SB	Open before	1872
Replacement box	Opened	23.12.1877
Replacement box	Opened	7.2.1909
***	Closed	29.4.1967
Wortley Jcn with the North Eastern Railway	Opened	1862
Double junction connecting the down slow line to the North Eastern line and the North Eastern line to the up slow line	Into use	25.4.1909
Double junction (DSL-DFL, UFL-USL)	Into use	25.4.1909
Double junction taken out of use and replaced by two double junctions near the site of Armley SB (ex-North Eastern line)	... ...	1967
Double junction DSL-DFL, UFL-USL	t.o.u.	5.3.1988

The 1862 junction replaced Holbeck Junction when the Holbeck joint station was built.
Between Wortley Junction and Armley North Eastern Sidings, and between Wortley Junction and Wellington Street Goods Station (over the North Eastern & Great Northern Joint line) the Midland possessed running powers for the exchange of through goods traffic with the North Eastern and Great Northern companies. The Midland company was also allowed to use the North Eastern line between Wortley Junction and Armley Junction to obtain access to the Great Northern's Wellington Street Goods Yard.

Wortley Jcn to Armley Station Jcn: up and down slow lines (down side)	Into use	25.4.1909
West of Wortley Jcn (point of slue into the Harrogate line) to Kirkstall Jcn: up and down fast lines	Abandoned	12.3.1967
Armley Bridge Sidings SB	Open before	16.8.1877
***	Closed	25.4.1909
Armley Jcn with the North Eastern Railway	Opened	....
ARMLEY EXCHANGE SIDINGS	Opened	18.11.1889
Closed for exchange, but continuing in use as sidings	... ...	4.3.1907
Sidings removed	... ...	1967

On the opening of Armley Exchange Sidings the exchange of goods traffic with the North Eastern Railway at Wortley Sidings ceased.

Armley Station SB	Open before	16.8.1877
Re-named Armley Station Junction SB	... ...	....
Replacement box	Opened	16.6.1901
***	Raised	20.6.1920
Replacement box	Opened	25.4.1909
Re-named Armley Canal Road No. 1 SB	... ...	5.1953
***	Closed	23.4.1967
Armley Station Jcn: double junction (DFL-DSL, USL-UFL)	Into use	....
Armley Station Jcn to Kirkstall Jcn: up and down fast lines	Into use	29.5.1910

Leeds Forge Company's Branch

Powers: --

Leeds Forge Company's Branch	Opened	1892
Working by staff without tickets	Commenced	19.9.1892
New connections	Into use	25.10.1909
***	Closed	2.12.1963 ?
ARMLEY	Opened	9.1847
Altered to ARMLEY CANAL ROAD	... ...	25.9.1950
***	CG	2.12.1963
***	CP	22.3.1965

Armley: position of the up main line at the station	Altered	19.9.1909
Position of the down main line on the north side of the station	Altered	26.9.1909
Armley Cutting SB	Opened	3.2.1908
***	Closed	30.5.1909
Armley Canal Junction SB	Opened	1.12.1889
Replacement box	Opened	20.10.1907
***	Re-framed	3.4.1910
Re-named Armley Canal Road No. 2 SB	... ...	5.1953
***	Closed	23.4.1967
Armley Canal Jcn to Kirkstall: up goods line	Into use	1.12.1889
Down goods line	Into use	8.12.1889
Redcote Lane bridge: Armley Canal Jcn moved west to this point	... ...	20.10.1907
Redcote Lane bridge to Kirkstall Jcn: second up goods line	Into use	20.10.1907
Armley Canal Jcn to Kirkstall Jcn: pairing by use of passenger lines with down and first up goods lines	Completed	24.4.1910
First up goods line	t.o.u.	3.4.1910
Replacement first up goods line	Into use	24.4.1910
***	t.o.u.	23.4.1967
Armley Canal Road No. 2 to Kirkstall Jcn: down goods line and second up goods line made down and up goods loops	... ...	1.5.1967
Kirkstall Station SB	Open before	1875
Replacement box named Kirkstall Station Junction SB	Opened	8.12.1889
***	Re-framed	25.7.1897
Replacement box	Opened	24.4.1910
Re-named Kirkstall Junction SB	... ...	....
***	Closed	....
Kirkstall Jcn: double junction (DGL-DFL, UFL-UGL)	Into use	29.5.1910
Kirkstall Jcn to Newlay: position of main lines	Altered	30.4.1905
Up slow line	Into use	4.3.1906
Down slow line (up side)	Into use	26.8.1906
Kirkstall Jcn: down sidings	t.o.u.	18.2.1973
Kirkstall Jcn to Apperley Jcn: up and down fast lines	Abandoned	23.4.1967
KIRKSTALL	Opened	16-30.7.1846
Replacement station	Opened	9.7.1905
***	CP	22.3.1965
***	CG	5.10.1970
KIRKSTALL FORGE	OG before	1.10.1853 *
***	OP	1.7.1860
***	CP	1.8.1905
***	CG	1959
There is some evidence to suggest a brief earlier opening of this station for passenger traffic, in February and March 1852.		
Kirkstall Forge to Newlay: position of main lines	Altered	2.4.1905
Kirkstall Forge: main lines placed in their permanent position	... ...	1.10.1905
Kirkstall Forge SB (first box)	Open before	1.11.1875
Replacement box	Opened	16.7.1893
Kirkstall Forge SB (second box)	Opened	15.10.1905
***	Closed	26.8.1906
Kirkstall Forge SB (third box)	Opened	28.3.1909
***	Closed	13.6.1909
Newlay South Sidings SB	Open before	16.8.1877
Replacement box	Opened	1.10.1893
Replacement box named Newlay Station SB	Opened	21.8.1904
***	Re-framed	20.5.1962
***	Closed	16.8.1976
Newlay (south) to Calverley Jcn: up and down slow lines (up side)	Into use	21.8.1904
NEWLAY	Opened	1.9.1846
Altered to NEWLAY FOR HORSFORTH	... ...	1.4.1875 *
Altered to NEWLAY & HORSFORTH	... ...	4.10.1889
Altered to NEWLAY	... ...	12.6.1961
***	CG	30.9.1963
***	CP	22.3.1965
Newlay Station SB	Open before	16.8.1877
Replacement box	Opened	20.10.1895
***	Closed	21.8.1904
Newlay North SB	Opened	17.11.1902
***	Closed	21.8.1904
Laithes Tunnel SB	Opened	7.4.1903
***	Closed	27.6.1903 ?
Calverley & Rodley Station SB	Open before	16.8.1877
***	Re-framed	16.6.1895
Replacement box	Opened	21.8.1904 ?
***	Re-framed	22.11.1959
***	Closed	9.3.1969
CALVERLEY	Opened	16-30.7.1846
Altered to CALVERLEY & RODLEY	... ...	1.10.1889
***	CP	22.3.1965
***	CG	7.10.1968
Calverley: fast lines near to the old Calverley Junction	Slued	28.8.1904

Calverley Junction SB	Opened	4.10.1896
Replacement box	Opened	11.8.1901
***	Alt.levers	17.11.1902
***	Closed	21.8.1904
Calverley (north) to Apperley Jcn: up and down slow lines	Into use	4.10.1896
Calverley Jcn to Apperley Jcn: position of lines	Altered	20.10.1901
Calverley Jcn to Leeds Jcn (Shipley)	Inspected	9.2.1902
Apperley Jcn: double junction (DFL-DSL, USL-UFL)	Into use	21.8.1904
Apperley Junction SB	Open before	1866
Replacement box	Opened	....
Replacement box	Opened	4.10.1896
Replacement box	Opened	27.11.1927
***	Closed	....
Apperley Jcn: layout at junction	Altered	10.11.1901
Single leads junction	Into use	14.11.1976

Otley & Ilkley Extension line

See page 168

Apperley Jcn to Apperley: down goods line	Into use	1897
Apperley Jcn to Guiseley Jcn: quadrupling completed and pairing by use of the fast lines and slow lines introduced	... ...	17.11.1901
Apperley Jcn to Thackley Jcn: up and down fast lines	Abandoned	12.3.1967
Apperley Bridge SB	Open before	16.8.1877
Re-named Apperley Bridge & Rawdon SB	... ...	....
Replacement box	Opened	6.10.1901
***	Closed	15.12.1968
APPERLEY BRIDGE	Opened	16-30.7.1846
Altered to APPERLEY	... ...	Late 1847
Altered to APPERLEY & RAWDON	Passenger	1.10.1890
***	Goods	24.12.1890
Altered to APPERLEY BRIDGE & RAWDON	... ...	1.5.1893 *
Altered to APPERLEY BRIDGE	... ...	12.6.1961
***	CG	1.6.1964
***	CP	22.3.1965
Apperley Bridge North SB	Opened	4.6.1899
***	Closed	17.11.1901
Apperley Bridge North SB to Thackley Jcn: up goods line (through the Thackley new tunnel)	Into use	27.1.1901
Apperley Viaduct SB	Opened	14.6.1908
***	Closed	29.6.1908
Apperley Viaduct SB	Opened	6.3.1910
***	Closed	10.10.1976
Apperley viaduct	Fell	16.11.1866
***	Re-opened	1.1.1867
Thackley Tunnel SB	Opened	6.11.1898
***	Closed	2.2.1902
***	Demolished	30.7.1905
Thackley new tunnel	Opened	1.1.1901
Thackley Sidings SB	Open before	16.8.1877
Re-named Thackley Junction SB	... ...	c.11.1881
Replacement box	Opened	3.12.1893
Replacement box	Opened	28.10.1900
***	Closed	8.1.1984
Thackley Jcn: up goods line to up passenger line crossover	Into use	27.1.1901
Down fast line to down slow line crossover	Removed	24.5.1908
Down slow line to down fast line crossover	Into use	31.5.1908
New junction from down main line to down fast line	Into use	12.3.1967
Thackley Jcn to Guiseley Jcn: up goods line	Into use	14.11.1881
Down goods line	Into use	12.12.1881
Down slow line taken out of use until further notice	... ...	1.2.1981
Former down slow line re-instated as down main line	... ...	15.3.1981
Up and down fast lines	t.o.u.	15.3.1981
Former down fast line re-instated as down loop line	... ...	12.4.1981
Down loop line	t.o.u.	27.9.1982
***	Abolished	30.1.1983
IDLE	OP by	1.9.1847 *
***	CP(All)	1.10.1848 *
Guiseley Junction SB	Opened	1876 ?
Replacement box	Opened	1.11.1891
Replacement box	Opened	23.6.1901
***	Closed	....

Between Guiseley Junction and Bradford the North Eastern Railway possessed running powers for alltraffic over the Midland line.

Shipley & Guiseley line

See page 169

Guiseley Jcn: double junction (DSL-DFL, UFL-USL)	Opened	....
Guiseley Jcn to Leeds Jcn: up and down slow lines	Into use	24.11.1901
***	t.o.u.	11.5.1975

Guiseley Jcn to Bingley Jcn: down main line made bi-directional	... ...	9.3.1980
Leeds Junction SB	Opened	1867
Replacement box	Opened	c.1874 ?
Replacement box	Opened	17.11.1901
***	Closed	20.7.1975
Leeds Jcn: double junction (DFL-DSL, USL-UFL)	Into use	1.12.1901
Shipley: junction with the Great Northern Railway	Opened	1.11.1875
***	t.o.u.	22.6.1969
Leeds Jcn to Bradford Jcn: up and down goods lines (down side)	Into use	7.2.1904
***	t.o.u.	22.6.1969
SHIPLEY	Opened by	16.7.1846
Replacement station about 1/8 mile to the north	Opened	1871-1873
Goods station altered to SHIPLEY TOWN GOODS STATION	By	6.4.1951
***	CG	1.9.1980
Bradford Junction SB	Open before	16.8.1877
Replacement box	Opened	27.9.1903
***	Re-framed	....
Panel added on the block shelf to work Forster Square station	... ...	21.10.1984
Bradford Jcn: double junction (DPL-DGL, UGL-UPL)	Into use	....
Through goods siding	In use by	1.7.1870 *
Bradford Jcn to Manningham Station: up and down goods lines	t.o.u.	24.5.1970
Shipley South Sidings SB to Manningham: down goods line	Into use	20.8.1876
Up goods line (down side)	Into use	3.12.1876
Shipley Goods Sidings SB	Open before	16.8.1877
***	Re-framed	1.11.1896
Replacement box	Opened	9.8.1903
***	Closed	3.9.1972
Frizinghall Station SB	Open before	16.8.1877
Replacement box	Opened	9.12.1906
***	Closed	24.5.1970
FRIZINGHALL	OP	1.2.1875
***	OG	22.5.1882
***	CP	22.3.1965
***	CG	6.7.1970
***	RO(P)	7.9.1987
Manningham Sidings SB	Open before	16.8.1877
Replacement box	Opened	14.11.1886
Replacement box	Opened	27.8.1916
***	Burnt out	23.2.1969
Manningham Sidings to Manningham Station: up goods line	Into use	11.1875-10.1876
Engine Shed Sidings SB	Opened	c.9.1886
Replacement box	Opened	30.6.1889
Replacement box	Opened	19.2.1899
***	Closed	4.4.1932
Manningham engine shed	Opened	1872
Additional shed	Opened	1888
***	Closed	30.4.1967
This shed replaced an earlier one at Bradford, opened in about 1853.		
Manningham Station SB	Open before	16.8.1877
***	Closed	30.6.1889
Manningham: up and down goods lines past the station (down side)	Into use	6.1881-4.1883
Manningham to Bradford: up and down goods lines	t.o.u.	24.5.1970
MANNINGHAM	OP	17.2.1868 *
***	OG	....
***	CP	22.3.1965
***	CG	7.10.1968
Manningham to Bradford No. 2 SB: block telegraph working	Introduced	1877
Manningham to Bradford Yard: down goods line	In use by	1.1.1872 *
Manningham Station Jcn: double junction (DGL-DPL, UPL-UGL)	Into use	30.6.1889
Manningham Station Jcn to Bradford: up and down goods lines	Into use	10.1876-8.1877
Manningham Station Junction SB	Opened	7.7.1889
***	Re-framed	....
***	Closed	21.10.1984
Manningham Station Jcn: arrival line	t.o.u.	19.2.1976
Manningham Station Jcn: Frizinghall siding, arrival line, and middle line abolished and new Valley arrival & departure line brought into use	... ... or	26.10.1980 ? 9.11.1980 ?
Manningham Station Jcn to Bradford Forster Square: west departure line taken out of use and east departure line re-named up main line	... ...	5.10.1980
East arrival line taken out of use and west arrival line re-named down main line	... ...	19.10.1980
Manningham Temporary Passenger SB	Opened	30.6.1889
***	Closed	7.7.1889
Manningham Temporary Goods SB	Opened	30.6.1889
***	Closed	7.7.1889
Manningham Passenger Lines Jcn to Bradford: two additional passenger lines	Into use	12.1888-8.1893
Manningham Passenger Lines Jcn to Bradford new station: working by train staff without tickets	Commenced	2.9.1889

Bradford Passenger Station SB	Opened	2.3.1890
***	Re-framed	1920
Re-named Bradford Forster Square SB	... ...	....
***	Re-framed	1943
Box closed, running lines brought under control of Shipley Bradford Junction SB, and a ground frame provided	... ...	21.10.1984
BRADFORD	OP	2.3.1890
Altered to BRADFORD FORSTER SQUARE	... ...	2.6.1924
Both the remaining platform lines and the siding shortened	... ...	13.1.1985
Bradford: Midland Hotel	Opened	1.7.1890
***	Sold	....
Bradford No. 3 SB	Open before	16.8.1877
Re-named Bradford Goods Yard SB	... ...	10.5.1890
***	Re-framed	30.6.1895
Replacement box	Opened	7.10.1906
***	Re-framed	21.2.1954
Box closed and ground frame provided in lieu	... ...	28.6.1961
***	t.o.u.	10.4.1976
TRAFALGAR STREET GOODS DEPOT	Opened	1877-1893
Amalgamated with VALLEY GOODS DEPOT	... ...	22.10.1962
***	CG&Coal	6.8.1984
Trafalgar Street Crossing SB	Opened	30.6.1895
***	Closed	1937 ?
Bradford No. 2 SB	Open before	16.8.1877
***	Closed	2.3.1890
From Bradford No. 2 SB into the station remained station-yard working until the opening of the new passenger station.		
VALLEY GOODS DEPOT	Open before	....
BRADFORD: new goods shed	Opened	1893
Bradford No. 1 SB	Open before	16.8.1877
***	Closed	2.3.1890
BRADFORD MARKET STREET	Opened	1.7.1846
***	Closed	2.3.1890

APPERLEY JUNCTION TO SKIPTON VIA ILKLEY

Otley & Ilkley Extension line

Powers: Midland Railway (Otley and Ilkley Extension) Act 1861

Apperley Jcn to Burley Jcn	OP	1.8.1865
Apperley Jcn to Menston Jcn	OG	1.10.1866
Apperley Jcn to Ilkley: block telegraph working	Intro. by	1873
Apperley Jcn to Guiseley	Singled	20.2.1983
Esholt Junction SB	Opened	1876 ?
Replacement box	Opened	15.10.1899
***	Closed	27.2.1983

Between Esholt Junction and Milner Wood Junction the North Eastern Railway possessed running powers for all traffic over the Midland line.

Shipley & Guiseley line

See page 169

Rawdon Junction SB	Opened	10.5.1892
***	Closed	12.4.1965

Guiseley & Yeadon branch

See page 169

GUISELEY	OP	1.8.1865
***	OG	1.10.1866
***	CG	7.10.1968
***	RO(Coal)	12.1969
***	C.Coal before	3.1983
Guiseley Station SB	Open before	1.11.1875
Replacement box	Opened	18.3.1906
Panel installed	... ...	27.2.1983
Menston Station SB	Open before	1.10.1876
Replacement box	Opened	1.2.1903
***	Re-framed	....
***	Closed	22.10.1951
MENSTON	OP	1.3.1873
***	CP(All)	1.3.1876
Replacement station 34 chains to the south	OP	1.11.1875
***	OG	1.3.1876
Menston Junction SB	Opened	1865 ?
Replacement box	Opened	....
Replacement box	Opened	24.3.1895
Box closed and ground frame provided in lieu	... ...	24.7.1966

Menston Jcn to Burley Jcn	OG	1.11.1866 *
Between Menston Junction and Burley Junction the North Eastern possessed running powers for all traffic over the Midland line.		

Otley Curve

Powers: Midland Railway (Otley and Ilkley Extension) Act 1861

Menston Jcn to Milner Wood Jcn	OP	1.8.1865
***	OG	1.10.1866
***	CP	25.2.1957
***	C.Tfc	5.7.1965
***	Closed	24.7.1966

Shipley & Guiseley line

Powers: Midland Railway (Additional Powers) Act 1872

Guiseley Jcn (Shipley) to Esholt Jcn	OP	4.12.1876
***	OG	13.12.1876
Working was by the block telegraph system from the opening. Between Guiseley Junction and Esholt Junction the North Eastern possessed running powers for all traffic over the Midland line.		
Guiseley Junction to Guiseley	Singled	27.2.1983
Baildon Station SB	Opened	4.12.1876
Replacement box	Opened	20.7.1902
***	Closed	24.2.1957
BAILDON	OP	4.12.1876
***	OG	13.12.1876
***	CP	5.1.1953
***	RO(P)	28.1.1957
***	CP	29.4.1957
***	CG	27.4.1964
***	RO(P)	5.1.1973
ESHOLT	OP	4.12.1876
***	OG	13.12.1876
***	CP&G	28.10.1940
Esholt Station SB	Opened	4.12.1876
***	Closed	25.1.1887

Guiseley & Yeadon branch

The Guiseley, Yeadon & Rawdon Railway changed its name to the Guiseley, Yeadon & Headingley Railway under the Leeds & Yeadon Railway Act 1891. Part of the line was vested in the Midland under the Midland Railway Act 1892 and the remainder was abandoned under the Guiseley, Yeadon, and Headingley Railway (Abandonment) Act 1893.

Powers: Guiseley, Yeadon and Rawdon Railway Act 1885
Guiseley, Yeadon and Rawdon Railway Act 1890
(Alteration of levels at Rawdon)

Yeadon to Rawdon Jcn	OG	26.2.1894
***	Closed	12.4.1965
The line was worked by the electric train token block system during the period when Yeadon Station SB was open, and otherwise by train staff without tickets.		
Yeadon to Rawdon Jcn: one engine in steam working	Commenced	2.8.1962
Yeadon Station SB	Opened	25.2.1894
Box closed and block telegraph working for up trains discontinued	... ...	2.7.1907
YEADON	OG	26.2.1894
***	CG	10.8.1964
YEADON (excursion traffic only)	OP(NA)	....
***	CP	....
Rawdon Jcn: down-line junction removed	... ...	1925

Otley & Ilkley Joint Line (Midland & North Eastern)

The Otley & Ilkley Joint Line Committee was constituted on 11 July 1861.

Otley to Ilkley	OP	1.8.1865
***	OG	1.10.1866
Between Otley and Harrogate the Midland possessed running powers for all traffic over the North Eastern line.		
Otley to Ilkley: block telegraph system	Installed	1873
Between Ilkley Junction and Bolton Abbey the North Eastern Railway possessed running powers for passenger traffic over the Midland line.		
(Arthington to) Otley to Burley Jcn	CP	22.3.1965
***	Closed	5.7.1965

OTLEY	OP	1.2.1865	
***	OG	1.10.1866	
***	CP	22.3.1965	
***	CG	5.7.1965	
Otley Station SB	Open before	1.11.1875	
Replacement box	Opened	....	
***	Re-framed	22.3.1902	
***	Closed	5.7.1965	
Otley Goods Yard SB	Open before	1.11.1875	
Replacement box	Opened	3.2.1913	
***	Closed by	16.4.1938	
***	Removed	4.12.1939	
Milner Wood Junction SB	Opened	1865	
Replacement box	Opened	....	
***	Re-framed	10.7.1910	
***	Closed	5.7.1965	

Otley & Ilkley Extension line

See page 168

Burley Junction SB	Opened	1865	
Replacement box	Opened	....	
Replacement box	Opened	25.2.1906	
***	Closed	23.1.1986	
BURLEY	OP	1.8.1865	
***	OG	1.10.1866	
Altered to BURLEY IN WHARFEDALE	By	9.7.1923	*
***	CG	27.4.1964	
BEN RHYDDING	Private stn	1.8.1865	*
***	OP	1.7.1866	
***	OG	1.10.1866	?
	or	1888	?
***	CG	5.7.1965	
Ben Rhydding Station SB	Opened	8.1877-4.1878	
Replacement box	Opened	6.1.1901	
***	Closed	4.12.1965	
Ilkley engine shed	Opened	1.7.1866	
***	Replaced	1892	
***	Closed	5.1.1959	
Ilkley Station SB	Open before	16.8.1877	
Replacement box	Opened	10.5.1887	
Replacement box	Opened	16.5.1888	
Replacement box	Opened	20.7.1913	
Box provided with a switch-panel	... ...	25.9.1983	
ILKLEY	OP	1.8.1865	
***	OG	1.10.1866	
***	CG	7.8.1967	
Middle siding	t.o.u.	11.3.1976	
Platforms 1 and 2 shortened by 45 yards	... ...	Mid-1987	

Skipton & Ilkley line

Powers: Midland Railway (Additional Powers) Act 1883

Ilkley to Bolton Abbey	OP	16.5.1888
***	OG	27.8.1888
Working was by the block telegraph system from the opening.		
Ilkley to Skipton	CP	22.3.1965
Ilkley to Embsay	C.Tfc	5.7.1965
***	t.o.u.	3.1.1966
Line severed at 211m 67ch (Ilkley)	... ...	12.1965
Addingham Station SB	Opened	16.5.1888
***	Closed	5.7.1965
Addingham to Embsay: single-line working	Introduced	31.12.1916
Double-line working	Restored	21.3.1921
ADDINGHAM	OP	16.5.1888
***	OG	27.8.1888
***	CP	22.3.1965
***	CG	5.7.1965
Bolton Abbey Station SB	Opened	16.5.1888
***	Closed	12.11.1964
BOLTON ABBEY	OP	16.5.1888
***	OG	27.8.1888
***	CP&G temp.	17.6.1940
***	Re-opened	17.3.1941
***	CG	27.4.1964
***	CP	22.3.1965
Bolton Abbey to Skipton	OP&G	1.10.1888
Skibeden to Embsay re-opened by the Yorkshire Dales Railway	... ...	....

Embsay Station SB	Opened	1.10.1888
Replacement box	Opened	24.7.1923
***	Closed	4.3.1969
EMBSAY	OP	1.10.1888
***	OG	11.1888
***	CG	27.4.1964
***	CP	22.3.1965
Embsay Station to Embsay Jcn line severed at the junction	... ...	21.10.1968
***	t.o.u.	4.3.1969
Embsay Junction SB	Opened	23.2.1902
***	Closed	6.7.1969

Yorkshire Dales Railway
See below.

Line severed at 219m 60ch (Embsay)	......	12.1965
Embsay to Skipton Station North Jcn transferred from North Eastern Region to London Midland Region	... ...	7.10.1968

Yorkshire Dales Railway

The Yorkshire Dales Railway was leased by the Midland Railway under an agreement of 5 July 1897. The Midland was given powers to subscribe under the Midland Railway Act 1900.

Powers: Yorkshire Dales Railway Act 1897

Embsay Jcn to Grassington	O.Formal	29.7.1902
***	OP	29.7.1902
***	OPG&M	30.7.1902
Electric train tablet block in place of train staff working	Commenced	26.6.1904
***	CP	22.9.1930
One engine in steam working	Commenced	20.9.1962
Transferred from North Eastern Region to London Midland Region	... ...	7.10.1968
Branch severed 312 yards north of Swinden "A" GF	... ...	25.8.1969
Branch cut back by a further 105 yards	... ...	31.5.1971
Branch re-named the Rylstone Branch and method of working changed to electric train token	... ...	18.8.1974
RYLSTONE	OPG&M	30.7.1902
***	CP	22.9.1930
***	CG	11.8.1969
Rylstone (Swinden Lime Works Siding) to Grassington & Threshfield	Closed	11.8.1969
Grassington Station SB	Opened	26.6.1904
***	Closed	20.9.1962
GRASSINGTON	OPG&M	30.7.1902
Altered to GRASSINGTON & THRESHFIELD	... ...	10.1902
***	CP	22.9.1930
***	CG	11.8.1969
Excursion trains continued to call at this station.		

LEEDS & BRADFORD EXTENSION LINE

Powers: Leeds and Bradford Railway Act 1845
Leeds and Bradford Railway Act 1846 (Alteration of levels at Bingley)
Midland Railway Act 1898 (Bingley & Thwaites Widening)
Midland Railway (Additional Powers) Act 1873 (Keighley - Land Powers only)

Leeds Jcn (Shipley) to Keighley	Opened	16.3.1847
***	OP	....
Shipley Jcns to Saltaire: block telegraph working	Intro. by	1873
Leeds Jcn to Bingley Jcn curve re-alignment	Into use	10.6.1883
SHIPLEY: new No. 5 platform on the down north curve line	Into use	....
Bi-directional working through platform 5 on the down curve line	Commenced	9.3.1980

Shipley West Curve
Powers: Leeds and Bradford Railways Act 1845

Bradford Jcn to Bingley Jcn	Opened	16.3.1847
Up main line of curve signalled as a terminal station	... ...	27.9.1903
***	Singled	9.3.1980

Skipton Junction SB	Opened	1867
Replacement box	Opened	c.1874 ?
Re-named Bingley Junction SB	... ...	....
Replacement box	Opened	3.3.1907
***	Re-framed	1979
***	Closed	....
Shipley Stone Sidings SB	Open before	16.8.1877
***	Closed	26.2.1905

Saltaire South SB	Open before	16.8.1877
Replacement box	Opened	26.11.1893
Re-named Saltaire SB	... ...	....
***	Closed	26.9.1964
SALTAIRE	OP	1.5.1856 *
***	OG	1.1.1859 ?
***	CG	1912-1925
***	CP	22.3.1965
***	RO(P)	9.4.1984
Saltaire to Keighley (Worth Valley Jcn): block telegraph working	Introduced	1874
Hirst Wood SB	Opened	10.1884
Replacement box	Opened	1901-1906
***	Closed	23.10.1972
BINGLEY	Opened	16.3.1847
Replacement station	Opened	24.7.1892
***	CG	28.6.1965
Bingley: work on the improvement of the station curve	Commenced	28.3.1920
Bingley South SB	Opened	1879
Replacement box	Opened	31.7.1892
***	Closed	23.10.1932
Bingley Station SB	Open before	16.8.1877
***	Closed	1879
Bingley SB	Opened	23.10.1932
Bingley North SB	Opened	1879
Replacement box	Opened	19.10.1890
Replacement box	Opened	21.10.1900
***	Closed	23.10.1932
Bingley North to Marley: down slow line and up goods line	Into use	21.10.1900
Bingley to Thwaites Jcn: slow/goods lines made goods lines throughout	... ...	4.10.1964
Up and down goods lines	t.o.u.	25.6.1967
CROSSFLATTS	OP	17.5.1982
Marley SB	Opened	5.2.1899
Replacement box named Marley Junction SB about 1/4 mile north	Opened	27.5.1900
***	Closed	4.10.1964
Marley Jcn: down main line to down goods line connection	Removed	21.10.1900
Down slow line to down passenger line crossover	Into use	21.10.1900
Up slow line to up passenger line crossover	Into use	21.10.1900
Marley to Thwaites Jcn: down goods line	Into use	27.5.1900
Up slow line	Into use	21.10.1900
Thwaites Crossing SB	Open before	16.8.1877
Replacement box	Opened	8.11.1891
Re-named Thwaites Station SB	... ...	1.6.1892
Re-named Thwaites Junction SB	... ...	1900
***	Closed	2.7.1967
THWAITES	OP	1.6.1892
***	CP(All)	1.7.1909
Keighley South SB	Opened	1882
Replacement box	Opened	9.11.1919
***	Closed	2.7.1967
Worth Valley Junction SB	Open before	16.8.1877
***	Closed	9.7.1882

Keighley & Worth Valley Railway
See page 175

Worth Valley Jcn to Keighley North: block telegraph working	Introduced	1878
Keighley: replacement junction with the Worth Valley line at the north end of the station instead of at the south end	Into use	9.7.1882
KEIGHLEY	Opened	16.3.1847
Replacement station	Opened	6.5.1883
Goods station altered to KEIGHLEY NORTH GOODS STATION	By	6.4.1951
***	CG	6.9.1982
Keighley Station SB	Open before	16.8.1877
***	Closed	c.10.1884
Keighley Station Junction SB: temporary box	Opened	1884
Permanent box	Opened	c.10.1884
***	Re-framed	13.9.1914
Keighley Station Jcn: trailing points between the down main line and the down branch	t.o.u.	23.3.1976
Keighley engine shed	Opened	1869
***	Replaced	1892
***	Closed	18.6.1962
Keighley: Queen's Hotel	Opened	....
***	Sold	....

Keighley to Skipton	Opened	8.9.1847
Keighley North SB	Open before	16.8.1877
***	Re-framed	6.12.1908
Replacement box	Opened	24.4.1927
***	Closed	19.6.1960
Keighley North to Robinson's Sidings: block telegraph working	Introduced	1875

Utley automatic signals (intermediate block signals)	Into use	8.8.1909
Replaced by three-aspect colour-light signals	... ...	19.6.1960
Steeton South SB	Open before	16.8.1877
Replacement box	Opened	24.7.1898
***	Re-framed	6.12.1908
***	Closed	22.4.1923
Steeton North SB	Open before	16.8.1877
Replacement box	Opened	18.2.1923
Re-named Steeton Station SB	... ...	22.4.1923
***	Re-framed	1940
STEETON	Opened	c.12.1847
Altered to STEETON & SILSDEN	... ...	1.9.1868 *
Replacement passenger station north of the level crossing	Opened	28.2.1892
***	CP	22.3.1965
***	CG	28.6.1965
Ballast Sidings SB (not a block post)	Opened	8.1877-4.1888
***	Closed	1889-1893
Kildwick Station SB	Opened	11.1875
Replacement box	Opened	20.6.1895
***	Re-framed	1965
***	Closed	....
KILDWICK	Opened by	4.1848
Altered to KILDWICK & CROSS HILLS	By	1.1.1863 *
Altered to KILDWICK & CROSSHILLS	After	1.10.1884 *
Replacement station 16 chains to the west	Opened	7.4.1889
***	CP	22.3.1965
***	CG	28.6.1965
CONONLEY	Opened	c.12.1847
***	CG	27.4.1964
***	CP	22.3.1965
***	RO(P)	20.4.1988
Cononley Station SB	Open before	16.8.1877
Replacement box	Opened	9.12.1894
Replacement box	Opened	28.6.1964
Snaygill SB	Open before	16.8.1877
Replacement box	Opened	5.7.1896
Replacement box	Opened	20.2.1898
***	Closed	15.9.1968
Snaygill to Skipton South Jcn: up goods line	Into use	15.1.1899
Down goods line	Into use	19.2.1899
Up and down slow lines	t.o.u.	15.9.1968
Snaygill to Skipton South SB: goods lines made slow lines and passenger lines designated fast lines	... ...	8.5.1904
Robinson's Sidings SB	Opened	26.7.1875
***	Closed by	16.8.1877
Robinson's Sidings to Skipton Station North: block telegraph system	Installed	1877
Skipton South Junction SB	Opened	c.12.1876
Replacement box	Opened	15.8.1886
***	Re-framed	15.1.1899
***	Re-framed	8.5.1904
Replacement box on south side of Skipton & Ilkley overbridge	Opened	27.7.1919
***	Closed	15.9.1968
Skipton South Jcn: connection from down main line to down goods line	Removed	19.2.1899
Down goods line to down passenger line crossover	Into use	19.2.1899
Skipton South Jcn to Skipton North Jcn: down goods line	Into use	31.12.1876
Working of down goods line by telegraph bell	Commenced	11.8.1895
Skipton Station South SB	Open before	1.11.1875
Replacement box	Opened	c.4.1876
Replacement box	Opened	18.2.1906
Skipton Level Crossing SB	Open before	10.1870
***	Closed	c.4.1876
SKIPTON	Opened	8.9.1847
Replacement station 10 chains further north	Opened	30.4.1876
Down back platform line made into down loop platform line	... ...	11.3.1906
No. 1 bay	t.o.u.	12.11.1978
Down back platform blocked at south end	... ...	12.11.1978
Down back platform made down siding	... ...	18.5.1986
***	CG	1.3.1982
SKIPTON NEW SIDINGS	Opened	27.9/18.10.1875
SKIPTON EXCHANGE SIDINGS	In use by	18.3.1876
***	Closed	....
Skipton Station North Junction SB	Open before	10.1870
Replacement box	Opened	c.4.1876
***	Slued	13.3.1887
Replacement box	Opened	12.8.1888
Replacement box	Opened	24.10.1915

Skipton & Ilkley line

See page 170

Skipton Station North to Colne: block telegraph system	Installed	1876

Skipton Station North Jcn to Skipton North Jcn: up goods line	Into use	11.1874-11.1875
Working of up goods line by telegraph bell	Commenced	11.8.1895
Down goods line made down through siding	... ...	6.7.1969
Down through siding	t.o.u.	....
Up goods line made up goods loop	... ...	30.12.1973
Skipton Station North Jcn to Engine Shed SB: down goods line made second line from down passenger line and existing down goods line made a siding	... ...	16.9.1888
Engine Shed SB	Open before	16.8.1877
Replacement box	Opened	13.11.1888
***	Re-framed	23.4.1916
***	Closed	7.1.1968
Skipton engine shed	Opened	1850
Second engine shed	Opened	1892
Facilities for steam	Withdrawn	3.4.1967
***	Closed	10.12.1967
Skipton North West Jcn moved 7 chains nearer to Leeds	... ...	1.2.1876
Skipton North Jcn: improved curve to the North Western line	Into use	1877
Up passenger line to up goods line crossover	Into use	....
Up goods line extension 330 yards towards Gargrave	Into use	10.8.1941
North West Junction SB	Open before	1.11.1875
Re-named Skipton North Junction SB	Before	16.8.1877
Replacement box	Opened	8.2.1891
***	Re-framed	11.4.1906
***	Raised	3.11.1912
***	Re-framed	10.11.1912
***	Closed	30.12.1973

North Western Railway

See page 176

Skipton to Colne	Opened	2.10.1848
Skipton North Jcn to Colne	CP&G	2.2.1970
Aire Bridge SB	Opened	11.10.1925
***	Closed	22.11.1925
Elslack Station SB	Open before	1.11.1875
Replacement box	Opened	23.4.1907
***	Closed	2.3.1952
ELSLACK	Opened	1.1.1849 *
***	CP&G	3.3.1952
Thornton-in-Craven Station SB	Open before	1.11.1875
Replacement box	Opened	19.5.1901
Box closed and ground frame on the platform provided in lieu	... ...	1.9.1929
***	t.o.u.	....
THORNTON	Opened	2.10.1848
Altered to THORNTON-IN-CRAVEN	... ...	27.9.1937 *
***	CG	30.7.1951
***	CP	2.2.1970
Earby Crossing SB	Open before	16.8.1877
***	Made NBP	6.12.1886
Replacement box	Opened	24.3.1895
Replacement box	Opened	16.9.1923
***	Closed	2.2.1970
EARBY	Opened	2.10.1848
***	CG	1.3.1965
***	CP	2.2.1970
Earby Station SB	Open before	16.8.1877
Replacement box	Opened	1885
Replacement box	Opened	5.6.1921
***	Closed	2.2.1970
Barnoldswick Junction SB	Opened	c.2.1871
Replacement box	Opened	3.12.1893
Replacement box 200 yards nearer to Colne	Opened	30.4.1916
Replacement box	Opened	20.2.1924
***	Closed	26.2.1967

Barnoldswick branch

Powers: Barnoldswick Railway Act 1867.
Worked by Midland from its opening, the company was vested in the Midland by the Midland Railway Act 1899 with effect from 1 July 1899.

Earby Jcn to Barnoldswick	OP&G	13.2.1871
***	CP	27.9.1965
***	C.Tfc	1.8.1966
Line severed at the junction	... ...	26.2.1967
Barnoldswick engine shed	Open before	1880
***	Closed by	7.1926
BARNOLDSWICK	OP&G	8.2.1871
***	CP	27.9.1965
***	CG	1.8.1966

FOULRIDGE	Opened	2.10.1848
***	CP&G	5.1.1959
Foulridge Viaduct SB	Opened	12.11.1893
***	Closed	3.12.1893
Foulridge SB	Open before	1.11.1875
Replacement box	Opened	28.5.1905
***	Closed	25.1.1960
Colne engine shed	Opened	....
***	Closed	28.9.1936
Engine Shed SB	Open before	16.8.1877
Re-named Colne North SB	... ...	c.1882
Replacement box	Opened	19.1.1902
Re-named Colne SB	... ...	7.4.1968
***	Closed	2.2.1970 ?
COLNE	Opened	2.10.1848
Enlargement of joint goods station	Into use	1904
Station transferred to the Central Division	... ...	15.11.195. ?
***	CG	8.1.1968
Between Leeds and Colne and Petteril Junction the North British Railway possessed running powers over the Midland line.		
Colne Station SB	Open before	16.8.1877
Re-named Colne South SB	... ...	....
***	Closed	17.5.1903
Colne Jcn with the Lancashire & Yorkshire Railway	Opened	1.2.1849
Colne No. 1 SB (about 570 yards south of Colne South SB)	Opened	27.8.1900
***	Closed	4.9.1967
Colne No. 2 SB (not at first a block post)	Opened	17.5.1903
***	Closed	7.4.1968

KEIGHLEY & WORTH VALLEY RAILWAY

The Keighley & Worth Valley Railway was worked by the Midland from its opening. It was vested in the Midland with effect from 1 July 1881 by the Midland Railway (Additional Powers) Act 1881, and it dissolved under the Midland Railway Act 1886.

Powers: Keighley and Worth Valley Railway Act 1862
Midland Railway (Additional Powers) Act 1882
(Keighley to Ingrow alterations)
Midland Railway Act 1891 (Oakworth Deviation: New Vale Viaduct)

Keighley to Oxenhope	OP	15.4.1867
***	OG	1.7.1867 *
***	CP	1.1.1962
***	CG(All)	18.6.1962
Line re-opened by the Keighley & Worth Valley Railway Preservation Society	... ...	29.6.1968
Between Keighley station and Keighley Junction the Great Northern possessed running powers over the Midland line.		
Keighley station to Great Northern Jcn	Doubled	8.6.1884
Keighley to Keighley Single Line Jcn: block telegraph working	Introduced	1884
Keighley West SB	Opened	1884
Replacement box	Opened	23.8.1921
Box made a shunting frame	... ...	18.6.1962
***	t.o.u.	28.6.1965
Great Northern Junction SB	Opened	1884
Replacement box 220 yards nearer Ingrow	Opened	24.8.1924
Box made a shunting frame	... ...	18.6.1962
***	t.o.u.	28.6.1965
Great Northern Jcn: double-line connection between the Worth Valley line and the LNER goods lines converted to a single line	... ...	11.10.1942
Single Line Junction SB	Opened	1884
***	Closed	24.8.1924
Keighley Single Line Jcn to Ingrow: block telegraph working in addition to the train staff	Introduced	1884
Keighley to Haworth: electric train tablet working	Commenced	22.4.1900
One engine in steam working	Commenced	25.3.1956
Ingrow SB	Open before	1.11.1875
***	Closed	8.2.1887
Ingrow Crossing SB	Opened	8.2.1887 ?
***	Closed	....
INGROW	OP	15.4.1867
***	OG	1.7.1867 *
Altered to INGROW WEST	... ...	2.3.1951
Altered to INGROW	... ...	12.6.1961
***	CP	1.1.1962
***	CG	18.6.1962

The section from Ingrow to the end of the branch was worked at first by one engine in steam, with train staff too from 1884.

DAMEMS	OP	1.9.1867	
***	OG	1.1.1869	?*
***	CP&G	23.5.1949	
Damems SB	Open before	1.11.1875	
***	Closed	....	
Damems, Oakworth, Haworth, and Oxenhope appear in a list of "signal posts" returned to the Board of Trade in November 1880, but they may not have been elevated signalbox structures. As new boxes were provided at Oakworth and Haworth in 1900, the return seems especially suspect in relation to these two locations.			
Mytholmes tunnel deviation (to avoid a timber viaduct)	Into use	6.11.1892	
Oakworth: passing-loop for goods traffic only	Into use	22.4.1900	
Oakworth Station SB	Open before	1.11.1875	
Oakworth Station SB	Opened	22.4.1900	
***	Closed	25.3.1956	
OAKWORTH	OP	15.4.1867	
***	OG	1.7.1867	*
***	CP	1.1.1962	
***	CG	18.6.1962	
HAWORTH	OP	15.4.1867	
***	OG	1.7.1867	*
***	CP	1.1.1962	
***	CG	18.6.1962	
Haworth Goods Yard: passing-loop for goods traffic only	Into use	22.4.1900	
Haworth Station SB	Open before	1.11.1875	
Haworth Station SB	Opened	22.4.1900	
***	Closed	25.3.1956	
Haworth to Oxenhope remained always one engine in steam.			
OXENHOPE	OP	15.4.1867	
***	OG	1.7.1867	*
***	CP	1.1.1962	
***	CG	18.6.1962	
Oxenhope Station SB	Open before	1.11.1875	
Keighley & Worth Valley Railway	Re-opened	29.6.1968	

NORTH WESTERN RAILWAY

The Midland began to work the North Western on 1 June 1852 under powers in the North-western Railway (Extension of Lancaster Branch, &c.) Act 1849. The North-western Railway Act 1852 dissolved and re-incorporated the company, repealing all previous Acts and authorising works and lands at Morecambe. The North-Western Railway Act 1857 authorised the lease or sale of the company to one or both of the Midland and the Lancaster & Carlisle Railways, and the Midland leased the line for 999 years. The company was conveyed to the Midland (under the powers of the 1857 Act) with effect from 1 January 1871, and stocks of the companies were consolidated from 1 January 1875 under the Midland Railway (Additional Powers) Act 1874.

Powers: North Western Railway Act 1848 (Skipton North Junction to Gargrave)
North Western Railway Act 1846 (Gargrave to Ingleton)

Skipton to Ingleton	Opened	30.7.1849	
Skipton to Bell Busk	Doubled by	8.1853	
Skipton to Clapham Jcn: block telegraph working	Introduced	1875	
Delaney's Sidings SB	Opened	5.3.1899	
***	Closed	15.12.1968	
Delaney's Sidings: down loop	Into use	26.10.1941	
***	t.o.u.	....	
GARGRAVE	Opened	1.8.1849	
***	CG	1.3.1965	
Gargrave Station SB	Open before	16.8.1877	
Replacement box	Opened	22.7.1900	
***	Re-framed	10.1.1909	
Box ceased to signal the up line and up IBS provided in lieu	... ...	11.11.1973	
Signalbox	Closed	30.12.1973	
Robinson's Sidings SB (not a block post)	Open before	1.11.1875	
***	Closed	2.1880-6.1881	
Ingber intermediate block signals	Into use	15.1.1911	
***	t.o.u.	19.12.1971	
Bell Busk to Hellifield	Doubled	1.6.1852	
Bell Busk Station SB	Open before	1.11.1875	
Replacement box	Opened	18.6.1899	
***	Re-framed	10.1.1909	
***	Closed	19.12.1971	
Bell Busk level crossing	Closed	19.12.1971	
BELL BUSK	Opened	1.8.1849	
Altered to BELL BUSK FOR MALHAM	... ...	1.10.1850	*
Altered to BELL BUSK	... ...	1.5.1889	?*
BELL BUSK FOR MALHAM	CP&G	4.5.1959	
Otterburn automatic signals (intermediate block signals)	Into use	15.1.1911	
***	t.o.u.	19.12.1971	

Hellifield Old Station SB	Open before	16.8.1877
Re-named Hellifield Goods Station SB	... ...	....
Replacement box	Opened	1.11.1908
Box closed and Hellifield Up IBS provided in lieu	... ...	2.10.1938
***	Abolished	11.11.1973
HELLIFIELD	Opened	1.8.1849
Replacement station 35 chains north of the old one and north of the junction with the Lancashire & Yorkshire line	Opened	1.6.1880
Time during which station was "closed" for tickets altered from 11 p.m. to 7 a.m. to 8.30 p.m. to 7.30 a.m.	... ...	12.5.1928
***	CG	20.4.1964
South (up) bay line, and connections	Removed	11.4.1965
North (down) bay line, and connections	Removed	2.1.1966
The new station was built with a through line on each side, outside the main lines through the platforms.		
Hellifield South Junction SB	Opened	c.1.1880
Replacement box	Opened	11.6.1911
Re-named Hellifield SB	... ...	27.3.1966
HELLIFIELD EXCHANGE SIDINGS (on the Lancashire & Yorkshire curve)	Opened	1.3.1880
***	Closed	....
Between Hellifield Junction and Ingleton and Wennington the Lancashire & Yorkshire Railway possessed running powers over the Midland line.		
Between Hellifield Junction and Ancoats Junction the Nidland possessed running powers over the Lancashire & Yorkshire line.		
Hellifield North Junction SB	Opened	c.6.1880
Replacement box	Opened	25.6.1905
27.3.1966	***	Closed
Hellifield engine shed	Opened	1880
***	Closed	17.6.1963
Motive power depot	Closed	9.2.1970
Hellifield to Hornby	Doubled	Late 1850
LONG PRESTON	Opened	1.8.1849
***	CG	4.11.1963
Long Preston Station SB	Open before	1.11.1875
Replacement box	Opened	8.5.1892
***	Closed	21.9.1971
Settle South Up IBS (semaphores)	Into use	1.6.1941
***	t.o.u.	....
Settle Junction South SB	Opened	1874
Replacement box	Opened	18.11.1894
***	Closed	4.4.1923
SETTLE JUNCTION	OP	2.10.1876
***	CP(All)	1.11.1877
Settle Junction SB	Opened	c.1875
Replacement box	Opened	30.10.1892
Replacement box	Opened	14.9.1913
***	Re-framed	1960
Settle Junction re-modelling	Commenced	13.10.1895

Settle & Carlisle line

See page 182

SETTLE	Opened	1.8.1849
Altered to SETTLE (OLD STATION) and closed for goods traffic	... ...	1.5.1876
***	RO(G)	1877 ?
Altered to GIGGLESWICK	... ...	1.11.1877
***	CG	9.9.1963
Settle Station SB	Open before	1.10.1876
Re-named Giggleswick Station SB	... ...	1.11.1877
Replacement box	Opened	31.12.1906 ?
***	Closed	16.11.1971
Eldroth SB	Opened	c.7.1885
Replacement box	Opened	28.1.1900
***	Closed	11.10.1966
LANESIDE	OG	....
***	CG(All)	1.1.1862 *
CLAPHAM	Opened	1.8.1849
***	CG	25.1.1965
Clapham Junction SB	Open before	16.8.1877
Replacement box	Opened	27.6.1915
***	Closed	22.9.1968
Clapham to Ingleton	Opened	30.7.1849
***	Closed	1.6.1850
***	Doubled	17.8.1861
***	Re-opened	1.10.1861
***	CP	1.2.1954
Clapham to Ingleton (London & North Western station)	Tfc ceased	1.3.1965
***	CG	19.6.1966
***	t.o.u.	26.7.1966
Clapham Jcn to Ingleton: block telegraph system	Installed	1882

Clapham to Barker's Siding: single-line working	Intro. by	18.6.1913
Double-line working	Restored	12.4.1920
Newby Moor Crossing SB	Opened	9.2.1892
***	Closed	14.6.1908
Ingleton engine shed	Opened	1878
***	Closed	30.1.1954
Ingleton Station SB	Open before	1.10.1876
Replacement box	Opened	25.8.1912
***	Closed	2.3.1965
INGLETON	Opened	1.8.1849
***	Closed	1.6.1850
***	Re-opened	1.10.1861
***	CP	1.2.1954
***	CG	1.3.1965

A new passenger station was opened soon after the re-opening of the line in 1861.
Excursion trains continued to use Ingleton station after closure.
Between Ingleton Junction and Ingleton station the Midland Railway possessed running powers over the London & North Western line for all traffic.
Between Ingleton Junction and Carlisle the Midland Railway possessed running powers over the London & North Western line.

Clapham & Lancaster Branch

Powers: North Western Railway Act 1846 (Clapham Junction to Halton)
North Western Railway Act 1848 (Halton to Lancaster)
North Western Railway Act 1846 (At Lancaster)

Clapham to Bentham	Opened	1.6.1850
Clapham Jcn to Ladies' Walk: block telegraph system	Installed	1876
Skew Crossing SB	Opened	c.7.1885
Replacement SB	Opened	14.8.1906
***	Closed	8.2.1966
Wenning Viaduct SB	Opened	30.5.1887
***	Closed	20.7.1887
BENTHAM	Opened	1.6.1850
Altered to BENTHAM HIGH	... ...	1.11.1851 *
Altered to BENTHAM	... ...	1.5.1876 *
***	CG	17.6.1968
High Bentham Station SB	Open before	16.8.1877
Replacement box	Opened	27.1.1895
***	Closed	11.4.1976
High Bentham: up refuge siding made up goods loop	... ...	29.3.1942
***	t.o.u.	11.4.1976

Bentham to Wennington	Opened	2.5.1850
Low Bentham Station SB	Open before	16.8.1877
Replacement box	Opened	25.8.1907
***	Closed	25.2.1964
LOW BENTHAM	Opened	2.5.1850
***	CP	1.8.1853
***	CG	24.12.1964
Wennington Sidings SB	Opened	....
***	Closed	....
WENNINGTON: permanent station	Opened	2.5.1850
***	CG	9.9.1963
Wennington Junction SB	Open before	16.8.1877
Replacement box	Opened	31.5.1890
Wennington: No. 1 down siding made into a loop	By	22.11.1941
Bay siding and connection	Taken away	8.3.1964
Up ground frame removed and up bay connection worked from the box	... ...	4.7.1965
Up-side bay	t.o.u.	19.1.1970
Down goods line	t.o.u.	27.2.1977

Furness & Midland Joint Line
See page 182

Wennington to Morecambe	CP	3.1.1966
***	CG	5.6.1967
Wennington to Lancaster Green Area	Opened	17.11.1849
WENNINGTON: Tatham Bridge temporary station, 3/4 of a mile to the west of the permanent station, probably for passenger traffic only	Opened	17.11.1849
***	Closed	1.5.1850
WRAY	OP	17.11.1849
***	CP(All)	1.6.1850
Hornby Station SB	Open before	16.8.1877
Replacement box	Opened	2.6.1889
***	Closed	26.4.1964

HORNBY	Opened	17.11.1849
Altered to HORNBY FOR KIRKBY LONSDALE	... ...	1.4.1851 *
Altered to HORNBY	... ...	1.1.1863 *
***	CP	16.9.1957
***	CG	20.4.1964
Hornby to Crook o' Lune (Caton side)	Doubled	2.6.1889
The line between Hornby and Ladies' Walk was worked by train staff and tickets when still single.		
CLAUGHTON		
***	OP	1.11.1851 *
Claughton Manor SB	CP(All)	1.8.1853
***	Opened	16.10.1898
Ashwell Sidings SB	Closed	18.12.1960
***	Open before	1.11.1875
Lunesdale Brick & Tile Company's Sidings SB (not a block post)	Closed	10.1876–8.1877
***	Open before	1.10.1876
The two signalboxes were probably the same location.	Closed	12.1888–8.1893
Caton Station SB	Open before	1.11.1875
Replacement box	Opened	21.5.1889
***	Closed	4.6.1967
CATON	Opened	17.11.1849
***	CP&G	1.5.1961
Crook o' Lune East SB	Opened	2.6.1889
***	Closed	27.10.1889
Crook o' Lune: remaining 600 yards of single line	Doubled	27.10.1889
Crook o' Lune SB	Opened	5.2.1889
Re-named Crook o' Lune West SB	... ...	2.6.1889
***	Closed	27.10.1889
Crook o' Lune to Halton	Doubled	3.3.1889
HALTON	Opened	17.11.1849
***	CG	11.1962
***	CP	3.1.1966
Halton Station SB	Open before	1.11.1875
Replacement box at Lancaster end of station	Opened	7.4.1889
***	Closed	4.6.1967
Halton to Ladies' Walk Sidings	Doubled	7.4.1889
Ladies' Walk: 2 new platform lines	Into use	10.7.1916
***	t.o.u.	....
Ladies' Walk SB	Open before	1.11.1875
Replacement box	Opened	17.3.1889
Replacement box	Opened	25.6.1916
***	Closed	4.6.1967
Ladies' Walk to Lancaster: block telegraph working	Introduced	1875
Ladies' Walk Sidings to Lancaster Green Ayre	Doubled	1880
Lancaster South SB	Open before	16.8.1877
Replacement box	Opened	20.10.1889
***	Closed	13.3.1932
LANCASTER	Opened	12.6.1848
Altered to LANCASTER (GREEN AREA)	... ...	1.6.1850
Altered to LANCASTER (GREEN AYRE)	... ...	1.11.1870 *
New station	Opened	1873
New portion of station (on up side)	Into use	23.3.1902
***	CP	3.1.1966
***	CG	8.1.1968
The station at Lancaster was opened with the line to Morecambe, seventeen months before the line from the east was opened.		
Lancaster Green Ayre: goods sidings	t.o.u.	4.5.1970
New Zealand Sidings	t.o.u.	12.8.1970
Parliament Street coal sidings	t.o.u.	7.10.1968
Lancaster engine shed	Opened	....
***	Closed	18.4.1966

Lancaster Castle Station Branch

Powers: North Western Railway Act 1849

Lancaster Green Area to Castle Jcn (Lancaster & Carlisle Railway)	Opened	18.12.1849
***	Closed	1.11.1876
***	Re-opened	1.2.1881
***	CP	1.1.1917 *
***	RO(P)	....
Working by interlocked lever (no token)	Commenced	14.1.1934
***	CP	3.1.1966
Section made up & down siding	... ...	4.6.1967
***	t.o.u.	17.3.1976
***	Closed	1.10.1976

Between Lancaster Junction and Lancaster Castle station the Midland possessed running powers over the London & North Western line for coaching traffic. Between Lancaster Junction and Goods Depot the Midland possessed running powers by arrangement for the exchange of merchandise traffic.

MORECAMBE HARBOUR & RAILWAY

The Morecambe Harbour & Railway Company was vested in the North Western Railway with effect from 29 October 1846 under the provisions of the incorporating Act.

Powers: Morecambe Harbour and Railway Act 1846
Midland Railway (Additional Powers) Act 1861
(Lancaster - Ends of Old Lune Viaduct)
Midland Railway Act 1909 (Lancaster - New Lune Viaduct)
North Western Railway Act 1852 (Morecambe Harbour)

Lancaster to Poulton-le-Sands	Opened	12.6.1848
The line was worked by train staff and tickets prior to doubling.		
Lancaster to Morecambe: block telegraph working	Introduced	14.1.1876
Lancaster to Morecambe	CP	3.1.1966
LANCASTER	Opened	12.6.1848
Lancaster to Heysham: experimental electric working	Commenced	24.5.1908
Lancaster Green Ayre SB	Opened	13.3.1932
***	Closed	4.6.1967
Lancaster North SB	Open before	1.11.1875
Replacement box	Opened	12.3.1899
***	Slued	24.9.1911
***	Enlarged & alt.levers	15.10.1911
***	Closed	13.3.1932
Lancaster North to Hest Bank Jcn	Doubled	3.4.1887
Lancaster: Lune bridge	Opened	1864
Lune SB	Opened	2.2.1908
***	Closed	15.3.1908
Lancaster earth siding (near Lune SB) to Torrisholme No. 1 Jcn:		
Single-line working on up main line	Introduced	2.2.1908
Single-line working on down main line	Introduced	23.2.1908
Double-line working	Restored	15.3.1908
Lancaster: up and down lines diverted to the new Lune viaduct	... ...	15.10.1911
Scale Hall Up IBS	Into use	2.11.1947
***	t.o.u.	....
SCALE HALL	OP	8.6.1957
***	CP(All)	3.1.1966
Torrisholme Factory Sidings SB	Opened	5.3.1916
Box closed and ground frame provided in lieu	... ...	21.6.1932
***	Recovered	27.10.1936
TORRISHOLME FACTORY PLATFORM	Opened	1915
***	Closed	1920
Torrisholme No. 1:		
line severed 542 yards on Lnacaster side of White Lund GF	... ...	4.6.1967
Torrisholme No. 1 SB	Opened	30.5.1897
***	Made BP	4.4.1898
***	Closed	....
***	Re-opened	29.4.1903
***	Closed	1.10.1903
***	Re-opened	....
***	Closed	22.10.1967

Heysham branch

See page 181

Torrisholme No. 1 Jcn to Hest Bank Jcn	t.o.u.	22.10.1967
***	Closed	23.10.1967
Hest Bank Junction SB	Opened	1875
Replacement box	Opened	27.7.1902
***	Closed	22.10.1911
Hest Bank Jcn with the London & North Western Railway	OG	1.10.1861 *
***	OP	8.8.1864
***	Removed	22.10.1911
***	Restored	15.4.1928

Between Morecambe Junction and Carnforth Joint Line Junction the Midland possessed running powers over the London & North Western line for merchandise traffic.

Between Morecambe Junction and Harbour the London & North Western possessed running powers over the Midland line for all traffic.

POULTON-LE-SANDS	Opened	12.6.1848
Re-located (?) and altered to MORECAMBE	... ...	1.8.1850 *
Replacement station	Opened	1873
Excursion platform line	t.o.u.	16.9.1906
Temporary station brought into use	... ...	4.11.1906
Temporary station closed and new terminus opened	... ...	24.3.1907
Refreshment rooms	Opened	8.7.1907
Altered to MORECAMBE PROMENADE	... ...	2.6.1924
***	CG	19.6.1967
Altered to MORECAMBE	... ...	6.5.1968

Morecambe Station SB	Open before	1.11.1875
Replacement box	Opened	7.2.1892
Replacement box	Opened	24.3.1907 ?
***	Re-framed	11.5.1919
***	Closed	....
Morecambe: North Western Hotel	Opened	11.9.1848
North Western Hotel re-named Midland Hotel	... ...	1871
Rebuilt station hotel	Re-opened	12.7.1933
***	Sold	....
MORECAMBE MARKET STREET COAL DEPOT	Opened	....
***	Closed	19.6.1967
MORECAMBE PIER	Opened	....
Altered to MORECAMBE HARBOUR	... ...	15.12.1854
***	CP	1.9.1904
***	CG	6.1933

HEYSHAM BRANCH

Powers: Midland Railway Act 1892 (Torrisholme end)
Midland Railway Act 1895 (Deviation of Branch)
Midland Railway Act 1892 (Heysham end)
Midland Railway Act 1896 (Heysham Harbour)

Heysham branch: working by Midland trains	Commenced	1.11.1898
***	Ceased	21.10.1899
Working between Hest Bank Jcn and Heysham was by train staff without tickets, but trains were to run on the correct line.		
Hest Bank Jcn to Heysham Harbour Station	OP	11.7.1904
***	OG	....
***	CP	8.10.1975
***	RO(P)	11.5.1987
The direction of the line was DOWN from Torrisholme Junction No. 2 to Morecambe station.		
Working was by the block telegraph system from the opening.		
Experimental electric trains between Morecambe and Heysham	Commenced	26.1.1908

Torrisholme Curve

Powers: Midland Railway Act 1892

Torrisholme No. 1 Jcn to Torrisholme No. 2 Jcn	OG	22.8.1904
***	OP	1.9.1904
***	CP	3.1.1966
Curve made a siding	... ...	22.10.1967
Torrisholme No. 2 SB	Opened	4.7.1904
Re-named Torrisholme SB	... ...	22.10.1967
Box closed and ground frame provided in lieu	... ...	20.7.1969
***	t.o.u.	21.2.1971
Torrisholme GF to White Lund Gas Works	Closed	2.2.1970
White Lund Sidings	Into use	....
***	t.o.u.	21.2.1971
Torrisholme No. 2 Jcn to Heysham Harbour: single-line working	Introduced	22.4.1917
Double-line working	Restored	10.4.1921
MIDDLETON ROAD	OP	11.7.1904
***	CP(All)	6.1905
MIDDLETON ROAD GOODS DEPOT, and ground frame	Opened	1904-1910
***	Closed	19.7.1965
Heysham Moss Sidings SB	Opened	3.12.1939
***	Closed	28.4.1987
Heysham Moss Sidings to Heysham Harbour: up line	t.o.u.	30.1.1977
Heysham Harbour Junction SB	Opened	4.7.1904
***	Closed	3.5.1970
Heysham Harbour Station SB	Opened	4.7.1904
Replacement box named Heysham Harbour SB 58 yards to the west	Opened	3.5.1970
***	Closed	30.1.1977
HEYSHAM HARBOUR	OP	11.7.1904
***	CP(All)	4.5.1970
Replacement station adjacent to the east	OP	4.5.1970
***	CP	6.10.1975
***	RO(P)	11.5.1987
There was some use of the station between its closure and re-opening.		
Heysham Goods Shed SB	Opened	1904
Box closed and ground frame provided in lieu	... ...	27.2.1905
***	t.o.u.	....
Heysham Tower Residential Hotel	Bought	1896
***	Closed	1919

FURNESS & MIDLAND JOINT LINE

Powers: Furness and Midland Railways Act 1863

Wennington Jcn to Carnforth East Jcn	OG	10.4.1867
***	OP	6.6.1867
Wennington to Melling: block telegraph working	Intro. by	1873
Melling Station SB	Open before	1.11.1875
Replacement box	Opened	21.1.1894
***	Closed	17.1.1960
MELLING	OP	6.6.1867
***	OG	17.2.1868
***	CP	5.5.1952
***	CG	12.9.1960
Melling to Arkholme: block telegraph working on one line	Intro. by	1873
Block telegraph working on the other line	Introduced	1875
ARKHOLME	OP	6.6.1867
***	OG	17.2.1868
Altered to ARKHOLME FOR KIRKBY LONSDALE	... ...	1.12.1869
***	CP&G	12.9.1960
Arkholme Station SB	Open before	1.10.1876
Replacement box	Opened	27.11.1898
***	Closed	18.7.1965
Arkholme to Kier Bridge: block telegraph working	Introduced	1875
BORWICK	OP	6.6.1867
***	OG	17.2.1868
***	CP&G	12.9.1960
Borwick Station SB	Open before	1.10.1876
Replacement box	Opened	15.5.1904
***	Closed	25.7.1965
Carnforth engine shed	Opened	1874
***	Closed	1944
Carnforth Engine Shed Sidings SB	Open before	16.8.1877
Replacement box	Opened	6.11.1898
***	Closed	27.2.1949
This signalbox was closed temporarily when the shed was closed in 1944, but not officially until considerably later.		
Carnforth East Junction SB	Opened	2.8.1880
Replacement box	Opened	19.1.1902
***	Closed	....
CARNFORTH	OP	6.6.1867
***	OG	....
Carnforth East Jcn to Carnforth Furness & Midland Jcn	Opened	1.7.1868
***	CP	2.8.1880
***	RO(P)	12.11.1972
***	CP	....
Kier Bridge SB	Open before	16.8.1877
***	Closed	1880
CARNFORTH	Opened	1.7.1868
***	Closed	2.8.1880
Carnforth Furness & Midland Junction SB	Opened	....
Replacement box	Opened	29.3.1896

Carnforth Curve

Powers: Furness Railway Act 1879

Carnforth East Jcn to Carnforth Station Jcn	Opened	2.8.1880
The opening of this curve, with access to the London & North Western and Furness joint station, allowed the closure of the Furness & Midland station.		
CARNFORTH	CG	7.10.1968
Carnforth: Furness & Midland Sidings (west-to-north curve)	Opened	....
***	Closed	....

SETTLE & CARLISLE LINE

Powers: Midland Railway (Settle and Carlisle) Act 1866
(Settle Junction to Dent)
Midland Railway (Additional Powers) Act 1871 (Arten Gill Deviation)
Midland Railway (Settle and Carlisle) Act 1866 (Dent)
Midland Railway (Additional Powers) Act 1871 (Cow Gill Deviation)
Midland Railway (Settle and Carlisle) Act 1866
(Hawes Junction to Cotehill)
Midland Railway (Additional Powers) Act 1875
(Appleby: southern junction with the North Eastern Railway)
Midland Railway (Additional Powers) Act 1874 (Cotehill)
Midland Railway (Settle and Carlisle) Act 1866
(Cotehill to Petteril Junction)

Settle Jcn to Petteril Jcn with the North Eastern Railway	OG (thro')	2.8.1875
***	OP&G	1.5.1876

Working was by the block telegraph system from the opening.

Settle Jcn to Appleby North Jcn	CG	16.5.1983
Settle (New Station) SB	Opened	2.8.1875
Replacement box	Opened	12.4.1891
***	Closed	13.5.1984
SETTLE (NEW STATION)	OP&G	1.5.1876
Altered to SETTLE	... ...	1.7.1879 *
***	CG	12.10.1970
Stainforth Sidings SB	Opened	2.8.1875
Replacement box	Opened	11.9.1898
Replacement box	Opened	3.1950
***	Re-framed	28.9.1961
Box closed and down IBS provided in lieu	... ...	29.9.1963
***	t.o.u.	....
Helwith Bridge SB	Opened	11.4.1876
Replacement box	Opened	23.8.1896
***	Closed	7.9.1969
Horton Station SB	Opened	2.8.1875
Replacement box	Opened	9.8.1896
***	Closed	13.5.1984
RIBBLESDALE SIDING	Opened	5.1.1877
***	Closed	....
HORTON	OP	1.5.1876
***	OG	1.8.1876 *
Altered to HORTON-IN-RIBBLESDALE	... ...	26.9.1927
***	CG	1.2.1965
***	CP	4.5.1970
***	RO(P)	29.9.1986

Horton-in-Ribblesdale, Ribblehead, Dent, Garsdale, and Kirkby Stephen stations were re-opened for weekend Dales Rail services in the summer of 1975, and Langwathby, Lazonby, and Armathwaite were added to the list in the summer of 1976. These summer weekend services continued until the re-opening of 29 September 1986.

Selside SB	Opened	10.1876-8.1877
Replacement box	Opened	16.6.1907
***	Closed	30.11.1975
Craven Lime Company's Sidings SB	Opened	c.6.1877
***	Closed	28.7.1879
***	Re-opened	....
***	Closed	15.7.1901
Salt Lake Sidings SB	Opened	2.8.1875
***	Closed	28.7.1879
Ribblehead Station SB	Opened	c.12.1876
Replacement box	Opened	10.7.1898
***	Closed	17.8.1969
BATTY GREEN	OP	4.12.1876
***	OG	1877
Altered to RIBBLEHEAD	... ...	1.5.1877 *
***	CG	7.11.1966
***	CP	4.5.1970
***	RO(P) [Up]	29.9.1986
Ribblehead viaduct: temporary single-line working	Commenced	1.10.1978
***	Withdrawn	17.12.1978
***	Commenced	14.1.1979
***	Withdrawn	29.4.1979
***	Commenced	6.4.1980
***	Withdrawn	8.6.1980
***	Commenced	21.9.1980
***	Withdrawn	2.11.1980
Line across the viaduct permanently singled	... ...	13.1.1985
Blea Moor SB	Opened	2.8.1875
Replacement box	Opened	4.12.1892
Replacement box	Opened	28.6.1914
Replacement box	Opened	16.12.1941
Blea Moor: up lie-by siding made up goods loop	... ...	16.12.1941
Down No. 1 lie-by siding made down goods loop	... ...	21.12.1941
Down goods loop	t.o.u.	13.1.1985
Blea Moor tunnel: approach-lit up outer distant, and gong	Into use	23.9.1943
Dent Head SB	Open before	1.11.1875
Replacement box	Opened	1892-1901
***	Closed	12.4.1965
Rise Hill Siding SB	Opened	2.8.1875
***	Closed	6.8.1877

It is possible that Rise Hill Siding and Dent Head station were one and the same location. If this was in fact the case, then there will have been no renewal in 1877.

Dent Station SB	Opened	6.8.1877
Replacement box	Opened	9.8.1891
***	Closed	28.1.1981

DENT	OP&G	6.8.1877
***	CG	1.10.1964
***	CP	4.5.1970
***	RO(P)	29.9.1986
Rise Hill to Hawes Jcn	Doubled	20.3.1876
The section between Rise Hill and Mallerstang was single when the line was opened for goods traffic.		
South End of Rise Hill Tunnel SB	Open before	16.8.1877
***	Closed	8.1877-4.1878
North End of Rise Hill Tunnel SB	Open before	16.8.1877
***	Closed	8.1877-4.1878
Hawes Junction water troughs	Into use	22.10.1907
***	Abandoned	3.1968
Hawes Junction South SB	Opened	2.8.1875
Replacement box	Opened	3.7.1892
***	Closed	10.7.1910
HAWES JUNCTION	OG	1.5.1876 ?
***	OP	1.8.1876
Altered to HAWES JUNCTION & GARSDALE	... ...	20.1.1900
Altered to GARSDALE	... ...	1.9.1932
***	CG	6.4.1964
Back platform	t.o.u.	17.1.1965
***	CP	4.5.1970
***	RO(P)	29.9.1986
Hawes Junction Station SB (on down platform)	Opened	10.7.1910
Re-named Garsdale Station SB	... ...	1.9.1932
***	Closed	....
Hawes Junction engine shed	Opened	1879
***	Closed	....
Hawes Junction North SB	Opened	2.8.1875
Replacement box	Opened	16.8.1891
***	Closed	10.7.1910

Hawes Branch

Powers: Midland Railway (Additional Powers) Act 1875 (Hawes Branch Deviation No. 1)
Midland Railway (Settle and Carlisle) Act 1866 (Hawes Branch: West of Moss Dale Head Tunnel)
Midland Railway (Additional Powers) Act 1875 (Hawes Branch Deviation No. 2)
Midland Railway (Settle and Carlisle) Act 1866 (Hawes Branch - Hawes end)
Midland Railway (Settle and Carlisle) Act 1866, and North Eastern Railway (Leyburn and Hawes Etc) Act 1870 (Hawes Joint Station Line)

Hawes Junction to Hawes	OG	1.8.1878
***	Closed	16.3.1959
***	t.o.u.	8.12.1963
Hawes branch, and junction with the North Eastern Railway	OP	1.10.1878
Working was by block telegraph and train staff. The North Eastern possessed running powers for all traffic between Hawes Joint Station and Settle Junction.		
Hawes West SB	Opened	1.10.1878
Replacement box	Opened	9.9.1900
***	Closed	14.4.1907
HAWES (Midland and North Eastern joint station)	OG (MR)	1.8.1878
***	OP	1.10.1878
***	CP	16.3.1959
***	CG	27.4.1964
Hawes East SB	Opened	1.10.1878
Replacement box	Opened	12.8.1900
Re-named Hawes Station SB	... ...	14.4.1907
***	Closed	1959 ?
The Midland Railway possessed running powers for all traffic over the North Eastern line between Hawes and Leyburn.		

Hawes Junction to Mallerstang Sidings	Doubled	4.10.1875
Ais Gill SB	Opened	2.8.1875
Replacement box	Opened	24.6.1900
***	Closed	28.1.1981
Mallerstang SB	Opened	2.8.1875
Replacement box	Opened	9.9.1894
***	Closed	31.8.1969
Kirkby Stephen Station SB	Opened	2.8.1875
Replacement box	Opened	6.5.1894
Re-named Kirkby Stephen West SB	... ...	....
Replacement box	Opened	27.10.1974
KIRKBY STEPHEN	OP&G	1.5.1876
Altered to KIRKBY STEPHEN & RAVENSTONEDALE	... ...	1.10.1900
Altered to KIRKBY STEPHEN WEST	... ...	8.6.1953 *
***	CG	28.9.1964
***	CP	4.5.1970
***	RO(P)	29.9.1986

Location / Event	Status	Date
CROSBY GARRETT	OP&G	1.5.1876
***	CP&G	6.10.1952
Crosby Garrett Station SB	Opened	2.8.1875
Replacement box	Opened	16.4.1899
***	Closed	12.4.1965
Griseburn Ballast Sidings SB	Opened	2.8.1875
Replacement box	Opened	10.12.1905
***	Closed	28.1.1981
ORMSIDE	OP	1.5.1876
***	OG	1.4.1880
***	CP&G	2.6.1952
Ormside SB	Opened	1876
Replacement box	Opened	11.8.1907
***	Closed	8.3.1960
Appleby South Junction SB	Opened	2.8.1875
***	Closed	26.10.1886
Appleby South Junction with the North Eastern Railway was completed by June 1877, but was apparently never connected up at the North Eastern end. The rails were taken out in 1901.		
Appleby Station SB	Opened	1876
Replacement box	Opened	26.10.1886
Re-named Appleby West SB	... ...	1951
Box closed and new ground frame provided at the junction with the spur to the former North Eastern Railway line	... ...	14.10.1973
APPLEBY	OP&G	1.5.1876
Altered to APPLEBY WEST	Goods	1.7.1950
***	Passenger	1.9.1952
Altered to APPLEBY	... ...	5.5.1968
***	CG	18.10.1971
Appleby North Junction SB	Opened	2.8.1875
Replacement box	Opened	26.10.1890
***	Raised	17.7.1904
***	Burnt out	4.6.1951
Replacement box named Appleby North SB 120 yards further north	Opened	6.1951
Appleby North Jcn with the North Eastern Railway	Inspected	6.8.1878
Between Appleby North (or Midland) Junction and Appleby Midland station the North Eastern possessed running powers for goods and mineral traffic over the Midland line.		
Between Appleby North Junction and Appleby North Eastern station the Midland possessed running powers over the North Eastern line.		
Appleby North Jcn connections: up line	t.o.u.	26.9.1954
Down line made down & up through siding	... ...	20.10.1957
***	Closed	31.3.1989
Appleby North Jcn to Petteril Bridge Jcn	CG	31.3.1989
Appleby engine shed	Opened	1881
***	Closed	....
Long Marton Station SB	Opened	2.8.1875
Replacement box	Opened	29.7.1900
***	Closed	22.3.1970
LONG MARTON	OP&G	1.5.1876
***	CG	6.4.1964
***	CP	4.5.1970
NEW BIGGIN	OP&G	1.5.1876
***	CG	7.11.1966
***	CP	4.5.1970
New Biggin Station SB	Opened	2.8.1875
Replacement box	Opened	29.7.1900
***	Closed	16.12.1973
Culgaith Station SB	Opened	c.1.1880
***	Re-framed	20.9.1896
Replacement box	Opened	4.10.1908
***	Closed	....
CULGAITH	OP&G	1.4.1880
***	CG	5.10.1964
***	CP	4.5.1970
Staingill SB	Opened	2.8.1875
***	Closed	2.1879-2.1880
Long Wathby Station SB	Opened	2.8.1875
Re-named Longwathby Station SB	... ...	....
Re-named Langwathby Station SB	Before	16.8.1877
Replacement box	Opened	5.7.1903
***	Closed	27.10.1968
LONGWATHBY	OP&G	1.5.1876
Altered to LANGWATHBY	... ...	1.10.1876 *
***	CG	6.7.1964
***	CP	4.5.1970
***	RO(P)	29.9.1986
LITTLE SALKELD	OP&G	1.5.1876
***	CG	6.7.1964
***	CP	4.5.1970

Little Salkeld Station SB	Opened	2.8.1875
Replacement box	Opened	13.8.1899
***	Closed	6.7.1964
Long Meg Sidings SB	Open before	1894
***	Re-framed	28.6.1896
***	Closed	13.3.1915
Long Meg Sidings GF replaced by a signalbox	... ...	3.7.1955
***	Closed	....
Ballast Sidings SB	Opened	10.1876-8.1877
***	Closed	4.1878-2.1879
LAZONBY	OP&G	1.5.1876
Altered to LAZONBY & KIRKOSWALD	... ...	22.7.1895
***	CG	2.11.1964
***	CP	4.5.1970
***	RO(P)	29.9.1986
Lazonby Station SB	Opened	2.8.1875
Replacement box	Opened	21.7.1895
***	Closed	12.4.1965
Baron Wood Siding SB	Opened	1877
***	Closed	20.11.1888
ARMATHWAITE	OP&G	1.5.1876
***	CG	6.4.1964
***	CP	4.5.1970
***	RO(P)	29.9.1986
One source suggests there may have been goods traffic here from 2 August 1875 and at Knot Hill from 4 October 1875.		
Armathwaite Station SB	Opened	2.8.1875
Replacement box	Opened	14.7.1899
***	Closed	5.1.1983
Low House Crossing SB	Opened	2.8.1875
Replacement box	Opened	14.10.1900
***	Closed	....
Highstand Gill SB	Opened	2.8.1875
Re-named Knott Hill SB	... ...	....
Re-named Cotehill Station SB	... ...	1876
Replacement box	Opened	14.8.1904
***	Closed	30.6.1952
KNOT HILL (OR HIGH STAND GILL) altered to COTEHILL	After	1.2.1876
***	OP&G	1.5.1876
***	CP&G	7.4.1952
Howe & Company's Sidings SB	Opened	1876
***	Re-framed	8.9.1895
Replacement box 100 yards to the north	Opened	17.12.1916
***	Re-framed	1943
***	Closed	....
Howe's Sidings: down siding made up & down reception line	... ...	2.5.1943
***	t.o.u.	....
CUMWHINTON	OP&G	1.5.1876
***	CP&G	5.11.1956
Cumwhinton Station SB	Opened	2.8.1875
Replacement box	Opened	1897
***	Closed	24.2.1957
SCOTBY	OP&G	1.5.1876
***	CP&G	1.2.1942
Scotby Station SB	Opened	2.8.1875
Replacement box	Opened	1897
***	Closed	31.10.1909
Durran Hill South Sidings SB	Open before	16.8.1877
Replacement box	Opened	8.11.1891
***	Re-framed	....
***	Closed	12.5.1963
Durran Hill South Sidings to Durran Hill Jcn: up goods line	Into use	11.1875-10.1876
Up goods line made bi-directional	... ...	31.12.1916
***	t.o.u.	....
Durran Hill South Sidings: two down reception lines	Into use	15.10.1944
DURRAN HILL SIDINGS	Opened	....
***	t.o.u.	....
Durran Hill Jcn to Petteril Goods Yard SB: reception lines	t.o.u.	19.1.1964
Durran Hill engine shed	Opened	1875
***	Closed	16.2.1936
***	RO temp.	1943
***	Closed	....
Durran Hill Junction SB	Open before	16.8.1877
Replacement box	Opened	17.11.1895
***	Closed	25.4.1971
Durran Hill Jcn: up goods line to up passenger line crossover	Into use	....
Durran Hill Jcn to Petteril Jcn: up goods line	Into use	11.1874-11.1875
Down goods line	Into use	11.1875-10.1876
Up and down goods lines	t.o.u.	....

Durran Hill Jcn to Petteril Goods Yard SB:		
up goods line on the down side of the down goods line	Into use	12.1888-8.1893
Second up goods line made bi-directional and named the independent line	... ...	8.2.1914
***	t.o.u.	....
PETTERIL GOODS DEPOT (CARLISLE MIDLAND GOODS STATION)	Opened	2.8.1875
Altered to PETTERIL BRIDGE GOODS DEPOT	... ...	3.9.1909
***	Closed	1.2.1966

Between Petteril Goods Depot and Petteril Junction the London & North Western possessed running powers over the Midland line for the exchange of merchandise traffic. The North Eastern also exercised running powers over this section of the Midland line for the exchange of traffic.

Between Petteril Goods Depot and Petteril Junction the Glasgow & South Western Railway possessed running powers over the Midland line.

Petteril Goods Yard SB	Opened	1876 ?
Replacement box	Opened	18.10.1891
***	Re-framed	....
***	C. temp	4.9.1960
***	Made NBP	12.11.1961
***	Abolished	19.1.1964 ?
	or	16.7.1965 ?
Petteril Junction SB	Opened	....
Replacement box	Opened	20.6.1891
Re-named Petteril Bridge Junction SB	... ...	....
***	Closed	3.6.1973

Between Petteril Junction and the junction with the Citadel Station lines the Midland possessed running powers for all traffic over the North Eastern line.

Between Petteril Junction and Canal Junction the Midland exercised running powers for goods, coal, coke, and livestock traffic.

Between Petteril Junction and London Road Goods Station the Midland exercised running powers over the North Eastern line for the exchange of goods, coal, coke, and livestock traffic.

Between Petteril Junction and Rome Street Junction the Midland possessed running powers over the North Eastern line for all traffic and exercised them for goods, coal, coke, and livestock traffic.

From London Road Junction the Midland Railway possessed running powers over the Carlisle Citadel Station Committee's lines.

Between Rome Street Junction and Crown Street Goods Station the Midland possessed running powers over the Maryport & Carlisle line.

CARLISLE: rebuilt and enlarged Citadel passenger station	Opened	4.7.1880
Station made "closed" for tickets 10 p.m. to 7 a.m. nightly	... ...	4.2.1929
Entirely "closed"	... ...	25.7.1938
Carlisle No. 12 SB: connection from shunting neck to Up Goods Line to give direct access to the carriage shed	Into use	11.5.1896

Between London Road Junction and the Carlisle goods and livestock stations the Midland Railway possessed running powers over the London & North Western line for the exchange of merchandise traffic.

Between Carlisle and Glasgow Buchanan Street, Edinburgh, Dundee, and Aberdeen the Midland Railway possessed running powers for all traffic over the Caledonian line.

Between Canal Junction and Edinburgh, Leith, Granton, Greenhill Junction, Larbert Junction, Perth, and Dundee the Midland possessed running powers for all traffic over the North British line.

From Gretna Junction the Midland Railway possessed running powers for all traffic over the whole line of the Glasgow & South Western Railway.

CARLISLE JOINT GOODS LINES

Land Powers for Dentonholme Joint Station:
North British Railway (Carlisle Citadel Station Branches) Act 1865

DENTONHOLME GOODS DEPOT, with branch	Opened	1.10.1883
Dentonholme Goods Yard SB	Opened	....
***	Closed	22.11.1903
Dentonholme Goods Yard North SB	Opened	22.11.1903
***	Closed	11.2.1973
Rome Street to Dentonholme Goods Yard North	Closed	24.9.1972
Dentonholme Goods Yard North to Dentonholme North Jcn	Closed	11.2.1973

The Maryport & Carlisle Railway possessed running powers over the Dentonholme Station lines, the Carlisle Goods Traffic Committee lines, and between the junction with the North Eastern Railway and Durran Hill Sidings.

Powers: Carlisle Citadel Station Act 1873 (Citadel Station Goods Lines)

Carlisle Goods Traffic Committee: new Carlisle goods lines	Into use	7.8.1877
Carlisle Goods Lines:		
Rome Street Jcn to Caldew Jcn; Rome Street Jcn to Forks Jcn	Off. closed	15.12.1985

These lines had been out of use for some time as a result of damage caused by a runaway train.

VII. THE MANCHESTER LINE

MANCHESTER, BUXTON, MATLOCK & MIDLANDS JUNCTION RAILWAY

The Manchester, Buxton, Matlock & Midlands Junction Railway was worked by the Midland from its opening, and then by the Midland and London & North Western Railways under an arrangement for nineteen years with effect from 1 July 1852 under the Manchester, Buxton, Matlock, and Midlands Junction Railway, and Cromford Canal Leasing Act 1852. The Midland Railway (Additional Powers) Act 1870 vested the company in the Midland with effect from 1 July 1871.

Powers: Manchester, Buxton, Matlock and Midland Junction Railway Act 1847
(Ambergate [North] Junction to Ambergate [West Junction])
Manchester, Buxton, Matlock and Midland Junction Railway Act 1846
(Ambergate to Whatstandwell)
Manchester, Buxton, Matlock and Midland Junction Railway Act 1847
(Whatstandwell to Cromford)
Manchester, Buxton, Matlock and Midland Junction Railway Act 1846
(Cromford to Matlock Bath)
Manchester, Buxton, Matlock and Midland Junction Railway Act 1847
(Matlock Bath to Darley Dale)
Manchester, Buxton, Matlock and Midland Junction Railway Act 1848
(Darley Dale to Rowsley)
Midland Railway (Additional Power) Act 1874
(Widening at Rowsley - Land Powers only)

Ambergate to Rowsley	OP	4.6.1849
***	O.Coal	20.8.1849
***	OG	End 12.1849
It is believed that there was at first no through passenger working between the main line at Ambergate (North) Junction and the Rowsley line. Goods traffic was, of course, worked through.		
Ambergate to Rowsley: block telegraph system	Installed	c.1866
Between Ambergate and Matlock Bath the London & North Western possessed running powers for all traffic passing to and from the Cromford & High Peak Railway (but not beyond).		
Ambergate West Jcn to Ambergate North Jcn (Ambergate North Curve)		
***	CP	1.6.1863
***	RO(P)	1.5.1877 *
***	CP	1.10.1877 *
***	RO(P)	1.7.1878 *
***	CP	1.1.1917 *
***	RO(P)	1.10.1919 *
***	CP	16.6.1947
***	Tfc ceased	3.10.1966
***	t.o.u	26.2.1967

Ambergate South Curve

Powers: Midland Railway (Additional Powers) Act 1862

Ambergate South Jcn to Ambergate West Jcn	OP&G	1.6.1863
***	Singled	11.8.1968
Ambergate South Jcn to Matlock: one engine in steam working	Commenced	11.5.1969
Electric key token working	Commenced	1.8.1976

Ambergate Middle Curve

Powers: Midland Railway (Additional Powers) Act 1873 (Land Powers only)

Ambergate Station Jcn to Ambergate North Jcn	Opened	10.12.1876
***	Tfc ceased	2.1.1967
***	t.o.u.	26.2.1967
***	Closed	12.5.1968

Ambergate West Junction SB	Open before	16.8.1877
Replacement box	Opened	21.5.1893
Box closed when the location ceased to be a junction	... ...	26.2.1967
***	Re-opened	11.8.1968
***	Closed	11.5.1969
Ambergate West Jcn to Matlock	Singled	11.5.1969
Johnson's Sidings SB	Opened	4.6.1883
Replacement box	Opened	4.9.1920
***	Closed	9.4.1933
WHATSTANDWELL BRIDGE	Opened	1.9.1853 *
Replacement passenger station south of the tunnel	Opened	11.11.1894
Altered to WHATSTANDWELL	... ...	1.7.1896 *
***	CG	6.4.1964
There may have been an earlier stopping-place at Whatstandwell.		
Whatstandwell Station SB	Open before	1.11.1875
Re-named Whatstandwell Sidings SB	... ...	11.11.1894
Replacement box	Opened	28.4.1895
***	Re-framed	17.9.1906
Replacement box	Opened	18.6.1922
***	Closed	24.7.1966

Whatstandwell to Cromford: curves altered	... ...	1884
High Peak Junction SB	Open before	1.11.1875
Replacement box	Opened	18.8.1901
***	Closed	29.10.1967
High Peak Jcn with the Cromford & High Peak Railway	Opened	21.2.1853
***	Closed	6.3.1967
High Peak North SB	Opened	17.4.1887
***	Closed	21.5.1887
Lea Wood SB	Opened	17.4.1887
***	Closed	21.5.1887
Cromford Sidings SB	Opened	1.9.1890
***	Closed	19.12.1965
CROMFORD	OP	4.6.1849
Matlock Bath SB	Open before	16.8.1877
Replacement box	Opened	15.3.1891
***	Raised	13.3.1910
***	Closed	19.12.1965
MATLOCK BATH	Opened	4.6.1849
***	CG	6.4.1964
***	CP	6.3.1967
***	RO(P)	27.5.1972
High Tor Tunnels SB	Opened	28.5.1888
***	Closed	1.7.1889
Matlock Bridge South SB	Open before	1875
Replacement box	Opened	3.12.1899
Re-named Matlock South SB	... ...	5.7.1905
***	Closed	27.2.1910
MATLOCK BRIDGE	Opened	4.6.1849
Altered to MATLOCK	... ...	1.7.1905
***	CG	4.9.1972
Matlock SB	Opened	27.2.1910
***	Closed	11.5.1969
Matlock Bridge North SB	Open before	1875
***	Re-framed	21.9.1890
Replacement box	Opened	7.1.1900
Re-named Matlock North SB	... ...	5.7.1905
***	Closed	27.2.1910
Matlock: line beyond bridge No. 35 towards Darley Dale re-opened as Research Department test track	... ...	7.2.1971
***	Lifted by	1974
Matlock: line severed at 146m 840yds	... ...	28.1.1974
Matlock to Rowsley	Closed	1.7.1968
Peak Rail intends to re-open the section between Matlock and Buxton to passenger traffic.		
Cawdor Bridge SB	Opened	13.2.1887
***	Closed	9.4.1887
Darley South SB	Open before	1.11.1875
***	Closed	6.1881-4.1883
DARLEY	Opened	4.6.1849
Altered to DARLEY DALE	... ...	1.10.1890
***	CG	6.4.1964
***	CP	6.3.1967
Darley Station SB	Open before	16.8.1877
Re-named Darley North SB	... ...	2.1879-2.1880
Re-named Darley Station SB	... ...	6.1881-4.1883
Re-named Darley Dale Station SB	... ...	10.1890 ?
Replacement box south of the station	Opened	24.5.1891
***	Re-framed	14.4.1901
***	Closed	7.7.1968
Darley Dale to Church Lane Crossing: up slow line	Into use	12.5.1901
Down slow line	Into use	18.8.1901
Up and down slow lines	t.o.u.	1.7.1968
Church Lane Crossing SB	Open before	16.8.1877
Replacement box	Opened	1892-1901
***	Alt.levers	12.11.1911
***	Closed	7.7.1968
Rowsley South Junction SB	Opened	c.3.1877
Replacement box	Opened	20.6.1915
***	Closed	11.6.1967
Rowsley South Jcn to Rowsley North Jcn: up and down goods lines	Into use	19.3.1877
***	t.o.u.	....
Rowsley South Jcn to Rowsley Sidings: down coal line	Into use	11.8.1889
***	t.o.u.	....
ROWSLEY SIDINGS	Opened	19.3.1877
Additional sidings (down sidings)	Into use	9.9.1928
***	Closed	27.4.1964
Rowsley Up Sidings SB (not a block post)	Opened	c.3.1877
Replacement box	Opened	2.5.1892
***	Re-framed	16.9.1917
Replacement box (second hand from another location)	Opened	7.9.1952
***	Closed	4.5.1964

Rowsley Down Sidings SB (not a block post)	Opened	c.3.1877
Replacement box	Opened	16.5.1892
Replacement box named Rowsley Down Sidings No. 1 SB	Opened	9.9.1928
***	Closed	20.12.1964
Rowsley Down Sidings No. 2 SB (not a block post)	Opened	9.9.1928
***	Closed	16.8.1964
Rowsley North Junction SB	Opened	c.3.1877
Replacement box	Opened	3.11.1889
Replacement box	Opened	17.4.1910
***	Closed	7.7.1968
Rowsley North Jcn to Rowsley goods depot	Closed	1.7.1968
ROWSLEY TICKET PLATFORM	Closed	....
Rowsley engine shed	Opened	1849
***	Enlarged	1879-1880
Replacement shed south of Rowsley South Junction SB	Replaced	1923
***	Closed	4.5.1964

Rowsley shed may have been closed for a period from 1863, but it was certainly in use again by 1869. The 1923 shed was not brought into use till 1926.

Rowsley MPD closed except as a signing-on point	... ...	4.1.1965
ROWSLEY	Opened	6.4.1849
***	CP	1.8.1862
***	CG	1.7.1968

ROWSLEY & BUXTON LINE

Powers: Midland Railway (Rowsley and Buxton) Act 1860
Midland Railway Act 1903 (Miller's Dale Loop)

Rowsley to Hassop	OP	1.8.1862
***	OG	1.11.1862

The old Rowsley terminus pointing into the Derwent valley was retained as the goods station and a new passenger station was opened on the line towards Buxton.

Rowsley to Buxton: block telegraph system	Installed	Late 1860s
Rowsley to Buxton Jcn	Closed	1.7.1968
Rowsley Station SB	Opened	....
Replacement box south of the station	Open before	16.8.1877
***	Closed	17.4.1910
ROWSLEY	OP	1.8.1862
Altered to ROWSLEY FOR CHATSWORTH	... ...	1.9.1867 *
Altered to ROWSLEY	... ...	14.6.1965 *
***	CP	6.3.1967
Haddon SB	Opened	15.12.1889
Box closed and down IBS provided in lieu	... ...	13.12.1964
***	t.o.u.	....
BAKEWELL	OP	1.8.1862
***	OG	1.11.1862
***	CP	6.3.1967
***	CG	1.7.1968
Bakewell Station SB	Open before	1.11.1875
Replacement box	Opened	16.1.1921
***	Closed	7.7.1968
Hassop Station SB	Opened	1876
Replacement box	Opened	21.7.1895
***	Closed	8.5.1966
HASSOP	OP	1.8.1862
***	OG	1.11.1862
Altered to HASSOP FOR CHATSWORTH	... ...	3.1870-5.1871 *
Altered to HASSOP	... ...	7.1906-7.1907 *
***	CP	17.8.1942
***	CG	5.10.1964

Hassop to Buxton	OP	1.6.1863
***	OG	1.7.1863
LONGSTONE	OP	1.6.1863
Altered to GREAT LONGSTONE FOR ASHFORD	... ...	1.10.1913 *
***	CP(All)	10.9.1962

One train in each direction continued to call after closure to meet the needs of one passenger. This unadvertised service lasted until the closure of the line.

Longstone Station SB	Open before	16.8.1877
***	Alt.levers	1.6.1892
Replacement box	Opened	15.3.1903
Re-named Great Longstone Station SB	... ...	....
***	Closed	....
***	RO(IBTSP)	9.2.1920
***	Closed	1.7.1931

CRESSBROOK SIDING	OM	1.5.1866 *
Altered to MONSAL DALE	... ...	1.9.1866 *
***	OP	1.9.1866
***	OG	1914
***	CP&G	10.8.1959
Ramblers' special trains continued to call for at least another year.		
Monsal Dale Station SB	Open before	1.10.1876
Replacement box	Opened	25.10.1896
***	Closed	15.1.1967
Litton Tunnel SB	Opened	1885
***	Closed	12.10.1886
Oldham Lime Company's Sidings SB	Open before	1.11.1875
Re-named Miller's Dale Lime Company's Sidings SB	... ...	7.2.1887
Replacement box	Opened	21.4.1890
Replacement box	Opened	16.4.1905
***	Closed	6.3.1967
Miller's Dale Lime Company's Sidings to Miller's Dale station: new up and down main lines over the new viaduct <u>AND</u> two new lines and platforms in the station	Into use	20.8.1905
Up slow line	Into use	1.4.1906
Down slow line	Into use	2.4.1906
Up and down slow lines	t.o.u.	6.3.1967
MILLER'S DALE	OP	1.6.1863
***	OG	1.10.1863 *
Altered to MILLER'S DALE FOR TIDESWELL	... ...	1.5.1889 *
Altered to MILLER'S DALE	... ...	14.6.1965 *
***	CG	27.8.1966
***	CP	6.3.1967
Miller's Dale Station SB	Open before	16.8.1877
Replacement box	Opened	25.1.1891
***	Re-framed	20.8.1905
***	Closed	6.3.1967
East Buxton Lime Sidings SB	Open before	16.8.1877
***	Re-framed	3.11.1895
Replacement box	Opened	11.10.1901
***	Closed	25.6.1933
Chee Tor Tunnel SB	Opened	4.8.1886
***	Closed	18.5.1888
Blackwell Mill Junction	Opened	1.10.1866
Re-named Peak Forest Junction	... ...	1.7.1871 *
Re-named Miller's Dale Junction	After	6.1875 *
Miller's Dale Junction SB	Open before	16.8.1877
Replacement box	Opened	10.1.1915
***	Closed	6.3.1967

<u>Rowsley & Buxton Extension line</u>
See page 193

Miller's Dale Jcn to Buxton	CP	6.3.1967
Miller's Dale Jcn to Buxton Jcn	Closed	6.3.1967
Buxton Junction SB	Open before	1.11.1875
Replacement box	Opened	11.3.1917
***	Closed	7.7.1968
(Great Rocks Jcn to) Buxton Jcn to Buxton No. 1 (Stockport line)	Singled	21.6.1970
Buxton Jcn to Buxton No. 1: direction changed from DOWN to UP	... ...	7.7.1968
BLACKWELL MILL	OP(NA)	1.11.1874 *
***	CP(All)	6.3.1967 *
Newton & Chambers Sidings SB	Open before	1.11.1875
Re-named Topley Pike SB	... ...	c.1876
Replacement box	Opened	3.2.1901
Box closed and ground frame provided in lieu	... ...	21.1.1969
***	t.o.u.	31.5.1970
Topley Pike: bridge No. 6	Singled	30.10.1960
***	Re-doubled	4.12.1960
During the period when the line was singled working was by electric train staff.		
Ashwood Dale SB	Opened	1877
Replacement box	Opened	2.2.1902
***	Closed	28.10.1968
Buxton Gas Works Sidings SB (not a block post)	Open before	16.8.1877
Box closed and ground frame provided in lieu	... ...	1937-1945
***	t.o.u.	14.10.1956
Buxton L. & N. W. Junction SB	Open before	16.8.1877
***	Closed	6.1881-4.1883
Buxton East Junction SB	Opened	20.11.1892
Replacement box	Opened	1906-1917
***	Closed	10.9.1967

Buxton Curve

Powers: Midland Railway (Rowsley and Buxton) Act 1860

Buxton East Jcn to Buxton North Jcn with the London & North Western Railway	Opened	1.7.1863 ?
***	Closed after	1870
***	Restored	12.7.1875
Facing connection to curve-line at Buxton East Jcn	Into use	17.5.1908
***	Singled	21.6.1970

Between Buxton Junction and Buxton Goods Station the Midland possessed running powers over the London & North Western line for merchandise traffic for exchange.
Between Buxton Junction and Cheadle Village Junction the Midland possessed running powers over the London & North Western line.

Buxton East Jcn to Buxton Midland SB	C.Tfc	6.3.1967
***	Closed	10.9.1967
Buxton engine shed	Opened	1862-1863
***	Closed	19.8.1935
Buxton Station SB	Open before	16.8.1877
***	Re-framed	18.6.1899
Replacement box	Opened	28.6.1908
***	Closed	10.9.1967
Buxton station: layout and signalling altered	... ...	28.6.1908
BUXTON	OP	1.6.1863
***	OG	1. 7.1863
Goods depot re-named to BUXTON CENTRAL GOODS DEPOT	... ...	1924
***	CP(All)	6.3.1967
***	CG	1.4.1967

ROWSLEY & BUXTON EXTENSION LINE

Powers: Midland Railway (Rowsley and Buxton Extension) Act 1862
Midland Railway Act 1900 (Chinley & New Mills Widening)
Midland Railway Act 1891 (New Mills Widening)

Blackwell Mill Jcn to New Mills Jcn with the Manchester, Sheffield & Lincolnshire Railway	OG	1.10.1866
***	CG	1.11.1866
***	RO(G)	24.1.1867
Blackwell Mill Jcn to New Mills Jcn	OP	1.2.1867

The line was closed because of a land-slip at Bugsworth. It was necessary to build a deviation before it could be brought back into use. It had been intended to open the line for passenger traffic on 1 November 1866, but the blockage prevented this.

Blackwell Mill Jcns to New Mills Jcn: block telegraph system	Installed by	1870
Miller's Dale Jcn to Peak Forest Jcn	Closed	1.7.1968

Blackwell Mill Curve

Powers: Midland Railway (Rowsley and Buxton Extension) Act 1862

Peak Forest Jcn to Buxton Jcn (these are the later names)	OG	1.10.1866
***	OP	1.5.1867
***	CP	6.3.1967
***	Singled	21.6.1970

Peak Forest Junction SB	Open before	16.8.1877
Replacement box	Opened	1906-1916 ?
Replacement box	Opened	....
***	Closed	7.7.1968
Peak Forest Jcn to Chinley North Jcn	CP	1.7.1968
Peak Forest Jcn to Great Rocks Jcn	Singled	21.6.1970

The direction of running became DOWN right through from Chinley North Junction to Buxton and the line was designated a goods line.

Tunstead SB	Opened	26.10.1930
***	Closed	21.6.1970
Tunstead to Great Rocks Jcn: former down main line made up & down through siding	... ...	21.6.1970
Great Rocks SB	Opened	24.5.1888 ?
Replacement box	Opened	20.10.1890
Replacement box named Great Rocks Junction SB about 700 yards north	Opened	23.2.1891
Replacement box	Opened	11.3.1923
Great Rocks Jcn: new fan of sidings	Into use	4.11.1895
Great Rocks Jcn to Peak Forest South: down goods line	Into use	26.7.1891
Down goods line made up & down through siding	... ...	21.6.1970
Peak Forest South SB	Open before	16.8.1877
Replacement box	Opened	12.4.1891
Replacement box	Opened	5.7.1925
***	Re-framed	21.7.1974

PEAK FOREST	OG	1.10.1866
***	OP	1.2.1867
Altered to PEAK FOREST FOR PEAK DALE	... ...	26.9.1893
Altered to PEAK FOREST	... ...	14.6.1965 *
***	CG	15.6.1964
***	CP	6.3.1967
Between Peak Forest and New Mills Junction the Manchester, Sheffield & Lincolnshire possessed running powers for coal, limestone, lime, and mineral traffic over the Midland line.		
Peak Forest North SB	Open before	16.8.1877
Replacement box	Opened	27.1.1901
Replacement box	Opened	1.3.1925
***	Closed	25.8.1968
South End of Dove Holes Tunnel SB	Opened	2.1880-6.1881
***	Closed	6.1881-4.1883
***	Re-opened	19.6.1892
***	Closed	1892-1893
Dove Holes South SB	Opened	19.6.1892
***	Closed	5.3.1967
Dove Holes Tunnel Central SB	Opened	2.1879-2.1880
***	Closed	2.1880-6.1881
Replacement box	Opened	6.7.1890
***	Closed	19.6.1892
North End of Dove Holes Tunnel SB	Open before	1.10.1876
Replacement box	Opened	8.6.1902
***	Closed	5.3.1967
Dove Holes Tunnel: tunnel fell in at the Manchester end	... ...	7.2.1904
***	RO(G)	17.3.1904
***	RO(P)	21.3.1904
Obstruction-warning wires	Installed	4.1904
Chapel-en-le-Frith landslip (at Dove Holes tunnel)	... ...	18.6.1872
***	RO(G)	28.7.1872
***	RO(P)	20.8.1872
Chapel-en-le-Frith South SB	Opened	10.12.1893
***	Closed	25.6.1905
Chapel-en-le-Frith South to North: down goods line	Into use	10.12.1893
***	t.o.u.	....
Chapel-en-le-Frith Station SB (first box)	Open before	16.8.1877
***	Closed	10.12.1893
Chapel-en-le-Frith Station SB (second box - on up platform)	Opened	25.6.1905
***	Closed	30.6.1968
CHAPEL-EN-LE-FRITH	OG	1.10.1866
***	OP	1.2.1867
Altered to CHAPEL-EN-LE-FRITH CENTRAL	... ...	2.6.1924
***	CG	2.12.1963
***	CP	6.3.1967
Chapel-en-le-Frith North SB	Opened	10.12.1893
***	Closed	25.6.1905
Chapel-en-le-Frith North: down goods line to down passenger line crossover	Into use	7.3.1894
***	t.o.u.	25.6.1905
Chapel-en-le-Frith North to Chinley South Jcn: up goods line	Into use	10.12.1893
Down goods line	Into use	7.3.1894
Up and down goods lines	t.o.u.	30.6.1968
Chinley South Junction SB	Opened	21.5.1893
***	Alt.levers	3.12.1893
***	Closed	17.5.1970

Chinley South Curve

See page 197

Chinley South Jcn to Chinley North Jcn	Singled	21.12.1980
Chinley North Junction SB	Opened	21.10.1893
Replacement box	Opened	26.10.1902
Replacement box named Chinley SB	Opened	14.12.1980
Chinley North Jcn: double junction (DSL-DFL, UFL-USL)	Into use	29.3.1903
Double junction (DFL-DSL, USL-UFL)	Into use	29.3.1903
Layout at the junction, and between Chinley North Junction and Chinley Station North	Re-modelled	6.12.1981

Dore & Chinley Line

See page 196

Chinley North Jcn to Chinley Station South Jcn: up goods line	Into use	19.10.1902
Chinley North Jcn to Chinley Station North Jcn: up and down slow lines (up side)	Into use	29.3.1903
Chinley Station SB (old station)	Open before	1.10.1876
Replacement box	Opened	5.10.1890
***	Closed	22.6.1902
Chinley Station South SB	Opened	22.6.1902
***	Re-framed	1.3.1903
***	Closed	29.9.1968

Chinley Station South: up slow line to up fast line crossover	Into use	29.3.1903 ?
***	t.o.u.	....
CHINLEY	OG	1.10.1866
***	OP	1.2.1867
Replacement passenger station further to the north	Opened	1.6.1902
Down loop outside the down platform	Into use	22.6.1902
Bay at the south end of the up platform	Into use	22.6.1902
Up loop on outside of the up island platform	Into use	22.6.1902
***	CG	7.10.1963
Chinley Station North SB	Opened	22.6.1902
***	Closed	6.12.1981
Chinley Station North: double junction (DSL-DFL, UFL-USL)	Into use	28.6.1903
***	t.o.u.	....
Chinley to Bugsworth Jcn: up and down slow lines (up side)	Into use	28.6.1903
Chinley Station Jcn to New Mills South Jcn: up and down slow lines	t.o.u.	28.1.1973
Bugsworth new line	Into use	22.3.1885
BUGSWORTH	OP	1.2.1867
Altered to BUXWORTH	... ...	4.6.1930
***	CP(All)	15.9.1958
Bugsworth Station SB	Open before	1.10.1876
Replacement box	Opened	1884
Replacement box (second-hand, from the Radlett area)	Opened	26.11.1893
Replacement box	Opened	2.9.1894
Replacement box named Bugsworth Junction SB 48 chains north	Opened	24.5.1903
***	Raised	26.10.1913
Re-named Buxworth Junction SB	... ...	4.6.1930
***	Closed	9.10.1966
Bugsworth Jcn: double junction (DFL-DSL, USL-UFL)	Into use	28.6.1903
Double junction (DSL-DFL, UFL-USL)	Into use	28.6.1903
Double junctions	Removed	24.10.1965
Bugsworth Jcn: new goods sidings	Into use	5.1908 *
Bugsworth Jcn to Gowhole Goods Jcn:		
position of the up and down main lines	Altered	31.5.1903
Bugsworth Jcn to New Mills South Jcn:		
up and down goods lines (up side)	Into use	14.6.1903
Goods lines made slow lines	... ...	3.7.1904
GOWHOLE UP SIDINGS	Opened	1.3.1903
DOWN SIDINGS	Opened	11.5.1903
***	Closed	18.5.1969
Gowhole Down Sidings SB	Opened	28.6.1903
Box closed and ground frame provided in lieu	... ...	19.12.1909
***	t.o.u.	18.5.1969
L. & E. Hall's Sidings SB	Open before	1.11.1875
Replacement box	Opened	21.8.1892
Re-named Gowhole Goods Junction SB	... ...	23.10.1892
***	Re-framed	28.6.1903
Replacement box	Opened	19.12.1920
***	Closed	18.5.1969
L. & E. Hall's Sidings SB to Midland Goods Yard SB:		
up and down goods lines	Into use	23.10.1892
New Mills South Jcn (south of): up Romiley goods loop	Into use	22.2.1981
New Mills South Jcn: double junction (DFL-DSL, USL-UFL)	Into use	14.6.1903
Double junction (DSL-DFL, UFL-USL)	Into use	14.6.1903
New Mills South Jcn to New Mills Central: line named "Romiley lines"	... ...	6.12.1981
New Mills South Jcn: junction with down Romiley line	Altered	30.9.1984
New Mills South Junction SB	Opened	4.5.1902
Replacement box	Opened	14.6.1903
***	Re-framed	....
***	Closed	....

New Mills & Heaton Mersey line

See page 197

New Mills South Jcn: up passenger line and up goods line	Slued	24.5.1903
New Mills South Jcn to New Mills Goods Jcn: up goods line	t.o.u.	4.6.1969
NEW MILLS GOODS DEPOT	Opened	....
Altered to NEW MILLS EAST GOODS DEPOT	... ...	2.6.1924 ?
***	Closed	9.9.1968
New Mills Goods Yard SB	Open before	16.8.1877
Replacement box named New Mills Goods Junction SB	Opened	21.8.1892
Replacement box	Opened	16.12.1928
***	Closed	4.6.1969

DORE & CHINLEY RAILWAY

The Dore & Chinley Railway was dissolved, its powers being transferred to the Midland, under the Midland Railway (Additional Powers) Act 1888 with effect from 2 April 1894.

Powers: Dore and Chinley Railway Act 1884 (Dore & Totley to East End of Totley Tunnel)
Dore and Chinley Railway Act 1885 (East End of Totley Tunnel to Hathersage)
Dore and Chinley Railway Act 1884 (Hathersage to East End of Cowburn Tunnel)
Midland Railway Act 1892 (Alteration of levels at Bamford and at Hope)
Dore and Chinley Railway Act 1885 (Cowburn Tunnel)
Dore and Chinley Railway Act 1884 (West End of Cowburn Tunnel to Chinley North Junction)

Dore Station Jcn to Chinley North Jcn	OG	6.11.1893	
Totley Tunnel East to Grindleford: block telegraph working in place of working by pilot engine and guard	Commenced	19.11.1893	
Dore Station Jcn to Chinley North Jcn	O. excursions	14.5.1894	
***	OP (thro')	1.6.1894	
***	OP (all)	25.6.1894	
Dore Station Jcn re-located 55 yards further north	... ...	8.4.1985	
Dore Station Jcn to Dore West Jcn (north of)	Singled	31.3.1985	
DORE & TOTLEY: Manchester-bound platform	t.o.u.	31.3.1985	
Dore South Junction Curve			
Powers: Dore and Chinley Railway Act 1885			
Dore South Jcn to Dore West Jcn	OG	11.6.1894	
***	OP	7. 2.1904	
***	CP	21. 3.1904	
***	RO(P)	1.4.1904	*
***	CP	1.7.1908	*
***	RO(P)	1.10.1911	
***	CP	1.1.1917	*
***	RO(P)	3.10.1966	
***	CP	2.5.1977	
***	Singled	23.1.1983	
***	RO(P)	11.5.1987	
Dore West Junction SB	Opened	29.10.1893	
Box closed and ground frame provided in lieu	Closed	16.1.1972	
***	Abolished	9.1.1983	
Totley Tunnel East SB	Opened	29.10.1893	
Totley Tunnel SB	Opened	13.1.1895	
***	Closed	1895	
This signalbox was on the down side of the line on the Grindleford side of the central ventilating shaft, to protect engineering operations at the shaft.			
GRINDLEFORD	OP&G	25.6.1894	
***	CG	3.1984	
Grindleford Station SB	Opened	29.10.1893	
Replacement box 270 yards to the west	Opened	20.11.1938	
Hathersage Station SB	Opened	29.10.1893	
***	Closed	19.11.1967	
HATHERSAGE	OP&G	25.6.1894	
***	CG	30.1.1965	
Bamford Station SB	Opened	29.10.1893	
BAMFORD	OP&G	25.6.1894	
***	CG	31.1.1966	
Water Works Sidings SB	Opened	16.2.1902	
***	Closed	8.4.1919	
Water Board's Sidings SB	Opened	2.12.1935	
***	Closed	16.10.1949	
Photographs suggest that the signalbox was the same one as before, re-opened after thirty years.			
Hope Station SB	Opened	29.10.1893	
***	Closed	5.8.1964	
HOPE FOR CASTLETON	OP&G	25.6.1894	
Altered to HOPE FOR CASTLETON & BRADWELL	By	1.4.1895	
***	CG	20.4.1964	
Altered to HOPE	... ...	14.6.1965	*
Earle's Sidings SB	Opened	14.4.1929	
Norman's Bank SB	Opened	8.2.1904	
***	Closed	17.5.1904	
***	Re-opened	18.7.1904	
Box closed and IBS provided in lieu	... ...	24.4.1960	
***	t.o.u.	....	
EDALE	OP&G	25.6.1894	
***	CG	7.10.1963	
Edale Station SB	Opened	29.10.1893	
Cowburn Tunnel East SB	Opened	29.5.1894	
***	Closed	13.1.1957	
Cowburn Tunnel West SB	Opened	29.10.1893	
***	Closed by	13.11.1966	

Chinley East Junction SB	Opened	29.10.1893
***	Raised	29.4.1894
***	Closed	27.2.1966

Chinley South Curve

Powers: Midland Railway Act 1889

Chinley East Jcn to Chinley South Jcn	OG	6.11.1893
***	O. excursions	14.5.1894 ?
***	OP	25.6.1894
***	CP	1.10.1904 *
***	RO(P)	1.7.1912 *
***	CP	1.1.1917 *
***	Closed	21.9.1964
***	t.o.u.	27.2.1966
Single-line curve	Restored	21.12.1980

Other sources give a date a week earlier for the restoration.

NEW MILLS & HEATON MERSEY LINE

Powers: Midland Railway Act 1897

New Mills South Jcn to Cheadle Heath	OG	4.5.1902
***	OP	1.7.1902
New Mills South Jcn to Heaton Mersey Jcn	CP	5.5.1969
New Mills South Jcn to Cheadle Jcn: line named "Cheadle lines"	... ...	6.12.1981
New Mills South Jcn to Northenden Jcn	Singled	19. 5.1984
New Mills South Jcn to Cheadle Jcn	C. temp.	11.1.1986
New Mills South Jcn to Edgeley Jcn No. 1: line named "up & down Hope Valley lines"	... ...	15.2.1986
New Mills South Jcn to Hazel Grove High Level Jcn re-opened double and thence to Cheadle Jcn single	RO(G)	9. 3.1986
New Mills South Jcn to Hazel Grove High Level Jcn	RO(P)	12.5.1986
Knat Hole Wood SB	Opened	4.5.1902
Closed experimentally (and never re-opened)	After	21.1.1905
***	Demolished	12.7.1909
Disley SB	Opened	4.5.1902
***	Re-framed	....
***	Closed	9.6.1968
Disley: down lie-by siding made a down goods loop	... ...	26.6.1955
***	t.o.u.	....
Disley tunnel: telephone communication through the tunnel	Introduced	6.1904
Telegraph communication for the Engineer's staff	Introduced	8.1904
Hazel Grove Station SB	Opened	24.3.1902
***	Closed	27.3.1977
HAZEL GROVE	OP	1.7.1902
***	CP(All)	1.1.1917
Hazel Grove: down loop	t.o.u.	12.11.1972

Hazel Grove Chord

Powers: British Railways Act 1984

Hazel Grove High Level Jcn to Hazel Grove East Jcn	Into use	9.3.1986
***	OP	12.5.1986

Bramhall Moor Lane Goods SB	Opened	4.5.1902
***	Closed	12.11.1967
BRAMHALL MOOR LANE GOODS DEPOT	OG	1.7.1902
***	OM	1903
***	CG	30.1.1965

Cheadle Heath to Heaton Mersey	OP	1.10.1901
***	OG	4.5.1902
***	Closed	1.1.1968

Cheadle Heath station had slow lines paired by use on the west side of the fast lines.

Cheadle Heath South Jcn: connection to down Liverpool line	t.o.u.	15.3.1966
Cheadle Heath South Junction SB	Opened	24.3.1902
***	Closed	17.8.1969
Cheadle Heath South Jcn to Cheadle Heath North Jcn: fast lines	Tfc ceased	5.5.1969
***	t.o.u.	17.8.1969
Fast lines re-instated and connected to the Liverpool Curve and the slow lines abandoned	... ...	25.10.1970
CHEADLE HEATH	OP	1.10.1901
Altered to CHEADLE HEATH FOR STOCKPORT	... ...	1.5.1902 *
***	OG	4.5.1902
Altered to CHEADLE HEATH STOCKPORT	... ...	1.10.1908 *
Altered to CHEADLE HEATH	... ...	14.6.1965 *
***	CP	2.1.1967
***	CG	1.7.1968

Cheadle Heath North Junction SB	Opened	24.3.1902
***	Closed	21.1.1968

Liverpool Curve

Powers: Midland Railway Act 1897

Cheadle Heath North Jcn to Cheadle Jcn with the Cheshire Lines	OG	4.5.1902
***	OP	1.7.1902
Cheadle Jcn: connection with the Cheshire Lines	Singled	9.5.1976
CHEADLE JUNCTION EXCHANGE SIDINGS	Opened	1.7.1902
***	Closed	31.1.1971

Cheadle Heath North Jcn to Chorlton Jcn	Tfc ceased	5.5.1969
***	t.o.u.	17.8.1969

MANCHESTER SOUTH DISTRICT RAILWAY

This company was vested in the Sheffield & Midland Committee under the Midland Railway (Further Powers) Act 1876. All powers and rights of the Manchester South District Railway were then transferred to the Midland Railway under the Midland Railway (Further Powers) Act 1877. Under powers of the Manchester, Sheffield & Lincolnshire Railway (Additional Powers) Act 1886 and the Midland Railway (Additional Powers) Act 1887 the section of the line north of Chorlton Junction was transferred by the Midland to the Cheshire Lines Committee on the opening on 1 October 1891 of the Fallowfield to Chorlton Junction section of the Manchester, Sheffield & Lincolnshire Railway's Manchester Central Station line.

Powers: Manchester South District Railway Act 1874 (Heaton Mersey East Junction to Didsbury)
Manchester South District Railway Act 1873 (Didsbury to Throstle Nest Junction)

Heaton Mersey (East) Jcn with the Cheshire Lines to Throstle Nest (East) Jcn with the Cheshire Lines	OP&G	1.1.1880
Working was by the block telegraph system from the opening.		
Heaton Mersey East Jcn to Throstle Nest East Jcn	CP	1.1.1968
Heaton Mersey East Jcn to Heaton Mersey Station Jcn	Closed	2.1.1967
***	Closed	4.1.1967
Heaton Mersey Station SB	Opened	1.1.1880
Replacement box	Opened	22.9.1901
Re-named Heaton Mersey Station Junction SB	... ...	29.9.1901
***	Closed	5.3.1967
Heaton Mersey Jcn to Chorlton-cum-Hardy Jcn	CP&G	5.5.1969
***	Off. t.o.u.	17.8.1969
HEATON MERSEY	OP	1.1.1880
***	OG	1905
***	CP	3.7.1961
***	CG	7.10.1963
Didsbury Goods Yard SB	Opened	1.1.1880
Replacement box	Opened	17.12.1899
***	Closed	5.3.1967
DIDSBURY	OP&G	1.1.1880
***	CG	2.11.1964
***	CP	2.1.1967
WITHINGTON	OP	1.1.1880
Altered to WITHINGTON & ALBERT PARK	... ...	1.7.1884 *
Altered to WITHINGTON & WEST DIDSBURY	... ...	1.4.1915
***	CP(All)	3.7.1961
Withington Station SB	Opened	1.1.1880
Replacement box	Opened	4.5.1924
***	Closed	21.6.1964
Chorlton Junction SB	Opened	12.8.1889
***	Closed	2.8.1971
Chorlton Jcn to Throstle Nest section transferred to the Cheshire Lines Committee on opening of the Fallowfield to Chorlton line	... ...	1.10.1891
Chorlton Jcn to Throstle Nest East Jcn	CP	5.5.1969
CHORLTON-CUM-HARDY	OP&G	1.1.1880
***	CG	30.11.1964
***	CP	2.1.1967
Chorlton-cum-Hardy Station SB	Opened	1.1.1880
Replacement box	Opened	9.8.1903
***	Closed	5.3.1967
Seymour Road SB	Opened	....
Box closed and IBS provided in lieu	... ...	16.9.1928
***	t.o.u.	5.3.1967
Throstle Nest South Junction SB	Opened	1879
Replacement box	Opened	30.9.1906
Re-named Throstle Nest Junction SB	... ...	30.8.1969
***	Closed	5.4.1970
Throstle Nest South Jcn to Throstle Nest East Jcn	t.o.u.	4.5.1969
***	Closed	5.5.1969

Throstle Nest Junction to Manchester Central (Cheshire Lines Committee)

(Glazebrook Jcn to) Throstle Nest Jcn to Cornbrook East Jcn	OP	2.9.1873
Cornbrook West Jcn to Manchester Central (temporary station)	OP	9.7.1877
MANCHESTER CENTRAL:		
Temporary station	OP	9.7.1877
Permanent station	OP	1.7.1880
Midland use of Manchester Central for main-line trains	Commenced	2.8.1880

MANCHESTER BRANCHES

Ancoats Goods Station Branch

Powers: Midland Railway (New Lines and Additional Powers) Act 1865

Midland Goods Jcn to Ancoats Goods Depot	OG	2.5.1870
Midland Jcn at Ardwick with the Manchester, Sheffield & Lincolnshire	Opened	16.4.1870
Midland Goods Junction SB (Manchester, Sheffield & Lincolnshire box)	Opened	....
Replacement box named Ashbury's West Junction SB	Opened	6.1889
Replacement box	Opened	30.7.1905
***	Closed	5.5.1984
Midland Viaduct SB	Opened	4.1.1887
***	Closed	7.8.1887
Ancoats Junction SB	Opened	30.7.1888
Replacement box	Opened	30.10.1927
***	Closed	27.2.1972
Ancoats Jcn to Palmerston Road GF: sidings Nos. 1 and 2	t.o.u.	5.12.1971
Ancoats branch: remainder made sidings and controlled from Ashburys West Junction SB	... ...	27.2.1972
Ashton Road No. 1 SB	Open before	16.8.1877
Re-named Ashton Road SB	... ...	6.1881-4.1883
Replacement box	Opened	8.10.1905
Box made a shunting frame	... ...	18.9.1966
***	t.o.u.	4.11.1972
	or	15.1.1972
Ashton Road No. 2 SB	Open before	16.8.1877
***	Closed	6.1881-4.1883

Ashton Road Depot Branch

Powers: --

ASHTON ROAD GOODS & COAL DEPOT	Open before	1877
***	Closed	10.9.1966
Ashton Road to Ancoats goods depot	Closed	17.7.1972
Ashton Road to Ancoats Yard: arrival and departure roads	t.o.u.	4.11.1972
Palmerston Bridge SB	Open before	16.8.1877
Replacement box	Opened	12.11.1893
Re-named Palmerston Road SB	... ...	....
***	Re-framed	16.5.1920
Box closed and lines worked as sidings from a ground frame	... ...	15.2.1959
***	t.o.u.	4.11.1972
ANCOATS GOODS DEPOT	OG	2.5.1870
***	Closed	17.7.1972

Ancoats Curve to the Lancashire & Yorkshire Railway

Powers: Midland Railway (Additional Powers) Act 1885 (Ancoats Junction Line)
Midland Railway Act 1888 (Ancoats Passenger Junction)

Ancoats Jcn to Midland Jcn with the Lancashire & Yorkshire Railway	OG	1.8.1888
***	O. excursions	6.1889
***	OP	1.7.1889

Between Ancoats Junction and Hellifield Junction the Midland possessed running powers for all traffic over the Lancashire & Yorkshire line. The company also possessed running powers over the branch from Bolton to Astley Bridge and over the main line between Clifton Junction and Colne.

Ashburys West Jcn to Philips Park No. 1	RO(P)	17.5.1982
Lines officially designated passenger lines again	... ...	29.4.1984
***	CP	16.5.1988

Working between the Midland Railway and the Lancashire & Yorkshire Railway was by block telegraph.

Midland Junction SB (Lancashire & Yorkshire box)	Closed	21.11.1965

Between Ashbury's West Junction and Ancoats Junction the Manchester, Sheffield & Lincolnshire Railway possessed running powers for all traffic over the Midland line.

WIDNES BRANCHES

Powers: No powers

Ditton Brook Iron Works branch	Open before	1882
Ditton Marsh branch: electric train tablet block working in place of pilot guard	Commenced	1926
Moor Lane Jcn to Ditton Marsh Shunter's Cabin: one engine in steam working in place of working by electric train tablet block	Commenced	15.10.1945
Ditton Marsh branch	Closed	8.1960
Hutchinson's branch	Open before	1882
This was a privately-owned line off the Marsh branch to West Bank Dock.		
Landowners' branches: Muspratt's branch	Opened	1881-1883
***	Closed	....
Landowners' branches: Blundell's branch	Open before	1883
***	Closed	....

LIVERPOOL BRANCHES

Sandon & Canada Docks Goods Station

Powers: Midland Railway (Additional Powers) Act 1883 (Land Powers only)
Midland Railway Act 1892 (Southerly Extension - Land Powers only)

SANDON & CANADA DOCK	OG	2.6.1873
***	OM	1891 **or** 1899 ?
***	CG	24.2.1969
Huskisson Goods Depot to Sandon Dock, junction with Mersey Docks & Harbour Board lines	OG	1.11.1882
***	Closed	21.7.1969
The line was worked by horse from Huskisson. A connection between Huskisson and Clarence Dock was established on 6 November 1882.		

Bootle Goods Branch OR Langton Branch

Powers: Midland Railway (Additional Powers) Act 1880
(Fazakerley Junction end)
Midland Railway (Additional Powers) Act 1881
Midland Railway (Additional Powers) Act 1880
(Alexandra & Langton Dock end)
Midland Railway (New Works Etc) Act 1877
(Alexandra & Langton Dock goods station - Land Powers only)
Midland Railway (Additional Powers) Act 1881
(Southerly Extension of goods station - Land Powers only)

Fazakerley North Jcn with the Cheshire Lines to Alexandra Dock	OG	1.6.1885
***	C.Tfc	20.11.1967
***	Off. closed	1.1.1968
***	Closed	22.9.1968
Fazackerley North Jcn to Langton Dock Goods Yard: down line made single line worked by train staff and ticket until further notice	By	5.11.1940
Normal working	Restored	11.11.1940
North Mersey High Level Yard to Langton Dock Goods Depot	Tfc ceased	5.1.1970 ?
LANGTON DOCK GOODS DEPOT	Opened	....
***	Closed	5.1.1970 ?
ALEXANDRA DOCK	OG	1.12.1882
***	OM	1885
***	CG	....
Alexandra & Langton Dock SB	Opened	....
***	Closed	c.1908

Linacre Branch (off the Bootle branch)

Powers: Midland Railway Act 1889

Linacre gas works branch	OG	20.5.1891
Linacre Gas Works Sidings SB	Opened	....
***	Re-framed	27.2.1906
***	Closed	....
Lancashire Tar Distillers Sidings to Linacre gas works	Closed	21.8.1934
Linacre gas works: points for tar works sidings clipped for the tar works, ground frame removed, and branch thence to the gas works taken away	... ...	9.5.1966
Linacre Branch GF to Lancashire Tar Distillers Sidings	Off. closed	1.1.1968
Linacre Dock Goods Yard SB	Opened	....
***	Closed	....

SHEFFIELD & MIDLAND: APPROACHES TO MANCHESTER

The Manchester, Sheffield & Lincolnshire line between Hayfield and the junction with that company's main line at Hyde Junction was made joint between the Sheffield and the Midland under the Manchester Sheffield and Lincolnshire Railway and Midland Railway Companies (Joint Lines) Act 1869.

Hayfield to New Mills Branch

Powers: Marple, New Mills and Hayfield Junction Railway Act 1864

Hayfield to New Mills Jcn	OP	1.3.1868
***	O.Coal	7.4.1870
***	OG	18.3.1872
***	CG	2.11.1964
***	CP	5.1.1970
The line was originally worked by train staff.		
Block telegraph working	Commenced	26.2.1889
HAYFIELD	OP	1.3.1868
***	O.Coal	7.4.1870
***	OG	18.3.1872
***	CG	15.4.1963
***	CP	5.1.1970
Hayfield to Tunnel End: electric train tablet block working	Commenced	4.12.1910
Hayfield SB	Open before	16.8.1877
Replacement box on New Mills side of level crossing	Opened	20.1.1925
***	Closed	5.1.1970
Slacks Crossing SB	Open before	16.8.1877
Replacement box	Opened	13.9.1892
Box closed and ground frame provided in lieu	... ...	13.11.1927
***	t.o.u.	10.10.1965
BIRCH VALE	OP&G	Mid-1868
***	CG	2.11.1964
***	CP	5.1.1970
Birch Vale SB	Opened	19.2.1889
***	Closed	4.12.1910
New Mills Tunnel End SB	Open before	16.8.1877
Box made the train staff signal box in place of New Mills Station Junction SB	... ...	21.8.1907
Replacement box	Opened	16.12.1924
***	Closed	5.1.1970
New Mills Junction SB	Open before	16.8.1877
Replacement box	Opened	2.11.1924
***	Closed	....

New Mills to Hyde Junction

Powers: Marple, New Mills and Hayfield Junction Railway Act 1860 (New Mills to Marple)
Manchester, Sheffield and Lincolnshire Railway (Newton and Compstall) Act 1858 (Marple to Hyde Junction)

New Mills to Compstall	Opened	1.7.1865
New Mills to Hyde Jcn / Ashburys East Jcn, and Romiley Curve: block telegraph system	Installed by	1873
NEW MILLS	OP	1.7.1865
***	OG	1906
Altered to NEW MILLS CENTRAL	... ...	25.8.1952
Strines Station SB	Open before	1.11.1875
Replacement box	Opened	19.11.1893
***	Re-framed	26.6.1904
***	Closed	27.7.1980
STRINES	OP	8.1866
***	OG	13.2.1872
***	CG	12.8.1963
Goyt Viaduct SB (signalling the down line only)	Opened	24.5.1888 ?
Replacement box	Opened	18.12.1904
Box closed and IBS provided in lieu	... ...	8.4.1934
***	t.o.u.	....
Usage of this signalbox was intermittent at first.		
Marple tunnel: double line through the tunnel	Into use	31.1.1875
Marple Cutting SB	Opened	c.1.1.1894
***	Closed	22.7.1894
Marple South SB	Opened	1875
Replacement box	Opened	16.8.1896
***	Closed	12.3.1905
Marple Goods Yard SB	Opened	1875
***	Closed	14.10.1894
Marple Platform SB	Opened	14.10.1894
***	Closed	12.3.1905

MARPLE	OP	1.7.1865
***	OG	2.9.1872
***	CG	5.10.1964
The station at Marple replaced the Compstall temporary station on completion of the Goyt viaduct.		
Marple: down loop platform and facing connection in down main line	Removed	1.12.1963
Up loop platform and connections	Removed	19.10.1964
Marple Station SB	Opened	....
***	Closed	1875
Marple Station SB (on up platform north of station buildings)	Opened	12.3.1905
***	Closed	27.7.1980
Marple North SB	Opened	1875
Replacement box	Opened	25.10.1903
***	Closed	12.3.1905
Marple Wharf Junction SB	Open before	16.8.1877
***	Re-framed	18.8.1901
Replacement box	Opened	11.12.1927
***	Closed	27.7.1980
Marple Wharf Jcn: connection with Marple Wharf branch severed	... ...	10.4.1899
Junction with Manchester, Sheffield & Lincolnshire and North Staffordshire Joint Line	OP	2.8.1869
***	OG	1.3.1870

Compstall to Hyde	OP&G	5.8.1862
COMPSTALL (temporary station)	OP	5.8.1862
***	CP(All)	1.10.1865
Oakwood SB (signalling the down line only)	Opened	24.5.1888 ?
Replacement box	Opened	8.5.1892
Replacement box	Opened	22.9.1907
Box closed and up and down IBS provided in lieu	... ...	18.6.1933
***	t.o.u.	....
ROMILEY	OP	5.8.1862
***	OG	2.9.1872
***	CG	30.1.1965
Romiley Junction SB	Open before	16.8.1877
Replacement box	Opened	1899
Box provided with a switch-panel and TCB working introduced between Romiley and Ashbury's East Jcn	... ...	18.11.1973
***	Re-framed	27.7.1980
***	Closed	....

Manchester & Stockport line

See page 202

Romiley Curve

Powers: Manchester, Sheffield and Lincolnshire Railway and Midland Railway Companies (Joint Lines) Act 1869

Romiley Jcn to Bredbury Jcn	OG	15.2.1875
***	OP	1.4.1875
***	Tfc ceased	2.1.1967
***	CP&G	6.3.1967

Woodley South SB	Open before	16.8.1877
Replacement box	Opened	15.6.1919
***	Closed	7.6.1936
Woodley Junction SB	Opened	....
Replacement box	Opened	15.12.1895
***	Re-framed	....
***	Re-framed	18.3.1984
***	Closed	21.9.1985
On 18 March 1984 the temporary panel from Chinley Junction SB was fitted into Woodley Junction SB in place of the frame.		
Woodley Jcn to Hyde North: line temporarily singled, Hyde Jcn taken out of use, and temporary platforms provided there	... ...	14.10.1984
Facilities restored on conversion to 25 kV of Glossop line	... ...	9.12.1984
WOODLEY	OP	5.8.1862
***	OG	2.9.1872
***	CG	17.5.1965
Apethorne Junction SB (Manchester, Sheffield & Lincolnshire box)	Closed	12.6.1966
Apethorne Jcn: connection between branch and main line	t.o.u.	27.2.1966
HYDE (second station)	OP	5.8.1862
***	OG	1.8.1873
***	CG	21.5.1966
Altered to HYDE CENTRAL	Goods	1.7.1950
***	Passenger	17.9.1951

Hyde (first station) to Hyde Jcn with the Manchester, Sheffield & Lincolnshire Railway	OP&G	1.3.1858
HYDE	OP	1.3.1858
***	CP(All)	5.8.1862

Hyde Station SB (Manchester, Sheffield & Lincolnshire box)	Closed	23.3.1969
HYDE JUNCTION	Opened	2.1863
Altered to HYDE NORTH	... ...	17.9.1951

Between Hyde Junction and Manchester the Midland possessed no running powers over the Manchester, Sheffield & Lincolnshire line save under the agreement of 28 August 1863 scheduled to the Manchester, Sheffield & Lincolnshire Railway (Purchase, Etc.) Act 1865 which permitted the Midland to work its traffic between Barnsley and Manchester, but it was allowed to work merchandise trains between Hyde Junction and Ashbury's Junction on payment of a bonus mileage of 3 miles in addition to the ordinary mileage proportion less 33.3% for working expenses.

Manchester & Stockport Line

Powers: Manchester and Stockport Railway Act 1866
Sheffield and Midland Railway Companies Committee Act 1873 (Alteration of levels between Bredbury and Reddish Junction)

Romiley Jcn to Ashbury's Jcn	OG	17.5.1875
***	OP	2.8.1875
Romiley to Ashbury's East Jcn: TCB working	Commenced	18.11.1973
Bredbury Station SB	Open before	1.11.1875
Replacement box	Opened	5.6.1904
Box closed and 2 ground frames provided in lieu	... ...	18.11.1973
Bredbury No. 1 GF	t.o.u.	....
Bredbury No. 2 GF	t.o.u.	6.6.1978
BREDBURY	OP	1.9.1875
***	OG	18.12.1876
***	CG	29.1.1968
Lingard's Lane Colliery Siding SB (not a block post)	Opened	30.10.1893
***	Closed	....
Box re-opened as a block post	... ...	23.7.1900
Replacement box	Opened	17.6.1924
***	Closed	16.10.1966
Reddish Junction SB	Open before	1.11.1875
Replacement box	Opened	1890 ?
Replacement box	Opened	29.4.1923
***	Closed	18.11.1973
BRINNINGTON	OP	12.12.1977

Brinnington Branch

Powers: Manchester, Sheffield, and Lincolnshire Railway (Additional Powers) Act 1872 (Brinnington Junction end)
Manchester and Stockport Railway Act 1866 (Reddish Junction end)

Brinnington Jcn to Reddish Jcn	OG	17.5.1875
***	OP	2.8.1875
***	C.Tfc	6.9.1965
***	Severed	3.1.1966
***	Off. closed	12.2.1966
***	Lifted	8.1966

Reddish Station SB	Open before	16.8.1877
Replacement box at Stockport end of up platform	Opened	25.6.1911
***	Closed	5.7.1964
REDDISH	OP&G	1.12.1875
Altered to REDDISH NORTH	Goods	1.7.1950
***	Passenger	24.7.1951
***	CG	5.9.1955
RYDER BROW	OP	4.11.1985
Belle Vue South SB	Open before	16.8.1877
***	Closed	14.1.1917
Belle Vue Station SB (on down platform near the south end)	Opened	14.1.1917
***	Closed	18.11.1973
BELLE VUE	OP	1.9.1875
***	OG	1.5.1897
Down-side bay	t.o.u.	7.7.1963
***	CG	15.6.1964
Old station entrance closed, buildings demolished, and the southern sections of very long platforms taken out of use; new entrance further north opened	... ...	12.5.1986
Belle Vue North SB	Open before	16.8.1877
***	Closed	14.1.1917
Belle Vue engine shed	Opened	1872
***	Closed	16.4.1956
All points clipped and signals removed	... ...	23.8.1964
Belle Vue Engine Shed SB	Open before	16.8.1877
Replacement box	Opened	....
***	Closed	7.3.1965
Ashbury's Engine Shed Jcn (for Belle Vue engine shed)	Opened	7.6.1871

Ashbury's East Junction SB re-named Ashbury's SB	... ...	5.5.1984

Between Ashbury's East Junction and Ardwick Junction the Midland possessed running powers for all traffic over the Manchester, Sheffield & Lincolnshire line.
Between Ardwick Junction and Manchester London Road Station the Midland possessed running powers over the London & North Western line, with use of the station and power to employ staff.

SHEFFIELD & MIDLAND: WIDNES LOOP

Eastern end

Powers: --

Widnes East Jcn to Widnes	OG	3.4.1877
***	OP	1.8.1879
Widnes East Jcn to Hough Green Jcn	Closed	5.10.1964
Widnes East Jcn to Widnes Jcn	Closed	13.12.1964

Widnes Curve

Powers: --

Widnes West Jcn to Widnes South Jcn	OG	3.4.1877
***	OP	1.8.1879
***	Closed	29.2.1880

WIDNES	OG	3.4.1877
***	OP	1.8.1879
East end of down platform shortened by 71 yards	... ...	5.4.1936
***	CG	....
***	CP	5.10.1964
Widnes Station SB	Opened	....
***	Closed	31.10.1954

Western end

Widnes to Hough Green Jcn	OG	1.7.1879
***	OP	1.8.1879
Moor Lane SB	Opened	....
***	Closed	13.12.1964
TANHOUSE LANE	OP&G	1.9.1890
***	CP	5.10.1964
***	CG	....
Tanhouse Lane SB made a ground frame	... ...	13.12.1964
Sullivan's Crossing SB closed and IBS provided in lieu	... ...	22.5.1938

HOTELS IN MANCHESTER AND LIVERPOOL

Manchester: Midland Hotel	Opened	7.9.1903
***	Sold	....
Liverpool: Adelphi Hotel	Opened	....
Extension to the hotel	Opened	3.1912
Rebuilt section	Opened	14.3.1914
Adelphi Hotel	Sold	....

VIII. BETWEEN DERBY AND BIRMINGHAM

BIRMINGHAM & DERBY JUNCTION RAILWAY

The Birmingham & Derby Junction Railway was amalgamated with the North Midland Railway and the Midland Counties Railway as the Midland Railway on 10 May 1844.

Powers: Birmingham and Derby Junction Railway Act 1836
Midland Railway Act 1891
(Melbourne Junction to Stenson Junction Widening)
Midland Railway (Ripley Branches) Act 1848
(Horninglow Bridge to Burton Passenger Station Widening)
Midland Railway (Burton Branches) Act 1860
(Burton Passenger Station to Leicester Junction Widening)
Midland Railway Act 1898 (Widening at Whitacre)
Midland Railway (New Lines) Act 1861
(Whitacre: new curves, and abandonment of the old alignment)
Birmingham and Derby Junction Railway Act 1838 (Hampton-in-Arden)

Derby to Hampton-in-Arden Jcn with the London & Birmingham Railway	O.Formal	5.8.1839
***	Opened	12.8.1839
DERBY - see SECTION V (North Midland Railway)		
DERBY (temporary station)	OP	12.8.1839
***	CP(All)	11.5.1840
Between Derby and Tamworth Junction the London & North Western possessed running powers over the Midland line for all traffic, with the use of stations other than the Midland's goods stations at Burton and Derby.		
Between Chaddesden and Derby and Willington Junction the North Staffordshire possessed running powers for all traffic over the Midland line.		
London Road Junction SB	Opened	1869
Replacement box	Opened	c.1877
Replacement box	Opened	6.12.1925
***	Closed	14.7.1969
Derby London Road Jcn to Melbourne Jcn: block telegraph working	Introduced	1869
London Road Jcn: down goods line	In use by	1.1.1869
Litchurch Junction SB	Opened	....
***	Closed by	16.8.1877

Litchurch Wagon Branch

Powers: Midland Railway (Additional Powers) Act 1874

Litchurch wagon branch	Opened by	1.1.1877
Partial use of yard	Comm. by	2.1877
Litchurch Jcn to L. & N. W. Jcn: down goods line	Into use	2.8.1874
Up goods line	Into use	20.11.1874
Goods lines	Re-modelled	15.10.1876
Ticket Platform Temporary SB	Opened	1876
***	Closed	1877
DERBY WEST TICKET PLATFORM	Closed	1.12.1900
LONDON ROAD WHARF	Opened	....
***	Closed	4.1.1965
Osmaston Road SB	Opened	1877
Replacement box	Opened	24.5.1903
Box closed and IBS provided in lieu	... ...	30.10.1932
***	t.o.u.	....
Cotton Lane SB	Opened	c.6.1868
Replacement box named Cotton Lane Junction SB	Opened	1871 ?
***	Closed	c.1874 ?
Junction for the London & North Western Railway goods depot	Opened	1.7.1871
L. & N. W. Junction SB	Opened	c.1874
Replacement box	Opened	19.4.1891
***	Closed	29.6.1969
PEAR TREE & NORMANTON	OP	2.6.1890
***	OG	1.1.1891
***	CG	4.1.1965
***	CP	4.3.1968
Station re-opened to passenger traffic as PEARTREE	... ...	4.10.1976
Melbourne Junction SB	Opened	1.9.1868
Replacement box	Opened	1869 ?
Replacement box	Opened	16.4.1888
***	Alt.levers	30.3.1890
Replacement box	Opened	12.10.1890
***	Re-framed	8.4.1906
***	Closed	29.6.1969

Derby & Melbourne line

See page 216

Melbourne Jcn to Willington Jcn: block telegraph working	Introduced	1873
Melbourne Jcn to Sunny Hill Goods Jcn: up and down goods lines	Into use	10.7.1892
***	t.o.u.	....
Sunny Hill SB	Open before	1.11.1875
Replacement box about half a mile nearer Derby	Opened	8.11.1891
Re-named Sunny Hill Goods Junction SB	... ...	....
***	Raised	24.7.1892
Replacement box	Opened	8.3.1925
Box closed and ground frame provided in lieu	... ...	15.11.1931
Ground frame taken out of use and signalbox provided in lieu	... ...	27.4.1941
Box closed and 2 ground frames provided in lieu	... ...	29.6.1969
Sunny Hill West GF	t.o.u.	22.5.1974
Sunny Hill East GF	t.o.u.	13.8.1983
Sunny Hill: up goods line to up passenger line crossover	Into use	10.7.1892
Down goods line to down passenger line crossover	Into use	10.7.1892
Crossovers	t.o.u.	....
Sunny Hill Goods Jcn: reception line and new sidings	Into use	27.4.1941
Sunny Hill Goods Jcn to Stenson Crossing: up and down goods lines	Into use	8.11.1891
Sunny Hill Goods Jcn to Stenson Jcn: down goods line	t.o.u.	23.2.1969
Up goods line	t.o.u.	16.3.1969
Stenson Crossing Goods Junction SB	Opened	26.10.1890
***	Closed	26.6.1932
Stenson Junction SB	Opened	3.11.1873
Replacement box	Opened	26.6.1892
Replacement box 146 yards nearer to Derby	Opened	28.3.1954
***	Closed	29.6.1969

Stenson & Weston line

See page 218

North Stafford Junction SB	Open before	16.8.1877
Replacement box	Opened	26.6.1892
***	Closed	26.6.1932
Willington Jcn with the North Staffordshire Railway	Opened	13.7.1849
Between Willington Junction and Stoke-on-Trent the Midland possessed running powers over the North Staffordshire line.		
Willington Jcn to Wetmore Jcn: block telegraph working	Introduced	18.3.1872
Willington Station SB	Open before	1875
Replacement box	Opened	12.6.1892
***	Closed	29.6.1969
WILLINGTON	Opened	12.8.1839
Altered to WILLINGTON & REPTON	... ...	1.10.1855
Altered to REPTON & WILLINGTON	... ...	1.5.1877 *
Altered to WILLINGTON FOR REPTON	... ...	1.10.1889
Altered to REPTON & WILLINGTON	... ...	....
***	CG	6.7.1964
***	CP	4.3.1968
Hargate SB	Opened	1875
Replacement box	Opened	10.7.1887
Box closed and approach-lit IBS provided in lieu	... ...	17.4.1932
***	t.o.u.	....
Fleam Bridge SB	Opened	11.9.1887
***	Closed	1.10.1887
Clay Mills Junction SB	Opened	1874
***	Alt.levers	1.3.1891
Replacement box	Opened	17.9.1899
Box made a ground frame	... ...	15.6.1969
***	t.o.u.	27.9.1987
Clay Mills to Wetmore: up and down goods lines	In use by	1.12.1873
***	t.o.u.	....

Wetmore Branch

Powers: --

Branch to the English Grain Company's works	Opened	4.2.1894
***	Closed	....

Wetmore Sidings: up passenger line to up goods line crossover	Into use	....
Down goods line to down passenger line crossover	Into use	....
Crossovers	t.o.u.	....
Wetmore Sidings SB	Opened	c.2.1873
Replacement box	Opened	12.7.1891
***	Re-framed	21.10.1900
Replacement box	Opened	12.6.1949
Box made a shunting frame	... ...	15.6.1969
***	t.o.u.	13.10.1985
WETMORE SIDINGS (= BURTON-ON-TRENT SIDINGS ?)	Opened	2.11.1873
Additional sidings	Into use	4.11.1873
***	Altered	19.11.1874
***	Closed	....
Wetmore Jcn to Horninglow Bridge: block telegraph working	Introduced	1874
Wetmore to Burton station: down goods line	Into use	4.11.1873

Wetmore to North Stafford Jcn: up goods line	Into use	4.11.1873
Wetmore to Horninglow Bridge: down goods line made through siding	... ...	....
Through siding	t.o.u.	1.10.1973
North Stafford Jcn: up passenger line to up goods line crossover	Into use	....
***	t.o.u.	....
North Stafford Junction SB	Opened	1861 ?
Replacement box	Opened	6.1873
Replacement box	Opened	29.9.1907
***	Closed	17.4.1966
North Stafford Jcn: junction with the North Staffordshire Railway	Opened	11.9.1848
***	CP	13.6.1960
***	t.o.u.	4.4.1966
Between North Stafford Junction and Burton station the North Staffordshire Railway possessed running powers for all traffic over the Midland line. The company also possessed running powers between North Stafford Junction and Wellingborough.		
Between North Stafford Junction and Burton station the Great Northern possessed running powers for all traffic over the Midland line.		
Between North Stafford Junction and Stoke-on-Trent the Midland possessed running powers over the North Staffordshire line.		
North Stafford Jcn (south of): new sidings	Into use	30.10.1874
North Stafford Jcn to Horninglow Bridge: up goods line	Into use	18.2.1883
Horninglow Bridge: up passenger line to up goods line crossover	Into use	....
Down goods line to down passenger line crossover	Into use	4.5.1902
Up goods line to up passenger line crossover	Into use	....
Down passenger line to down goods line crossover	Into use	....
Crossovers	t.o.u.	....
Horninglow Bridge SB	Opened	1864
Replacement box	Opened	....
Replacement box	Opened	1882
Replacement box	Opened	11.9.1898
***	Closed	26.11.1933

Burton branches

See page 219

Horninglow Bridge to Leicester Jcn: block telegraph system	Installed	1877
Top of Guild Street Branch SB (not a block post)	Open before	12.1888
***	Closed	6.8.1893
Guild Street No. 1 SB	Opened	6.8.1893
***	Slued	9.3.1902
Box re-framed and re-named Horninglow Bridge SB	... ...	26.11.1933
Box made a shunting frame	... ...	15.6.1969
***	t.o.u.	2.12.1973
Lines from Hawkins Lane Jcn made sidings	... ...	18.7.1965
***	C.Tfc	1.1.1968
Burton Yard SB	Open before	16.8.1877
***	Closed	1882
Burton Goods Yard SB	Opened	....
***	Closed	18.7.1965
Derby Road: new grain warehouse	Opened	21.9.1901
New bonded warehouse	Opened	4.12.1901
Derby Road warehouses	Closed	....
DERBY STREET GOODS DEPOT	Opened	....
Altered to BURTON-ON-TRENT FREIGHT TERMINAL	... ...	....
***	Closed	2.7.1979
Burton Station North SB	Opened	c.3.1882
***	Re-framed	12.7.1896
Replacement box	Opened	21.2.1915
***	Closed	17.10.1965
Burton: up and down goods lines through the station to join up at Leicester Jcn with the existing up and down goods lines	Into use	26.3.1882
Burton Level Crossing SB	Opened	....
Replacement box	Open before	16.8.1877
***	Closed	c.3.1882
BURTON	Opened	8.12.1839
Replacement station 7 chains to the south	Opened	29.4.1883
Station made "closed" for tickets	... ...	1.10.1899
Altered to BURTON-ON-TRENT	... ...	1.7.1903 *
***	CG	6.10.1975
Burton: new sidings	Into use	2.11.1873
New sidings	Into use	2.10.1876
New sewage siding	Into use	12.7.1875
New goods lines and sidings	Into use	21.2.1875
Burton: new down goods line	Into use	23.11.1873
New up and down goods lines	Into use	2.2.1874
New up goods line	Into use	30.10.1874
New down goods line	Into use	30.10.1876
It has not proved possible to determine exactly where the above sidings and goods lines were located.		

Moor Street SB	Open before	16.8.1877
Re-named Burton Station South SB	... ...	....
Replacement box	Opened	c.3.1882
***	Re-framed	19.7.1896
Replacement box	Opened	20.12.1914
***	Closed	15.6.1969
Burton Station South: down goods line to down passenger line crossover	Into use	....
***	t.o.u.	....
Leicester Jcn: additional sidings	Into use	1.10.1874
Leicester Junction SB	Opened	1847
Replacement box	Opened	....
Replacement box	Opened	1884 ?
Replacement box	Opened	9.2.1902
***	Re-framed	29.6.1924
***	Closed	15.6.1969

Leicester & Burton line

See page 75

Between Burton South Junction and Dixie Sidings the Great Northern possessed running powers over the Midland line.

Leicester Jcn to Wichnor Jcn: block telegraph working	Introduced	18.3.1872
Burton engine shed	Opened	6.1859
***	Replaced	29.4.1870
No. 2 engine shed	Opened	1892
Both engine sheds	Closed	....
Leicester Jcn to Branstone Bridge Jcn: up and down goods lines	Into use	22.2.1874
Branstone Junction SB	Opened	....
Replacement box	Opened	1874
Replacement box	Opened	15.9.1889
Replacement box	Opened	28.1.1923
***	Closed	15.6.1969

Birmingham Curve

See page 77

Branston Jcn to Dunstall SB: down goods line	Into use	10.11.1901
***	t.o.u.	29.9.1968
Branston Jcn: down goods line to down passenger line crossover	Into use	10.11.1901
Up main line to up goods line connection	t.o.u. by	22.3.1989
Branston: additional sidings	Into use	3.11.1875
BRANSTON	OP	1.10.1889
***	CP(All)	22.9.1930
Dunstall SB	Opened	1875
Replacement box	Opened	1877
***	Re-located	1889-1893
Replacement box on new site	Opened	20.1.1907
Box closed and IBS provided in lieu	... ...	28.4.1935
***	t.o.u.	....
Barton & Walton Station SB	Open before	1875
***	Re-framed	8.11.1896
Replacement box	Opened	22.12.1907
***	Closed	15.6.1969
BARTON & WALTON	Opened	12.8.1839
***	CP	5.8.1958
***	CG	6.7.1964
Barton & Walton: down goods loop	Into use	8.3.1908
***	t.o.u.	17.4.1968
Wichnor Jcn to Wichnor South Sidings: down goods line	Into use	27.10.1907
***	t.o.u.	25.2.1968
Wichnor Junction SB	Opened	....
Replacement box	Opened	1873
***	Re-framed	9.8.1896
Replacement box	Opened	24.9.1899
Replacement box	Opened	9.8.1953
Box closed and ground frame provided in lieu	... ...	15.6.1969
***	t.o.u. by	5.9.1986
Wichnor Jcn to Tamworth Curve Jcn: block telegraph working	Introduced	1873
Wichnor Jcn with the South Staffordshire Railway	OP	9.4.1849
***	OG	7-8.1849
***	CP	18.1.1965

The Midland Railway possessed running powers for all traffic over the South Staffordshire Railway including stations between Wichnor Junction and Dudley (with the Sedgley Loop, the Princes End Branch, the Darlaston Branch, and the Bescot Loops) and between Walsall and Cannock (with the Norton branch and the Lichfield Curve).

WICHNOR JUNCTION	OP	2.4.1855
***	CP (Mid.)	1.8.1856
***	OG before	1872
***	CG	1890
***	CM	1894

Wichnor South Sidings SB	Open before	1.11.1875
***	Re-framed	23.8.1896
Replacement box named Wichnor Sidings SB	Opened	25.11.1923
***	Closed	26.5.1968
WICHNOR JUNCTION SIDINGS	Opened	....
***	Closed	....
Wichnor Jcn with the South Staffordshire Railway (goods junction)	Opened	....
***	Closed	....
OAKLEY & ALREWAS	OP	15.6.1840
Altered to OAKLEY	... ...	1.11.1849 *
Altered to CROXALL	... ...	1.12.1856 *
***	CP(All)	9.7.1928
This station handled goods traffic from 1889 to 1894 inclusive, and it handled mineral traffic from 1917.		
Croxall Station SB	Open before	1.11.1875
***	Re-framed	28.6.1896
Replacement box	Opened	28.1.1906
Box closed and approach-lit IBS provided in lieu	... ...	27.8.1933
IBS made continuously lit	... ...	5.12.1943
***	t.o.u.	....
HASELOUR	Opened	1.7.1850 *
Altered to HASELOUR & ELFORD	... ...	1.11.1855 *
Altered to ELFORD & HASELOUR	... ...	1.9.1864 *
Altered to HASELOUR	... ...	1.4.1904
Altered to ELFORD	... ...	5.5.1914
***	CP&G	31.3.1952
***	RO(G) – PS	7.1954
***	CG	1.11.1973
Haselour Station SB	Open before	1.11.1875
Replacement box	Opened	24.1.1904
Replacement box	Opened	26.4.1908
Replacement box	Opened	5.11.1911
Re-named Elford Station SB	... ...	....
Replacement box 265 yards to the north	Opened	24.5.1959
***	Closed	15.6.1969
Elford: down goods loop	Into use	5.4.1942
Haselour: down goods loop	Into use	26.4.1908
Carter's Bridge down-line IBS	Into use	5.4.1942
Wigginton SB	Opened	2.1880-6.1881
Replacement box	Opened	7.2.1904
Box closed and up and down approach-lit IBS provided in lieu	... ...	26.2.1933
IBS made continuously lit	... ...	5.12.1943
***	t.o.u.	....
Tamworth troughs	Into use	4.1909
Tamworth Curve Junction SB	Opened	c.1.1873
***	Closed	1880
Tamworth Curve Jcn to Whitacre Jcn: block telegraph working	Introduced	....

Tamworth East Curve to the London & North Western Railway

Powers: Midland Railway (Branches Etc.) Act 1866

Tamworth Curve Jcn to the junction with the Trent Valley line	... ...	....

This curve was apparently complete except for the junction with the London & North Western Railway by September 1872. Although ready to open on 7 July 1873, it was never connected up. The rails were removed about 1878.

Tamworth North SB	Open before	16.8.1877
Replacement box	Opened	28.5.1899
***	Closed	8.8.1925

Tamworth West Curve to the London & North Western Railway

Powers: --

Tamworth north-to-west curve	Opened	12.6.1847
***	Closed	10.3.1969
Tamworth High Level SB	Opened	8.8.1925
***	Closed	10.8.1969
TAMWORTH	Opened	12.8.1839
Altered to TAMWORTH HIGH LEVEL	... ...	2.6.1924
Extended platforms	Off. opened	24.9.1962
Altered to TAMWORTH	... ...	3.5.1971
Tamworth South SB	Open before	16.8.1877
Replacement box	Opened	9.7.1899
***	Closed	8.8.1925
Glascote SB	Open before	1.11.1875
Re-named Kettlebrook Sidings SB	... ...	1.3.1881 ?
Replacement box	Opened	27.5.1900
***	Closed	3.11.1968
GLASCOTE	OG by	1877
Glascote (Siding) altered to KETTLEBROOK (Station)	... ...	1.3.1881
New sidings	Into use	7.4.1884
***	CG	4.1.1965

Perrin & Harrison's Sidings SB	Open before	1.11.1875
Replacement box	Opened	17.6.1900
***	Re-framed	....
***	Closed	10.8.1969
Wilnecote Station SB	Open before	1.11.1875
Replacement box	Opened	8.6.1902
***	Closed	11.1951
WILNECOTE & FAZELEY	Opened	16.5.1842
Altered to WILNECOTE	... ...	1.4.1904
***	CG	6.7.1964
Tame Valley Colliery Sidings SB	Open before	1.11.1875
Replacement box	Opened	22.7.1894
***	Closed	7.5.1933
Hockley Hall Colliery Sidings SB	Open before	16.8.1877
Replacement box	Opened	13.8.1899
***	Closed	10.6.1918
Whateley Colliery Sidings SB	Open before	1.11.1875
Replacement box	Opened	17.8.1890
***	Raised	11.8.1895
***	Raised	17.2.1900
***	Raised	30.10.1904
Replacement box	Opened	24.2.1946
Box closed and ground frame provided in lieu	... ...	28.10.1962
***	t.o.u.	1.2.1965
Cliff Sidings SB	Open before	16.8.1877
Replacement box	Opened	24.6.1900
***	Closed	28.10.1962
Kingsbury Branch Sidings SB	Opened	23.11.1877
***	Re-framed	8.12.1895
Replacement box	Opened	16.4.1899
***	Re-framed	10.9.1899
Replacement box 6 chains to the south	Opened	16.12.1906
Box closed and shunting frame provided in lieu	... ...	10.8.1969
***	t.o.u.	....

Kingsbury Branch

Powers: Midland Railway (Additional Powers) Act 1873

Kingsbury Jcn to Baddesley (OR Baxterley Park) Colliery Sidings	OG	28.1.1878
About 500 yards at Kingsbury Branch Sidings	Re-aligned	10.9.1899
Working by by pilot guard without tickets	By	24.10.1906
***	OP before	3.1914
***	CP	7.12.1928
***	CG	3.1989

Birch Coppice Colliery Branch

Powers: Midland Railway (Additional Powers) Act 1873 (Land powers only)

Birch Coppice Colliery branch	In use by	1882
***	t.o.u. by	29.1.1988
Hall End Sidings (OR Birch Coppice Colliery Sidings)	In use by	1882
***	t.o.u.	28.3.1983

KINGSBURY COLLIERY SIDINGS WORKMEN'S PLATFORM	OP(NA) before	3.1914
***	CP(All)	7.12.1928

KINGSBURY	Opened	12.8.1839
***	CG	6.7.1964
***	CP	4.3.1968
Kingsbury Station SB	Open before	1.11.1875
Replacement box	Opened	2.10.1898
Replacement box named Kingsbury Station Junction SB	Opened	6.9.1908
***	Closed	10.8.1969
Whitacre North SB	Opened	7.11.1897
***	Re-framed	27.5.1900
***	Closed	23.3.1958
Whitacre North Jcn to Whitacre: up and down goods lines	Into use	27.5.1900
Up goods line made Engineer's siding	... ...	28.7.1968
Down derby goods line	t.o.u.	4.4.1982
Whitacre Junction SB	Open before	16.8.1877
Replacement box	Opened	30.4.1899
Replacement box	Opened	17.12.1939
***	Closed	10.8.1969
WHITACRE JUNCTION (first station)	Opened	10.2.1842
***	CP&G	1.11.1864

Kingsbury & Water Orton line

See page 211

Nuneaton & Whitacre line

See page 225

Whitacre to Hampton Jcn	CP	1.1.1917 *
***	Singled	8.1842-3.1843
At the singling, time-interval working was still in operation. The branch was later worked by train staff without tickets.		
Whitacre to Maxstoke	CG(All)	1.5.1939
Line severed 300 yards from its start	... ...	12.12.1970
Line reduced to a 1 1/2 mile siding	... ...	26.11.1951
Maxstoke Crossing: stop block provided 50 yards on the Whitacre side	... ...	7.9.1943
Line cut 870 yards north of bridge No. 16 and stop block provided	... ...	15.9.1942
Bridge No. 16 to Hampton: line made a siding	... ...	12.1.1935
COLESHILL	Opened	12.8.1839
Altered to COLESHILL (HAMPTON LINE)	... ...	1.11.1849 *
Altered to COLESHILL	... ...	1.12.1872 *
***	CP	1.1.1917
Altered to MAXSTOKE	... ...	9.7.1923
***	CG	1.5.1939
Coleshill Station SB	Opened	....
***	Closed	....
This location is named in a list of "signal posts" returned to the Board of Trade in November 1880, but it is possible that there was never a signalbox structure.		
Maxstoke to Hampton-in-Arden	CG	24.4.1930
Hampton end of Whitacre & Hampton branch worked as a siding	... ...	22.9.1930
Hampton Station SB	Open before	1885
***	Closed	1916-1960
HAMPTON	Opened	12.8.1839
Altered to HAMPTON JUNCTION	... ...	1.11.1849 *
Altered to HAMPTON	... ...	1.12.1872 *
***	CP	1.1.1917
***	CG	4.1.1965
After the withdrawal of the Midland-line goods service the goods depot was treated as part of the London & North Western station.		

Kingsbury & Water Orton Line

Powers: Midland Railway Act 1906

Kingsbury Jcn to Water Orton Station Jcn	OG	22.3.1909
***	OP	3.5.1909
Working was by the block telegraph system from the opening. On 22 March 1909 the new lines were designated the fast lines; the old route between these two points became the slow lines.		
Kingsbury Jcn to Water Orton East Jcn: closure of the line for renewal of the formation	... ...	3.1980
***	RO(G)	18.8.1980
***	RO(P)	22.8.1980

Whitacre & Birmingham Line

Powers: Birmingham and Derby Junction Railway Act 1840
(This Act also authorised the abandonment of the Whitacre to Stechford line authorised in 1836.)
Midland Railway (New Works Etc) Act 1876
(Widening at Water Orton - Land powers only)
Midland Railway Act 1899
(Water Orton & Castle Bromwich Widening - Land powers only)
Midland Railway (Additional Powers) Act 1875
(Castle Bromwich & Saltley Widening - Land powers only)
Midland Railway Act 1893 (Widening at Saltley)

Whitacre Jcn to Birmingham Lawley Street	O.Formal	9.2.1842
***	OP	10.2.1842
***	OG	11.4.1842
Whitacre Jcn to Birmingham: block telegraph system	Installed by	1873
WHITACRE JUNCTION	Opened	10.2.1842
Replacement station 60 chains to the south on the deviation line	Opened	1.11.1864
Altered to WHITACRE	... ...	1.10.1904 *
***	CG	1.3.1965
***	CP	4.3.1968
Forge Mills Station SB	Open before	1.11.1875
Replacement box	Opened	26.2.1893
Re-named Coleshill Station SB	... ...	1923
Replacement box 270 yards to the east	Opened	3.12.1939
***	Closed	10.8.1969
FORGE MILLS	OP	10.2.1842
***	OG	....
Altered to FORGE MILLS (FOR COLESHILL)	... ...	1.11.1849 *
Altered to FORGE MILLS	... ...	1.4.1904
Altered to COLESHILL	... ...	9.7.1923

COLESHILL (continued)	CG	6.7.1964
***	CP	4.3.1968
Water Orton Station SB	Open before	16.8.1877
Replacement box	Opened	1879
Replacement box named Water Orton Station Junction SB	Opened	6.7.1890
***	Re-located	15.9.1907
Replacement box	Opened	31.5.1908
Replacement box named Water Orton East Junction SB	Opened	12.5.1963
***	Closed	10.8.1969
Water Orton Station Jcn to Water Orton Jcn: down goods line	Into use	6.7.1890
Second up goods line	Into use	13.12.1891
Water Orton East Jcn to Castle Bromwich Jcn: down goods line	t.o.u.	4.11.1984
Water Orton East Jcn to Water Orton West Jcn: down slow line (the former down goods line)	Into use	2.12.1984
Up goods line	t.o.u.	20.2.1983
Down main line made down & up fast line	... ...	2.12.1984
Water Orton Station Jcn: up passenger line to up goods line crossover	Into use	....
Down goods line to down passenger line crossover	Into use	....
WATER ORTON	OP	10.2.1842
***	OG	....
Replacement goods yard and sidings on the down side	Opened	17.5.1908
Replacement passenger station 10 chains to the west	Opened	3.5.1909
***	CG	7.3.1966
Water Orton Station to Water Orton Jcn: up goods line	Into use	19.5.1879
Water Orton Sidings SB	Opened	8.1.1893
Replacement box	Opened	18.4.1943
Replacement box	Opened	10.6.1956
***	Closed	27.4.1969
WATER ORTON NEW SIDINGS	Opened	12.12.1892
Arrival line from Water Orton West Jcn	t.o.u.	27.4.1969
Departure line to Water Orton East Jcn	t.o.u.	27.4.1969
Water Orton Sidings	Closed	....
Water Orton Junction SB	Opened	1879
Replacement box	Opened	25.1.1891
***	Re-framed	30.9.1900
Replacement box	Opened	18.4.1943
Re-named Water Orton West Junction SB	... ...	12.5.1963
***	Closed	10.8.1969

Walsall, Wolverhampton & Midland Junction Railway
See page 226

Water Orton Jcn: down goods line to down passenger line crossover	Into use	30.9.1900
***	t.o.u.	7.1.1968
Water Orton West Jcn: down passenger line to up passenger line crossover	Into use	7.1.1968
Water Orton Jcn to Castle Bromwich Jcn: up goods line	Into use	30.7.1899
Down goods line	Into use	30.9.1900
Water Orton West Jcn to Castle Bromwich: up goods line made up & down slow line	... ...	2.12.1984
Water Orton West Jcn to ......: down goods line	t.o.u.	....
Castle Bromwich North SB	Opened	30.7.1899
***	Closed	30.9.1900
Castle Bromwich Junction SB	Opened	1879
Replacement box	Opened	30.7.1899
***	Raised	21.4.1907
Replacement box	Opened	12.8.1945
***	Closed	10.8.1969

Castle Bromwich Curve
See page 227

Castle Bromwich Jcn: continuation of main lines of Walsall branch to new junction at north end of Castle Bromwich station	Into use	30.7.1899
Down goods line to down passenger line crossover	Into use	7.4.1907
Up goods line to up passenger line crossover	Into use	16.6.1901
Down passenger line to down goods line crossover	Into use	13.10.1901
Castle Bromwich Jcn to Bromford Bridge: up goods line made up & down goods line	... ...	2.12.1984
Castle Bromwich Jcn to Castle Bromwich Station Jcn: up goods line	Into use	16.6.1901
Down goods line	Into use	13.10.1901
CASTLE BROMWICH	OP	10.2.1842
***	OG	....
New station building	Opened	End 1901
***	CG	1.6.1964
***	CP	4.3.1968
Excursion trains continued to call at this station.		
Castle Bromwich Station SB	Open before	1.11.1875
Replacement box	Opened	19.6.1892
Re-named Castle Bromwich Station Junction SB	... ...	3.10.1893
***	Raised	18.2.1894
***	Closed	13.10.1901

Castle Bromwich Station (south) Jcn to Bromford Jcn: up goods line	Into use	3.10.1893
Down goods line	Into use	8.10.1893
Castle Bromwich South SB	Opened	13.2.1916
***	Closed	12.10.1932
Bromford SB	Opened	24.11.1889
Re-named Bromford Junction SB	... ...	28.9.1890
***	Closed	8.10.1893
Bromford Jcn to Washwood Heath Jcn: up and down goods lines	Into use	28.9.1890
Bromford Bridge North SB	Opened	23.2.1896
***	Closed	24.12.1917
Bromford Bridge North:		
down passenger line to down goods line crossover	Into use	....
Up goods line to up passenger line crossover	Into use	....
BROMFORD FORGE	OP	16.5.1842
***	CP(All)	1.6.1843 *
BROMFORD BRIDGE: new racecourse station on site of Forge station	OP(NA)	9.3.1896
***	CP(All)	28.6.1965
Bromford Bridge was provided with platforms on the goods lines. Special block-posts at Bromford Bridge North and Bromford Bridge South were brought into use only when passenger race-traffic was to be run and when passenger trains were operated the section of line between the two block posts was worked by block telegraph.		
Bromford Bridge Station SB	Opened	16.12.1917
***	Closed	24.8.1969
Bromford Bridge South SB	Opened	23.2.1896
***	Closed	16.12.1917
Bromford Bridge South:		
down goods line to down passenger line crossover	Into use	....
Up passenger line to up goods line crossover	Into use	....
Down platform line to down passenger line connection	Removed	13.8.1967
Up passenger line to up platform line connection	Removed	....
Up goods line to up passenger line crossover	Into use	10.12.1967
Various connections	Removed	15.4.1984
Bromford Bridge to Washwood Heath No. 1 SB:		
up goods line made up & down goods line	... ...	12.5.1984
Washwood Heath Junction SB	Opened	c.8.1876
Replacement box	Opened	29.12.1889
***	Re-framed	28.9.1890
Replacement box	Opened	8.9.1918
***	Closed	24.8.1969
Washwood Heath Jcn: down passenger line to down goods line crossover	Into use	14.4.1907
First down goods line to down passenger line crossover	Into use	16.6.1912
Up goods line to up passenger line crossover	Into use	28.9.1890
Down goods line to down passenger line crossover	Into use	....
Down reception line and sidings	Into use	17.2.1935
Washwood Heath Jcn to Church Road Crossing (Saltley): down goods line	Into use	11.1874-11.1875
Second down goods line	Into use	16.9.1888
Up goods line	Into use	29.12.1889
Washwood Heath Jcn to Washwood Heath Sidings (north end):		
Nos. 1, 2, and 3 reception lines (down side)	Into use	9.9.1900
On the same day Nos 10, 11, and 12 marshalling sidings were made Nos. 4, 5, and 6 reception lines.		
Washwood Heath Jcn to Washwood Heath Sidings No. 1:		
No. 1 reception siding made bi-directional	... ...	12.12.1909
Washwood Heath Jcn to Washwood Heath No. 2 SB:		
working of down goods line No. 2 by "No Block" regulations	Commenced	13.8.1967
Washwood Heath Up Sidings North Stage taken out of use and signalbox (not a block post) provided in lieu	... ...	....
Washwood Heath Up Sidings North SB	Re-framed	2.3.1924
***	Closed	....
WASHWOOD HEATH SIDINGS	Opened	1.10.1877
Additional down-side fan of sidings	Into use	15.11.1891
Additional sidings on the down side	Into use	17.2.1935
Down gravitation sidings	Into use	5.8.1923
Nos. 1 to 23 marshalling sidings and 2 carriage & wagon sidings	t.o.u.	18.11.1973
WASHWOOD HEATH UP SIDINGS	Opened	7.1.1918
Additional sidings on the up side	Into use	24.5.1930
Washwood Heath Up Sidings: up reception line No. 3	Into use	19.8.1930
Hump shunting	Ceased	9.12.1972
Washwood Heath Up Sidings SB		
re-named Washwood Heath Up Sidings South SB	... ...	17.6.1918
Washwood Heath Sidings No. 6 SB (not a block post)	Opened	24.5.1930
Box made a shunting frame	... ...	24.8.1969
***	t.o.u.	16.12.1973
Washwood Heath Sidings No. 5 SB (not a block post)	Opened	24.5.1930
Box made a shunting frame	By	24.8.1969
Shunting frame made a points cabin	... ...	16.12.1973
Washwood Heath No. 5 to Washwood Heath No. 2:		
up sidings 2, 3, & 4 made into reception lines 2, 3, and 4	... ...	18.6.1978
Washwood Heath Sidings No. 4 SB (not a block post)	Opened	5.8.1923
Box made a shunting frame	... ...	24.8.1969
***	t.o.u.	18.11.1973

Washwood Heath Sidings No. 3 SB (not a block post)	Opened	9.9.1900
***	Re-framed	....
Box ceased to signal the second down goods line	... ...	13.8.1967
Box made a shunting frame	... ...	24.8.1969
***	t.o.u.	9.12.1973
Washwood Heath Sidings SB (not a block post)	Opened	....
Replacement box	Opened	14.3.1892
Re-named Washwood Heath Sidings No. 2 SB	... ...	18.8.1895
***	Raised	5.5.1914
Replacement box	Opened	....
Box made a shunting frame	... ...	24.8.1969
Shunting frame taken out of use and replaced by Metropolitan Cammell GF (power worked)	... ...	3.8.1986
Washwood Heath Sidings to Saltley Sidings: first and second down goods lines	Into use	18.8.1895
Washwood Heath Sidings No. 1 SB	Opened	18.8.1895
Replacement box	Opened	19.3.1899
***	Re-framed	6.4.1924
Box made a shunting frame	... ...	24.8.1969
***	t.o.u.	....
Washwood Heath Sidings No. 1: down goods line to down passenger line crossover	Into use	....
Up passenger line to up goods line crossover	Into use	....
Washwood Heath Sidings No. 1 to Saltley Sidings: up goods line	Into use	25.8.1895
***	t.o.u.	28.5.1899
Washwood Heath Sidings No. 1 to Saltley Jcn: independent up Lawley Street goods line	Into use	4.6.1899
Independent down Lawley Street goods line	Into use	18.6.1899
Washwood Heath Sidings No. 1 to Landor Street Jcn: independent up and down Camp Hill goods lines	Into use	3.9.1899
Washwood Heath Sidings No. 1 to Duddeston Road: down Lawley Street line	t.o.u.	9.4.1967
Up Lawley Street line made up & down Lawley Street line	... ...	9.4.1967
Down Lawley Street line re-opened as up Lawley Street line	On	7.5.1967
Down Camp Hill goods line made up & down through siding	... ...	23.7.1967
Up Camp Hill goods line made down Camp Hill goods line	... ...	23.7.1967
Church Road Crossing SB	Open before	16.8.1877
Replacement box	Opened	c.8.1878
Replacement box	Opened	29.12.1889
Replacement box	Opened	9.9.1894
***	Closed	18.8.1895
SALTLEY WHARF	Opened	....
***	Closed	4.11.1963
Saltley Sidings SB	Open before	16.8.1877
Replacement box	Opened	11.8.1895
***	Moved	12.3.1899
Replacement box	Opened	18.6.1899
***	Closed	24.8.1969
Saltley level crossing	Removed	5.1895
SALTLEY	OP	1.10.1854
Replacement station: up side of new island platform	Into use	4.6.1899
Replacement station: down side of new island platform	Into use	2.7.1899
***	CP(All)	4.3.1968
Saltley: down goods line	Into use	31.10.1875
Saltley to Duddeston Road: independent siding made down goods line	... ...	6.12.1936
Saltley Junction SB	Opened	....
Replacement box	Opened	c.11.1866
Replacement box	Opened	c.8.1878
***	Re-framed	11.10.1896
Replacement box	Opened	4.6.1899
***	Re-framed	....
***	Closed	24.8.1969
Saltley Jcn to Landor Street Jcn: up Camp Hill goods line made back engine siding	... ...	23.7.1967
Saltley Jcn to Lawley Street: up and down goods lines	Into use	19.11.1876
Second up goods line (up side)	Into use	12.1888-8.1893
On the opening of the new goods lines in November 1876 Duddeston Road ceased to be the point of divergence for passenger trains running over the Birmingham Extension Line (Derby Curve) to New Street station.		
Saltley engine shed	Opened	1854
***	Completed by	2.1856
***	Replaced	1868
No. 2 engine shed	Opened	1876
No. 3 engine shed	Opened	1900
Engine sheds	C.Steam	6.3.1967
Duddeston Road SB	Open before	16.8.1877
Replacement box	Opened	c.1.1878
Replacement box	Opened	23.9.1888
***	Re-framed	26.7.1914
Replacement box	Opened	2.10.1955
***	Closed	24.8.1969

Aston Curve

Powers: Midland Railway (Additional Powers) Act 1862

Duddeston Road to St Andrew's Jcn	OG	2.1866 *
***	Approved	28.7.1866
***	OP	1.11.1866 *
Block telegraph system	Installed by	1873
***	CP	1.5.1900
Brick Yard Crossing SB	Open before	1.10.1876
Replacement box	Opened	15.5.1904
***	Closed	20.2.1966
Duddeston Road: down New Street line to up Camp Hill line crossover	Into use	12.1.1908
Saltley PSB:		
1. Tamworth / Abbey Jcn / Sutton Park to Bromford Bridge (exc)	Into use	9-11.8.1969
2. Bromford Bridge to King's Heath / Bordesley South	Into use	23-25.8.1969
3a. Moor Street to Leamington (exc) / Hall Green, and Hatton to Bearley Jcn	Into use	30.8-1.9.1969
3b: King's Heath / Church Road Jcn to Barnt Green Main Line Jcn, and Barnt Green Main Line Jcn to Redditch	Into use	6-8.9.1969
SALTLEY FREIGHTLINER TERMINAL	Opened	....
Landor Street Junction: new running junction	Into use	15.11.1896

On the same day block telegraph working was withdrawn on the up and down Camp Hill Lines between Saltley Junction and Duddeston Road, but it was retained on the down line between Duddeston Road and the new Landor Street Junction.

Landor Street Junction SB	Opened	15.11.1896
***	Closed	24.8.1969
Lift Sidings SB	Opened	1852
Replacement box in the centre of the exchange sidings	Opened	1878
***	Closed	2.9.1894

Spur to the Grand Junction Railway

Powers: --

Inclined spur from Lawley Street to the Grand Junction Railway	OG	11.4.1842
***	CG(All)	1.11.1850

The Lift

Powers: --

Lift connection to a point near the junction of the Birmingham & Gloucester line with the London & Birmingham line	Into use	7.1843
***	Removed	Mid-1853
BIRMINGHAM LAWLEY STREET	Opened	10.2.1842
***	CP	1.5.1851
Lawley Street to London Yard	Opened	1.3.1860
Lawley Street "A" SB	Opened	13.9.1891
Replacement box	Opened	13.3.1927
***	Closed	25.11.1973
Lawley Street No. 1 SB	Opened	....
Re-named Lawley Street "B" SB	... ...	4.9.1892
Replacement box	Opened	28.5.1893
***	Closed	16.8.1970
Lawley Street No. 2 SB	Opened	....
***	Closed	24.1.1892
Lawley Street No. 3 SB	Opened	12.1896-5.1899
***	Closed	8.5.1966
LAWLEY STREET GOODS YARD	Re-modelled	1892-1893
New goods shed	Opened	29.10.1945
Major alterations to sidings	... ...	29.9.1968
BIRMINGHAM INLAND PORT and LANDOR STREET FREIGHT DEPOT	Closed	6.2.1987

Birmingham Extension

Powers: Midland Railway (Birmingham Extension) Act 1846
London and North Western Railway (New Railways) Act 1892

Duddeston Road to Derby Jcn (first Aston Curve)	Completed	1.11.1850
***	OG by	2.1851
***	OP	1.5.1851
***	Closed	17.5.1896
Derby Junction SB	Open before	16.8.1877
***	Closed	26.4.1895

Between Derby Junction and New Street Junction the Midland possessed running powers for passenger traffic, together with powers to use New Street station. Merchandise traffic to and from the Exchange Sidings was also worked.

Independent lines for Midland trains through new south tunnel and underpass line from Derby Jcn to Grand Jcn	Into use	17.5.1896
BIRMINGHAM EXCHANGE SIDINGS	Into use	7.1878
Exchange of traffic	Commenced	2.9.1878
***	Ceased	27.4.1896
Replacement exchange sidings	Into use	19.7.1896

Gloucester Junction SB	Opened	....
Re-named Exchange Sidings SB	By	20.5.1896
***	Closed	24.8.1969
Grand Junction SB	Closed	4.6.1966
BIRMINGHAM altered to BIRMINGHAM CURZON STREET	... ...	11.1852
***	CP	1.7.1854
Proof House Junction SB	Closed	4.6.1966
BIRMINGHAM BANBURY STREET TICKET PLATFORM	Closed	1.7.1885
BIRMINGHAM NEW STREET: user by Midland passenger trains	Commenced	1.7.1854
Midland platforms	Into use	8.2.1885
Midland express passenger trains running through New Street	Commenced	1.10.1885
Use of the new side by all Midland passenger trains	Commenced	1.10.1889
Passenger station made joint between the London & North Western and Midland Railway Companies	... ...	1.4.1897
Some Midland goods trains began to work through the station between Saltley and Birmingham Central Goods Depot	... ...	1.4.1897

DERBY & MELBOURNE LINE

Powers: Midland Railway (New Lines and Additional Powers) Act 1864

The direction of the line was DOWN from Trent to Melbourne Junction.

Melbourne Jcn to Melbourne	OP&G	1.9.1868
Derby to Melbourne: block telegraph system	Installed	1882
Derby and Ashby-de-la-Zouch; Derby and Trent via Castle Donington	CP	22.9.1930
Melbourne Jcn to Sinfin Sidings: additional running line	Into use	18.12.1921
***	t.o.u.	....
Melbourne Jcn to Chellaston Jcn	Singled	8.6.1969
Line designated a siding	... ...	29.6.1969
Melbourne Jcn to Rolls Royce Siding (1m 249yds from Melbourne Jcn) made a passenger line as the Sinfin branch	... ...	27.9.1976
SINFIN NORTH	OP(NA)	4.10.1976
SINFIN CENTRAL	OP	4.10.1976
Sinfin Sidings SB	Opened	2.12.1921
***	Closed	1937-1945
Line severed 1m 249yds from Melbourne Jcn at Rolls Royce Siding	... ...	30.12.1973
CHELLASTON & SWARKESTONE	OP&G	1.9.1868
***	CP	22.9.1930
***	CG	13.6.1966
Excursion trains continued to call at this station.		
Chellaston Station SB	Open before	1.11.1875
Replacement box	Opened	19.9.1910
***	Closed	10.7.1966
Chellaston West Junction SB	Open before	1.11.1875
Replacement box	Opened	6.1.1901
Re-named Chellaston Junction SB	... ...	24.5.1932
***	Closed	29.6.1969
Chellaston West Jcn	t.o.u.	30.12.1973

Stenson & Weston line

See page 218

Chellaston East Junction SB	Open before	1.11.1875
Replacement box	Opened	19.9.1887
***	Closed	24.5.1932
Chellaston East Jcn (location) re-named Worthington Jcn	... ...	29.6.1969

Sawley & Weston line

See page 218

Chellaston East Jcn to Worthington	Singled	26.2.1967
Electric train token replaced by working one engine in steam	... ...	8.9.1968
Traffic ceased (but the line is still not officially closed)	... ...	21.5.1980
Chellaston Quarry SB	Opened	17.12.1939
Replacement box	Opened	22.12.1944
***	Closed	13.3.1966
King's Newton SB	Opened	8.7.1940
***	LMS worked	17.12.1944
***	Closed	2.9.1962
Melbourne Brick Sidings SB	Open before	16.8.1877
***	Closed	11.1885-12.1888
MELBOURNE	Opened	1.9.1868
***	CP	22.9.1930
***	CG	5.7.1965
Excursion trains continued to call at least until 1939.		
Melbourne Station SB	Opened	1872
Replacement box	Opened	11.1.1914
***	Closed	26.2.1967

WORTHINGTON EXTENSION

Powers: Midland Railway (New Lines and Additional Powers) Act 1864

Melbourne to Worthington Extension	OM	1.9.1869
***	OG	1.10.1869 ?
***	OP	1.10.1869
Working by train staff and ticket instead of by train staff without tickets	Commenced	1.1.1874
Working by train tablet instead of by train staff and ticket	Commenced	26.7.1891
One engine in steam working	Commenced	8.9.1968
Closed to traffic (closure not yet official)	CG(All)	21.5.1980
WILSON	Opened	1.10.1869
***	CP	1.6.1871
***	CG	....
TONGE & BREEDON	Opened	1.9.1869
Altered to TONGE & BREEDON	... ...	1.5.1897
***	CP	22.9.1930
***	CG	7.9.1959
Excursion trains continued to call at this station.		
Tonge & Breedon Station SB (not a block post)	Open before	16.8.1877
***	Closed	1937-1945
Worthington Station SB	Open before	16.8.1877
Box closed and 2 ground frames provided in lieu	... ...	8.9.1968
WORTHINGTON	OM	1.9.1869
***	OP	1.10.1969
***	CP	22.9.1930
***	CG	4.5.1964

Excursion trains continued to call at this station.

The line between Chellaston East Junction and Swisby Road (north end of Ashby tunnel) was occupied by the War Department for the Melbourne Military Railway between 19 November 1939 and 31 December 1944. On 1 January 1945 the LMS took over operation of the line from the Melbourne Military Railway.

Ticknall Tramway	Opened	1802-1836
Taken over by the Midland Railway	... ...	1846
Abandoned piecemeal after	... ...	1850
Finally closed	... ...	1913

ASHBY & BREEDON LINE

Powers: Ashby-de-la-Zouch Canal Act 1794
Midland Railway (New Lines and Additional Powers) Act 1865

Ashby to Worthington	OP&G	1.1.1874
Working by train tablet instead of by train staff and ticket	Commenced	26.7.1891
Ashby to Burton Road Crossing (Standard Soap Company's Siding)	Closed	8.1.1964 ?
	or	9.2.1964 ?
ASHBY (branch station)	OP	1.1.1874
Altered to ASHBY-DE-LA-ZOUCH	... ...	2.6.1924 ?
***	CP	22.9.1930
Tamworth Road Crossing SB	Open before	16.8.1877
Replacement box	Opened	26.7.1891
***	Closed	7.7.1931
High Street Crossing SB	Open before	16.8.1877
Replacement box	Opened	26.7.1891
***	Closed	7.7.1931
Burton Road Crossing SB	Open before	16.8.1877
Replacement box	Opened	26.7.1891
***	Re-framed	11.2.1906
***	Closed	7.7.1931
Burton Road Crossing (Holywell Siding) to New Lount Colliery Empty Wagon Sidings (scotch-block put in at Ticknall siding)	Closed	11.12.1949
Line severed at Burton Road Crossing	... ...	9.5.1955
Scotch-blocks were put at both ends of the Ashby tunnel on 11 December 1949.		
Love's Brick Yard SB	Open before	16.8.1877
***	Closed	4.1883-11.1885
Ticknall Wharf SB	Open before	16.8.1877
***	Closed	4.1883-11.1885
Heath End Colliery Sidings SB	Open before	16.8.1877
***	Closed	4.1883-11.1885
Lount SB	Opened	1873
***	Closed	4.1883-11.1885
The four locations immediately above, together with Coleorton Junction, are named in a list of "signal posts" returned to the Board of Trade in November 1880, but there may not actually have been signalbox structures.		
New Lount Colliery: line severed	... ...	9.5.1955

New Lount Colliery to Worthington West GF	t.o.u.	27.11.1968
Coleorton Junction SB	Opened	1873
***	Closed by	16.8.1877
Between Coleorton Colliery Sidings and Ashby-de-la-Zouch the London & North Western Railway possessed running powers over the Midland line.		
Coleorton Tramway	Opened	1833
***	Closed	1872
Lount to Newbold section of Coleorton Tramway relaid for colliery use	... ...	1925

SAWLEY & WESTON LINE

Powers: Midland Railway (New Lines and Additional Powers) Act 1865

Sheet Stores Jcn to Chellaston East Jcn	OP	6.12.1869
***	OG	20.12.1869
Block telegraph system	Installed	1882
***	CP	22.9.1930
Between Chellaston East Junction and Sheet Stores Junction the London & North Western possessed running powers by arrangement over the Midland line for merchandise traffic as part of a running powers route between Stenson Junction and Sneinton Junction (Nottingham). Between Chellaston East Junction and Sheet Stores Junction the North Staffordshire possessed running powers over the Midland line as part of a running powers route between Stenson Junction and Nottingham.		
Lock Lane Crossing SB	Open before	1.10.1876
Replacement box	Opened	9.11.1902
Replacement box	Opened	1961-1969
Box made a gate box	... ...	28.9.1969
Castle Donington Ballast Pit Sidings SB	Opened	3.11.1879
Re-named Hemington Ballast Sidings SB	... ...	....
***	Closed	6.1881-4.1883
This signalbox is already shewn as temporarily closed in the Appendix of 1 February 1880.		
Castle Donington Station SB	Open before	1.11.1875
Replacement box	Opened	28.4.1901
***	Re-framed	....
***	Closed	28.9.1969
CASTLE DONINGTON	OP	6.12.1869
***	OG	20.12.1869
Altered to CASTLE DONINGTON & SHARDLOW	... ...	1.5.1898 *
***	CP	22.9.1930
***	CG	1.5.1967
Excursion trains continued to call at this station.		
Canal Bridge SB	Opened	17.12.1924
***	Closed	8.2.1925
Weston-on-Trent Station SB	Open before	1.11.1875
Replacement box	Opened	2.10.1898
***	Closed	24.4.1966
WESTON-ON-TRENT	OP	6.12.1869
***	OG	20.12.1869
***	CP	22.9.1930
***	CG	7.9.1959
Chellaston Ballast Pit Sidings SB	Opened	3.11.1879
***	Closed	....

STENSON & WESTON LINE

Powers: Midland Railway (Branches Etc) Act 1866

Chellaston West Jcn to Stenson Jcn	OG	3.11.1873
***	OP	1.5.1874 *
The passenger opening was for North Staffordshire trains only. Working was by the block telegraph system from the opening. Between Chellaston West Junction and Stenson Junction the London & North Western possessed running powers by arrangement over the Midland line for merchandise traffic as part of a running powers route between Stenson Junction and Sneinton Junction (Nottingham). Between Chellaston West Junction and Stenson Junction the North Staffordshire possessed running powers over the Midland line as part of a running powers route between Stenson Junction and Nottingham.		

BURTON GOODS BRANCHES

The London & North Western possessed running powers over the Midland lines in Burton.

Hay Branch

Powers: Midland Railway and Burton-upon-Trent Bridge Act 1859

Wetmore Sidings to Hawkins Lane Jcn: inwards and outwards lines	t.o.u.	26.9.1965
New connecting line	Into use	23.1.1966
Horninglow Bridge to Hawkins Lane Sidings: up & down goods line	Into use	26.1.1966
Up & down goods line made a siding	... ...	15.11.1970
Burton North Junction SB (Great Northern and North Staffordshire)	Opened	....
***	Closed	9.5.1954
Burton South Junction SB (Great Northern and North Staffordshire) re-named Hawkins Lane Sidings SB	... ...	9.5.1954
***	Closed	15.11.1970
North Stafford Jcn to Anderstaff Lane	Opened	11.1861
North Stafford Jcn to Hawkins Lane Jcn	Closed	23.1.1966
Hawkins Lane Jcn with the London & North Western Railway and the North Staffordshire Railway	Opened	1.4.1868
Hawkins Lane Jcn with the Great Northern Railway	Opened	1.8.1878 ?
Hawkins Lane Junction SB	Opened	....
Replacement box	Opened	1883
***	Alt.levers	5.3.1893
Replacement box	Opened	8.12.1929
***	Closed	2.2.1966
Hawkins Lane Jcn to Anderstaff Lane	Closed by	5.2.1966
Line made a siding	... ...	1.3.1969
Salt's Maltings SB	Opened	30.7.1877
Replacement box	Opened	21.1.1901
***	Closed	12.4.1932
Anderstaff Lane to the Hay	Opened	6.11.1864
Anderstaff Lane SB	Opened	14.10.1867
Replacement box	Opened	1881
Replacement box	Opened	17.7.1904
***	Closed	1.3.1969
Anderstaff Lane: line southwards made a siding	... ...	31.3.1963
Salt's Engine Shed SB	Opened	....
Replacement box	Opened	21.4.1907
***	Closed	31.3.1963
Trent Bridge SB	Opened	....
Replacement box	Opened	24.2.1908
***	Closed	18.6.1934
Hay SB	Opened	....
***	Re-located	20.5.1889
Replacement box	Opened	22.10.1905
***	Closed	27.10.1930
HAY WHARF	Opened	....
***	Closed	6.7.1984

Sanders Branch

Powers: --

Hawkins Lane Jcn to end of Allsopp's Cooperage Branch	Opened	11.1861
***	Closed	....

Guild Street Branch

Powers: No Construction Powers (Junction of Guild Street and Hay Branches)
Midland Railway (Burton Branches) Act 1860 (Hay end)
Midland Railway and Burton-upon-Trent Bridge Act 1859 (Crossing of Guild Street)
Midland Railway (Burton Branches) Act 1860 (Guild Street Junction end)

Hay SB to Horninglow Bridge	Opened	4.10.1862
***	Closed	31.3.1973
Hay SB to High Street Crossing: working of up line as single line by train staff without tickets	Commenced	2.7.1893
High Street Crossing SB	Opened	14.10.1867
Replacement box	Opened	1889
***	Closed	c.1964
Church Croft Junction SB	Opened	14.10.1867
Replacement box	Opened	8.3.1892
***	Closed	31.3.1963
Guild Street SB	Opened	....
Replacement box	Opened	1889
***	Closed	c.1964

Allsopp's Crossing SB	Opened	....
Replacement box	Opened	6.2.1893
***	Closed	16.7.1967
Brook Street Crossing SB	Opened	....
***	Closed	1937-1945
It is known that there were signals in this location, but the existence of a signalbox is uncertain.		
Allsopp's Siding to Horninglow Bridge	t.o.u.	4.1973

Horninglow Branch

Powers: Midland Railway (Additional Powers) Act 1867

Horninglow Bridge to Horninglow Wharf	OG	27.2.1873
Line made a siding	... ...	15.8.1969
***	Closed	1.1.1970 ?
***	Recovered	5.1970 ?
Horninglow Bridge to Bass Sidings	Closed	14.7.1970 ?
Horninglow Bridge: junction	Altered	30.4.1882
Bass Sidings to Truman, Hanbury & Buxton Sidings	Closed	22.8.1970
Horninglow Wharf (Cyclops Engineering Siding) to Victoria Street level crossing	t.o.u.	28.2.1969
The line was cut at Victoria Street level crossing.		
Derby Street Crossing SB	Opened	....
***	Closed	1937-1945
It is known that there were signals in this location, but the existence of a signalbox is uncertain.		
HORNINGLOW WHARF	Opened	....
***	Closed	6.7.1964
Horninglow Wharf Extension	Into use	4.12.1890
HORNINGLOW GOODS DEPOT (Great Northern Railway)	Opened	1.7.1878
***	Closed	....
Horninglow Bridge SF to Wetmore SF: through siding severed	... ...	1.10.1973

Mosley Street Branch

Powers: Midland Railway (New Lines and Additional Powers) Act 1864

Burton Station South to Ind Coope & Co. on Station Street	Opened	13.3.1865
***	Closed	....

Shobnall Branch

Powers: Midland Railway (Additional Powers) Act 1874
(There were no construction powers for Shobnall Wharf, but land was purchased under the 1874 Act)

South end of Burton station to Shobnall Wharf (Bass & Co's Maltings)	Opened	28.4.1873
Leicester Jcn to Wellington Street Jcn: new curve	Opened	27.11.1876
The new curve replaced the curve from Burton Station South SB, which was abandoned as a running line on its opening.		
Branch doubling and extension to canal and new ale dock	Into use	2.11.1874
Leicester Jcn to Wellington Street: line singled and made siding	... ...	17.3.1968
Leicester Jcn to Wellington Street	Closed	10.2.1979
Shobnall Junction SB	Opened	3.7.1882 ?
Replacement box	Opened	17.12.1917
***	Closed	24.4.1966
Wellington Street Junction SB	Opened	27.11.1876 ?
Replacement box	Opened	24.2.1901
Box made a gate box only	... ...	17.3.1968
***	t.o.u.	10.6.1968
Wellington Street to Shobnall Jcn: line singled and made siding	... ...	24.4.1966
Wellington Street Jcn to Shobnall Maltings	Closed	20.1.1968
Timber Wharf SB	Opened	1876
***	Closed	....
SHOBNALL WHARF	Opened	28.4.1873
***	Closed	6.7.1964
Shobnall Maltings SB	Opened	1897
Box moved to the west side of the level crossing	... ...	8.1.1923
***	Closed	1945-1960
Shobnall Junction SB	Opened	....
Replacement box	Opened	17.12.1917
***	Closed	24.4.1966
Allsopps Sidings SB made a ground frame	... ...	7.10.1963
Branch extended to Bass & Company's Maltings		1.12.1875
and to Perks & Sons Timber Yard at Bond End	... ...	2.12.1875
Branch extended to Mann & Crossman's Brewery and opened for traffic	... ...	29.12.1876
Shobnall Maltings Branch (last Burton branch)	Closed	31.10.1979

Shobnall branch:		
London & North Western extension to Dallow Lane (Horninglow)	Opened	3.7.1882 ?
Extension from Dallow Lane to Stretton Jcn with the North Staffordshire Railway	Opened	1.9.1882
Branch made a siding	... ...	7.10.1963

Duke Street Branch (from Uxbridge Street Junction)

Powers: Midland Railway (Additional Powers) Act 1874
(Dale Street Branch)
Midland Railway (Additional Powers) Act 1879
(Uxbridge Street Junction to Wood Street)
Midland Railway (Additional Powers) Act 1879
(Duke Street Branch to Eadie's Brewery)

James Street Junction SB	Opened	26.4.1880
***	Alt.levers	28.3.1887
***	Re-framed	23.1.1898
Replacement box	Opened	13.1.1929
***	Closed	20.1.1968
James Street Jcn to New Street No. 2 SB: one engine in steam working	Commenced	7.5.1928
Park Street No. 1 SB	Opened	2.12.1875
Replacement box	Opened	13.12.1902
***	Closed	20.1.1968
New Street No. 1 SB	Opened	2.12.1875
Replacement box	Opened	15.11.1891
***	Closed	20.1.1968
Duke Street Crossing SB	Opened	2.12.1875
***	Alt.levers	29.3.1887
Replacement box	Opened	16.3.1907
***	Alt.levers	23.2.1916
***	Closed	20.1.1968

Dale Street Branch

Powers: --

Dale Street Jcn to Leicester Jcn Loop Line	Opened	25.2.1884
***	Closed	....

Bond End Branch (from Wellington Street Junction)

Powers: Midland Railway (Additional Powers) Act 1874

Dale Street SB	Opened	1882 ?
***	Re-framed	5.12.1920
***	Closed	20.1.1968
Uxbridge Street Crossing SB	Opened	2.12.1875
Replacement box	Opened	20.6.1910
***	Closed	20.1.1968
Line cut at Uxbridge Street Jcn and section from Uxbridge Street Jcn to Bond End Wharf closed	... ...	2.3.1964
Bond End branch to Perks & Sons timber yard	Opened	2.12.1875
BOND END WHARF	Opened	2.12.1875
***	Closed	2.3.1964
Branch, together with Shobnall branch extension	Closed	20.1.1968
James Street to Wood Street connection	Into use	4.10.1886
***	t.o.u.	....
There were no construction powers for this line, and no authority is cited for the land purchase either.		
James Street to New Street No. 2 SB made one engine in steam, but using both lines in the correct direction	... ...	7.5.1928
James Street to New Street No. 2 SB: up line	Removed	2.7.1935
Extension from James Street Jcn to Thornewill & Warham, other premises, and various breweries	Opened	26.4.1880
Branston Road Crossing SB	Opened	2.12.1875
***	Alt.levers	31.3.1887
Replacement box	Opened	6.7.1902
***	Closed	2.3.1964

New Branch (from James Street Junction)

Powers: --

Park Street No. 2 SB	Opened	26.4.1880
Replacement box	Opened	15.5.1909
Box closed and ground frame provided in lieu	... ...	2.7.1935
New Street No. 2 SB	Opened	26.4.1880
Replacement box	Opened	1.7.1905
Box made a ground frame	... ...	2.7.1935
***	Demolished	1968

Lichfield Street Crossing SB	Opened	1880 ?
Replacement box	Opened	11.3.1905
***	Closed	2.7.1935

Robinson's Brewery Branch

Powers: Midland Railway (Additional Powers) Act 1878

Brewery branch	Opened	....
***	Closed	....

The Midland possessed running powers for all traffic over London & North Western sidings at Burton, and exercised these powers over the Dallow Lane Branch and the Kottingham and Moor Street Branch.

KOTTINGHAM & MOOR STREET WHARF re-named MOOR STREET WHARF	... ...	1918-1929
MOOR STREET WHARF (London & North Western Railway)	Opened	10.1884
***	Closed	6.7.1964

SOUTH LEICESTERSHIRE RAILWAY (London & North Western Railway)

The Nuneaton & Hinckley Railway Act 1860 gave the London & North Western running powers for all traffic into Leicester and the Midland similar running powers over the South Leicestershire line and over the London & North Western's Coventry & Nuneaton line.

Coventry Midland engine shed	Opened	....
***	Closed	1904

ENDERBY BRANCH (Midland & London & North Western Joint Line)

Powers: Midland Railway (Additional Powers) Act 1890

Narborough Jcn (South Leicestershire line) to Enderby	OG	24.7.1893
Working was by train staff without tickets.		
The line was worked by each company in alternate years.		
Enderby branch extension (2m 18ch to 2m 31ch)	OG	1.1.1912
Enderby branch: Midland trains	Withdrawn	1908
***	Tfc ceased	Late 1976
***	t.o.u.	2.1977
***	Off. closed	30.4.1980
***	Severed	25.5.1980
Asylum sidings (Enderby & Stoney Stanton Granite Company)	In use by	19.10.1904
Ground frame and connection	Removed	11.10.1942

ASHBY & NUNEATON JOINT RAILWAY (Midland and London & North Western)

The Ashby Canal & Tramways undertaking was vested in the Midland Railway in 1846.

The main line from the junctions at Nuneaton to the junctions at Moira was worked by the block telegraph system from its opening.

Abbey Junction to Weddington Junction Curve

Powers: Midland and London and North Western Railway Companies (Ashby and Nuneaton Railway) Act 1868

Nuneaton Abbey Jcn to Weddington Jcn	OG	18.8.1873
***	OP	1.9.1873
***	CP	13.4.1931
Judkin's Siding to Weddington Jcn	t.o.u.	19.7.1971
***	Closed	18.7.1971

Nuneaton to Overseal

Powers: Midland and London and North Western Railway Companies
(Ashby and Nuneaton Railway) Act 1868
(Nuneaton Ashby Junction to Stoke Golding)
Midland Railway (Ashby and Nuneaton Etc) Act 1866
(Hinckley to Shackerstone)
Midland and London and North Western Railway Companies
(Ashby and Nuneaton Railway) Act 1868 (Shackerstone to Snarestone)
Midland Railway (Ashby and Nuneaton Etc) Act 1866
(Snarestone to Moira West Junction)

Nuneaton Ashby Jcn to Moira West Jcn	OM	1.8.1873
***	OG	18.8 1873
***	OP	1.9.1873
***	CP	13.4.1931
Between Nuneaton (Trent Valley line) station and Ashby Junction the Midland possessed running powers over the London & North Western line for coaching traffic.		
Nuneaton: joint-line junction restored to about its pre-1892 place	... ...	4.4.1909
Ashby Jcn to Weddington Jcn line severed	... ...	17.8.1969
Ashby Jcn to Market Bosworth	t.o.u.	19.7.1971
***	Closed	18.7.1971
Weddington Junction SB	Opened	1872
Replacement box	Opened	7.1887
***	Closed	18.7.1971
Higham SB	Opened	1872
***	Closed	1876
HIGHAM-ON-THE-HILL	OP	1.9.1873
***	CP(All)	13.4.1931

Hinckley & Stoke Golding Line

Powers: Midland Railway (Ashby and Nuneaton Etc) Act 1866
Midland Railway Act 1914 (Abandonment)

Hinckley to Stoke Golding	Completed	31.8.1873
RCH distances amended on abandonment of the line	... ...	1.10.1889
Formal decision to lift the line	... ...	16.10.1889
This line was never opened to public traffic.		
STOKE GOLDING	OG	18.8.1873
***	OP	1.9.1873
***	CP	13.4.1931
***	C.Parcels	2.7.1951
***	CG	6.8.1962
Stoke Golding Station SB	Opened	1872
Replacement box	Opened	....
***	Closed	7.8.1962
Shenton Station SB	Opened	1872
***	Closed	....
SHENTON	OG	18.8.1873
***	OP	1.9.1873
***	CP	13.4.1931
***	C.Parcels	2.7.1951
***	CG	4.6.1956
Market Bosworth Station SB	Opened	1872
Replacement box	Opened	1.1899
***	Closed	18.7.1971
MARKET BOSWORTH	OG	18.8.1873
***	OP	1.9.1873
***	CP	13.4.1931
***	C.Parcels	2.7.1951
***	CG	4.3.1968
Market Bosworth to Shackerstone Jcn	Singled	29.11.1964
Market Bosworth to Measham	t.o.u.	12.11.1971
Market Bosworth to Shackerstone re-opened for seasonal passenger use by the Shackerstone Railway Society	... ...	26.3.1978
SHACKERSTONE	OG	18.8.1873
***	OP	1.9.1873
***	CP	13.4.1931
***	C.Parcels	2.7.1951
***	CG	2.3.1964
Shackerstone Junction SB	Opened	1872
***	Re-framed	1881
Replacement box	Opened	24.6.1890
***	Closed	29.11.1964

Coalville branch

See page ...

Shackerstone Jcn to Measham	Singled	1.4.1934
Hill Bridge Crossing SB	Open before	1.11.1875
***	Closed by	16.8.1877
Snarestone SB	Opened	1872
***	Closed	4.1883-11.1885
SNARESTONE	OG	18.8.1873
***	OM	1874
***	OP	1.9.1873
***	CP	13.4.1931
***	C.Parcels	2.7.1951
***	CG	7.8.1967
Measham Colliery Sidings SB	Opened	29.9.1902
***	Closed	1.4.1934

Measham Station SB	Opened	1872
Replacement box	Opened	16.7.1899
Replacement box	Opened	1.4.1934
***	Closed	6.8.1972
MEASHAM	OG	18.8.1873
***	OP	1.9.1873
***	CP	13.4.1931
***	C.Parcels	2.7.1951
***	CG	6.7.1964
Measham to Moira West Jcn	Singled	6.8.1972
DONISTHORPE	OP&M	1.5.1874
***	OG	1-4.1883
***	CP	13.4.1931
***	CG	6.7.1964
Donisthorpe Station SB	Opened	1872
Replacement box	Opened	19.4.1896
***	Raised	26.10.1913
***	Closed	6.8.1972

Donisthorpe Colliery Branch

Powers: No construction powers

Donisthorpe Colliery branch	Opened	1873
Donisthorpe Colliery	Closed	19.7.1980

Line severed 500 yards south of former Overseal GF and section from Donisthorpe Colliery and Measham closed	... ...	20.6.1981
End of remaining branch to Moira West Jcn	t.o.u.	27.1.1985
Moira South Junction SB	Opened	1872
Replacement box	Opened	14.8.1892
***	Closed	21.7.1968

Moira East Curve

Powers: Midland Railway (Ashby and Nuneaton Etc) Act 1866

Moira South Jcn to Moira East Jcn	OG	....
***	OP	1.9.1873
***	CP	13.4.1931
***	Closed	27.7.1967
***	t.o.u.	28.1.1968

Overseal MPD	Lifted	7.9.1964
OVERSEAL & MOIRA	OG	18.8.1873
***	OP	1.9.1873
***	CP	1.7.1890
Goods depot altered to OVERSEAL GOODS SIDINGS	... ...	1915
***	CG	1917 ?
Platforms removed	... ...	11.1918
Goods shed and station buildings removed	... ...	1920
***	Closed	5.1946

Coalville Branch

Powers: Midland Railway (Ashby and Nuneaton Etc) Act 1866

Shackerstone Jcn to Coalville Jcn	OM	1.8.1873
***	OG	18.8.1873
***	OP	1.9.1873
***	CP	13.4.1931
The single line was worked by train staff and tickets.		
Shackerstone Jcn to Hugglescote	Closed	6.4.1964
Shackerstone Jcn to Charnwood Forest Jcn: train tablet working	Commenced	3.5.1891
Helpout Mill SB	Opened	1872
***	Closed	1881
Heather (South ?) SB	Opened	1878
***	Closed	c.1933
HEATHER	OG	18.8.1873
***	OP	1.9.1873
Altered to HEATHER & IBSTOCK	... ...	1.9.1894
***	CP	13.4.1931
***	C.Parcels	2.7.1951
***	CG	7.6.1954
Heather Colliery South SB	Opened	1877
***	Closed	1881
Heather Colliery North SB	Opened	1877
***	Closed	3.5.1891
Hugglescote Station SB	Opened	1872
Replacement box	Opened	11.3.1894
***	Closed	4.7.1965

HUGGLESCOTE	OG	18.8.1873
***	OP	1.9.1873
***	CP	13.4.1931
***	C.Parcels	2.7.1951
***	CG	6.4.1964
Hugglescote to Coalville	CP	1.1.1917 *
***	RO(P)	....
Hugglescote to Charnwood Forest Jcn	Closed	17.8.1964
South Leicestershire Colliery Sidings SB	Opened	1879
***	Closed	3.5.1891
Line severed 300 yards west of Charnwood Forest Jcn	... ...	4.7.1965
Charnwood Forest Junction SB	Opened	c.3.1883
Replacement box	Opened	9.2.1908
***	Closed	4.7.1965
Charnwood Forest Jcn to Coalville Jcn	Closed	17.4.1967
Coalville Sidings SB	Opened	1872
***	Closed	c.3.1883

NUNEATON & WHITACRE LINE

Nuneaton Loop Line

Powers: Midland Railway (New Lines) Act 1861

Nuneaton (London & North Western station) to Nuneaton Abbey Jcn	OG	21.3.1867
***	OP	1.1.1909
***	CP	....
***	RO(P)(Suns)	15.9.1963
***	RO(P) Daily	6.6.1966
Loop line designated a passenger line	... ...	23.3.1969
Nuneaton Trent Valley Line Jcn: amended distances	... ...	1.1.1882
Further amended distances	... ...	1.7.1911

Main line

Powers: Midland Railway (New Lines) Act 1861

Midland (<u>OR</u> South Leicestershire) Jcn to Whitacre Jcn	OP	1.11.1864
***	OG	1.12.1864
Nuneaton to Stockingford: block telegraph system	Installed	1873
Between Nuneaton and Stockingford, including Haunchwood Works and the Stockingford branch, the London & North Western possessed running powers over the Midland line for all traffic.		
Midland Jcn to Abbey Jcn	CP	4.3.1968
***	RO(P) Sats.	29.5.1976
***	RO(P) daily	2.5.1977
***	CP daily	17.5.1982
***	RO(P) Suns.	25.5.1982
***	CP Sats.	4.9.1982
***	CP Suns.	19.9.1982
NUNEATON BRIDGE	OP	1.3.1866 *
***	CP (LNWR)	1.4.1868 *
***	CP(All) (MR)	1.10.1887 *
No evidence for the existence of Nuneaton Bridge station has been found in any issue of the Public Time Tables.		
Nuneaton Sidings SB	Opened	14.7.1907
Box closed and ground frame provided in lieu	... ...	17.3.1935
NUNEATON SIDINGS	Opened	....
New up sidings	Into use	28.1.1894
Up shunting siding and 2 reception lines	Into use	1.12.1907
***	Closed	....
Abbey Junction SB	Open before	16.8.1877
***	Re-framed	c.3.1894
Replacement box	Opened	1.11.1925
***	Closed	....
NUNEATON	OP	1.11.1864
***	OG	1.12.1864
Replacement station 7 chains to the west	Opened	1.9.1873
Altered to NUNEATON ABBEY STREET	... ...	2.6.1924
***	CP	4.3.1968
***	CG	2.8.1982
Nuneaton Station SB	Open before	16.8.1877
Replacement box	Opened	2.12.1906
***	Closed	22.11.1925
Nowell's Sidings SB	Open before	1.11.1875
Replacement box	Opened	19.12.1905
***	Closed	2.12.1934
STOCKINGFORD	OP	1.11.1864
***	OG	1.12.1864
***	CG	11.4.1960
***	CP	4.3.1968

Stockingford Station SB	Open before	1.11.1875
Replacement box	Opened	25.5.1902
***	Closed	2.12.1934
Stockingford engine shed	Opened	12.1.1903
***	Closed	7.11.1932
Stockingford Branch Junction SB	Opened	....
Replacement box named Stockingford Sidings SB 24 chains west	Opened	7.3.1897
Re-named Stockingford Station SB	... ...	2.12.1934
***	Closed	10.8.1969
Stockingford to Arley: block telegraph system	Installed by	1873

Stockingford Branch
Powers: Midland Railway (Additional Powers) Act 1873

Stockingford Sidings to Stockingford Colliery	Opened	3.4.1876
***	Closed	17.11.1964
TUNNEL PIT WORKMEN'S PLATFORM	OP(NA) before	7.1915 *
***	CP(All)	....
ANSLEY HALL GOODS WHARF (at the top of the branch)	Opened	10.5.1886
***	Closed	....
Stockingford Colliery Siding and ground frame	Recovered	14.6.1933

Ansley Hall Colliery Branch
Powers: No Construction or Land Powers

Ansley Hall Colliery branch	Opened	9.1876
***	Closed	17.11.1964
Stockingford Colliery to Ansley Hall Colliery	Closed	2.11.1959

Stockingford Tunnel SB	Opened	16.12.1894
Re-named Stockingford Tunnel Sidings SB	... ...	....
Replacement box	Opened	29.2.1948
***	Closed	10.8.1969
Stockingford Tunnel Pit Sidings to Arley Colliery Sidings	C. temp.	10.1.1949
***	Re-opened	9.4.1949
***	C. temp.	11.5.1949
***	Re-opened	24.10.1949
Stockingford tunnel: single-line working for repairs	Commenced	21.11.1948
Double-line working	Restored	4.1953
Single-line working for repairs	Commenced	6.10.1968
Double-line working	Restored	23.3.1969
Arley Tunnel SB	Opened	5.12.1948
***	Closed	17.5.1953
Arley Colliery Sidings SB	Opened	13.7.1902
Box made a ground frame	... ...	10.8.1969
***	t.o.u.	22.5.1977
ARLEY COLLIERY SIDINGS WORKMEN'S PLATFORM	OP(NA) before	7.1915 *
***	CP(All)	....
Arley Station SB	Open before	1.11.1875
Replacement box	Opened	13.3.1898
***	Closed	6.10.1968
Arley to Whitacre Jcn: block telegraph system	Installed	1873
ARLEY	OP	1.11.1864
***	OG	1.12.1864
Altered to ARLEY & FILLONGLEY	... ...	1.3.1867 *
***	CG	4.1.1965
***	CP	7.11.1960
SHUSTOKE	OP	1.11.1864
***	OG	1.12.1864
***	CG	24.7.1961
***	CP	4.3.1968
Shustoke Station SB	Open before	1.11.1875
Replacement box	Opened	16.4.1899
***	Re-framed	....
***	Closed	10.8.1969
Whitacre: down Leicester-line goods line	Into use	29.9.1968
***	t.o.u.	....

WALSALL, WOLVERHAMPTON & MIDLAND JUNCTION RAILWAY

The Wolverhampton, Walsall & Midland Junction Railway's powers were transferred to the Midland by an Act of 30 July 1874.

Powers: Wolverhampton, Walsall and Midland Junction Railway Act 1872

Water Orton Jcn to North Walsall Jcn	OG	19.5.1879
Water Orton Jcn to Ryecroft Jcn (London & North Western Railway)	OP	1.7.1879
Working was by the block telegraph system from the opening.		
Water Orton Jcn to Park Lane Jcn	CP	1.4.1907 *
***	Singled	7.1.1968
Water Orton Jcn to Ryecroft Jcn made goods lines	... ...	7.1.1968
Lines made passenger lines again	... ...	2.12.1984

Castle Bromwich Curve

Powers: Wolverhampton, Walsall and Midland Junction Railway Act 1873

Castle Bromwich Jcn to Park Lane Jcn	OG	19.5.1879
***	OP	1.7.1879
***	CP	18.1.1965
Lines made goods lines (worked absolute block)	... ...	7.1.1968
***	Singled	3.8.1969
Line made a passenger line again	... ...	2.12.1984

Between 1970 and 1983 the Castle Bromwich Junction to Ryecroft Junction line was used by certain seasonal passenger trains on Friday evenings and Saturdays in summer.

Park Lane Junction SB	Opened	1.7.1879 ?
Replacement box	Opened	18.1.1903
Replacement box	Opened	5.9.1933
***	Closed	10.8.1969
Park Lane Jcn to Ryecroft Jcn	CP	18.1.1965
Penns Goods SB	Opened	19.5.1879
***	Re-framed	7.6.1896
***	Closed	7.5.1922

This box was revived as a temporary block post on 21 July 1957 for a jamboree at Sutton Park.

Penns Passenger Station SB	Opened	19.6.1898
***	Closed	26.6.1898
PENNS	OG	19.5.1879
***	OP	1.7.1879
Altered to PENNS FOR WALMLEY	By	17.10.1936
***	CP	18.1.1965
***	CG	1.2.1965
Sutton Town SB	Opened	19.6.1898
***	Closed	26.6.1898
SUTTON COLDFIELD	OP	1.7.1879
Altered to SUTTON COLDFIELD TOWN	... ...	1.5.1882 *
Altered to SUTTON COLDFIELD	... ...	1.4.1904
Altered to SUTTON COLDFIELD TOWN	... ...	2.6.1924
***	CP(All)	1.1.1925
SUTTON PARK	OG	19.5.1879
***	OP	1.7.1879
***	CG	7.12.1964
***	CP	18.1.1965
Back platform	t.o.u.	1.2.1965
Sutton Park SB	Opened	19.5.1879
Replacement box	Opened	9.1.1898
***	Re-framed	5.6.1898
***	Closed	10.8.1969
Sutton Park Goods Yard SB	Opened	5.6.1898
***	Closed	2.7.1898
Sutton Park to Aldridge: single-line working by tablet	Introduced	7.1.1917
Double-line working	Restored	20.3.1921
JERVIS TOWN	OP	....
Altered to STREETLY	... ...	c.7.1879
STREETLY	CP(All)	18.1.1965
Streetley Station SB	Opened	19.5.1879
***	Closed	26.10.1925

This box was revived as a temporary block post on 21 July 1957 for a jamboree at Sutton Park.

ALDRIDGE	OG	19. 5.1879
***	OP	1.7.1879
***	CG	7.12.1964
***	CP	18.1.1965
Aldridge Junction SB	Opened	19.5.1879 ?
Replacement box	Opened	4.5.1919
***	Closed	18.5.1969

Walsall Wood branch

See page 228

Lichfield Road Junction SB	Opened	19.5.1879
Replacement box	Opened	1.7.1900
***	Closed	4.6.1967

Walsall Curve

Powers: Wolverhampton, Walsall and Midland Junction Railway Act 1872

Lichfield Road Jcn to Ryecroft Jcn	OG	19.5.1879
***	OP	1.7.1879
***	CP	18.1.1965

Lichfield Road Jcn to North Walsall Jcn	OG	19.5.1879
***	Tfc ceased	7.1.1965
***	t.o.u.	30.4.1967
***	Closed	1.5.1967

WALSALL WOOD BRANCH AND EXTENSION

Powers: Midland Railway (Additional Powers) Act 1878 (Aldridge)
Midland Railway (New Works Etc) Act 1876 (Walsall Wood)
Midland Railway (Additional Powers) Act 1880 (Brownhills)

Aldridge to Brownhills	OG	1.4.1882
***	OP	1.7.1884
***	CP	31.3.1930
Working was by the block telegraph system from the opening.		
Aldridge Jcn to Aldridge Colliery Sidings	Singled	30.6.1940
Aldridge Jcn to Aldridge BICC Siding	Closed	10.2.1969
Branch shortened by 3/4 mile (with buffers at the 48 milepost)	w.e.f	23.3.1957
Branch further shortened	... ...	3.6.1962
Branch closed to traffic and made the BICC Siding	... ...	2.8.1965
BICC Siding	Closed	9.2.1969
Aldridge BICC Siding to Walsall Wood	Closed	5.7.1965
Aldridge Temporary SB	Opened	19.6.1898
***	Closed	26.6.1898
Aldridge Colliery Sidings SB	Opened	1883
Replacement box	Opened	30.1.1906
Box closed and 2 ground frames (north and south) provided in lieu	... ...	3.3.1946
Aldridge Colliery Sidings to Conduit Colliery Sidings: one engine in steam working	Commenced	31.3.1930
Aldridge Colliery Sidings to Walsall Wood	Singled	7.7.1940
WALSALL WOOD	OG	7.1883
***	OP	1.7.1884
***	CP	31.3.1930
***	CG	3.9.1962
Walsall Wood SB	Opened	1883
***	Burnt out	25.3.1932
Walsall Wood to Brownhills (junction with NCB near Chasewater)	Closed	31.3.1930
***	Closed by	9.1960
BROWNHILLS	OG	7.1883
***	OP	1.7.1884
Altered to BROWNHILLS (WATLING STREET)	... ...	2.6.1924
***	CP&G	31.3.1930
Brownhills Station SB	Opened	1883
Replacement box	Opened	1906
***	Closed	31.3.1930
Brownhills to Cannock Chase	OM	1.11.1882
Brownhills to Cannock Chase Sidings: one line of rails removed to create a single line (to continue to be worked by train staff without tickets) (49m 46ch to 50m 10ch)	... ...	13.1.1924
Conduit Colliery Sidings SB	Opened	10.3.1895
***	Closed	31.3.1930 ?

WALSALL & WOLVERHAMPTON LINE

Between Wolverhampton Junction and Ryecroft Junction the Great Western possessed running powers for all traffic.

Walsall & Wolverhampton Line:		
Sold by the London & North Western to the Midland	... ...	1.7.1876
Passenger service, worked with Midland engines and carriages	Commenced	1.8.1876
Wichnor Jcn and Dudley: Midland goods trains	Commenced	1.9.1867
***	Ceased	19.5.1879
Walsall and Dudley: Midland goods trains	Withdrawn	1.1.1909
Walsall and Wolverhampton: goods service over the London & North Western via Bescot	Commenced	1.9.1867
Between Bescot Junction with the South Staffordshire Railway and Wolverhampton via Bushbury the Midland possessed running powers for all traffic over the London & North Western line.		
Between Walsall station and Heath Town Junction the Midland possessed running powers for coaching traffic over the London & North Western line.		
Midland and London & North Western: reciprocal user of this line	Commenced	1.1.1909

Walsall Engine Shed Branch

Powers: Midland Railway (Additional Powers) Act 1880 (Land Powers only)

Walsall engine shed	Opened	1880
***	Closed	2.9.1925

Walsall Goods Station Branch

Powers: Midland Railway (New Works Etc.) Act 1877

WALSALL GOODS DEPOT, and branch	Opened	27.9.1880
Altered to WALSALL TASKER STREET	... ...	....
***	CG(All)	3.8.1981
Walsall Midland Goods Yard SB	Opened	1880 ?
Replacement box	Opened	27.8.1905
***	Closed	3.1.1927

The London & North Western Railway possessed running powers for merchandise traffic over the Midland's Walsall Goods Branch.

The Wolverhampton, Walsall and Midland Junction Railway Act 1872 gave running powers for all traffic between Walsall station and the junction with that line, with use of stations.

Walsall & Wolverhampton Line

Powers: Wolverhampton and Walsall Railway Act 1867
(Walsall to Short Heath)
Wolverhampton and Walsall Railway Act 1865 (Short Heath)
Wolverhampton and Walsall Railway Act 1866
(Wednesfield to Wolverhampton)
Wolverhampton and Walsall Railway Act 1870 (junction at Wolverhampton with the London & North Western Railway)

Ryecroft Jcn to Wolverhampton Crane Street Jcn	Opened	1.11.1872

The block telegraph system was installed on this line by the London & North Western company prior to the sale of the line to the Midland company. What signalling was transferred to the Midland at the sale is not known.
Between Ryecroft Junction and Heath Town Junction the London & North Western Railway possessed running powers over the Midland line for coaching traffic.

Walsall & Wolverhampton line transferred to supervision of Western Division for control	... ...	22.8.1927
Walsall & Wolverhampton line transferred to supervision of Western Division for timetables	... ...	26.9.1927
Ryecroft Jcn to Crane Street Jcn	CP	5.1.1931
Ryecroft Jcn to Heath Town Jcn: line closed to through traffic	... ...	10.8.1964
Ryecroft Jcn to Birchills Power Station (Birchills branch)	Closed	12.5.1980
North Walsall Junction SB	Opened	1879
***	Re-framed	31.5.1896
Replacement box	Opened	28.10.1906
***	Closed	4.6.1967
NORTH WALSALL	OP	1.11.1872
***	CP(All)	13.7.1925
North Walsall to Willenhall: single-line working	Introduced	4.2.1917
Double-line working	Restored	8.5.1921
Birchills Sidings SB	Opened	19.2.1911
Replacement box named Birchills Power Station Sidings SB 77 yards nearer to Willenhall	Opened	20.11.1949
***	Closed	1964 ?
Box made a ground frame	... ...	4.6.1967
Birchill's Sidings to Willenhall: single-line working	Introduced	2.8.1922
Near 49 milepost (north of Birchills Power Station Siding SB): line severed and section from stop-block to Willenhall Stafford Street worked as a siding	... ...	28.9.1964
Birchills Power Station Sidings SB to Short Heath	Off. closed	1.11.1965
BENTLEY	Opened	1.11.1872
***	CP&G	1.10.1898
Bentley SB (not a block post)	Open before	16.8.1877
***	Closed	12.1896-5.1899
Short Heath Station SB (not a block post)	Opened	17.11.1903
***	Closed	....
SHORT HEATH CLARK'S LANE	OP	1.11.1872
***	OG	1877
***	CP	5.1.1931
***	CG	7.12.1964
Short Heath to Willenhall Stafford Street	Closed	7.12.1964
***	Off. closed	1.11.1965
WILLENHALL MARKET PLACE	OP	1.11.1872
***	OG	1876
Altered to WILLENHALL	... ...	1.4.1904
Altered to WILLENHALL STAFFORD STREET	... ...	2.6.1924
***	CP	5.1.1931
***	CG	1.11.1965
Willenhall Station SB	Open before	1880
***	Closed	26.11.1893 ?
Replacement box	Opened	26.10.1893
***	Closed	1.8.1965

Willenhall Stafford Street to Wednesfield: working as a siding	Commenced	15.8.1965
***	Closed	1.11.1965
WEDNESFIELD	OP	1.11.1872
***	OG	1876
***	OM	1877
***	CP	5.1.1931
***	CG	4.10.1965
Wednesfield Station SB	Open before	1880
Replacement box	Opened	23.10.1898
***	Closed	1.8.1965
Wednesfield to Heath Town Siding: one engine in steam working	Introduced	15.8.1965
Wednesfield: line severed	... ...	18.12.1971
Heath Town Sidings: line severed 550 yards south of this point	... ...	19.11.1983
HEATH TOWN	OP	1.11.1872
***	CP(All)	1.4.1910
Heath Town Junction SB	Open before	1880
Replacement box	Opened	19.5.1912
***	Closed	15.8.1965
Heath Town Jcn with the London & North Western Railway	OP	1.3.1881

Between Heath Town Junction and Crane Street Junction the London & North Western possessed running powers for all traffic over the Midland line.
Between Crane Street Junction and Wolverhampton station the Midland possessed running powers for coaching traffic over the London & North Western line.

Wolverhampton Curve

Powers: Wolverhampton and Walsall Railway Act 1865

Heath Town Jcn to junction with the Great Western Railway	Open before	7.1873

Wolverhampton Goods Station Branch

Powers: Midland Railway (New Works Etc) Act 1877 (Land Powers only)

WOLVERHAMPTON GOODS SHED, and goods station branch	Opened	4.10.1880
Vialit & Company's Sidings	Removed by	17.7.1966
Wednesfield: loading-dock siding	Removed	1.5.1967
WOLVERHAMPTON WEDNESFIELD ROAD	C.Coal	11.1983

IX. BETWEEN BIRMINGHAM AND GLOUCESTER

BIRMINGHAM & GLOUCESTER RAILWAY

Section 21 of the Birmingham and Gloucester Railway Act 1836 gave the company the right of user of the London & Birmingham station "or any future terminus of that Company in or near Birmingham". It was by these powers that the Midland Railway gained access first to Curzon Street and then to New Street station.

By an agreement of 14 January 1845 the Birmingham & Gloucester and Bristol & Gloucester Railways were "worked as one" as the Birmingham & Bristol Railway. The Midland took over working the lines on 7 May 1845 and entered into a perpetual lease with effect from 1 July 1845. The companies were amalgamated in 1846.

Birmingham to Cheltenham

Powers: Birmingham and Gloucester Railway Act 1836
(Gloucester Junction to Cheltenham High Street)
Birmingham and Gloucester Railway Act 1836,
Midland Railway (New Lines and Additional Powers) Act 1864,
and Midland Railway (New Works Etc) Act 1877 (Camp Hill Goods Depot)
London Midland and Scottish Railway Act 1923 (King's Norton widening)
London Midland and Scottish Railway Act 1923
(Barnt Green & Longbridge widening)
London Midland and Scottish Railway (No. 1) Act 1930
(Bromsgrove & Stoke Works Widening)
Cheltenham Station Act 1890 (Midland and South Western Junction Railway engine shed and sidings)
Birmingham and Gloucester Railway Act 1837 (Cheltenham)

Gloucester Jcn (London & Birmingham Railway) to Camp Hill	Opened	17.8.1841	
Camp Hill to Cofton Farm temporary station	OP	17.12.1840	
Camp Hill to Gloucester	OG	10.1841	?
Cofton Farm temporary station to Bromsgrove	OP	17.9.1840	
Bromsgrove to Cheltenham	OP	24.6.1840	
Birmingham: new junction with the London & North Western Railway	Opened	19.2.1855	
Birmingham to Stoke Works Jcn: block telegraph system	Installed	1869–1872	
Grand Jcn to St Andrew's Jcn	CP	27.1.1941	
***	RO(P)	6.3.1967	
Garrison Lane SB	Open before	16.8.1877	
***	Closed	17.5.1896	
St Andrew's Junction SB	Opened	1869	
Replacement box	Opened	....	
Replacement box	Opened	27.8.1916	
***	Closed	13.11.1966	
Bordesley Junction SB	Opened	1869	
Replacement box	Opened	20.2.1898	
Replacement box	Opened	6.4.1941	
***	Closed	24.8.1969	

Bordesley Curve

Powers: No Powers

Bordesley Jcn to the junction with the Great Western Railway	Opened	1.11.1861	
***	Doubled	13.7.1941	
Working by staff without tickets between 6 a.m. Sundays and 6 a.m. Mondays	Commenced	12.9.1909	
Electric key token working in place of pilot guard working on weekdays and train staff working on Sundays	Commenced	24.9.1928	
Absolute block working	Commenced	14.5.1966	
***	OP	6.3.1967	?

CAMP HILL (first station)	Opened	17.12.1840	
***	CP	17.8.1841	
***	RO(P)	15.11.1841	
***	CP	....	
***	CG	7.2.1966	
Camp Hill Station SB	Opened	1869	
Replacement box	Opened	4.5.1890	
Replacement box	Opened	23.2.1941	
Box closed and 2 ground frames provided in lieu	... ...	24.8.1969	
Nos. 1 and 2 GFs	t.o.u.	5.12.1971	
CAMP HILL (second station)	OP	....	
Altered to CAMP HILL & BALSALL HEATH	... ...	1.12.1867	*
Altered to CAMP HILL	... ...	1.4.1904	
***	CP(All)	27.1.1941	
BRIGHTON ROAD	OP	1.11.1875	
***	CP(All)	27.1.1941	

Brighton Road SB	Open before	16.8.1877
Replacement box	Opened	25.6.1899
Box closed and semaphore IBS provided in lieu at Brighton Road on the down line and Moseley on the up line	... ...	4.5.1941
Intermediate block signals	t.o.u.	....
MOSELEY (new second station)	OP	1.11.1867
***	CP(All)	27.1.1941
This station was provided under the terms of an Act or agreement.		
MOSELEY (first station)	OP	11.1841
***	OG	....
Altered to KING'S HEATH	... ...	1.11.1867
***	CP	27.1.1941
***	CG	2.5.1966
King's Heath Station SB	Open before	1.11.1875
Replacement box	Opened	30.4.1906
***	Closed	7.9.1969
HAZELWELL	OP&G	1.1.1903
***	CP	27.1.1941
***	CG	1.3.1965
Hazelwell Station SB	Opened	6.4.1902
***	Closed	7.9.1969 ?
	or	15.12.1968 ?
LIFFORD (first station)	Opened	17.12.1840
***	Closed	1.12.1844 *
The second Lifford station was on the Birmingham West Suburban line.		
LIFFORD (third station)	OP&G	28.9.1885
***	CP	30.9.1940
***	CG	6.7.1964
Lifford Bridge SB	Opened	5.4.1891
***	Closed	19.4.1891
Lifford Junction SB	Open before	16.8.1877
Re-named Lifford Station Junction SB	... ...	....
Replacement box	Opened	8.5.1892
Box closed and ground frame provided in lieu	... ...	7.9.1969
***	t.o.u.	3.11.1984

Lifford Curve

Powers: Midland Railway Act 1888

Lifford Station Jcn to Lifford West Jcn	Into use	16.5.1892
***	OP	1.7.1892
***	CP	27.1.1941
***	RO(P)	6.3.1967
***	CP	....

Birmingham West Suburban line

See page 238

King's Norton Junction SB	Opened	9.1885 ?
***	Closed	14.3.1926
KING'S NORTON	Opened	1.5.1849 *
***	CG	1.9.1964
New station (with extra platforms) and junction	Into use	14.3.1926
King's Norton SB	Open before	16.8.1877
Replacement box	Opened	3.1.1892
Re-named King's Norton Station Junction SB	... ...	....
Replacement box named King's Norton Station SB	Opened	14.3.1926
Box made a shunting frame	... ...	7.9.1969
Shunting frame and Down Sidings GF taken out of use and new East and West GFs provided	... ...	23.4.1978
King's Norton Station SB: up goods line between the connection to the up main line south of the box and that to the up New Street line north of the box	Recovered	28.5.1967
King's Norton to King's Norton Earth Siding SB: down goods line	Into use	18.10.1891
King's Norton to Northfield Goods Jcn: up and down goods lines	Into use	1.5.1892
King's Norton to Halesowen Jcn: goods lines made slow lines	... ...	23.4.1978
King's Norton Earth Sidings SB	Opened	6.10.1890
***	Closed	1.5.1892
Northfield Goods Junction SB	Opened	1.5.1892
***	Closed	2.9.1894
Northfield Goods Jcn to Halesowen Jcn: down goods line	Into use	8.7.1894
Up goods line	Into use	2.9.1894
NORTHFIELD	Opened	1.9.1870
Replacement station with a single island platform	Into use	Early 1893
***	CG	6.7.1964
Outside platforms	Into use	8.5.1978
Northfield Station SB	Open before	1.11.1875
***	Alt.levers	24.3.1890
Replacement box	Opened	1.5.1892
Replacement box 123 yards to the north	Opened	11.3.1934
***	Closed	2.3.1969

Northfield Station: up goods line to up passenger line crossover	Into use	....	
Down goods line to down passenger line crossover	Into use	....	
Up passenger line to up goods line crossover (slip-points)	Into use	24.2.1918	
Running-line crossovers	t.o.u.	23.3.1967	
Halesowen Junction SB	Opened	8.9.1881	
Replacement box	Opened	10.4.1892	
Replacement box	Opened	5.1.1930	
Box made a shunting frame	... ...	7.9.1969	
***	t.o.u.	4.11.1973	

Halesowen branch

See page 240

Halesowen Jcn: new junction layout and reversing siding	Into use	23.4.1978	
Halesowen Jcn to Barnt Green: up and down goods lines	Into use	25.5.1930	
LONGBRIDGE	OP	11.1841	
***	CP	1.5.1849	*
Platforms alongside the up and down main lines	OP(NA)	1.7.1918	?
	or	1.2.1918	?
***	CP by	1922	
New station on site of the 1840s station	Opened	8.5.1978	
Cofton SB	Opened	6.7.1926	?
***	Closed	10.11.1929	
Cofton tunnel	Demolsihed	26-28.1.1929	
Cofton to Barnt Green Main Line Jcn: down goods line	t.o.u.	7.6.1969	
***	or	5.1969	
COFTON FARM (temporary station)	Opened	17.9.1840	
***	Closed	17.12.1840	
COFTON	Opened	Late 1840	
***	Closed after	12.1843	
BARNT GREEN	Opened	1.5.1844	*
Altered to BARNT GREEN FOR REDDITCH	... ...	1.6.1857	*
Altered to BARNT GREEN FOR BROMSGROVE LICKEY	Before	1.1.1863	*
***	CG	6.7.1964	
Altered to BARNT GREEN	... ...	1.7.1868	*
Barnt Green Main Line Junction SB	Opened	1869	
Replacement box	Opened	7.12.1890	
Replacement box	Opened	28.11.1897	
Replacement box 100 yards to the north	Opened	15.9.1929	
Box closed and ground frame provided in lieu	... ...	7.9.1969	
***	t.o.u.	11.9.1982	

Redditch branch

See page 241

Barnt Green Main Line Jcn: up refuge siding (south of the junction) removed to make way for the new up platform	... ...	13.3.1927
Section of up slow line	Recovered	15.10.1967
Linthurst IBS	Into use	7.7.1930
***	t.o.u.	....
Blackwell: centre bank-engine siding	Into use	27.4.1930
Down refuge siding made down goods loop	... ...	21.6.1931
***	Extended	23.7.1967
Blackwell SB	Opened	1869
Replacement box	Opened	7.11.1897
Replacement box	Opened	27.4.1930
***	Closed	20.4.1969
BLACKWELL	Opened	5.6.1841
***	CG	3.2.1964
***	CP	18.4.1966
Blackwell: facing crossover and ground frame	Into use	21.4.1969
TOP OF LICKEY INCLINE	OP	11.1841
***	CP	....
Lickey Incline: time-rules for descent of incline	Introduced	11.2.1889
New regulations brought into force	... ...	27.10.1889
Compulsory stop for down passenger trains superseded by a requirement to reduce speed to 10 miles per hour	... ...	10.11.1941
BROMSGROVE	Opened	24.6.1840
***	CG	5.6.1967
Down platform taken out of use and up platform made bi-directional	... ...	20.4.1969
There were from the beginning three tracks between the platforms of Bromsgrove station, that in the centre being used for the stabling of banking engines.		
Bromsgrove East SB	Opened	1869
Replacement box	Opened	....
Re-named Bromsgrove Station SB	... ...	6.1881-4.1883
Replacement box	Opened	18.1.1914
Box made Bromsgrove Station GF	... ...	20.4.1969
Replacement Bromsgrove No. 1 GF	Into use	7.5.1969

Bromsgrove to Bromsgrove South: down platform line and down goods line made into down slow line	... ...	26.10.1924
(The down middle line and the down passenger line between these points were re-named the down fast line.)		
Bromsgrove Station to Bromsgrove South: up goods line	Into use	20.4.1885
Down goods line	Into use	10.5.1885
Bromsgrove Station to Bromsgrove South: up and down goods lines	t.o.u.	....
Bromsgrove engine shed	Opened	1840
***	Closed	27.9.1964
Bromsgrove: banking from the South Box instead of from the station for trains not booked to stop	Commenced	2.2.1914
Bromsgrove South to Stoke Works Jcn quadrupling:		
down fast and slow lines	Into use	7.5.1933
Up fast and slow lines	Into use	28.5.1933
Bromsgrove West SB	Opened	1869
Replacement box	Opened	25.5.1883
Re-named Bromsgrove South Junction SB	... ...	27.6.1885
Replacement box	Opened	24.9.1922
***	Closed	20.4.1969
Bromsgrove South: down slow line to down fast line crossover	Into use	....
Down fast line to down slow line crossover	Into use	11.2.1968
Bromsgrove South to Stoke Works Jcn:		
up slow line made up & down branch as a continuation of the Droitwich line (no connection from the Gloucester direction)	... ...	23.2.1969
Up & down branch line made up branch line and down slow line made down goods loop	... ...	9.3.1969
Up branch line	t.o.u.	23.3.1969
Down goods loop made down goods line	... ...	20.4.1969
Stoke Works Junction SB	Open before	16.8.1877
Replacement box	Opened	16.10.1892
Replacement box 144 yards to the north	Opened	5.3.1933
***	Closed	23.3.1969
	<u>or</u>	10.3.1969

The Oxford, Worcester & Wolverhampton Railway possessed running powers for merchandise traffic across the Midland line at Stoke Prior Junction into the Imperial Salt and Alkali Works (Salt Union) Ltd, the Midland possessing similar powers both at Stoke Works and into the British Alkali Works (Salt Union Ltd) over the Oxford, Worcester & Wolverhampton sidings on the down side of the Midland line.

Stoke Prior Jcn with the Oxford, Worcester & Wolverhampton Railway	Opened	18.2.1852
Junction re-named Stoke Works Junction	... ...	....

<u>Worcester Loop</u>
See page 245

Stoke Works Jcn: facing crossover (part of new junction layout), and trailing crossover worked from a new ground frame	Into use	10.3.1969	
Stoke Works Jcn to Abbot's Wood Jcn	CP	1.10.1855	
***	RO(P)	1.6.1880	*
Stoke Works Jcn to Abbott's Wood Jcn: block telegraph system	Installed	1878	
Stoke Works Station SB	Open before	16.8.1877	
Re-named Stoke Works Goods Sidings SB	... ...	....	
***	Re-framed	22.11.1896	
Replacement box	Opened	10.9.1905	
***	Closed	2.4.1933	
STOKE	Opened	24.6.1840	
Altered to STOKE WORKS	By	31.10.1840	
***	CP	1.10.1855	
DODDERHILL	OP	11.1841	
***	CP(All)	5.3.1844	?
Droitwich Road SB	Open before	16.8.1877	
Replacemeent box	Opened	1878	?
Replacement box	Opened	27.12.1881	
***	Re-framed	13.12.1896	
Replacement box	Opened	31.10.1905	
***	Closed	30.5.1954	
DROITWICH	Opened	24.6.1840	
Altered to DROITWICH ROAD	... ...	10.2.1852	
***	CP	1.10.1855	
***	CG	1.12.1858	
***	RO(G)	2.4.1866	?
***	CG	1.10.1952	
Canal Bridge SB	Opened	....	
***	Closed	....	
Dunhampstead SB	Open before	16.8.1877	
Replacement box	Opened	1878	?
Replacement box	Opened	27.12.1881	
Replacement box	Opened	23.11.1902	
Box made a ground frame for the level crossing	... ...	9.3.1969	
AHBs installed	... ...	31.5-13.7.1986	

DUNHAMPSTEAD	OP	11.1841	
***	OG	....	
***	CP	1.10.1855	
***	CG	1.10.1949	
ODDINGLEY	OP	9.1845	
***	CP(All)	....	
Oddingley Crossing SB (not a block post)	Opened	....	
Replacement box	Opened	17.3.1908	
New ground frame and crossover	Into use	10.3.1969	
***	t.o.u.	1.6.1986	
BREDICOT	OP	11.1845	
***	CP(All)	....	
SPETCHLEY	Opened	24.6.1840	
***	CP	1.10.1855	
***	CG	2.1.1961	
Some special trains continued to serve Spetchley after closure, conveying excursion traffic to Spetchley Park.			
Spetchley SB	Open before	16.8.1877	
Replacement box	Opened	1878	?
Replacement box	Opened	27.12.1881	
***	Re-framed	20.12.1896	
Replacement box	Opened	12.6.1904	
Replacement box	Opened	13.4.1930	
Box closed, Spetchley Sidings GF brought into use, and up refuge siding converted into up goods loop	... ...	9.3.1969	
Spetchley: down goods loop	Into use	9.12.1930	
***	t.o.u.	10.1.1969	
NORTON	OP	11.1841	
***	CP(All)	1.9.1846	*
Norton Crossing GF and home and distant signals	Into use	....	
***	t.o.u.	27.6.1937	
Abbot's Wood Junction SB	Open before	16.8.1877	
Replacement box	Opened	25.9.1892	
Replacement box	Opened	15.10.1933	
Box closed and ground frame provided in lieu	... ...	9.3.1969	
***	t.o.u.	20.10.1978	
Abbot's Wood Jcn with the Oxford, Worcester & Wolverhampton Railway	Opened	5.10.1850	

Worcester Loop

See page 245

WORCESTER JUNCTION	OP	11.1850	
***	Opened	1.8.1851	?
Altered to ABBOT(T)'S WOOD JUNCTION	... ...	1.3.1852	*
***	CP(All)	1.10.1855	
This was an exchange station only, but was advertised in public timetables and in Bradshaw.			
Abbott's Wood Jcn to Defford: block telegraph system	Installed	1873	
Abbot's Wood Jcn: down refuge siding extended 170 yards north and made into a loop	... ...	30.3.1930	
Extended 166 yards at north end	... ...	22.10.1967	
Extended at south end	... ...	5.1968	
WADBOROUGH	OP	11.1841	
***	CP(All)	4.1.1965	
PIRTON SIDINGS	Open before	1872	
***	Closed	1964	
Pirton Sidings: trailing crossover and ground frame	Into use	5.5.1968	
Facing crossover	Into use	9.3.1969	
Pirton Sidings SB	Open before	1.11.1875	
Replacement box	Opened	7.9.1902	
Replacement box	Opened	15.10.1933	
Box made a ground frame for the level crossing	... ...	9.3.1969	
***	t.o.u.	4/18.5.1986	
PIRTON	OP	11.1841	
***	CP	c.1846	
BESFORD	OP	11.1841	
***	CP(All)	1.9.1846	
Defford: aerodrome emergency colour-light signals (normally out)	Into use	3.9.1944	
***	Removed	....	
Defford SB	Open before	16.8.1877	
Replacement box	Opened	31.1.1897	
***	Closed	3.5.1964	
Defford to Cheltenham: block telegraph system	Installed	1874	
DEFFORD	Opened	24.6.1840	
***	CG	1.7.1963	
***	CP	4.1.1965	
Avon Bridge SB opened to control temporary single-line working	... ...	12.4.1931	
Box closed and double-line working restored	... ...	19.7.1931	

Eckington SB	Opened	1874
Replacement box	Opened	11.9.1892
Box made a ground frame for the level crossing	... ...	16.2.1969
Ground frame and level crossing	t.o.u.	19.12.1972
ECKINGTON	Opened	24.6.1840
***	CG	1.7.1963
***	CP	4.1.1965
Eckington: up refuge siding made up goods loop	By	3.1.1942
Facing and trailing crossovers and ground frame	Into use	17.2.1969
BREDON	Opened	24.6.1840
***	CG	1.7.1963
***	CP	4.1.1965
Bredon SB	Open before	1.11.1875
Replacement box	Opened	8.1.1905
***	Closed	16.2.1969
Ashchurch level crossing: down lie-by siding converted to down goods loop	... ...	28.9.1941
Ashchurch Level Crossing SB	Open before	16.8.1877
Replacement box	Opened	16.9.1900
Replacement box at the north end of the station also taking on the functions of Evesham Junction SB and Tewkesbury Junction SB	Opened	16.10.1927
***	Closed	27.7.1958
Ashchurch level crossing	t.o.u.	5.5.1957
***	Recovered	12.5.1957 ?
	<u>or</u>	27.7.1958 ?
Ashchurch engine shed	Opened	1863
***	Closed	....
ASHCHURCH	Opened	24.6.1840
***	CG	1.6.1964
***	CP	15.11.1971
Ashchurch Junction SB	Open before	16.8.1877
Replacement box	Opened	16.12.1900
Replacement box named Ashchurch SB	Opened	27.7.1958
***	Closed	16.2.1969

<u>**Ashchurch & Evesham line**</u>

See page 243

<u>**Tewkesbury branch**</u>

See page 244

Ashchurch: facing crossover and ground frame. The trailing crossover at this point already existed.	Into use	16.2.1969
Cleeve: facing and trailing crossovers and ground frame	Into use	16.2.1969
CLEEVE	Opened	14.2.1843
***	CP	20.2.1950
***	CG	4.4.1960
Cleeve SB	Open before	1.11.1875
Replacement box	Opened	8.8.1897
Replacement box	Opened	19.11.1944
***	Closed	16.2.1969
SWINDON	OP	5.1842
***	CP(All)	1.10.1844
CHELTENHAM TEWKESBURY ROAD BRIDGE COAL WHARF	Opened	....
***	Closed	3.1.1966
The yard itself was completely taken out of use on 10 July 1964. A coal depot remained amongst the High Street sidings.		
Cheltenham High Street: down refuge siding made into down goods loop	... ...	14.9.1941
Down goods loop converted to a down refuge siding	... ...	27.11.1960
***	t.o.u.	17.3.1967
Cheltenham High Street North SB	Opened	1882
***	Closed	11.6.1911
Cheltenham High Street SB (first box)	Open before	16.8.1877
***	Closed	1882
Cheltenham High Street SB (second box)	Opened	11.6.1911
Box closed, existing ground frame taken out of use, and a new ground frame provided	... ...	24.11.1968
CHELTENHAM TEWKESBURY ROAD BRIDGE	OP	1.9.1862
Altered to CHELTENHAM HIGH STREET	... ...	1.10.1862
***	OG	1890-1891
***	CP	1.7.1910
The Cheltenham Station Company was incorporated in 1890 and the station was worked by the Midland & South Western Junction Railway with effect from 10 July 1890. The Cheltenham Station Company was vested in the Midland with effect from 10 June 1895 by an Act of that year. Between Cheltenham High Street Goods Station and Cheltenham Lansdown Passenger Station and Lansdown Junction the Midland & South Western Junction Railway possessed running powers respectively for goods and mineral traffic and for all traffic over the Midland line.		
CHELTENHAM COAL CONCENTRATION DEPOT	Closed by	15.4.1988

Cheltenham High Street South SB	Opened	1882
***	Alt.levers	8.6.1890
***	Closed	11.6.1911
Cheltenham High Street to Alston Jcn: up lie-by made up goods line	... ...	14.9.1941
Permissive working on the new up goods line	Commenced	13.10.1941
Alstone Junction SB	Opened	3.5.1891
Re-named Alston Junction SB	... ...	....
Box made a ground frame named Alstone Junction GF	... ...	24.11.1968
Alstone Jcn: facing and trailing crossovers	Into use	22/23.1.1966
Alstone Jcn to Cheltenham Lansdown: down goods line	Into use	28.6.1891
Line made a carriage siding by removal of the facing points	... ...	6.11.1967
ALSTONE WHARF	OM	7.1842
Altered to ALSTON WHARF	... ...	....
***	Closed	3.1.1966
Cheltenham Lansdown Station SB	Open before	16.8.1877
Replacement box	Opened	28.6.1891
***	Closed	24.11.1968
CHELTENHAM	OP	24.6.1840
Altered to CHELTENHAM SPA (LANSDOWN)	... ...	1.2.1925
South-end bay platform	Into use	14.1.1900
Connection between down main line and bay line	t.o.u.	2.12.1964

Cheltenham to Gloucester

Powers: Cheltenham and Great Western Union Railway Act 1836

Under the terms of the 1836, 1838, and 1842 Acts the line between Lansdown Junction and Tramway Junction was built at equal expense and for the equal use of the Cheltenham & Great Western Union and the Birmingham & Gloucester companies, the former to maintain from Lansdown Junction to the Midway Board at Churchdown, and the latter thence to Tramway Junction. Churchdown station was treated as a joint station. Signalling between Cheltenham and Gloucester provided and maintained by the Great Western.

Cheltenham to Gloucester:		
narrow gauge line opened by the Birmingham & Gloucester Railway	... ...	4.11.1840
Block telegraph system	Installed	1873
Lansdown Jcn with the Great Western line to St James's Station	Opened	23.10.1847
***	Closed	....
Lansdown Junction SB	Opened	....
Replacement box	Opened	10.5.1914
Replacement box	Opened	26.7.1942
***	Closed	12.11.1977
Lansdown Jcn with the Banbury & Cheltenham Direct Railway	Opened	1.6.1881
***	Closed	15.10.1962
***	t.o.u.	16.5.1965

Between Andoversford Junction and Red Posts Junction the Midland possessed running powers for all traffic over the Midland & South Western Junction line. However, as the company possessed no powers over the Great Western line between Lansdown Junction and Andoversford Junction, these powers line were inoperative.

Lansdown Jcn to Hatherley Jcn: up and down relief lines	Into use	23-30.8.1942
Lansdown Jcn to Churchdown: down relief line	t.o.u.	30.8.1966
Up relief line	t.o.u.	5.9.1966
Hatherley Jcn with the Great Western Railway	Laid in	6/13.11.1904
Facing points at both ends of the curve	Into use	2.7.1905
Hatherley Jcn with the Great Western Railway	Opened	1.1.1906
	<u>or</u>	8.1.1906
***	Closed	28.8.1956
Hatherley Junction SB	Opened	2.10.1899
Replacement box	Opened	26.7.1942
***	Closed	20.11.1966
Hatherley Jcn to Churchdown: up and down relief lines	Into use	9.8.1942
The existing connections at Churchdown were retained as crossovers.		
BADGWORTH	OP	22.8.1843
***	CP(All)	1.11.1846 *
Badgworth SB	Opened by	20.4.1940
***	Closed	26.10.1952
Churchdown SB	Opened	....
***	Re-framed	27.7.1902
Replacement box	Opened	14.12.1913
Replacement box	Opened	28.6.1942
Box closed, and facing and trailing crossovers controlled from a new ground frame brought into use	... ...	26.2.1967
CHURCHDOWN	OP	Mid 8.1842
***	CP(All)	End 9.1842
Second station	OP	2.2.1874
Platforms on the relief lines	In use by	1.4.1944
***	CP(All)	2.11.1964
Churchdown to Elm Bridge: up relief line	Into use	5.7.1942
Down relief line	Into use	12.7.1942

Churchdown to Engine Shed Jcn: up relief line	t.o.u.	15.1.1967
Down relief line	t.o.u.	5.2.1967
Elm Bridge SB	Opened	29.1.1940
***	Closed	5.6.1965
Elm Bridge to Engine Shed Sidings: up and down goods lines	Into use	3.5.1942
Up goods line made up relief line	... ...	5.7.1942 ?
Down goods line made down relief line	... ...	12.7.1942
Engine Shed Sidings to Barnwood Jcn: down goods line	Into use	24.10.1897
Engine Shed Sidings to Tramway Jcn: up goods line	Into use	27.10.1940
Engine Shed Sidings SB	Opened	24.6.1894
Replacement box	Opened	21.7.1901
Replacement box	Opened	22.2.1942
Re-named Engine Shed Junction SB	... ...	7.6.1942
***	Closed	26.5.1968
Engine Shed Junction re-named Barnwood Junction	... ...	26.5.1968
Gloucester (Barnwood) engine shed	Opened	2.7.1894
***	Closed	4.5.1964
The Barnwood engine shed replaced an earlier shed on the site of the new passenger station.		
Barnwood Junction SB	Open before	16.8.1877
Box closed and ground frame provided in lieu	... ...	10.11.1940
***	t.o.u.	26.5.1968
BARNWOOD SIDINGS	Opened	....
***	t.o.u.	....
Gloucester PSB	Opened	25-26.5.1968
1a. Lansdown Jcn to Churchdown	Into use	19-20.11.1966
1b. Churchdown to Engine Shed Jcn	Into use	25-26.2.1967
2. Engine Shed Jcn to Tuffley Jcn / Over Jcn / California Crossing	Into use	25-26.5.1968
3a. California Crossing to Naas Crossing	Into use	10-12.8.1968
3b. Tuffley Jcn to Standish Jcn	Into use	14-15.9.1968
3c. Standish Jcn to Charfield / Stonehouse (Great Western)	Into use	12-14.10.1968
4. Cleeve/Malvern Road East to Lansdown Jcn	Into use	23-25.11.1968
5. Pirton Sidings to Cleeve	Into use	15-17.2.1969
6. Bromsgrove South to Pirton Sidings / Droitwich, and Norton Jcn to Abbot's Wood Jcn	Into use	8-10.3.1969
7. Barnt Green Main Line Jcn (exc) to Bromsgrove South	Into use	19-21.4.1969
8. Over Jcn to Awre Jcn	Into use	31.5-2.6.1969
Tramway Junction SB	Open before	16.8.1877
Replacement box	Opened	30.8.1896
Replacement box	Opened	8.5.1927
***	Closed	26.5.1968
Tramway Crossing and Junction re-named Horton Road Crossing and Junction	... ...	26.5.1968
Tramway Jcn with the Great Western Railway	Opened	23.10.1847
At Tramway Junction the Midland Railway possessed running powers for merchandise traffic over a Great Western crossover road and siding giving access to the Emlyn Works.		
Tramway Jcn to Midland goods depot	Closed	1.8.1967
Tramway Jcn to Stroud Road Jcn: up and down goods lines	In use by	1.8.1863 *
***	t.o.u.	....
Gloucester Goods Junction SB	Open before	1869
Replacement box	Opened	....
Replacement box	Opened	6.6.1920
***	Closed	24.3.1968
Gloucester Passenger Station Junction SB	Open before	16.8.1877
Replacement box	Opened	6.3.1892
***	Closed	12.4.1896
Passenger Station Junction SB was replaced by Passenger Station SB on the opening of the new passenger station and its approach-lines.		
Gloucester Passenger Station SB (at the old passenger station)	Opened	4.1883-11.1885
***	Closed	12.1888-8.1893
GLOUCESTER	Opened	4.11.1840
***	CP	12.4.1896
***	CG	....

BIRMINGHAM WEST SUBURBAN RAILWAY

The West Suburban line was vested in the Midland Railway with effect from 1 July 1875 by Act of 1875.

Birmingham New Street to Church Road

Powers: Midland Railway (Additional Powers) Act 1881

New Street Jcn to Church Road Jcn	OP	1.7.1885
***	OG	.... ?
Five Ways Station SB	Opened	1.7.1885
Replacement box	Opened	8.11.1891
***	Closed	18.3.1923

FIVE WAYS	OP	1.7.1885
***	CP	2.10.1944
***	RO(P)	8.5.1978

Birmingham Granville Street to King's Norton

Powers: Birmingham West Suburban Railway Act 1871
Birmingham West Suburban Railway Act 1873
(Suffolk Street to Bridge Street - Land Powers only)
Midland Railway (Additional Powers) Act 1879
(Five Ways to Selly Oak Widening & Improvement)
Birmingham West Suburban Railway Act 1873
(Somerset Road to Bournville Deviation)
Midland Railway (Additional Powers) Act 1881
(Somerset Road to King's Norton Widening & Improvement)
Midland Railway (Additional Powers) Act 1874
(Lifford Canal Branch Junction to Lifford)

Granville Street to King's Norton	Opened	3.4.1876
BIRMINGHAM (GRANVILLE STREET)	OP	3.4.1876
***	CP(All)	1.7.1885

Worcester Wharf Goods Depot
Powers: Midland Railway (New Works Etc) Act 1876,
Midland Railway (Additional Powers) Act 1879, and
Midland Railway (Additional Powers) Act 1882
(All giving land powers only)

Worcester Wharf to Church Road Jcn	OG	1.7.1887
***	Doubled	6.12.1891
***	C.Tfc	6.3.1967
***	Closed	17.12.1967
The direction of the line was DOWN from Birmingham Central to Church Road Junction.		
The branch was worked by train staff without tickets as a single line and by block telegraph once it was doubled.		
WORCESTER WHARF GOODS DEPOT	OG	1.7.1887
***	OM	1888
Altered to BIRMINGHAM CENTRAL GOODS DEPOT	... ...	1.6.1892
***	Closed	6.3.1967
Worcester Wharf SB	Opened	6.12.1891
Re-named Birmingham Central Goods SB	... ...	31.7.1893
***	t.o.u.	6.3.1967
***	Closed	17.12.1967

Church Road Junction SB	Opened	12.3.1887
Replacement box 130 yards nearer Birmingham	Opened	18.3.1923
***	Closed	7.9.1969
Church Road Jcn to King's Norton	Doubled by	1885
CHURCH ROAD	OP	3.4.1876
***	CP(All)	1.1.1925
This station was provided under the terms of an Act or agreement.		
SOMERSET ROAD FOR HARBORNE	OP	3.4.1876
***	CP	28.7.1930
This station was provided under the terms of an Act or agreement.		
UNIVERSITY	OP	8.5.1978
Selly Oak: deviation replacing the line over the old canal viaduct	Into use	13.4.1885
SELLY OAK	OP	3.4.1876
***	OM	1883
***	OG by	4.1884
Replacement station	Opened	13.4.1885
Altered to SELLY OAK & BOURNBROOK	... ...	22.11.1898
Altered to SELLY OAK	... ...	1.4.1904
***	CG	2.11.1970
Selly Oak Station SB	Opened	13.4.1885
***	Re-framed	7.6.1914
Replacement box	Opened	19.1.1958
Box made a shunting frame	... ...	7.9.1969
***	t.o.u.	12.8.1973
Junction with Cadbury's internal railway	Opened	....
***	t.o.u.	9.6.1977
STIRCHLEY STREET	OP	3.4.1876
Altered to STIRCHLEY STREET & BOURNVILLE	... ...	4.3.1880
Altered to BOURNVILLE & STIRCHLEY STREET	... ...	1.7.1888 *
Altered to BOURNVILLE	... ...	1.4.1904

Lifford Canal Branch
Powers: Midland Railway (Additional Powers) Act 1874
After the building of the deviation line between Stirchley Street and King's Norton the old line became the Lifford Canal branch. The second Lifford station was situated on the section of line by-passed; it was replaced by the third Lifford station, on the Camp Hill line.

Lifford Canal branch made a through siding worked by telephone instead of single line worked by train staff only	... ...	25.1.1936
Section of the branch from the junction to bridge No. 135	Closed	4.9.1967
LIFFORD: second station	OP	1.6.1876
***	CP(All)	28.9.1885
Bournville & Stirchley Street SB	Opened	1885
***	Alt.levers	7.8.1892
Replacement box	Opened	13.1.1895
Replacement box	Opened	28.8.1932
***	Closed	7.9.1969
Bournville engine shed	Opened	12.3.1894
***	Closed	14.2.1960
Cadbury's Parkside Depot (on the site of Bournville engine shed)	Opened	....
***	t.o.u.	9.6.1977
Stirchley Street & King's Norton Deviation	Opened	26.9.1885
The section of line replaced became the Lifford Canal Branch.		
Lifford West Junction SB	Opened	3.5.1891
***	Closed	28.8.1932

HALESOWEN BRANCH

This line was worked by the Great Western and Midland jointly under an 1872 agreement and it was vested jointly in the Midland and Great Western companies with effect from 1 July 1906 by the Midland Railway Act 1906.

Powers: Halesowen and Bromsgrove Branch Railways Act 1865 (Halesowen Junction to Rubery)
Halesowen and Bromsgrove Branch Railways Act 1873 (Rubery to Hunnington)
Halesowen Railway Act 1879 (Hunnington to Halesowen)

Halesowen Jcn to Halesowen Jcn with the Great Western Railway	OP&G	10.9.1883
***	CP	4.1919
Halesowen Main Line Jcn to Halesowen Single Line Jcn	Singled	18.9.1892
Halesowen Jcn to Longbridge Platform: siding on up side of main line made a running line for non-passenger trains as a goods loop line	... ...	12.11.1916
Halesowen Jcn to Longbridge East: line made a siding	... ...	7.9.1969
***	Closed	27.9.1969
Halesowen Single Line Junction SB	Opened	10.9.1883
***	Closed	18.9.1892
Line severed at a point between bridge No. 1 and Longbridge East	... ...	16.7.1965
Longbridge SB	Opened	12.11.1916
***	Re-framed	18.3.1917
Re-named Longbridge East SB	... ...	15.4.1917
***	Closed	....
Longbridge: up loop line	Into use	15.4.1917
***	t.o.u.	....
LONGBRIDGE	OP(NA)	2.1915
***	OG	1917
***	CP	4.1.1960
***	C.Parcels	2.5.1978
Workmen's trains continued, from both ends of the line.		
Longbridge West SB	Opened	15.4.1917
***	Closed	10.8.1922
***	Re-opened	21.7.1923
***	Closed	29.10.1961
Longbridge West: all connections	t.o.u.	10.8.1922
The loop-points were retained, to be worked by hand, so that locomtives might run round their trains.		
Line severed 476 yards north of Longbridge East SB	... ...	1.8.1964
Longbridge West (BMC Sidings) to Rubery	Closed	6.7.1964
Birmingham Corporation Water Works Sidings (and private branch)	Into use	1897
Connection to the main line	t.o.u.	8.7.1917
Rubery SB	Opened	10.9.1883
Replacement box	Opened	27.7.1919
***	Closed	1964
RUBERY	OP&G	10.9.1883
***	CP	4.1919
***	CG	6.7.1964
***	C.Workmen by	9.1936
This station was provided under the terms of an Act or agreement.		
Rubery to Halesowen: temporary closure for engineering works	...	29.6.1891--7.7.1891
Line severed 200 yards north of Rubery SB	By	2.3.1964
FRANKLEY PUBLIC SIDING	Opened	10.9.1883
***	Recovered	13.10.1957
Hunnington SB	Opened	10.9.1883
***	Closed	24.5.1887
HUNNINGTON	OP&G	10.9.1883
***	CP	4.1919
***	CG	6.1.1964
***	C.Workmen	1.9.1958

Hunnington station was provided under the terms of an Act or agreement.		
Line severed 200 yards south of Halesowen SB	... ...	2.3.1964
HALESOWEN (Great Western station)	OP&G	....
***	CP	5.12.1927
***	CG	9.9.1968
***	C.Workmen	1.9.1958
The Midland Railway possessed running powers for all traffic into Halesowen station and the power to appoint staff. Midland staff were withdrawn on 1 July 1915. Excursion trains continued to call at this station.		

REDDITCH RAILWAY

Powers: Redditch Railway Act 1858

The company was leased to the Midland on incorporation. It was dissolved and transferred to the Midland in 1863, and merged with the Midland with effect from 1 January 1875 under the Midland Railway (Additional Powers) Act 1874.

Barnt Green to Redditch	OP	19.9.1859
***	OG	1.10.1859
Barnt Green Main Line Jcn to Barnt Green Single Line Jcn: additional 350 yards of double track	Into use	9.12.1894
Barnt Green Main Line Jcn to Redditch: one train working	Comm. by	5.9.1986
Barnt Green Single Line Junction SB	Opened	1883
Replacement box further south	Opened	9.12.1894
***	Closed	7.9.1969
Barnt Green Single Line Jcn to Redditch: electric train tablet working in place of train staff and ticket	Introduced	20.9.1891
ALVECHURCH	OP&G	1.11.1859 *
***	CG	6.7.1964
This station was provided under the terms of an Act or agreement.		
Alvechurch SB	Open before	1.11.1875
***	Closed	1885
Redditch Gas Works Sidings SB	Open before	16.8.1877
Replacement box 120 yards south	Opened	8.11.1925
Re-named Redditch North SB	... ...	17.1.1926
Re-named Redditch SB	... ...	....
***	Closed	10.8.1986
Redditch North SB (first box)	Opened	1885
***	Closed	17.1.1926
Redditch engine shed	Opened	1872-1873
***	Closed	1.6.1964
Redditch Gas Works Sidings SB to Redditch station: up loop line	Extended	17.1.1926
Up line made a siding and down line made up & down running line	... ...	29.1.1967
Redditch SB	Open before	1.11.1875
***	Closed	1885
REDDITCH (first station)	OP	19.9.1859
***	OG	1.10.1859
***	CP	4.5.1868
***	CG	8.9.1969

EVESHAM & REDDITCH RAILWAY

The Evesham & Redditch Railway leased on incorporation to the Midland and vested in the Midland by the Midland Railway (Additional Powers) Act 1882.

Powers: Evesham and Redditch Railway Act 1863

Redditch to Alcester	OPG&M	4.5.1868
***	CP	1.10.1962
***	CG	13.6.1964
***	Closed	6.7.1964
Redditch (third station) to Redditch (second station)	Closed	7.2.1972
REDDITCH (second passenger station, 22 chains south of the old one)	OP	4.5.1868
Replacement passenger station 8 chains to the north	Opened	7.2.1972
Redditch South SB	Opened	1885
Replacement box	Opened	23.8.1925
***	Closed	29.1.1967
Redditch South: line severed at the south end of the platforms	... ...	29.1.1967
The line between Redditch and Studley was worked by train staff and block telegraph by 1873. Between Studley and Evesham was worked by train staff only, with the addition of the block telegraph from 1880.		
Redditch South to Alcester Jcn: electric train token block working	Commenced	11.10.1891
Studley Station SB	Open before	1.11.1875
Replacement box	Opened	26.5.1891
***	Closed	1962-1964

STUDLEY & ASTWOOD BANK	OP&G	4.5.1868
***	CP	1.10.1962
***	CG	6.7.1964
Coughton SB	Open before	16.8.1877
	Closed	11.10.1891 ?
COUGHTON	OP&G	4.5.1868
***	CP&G	30.6.1952
This station was provided under the terms of an Act or agreement.		
Alcester to Evesham	OG	16.6.1866
***	OP	17.9.1866
***	C. temp.	1.10.1962
***	Off. closed	1.7.1963
Alcester to Evesham North made two staff & ticket sections	... ...	29.6.1891
Alcester Junction SB	Open before	16.8.1877
Replacement box	Opened	28.5.1922
Replacement box named Alcester SB 160 yards north of the station	Opened	24.4.1932
***	Closed	.... ?
Alcester Jcn to Broom Jcn North: electric train token block working	Commenced	7.8.1892
Alcester Jcn with Alcester Railway line to Bearley	Opened	4.9.1876
***	Closed	1.1.1917
***	Removed	25.3.1917
***	Restored	29.7.1923
***	CP	25.9.1939
***	CG	1.3.1951
***	t.o.u.	31.5.1953
The Alcester Railway, absorbed by the Great Western Railway, possessed running powers for all traffic into Alcester station.		
Alcester: station loop line	Into use	4.9.1876
ALCESTER	OG	16.6.1866
***	OP	17.9.1866
***	CP	1.10.1962
***	CG	6.7.1964
Alcester Station SB	Open before	16.8.1877
Replacement box	Opened	17.12.1905
***	Closed	24.4.1932
Alcester (exclusive) to Ashchurch	t.o.u.	8.3.1964
WIXFORD (temporary station)	Opened	17.9.1866
Permanent station	Opened	....
***	CP&G	2.1.1950
Broom Junction North SB	Opened	2.6.1879
Replacement box	Opened	3.9.1913
***	Closed	6.5.1934
Broom Junction: block working between North SB and South SB	Commenced	9.10.1892
BROOM JUNCTION (exchange station)	OP(NA)	2.6.1879
***	OP	1.11.1880
***	OG	2.1882
Station made joint	... ...	1896
***	CP&G	1.10.1962
Another source gives October 1881 for the passenger opening.		
Broom Junction South SB	Opened	2.6.1879
Replacement box	Opened	9.10.1892
Replacement box named Broom Junction SB	Opened	6.5.1934
Re-named Broom North Junction SB	... ...	17.5.1942
***	Closed	5.7.1962
Broom Jcn South to Evesham North: electric train token block working	Commenced	24.7.1892
Broom Jcn with the Stratford-on-Avon and Midland Junction Railway	OP&G	2.6.1879
***	t.o.u.	1.7.1962
***	Recovered	10.1962
Broom West Junction SB	Opened	27.9.1942
***	Closed	1.7.1962
Broom Curve		
Powers: --		
Broom West Jcn to Broom East Jcn	OG	27.9.1942
***	Closed	1.7.1962
Broom East Junction SB	Opened	17.5.1942
***	Closed	1.7.1962
SALFORD PRIORS	OG	16.6.1866
***	OP	17.9.1866
***	CP&G	1.10.1962
Harvington Station SB	Opened	2.6.1891
***	Closed	1.3.1964
HARVINGTON	OG	16.6.1866
***	OP	17.9.1866
***	CP&G	1.10.1962
Evesham North SB	Opened	23.9.1890
Replacement box 7 chains nearer Alcester	Opened	25.6.1905
***	Closed	20.1.1935
Evesham North: double line extended 180 yards towards Redditch	... ...	3.7.1904
Evesham North to Evesham South: block telegraph working	Introduced	23.9.1890

ASHCHURCH & EVESHAM LINE

Powers: Midland Railway (New Lines) Act 1861

Evesham to Ashchurch	OG	1.7.1864
***	OP	1.10.1864
***	CP	17.6.1963
The line between Evesham and Beckford was worked on the time interval system, and between Beckford and Evesham Junction (Ashchurch) by telegraph bells prior to the introduction of the block telegraph system. At the opening of this line there were temporary stations at both ends; the new station at Ashchurch was to be brought into use with the new junction at that place.		
Evesham to Ashchurch War Department Sidings	Closed	9.9.1963 ?
	or	8.3.1964 ?
Evesham to Evesham Jcn (Ashchurch): block telegraph working	Introduced	23.9.1890
EVESHAM (temporary station)	Opened	1.7.1864
Permanent station	OP&G	1.10.1864 ?
Goods Depot altered to EVESHAM SOUTH	... ...	4.9.1951
***	CP	17.6.1963
Evesham Station SB	Open before	1.11.1875
***	Closed	23.9.1890
Evesham South SB	Opened	23.9.1890
Replacement box	Opened	14.10.1934
Re-named Evesham SB	... ...	20.1.1935
***	Closed	8.3.1964
Evesham engine shed	Opened	1870-1871
***	Closed	14.9.1931
Evesham Jcn with the Great Western Railway	Open before	23.11.1868
New running junction with Western Region line	Into use	19.3.1957
***	Closed	....
The West Midland Railway possessed traffic facilities over the Evesham & Redditch line, with contingent running powers between Evesham Junction and Redditch if such facilities were not afforded. A similar arrangement applied over the Evesham & Ashchurch line.		
BENGEWORTH	OP	1.10.1864
***	OG	1.6.1867
***	CP&G	8.6.1953
Bengeworth Station SB	Opened	29.7.1890
***	Closed	8.6.1953
Bengeworth to Beckford: single-line working	Introduced	31.1.1917
Double-line working	Restored	22.2.1921
Hinton Station SB	Opened	29.7.1890
Replacement box	Opened	8.1.1924
***	Closed	1.3.1964
HINTON	OG	1.7.1864
***	OP	1.10.1864
***	CP	17.6.1963
***	CG	1.7.1963
Ashton-under-Hill Station SB	Opened	12.8.1890
Box closed and ground frame provided in lieu	... ...	25.1.1910
***	t.o.u.	....
ASHTON-UNDER-HILL	OG	1.7.1864
***	OP	1.10.1864
***	CP&G	17.6.1963
Beckford Station SB	Opened	12.8.1890
Replacement box	Opened	18.12.1923
***	Closed	1.3.1964
BECKFORD	OG	1.7.1864
***	OP	1.10.1864
***	CP	17.6.1963
***	CG	1.7.1963
Ashchurch East SB, with new sidings connections and sidings	Opened	13.9.1942
***	Closed	31.12.1949 ?
	or	2.1.1950 ?
Evesham Junction SB	Open before	1.11.1875
Replacement box	Opened	12.8.1900
***	Closed	16.10.1927
Ashchurch: all Evesham branch connections	t.o.u.	8.3.1964

Ashchurch Curve

Powers: Midland Railway (New Lines and Additional Powers) Act 1863

Evesham Jcn to Tewkesbury Jcn	Opened	1.10.1864
***	Singled by	1927
***	C.Tfc	5.5.1957
***	Closed	12.5.1957
***	Closed	24.5.1957

TEWKESBURY & MALVERN RAILWAY

The Tewkesbury & Malvern Railway was leased on incorporation to the Midland and was vested in the Midland from 1 July 1877 by the Midland Railway (Further Powers) Act 1876.

Powers: Midland Railway (New Lines and Additional Powers) Act 1865
(Malvern Wells sidings)
Tewkesbury and Malvern Railway Act 1862
(Malvern Wells Junction to Malvern Wells)
Tewkesbury and Malvern Railway Act 1860
(Malvern Wells to Tewkesbury)

Malvern & Tewkesbury Jcn to Malvern Wells	Opened	1.7.1862
The Tewkesbury and Malvern Railway Act 1860 provided for that company to have access to Great Malvern station. The Midland possessed running powers for all traffic between Malvern Link station and the Tewkesbury line junction. Excursion traffic was to be worked only to Malvern Link station. The Worcester & Hereford Railway possessed contingent running powers between Malvern Junction and Tewkesbury and Ashchurch in the event of the Midland company refusing to give through bookings and facilities.		
Working was by time interval prior to the introduction of the block telegraph on 8 August 1890.		
Malvern & Tewkesbury Jcn to Upton-on-Severn	CP	1.12.1952
Malvern & Tewkesbury Jcn to Malvern New Midland Sidings	Closed	1.5.1968
MALVERN JUNCTION SIDINGS	Opened	21.2.1877
Altered to MALVERN SIDINGS	By	1904
Altered to MALVERN NEW MIDLAND SIDINGS	... ...	1946
***	Closed	1.5.1968
Malvern New Midland Sidings to Upton-on-Severn	Closed	1.12.1952
***	Lifted	9.1953
Malvern engine shed	Opened	....
***	Closed	14.9.1931
Malvern Wells Sidings SB	Opened	1877
Old lever-frame moved into a replacement box	... ...	21.2.1905
***	Closed	20.10.1954
Malvern Sidings to Tewkesbury: block telegraph working	Commenced	8.7.1890
MALVERN WELLS	Opened	1.7.1862
Altered to MALVERN HANLEY ROAD	... ...	2.3.1951
***	CP&G	1.12.1952
Malvern Wells Station SB	Open before	1.11.1875
Replacement box	Opened	15.5.1945
***	Closed	1.12.1952
Malvern Wells to Tewkesbury	OP	16.5.1864
***	OG	1.9.1870
UPTON	OP	16.5.1864
***	OG	1.9.1870
Altered to UPTON-ON-SEVERN	... ...	4.1889
***	CP	14.8.1961
***	CG	1.7.1963
Upton-on-Severn Station SB	Opened	8.7.1890
Replacement box	Opened	26.5.1946
Box closed and 3 ground frames provided in lieu	... ...	20.7.1958
Upton-on-Severn to Tewkesbury:		
up line used for storing wagons and single-line working by pilotman introduced on down line	In w/e	9.7.1913
Double-line working re-instated	In w/e	27.8.1913
Single-line working by pilotman re-introduced	In w/e	18.2.1914
Mode of operation changed to pilot guard working	... ...	23.2.1914
Double-line working re-instated	In w/e	1.7.1914
Single-line working by train staff and ticket	Introduced	31.12.1916
***	Closed	1.7.1963
Upton-on-Severn to Ashchurch	CP	14.8.1961
One engine in steam working replaced electric train token working	... ...	17.12.1961
Ripple Station SB	Opened	....
Box closed and ground frame provided in lieu	... ...	18.1.1911
***	Removed	9.11.1942
RIPPLE	OP	16.5.1864
***	OG	1.9.1870
***	CP	14.8.1961
***	CG	18.12.1961
***	CG	1.7.1963 ?
Ripple to Tewkesbury: new alignment (for a motorway bridge)	In use by	19.5.1959
Tewkesbury Station SB	Open before	1.11.1875
***	Re-framed	6.4.1902
Replacement box	Opened	18.5.1920
Box closed and ground frame to control the Quay Branch provided in lieu	... ...	17.12.1961
***	t.o.u.	....

TEWKESBURY (temporary station)	OP	16.5.1864
Permanent station replacing the station on the Tewkesbury branch	Opened	....
***	CP	14.8.1861
***	CG	2.11.1964

TEWKESBURY BRANCH

Powers: Birmingham and Gloucester Railway Act 1837
Midland Railway (New Lines and Additional Powers) Act 1863 (Widening)

Tewkesbury Quay to Tewkesbury	Opened	c.1844
Tewkesbury Quay to Tewkesbury engine shed	Closed	1.2.1957
Tewkesbury to Ashchurch Jcn	Opened	21.7.1840

The Act of incorporation prohibited the use of locomotive power, but a locomotive-hauled train was used to take passengers from Tewkesbury to see the inaugural train on the Cheltenham to Bromsgrove section of the Birmingham & Gloucester line on 24 June 1840. No powers were ever taken to repeal the prohibition. However, from 18 February 1844 all traffic except for the night mail service was worked by locomotives. There were further periods of horse working.

TEWKESBURY	Opened	21.7.1840
***	CP	16.5.1864
Tewkesbury engine shed	Opened	....
***	Closed	14.8.1961
Tewkesbury engine shed (Oldbury Road LC) to Chance Street LC	Closed	17.12.1961
Junction line with the Tewkesbury & Malvern Railway	Opened	1863
Tewkesbury & Malvern Jcn to Tewkesbury Jcn (Ashchurch)	Doubled	1864
***	Singled	20.7.1958
***	Closed	2.11.1964
Tewkesbury Junction SB	Open before	1.11.1875
Replacement box	Opened	5.11.1893
***	Closed	16.10.1927
Tewkesbury to Ashchurch: block telegraph system	Installed	1876
ASHCHURCH: ticket platform on Tewkesbury line taken out of use	... ...	1.2.1901

WORCESTER LOOP

The Midland Railway possessed running powers over the Worcester Loop Line between Stoke Prior Junction and Abbotswood Junction for all traffic passing to or from the Birmingham & Gloucester Railway and for all traffic with places on or beyond the Midland Railway.

Stoke Works station on the Great Western line was never served by the trains of its owning company, but only by those of the Midland.

When the section of line between Worcester and Abbot's Wood Junction was opened on 5 October 1850 the Midland provided the service.

Worcester Midland Goods Station

Powers: Midland Railway (New Lines and Additional Powers) Act 1863

WORCESTER GOODS DEPOT	Opened	17.4.1868
***	t.o.u.	28.2.1988
Midland engine shed	Opened	1870
***	Closed	12.12.1932

X. WORCESTER, HEREFORD, & SOUTH WALES

WORCESTER & HEREFORD RAILWAY (GREAT WESTERN RAILWAY)

Between Worcester and Shelwick Junction, and between Barr's Court Junction (also known as Barton Junction) and Barton station the Midland Railway possessed running powers for all traffic over the Great Western line. The Midland also possessed the right to use with its engines and carriages or otherwise the Hereford and Newport sections of the West Midland Railway (i.e. the railway between Worcester and Middle Duffryn (Mountain Ash) via Pontypool) and all such other portions of the West Midland as lay between Worcester and any place in South Wales (inclusive of such place), together with the West Midland line between Stoke Prior Junction and Worcester. These powers were later limited to certain traffics only.

Between Shelwick Junction and Barr's Court Junction the Midland Railway, as a company using the Worcester & Hereford Railway, possessed running powers for all traffic over the Shrewsbury & Hereford line.

The Midland Railway possessed running powers for all traffic over the Vale of Neath line between Middle Duffryn and Swansea. Under the agreement by which the Midland was admitted to Barr's Court station in Hereford the company also received running powers between that station and Red Hill Junction via Rotherwas Junction if it exercised its powers towards Swansea.

HEREFORD, HAY & BRECON RAILWAY

Powers: Hereford, Hay and Brecon Railway (Deviation) Act 1860 (Hereford)
Hereford, Hay and Brecon Railway Act 1859 (Hereford to Moorhampton)
Hereford, Hay and Brecon Railway Act 1862 (Moorhampton to Kinnersley)
Hereford, Hay and Brecon Railway Act 1859 (Kinnersely to Whitney-on-the-Wye)
Hereford, Hay and Brecon Railway Act 1862 (Whitney-on-the Wye to Hay)
Hereford, Hay and Brecon Railway Act 1859 (Hay)
Hay Railway Act 1811, and Hay Railway Act 1812 (Land at Hay)
Hereford, Hay and Brecon Railway Act 1862 (Hay to Glasbury-on-Wye)
Hereford, Hay and Brecon Railway Act 1859 (Glasbury-on-Wye to Three Cocks Junction)

The Midland and the Hereford, Hay & Brecon companies entered into a working agreement for two-and-a-half years on 14 September 1869, an attempt to amalgamate having been rejected by parliament, and on 1 October 1869 the Midland took over the working of the line. The Hereford, Hay & Brecon was leased to the Midland with effect from 1 July 1874 under the Midland and Hereford, Hay & Brecon Railways Act 1874 and absorbed by the the Midland Railway (Additional Powers) Act, the company being dissolved under the Midland Railway (Additional Powers) Act 1886.

Hereford (Moorfields) to Moorhampton	OM	24.10.1862
***	OP	30.6.1863
Moorhampton to Eardisley	OP&G	30.6.1863
Eardisley to Hay	OP&G	11.7.1864
Hay to Three Cocks Jcn	OG	1.9.1864
***	OP	19.9.1864
Hereford, Hay & Brecon line	CP	31.12.1962
Hereford Barton Station and Junction		
HEREFORD (BARTON): Hereford, Hay & Brecon user	Commenced	1864
***	Ceased	1.7.1867
Mid Wales Railway user	Commenced	16.3.1868
***	Ceased	1.10.1869
Midland user for Hereford, Hay & Brecon trains	Commenced	1.4.1874
HEREFORD (BARTON)	CP	2.1.1893
Barton to Moorfields Goods Station	Closed	30.6.1894
HEREFORD (MOORFIELDS)	Opened	30.6.1863
***	CP	1.4.1874
Between Hereford and Three Cocks Junction running powers for all traffic were possessed by: "The Mid-Wales Railway Company and all persons and Corporations from time to time lawfully working the Railways of the Mid-Wales Company."		
HEREFORD: new Midland goods depot	Opened	2.1.1893
***	Closed	....
Moorfields Goods Station to Moorfield Jcn: lines made Moorfields Yard	... ...	30.6.1894
Moorfields to Brecon End of Moorfields: pilot guard working	Commenced	19.6.1892
Moorfields Goods Station SB	Open before	16.8.1877
***	Closed	30.6.1894
Moorfields Junction engine shed	Opened	30.6.1894
***	Closed	10.12.1924

Brecon Curve: Junction Curve at Hereford

Powers: Hereford, Hay and Brecon Railway Act 1859, and Hereford, Hay and Brecon Railway (Deviation) Act 1860 (No construction powers)

Barton & Brecon Curve Jcn to Moorfields Jcn	Into use	1.1.1893
***	OP&G	2.1.1893
***	Closed	1.8.1966

Access to Barr's Court Station

HEREFORD (BARR'S COURT): Midland user of the Great Western and London & North Western joint station	Commenced	2.1.1893
Brecon End of Moorfields Goods Yard SB	Open before	16.8.1877
Replacement box	Opened	19.6.1892
Re-named Moorfields Junction SB	... ...	1.1.1893
***	Closed	24.11.1963
Brecon End of Moorfields to Credenhill: working by electric train tablet block	Commenced	19.6.1892
Moorfields Jcn to Eardisley	Closed	28.9.1964
Credenhill SB	Open before	1.11.1875
Replacement box	Opened	3.11.1891
***	Re-framed	21.5.1911
Replacement box	Opened	8.4.1917
***	Closed	26.5.1929
Credenhill: bi-directional goods loop line (down side)	Into use	15.4.1917
***	t.o.u.	22.2.1927
CREDENHILL	Opened	30.6.1863
***	CP	31.12.1962
***	CG	28.9.1964
Credenhill to Moorhampton: working by electric train tablet block	Commenced	19.6.1892
WESTMOOR (private station)	OP(NA) before	1.10.1869 *
***	CP(All)	....
This station was provided under the terms of an Act or agreement, which also provided for stops to be made at the station.		
Moorhampton Station SB	Open before	1.11.1875
Replacement box	Opened	17.1.1892
***	Raised	9.9.1914
***	Closed	....
MOORHAMPTON	OP&G	30.6.1863
***	CP&G	31.12.1962
This station was provided under the terms of an Act or agreement.		
Moorhampton to Hay: staff & ticket working withdrawn, and electric train tablet block working between Moorhampton and Eardisley Junction and also between Eardisley West and Hay	Commenced	26.6.1892
Kinnersley Station SB	Open before	1.11.1875
***	Closed	26.6.1892
KINNERSLEY	OP&G	30.6.1863
***	CP&G	31.12.1962
Eardisley Junction SB	Open before	1.11.1875
Replacement box	Opened	18.6.1893
***	Re-framed	....
***	Closed	....
Eardisley Jcn with the Great Western Railway	Opened	3.8.1874
***	Closed	1.1.1917
***	Removed	17.4.1917
***	Restored	7-8.12.1922
***	Re-opened	11.12.1922
***	t.o.u.	21.8.1955
Between Eardisley Junction and Eardisley station the Great Western possessed and exercised running powers for all traffic over the Hereford, Hay & Brecon line.		
EARDISLEY	OP&G	30.6.1863
***	CP	31.12.1962
***	CG	28.9.1964
Eardisley to Three Cocks Jcn	Closed	31.12.1962
Eardisley West SB	Opened	10.9.1888
***	Raised	7.9.1915
***	Closed	15.10.1934 ?
WHITNEY	OP&G	11.7.1864
Altered to WHITNEY-ON-THE-WYE	... ...	4.3.1880
Altered to WHITNEY-ON-WYE	... ...	14.7.1924
***	CP&G	31.12.1962
Whitney Station SB	Open before	1.11.1875
***	Closed	26.6.1892
Hay Junction SB	Opened	21.4.1889
***	Closed	....
Hay Junction with the Golden Valley Railway	Opened	21.4.1889
***	Closed	1.1.1950
Between Hay Junction and Hay station the Great Western possessed running powers for all traffic over the Hereford, Hay & Brecon line.		
Hay Jcn to Hay: double-line working	Commenced	21.4.1889

HAY	OP&G	11.7.1864
Altered to HAY-ON-WYE	... ...	13.6.1955
***	CP&G	31.12.1962
Hay Station SB	Open before	1.11.1875
Replacement box	Opened	12.11.1888
***	Re-framed	9.8.1921
***	Closed	....
GLASBURY	OG	1.9.1864
***	OP	19.9.1864
Altered to GLASBURY-ON-WYE	... ...	1.2.1894
***	CP&G	31.12.1962
Glasbury Station SB	Open before	1.11.1875
***	Closed	3.7.1892
Three Cocks Junction SB	Opened	....
***	Closed	....

MID-WALES RAILWAY

Between Three Cocks Junction and Talyllyn Junction the Midland Railway possessed running powers for all traffic over the Mid-Wales line.

BRECON & MERTHYR TYDFIL JUNCTION RAILWAY

Between Talyllyn Junction and Brecon station and the junction with the Neath & Brecon Railway the Midland Railway possessed running powers for all traffic over the Brecon & Merthyr line.

BRECON JOINT PASSENGER STATION	Opened	1.3.1871
***	CP(All)	31.12.1962

This station was owned by the Brecon & Merthyr company and was used jointly by that company and by the Midland as successor to the Hereford, Hay & Brecon company.

Between Morlais Junction and the junctions at Merthyr with the Great Western and Taff Vale lines the Midland Railway possessed running powers for all traffic over the Brecon & Merthyr and London & North Western Joint Railway.

NEATH & BRECON RAILWAY

The Midland Railway possessed running powers for all traffic over the whole of the Neath & Brecon Railway.

SWANSEA VALE AND NEATH & BRECON JUNCTION RAILWAY (Neath & Brecon Railway)

The Swansea Vale and Neath & Brecon Junction Railway was vested in the Neath & Brecon Railway by Act of 1869.

SWANSEA VALE RAILWAY

Scott's Tramway, between Llansamlet and the coast and about three and a half miles in length, was brought into use in 1819. It was extended, probably in 1845 or shortly afterwards, by means of wayleaves as far as Graigola.

The Swansea Vale Railway was leased to the Midland with effect from 1 July 1874 by Act of that year, and the Midland took possession on 1 September 1874. Accounts were transferred on 1 November 1874. The company was vested in the Midland with effect from 11 August 1876 by Act of the same date.

The London & North Western Railway possessed running powers over the entire Swansea Vale Railway.

The Neath & Brecon Railway possessed running powers to work a minimum of three passenger trains and two goods trains each way on weekdays over the Swansea Vale line between Ynysygeinon Junction and Swansea. The Neath & Brecon company exercised its running powers for passenger trains between 1875 and June 1877, when an agreement arranged that as long as the Midland should work the Neath & Brecon line between Brecon and Ynysygeinon the Neath & Brecon should not exercise these running powers.

Powers: Swansea Vale Railway Act 1855
(Swansea to Pontardawe: acquisition of private railway)
Swansea Vale Railway Act 1855 (Swansea)
South Wales Railway Act 1855 (Six Pit)
Swansea Vale Railway Act 1856 (Pontardawe to Clayphon Wharf)

The direction of the line was DOWN from Brynamman to Swansea.

The block telegraph system was installed in 1874
and the train staff was added from 17 January 1875.

Swansea to Graigola (Glais)	OG	12.1852
Graigola (Glais) to Pontardawe	OG	24.12.1859
Swansea to Pontardawe	O.Formal	20.2.1860
***	OP	21.2.1860
Pontardawe to Ynisygeinon	OP&G	21.1.1861
Ynisygeinon to Ystalyfera	OP&G	20.11.1861
Ystalyfera to Yniscedwyn (Clayphon Wharf)	OG by	1864
Ystalyfera to Gurnos Jcn (and Brynamman)	OP	2.3.1868 ?

(Closing dates are given in the normal geographical order.)

Swansea Goods Depot

Powers: Swansea and Neath Railway Act 1861

SWANSEA GOODS DEPOT, and branch	OG	1.3.1876

The Midland possessed running powers for all traffic over the Vale of Neath line between St Thomas Junction and the Midland Goods Station, a distance of eight chains.

Swansea: junction with the Great Western Railway (broad gauge)	OG	2.1857
Converted to narrow gauge	... ...	11.5.1872
SWANSEA	OG	....
***	OP	21.2.1860
Altered to SWANSEA ST THOMAS	... ...	....
***	CG	26.8.1929
***	CP	25.9.1950
Swansea St Thomas to Swansea Vale Junction	Closed	25.9.1950
Swansea Station SB	Open before	1.11.1875
Replacement box	Opened	18.12.1892
***	Closed	27.5.1968
Swansea engine shed	Opened	....
***	Enlarged	1864
***	Closed	Late 1890s
ST THOMAS'S GOODS YARD	Opened	....
Sidings east of the main line	t.o.u.	7.5.1967
Sidings in outer group west of the main line	t.o.u.	27.5.1968
All remaining sidings	t.o.u.	28.10.1969
Swansea to Llansamlet: line relaid to mixed gauge	After	1.1856
	& by	2.1857
Swansea to Upper Bank Jcn	Doubled	18.12.1892
***	Singled	27.5.1968

Prior to 18 December 1892 there were two lines between Swansea and Upper Bank Junction, but these were worked as two parallel single lines, one to and from Clydach and one to and from Six Pit.

Swansea to Upper Bank: single running line from Eastern Depot to Morriston and Six Pit controlled by public telephone	... ...	27.5.1968
Swansea Eastern Depot to Morriston: one train working	Commenced	11.7.1976
***	CG(All)	24.5.1983
Harbour Branch Sidings SB	Open before	16.8.1877
Replacement box	Opened	18.12.1892
***	Closed	7.5.1967
Swansea: junction with Swansea Harbour Trust lines	Opened	....
***	t.o.u.	27.5.1968

Swansea Docks area

Powers: No Construction Powers - Prince of Wales Dock Coal Drops (Leasehold)
Midland Railway Act 1911 - King's Dock Lines
No Construction Powers - King's Dock Coal Hoist (Leasehold)

Midland coal drops (King's Dock)	Opened	....
Midland reception etc. sidings	Opened	....
Midland coal hoist sidings	Opened	....

King's Dock was opened on 23 November 1909 and the various Midland facilities were opened in 1909-10.

The Midland Railway possessed running powers for goods traffic between St Thomas Junction and Eastern Dock Junction over the Vale of Neath line and worked coal traffic between the Swansea Vale line and reception sidings at the rear of the coal tips at the Prince of Wales Dock, running over the Swansea Harbour Trust line between Eastern Dock Junction and its portion of those reception sidings.

Swansea: temporary closure of New Cut bridge for re-building; all traffic to and from the docks to run via the low-level sidings	... ...	1.6.1902

Swansea North Dock Branch

Powers: --

SWANSEA: NORTH DOCK GOODS DEPOT, and branch	OG by	1883
***	Re-modelled	9.1903
Ground frame, and signals controlling the drawbridge	t.o.u.	7.11.1954
Line to North Dock	t.o.u.	10.2.1955

Foxhole Sidings SB	Opened	18.12.1892	
***	Closed	18.2.1934	
White Rock Sidings SB	Open before	16.8.1877	
Box closed and ground frame provided in lieu	... ...	12.1888-8.1893	
***	t.o.u.	4.7.1966	
UPPER BANK	OG	....	
***	OP	1.9.1863	*
***	CP	25.9.1950	
***	CG	3.8.1964	
Upper Bank Junction SB	Open before	1.11.1875	
Replacement box	Opened	11.12.1892	
***	Closed	27.5.1968	
Upper Bank Jcn to Upper Bank Sidings	Doubled	11.12.1892	
Upper Bank Jcn to Glais Jcn (via Six Pit Jcn)	CP	1.3.1875	
Upper Bank Jcn to Six Pit Jcn (Imperial Smelting Company's Siding)	Tfc ceased	c.5.1973	
Upper Bank Jcn taken out of use and line to Six Pit closed	... ...	13.9.1982	
UPPER BANK SIDINGS	Into use	....	
***	Extended	1864	
Altered to UPPER BANK OLD YARD	... ...	....	
Outer four sidings	Recovered	1962	
Remaining sidings	t.o.u.	29.12.1967	
UPPER BANK SIDINGS: new up sidings	Into use	3.11.1907	
Altered to UPPER BANK NEW YARD	... ...	....	
Back sidings	Into use	c.8.1908	
***	Recovered	1962	
Upper Bank Sidings SB	Opened	11.12.1892	
Replacement box	Opened	3.11.1907	
***	Closed	1961	
Upper Bank Sidings to Glais Jcn: electric train tablet working working	Commenced	5.6.1898	
Upper Bank Sidings to north of Six Pit Jcn: through siding	Into use	12.1907	
***	t.o.u.	5.9.1965	
Six Pit Junction SB	Open before	1.11.1875	
Replacement box	Opened	15.3.1896	
***	Closed	6.1961	

Midland & Great Western Joint Junction Line

Powers: --

Six Pit Jcn to Swansea Valley Jcn	OG	2.1857	
***	Closed	7.1961	?

Broad gauge rails were added between the new junction and the terminus in Swansea.
Between Six Pit Junction and Swansea High Street station the Midland possessed contingent running powers for all general traffic over the South Wales Railway's line if facilities were not afforded.

Swansea Valley Junction SB (Great Western junction box)	Closed	3.2.1963	
Six Pit Jcn: new run-round connection	Into use	29.12.1967	
SIX PIT SIDINGS	Opened	....	
***	t.o.u.	....	
SIX PIT GOODS DEPOT	Opened	....	
Altered to SIX PIT JUNCTION GOODS DEPOT	... ...	....	
***	Closed	5.7.1965	
Six Pit Jcn to Yniscedwyn Colliery Exchange Sidings	Tfc ceased	23.3.1968	
***	t.o.u.	22.4.1968	
***	Off. closed	30.4.1968	
LLANSAMLET SIDINGS	Into use	....	
***	Extended	1864	
***	t.o.u.	....	
Llansamlet Station SB	Open before	1.11.1875	
Re-named Llansamlet Sidings SB	... ...	8.1877-4.1878	
***	Re-framed	15.8.1905	
Box closed and three ground frames provided in lieu	... ...	23.2.1932	
South ground frame and connection to siding	t.o.u.	9.8.1965	
LLANSAMLET	OG	....	
***	OP	21.2.1860	
***	CP	1.3.1875	
Altered to LLANSAMLET SOUTH	... ...	2.1950	
***	CG	12.7.1965	
BIRCHGROVE	OP	5.5.1866	*
***	CP(All)	1.3.1875	
Glais: loop at Glais Old Station	Into use	1.9.1907	
GLAIS	OG	....	
***	OP	21.2.1860	
***	CP	1.3.1875	
***	CG	8.11.1965	
Glais Junction SB	Open before	1.11.1875	
Replacement box	Opened	24.3.1890	
***	Closed	....	
Glais Jcn: facing connection to Clydach-on-Tawe South No. 2 SB, already secured out of use, replaced by plain line	... ...	12.2.1956	

Old Graigola Sidings & Boundary Sidings SB (not a block post)	Open before	1.11.1875
***	Closed	8.5.1892 ?

Bryncoch & Wernddu Branch

Powers: --

Bryncoch & Wernddu branch "has been brought into use"	... ...	7.1893
This branch, which was worked by train staff without tickets, left the main line immediately south of Pontardawe.		
Bryncoch & Wernddu branch	Closed	1932
***	Removed	26.9.1936
Pontardawe South SB	Open before	1.10.1876
Replacement box	Opened	6.11.1892
Re-named Pontardawe SB	... ...	7.11.1965
***	Closed	24.11.1967
Pontardawe: line through the station	Doubled	5.6.1876
***	Singled	7.11.1965 ?
	or	17.10.1965 ?
Pontardawe North SB	Open before	1.10.1876
Re-named Pontardawe Station SB	... ...	20.3.1892
***	Re-framed	18.9.1898
Replacement box	Opened	28.7.1912
***	Closed	7.11.1965 ?
	or	17.10.1965 ?
PONTARDAWE	OG	....
***	OP	21.2.1860
New goods yard and extension of up platform	Into use	7.1907
***	CP	25.9.1950
***	CG	12.7.1965
Pontardawe to Gurnos: section made a siding	... ...	18.3.1967
Pontardawe North SB (second box)	Opened	20.3.1892
***	Closed	6.1908-6.1911 ?
	or	12.5.1929 ?
Glantawe Sidings SB	Open before	1.10.1876
***	Closed	5.4.1887
Waenycoed Ynismedw Sidings SB (not a block post)	Open before	1.11.1875
***	Closed	15.5.1892 ?
Waun Coed Colliery Sidings	Into use	1864
***	t.o.u.	....
Cwm Click Sidings SB	Open before	1.11.1875
Re-named Cwmtawe Sidings SB	... ...	6.1881-4.1883
***	Closed	22.9.1891
YNYSYGEINON	OP	21.1.1861
***	CP	1.3.1862 *
Ynisygeinon Sidings SB	Opened	29.6.1891
***	Raised	16.8.1914
***	Closed	28.3.1965
Ynisygeinon Junction SB	Open before	1.11.1875
Replacement box	Opened	3.4.1910
***	Alt.levers	27.1.1914
***	Closed	20.2.1967
Ystalyfera Works Crossing SB (not a block post)	Open before	1.11.1875
Replacement box	Opened	22.7.1896
Replacement box	Opened	23.12.1918
***	Closed by	1937
Ystalyfera: goods-yard connections	Removed	27-29.5.1920
Ystalyfera Station SB	Open before	1.11.1875
Replacement box	Opened	22.1.1889
***	Closed	....
YSTALYFERA	OG	....
***	OP	20.11.1861
***	CP	25.9.1950
***	CG	26.5.1920
***	RO(G)	....
***	CG	11.1927
Ystalyfera: all facilities except the single running line	t.o.u.	7.8.1967
Gurnos Junction SB	Open before	1.11.1875
Replacement box	Opened	5.7.1896
***	Closed	27.9.1964
The section of the line between Gurnos Junction and the end of the original line became known as the Yniscedwyn Branch.		
Gurnos engine shed	Opened	1864
***	Replaced	1900
***	Closed	2.4.1962
Yniscedwyn branch: working by pilot guard without tickets	Commenced	17.12.1906
Ystradgynlais Colliery was originally called Hendrelais Colliery.		
Clayphon GF to Clayphon Wharf (siding)	t.o.u.	4.7.1966

Yniscedwyn Tin Plate Works Branch

Powers: --

Yniscedwyn Tin Plate Works branch	Opened	1864
***	Closed	....
Yniscedwyn Colliery to Easton Brothers Siding	Closed	13.6.1966

Wernplumis Branch

Powers: --

Clayphon Bridge Jcn to Gurnos Anthracite Colliery	Opened	....
***	Recovered	5.6.1956

Morriston Loop

Powers: Swansea Vale Railway Act 1867

Upper Bank to Morriston	OP&G	2.10.1871
Morriston to Glais (Clydach branch)	OP&G	1.3.1875
Upper Bank to Clydach: direction of UP and DOWN reversed	... ...	12.2.1956
Upper Bank Jcn to Morriston East No. 1 SB: electric train tablet working replaced by electric train token working	... ...	5.10.1958
Upper Bank Jcn to Clydach-on-Tawe South: one engine in steam working	Commenced	22.2.1965
Upper Bank engine shed	Opened	8.1893
***	Closed	4.2.1963
This shed replaced an earlier one at Swansea.		
Upper Bank engine shed sidings	t.o.u.	7.7.1963 ?
Steel Works Sidings & Beaufort Sidings SB	Open before	1.11.1875
***	Closed	9.4.1888
Morriston South SB	Opened	13.9.1891
***	Raised	7.5.1916
Re-named Morriston East No. 1 SB	... ...	c.1.1950
***	Closed	22.2.1965 ?
Morriston: down loop extension of about 140 yards towards Swansea	Into use	20.10.1907
Morriston Station SB	Open before	1.11.1875
***	Closed	13.9.1891
MORRISTON	OG	....
***	OP	1.3.1875
Altered to MORRISTON EAST	... ...	1.1950
***	CP	25.9.1950
***	CG	4.10.1965
Morriston North SB	Opened	13.9.1891
Re-named Morriston East No. 2 SB	... ...	c.1.1950
***	Closed	22.2.1965 ?
Line taken out of use at 3m 20ch	... ...	1.9.1965
Line severed at this point	... ...	10.11.1965
The line was further cut back to 3m 16ch, and the long siding which had run to the river bridge was taken out of use, on 23 July 1966. Alterations were made at Morriston on 5-6 February 1974. The former brickworks connection was re-instated and the connection to Birds (Swansea) Limited was removed on 15 June 1974, and the connection to the steel and tin-plate works was removed in August 1975.		
Morriston East to Clydach-on-Tawe South (5m 22ch)	Closed	12.7.1965 ?
	<u>or</u>	1.9.1965 ?
Tyrcenol Sidings SB	Open before	1.11.1875
***	Closed by	16.8.1877
Tyrcenol Sidings GF	t.o.u.	10.9.1961

Tyrcenol Branch

Powers: Agreement with the Great Western Railway dated 3 October 1881.

Tyrcenol Jcn with the Great Western Railway	Completed	9.5.1881
Junction never used: points removed	... ...	1885
Tyrcenol Junction SB	Ready	6.1881-4.1883
***	Removed by	4.1883

Tyrcenol (or Morriston) Junction SB	Opened	Never
Block instruments	Removed	1882
Points of the junction	Removed	1885
Signalbox and remaining signals	Removed	1893
Ynysforgan SB	Opened	....
***	Closed by	1899
Clydach-on-Tawe No. 3 GF	Into use	13.2.1956
***	t.o.u.	19.3.1964
Cwm Clydach South SB	Opened	10.8.1891
Re-named Clydach-on-Tawe South SB	... ...	1.11.1901
Re-named Clydach-on-Tawe No. 2 SB	... ...	c.1.1950
Box closed and ground frame provided in lieu	... ...	13.2.1956
CWM CLYDACH	OG	....
***	OP	1.3.1875
Altered to CLYDACH-ON-TAWE	... ...	1.10.1901
Altered to CLYDACH-ON-TAWE SOUTH	... ...	1.1950
***	CP	25.9.1950
***	CG	12.7.1965

Cwm Clydach SB	Open before	1.11.1875
Re-named Cwm Clydach North SB	... ...	10.8.1891
Replacement box	Opened	10.5.1896
Re-named Clydach-on-Tawe North SB	... ...	1.11.1901
Re-named Clydach-on-Tawe No. 1 SB	... ...	c.1.1950
Box closed and ground frame provided in lieu	... ...	13.2.1956
Clydach-on-Tawe North (5m 22ch) to 5m 39ch	Closed	19.3.1964
Clydach-on-Tawe (5m 39ch) to Glais Jcn	Closed	25.9.1950
***	t.o.u.	13.2.1956
GLAIS: second station	OG	....
***	OP	1.3.1875
***	CP	25.9.1950
***	CG	8.11.1965

Swansea Vale Extension Railway

Powers: Swansea Vale Railway (Extension) Act 1861
(Purchase of Palleg or Cwm Twrch Railroad, and authorisation of the Brynamman and Caelliau Branches)

Gurnos Jcn to Brynamman	OM	1.1.1864
***	OG	....
***	OP	2.3.1868
***	Closed	28.9.1964
Gurnos Jcn to 13m 20ch	Closed	7.1967
GURNOS JUNCTION GOODS STATION	Open before	1877
***	Closed	12.7.1965
Gurnos Jcn to Amman Sidings:		
staff & ticket working in place of working by train staff alone	Commenced	3.1.1893
Electric train tablet block working	Commenced	12.7.1896
GURNOS JUNCTION MARSHALLING SIDINGS	Opened	30.1.1907
Up reception siding	Into use	3.2.1907
Various sidings	t.o.u.	28.9.1964
Various sidings	t.o.u.	14.9.1965
Dead-end siding and brake-van siding	t.o.u.	18.10.1965
Cwmphil Sidings SB	Open before	16.8.1877
***	Closed	4.7.1887
Blaen-cwm Colliery Sidings SB	Opened	23.8.1908
Box closed and ground frame provided in lieu	... ...	1950-1956
***	t.o.u.	7.1967 ?
Blaen-cwm Colliery Sidings GF (13m 20ch) to Brynamman West	Closed	28.9.1964
CWMTWRCH WELL HALT	OP	14.12.1935
***	CP(All)	25.9.1950
GWYS	OG	....
***	OP	2.3.1868
***	CP	25.9.1950
***	CG	1.4.1963
Gwys SB	Open before	1.11.1875
***	Closed	....

Caelliau Branch

Powers: Swansea Vale Railway (Extension) Act 1861

Caelliau Colliery Branch Jcn to Brynhenllys Colliery Siding	Open before	1881
Brynhenllys to Black Mountain Colliery Sidings tramway converted to a railway	... ...	....
Caelliau branch: working by train staff without tickets	Commenced	5.11.1905
Caelliau Jcn (Gwys) to Brynhenllys Colliery	Closed	20.12.1962
	or by	5.1962
Brynhenllys Colliery to Black Mountain Colliery	Closed by	1940

Cwmllynfell & Hendreforgan Sidings SB	Open before	1.11.1875
***	Closed	12.1888-8.1893
GWAUN CAE GURWEN COLLIERS' PLATFORM	OP(NA)	7.12.1896
Altered to CWMLLYNFELL	... ...	1.7.1909
***	OP	1.7.1909
***	OG	1913
***	CP	25.9.1950
***	CG	28.9.1964
Various spellings of Gwaun cae Gurwen are found in the sources.		
Gwaen-cae-Gurwen Colliery Sidings: goods loop line	Into use	5.1.1908
***	t.o.u.	....
Gwaen-cwm-Gurwen Colliery Sidings SB	Opened	5.1.1908
***	Closed	27.9.1964
Waencaegerwen & Rhosamman Sidings SB	Open before	1.11.1875
***	Closed	20.6.1887
Amman Sidings SB	Opened	8.11.1891
***	Closed	16.8.1908
Amman Sidings to Brynamman Sidings: staff & ticket working	Commenced	12.7.1896

Brynamman Station SB	Open before	1.11.1875
Replacement box	Opened	5.1.1896
Replacement box about 200 yards nearer Gurnos	Opened	16.8.1908
***	Closed	27.9.1964
The Great Western Railway possessed running powers over 30 chains of the Midland line west of Brynamman.		
Bryanmman Jcn with the Great Western Railway	Opened	1869
The Midland possessed running powers over 118 yards of the Llanelly Railway & Dock Company's line at Brynamman for the purpose of obtaining access to the Amman Company's sidings through the lower connection.		
BRYNAMMAN	OG	....
***	OP	2.3.1868
LMS station master withdrawn and station placed under Great Western supervision	... ...	1.8.1929
Altered to BRYNAMMAN EAST	... ...	1.1950
***	CP	25.9.1950
***	CG	28.9.1964

XI. BETWEEN GLOUCESTER AND BRISTOL

BRISTOL & GLOUCESTERSHIRE RAILWAY

Powers: Bristol and Gloucestershire Railway Act 1828

Cuckold's Pill (Floating Harbour) to Mangotsfield	Opened	6.8.1835
Mangotsfield to Coalpit Heath	Opened	7.1832
CUCKOLD'S PILL altered to Avon Street Wharf	... ...	....
Keynsham Jcn (Mangotsfield) to Westerleigh Jcn	C. temp.	5.6.1844
Keynsham Jcn to Westerleigh Jcn: mixed-gauge line	Ready by	29.7.1844
This mixed-gauge section was to allow the continuing use of the line between Keynsham Junction and Coalpit Heath by trains to and from the Avon & Gloucestershire line. It was the earliest example of the provision of mixed-gauge track.		

BRISTOL & GLOUCESTER RAILWAY

The Bristol & Gloucester Railway Act 1839 empowered the new company to absorb the Bristol & Gloucestershire Railway and build a new line northwards from Westerleigh.

Powers: Bristol and Gloucester Railway Act 1843
(Great Western & Midland Junction to Lawrence Hill Junction)
Bristol and Gloucester Railway Act 1839 (Bristol to Mangotsfield)
Bristol and Gloucester Railway Act 1839
(Coal Pit Heath Branch Junction to Standish Junction)

Gloucester to Bristol (broad gauge)	O.Formal	6.7.1844
***	OP	8.7.1844
***	OG	2.9.1844
***	O.Coal	9.9.1844
Narrow gauge working	Commenced	29.5.1854
Under the Birmingham and Bristol and Midland Railways Act 1846 the broad gauge was to be maintained between the junctions at Bristol and Gloucester and running powers for all traffic were granted to the Great Western. Under the Midland Railway (Gloucester to Stonehouse) Act 1848 the laying of narrow-gauge rails between Bristol and Standish Junction was permitted. The use of the broad-gauge rails became impossible when the Great Western converted the Gloucester area to the narrow gauge in May 1872. Those at the southern end, to Westerleigh Junction, were retained until January 1882 for a daily coal train to and from Parkfield Colliery.		

Stonehouse Junction Railway

Powers: Midland Railway (Gloucester and Stonehouse Railway) Act 1848

Gloucester Passenger Jcn to Barton Street Jcn; **and** California Crossing Jcn to Standish Jcn	OP&G	29.5.1854
Gloucester Passenger Junction was 14 chains west of Tramway Crossing, which was the point of junction of the Gloucester Docks branch. The passenger lines rejoined the docks branch about 5 chains north of Barton Street level crossing, diverging from the branch again at California Crossing.		
Gloucester to Stonehouse: block telegraph system	Installed	1869–1872
Passenger Station Jcn to Barton Street Jcn: original route	Closed	12.4.1896
Gloucester Goods Jcn to Barton Street: up goods line made a siding	... ...	18.2.1968
Down goods line made a siding	... ...	25.2.1968
Horton Road Jcn to Tuffley Jcn	Closed	1.12.1975
Gloucester engine shed	Opened	....
***	Replaced	8.7.1851
***	Closed	2.7.1894
This original Gloucester engine shed stood on land required for the new passenger station. It was replaced by a shed at Barnwood.		
GLOUCESTER: temporary accommodation for Bristol & Gloucester trains	Into use	8.7.1844
Gloucester Passenger Station SB	Opened	12.4.1896
***	Closed	3.3.1968
GLOUCESTER: replacement passenger station	Opened	12.4.1896
Station made "closed" for tickets	Down side	23.11.1914
***	Entirely	17.4.1919
Altered to GLOUCESTER EASTGATE	... ...	17.9.1951
***	CG	1.8.1967
No. 1 shunting siding	Recovered	7.1.1968
Platform No. 4 (loop) made down main line	... ...	18.2.1968
Platform No. 3 (down main line)	t.o.u.	25.2.1968
Former down main line restored to use as up main line and former up platform and former up main line taken out of use	... ...	5.5.1968
EASTGATE and CENTRAL stations combined as GLOUCESTER	... ...	26.5.1968
Eastgate section of Gloucester passenger station	Closed	1.12.1975

Barton Street SB	Open before	16.8.1877
Replacement box	Opened	2.12.1894
Box made a ground frame	... ...	26.5.1968
***	t.o.u.	1.12.1975
Barton Street level crossing: lifting barriers	Into use	3.12.1960
Barton Street Jcn: connections	t.o.u.	28.1.1968
Stroud Road SB	Open before	16.8.1877
***	Closed	1878

Gloucester Docks branch

See page 261

California Crossing SB (not a block post)	Opened	8.1877-4.1878
Box made a block post for the up and down main lines	... ...	25.8.1890
Replacement box	Opened	24.7.1892
Replacement box	Opened	26.9.1920
Box made a ground frame	... ...	11.8.1968
***	t.o.u.	1.12.1975
Bowley's Crossing SB (not a block post)	Opened	8.1877-4.1878
***	Closed	....
Painswick Road Crossing SB	Opened	15.10.1893
Box made a ground frame	... ...	11.8.1968
***	t.o.u.	1.12.1975
Tuffley Sidings SB	Opened	8.7.1876
Replacement signalbox about a quarter of a mile to the south named Tuffley Junction SB	Opened	24.7.1898
Replacement box 96 yards to the south also signalling the adjacent Great Western lines	Opened	7.12.1941
Box closed and ground frame provided in lieu	... ...	11.8.1968
***	t.o.u.	5.12.1975

Gloucester New Docks branch

See page 261

Tuffley Jcn to Standish Jcn: independent Midland and Great Western pairs of running lines converted to a single two-track route	... ...	4.8-13.10.1968
TUFFLEY WHARF	Opened	....
***	Closed	....
Tuffley Jcn: up loop line	Into use	1941
Crossover and connections between up loop line and down main line	t.o.u.	7.3.1966
Single line to and from Quedgeley Depot provided in the course of simplification of the four-track layout	... ...	10.8.1968
Quedgeley Sidings SB	Opened	28.11.1915
***	Closed	25.4.1926
QUEDGELEY WORKMEN'S PLATFORM	Opened	13.12.1915
***	Closed	1925
Naas Crossing SB	Open before	16.8.1877
Naas Crossing SB: replacement box	Opened	21.12.1902
***	Re-framed	....
Box made a gate box and re-named Brookthorpe Crossing GB	... ...	15.9.1968
***	Burnt out	20.5.1977
Crossing closed to vehicles	... ...	23.12.1982
Haresfield SB	Open before	16.8.1877
Replacement box	Opened	18.11.1900
***	Raised	2.7.1911
***	Raised	7.10.1923
Box made a ground frame for the level crossing	... ...	15.9.1968
Level crossing closed to vehicles	... ...	11.1971
Ground frame	t.o.u.	19.12.1971
HARESFIELD	OP	29.5.1854
***	CP(All)	4.1.1965
This station was provided under the terms of the authorising Act.		
Standish Junction SB	Open before	16.8.1877
***	t.o.u.	1886
***	Closed	3.1.1887
Standish Junction SB (new box)	Opened	28.6.1908
***	Closed	13.10.1968
Standish Jcn with the Great Western Railway: first (end-on) junction	Opened	8.7.1844
***	Closed	29.5.1854
Connection with the Cheltenham & Great Western Union	Opened	12.5.1845
Second junction with the Great Western Railway	Opened	21.4.1873
***	Closed	30.1.1887
Third junction with the Great Western Railway	Prepared	28.6.1908
***	Opened	1.7.1908
Stonehouse Station SB	Open before	16.8.1877
Replacement box	Opened	5.9.1897
Box closed and ground frame provided in lieu	... ...	13.10.1968
***	t.o.u.	....

Stonehouse & Nailsworth branch

See page 261

Stonehouse to Berkeley Road: block telegraph system	Installed	1873
Stonehouse: branch connections made hand operated	... ...	4.12.1966
STONEHOUSE	Opened	8.7.1844
Altered to STONEHOUSE BRISTOL ROAD	... ...	17.9.1951
***	CP	4.1.1965
***	CG	3.1.1966
Stonehouse Viaduct SB	Opened	....
***	Closed	....
Switches and crossings	Taken out	10.6.1915
Signalbox	Removed	25.6.1916
Frocester: junction with Frampton Ballast Pit branch	Opened	20.5.1918
***	Removed	27.4.1924
Frocester Station SB	Open before	1.11.1875
Replacement box	Opened	22.10.1899
Lever-frame reversed	... ...	21.3.1920
***	Closed	11.5.1966
FROCESTER	Opened	8.7.1844
***	CP&G	11.12.1961
Coaley Junction SB	Open before	1.11.1875
Replacement box	Opened	26.10.1891
Replacement box	Opened	31.3.1935
Box closed and ground frame provided in lieu	... ...	13.10.1968
***	t.o.u.	5.4.1964

Dursley branch

See page 262

DURSLEY JUNCTION	OG	25.8.1856
***	OP	18.9.1856
Altered to COALEY	... ...	1.10.1870 *
***	CP	4.1.1965
***	CG	1.11.1966
Gossington SB	Opened	20.2.1916
Box took over working of the internal sidings connections	... ...	17.5.1916
***	Closed	21.2.1926
Berkeley Road Junction SB	Open before	1871
Replacement box	Opened	29.7.1900
***	Re-framed	....
Box made a ground frame	... ...	13.10.1968
***	t.o.u.	c.6.1972

Berkeley branch

See page 263

Berkeley Road to Bristol: block telegraph system	Installed	1869-1872
Berkeley Road: connection from down main line to down branch line taken out of use and junction layout altered	... ...	2.5.1965
DURSLEY & BERKELEY	Opened	8.7.1844
Altered to BERKELEY ROAD	... ...	1.6.1845 *
***	CP	4.1.1965
***	CG	1.11.1966
Berkeley Road South Junction SB	Opened	1.3.1908
***	Closed	12.4.1908
***	Re-opened	....
***	Closed	24.3.1963
Berkeley Road South Jcn with the Great Western Railway	Opened	9.3.1908
***	Closed	12.4.1908
***	Re-opened	....
***	Closed	24.3.1963
Berkeley Road South Jcn: connection in the down main line	t.o.u.	10.3.1963
Remaining connections	t.o.u.	17.3.1963
Wick up and down IBS	Into use	7.12.1941
***	t.o.u.	13.10.1968
Up and down IBS replaced by Wick Temporary SB	... ...	4.11.1951
Temporary signalbox closed and crossover taken out of use	By	1960
Bendall's Sidings SB	Opened	18.8.1890
***	Closed	15.3.1902
***	Re-opened	17.8.1903
Box to be open only when required for traffic	... ...	17.9.1906
Box closed and ground frame provided in lieu	... ...	12.3.1912
***	t.o.u.	17.6.1928
Charfield North SB	Opened	1.8.1897
***	Closed	18.4.1909
CHARFIELD	Opened	8.7.1844
Altered to CHARFIELD (FOR WOOTTON-UNDER-EDGE)	... ...	1.7.1879 *
***	CP	4.1.1965
***	CG	6.9.1965
This station was provided under the terms of an Act or agreement.		
Charfield Station SB	Open before	16.8.1877
***	Closed	1.8.1897
Charfield: up refuge siding made up goods loop	... ...	29.3.1942
Down refuge siding made down goods loop	... ...	19.4.1942

Charfield Station SB (new box on the down platform)	Opened	18.4.1909
***	Closed	16.5.1971
Charfield South SB	Opened	1.8.1897
***	Closed	18.4.1909
WICKWAR	Opened	8.7.1844
***	CG	10.6.1963
***	CP	4.1.1965
This station was provided under the terms of an Act or agreement.		
Wickwar Station SB	Open before	16.8.1877
Replacement box	Opened	4.10.1908
***	Closed	2.11.1965
Rangeworthy SB	Opened	25.1.1942
***	Closed	19.10.1969
Rangeworthy Colliery Sidings SB	Opened	4.1883–11.1885
***	Closed	19.5.1888
***	Removed	28.8.1893
Yate Colliery Sidings SB	Open before	1.11.1875
***	Closed	9.6.1888
***	Removed	28.8.1893
Yate Junction SB	Open before	16.8.1877
Replacement box named Yate Main Line Junction SB	Opened	9.3.1886
Box made a ground frame	... ...	19.10.1969
***	t.o.u.	10.5.1971

Thornbury branch
See page 267

Yate: main-line connection to and from Thornbury (and ground frame)	t.o.u.	18.12.1966
YATE	Opened	8.7.1844
***	CP	4.1.1965
***	CG	20.6.1966
New passenger station on approximately the same site	Opened	15.5.1989
Yate South Junction SB	Opened	28.11.1897
***	Closed	12.7.1903
***	Re-opened	1.3.1908
***	Closed	9.5.1971
Yate South Junction with the Great Western Railway	OG	9.3.1908
***	OP	2.11.1908
Yate South Jcn to Westerleigh West Jcn	RO(P)	5.5.1969
Yate South Jcn to Bristol Temple Meads	CP	27.12.1969
***	CP(off.)	29.12.1969
Yate South Jcn: Great Western flyover line	t.o.u.	18.1.1970
Yate South Jcn to Mangotsfield North Jcn	Singled	4.1.1970
Yate South Jcn to Bath Midland Bridge Road: one train working	Commenced	4.1.1970
***	Closed	31.5.1971
Yate South Jcn to Westerleigh Refuse Terminal	First train	19.11.1985

Coal Pit Heath Branch
Powers: Bristol and Gloucestershire Railway Act 1828
This was part of the original Bristol & Gloucestershire line.

Westerleigh North Jcn to Coal Pit Heath	OG by	17.7.1832
Working by locomotive power	By	9.6.1847
Branch ceased working on closure of the two remaining pits (Frog Lane, and Mayshill)	... ...	1949
Made a siding	... ...	21.11.1955
Westerleigh North Jcn: connection from the branch line to the down fast line and down goods lines	t.o.u.	27.10.1963
Westerleigh Junction SB	Open before	1866
Replacement box	Opened	....
Replacement box	Opened	28.1.1896
Replacement box	Opened	23.9.1900
Re-named Westerleigh North Junction SB	... ...	30.9.1900
***	Closed	22.2.1965
Westerleigh North Jcn to Parkfield Sidings North: first up goods line	Into use	30.9.1900
***	t.o.u.	....
Westerleigh North Jcn to Westerleigh South Jcn: first down goods line	Into use	28.7.1901
***	t.o.u.	....
Westerleigh North Jcn to Westerleigh Down Sidings SB: second down goods line	Into use	28.7.1901
***	t.o.u.	22.2.1965
Westerleigh Up Sidings SB (not a block post)	Opened	30.9.1900
***	Closed	22.2.1965
WESTERLEIGH UP SIDINGS	Into use	....
Additional and extended sidings	Into use	1942
***	t.o.u.	22.2.1965
Westerleigh Up Sidings to Parkfield Sidings North: second up goods line	Into use	30.9.1900
***	t.o.u.	22.2.1965
Westerleigh Down Sidings SB (not a block post)	Opened	28.7.1901
***	Closed	22.2.1965

WESTERLEIGH DOWN SIDINGS	Into use	7.8.1901
Additional and extended sidings	Into use	1942
***	t.o.u.	22.2.1965
Parkfield Colliery Sidings to Bristol: broad-gauge trains	Ceased	16.1.1882
Line made narrow-gauge only	... ...	1.2.1882
Parkfield Colliery Sidings SB	Open before	16.8.1877
Re-named Parkfield Colliery Sidings North SB	... ...	12.1888-8.1893
Replacement box	Opened	19.8.1900
Re-named Westerleigh South Junction SB	... ...	30.9.1900
***	Closed	22.2.1965
Brandy Bottom Sidings SB	Opened	1861
Re-named Parkfield Colliery Sidings South SB	... ...	....
Replacement box	Opened	....
***	Closed	10.12.1899
Shortwood Sidings SB	Opened	1865-1872
Replacement box	Opened	9.11.1890
***	Closed	22.2.1965
Mangotsfield North Junction SB	Opened	1869
Replacement box	Opened	3.11.1889
***	Re-framed	16.1.1921
***	Closed	4.1.1970
Keynsham Jcn re-named Mangotsfield North Jcn	... ...	4.8.1869 ?
Mangotsfield North Jcn to Lawrence Hill GF	Closed	3.1.1970 ?
***	Closed	4.1.1970 ?

Bath branch
See page 268

MANGOTSFIELD	Opened	1.5.1845 *
Replacement passenger station 40 chains to the south	Opened	4.8.1869 *
***	CG	10.6.1963
***	CP	7.3.1966
Mangotsfield South Junction SB	Opened	1869
Re-named Mangotsfield Station Junction SB	... ...	29.10.1877
***	Re-framed	29.3.1914
Replacement box	Opened	5.11.1922
***	Burnt out	22.1.1967
Mangotsfield Stone Siding SB	Opened	10.12.1877
Replacement box	Opened	8.12.1895
Box closed and semaphore IBS provided in lieu	... ...	21.7.1935
***	t.o.u.	....
STAPLE HILL	OP	1.11.1888
***	CP(All)	7.3.1966
FISHPONDS	OP	....
***	CP(All)	1.9.1850
FISH PONDS	Opened	3.1866
Altered to STAPLETON	... ...	1.4.1866
Altered to FISH PONDS	... ...	1.1.1867
***	OM before	1872
***	OG	1879
FISH PONDS altered to FISHPONDS	... ...	1.5.1939 ?
Down back platform bay line	t.o.u.	26.11.1961
***	CG	13.12.1965
***	CP	7.3.1966
Fishponds Station SB	Open before	16.8.1877
Replacement box	Opened	19.1.1896
***	Re-framed	15.10.1905
***	Closed	12.5.1968
Kingswood Junction SB	Opened	c.10.1874
Replacement box	Opened	12.6.1892
***	Raised	26.6.1904
***	Closed	14.6.1965

Bristol First Junction Line
See page 270

Kingswood Colliery branch, with the main-line connections	t.o.u.	25.10.1954
Wagon Works Siding SB	Opened	c.1867
Re-named Wagon Works Junction SB	By	16.8.1877
Replacement box	Opened	22.5.1892
Re-named Wagon Works Siding SB	......	c.9.1897
Box closed and ground frame provided in lieu	... ...	10.9.1911
***	t.o.u.	20.11.1955

Bristol Second Junction Line

Powers: Great Western and Midland Railway Companies (Clifton & Bristol) Act 1871

Wagon Works Jcn to Easton Road Jcn (Great Western Railway)	Inspected	28.5.1879
***	OG	19.5.1880
***	OP	1.9.1885
***	CP	1.10.1886
***	t.o.u.	12.9.1897

Lawrence Hill GF to Bristol East made a siding	... ...	4.1.1970
Lawrence Hill GF to Bristol East	t.o.u.	13.9.1974
The points at Lawrence Hill were damaged in a derailment on 13 September 1974, cutting access to this section from the north. The line was severed at 129 1/2 miles on 22 November 1977 and the section between the junction and the cut was officially closed.		
Lawrence Hill Junction SB	Open before	1858
Replacement box	Opened	....
Replacement box	Opened	29.3.1908
***	Closed	28.7.1968
Bristol engine shed	Opened	....
***	Replaced	1873
***	Closed	14.10.1965
Engine House Bridge SB	Open before	1858
Re-named Old Engine Shed SB	... ...	....
***	Closed	4.1883-11.1885
Ehgine Shed Sidings SB	Opened	4.1883-11.1885
Replacement box	Opened	15.12.1895
***	Raised	17.3.1901
***	Closed	14.5.1967
Bristol East SB (Great Western box): replacement box	Opened	29.11.1935
***	Closed	9.3.1970
Bristol Station "C" SB	Opened	5.5.1878
Box re-framed and re-named Bristol Old Station SB	... ...	c.10.1891
***	Closed	19.12.1965
Bristol Power Signal Box	Opened	9.3.1970
2a. Charfield to Yate South Jcn	Into use	18-20.10.1969
2b. Mangotsfield North Jcn to Lawrence Hill GF	Closed	3-4.1.1970
2c. Yate South Jcn to Westerleigh Jcn, with new layout	Into use	17-18.1.1970
TEMPLE MEADS: station made joint	... ...	1.1.1878
Old station	CP(All)	6.9.1965
***	Closed	22.2.1970 ?
***	Recovered	1966

Bristol St Philip's Station Branch

Lawrence Hill Jcn to Barrow Lane SB: up & down goods line redesignated a through siding	... ...	25.9.1949
Lawrence Hill Jcn to Bristol St Philip's	CP	21.9.1953
All signalling removed, all points made hand-worked, single goods line re-named branch siding	... ...	8.11.1964
Lawrence Hill Jcn to Bristol Midland Road	Closed	1.3.1967 ?
	<u>or</u>	1.4.1967 ?
All sidings were taken out of use on the date of closure, leaving only the line running through from Barrow Lane Junction to Avonside Wharf.		
Bristol Goods Junction SB	Open before	16.8.1877
***	Closed	4.1883-11.1885
Barrow Lane Junction SB	Opened	4.1888-11.1893
Replacement box	Opened	15.12.1912
***	Closed	1.8.1966
St Philip's SB	Opened	1870 ?
***	Re-framed	20.11.1905
***	Repaired	12.11.1911
Replacement box	Opened	14.6.1921
***	Closed	8.11.1964
ST PHILIP'S GOODS DEPOT	Opened by	1.12.1858 *
Altered to MIDLAND ROAD GOODS DEPOT	... ...	15.9.1952
***	Closed	1.4.1967
ST PHILIP'S	OP	2.5.1870
Station made "closed" for tickets	... ...	30.1.1928
***	CP(All)	21.9.1953
Bristol St Philip's: line designated goods line	... ...	6.12.1953

Avon Street Wharf Branch

Powers: Bristol and Gloucestershire Railway Act 1828, Bristol and Gloucester Railway Act 1839, Midland Railway (Additional Powers) Act 1890

AVON STREET WHARF (also: LOWER WHARF), and branch	Opened	6.8.1835
***	Closed	....
This was the original Bristol depot of the Bristol & Gloucestershire at Cuckold's Pill in the Floating Harbour.		

King's Wharf

KING'S WHARF came into Midland possession	... ...	12.1897

GLOUCESTER OLD DOCKS BRANCH or HIGH ORCHARD BRANCH

Powers: Birmingham and Gloucester Railway Act 1845

Tramway Jcn to High Orchard Yard/Albion Crossing	Opened	1848
Made a siding	... ...	21.9.1957
***	Closed	1.10.1971
Southgate Street Crossing SB	Opened	....
Replacement box	Opened	5.7.1904
***	Closed	21.9.1957

GLOUCESTER NEW DOCKS BRANCH or TUFFLEY BRANCH

Powers: Midland Railway Act 1893

Tuffley Jcn to Gloucester New Docks	OG	24.5.1900

This branch, also known as the Tuffley branch or the Hempste(a)d branch, was worked by train staff without tickets.

Tuffley Jcn to Hempstead gas works siding	Closed	14.1.1971
Gas works siding to canal bridge	Closed	1969
Canal Bridge SB	Opened	24.5.1900
***	Closed by	21.5.1938
Branch severed at the canal	By	21.5.1938

Hempste(a)d Wharf Branch

Hempste(a)d Wharf line	OG	....
Made a siding	... ...	11.8.1968
***	t.o.u.	....
HEMPSTE(A)D WHARF	Closed	1.8.1967

NAILSWORTH AND STROUD BRANCHES

Stonehouse & Nailsworth

Powers: Stonehouse and Nailsworth Railway Act 1863

The line was worked by the Midland under lease from its opening. The company was vested in the Midland by Act of 1878 with effect from 1 July 1878, being dissolved under the terms of the Midland Railway Act 1886.

Stonehouse to Nailsworth	OG	1.2.1867
***	OP	4.2.1867
***	CP	16.6.1947

Working was by train staff without tickets prior to the installation of the block telegraph between Stonehouse and Dudbridge in 1885.

Stonehouse Bristol Road to Nailsworth	C.Tfc	1.6.1966
Made a siding	... ...	4.12.1966
Stonehouse Wharf SB	Open before	16.8.1877
Box closed and ground frame provided in lieu	... ...	....
***	Recovered	7.9.1958
STONEHOUSE WHARF	Opened	....
***	Closed	8.10.1955
RYEFORD	OG	1.2.1867
***	OP	4.2.1867
***	CP	16.6.1947
***	CG	1.6.1964
Ryeford Station SB	Opened	1885
Replacement box	Opened	22.1.1924
Box closed and two ground frames provided in lieu	... ...	7.9.1958
Dudbridge Sidings SB	Opened	1885
Replacement box	Opened	1.1.1924
***	Closed	7.12.1957
DUDBRIDGE FOR STROUD	OG	1.2.1867
***	OP	4.2.1867
Up platform brought into use and down platform lengthened	... ...	7.1885
Altered to DUDBRIDGE	... ...	1.7.1886 *
***	CP	16.6.1947
***	CG	1.6.1966
Dudbridge station made the staff station (with hand-worked points) for the lines to Nailsworth and to Stroud	... ...	7.12.1957
Dudbridge Junction SB	Opened	1885
Replacement box	Opened	15.1.1924
***	Closed	7.12.1957

Stroud Branch

Powers: Midland Railway (Additional Powers) Act 1880,
Midland Railway (Additional Powers) Act 1882 (at Stroud)

Dudbridge to Stroud	OG	16.11.1885
***	OP	1.7.1886
***	CP	1.1.1917
***	RO(P)	....
***	CP	16.6.1947
***	Closed	1.6.1966
The Stroud branch was worked by train staff.		
STROUD	OG	16.11.1885
***	OP	1.7.1886
***	CP	16.6.1947
***	CG	1.6.1966
This station was briefly closed during January 1917.		
Stroud engine shed	Opened	....
***	Closed	....
WOODCHESTER	OG	1.2.1867
***	OP	1.7.1867
***	CP	16.6.1947
***	CG	1.6.1964
Nailsworth Station SB	Open before	1.11.1875
Box closed and ground frame provided in lieu	... ...	13.7.1886
***	Recovered	7.9.1958
Nailsworth: connections leading to the former passenger station	t.o.u.	13.7.1964
NAILSWORTH	OG	1.2.1867
***	OP	4.2.1867
***	CP	16.6.1947
***	CG	1.6.1966
Nailsworth engine shed	Opened	1867
***	Closed by	11.1895

DURSLEY & MIDLAND JUNCTION RAILWAY

The Dursley & Midland Junction Railway was incorporated in 1855, to be worked by the Midland. Working was by a contractor between September 1857 and April 1858, when the Dursley company began to work the line itself. The Midland took over the locomotive to work the line in May 1861. The Dursley company was vested in the Midland from October 1861 by Act of that year, the legal transfer being on 1 January 1861.

Dursley Jcn to Dursley	OG	25.8.1856
***	OP	17.9.1856
***	CP	10.9.1962
Made a siding	... ...	13.10.1968
The branch was worked by train staff without tickets.		
Dursley Jcn to Lister's Siding GF	Closed	13.7.1970
Cam Station SB	Open before	16.8.1877
***	Closed	12.1888-8.1893
Cam and Dursley are named in a list of "signal posts" returned to the Board of Trade in November 1880, but there may have been no actual signalbox structures.		
CAM	OG	25.8.1856
***	OP	17.9.1856
***	CP	10.9.1962
***	CG	12.8.1963
Line curtailed by 350 yards (Lister's Siding GF to Dursley)	... ...	27.7.1968
Dursley engine shed	Opened	1856
***	Closed	10.9.1962
This shed was an earlier building bought by the railway in 1856.		
Dursley Station SB	Open before	16.8.1877
***	Closed	12.1888-8.1893
DURSLEY	OG	25.8.1856
***	OP	17.9.1856
***	CP	10.9.1962
***	CG	1.11.1966

SEVERN & WYE AREA

The Severn & Wye, the Severn Bridge line, and the Midland Berkeley branch were made joint Midland and Great Western lines by Act of 1894. The Severn & Wye continued under its own management until 1 July 1895.

Between Berkeley Road Junction and Sharpness Docks Goods Station the Great Western possessed running powers for all traffic over the Midland line.

Between 1 July 1894 and 1906 all signalling on the joint lines was maintained by the Great Western company and it was during this period that the block system was introduced on the lines beyond Sharpness. from 1 January 1906 the Midland maintained the joint lines from Berkeley Road Junction to near Coleford Branch Junction, together with the loop line. Responsibility passed back to the Great Western in 1923.

Berkeley branch

Powers: Midland Railway (Additional Powers) Act 1872

Berkeley Road to Sharpness Docks	OG	2.8.1875
***	OP	1.8.1876
***	CP	2.11.1964
Berkeley Road to Sharpness: block telegraph system	Installed	1876
Berkeley Road Jcn to Sharpness South SB	Singled	26.7.1931
One engine in steam working replaced electric train token working	... ...	9.5.1965
Line made a siding	... ...	13.10.1968
Berkeley Loop Junction SB	Opened	29.11.1904
***	Closed	27.1.1963
***	Recovered	7.7.1963

Berkeley Loop (Great Western Railway)

Berkeley Loop Jcn to Berkeley South Jcn	OG	9.3.1908
***	Closed	27.1.1963
***	Recovered	7.7.1963
Berkeley Station SB	Opened	1876
***	Closed	26.7.1931
BERKELEY	OP&G	1.8.1876
***	CP	2.11.1964
***	CG	1.11.1966
Oldminster Junction SB	Opened	....
***	Closed by	1920

Oldminster Sidings

Powers: --

Oldminster Jcn to Sharpness South Jcn: Oldminster Sidings lines	Into use	....
Sharpness: goods avoiding lines through Oldminster Sidings made running lines instead of sidings	... ...	1.1.1901
Oldminster Sidings	t.o.u.	19.5.1964
OLDMINSTER WHARF	Opened	....
***	Closed	19.5.1964
Sharpness Station SB	Opened	1876
Re-named Sharpness Docks Junction SB	... ...	1879
Re-named Sharpness South Junction SB	... ...	....
***	Alt.levers	11.2.1890
Replacement box 150 yards nearer Sharpness	Opened	25.1.1914
***	Closed	9.5.1965
SHARPNESS	OG	2.8.1875
***	OP	1.8.1876
***	CP	16.10.1879
See below for the replacement station on the Severn Bridge line.		
SHARPNESS DOCKS GOODS STATION	Closed	3.1.1966

Severn Bridge Railway

Powers: Severn Bridge Railway Act 1872

Sharpness South Jcn to Lydney Tin Works Jcn	O.Formal	17.10.1879
***	OP&G	20.10.1879
***	CP	27.10.1960
A bonus mileage (3 miles additional) was allowed for the Severn bridge (actual length 55 chains) by Act of 1872.		
Sharpness South Jcn: junction to 3m 72ch	Singled	22.5.1965
Sharpness South Jcn to Sharpness North GF	Closed or	2.11.1964 ....
***	Recovered	5.1967
Sharpness South Jcn (3m 72ch) to Sharpness North GF	Singled	9.1956
Sharpness South SB	Opened	....
***	Closed	1903
SHARPNESS: replacement passenger station	Opened	16.10.1879
Revised layout	Into use	1903
***	CP	2.11.1964
Sharpness Docks Station SB	Opened	c.10.1879
***	Closed	27.10.1957
Sharpness East to Severn Bridge: working by train tablet in place of working by train staff with tickets	Commenced	19.8.1889

Sharness Dock North Branch		
Sharpness Dock North Branch	Opened	20.10.1879
Sharpness North GF to Sharpness Docks	Off. closed	2.11.1964
***	Recovered	5.1967
SHARPNESS DOCKS GOODS STATION	Closed	3.1.1966
Canal Swing Bridge SB	Opened	17.10.1879 ?
Ceased to signal trains	... ...	26.10.1960
Sharpness North GF to Severn Bridge	Off.closed	2.11.1964
Severn Bridge put out of action	... ...	25.10.1960
SEVERN BRIDGE	OP&G	20.10.1879
Station loop	Lengthened	1907
***	CG	4.3.1957
***	CP	26.10.1960
Severn Bridge Station SB	Opened	17.10.1879 ?
Replacement box	Opened	12.11.1911
Ceased to signal trains	... ...	26.10.1960
Lydney Junction "A" SB	Opened	1879
Box re-named Otter's Pool Junction SB and the junction with the Great Western Railway named Otter's Pool Jcn	... ...	1905
Replacement box	Opened	1.11.1914
***	Closed	14.2.1965
Otter's Pool Jcn: double junction	t.o.u.	8.3.1964
Lydney East Loop		
Powers: No Construction Powers		
Lydney Junction to Lydney Jcn with the Great Western Railway (Lydney East Loop)	Opened	20.10.1879
***	t.o.u.	8.3.1964
Lydney West Loop		
Powers: --		
Lydney Jcn with the Great Western Railway to Junction of West Loop (Lydney West [Mineral] Loop)	Opened	....
Lydney Avoiding Line treated as a running line instead of a siding	... ...	1.1.1901
Otter's Pool Jcn to Lydney Goods Yard SB	t.o.u.	14.2.1965
LYDNEY JUNCTION	OP&G	20.10.1879
***	CG	21.5.1955
***	CP	26.10.1960
Lydney to Cinderford and Coleford	CP	8.7.1929
Lydney Yard SB	Opened	1879 ?
Replacement box	Opened	16.12.1906
***	Closed	28.6.1960

Severn & Wye Railway

The basic Act for the Severn & Wye tramway system was the Lydney and Lidbrook Railway Act 1809, and the Acts of 1810 and 1853 referred to the tramways only. The Severn and Wye Railway and Canal Act 1869 was the basic Act for the railways, authorising retrospectively the existing broad-gauge line and giving additional powers, including abandonment of tramways only after the substitution of a new railway line.

Powers: Severn and Wye Railway and Canal Act 1810
(Lydney Harbour to Upper Forge)
Severn and Wye Railway and Canal Act 1853
(Lydney Harbour to Lydney Town Station)
Lydney and Lidbrook Railway Act 1809
(Upper Forge to Coleford Branch Junction)
Severn and Wye Railway and Canal Act 1853
(Upper Forge to Loop Line Junction)
Severn and Wye Railway and Canal Act 1853,
and Severn and Wye Railway and Canal Act 1869
(Loop Line Junction to Whitecroft Viaduct)

Lydney Jcn with the Great Western Railway to Wimberry Jcn (Speech House Road), and Wimberry branch: broad-gauge line alongside the tramroad	Into use	19.4.1869
Conversion to narrow gauge	OG	5.1872
Lydney Docks branch: south-side line to the outer and north-side line to the upper dock	OG	5.1872
Lower dock sidings	t.o.u.	18.11.1960
South-side line	Recovered by	1962
North-side line, and line from far side of Lydney Crossing	Closed	25.8.1963
Level crossing of the South Wales main line	Removed	9.1963
LYDNEY JUNCTION	OP	23.9.1875
***	CP(All)	16.10.1879

This first Lydney Junction station was a terminal, at right-angles to the Great Western station. For the replacement station on the line of the Severn Bridge Railway, see above.

Lydney Junction to Drybrook Road	OP	23.9.1875
Lydney to Parkend re-opened by the Dean Forest Railway	... ...	....
Lydney Engine Shed	Opened	....
***	Closed	3.1964
Lydney Engine Shed Junction SB	Opened	1889-1898
Replacement box	Opened	24.3.1918
***	Closed	2.10.1967
Engine Shed Jcn to Lydney Town SB: line singled in stages	Between &	14.2.1965 2.10.1967
LYDNEY TOWN	OG	....
***	OP	23.9.1875
***	CP	26.10.1960
***	CG	1.8.1967
Lydney Town to Coleford, Cinderford, and Lydbrook Junction	CP	8.7.1929
Lydney Town Station SB	Opened	1877-1889
Replacement box	Opened	1897
Box made a ground frame	... ...	2.10.1967
***	t.o.u.	16.7.1969
Lydney Town: main lines at north end slued to new position	... ...	6.7.1896
Lydney to Parkend: one engine in steam working	Commenced	2.10.1967
Tufts Junction SB	Opened	1875
Replacement box	Opened	1897
***	Re-framed	10.10.1948
***	Closed	2.10.1967
Oakwood Branch		
Powers: Severn and Way Railway and Canal Act 1872		
Tufts Jcn to Park Hill Level	Opened	1874
Extension to Dyke's (or Whitecroft) Level	... ...	1876
Extension to Parkgutter pit (Princess Royal Colliery Company)	... ...	1890-1891
Tufts Jcn to Princess Royal Colliery Empty Wagon Sidings	Tfc ceased	8.2.1965
***	Closed	17.5.1965
Mineral Loop Line		
Tufts North Jcn to Crump Meadow	OM	22.4.1872
Crump Meadow to Wimberry Jcn	OM	6.1872
Tufts Jcn to Pillowell	Closed	30.11.1957
***	Recovered	4.10.1959
Pillowell to Acorn Patch	Closed	13.3.1951
Moseley Green tunnel	Closed	1.4.1942
Moseley Green tunnel to Blakeney Road bridge	Recovered by	7.1943
***	Re-opened	29.12.1943
Acorn Patch to Drybrook Road	Last train	16.6.1953
***	Recovered	20.4.1958
Tufts Jcn to Parkend: electric train tablet block working in place of working by train staff and tickets	Introduced	19.8.1889
Down line	t.o.u.	30.11.1930
Tufts Jcn to Whitecroft	Doubled	6.1896
Siding (the former down line)	t.o.u.	30.6.1964
WHITECROFT	OP	23.9.1875
***	OG	1890
***	CP	8.7.1929
***	CG	1.8.1967
Whitecroft SB	Opened	1897 ?
Box made a ground frame	... ...	30.11.1930
***	t.o.u.	2.10.1967 ?
Whitecroft to Coleford Branch Jcn	Doubled	5.1897
Parkend Goods Station Branch		
Powers: No Construction Powers		
Parkend Goods branch	OG	1869
PARKEND GOODS DEPOT	OG	....
***	CG	1.8.1967
This goods station was known earlier as Parkend Marsh Sidings.		
PARKEND	OP	23.9.1875
***	CP	8.7.1929
Parkend SB	Open before	1889
Replacement box	Opened	1897 ?
***	Closed	2.10.1967
Parkend to Coleford Jcn (and through to Whitecliffe Sidings)	C.Tfc	4.8.1967
***	Closed	2.10.1967
Travellers' Rest Crossing SB	Opened	1897 ?
***	Closed	2.10.1967

Parkend Royal Colliery Branch		
Powers: No powers (?)		
Coleford Branch Junction to Parkend Royal Colliery	Opened	4.1869 ?
Coleford Branch Jcn to Traveller's Rest LC	Closed	16.5.1965
Traveller's Rest LC to 13m 33ch	Closed	19.5.1940
The section between the junction connection and the level crossing remained until 16 May 1965.		
13m 33ch to Parkend Royal Colliery	Tfc. ceased	1928
COLEFORD JUNCTION	OP(NA)	9.1878 ?
***	CP	1.11.1879 ?*
Coleford Branch Junction SB	Opened	1879 ?
***	Re-framed	c.1900
Replacement box	Opened	1.12.1925
***	Closed	2.10.1967
Coleford Branch		
Powers: Severn and Wye Railway and Canal Act 1872		
Coleford Jcn to Coleford	OG	19.7.1875
***	OP	9.12.1875
***	CP	8.7.1929
**	Last train	4.8.1967
***	Closed	2.10.1967
MILKWALL	OG	19.7.1875
***	OP	9.12.1875
***	CP	8.7.1929
***	CG	1.5.1944
Sling Branch		
Milkwall to Sling	OG	3.1876 ?
***	Closed	2.10.1967
Coleford: sidings connection with the Great Western Railway	OG	7.12.1885
Direct connection with the Great Western Railway	OG	21.10.1951
COLEFORD	OG	19.7.1875
***	OP	9.12.1875
***	CP	8.7.1929
***	CG	1.8.1967
Coleford Jcn to Speech House Road	Closed	12.8.1963
***	Lifted	25.7.1964
The last train actually ran the day after closure.		
SPEECH HOUSE ROAD	OG	....
***	OP	23.9.1875
***	CP	8.7.1929
***	CG	12.8.1963
Speech House Road SB	Opened	....
Replacement box	Opened	c.1893
***	Closed	....
Speech House Road to Serridge Jcn (and through to Mierystock)	Closed	21.11.1960
***	Recovered	2.1962
Severn & Wye line north of Speech House Road, and Wimberry branch	t.o.u.	8.11.1961
Wimberry Branch		
Wimberry Jcn to Wimberry	OG	....
***	Tfc ceased	9.1960
***	Last train	21.11.1960
***	Recovered	2.1962
Wimberry branch extended from junction at 15m_12ch to Speech House station at 14m_70ch	... ...	30.10.1912
Wimberry Jcn to Bilson North and South Junctions with the Great Western Railway	OG	15.9.1873
SERRIDGE PLATFORM	OP(NA)	9.1878 *
***	CP	1.11.1879 *
Serridge Junction SB	Opened	....
Box closed and ground frame provided in lieu	... ...	12.12.1951
***	t.o.u.	21.11.1960
Lydbrook Branch		
Serridge Jcn to Lydbrook Jcn (with the Great Western Railway)	OG	26.8.1874
***	OP	23.9.1875
***	CP	8.7.1929
Serridge Jcn to Mierystock	Last train	13.5.1961
***	Closed	8.11.1961
Mierystock to Lydbrook Jcn	Closed	30.1.1956
Upper Lydbrook South SB	Opened	....
Upper Lydbrook South SB and Upper Lydbrook North SB closed and replacement Lydbrook Station SB opened	... ...	10.1892
Replacement box	Opened	1912
Box made Lydbrook South GF and new Lydbrook North GF brought into use	... ...	1929

UPPER LYDBROOK	OG	26.8.1974
***	OP	23.9.1875
***	CP	8.7.1929
***	CG	30.1.1956
Upper Lydbrook North SB	Opened	....
***	Closed	10.1892
LOWER LYDBROOK	OP	23.9.1875
***	CP(All)	1.4.1903
Lower Lydbrook SB	Opened	....
Box made Lower Lydbrook North GF and new Lower Lydbrook South GF brought into use	... ...	....
***	t.o.u.	1938
LYDBROOK JUNCTION (Great Western station)	Opened	4.8.1873 ?
***	CP	5.1.1959
***	CG	2.11.1964
Trafalgar Colliery SB	Opened	....
Box closed and the ground frame on Drybrook Road platform converted into Drybrook Road SB	... ...	10.1892
Replacement signalbox named Drybrook Road Junction SB	Opened	....
Box made a ground frame	... ...	17.5.1927
***	t.o.u.	....
DRYBROOK ROAD	OG	....
***	OP	23.9.1875
***	CP	8.7.1929
***	CG	10.1949
Drybrook Road SB (at the level crossing)	Open	1892 ?
Drybrook Road to Cinderford	OP	9.12.1875 ?
Drybrook Road to Bilson Platform	OP	9.1876
Drybrook Road to Bilson South Jcn	Closed	9.12.1951
***	Last train	16.6.1953
BILSON PLATFORM	OP	9.1876
***	CP(All)	5.8.1878

Cinderford Extension Line

Powers: --

Laymoor Jcn to Cinderford new station	Opened	2.7.1900
Laymoor Jcn to Cinderford Jcn	Closed	9.12.1951
Cinderford Junction SB	Opened	29.3.1908
Box closed and line severed at the junction	Closed	31.12.1950

Cinderford Curve (Great Western Railway)

Powers: Great Western Railway (General Powers) Act 1909

Cinderford Jcn to Bilson Jcn	Opened	6.4.1908

Between Cinderford Junction and Cinderford joint passenger station the Great Western Railway possessed running powers for passenger traffic.

Cinderford Jcn to Cinderford	Closed	1.8.1967
***	Last train	3.8.1967
***	Recovered	1969
Cinderford Station SB	Opened	....
Box closed and two ground frames provided in lieu	... ...	17.5.1927
CINDERFORD: replacement station	OP&G	2.7.1900
Goods depot altered to CINDERFORD TOWN	By	1.8.1952
***	CP	3.11.1958
***	CG	1.8.1967
Cinderford South Loop Jcn to Bilson North Jcn	Closed	9.12.1951
***	Recovered	23.2.1958
CINDERFORD (located on the Bilson North Curve)	Opened	5.8.1878
***	Closed	2.7.1900

THORNBURY BRANCH

Powers: Midland Railway (Bath and Thornbury) Lines Act 1864

Yate to Iron Acton (for Frampton Cotterell)	OM by	8.1868
Iron Acton to Tytherington	OM by	8.1869
Yate to Thornbury	OP&G	2.9.1872
***	CP	19.6.1944
***	Off. closed	30.9.1967
***	Last Train	24.11.1967

The branch was worked by train staff between Yate and Iron Acton and by one engine in steam between Iron Acton and Thornbury until 1876-7, after which the whole branch was worked by train staff only.

Yate to Tytherington Quarry	Re-opened	3.7.1972
Key token operation in place of one train working	Commenced	30.11.1981
Yate Main Line Jcn: loop line between the junction and Yate Single Line Jcn and siding alongside the loop line between the same points extension about 200 yards towards Thornbury	Into use	8.10.1905

Yate Single Line Junction SB	Opened	9.3.1886	
Replacement box	Opened	8.10.1905	
***	Closed	14.11.1926	
Iron Acton Station SB	Open before	16.8.1877	
***	Re-framed	26.6.1907	
***	Closed	19.6.1928	
IRON ACTON	OP	2.9.1872	
***	OG	1880	
***	CP	19.6.1944	
***	CG	10.6.1963	

Frampton Cotterell branch

Powers: Midland Railway (New Lines and Additional Powers) Act 1865

Iron Acton to Frampton Cotterell	Opened by	8.1868	
***	Closed by	1.2.1877	*

Authorisation for the closure of the branch was given on 15 April 1878 and the track was recovered either before 1881 or in 1892.

Tytherington Quarry to Thornbury: line retained only for rounding	... ...	20.6.1966	
***	Last train	24.11.1967	
Tytherington SB	Open before	16.8.1877	
***	Closed	....	

This location is named in a list of "signal posts" returned to the Board of Trade in November 1880, but there may have been no actual signalbox structure.

TYTHERINGTON	OP	2.9.1872	
***	OG	1875	
***	CP	19.6.1944	
***	CG	10.6.1963	
THORNBURY	OP&G	2.9.1872	
***	CP	19.6.1944	
***	CG	20.6.1966	
Thornbury SB	Open before	16.8.1877	
***	Closed	26.10.1886	
Thornbury engine shed	Opened	1872	
***	Closed	19.6.1944	

BATH BRANCH

Powers: Midland Railway (Bath and Thornbury) Lines Act 1864
(There were no construction powers for the Rodway Hill Curve which formed that part of the main line between Mangotsfield South Junction (later Station Junction) and Mangotsfield East Junction (later South Junction).

Mangotsfield South Jcn to Bath (temporary station)	OP	4.8.1869	
***	OG	1.9.1869	
***	CP	7.3.1966	
Mangotsfield Junctions to Bath: block telegraph system	Installed	1869-1872	
Mangotsfield South Junction re-named Mangotsfield Station Junction	... ...	....	
Mangotsfield Station Jcn to Mangotsfield South Jcn	Closed	7.3.1966	
***	t.o.u.	22.1.1967	?
	or	29.1.1967	?

Mangotsfield North Curve

Mangotsfield North Jcn to Mangotsfield East Jcn	OG	1.7.1873	*
***	OP	1.7.1891	*
***	CP	1.1.1917	*
***	RO(P)	1.5.1919	*
***	CP	9.1939	
***	RO(P) by	5.1941	*
***	CP by	8.1944	*
***	RO(P) by	3.1945	*
***	CP	10.9.1962	
Line singled and worked one engine in steam	... ...	5.5.1968	
***	Closed	31.5.1971	

Mangotsfield East Junction SB	Opened	1869	
Re-named Mangotsfield South Junction SB	... ...	29.10.1877	
Replacement box	Opened	29.11.1896	
***	Closed	6.10.1935	
Mangotsfield South Jcn to Weston singled and worked one engine in steam from Mangotsfield North Junction	... ...	5.5.1968	
Mangotsfield South Jcn to Bath Midland Bridge Road	Closed	31.5.1971	
WARMLEY	OP	4.8.1869	
***	OG	1.9.1869	
***	CG	17.5.1965	
***	C.Coal & E.	5.1965	
***	CP	7.3.1966	

Warmley Station SB	Open before	16.8.1877
Replacement box	Opened	1.9.1918
Box made a ground frame	... ...	5.5.1968
***	t.o.u.	1.12.1968
OLDLAND COMMON HALT	OP/Pcls	2.12.1935
***	CP(All)	7.3.1966
Bitton Station SB	Open before	1.11.1875
Replacement box	Opened	29.4.1894
***	Closed	19.7.1965
BITTON	OP	4.8.1869
***	OG	1.9.1869
***	CG	5.7.1965
***	CP	7.3.1966
Boyd Avon SB opened and single-line working over Bridge No. 19 began	... ...	23.5.1937
Box closed and double-line working restored	... ...	25.7.1937
Box re-opened and single-line working resumed	... ...	3.10.1937
Box closed and double-line working restored	... ...	7.11.1937
Kelston Bridge SB opened and single-line working over Bridge No. 24 began	... ...	19.3.1939
Box closed and double-line working restored	... ...	11.6.1939
KELSTON FOR SALTFORD	OP	1.12.1869
***	CP(All)	1.1.1949
This station was provided under the terms of an Act or agreement.		
Kelston Station SB (not a block post, but used occasionally as such)	Opened	....
Replacement box adjacent to the ground frame on the down platform brought into use as a block post	... ...	30.5.1936
***	Closed	....
Newton SB opened and single-line working over Bridge No. 28 began	... ...	28.4.1935
Box closed and double-line working restored	... ...	28.7.1935
Rudmore Park SB opened and single-line working over Bridge No. 35 began	... ...	29.4.1934
Box closed and double-line working restored	... ...	2.9.1934
Weston Station SB	Open before	16.8.1877
***	Re-framed	14.5.1905
Replacement box	Opened	5.9.1920
***	Closed	5.5.1968
WESTON	OP	4.8.1869
***	OG	1.9.1869
Altered to WESTON (BATH)	... ...	1.10.1934
***	CP	21.9.1953
***	CG	29.11.1965
Weston to Bath up and down lines made sidings	... ...	12.9.1966
Bridge No. 40: single-line working between Weston and Bath Jcn	Commenced	3.5.1936
***	Ceased	26.7.1936
Bath Junction SB	Open before	16.8.1877
Replacement box	Opened	1.10.1911
Replacement box also taking over the work of the Somerset & Dorset Bath Single Line Junction SB	Opened	13.4.1924
***	Closed	12.9.1966
Bath Jcn with the Somerset & Dorset line	Opened	20.7.1874
***	Closed	30.11.1967
Between Bath Junction and Bath the Somerset & Dorset Railway possessed running powers over the Midland line.		
Bath Jcn to Bath Station SB: up goods line	Into use	4.1883-11.1885
***	t.o.u.	....

Bath Gas Works Branch

Powers: --

Bath gas works branch	Opened	1.9.1969
Bath gas works: production ceased	... ...	20.5.1971

Bath Riverside Branch

Powers: --

Branch to the river at Bladwells Yard	Opened	1887 ?
***	Closed	1922-1923
***	Recovered	c.1944
Bath engine shed	Opened	....
***	Closed	1928

Bath Station SB	Open before	1.11.1875
Replacement box	Opened	24.4.1892
***	Re-framed	1940
***	Closed	12.9.1966
BATH GOODS DEPOT	Opened	2.5.1870
Altered to MIDLAND BRIDGE ROAD GOODS DEPOT	... ...	18.6.1951
***	Closed	31.5.1971
Bath Midland Bridge Road (junction for depot) to Bath Green Park	Closed	7.3.1966 ?
	or	15.8.1966 ?
***	t.o.u.	12.9.1966

BATH (temporary station)	OP	4.8.1869
Permanent passenger station	Opened	7.5.1870
Altered to BATH GREEN PARK	... ...	18.6.1951
***	CP(All)	7.3.1966

The name Bath Queen Square, used by Bradshaw for many years, was never the official name of this station.

AVONMOUTH JOINT LINES

Clifton extension line

Powers: Great Western and Midland Railway Companies (Clifton and Bristol) Act 1871
Bristol Port Railway and Pier Company Act 1867

Kingswood Jcn to Ashley Hill Jcn (Midland First Junction Line)	OP	1.10.1874
***	OG	2.7.1877 ?
***	CP	1.1.1917 *
***	RO(P)	5.5.1919
***	Singled	30.3.1941
***	CP	31.3.1941
***	Re-doubled	....
***	Closed	14.6.1965

Between Kingswood Junction and Ashley Hill Junction the Great Western Railway possessed running powers for all traffic.

Kingswood Jcn to Clifton: block telegraph system	Installed	1874
Ashley Hill Jcn to Clifton Down	OG (GWR)	6.1874
***	OP	1.10.1874
***	OG (MR)	1.3.1875 *
Stapleton Road Gas Works SB	Opened	7.4.1895
***	Closed	14.6.1965
Ashley Hill Junction SB	Open before	16.8.1877
***	Re-framed	5.6.1904
Replacement box	Opened	10.5.1959
***	Closed	27.2.1966
(Narroways Hill Jcn to) Ashley Hill Jcn to Avonmouth Dock Jcn	Singled	18.10.1970
MONTPELIER	OG	6.1874 ?
***	OP	1.10.1874
***	OG (Mid.)	1.3.1875 *
***	CG	29.11.1965

Another source gives the dateof opening for passenger traffic as 1 March 1875 and for goods traffic as 1877.

Montpelier Station SB	Open before	16.8.1877
***	Re-framed	1.10.1899
Box closed and ground frame provided in lieu	... ...	10.5.1959
Redland Station SB	Opened	17.9.1899
***	Closed	21.6.1950
REDLAND	OP	12.4.1897
Clifton Down Temporary SB	Opened	1.1.1950
***	Closed	5.6.1950
Clifton Down: temporary single-line working on the down line	Commenced	1.1.1950
***	Ceased	25.5.1950
CLIFTON DOWN	OG (G.W.)	6.1874
***	OP	1.10.1874
***	OG (Mid.)	1.3.1875 *
***	CG	5.7.1965

Another source gives 1877 for the goods traffic opening.

Clifton Down Station SB	Open before	16.8.1877
***	Alt.levers	11.10.1914
***	Closed	18.10.1970
Clifton Down to Sneyd Park Jcn	OG	24.2.1877
Block telegraph system	Installed	1877
Clifton Tunnel West SB	Opened	20.5.1917
***	Closed	....
Clifton Tunnel West SB (second box)	Opened by	13.8.1924
***	Closed	....

Bristol Port, Railway & Pier

Working of the Bristol Port, Railway & Pier Company's line was taken over by the Midland and Great Western Railways jointly on 25 May 1871, and on 1 September 1890 the line became their joint property.

Powers: Bristol Port, Railway and Pier Act 1862,
Great Western Railway Act 1903 (Sneyd Park Junction & Avonmouth Widening)

Clifton to Avonmouth	OP	6.3.1865

CLIFTON	OP	6.3.1865
***	OG	....
Altered to HOTWELLS	... ...	1.9.1890
***	CG	1.9.1890
Station made "closed" for tickets	... ...	3.7.1917
***	CP(All)	19.9.1921
Hotwells SB	Opened	13.5.1917
***	Closed	14.10.1917
During the period when this signalbox was open the Hotwells branch was worked by electric train tablet block. At other times working was by train staff only.		
HOTWELLS HALT (on the west side of the tunnel)	OP	14.5.1917
***	CP(All)	3.7.1922
Hotwells to Sneyd Park Jcn	Closed	3.7.1922
Sneyd Park Junction SB	Open before	16.8.1877
Re-named Sneyd Park SB	... ...	1.2.1925
Box closed and Sea Mills IBS provided in lieu	... ...	26.5.1935
***	t.o.u.	....
Sneyd Park SB to Avonmouth Dock Jcn	Singled	18.10.1970
Sneyd Park Jcn to Shirehampton, and Shirehampton to Avonmouth Dock Jcn: electric train tablet block working in place of staff & ticket	Commenced	12.6.1892
Sneyd Park Jcn: junction with the Hotwells branch	Recovered	27.7.1924
Sneyd Park Jcn to Shirehampton	Doubled	6.1.1907
SEA MILLS	OP	6.3.1865
Horse Shoe Curve SB	Opened	14.2.1904
Box re-located 120 yards nearer Sneyd Park	... ...	20.11.1904
Box re-located 60 yards nearer Sneyd Park	... ...	3.9.1905
***	Closed	28.1.1906
Horse Shoe Point SB	Opened	22.4.1917
***	Closed	30.8.1924
Shirehampton Station SB	Open before	16.8.1877
Replacement box	Opened	13.8.1905
***	Re-framed	13.5.1906
Box closed and ground frame provided in lieu	... ...	18.10.1970
SHIREHAMPTON	OP	6.3.1865
***	OG	....
***	CG	29.11.1965
Shirehampton (Sea Mills end) to Avonmouth Dock	Doubled	13.5.1906
Crown Brickyard Crossing SB (not a block post)	Opened	16.2.1892
Replacement box	Opened	24.7.1904
***	Re-framed	14.2.1911
***	Made BP	28.2.1911
Re-named Avonmouth Dock Junction SB	... ...	14.5.1911
***	Closed	23.1.1988
Avonmouth Dock Junction SB (first box)	Opened	4.1883-11.1885
Replacement box	Opened	30.8.1903
Replacement box named Avonmouth Dock Sidings SB a little nearer Avonmouth Dock station	Opened	14.5.1911
***	Closed	19.1.1969
Avonmouth Dock Station SB	Opened	17.5.1903
***	Re-framed	4.12.1904
***	Moved	28.10.1917
***	Closed	19.1.1969
AVONMOUTH DOCK JOINT STATION	OP	1.9.1885
Line at back of platform into use as a passenger line	... ...	24.7.1904
New siding alongside back platform line	Into use	4.12.1904
Second siding from back platform line	Into use	16.7.1905
Station made "closed" for tickets	... ...	2.7.1917
New platform on the up side of the line	Into use	15.7.1918
Gloucester Road Crossing SB	Opened	....
Replacement box	Opened	25.6.1911
***	Closed	5.8.1967
AVONMOUTH DOCK (adjoining Gloucester Road level crossing)	CP	18.5.1903
Between Avonmouth Dock joint passenger station and St Andrew's Junction the Great Western Railway possessed running powers for "all traffic which has passed, or will pass over the Joint Line".		
AVONMOUTH DOCK	OG (MR)	7.1877
***	Enlarged	8.1904
Avonmouth Dock to Avonmouth Terminus	CP	1.10.1902
AVONMOUTH	OP	6.3.1865
***	CP	1.10.1902
Workmen's trains - final day of operation	... ...	15.5.1903
Avonmouth engine shed	Opened	1.1.1905
***	Closed	1924
Avonmouth Hotel and Pleasure Gardens (BPR&P)	Opened	10.4.1865
Avonmouth Pier (BPR&P)	Opened	3.6.1865

Construction of Avonmouth Dock	Commenced	26.8.1868
Avonmouth Dock	Opened	24.2.1877
It appears likely that during the construction of the dock a service was provided to an unadvertised halt - the navvies' platform - at the site of the works.		
Avonmouth Docks SB	Open before	16.8.1877
***	Closed	4.1883-11.1885
Avonmouth Terminus SB	Opened	4.1883-11.1885
***	Closed	17.5.1903

Avonmouth Docks

Powers: Bristol Docks and Railways Act 1901, Bristol Corporation Act 1902

King Edward Dock	Opened	9.9.1908
Line to St Andrew's Jcn	Opened	1905
Avonmouth Dock Jcn to Gloucester Road Jcn with the Great Western line from Pilning (using 47 chains of sidings laid in 1877)	OG	5.2.1900
Great Western Railway's Filton & Avonmouth line, with Avonmouth Dock station to St Andrew's Jcn connection to the Pilning line (joint)	Opened	9.5.1910

Between St Andrew's Junction and the Great Western junction with the dock lines the Midland Railway possessed certain powers: there were no separate powers for Midland traffic -- the Midland obtained powers only as partners with the Great Western in the Bristol Port & Pier Joint Railway and only for the traffic of the joint line.

TRACK DIAGRAMS
OF LINES COVERED
IN THE CHRONOLOGY

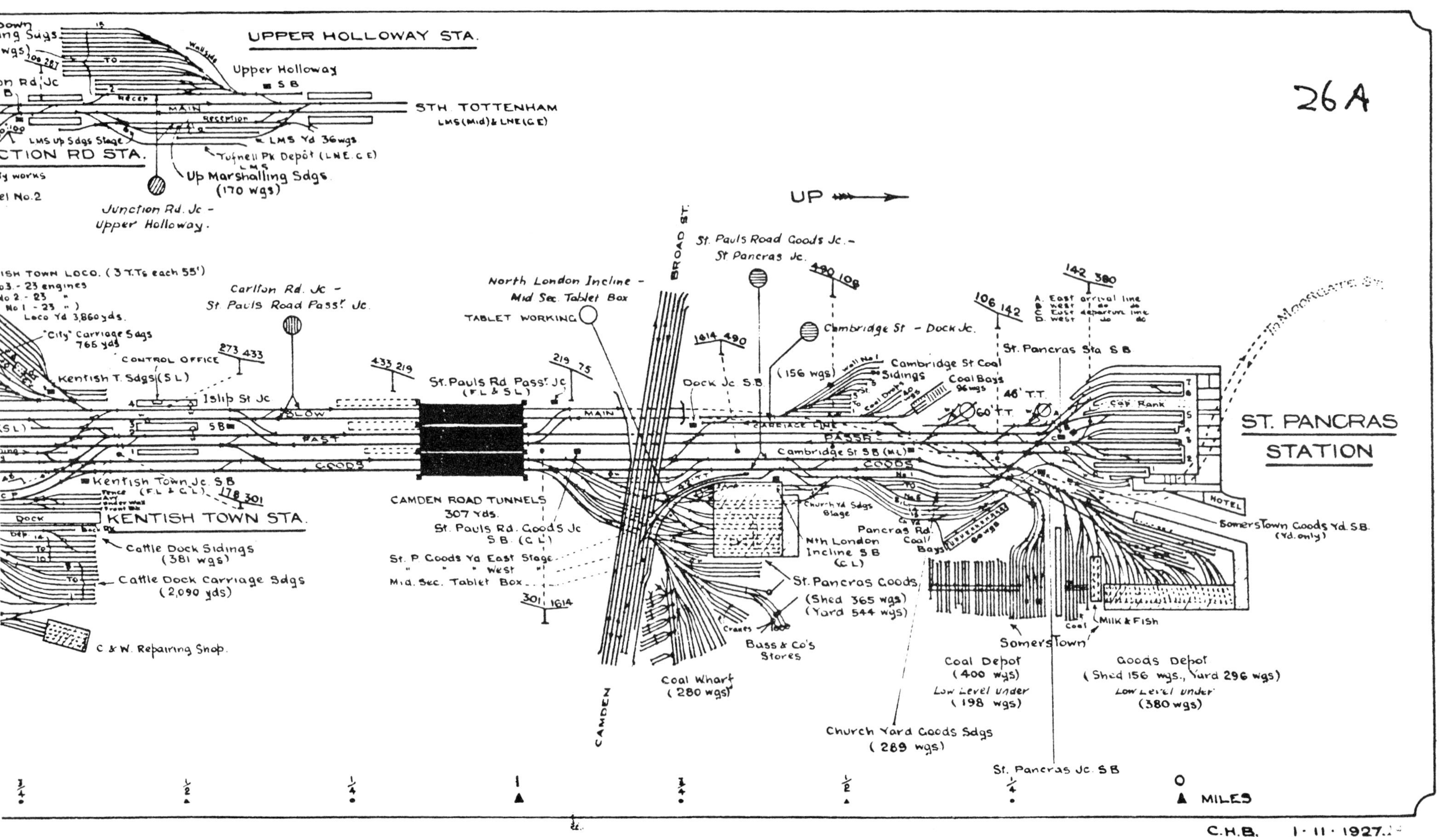
26A
UPPER HOLLOWAY STA.
Upper Holloway S B
STH. TOTTENHAM
LMS (Mid) & LNE (G E)
LMS Up Sdgs Stage
LMS Yd 36 wgs
Tufnell Pk Depôt (LNE. C.E) LMS
Up Marshalling Sdgs (170 wgs)
Junction Rd. Jc - Upper Holloway.
Carlton Rd. Jc - St Pauls Road Passr. Jc
"City" Carriage Sdgs 765 yds
CONTROL OFFICE
Kentish T. Sdgs (S L)
Islip St Jc
SLOW
FAST
GOODS
Kentish Town Jc. S B (F L & C L)
KENTISH TOWN STA.
Cattle Dock Sidings (381 wgs)
Cattle Dock Carriage Sdgs (2,090 yds)
C & W. Repairing Shop.
St. Pauls Rd Passr. Jc (F L & S L)
CAMDEN ROAD TUNNELS 307 Yds.
St. Pauls Rd. Goods Jc S B (C L)
St. P Goods Yd East Stage
" " " West "
Mid. Sec. Tablet Box
North London Incline - Mid Sec. Tablet Box
TABLET WORKING
MAIN
BROAD ST.
CAMDEN
UP
St. Pauls Road Goods Jc. - St Pancras Jc.
Dock Jc. S.B
(156 wgs)
Cambridge St - Dock Jc.
Cambridge St Coal Sidings
Coal Bays 96 wgs
CARRIAGE LINE
PASSR
Cambridge St. SB (ML)
GOODS
Church Yd Sdgs Stage
Nth London Incline S B (C L)
Pancras Rd. Coal Bays
St. Pancras Goods (Shed 365 wgs) (Yard 544 wgs)
Bass & Co's Stores
Coal Wharf (280 wgs)
Church Yard Goods Sdgs (289 wgs)
A. East arrival line
B. West do do
C. East departure line
D. West do do
St. Pancras Sta S B
46' T.T.
60' T.T.
Cab Rank
ST. PANCRAS STATION
HOTEL
SomersTown Goods Yd. S.B. (Yd. only)
Somers Town
Milk & Fish
Coal Depot (400 wgs) Low Level under (198 wgs)
Goods Depot (Shed 156 wgs., Yard 296 wgs) Low Level under (380 wgs)
St. Pancras Jc. S B
To Moorgate St.
¾ ½ ¼ 1 ¾ ½ ¼ 0 MILES
C.H.B. 1·11·1927.

274

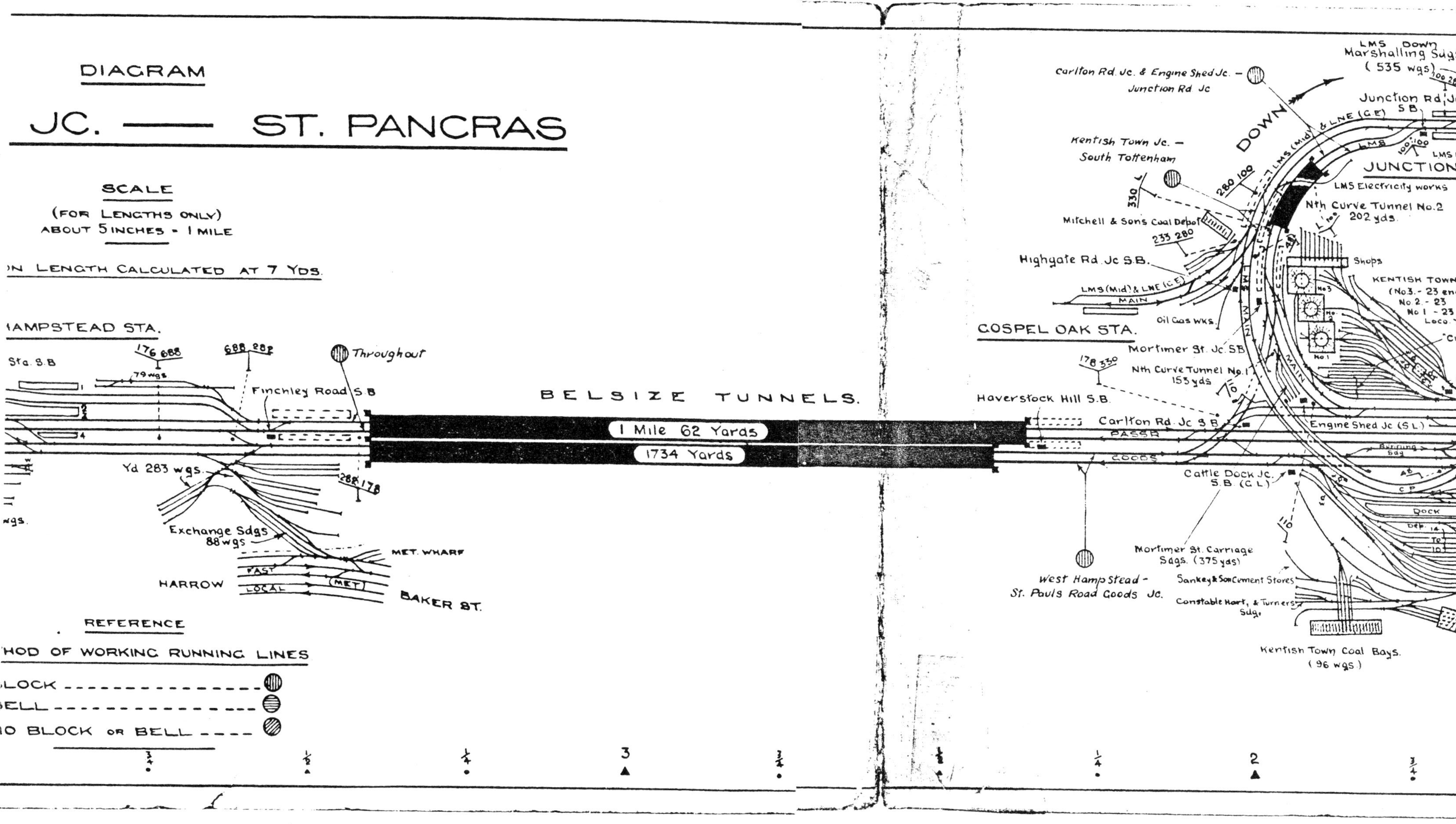
DIAGRAM
JC. —— ST. PANCRAS
SCALE
(FOR LENGTHS ONLY)
ABOUT 5 INCHES - 1 MILE
N LENGTH CALCULATED AT 7 YDS.
AMPSTEAD STA.
Sta. S.B
176 688
79 wgs
688 288
Throughout
Finchley Road S.B
BELSIZE TUNNELS.
1 Mile 62 Yards
1734 Yards
Yd 283 wgs.
288 178
Exchange Sdgs
88 wgs
MET. WHARF
HARROW
FAST
LOCAL
MET
BAKER ST.
REFERENCE
HOD OF WORKING RUNNING LINES
LOCK
ELL
IO BLOCK OR BELL
3
2
Carlton Rd. Jc. & Engine Shed Jc. -
Junction Rd Jc
Kentish Town Jc. -
South Tottenham
330
280 100
DOWN
LMS (Mid) & LNE (GE)
LMS
LMS Down
Marshalling Sdgs
(535 wgs)
Junction Rd Jc
S.B
JUNCTION
LMS Electricity works
Nth Curve Tunnel No.2
202 yds.
Mitchell & Sons Coal Depot
233 280
Highgate Rd. Jc S.B.
LMS (Mid) & LNE (C.E)
MAIN
Oil Gas Wks.
Shops
KENTISH TOWN
(No 3. - 23 eng
No 2. - 23
No 1 - 23
Loco. Y
GOSPEL OAK STA.
Mortimer St. Jc. SB
178 330
Nth Curve Tunnel No. 1
155 yds
Haverstock Hill S.B.
Carlton Rd. Jc S.B.
PASSR
GOODS
Engine Shed Jc (S.L)
Running Bay
Cattle Dock Jc.
S.B. (C.L)
Dock
Mortimer St. Carriage
Sdgs. (375 yds)
West Hampstead -
St. Pauls Road Goods Jc.
Sankey & Son Cement Stores
Constable Hart, & Turners Sdg.
Kentish Town Coal Bays.
(96 wgs.)

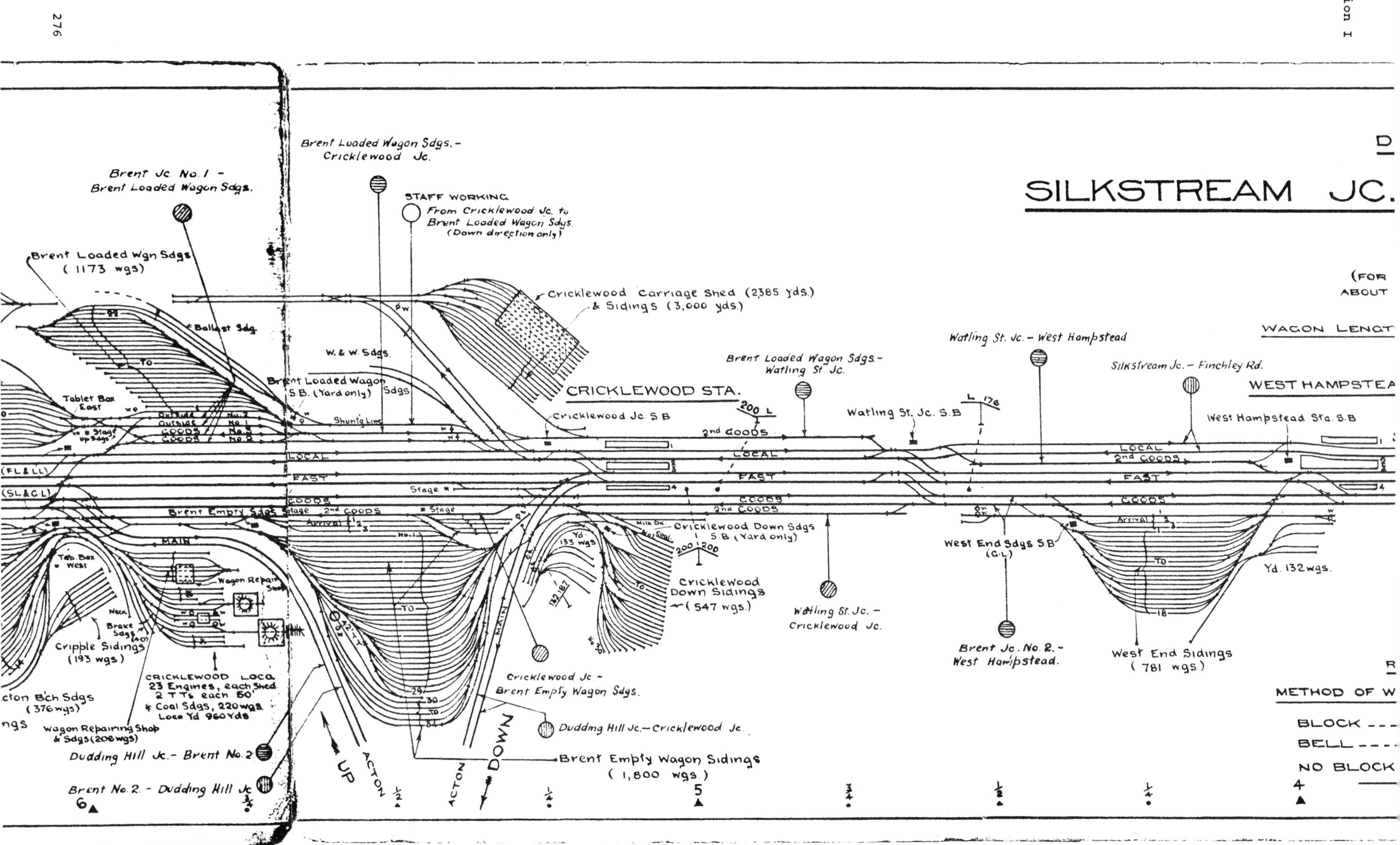
SILKSTREAM JC.
(FOR
ABOUT
WAGON LENGT
WEST HAMPSTEA
METHOD OF W
BLOCK
BELL
NO BLOCK
Brent Loaded Wagon Sdgs. - Cricklewood Jc.
Brent Jc. No. 1 - Brent Loaded Wagon Sdgs.
STAFF WORKING From Cricklewood Jc. to Brent Loaded Wagon Sdgs. (Down direction only)
Brent Loaded Wgn Sdgs (1173 wgs)
Ballast Sdg.
Cricklewood Carriage Shed (2385 yds.) & Sidings (3,000 yds.)
W. & W. Sdgs.
Brent Loaded Wagon S.B. (Yard only)
Sdgs
Shuntg Line
Tablet Box East
CRICKLEWOOD STA.
Cricklewood Jc. S.B
Brent Loaded Wagon Sdgs - Watling St. Jc.
Watling St. Jc. - West Hampstead
Silkstream Jc. - Finchley Rd.
Watling St. Jc. S.B
West Hampstead Sta. S.B
LOCAL
FAST
GOODS
2nd GOODS
(FL & LL)
(SL & C.L)
Brent Empty Sdgs
MAIN
Tab. Box West
Wagon Repair Shed
Cripple Sidings (193 wgs)
CRICKLEWOOD LOCO. 23 Engines, each Shed 2 T.T's each 50' * Coal Sdgs, 220 wgs Loco Yd 960 Yds
cton B'ch Sdgs (376 wgs)
Wagon Repairing Shop & Sdgs (208 wgs)
Dudding Hill Jc. - Brent No. 2
Brent No. 2 - Dudding Hill Jc.
UP
ACTON
DOWN
Cricklewood Down Sdgs 1 S.B (Yard only)
Yd. 133 wgs
Cricklewood Down Sidings (547 wgs.)
Watling St. Jc. - Cricklewood Jc.
Cricklewood Jc. - Brent Empty Wagon Sdgs.
Dudding Hill Jc. - Cricklewood Jc.
Brent Empty Wagon Sidings (1,800 wgs.)
West End Sdgs S.B (C.L.)
Brent Jc. No. 2 - West Hampstead.
West End Sidings (781 wgs)
Yd. 132 wgs.
6
5
4

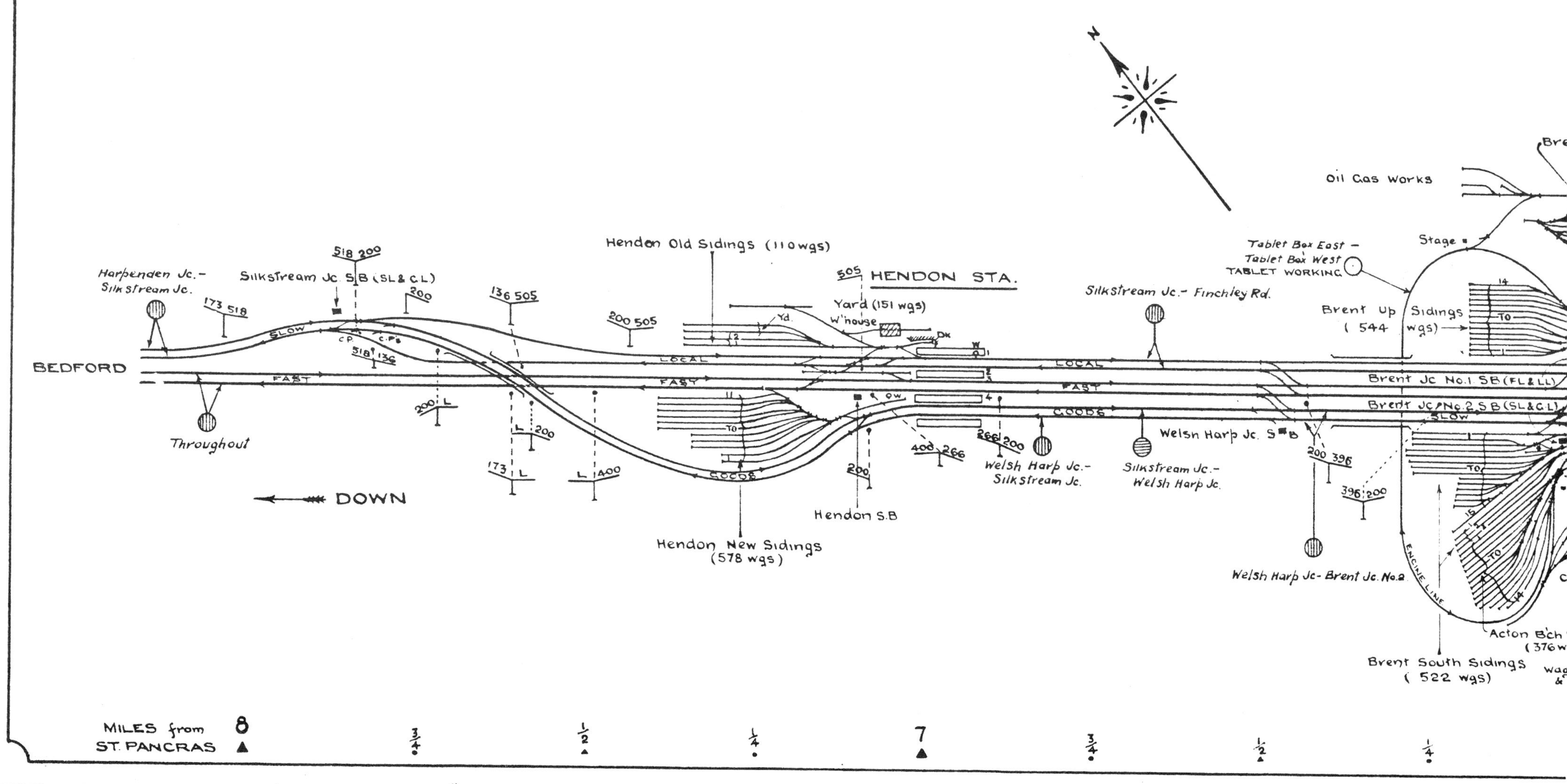
Oil Gas Works
Stage
Tablet Box East - Tablet Box West TABLET WORKING
Brent Up Sidings (544 wgs)
Brent Jc No.1 SB (FL&LL)
Brent Jc No.2 S.B (SL&CL)
SLOW
ENGINE LINE
Acton B'ch
Brent South Sidings (522 wgs)
Harpenden Jc.- Silkstream Jc.
Silkstream Jc S.B (SL & C.L)
SLOW
BEDFORD
FAST
Throughout
DOWN
Hendon Old Sidings (110 wgs)
505 HENDON STA.
Yard (151 wgs)
W'house
LOCAL
FAST
GOODS
Hendon New Sidings (578 wgs)
Hendon S.B
Welsh Harp Jc.- Silkstream Jc.
Silkstream Jc.- Welsh Harp Jc.
Silkstream Jc.- Finchley Rd.
Welsh Harp Jc. S.B
Welsh Harp Jc- Brent Jc. No.2
MILES from ST. PANCRAS
8
7

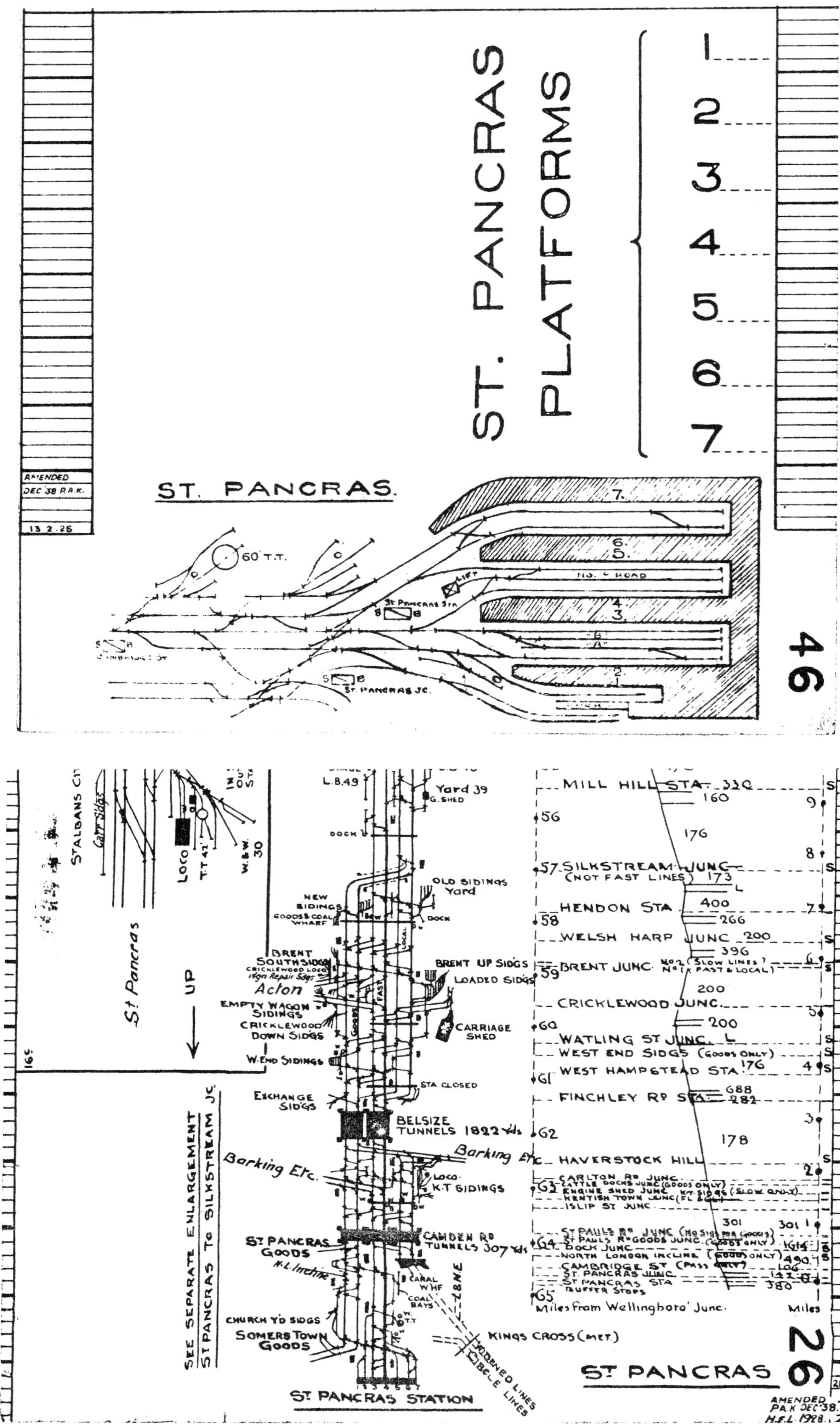
ST. PANCRAS PLATFORMS
1
2
3
4
5
6
7
AMENDED DEC 38 P.A.K.
13.2.26
ST. PANCRAS.
60' T.T.
NO. 6 ROAD
LIFT
St Pancras Sta
St. Pancras Jc.
46
MILL HILL STA
SILKSTREAM JUNC (NOT FAST LINES)
HENDON STA
WELSH HARP JUNC
BRENT JUNC
CRICKLEWOOD JUNC.
WATLING ST JUNC.
WEST END SIDGS (GOODS ONLY)
WEST HAMPSTEAD STA
FINCHLEY Rd STA
HAVERSTOCK HILL
CARLTON Rd JUNC
KENTISH TOWN JUNC
ISLIP ST JUNC
ST PAULS Rd JUNC
DOCK JUNC
NORTH LONDON INCLINE (GOODS ONLY)
CAMBRIDGE ST (PASS ONLY)
ST PANCRAS JUNC
ST PANCRAS STA BUFFER STOPS
Miles from Wellingboro' Junc.
Miles
Yard 39
OLD SIDINGS Yard
NEW SIDINGS
GOODS & COAL WHARF
BRENT SOUTH SIDGS
CRICKLEWOOD LOCO
Acton
EMPTY WAGON SIDINGS
CRICKLEWOOD DOWN SIDGS
W. END SIDINGS
BRENT UP SIDGS
LOADED SIDGS
CARRIAGE SHED
STA CLOSED
EXCHANGE SIDGS
BELSIZE TUNNELS 1822 Yds
Barking Etc.
LOCO K.T SIDINGS
ST PANCRAS GOODS
CAMDEN Rd TUNNELS 307 Yds
N.L. Incline
CANAL WHF
COAL BAYS
CHURCH Yd SIDGS
SOMERS TOWN GOODS
KINGS CROSS (MET.)
WIDENED LINES
CIBELE LINES
ST PANCRAS STATION
ST PANCRAS
26
St Pancras
UP
STALBANS CT
LOCO
SEE SEPARATE ENLARGEMENT ST PANCRAS TO SILKSTREAM JC
AMENDED P.A.K DEC '38.
H.F.L. 1928.

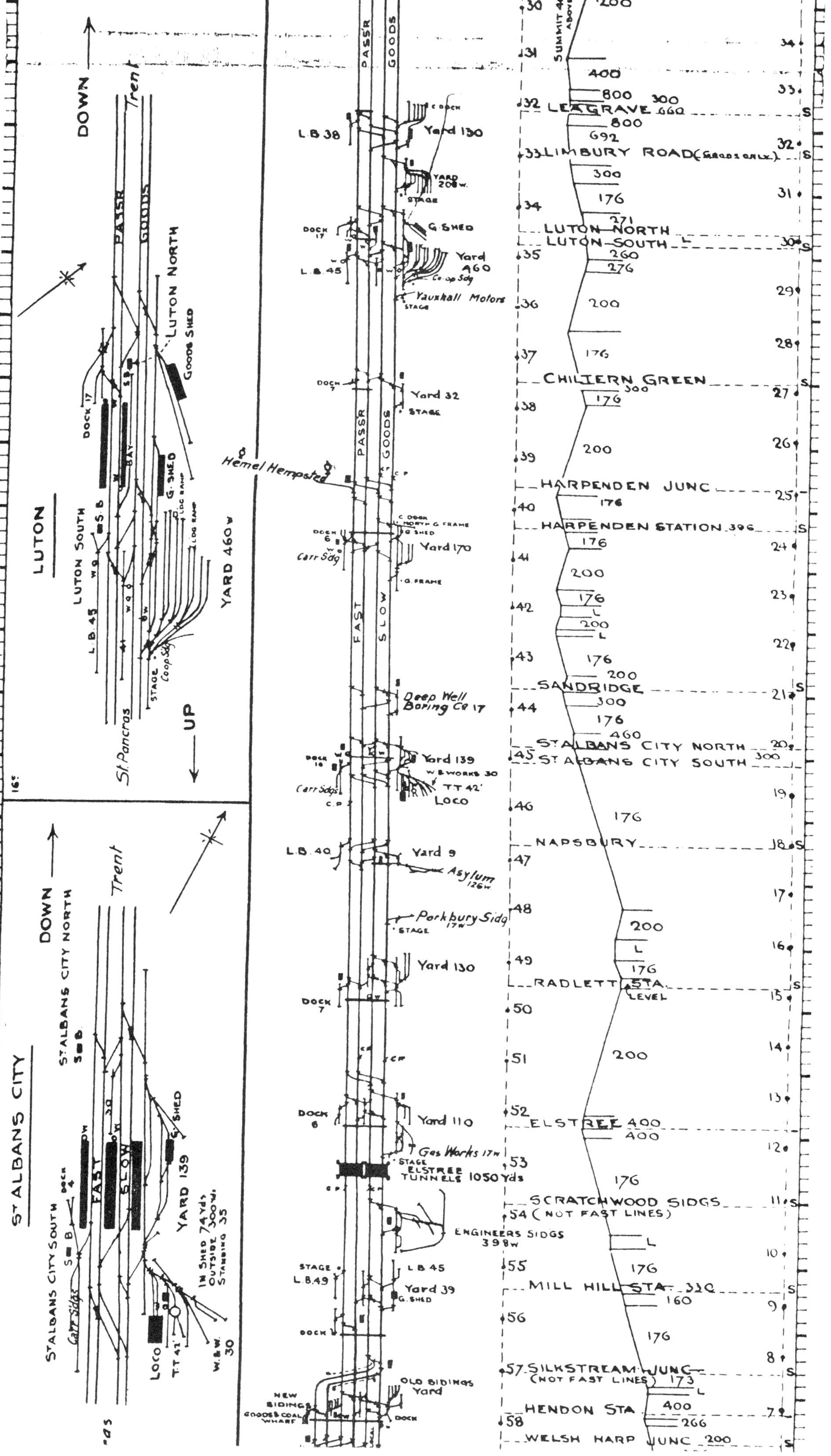
LUTON
DOWN
UP
Trent
PASSR
GOODS
LUTON NORTH
GOODS SHED
LUTON SOUTH
DOCK 17
L.B.45
YARD 460W
St. Pancras
ST ALBANS CITY
ST ALBANS CITY NORTH
ST ALBANS CITY SOUTH
FAST
SLOW
YARD 139
LOCO
T.T. 42
Carr Sidgs
IN SHED 74 Yds
OUTSIDE 300W
STANDING 35
SUMMIT 400 ABOVE
LEAGRAVE
LIMBURY ROAD (GOODS ONLY)
LUTON NORTH
LUTON SOUTH
CHILTERN GREEN
HARPENDEN JUNC
HARPENDEN STATION
SANDRIDGE
ST ALBANS CITY NORTH
ST ALBANS CITY SOUTH
NAPSBURY
RADLETT STA.
LEVEL
ELSTREE
SCRATCHWOOD SIDGS
(NOT FAST LINES)
MILL HILL STA.
SILKSTREAM JUNC
(NOT FAST LINES)
HENDON STA
WELSH HARP JUNC
L.B.38
Yard 130
YARD 208W.
G.SHED
Yard 460
Vauxhall Motors
Yard 32
Hemel Hempsted
Yard 170
Carr Sdg
Deep Well Boring Co 17
Yard 139
W.G. WORKS 30
TT 42'
Loco
L.B.40
Yard 9
Asylum 126W
Parkbury Sidg 17W
Yard 130
Yard 110
Gas Works 17W
ELSTREE TUNNELS 1050 Yds
ENGINEERS SIDGS 398W
L.B.45
L.B.49
Yard 39
OLD SIDINGS Yard
NEW SIDINGS
GOODS & COAL WHARF

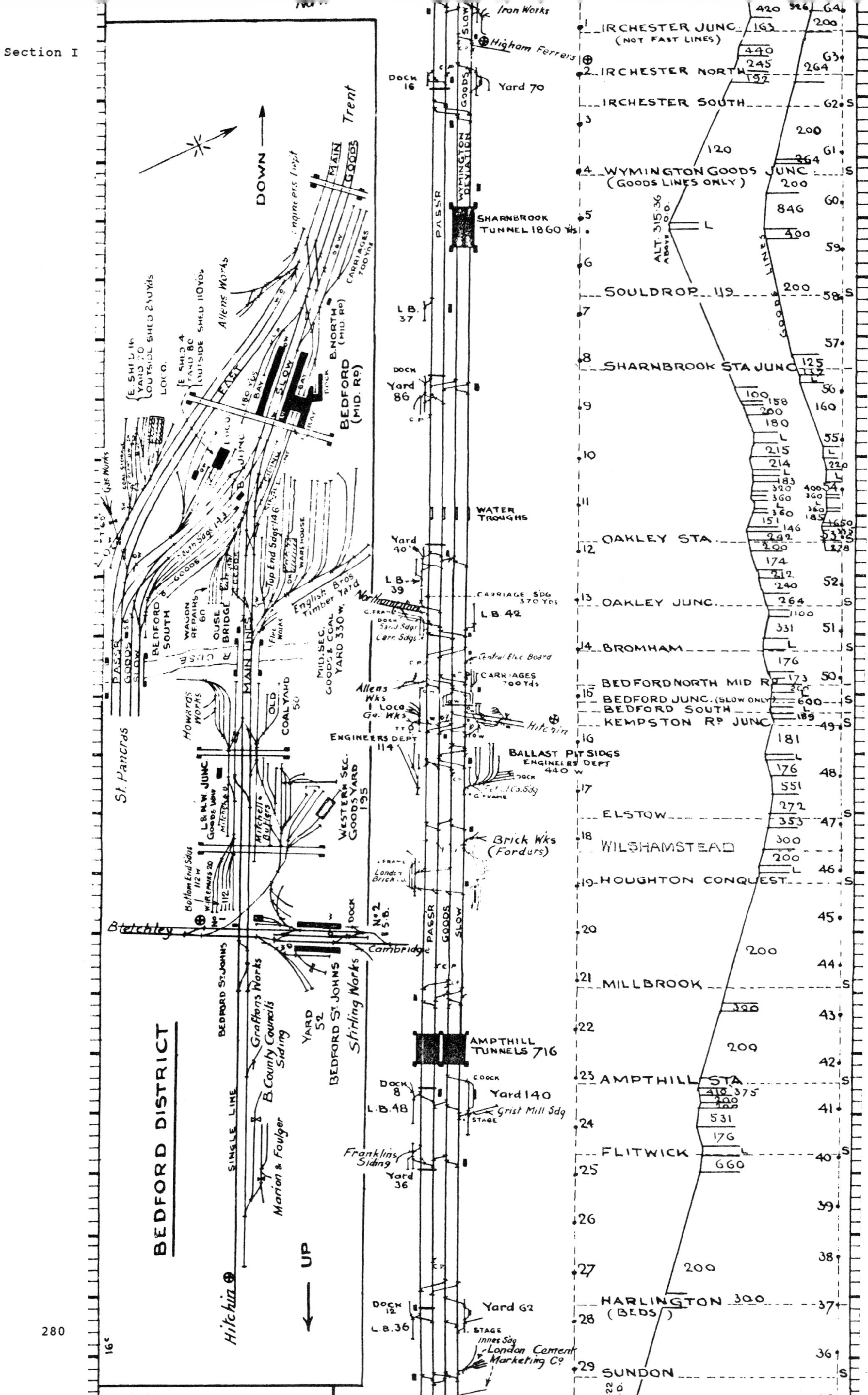
BEDFORD DISTRICT
DOWN
UP
Trent
St. Pancras
Hitchin
Bletchley
Cambridge
Northampton
BEDFORD (MID. RD)
B. NORTH (MID. RD)
BEDFORD SOUTH
OUSE BRIDGE
MAIN LINE
PASSR
GOODS
SLOW
FAST
MAIN
L.&N.W. JUNC
BEDFORD ST. JOHNS
SINGLE LINE
Allens Works
English Bros Timber Yard
MID. SEC. GOODS & COAL YARD 330 W.
WESTERN SEC. GOODS YARD 195
Howards Works
Mitchell Butlers
Graftons Works
B. County Councils Siding
Marion & Foulger
Stirling Works
OLD COALYARD 50
WAGON REPAIRS 60
Iron Works
Higham Ferrers
Yard 70
WYMINGTON DEVIATION
SHARNBROOK TUNNEL 1860 Yds
WATER TROUGHS
CARRIAGE SDG 370 Yds
Central Elec Board
CARRIAGES 700 Yds
BALLAST PIT SIDGS ENGINEERS DEPT 440 W
Brick Wks (Forders)
London Brick Co
AMPTHILL TUNNELS 716
Yard 140
Grist Mill Sdg
Franklins Siding
Yard 36
Yard 62
London Cement Marketing Co
IRCHESTER JUNC. (NOT FAST LINES)
IRCHESTER NORTH
IRCHESTER SOUTH
WYMINGTON GOODS JUNC (GOODS LINES ONLY)
SOULDROP 119
SHARNBROOK STA JUNC
OAKLEY STA
OAKLEY JUNC
BROMHAM
BEDFORD NORTH MID RD
BEDFORD JUNC. (SLOW ONLY)
BEDFORD SOUTH
KEMPSTON RD JUNC
ELSTOW
WILSHAMSTEAD
HOUGHTON CONQUEST
MILLBROOK
AMPTHILL STA
FLITWICK
HARLINGTON (BEDS) 300
SUNDON
ALT. 315.36 ABOVE O.D.
GOODS LINES

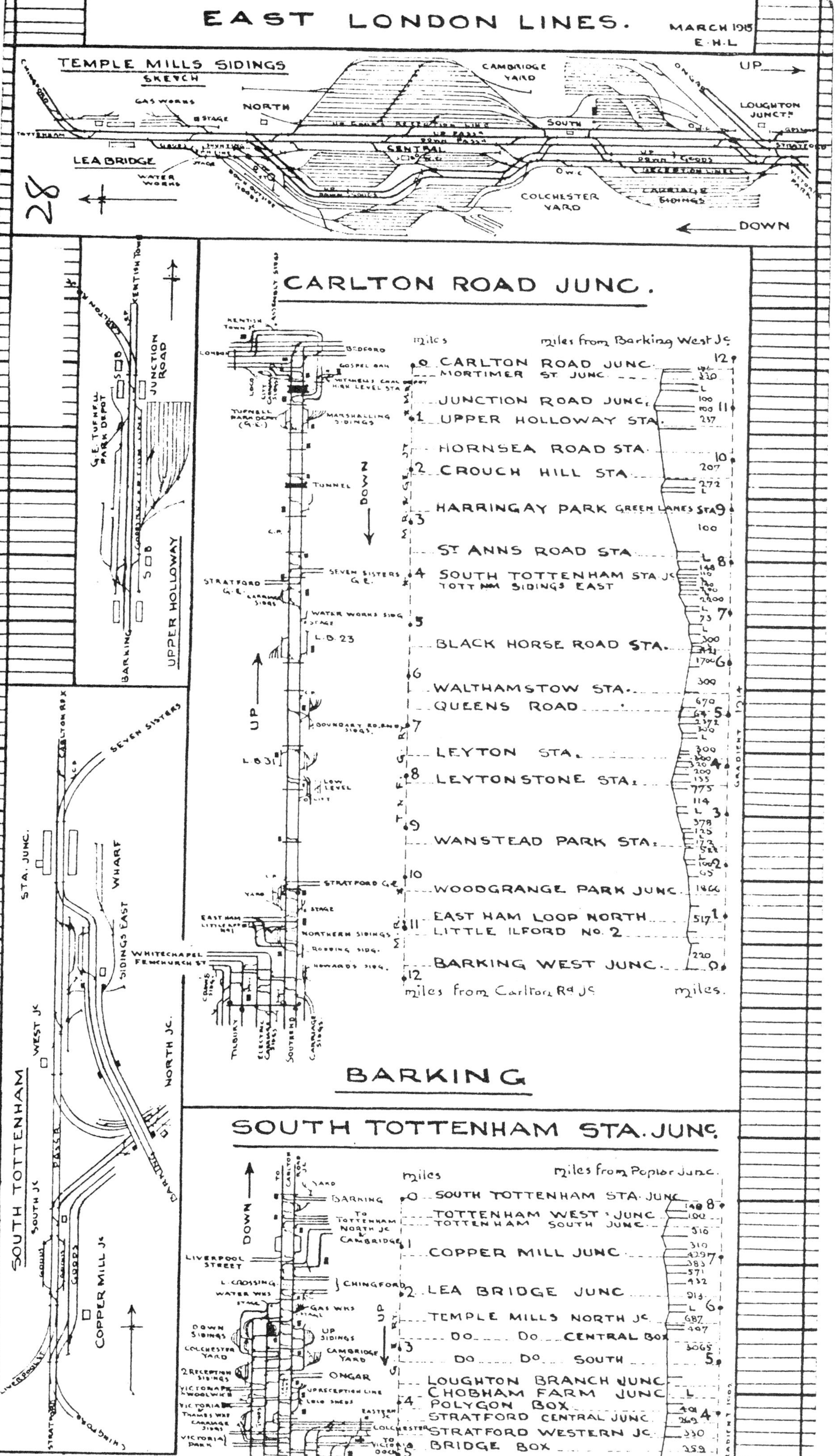
EAST LONDON LINES.
MARCH 1915
E.H.L.
TEMPLE MILLS SIDINGS
SKETCH
CAMBRIDGE YARD
NORTH
SOUTH
CENTRAL
LOUGHTON JUNCT.
UP
DOWN
LEA BRIDGE
COLCHESTER YARD
CARRIAGE SIDINGS
28
CARLTON ROAD JUNC.
miles
miles from Barking West Jc
CARLTON ROAD JUNC.
MORTIMER ST. JUNC.
JUNCTION ROAD JUNC.
UPPER HOLLOWAY STA.
HORNSEA ROAD STA.
CROUCH HILL STA.
HARRINGAY PARK GREEN LANES STA
ST ANNS ROAD STA.
SOUTH TOTTENHAM STA JC
TOTTENHAM SIDINGS EAST
BLACK HORSE ROAD STA.
WALTHAMSTOW STA.
QUEENS ROAD
LEYTON STA.
LEYTONSTONE STA.
WANSTEAD PARK STA.
WOODGRANGE PARK JUNC.
EAST HAM LOOP NORTH
LITTLE ILFORD No. 2
BARKING WEST JUNC.
miles from Carlton Rd Jc
miles.
GRADIENT
BARKING
UPPER HOLLOWAY
JUNCTION ROAD
SOUTH TOTTENHAM
SOUTH TOTTENHAM STA. JUNC.
miles
miles from Poplar Junc.
SOUTH TOTTENHAM STA. JUNC
TOTTENHAM WEST JUNC
TOTTENHAM SOUTH JUNC
COPPER MILL JUNC
LEA BRIDGE JUNC
TEMPLE MILLS NORTH JC
DO DO CENTRAL BOX
DO DO SOUTH
LOUGHTON BRANCH JUNC
CHOBHAM FARM JUNC
POLYGON BOX
STRATFORD CENTRAL JUNC
STRATFORD WESTERN JC
BRIDGE BOX
COPPER MILL JC
NORTH JC.
WEST JC
STA. JUNC.
WHARF
SEVEN SISTERS

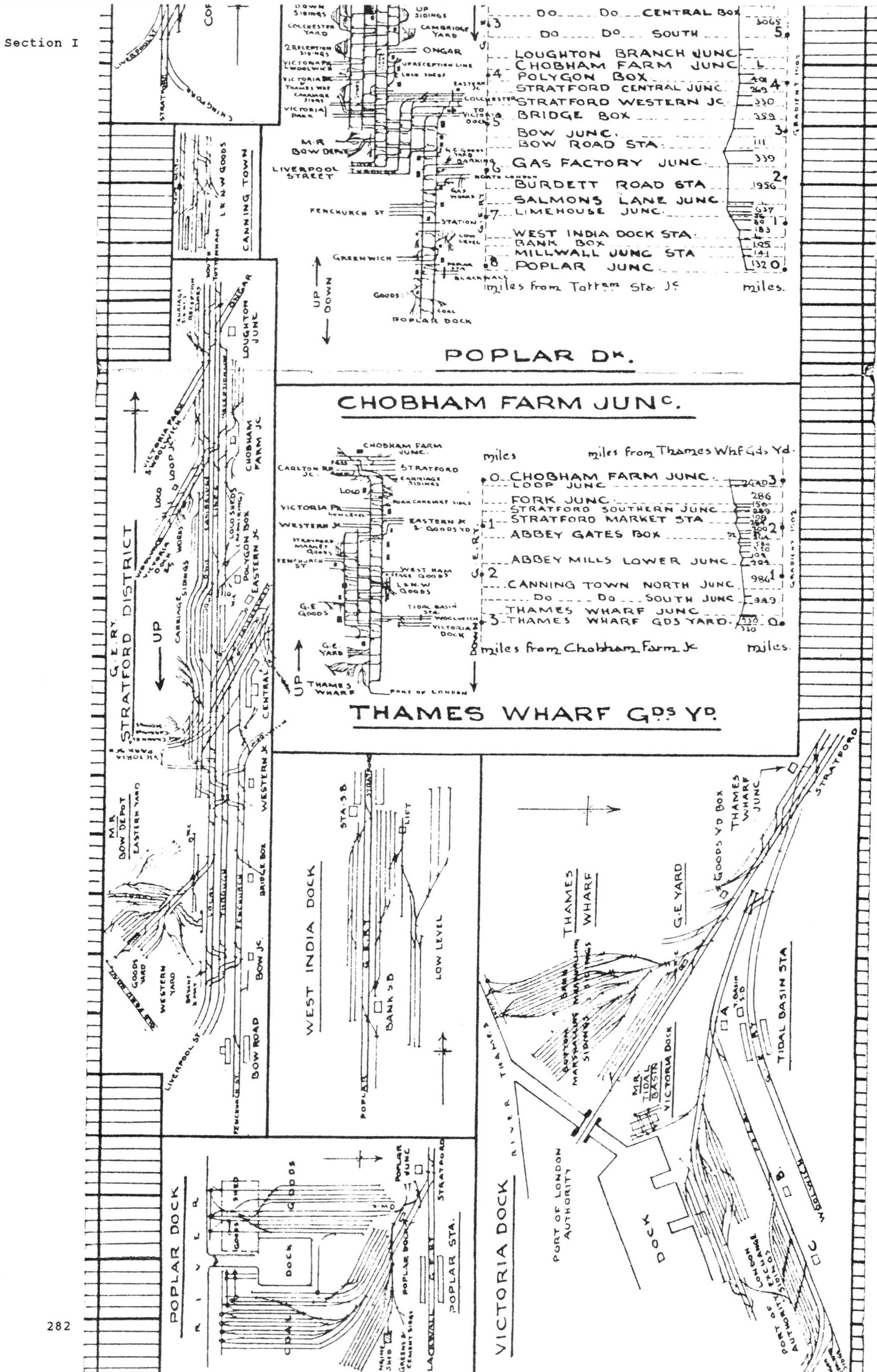
POPLAR Dk.
LOUGHTON BRANCH JUNC.
CHOBHAM FARM JUNC.
POLYGON BOX
STRATFORD CENTRAL JUNC.
STRATFORD WESTERN JC.
BRIDGE BOX
BOW JUNC.
BOW ROAD STA.
GAS FACTORY JUNC.
BURDETT ROAD STA.
SALMONS LANE JUNC.
LIMEHOUSE JUNC.
WEST INDIA DOCK STA.
BANK BOX
MILLWALL JUNC STA.
POPLAR JUNC.
miles from Totten Sta. Jc
miles.
CHOBHAM FARM JUNc.
miles from Thames Whf Gds Yd.
CHOBHAM FARM JUNC.
LOOP JUNC.
FORK JUNC.
STRATFORD SOUTHERN JUNC.
STRATFORD MARKET STA.
ABBEY GATES BOX
ABBEY MILLS LOWER JUNC.
CANNING TOWN NORTH JUNC.
Do Do SOUTH JUNC.
THAMES WHARF JUNC.
THAMES WHARF GDS YARD.
miles from Chobham Farm Jc
miles.
THAMES WHARF Gds Yd.
G.E.RY. STRATFORD DISTRICT
UP
DOWN
CANNING TOWN
WEST INDIA DOCK
LOW LEVEL
BANK S.D
M.R. BOW DEPOT
EASTERN YARD
WESTERN YARD
GOODS YARD
BOW JC.
BOW ROAD
LIVERPOOL ST
THAMES WHARF
G.E YARD
GOODS YD BOX
THAMES WHARF JUNC
STRATFORD
TIDAL BASIN STA
RIVER THAMES
VICTORIA DOCK
PORT OF LONDON AUTHORITY
DOCK
POPLAR DOCK
GOODS
COAL
POPLAR STA.
POPLAR JUNC
BLACKWALL

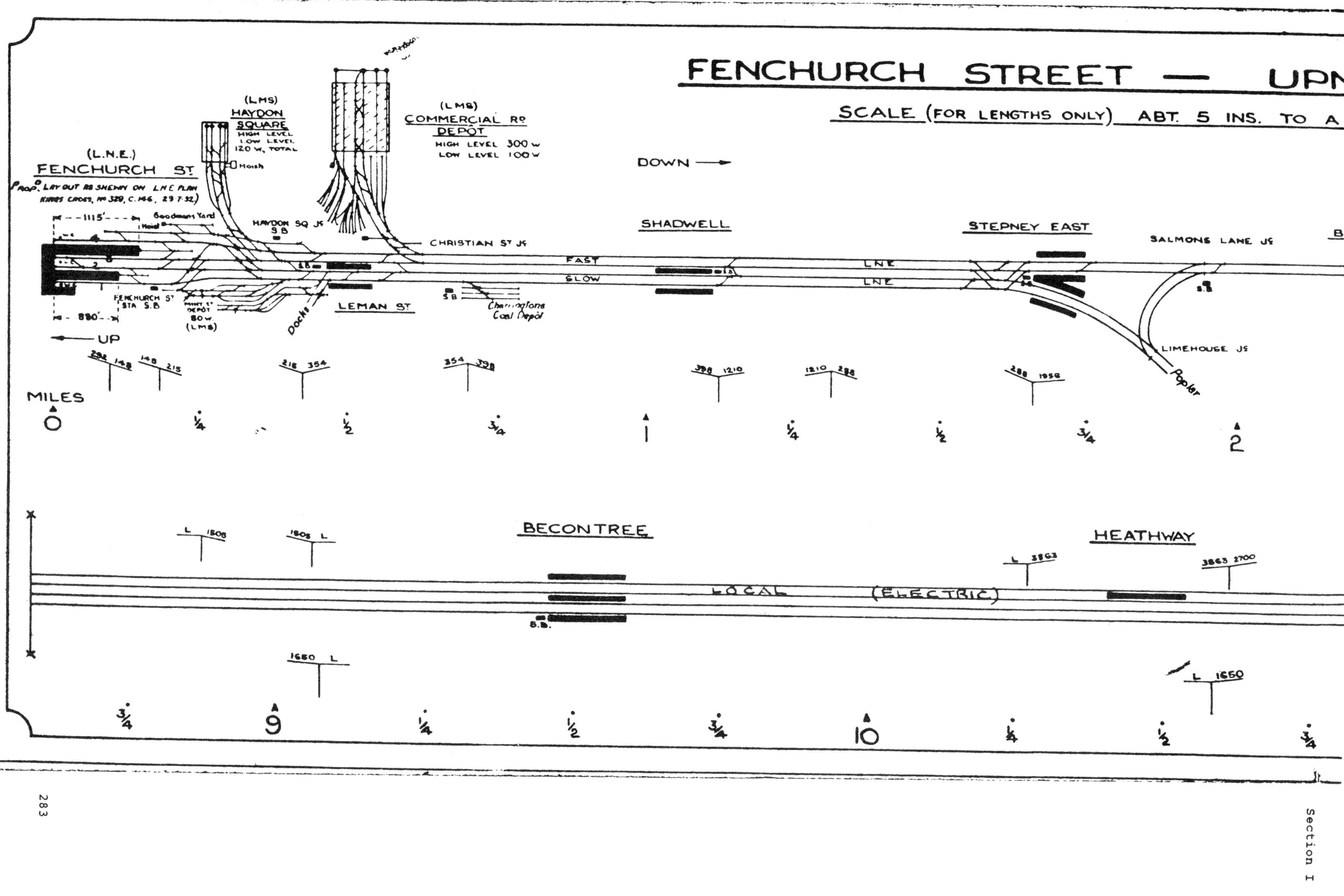
FENCHURCH STREET — UPM
SCALE (FOR LENGTHS ONLY) ABT. 5 INS. TO A
(L.N.E.)
FENCHURCH ST
(LMS)
HAYDON SQUARE
HIGH LEVEL
LOW LEVEL
120 W. TOTAL
Hoist
(LMS)
COMMERCIAL RD DEPOT
HIGH LEVEL 300 W
LOW LEVEL 100 W
DOWN
UP
Goodmans Yard
HAYDON SQ JC S.B
CHRISTIAN ST JC
FENCHURCH ST STA S.B
Docks
LEMAN ST
Charringtons Coal Depot
SHADWELL
FAST
SLOW
LNE
STEPNEY EAST
SALMONS LANE JC
LIMEHOUSE JC
Poplar
MILES
0
1
2
BECONTREE
HEATHWAY
LOCAL
(ELECTRIC)
9
10

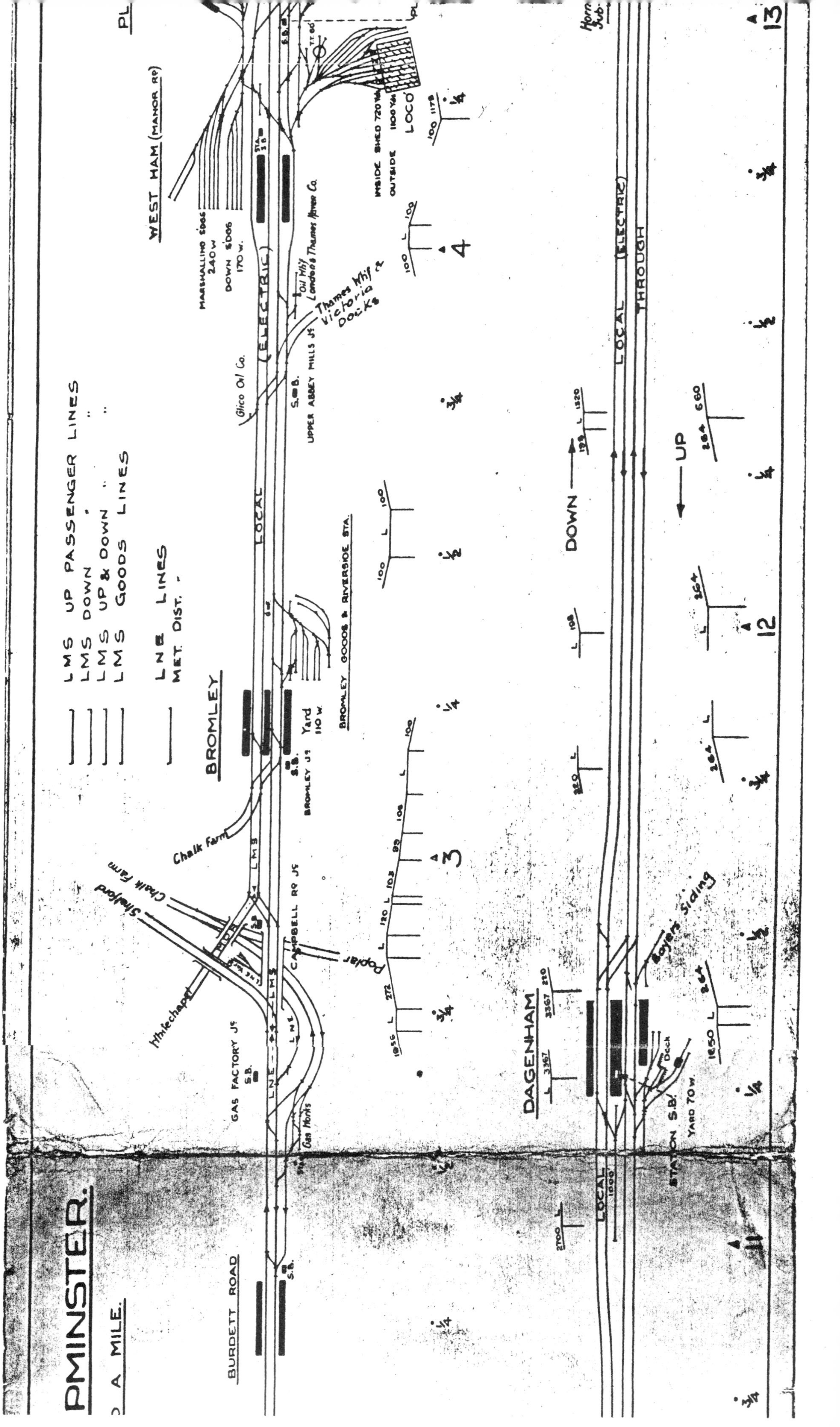

PMINSTER.

D A MILE.

LMS	UP PASSENGER LINES
LMS	DOWN " "
LMS	UP & DOWN " "
LMS	GOODS LINES
LNE	LINES
MET. DIST.	"

BURDETT ROAD

S.B.

Gas Works

GAS FACTORY Jc S.B.

Whitechapel

Shelford

Chalk Farm

Chalk Farm

LNE

LMS

CAMPBELL RD Jc

Poplar

BROMLEY

S.B.

BROMLEY Jc

Yard 110 w.

BROMLEY GOODS & RIVERSIDE STA.

LOCAL (ELECTRIC)

Glico Oil Co.

S.B.

UPPER ABBEY MILLS Jc

Thames Whf & Victoria Docks

Oil Whf

London & Thames Haven Co.

WEST HAM (MANOR RD)

MARSHALLING SDGS 240 w

DOWN SDGS 170 w.

STA. S.B.

S.B.

T.T. 60'

INSIDE SHED 720 Yds

OUTSIDE 1100 Yds

LOCO

PL

3

4

DAGENHAM

LOCAL 1000'

STATION S.B.

Dock

YARD 70 w.

Boyers Siding

DOWN →

← UP

LOCAL (ELECTRIC)

THROUGH

Horn Sub

11

12

13

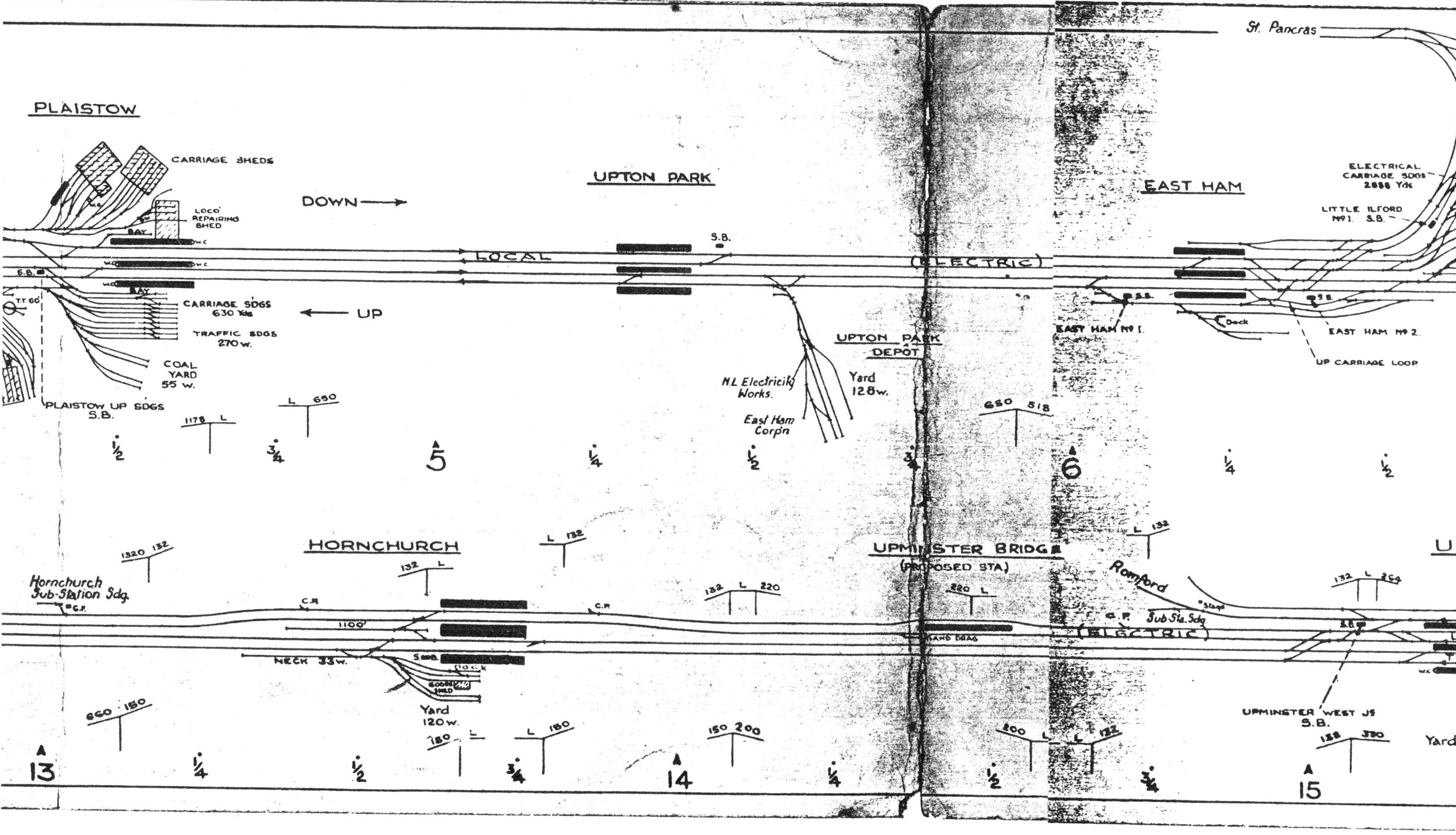

PLAISTOW
CARRIAGE SHEDS
LOCO REPAIRING SHED
BAY
DOWN
LOCAL
UP
CARRIAGE SDGS 630 Yds
TRAFFIC SDGS 270 W.
COAL YARD 55 W.
PLAISTOW UP SDGS S.B.
UPTON PARK
S.B.
(ELECTRIC)
UPTON PARK DEPOT
N.L. Electricity Works.
East Ham Corpn
Yard 128 W.
St. Pancras
EAST HAM
ELECTRICAL CARRIAGE SDGS 2888 Yds
LITTLE ILFORD No1. S.B.
EAST HAM No 1.
EAST HAM No 2.
UP CARRIAGE LOOP
Dock
HORNCHURCH
Hornchurch Sub-Station Sdg.
NECK 33 W.
Yard 120 W.
UPMINSTER BRIDGE
(PROPOSED STA)
Romford
Sub Sta. Sdg
UPMINSTER WEST JS S.B.
Yard
13
14
15
5
6

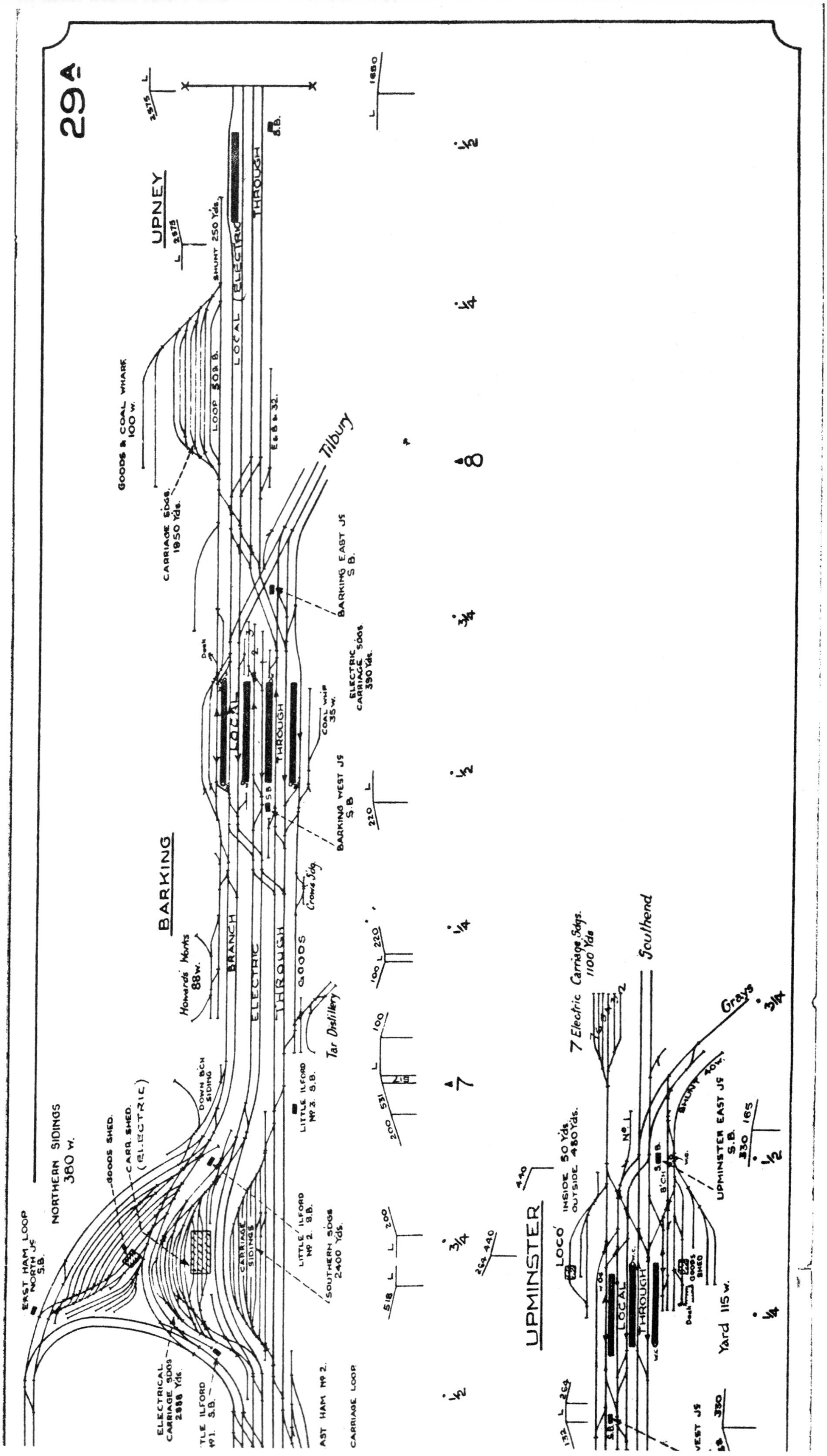

29A

EAST HAM LOOP NORTH J^N S.B.

NORTHERN SIDINGS 380 w.

GOODS SHED.

CARR. SHED. (ELECTRIC)

ELECTRICAL CARRIAGE SDGS 2888 Yds.

LITTLE ILFORD Nº1. S.B.

DOWN B'CH SIDING

CARRIAGE SIDINGS

LITTLE ILFORD Nº 2. S.B.

SOUTHERN SDGS 2400 Yds.

LITTLE ILFORD Nº 3. S.B.

EAST HAM Nº 2.

CARRIAGE LOOP

BARKING

Howards' Works 88w.

BRANCH

ELECTRIC

THROUGH

GOODS

Tar Distillery

Crow's Sdg.

Dock

LOCAL

THROUGH

SB

BARKING WEST J^N S.B

COAL WH^F 35 w.

ELECTRIC CARRIAGE SDGS 390 Yds.

BARKING EAST J^N S.B.

Tilbury

CARRIAGE SDGS. 1950 Yds.

GOODS & COAL WHARF 100 w.

LOOP 502 B.

E. & B. 32.

SHUNT 250 Yds.

UPNEY

L 2575

2575 L

LOCAL ELECTRIC

THROUGH

S.B.

L 1650

518 L L 200

200 531 L 100

517

100 L 220

220 L

½ ¾ 7 ¼ ½ ¾ 8 ¼ ½

264 440

UPMINSTER

440

132 L 264

LOCO'

INSIDE 50 Yds. OUTSIDE 480 Yds.

7 Electric Carriage Sdgs. 1100 Yds

7 6 5 4 3 2

W.C.

S.B.

LOCAL

THROUGH

W.C.

Nº 1

Southend

B'CH

S.B.

W.C.

Dock

GOODS SHED

WEST J^N

58 330

Yard 115 w.

UPMINSTER EAST J^N S.B.

330 165

SHUNT 40 w.

Grays

¼ ½ ¾

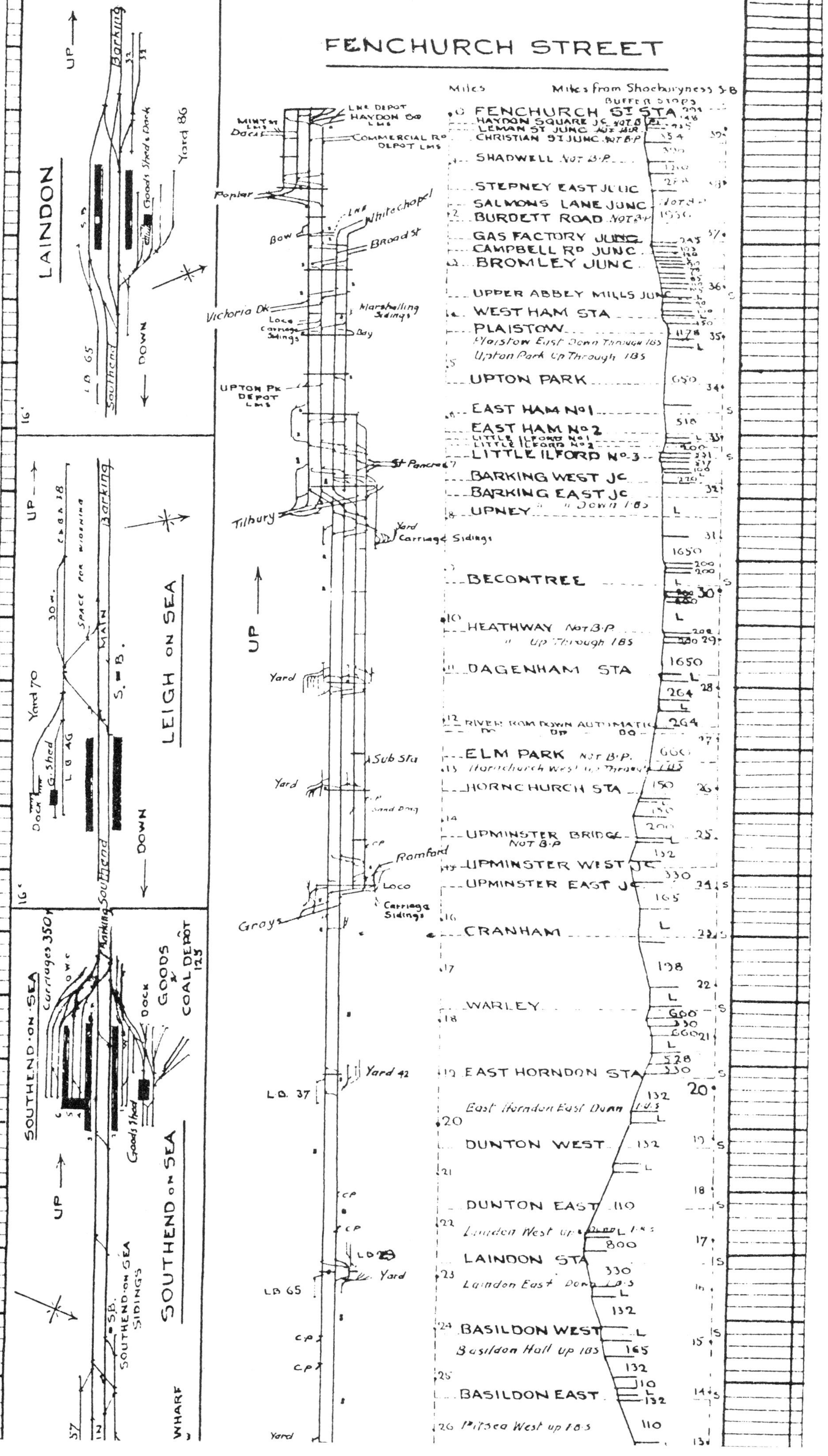
FENCHURCH STREET
Miles
Miles from Shoeburyness S.B.
FENCHURCH ST STA
SHADWELL Not B.P.
STEPNEY EAST JUNC
SALMONS LANE JUNC
BURDETT ROAD Not B.P.
GAS FACTORY JUNC
CAMPBELL RD JUNC
BROMLEY JUNC
UPPER ABBEY MILLS JUNC
WEST HAM STA
PLAISTOW
UPTON PARK
EAST HAM No 1
EAST HAM No 2
LITTLE ILFORD No 3
BARKING WEST JC
BARKING EAST JC
UPNEY
BECONTREE
HEATHWAY Not B.P.
DAGENHAM STA
ELM PARK Not B.P.
HORNCHURCH STA
UPMINSTER BRIDGE Not B.P.
UPMINSTER WEST JC
UPMINSTER EAST JC
CRANHAM
WARLEY
EAST HORNDON STA
DUNTON WEST
DUNTON EAST
LAINDON STA
BASILDON WEST
BASILDON EAST
LAINDON
LEIGH ON SEA
SOUTHEND ON SEA

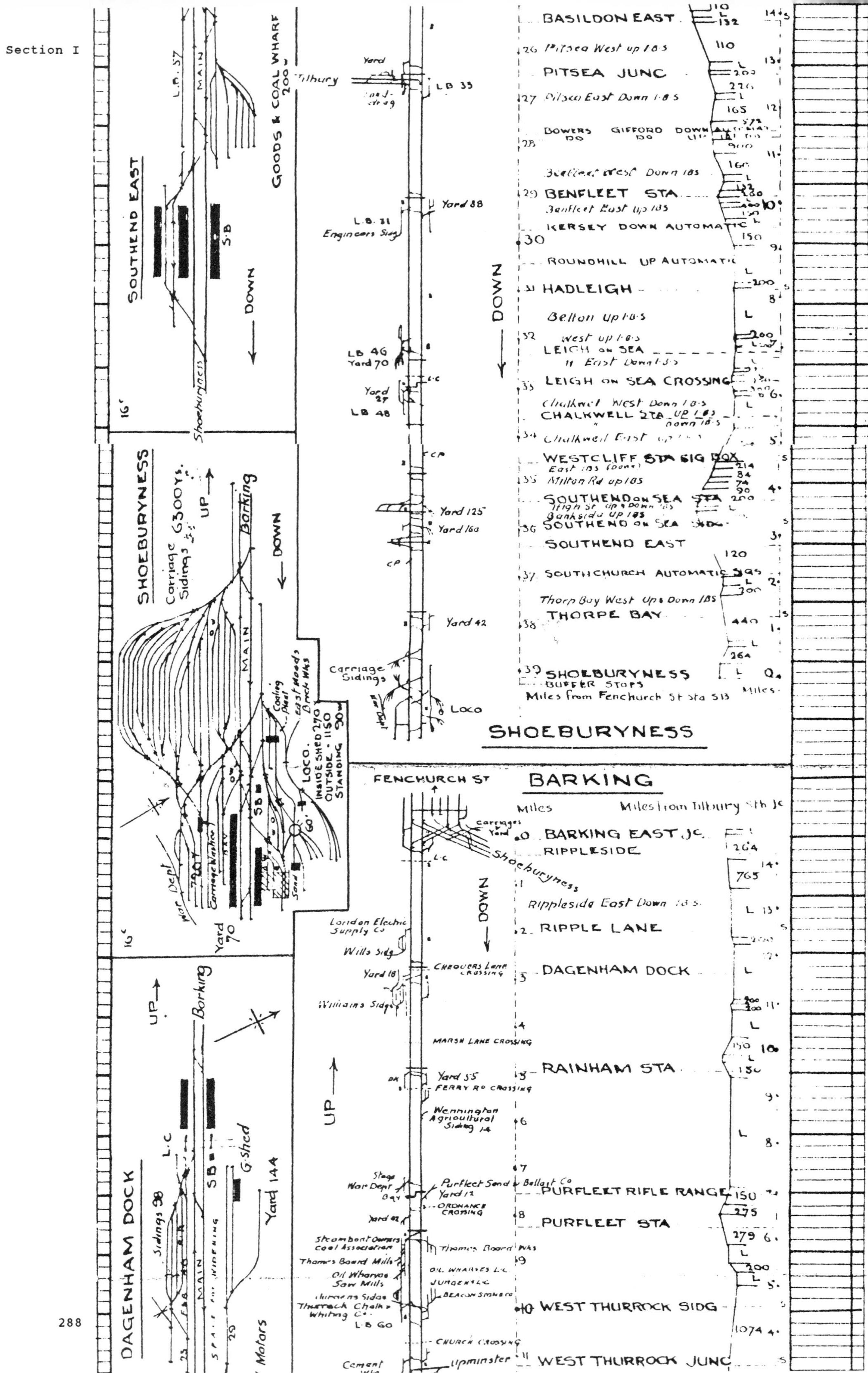
BASILDON EAST
Pitsea West up I.B.S
PITSEA JUNC
Pitsea East Down I.B.S
BOWERS DO
GIFFORD DO
BENFLEET STA
Benfleet East up IBS
KERSEY DOWN AUTOMATIC
ROUNDHILL UP AUTOMATIC
HADLEIGH
Belton Up I.B.S
LEIGH ON SEA
LEIGH ON SEA CROSSING
CHALKWELL STA
WESTCLIFF STA SIG BOX
Milton Rd up IBS
SOUTHEND ON SEA
SOUTHEND EAST
SOUTHCHURCH AUTOMATIC
Thorp Bay West Up & Down IBS
THORPE BAY
SHOEBURYNESS
BUFFER STOPS
Miles from Fenchurch St Sta SB
SHOEBURYNESS
BARKING
FENCHURCH ST
Miles
Miles from Tilbury Sth Jc
BARKING EAST Jc
RIPPLESIDE
Rippleside East Down IBS
RIPPLE LANE
DAGENHAM DOCK
RAINHAM STA
PURFLEET RIFLE RANGE
PURFLEET STA
WEST THURROCK SIDG
WEST THURROCK JUNC
SOUTHEND EAST
GOODS & COAL WHARF 200w
DOWN
UP
MAIN
Carriage Sidings G300Ys.
LOCO. INSIDE SHED 270 OUTSIDE 1150 STANDING 90w
DAGENHAM DOCK
Yard 144
G.Shed
Motors
Tilbury
Yard 88
Engineers Sidg
Carriage Sidings
Loco
Upminster
Cement

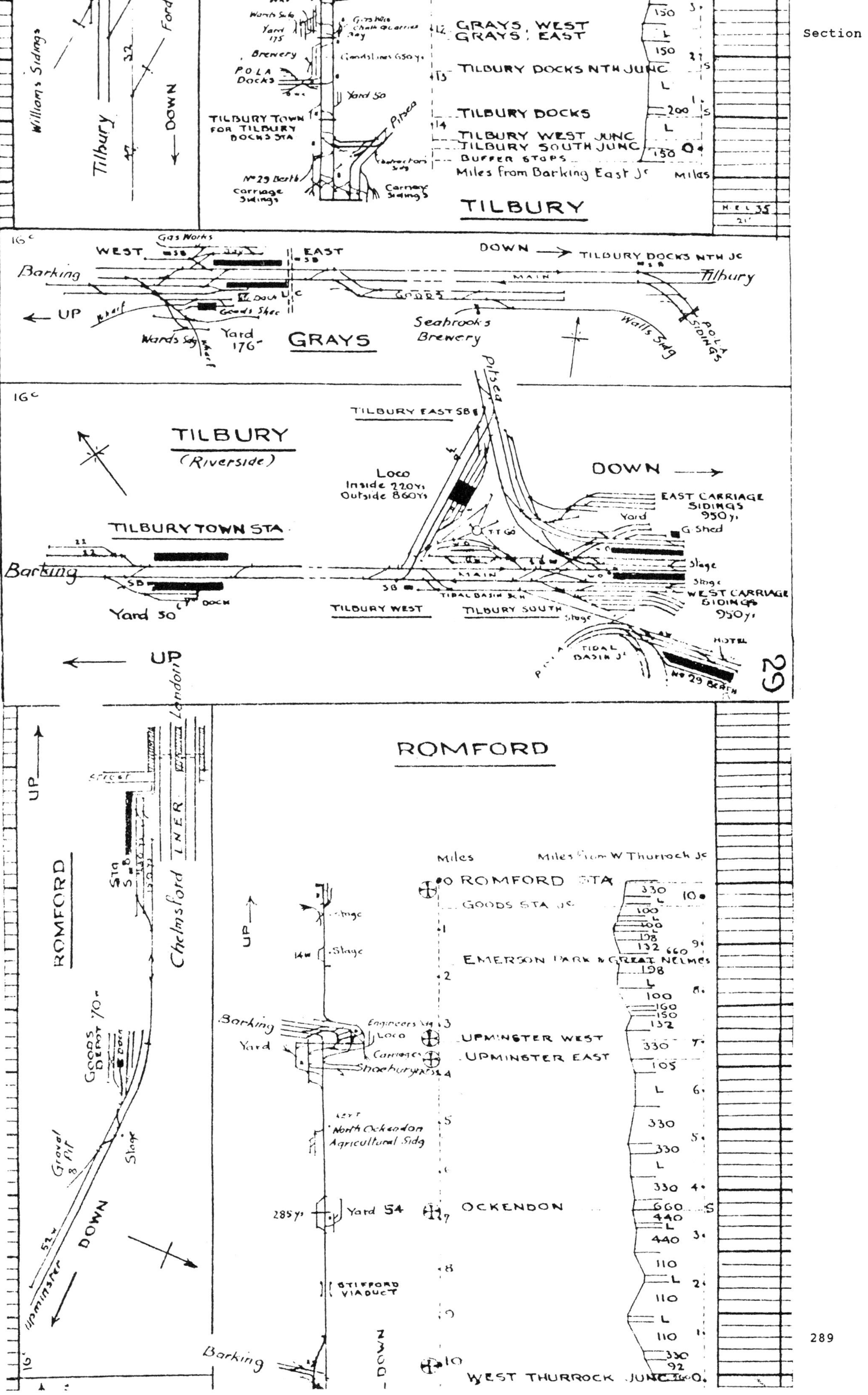
Williams Sidings
Tilbury
Ford
DOWN
Brewery
POLA Docks
Yard 50
TILBURY TOWN FOR TILBURY DOCKS STA
Pitsea
No 29 Berth
Carriage Sidings
GRAYS WEST
GRAYS EAST
TILBURY DOCKS NTH JUNC
TILBURY DOCKS
TILBURY WEST JUNC
TILBURY SOUTH JUNC
BUFFER STOPS
Miles from Barking East Jc
Miles
TILBURY
Gas Works
WEST
EAST
DOWN
TILBURY DOCKS NTH JC
Barking
MAIN
Tilbury
GOODS
UP
Goods Shed
Yard 176
Wards Sdg
Wharf
GRAYS
Seabrooks Brewery
Walls Sdg
POLA SIDINGS
TILBURY EAST SB
TILBURY
(Riverside)
Loco
Inside 220 Yds
Outside 860 Yds
DOWN
EAST CARRIAGE SIDINGS 950 Yds
Yard
G Shed
TILBURY TOWN STA
Barking
MAIN
Stage
WEST CARRIAGE SIDINGS 950 Yds
Yard 50
TILBURY WEST
TILBURY SOUTH
TIDAL BASIN Jc
HOTEL
No 29 BERTH
UP
London
62
ROMFORD
UP
Sta
Chelmsford
LNER
ROMFORD
GOODS DEPOT 70
Gravel Pit
DOWN
Upminster
Miles
Miles from W Thurrock Jc
ROMFORD STA
GOODS STA Jc
Stage
EMERSON PARK & GREAT NELMES
Barking
Yard
Engineers Sdg
Loco
Carriages
Shoeburyness
UPMINSTER WEST
UPMINSTER EAST
North Ockendon Agricultural Sdg
OCKENDON
Yard 54
STIFFORD VIADUCT
DOWN
Barking
WEST THURROCK JUNC

WEST THURROCK JUNC

Miles from Romford Sta — Miles

Miles	Location	Gradient	Miles
8	STIFFORD VIADUCT	110	2
9		L	
		110	
		L	1
		110	
		330	
		92	
10	WEST THURROCK JUNC		0

GRAYS

Yard 176 — Wharf — Quarries — Oil Depot — Wards Sidg — Stage — G Shed — Dock — Main — West S.B — East S.B — Brewery & Malls Sidg — Barking — Tilbury — UP — DOWN

TILBURY

Miles from Pitsea Jc — Miles

Miles	Location	Gradient	Miles
0	TILBURY SOUTH JC		
	TILBURY EAST JC	542 / 200 / L	10
1	Fort Rd Crossing	3550	9
2	LOW STREET		8
	Muckingford Crossing	340	
3		250	7
4	Mucking Crossing	250	
	THAMES HAVEN JC	200	6
	London Rd L.C.	195 / L	
5	STANFORD-LE-HOPE	200	5
6		L / 470 / 120 / L	4
7		200	
		L	3
8	Fobbing Rd Crossing	200	2
9	Vange Crossing	L / 200 / 200 / L / 200	1
10	PITSEA JUNC	L / 200	0

Miles from Tilbury Sth Jc — Miles

Carriages — No 29 Berth — Ballast Pit Yard — W & W Dept — Yard 50 — Yard 34 — Sand drag — Thames Haven — Barking — Shoeburyness — UP — DOWN

PITSEA JUNC

Tilbury — Stage — G Shed — Yard 67 — Barking — Sand drag — LB 33 — Shoeburyness — UP — DOWN

THAMES HAVEN JUNC

Miles — Miles from Thames Haven

Miles	Location	Gradient	Miles
0	THAMES HAVEN JC	116	
	MAYES CROSSING HALT	330	
1		L / 132 / L / 200	3
2	MINER'S SAFETY EXPLOSIVE CO / CURRY MARSH		2
		L	1
3	LONDON & THAMES HAVEN CO		
	LONDON & T. HAVEN OIL WHARVES HALT		
	THAMES HAVEN HALT (SHELL MEX)	343 / L	
	THAMES HAVEN		0

Miles from Thames Haven Jc — Miles

Barking — Pitsea — Stage — L.C. — European Petm Co — Oil Wharves Crossing Halt — Corringham Light Ry — Asiatic Petm Co / Shell Mex — Yard 100 — River Thames — UP — DOWN

THAMES HAVEN

Thames Haven Jc — Corringham Light Ry — Kynochs Sidgs — Manorway — Halt — Asiatic Petm Co (Shell Mex) — UP — DOWN

30

H.E.L 1935

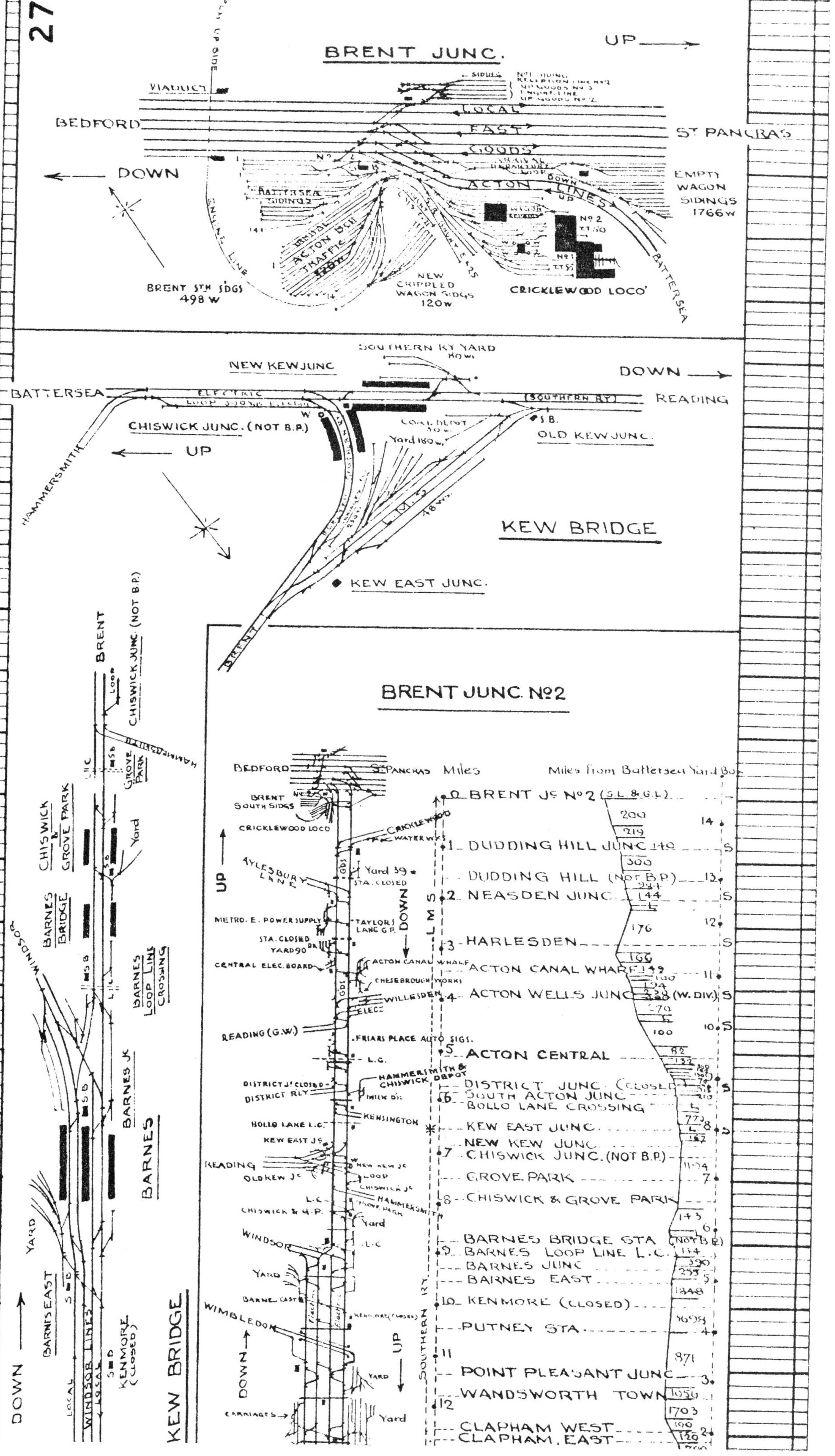
27
BRENT JUNC.
UP
BEDFORD
ST PANCRAS
DOWN
LOCAL
FAST
GOODS
ACTON LINES
EMPTY WAGON SIDINGS 1766 W
BRENT STH SDGS 498 W
NEW CRIPPLED WAGON SDGS 120 W
CRICKLEWOOD LOCO'
BATTERSEA
KEW BRIDGE
NEW KEW JUNC
SOUTHERN RY YARD
BATTERSEA
DOWN
READING
CHISWICK JUNC. (NOT B.P.)
OLD KEW JUNC.
UP
HAMMERSMITH
KEW EAST JUNC.
BRENT
BRENT JUNC. No 2
Miles
Miles from Battersea Yard Box
0 BRENT Jc No 2 (S.L. & G.L.)
1 DUDDING HILL JUNC
DUDDING HILL (Not B.P.)
2 NEASDEN JUNC.
3 HARLESDEN
ACTON CANAL WHARF
4 ACTON WELLS JUNC (W. DIV.)
5 ACTON CENTRAL
DISTRICT JUNC (CLOSED)
6 SOUTH ACTON JUNC
BOLLO LANE CROSSING
KEW EAST JUNC
NEW KEW JUNC
7 CHISWICK JUNC. (NOT B.P.)
GROVE PARK
8 CHISWICK & GROVE PARK
BARNES BRIDGE STA (NOT B.P.)
9 BARNES LOOP LINE L.C.
BARNES JUNC
BARNES EAST
10 KENMORE (CLOSED)
PUTNEY STA
11
POINT PLEASANT JUNC
WANDSWORTH TOWN
12
CLAPHAM WEST
CLAPHAM EAST
L M S
SOUTHERN RY
CHISWICK & GROVE PARK
BARNES BRIDGE
BARNES LOOP LINE CROSSING
BARNES JC
BARNES
BARNES EAST
KENMORE (CLOSED)
WINDSOR LINES
KEW BRIDGE
WINDSOR
DOWN
UP

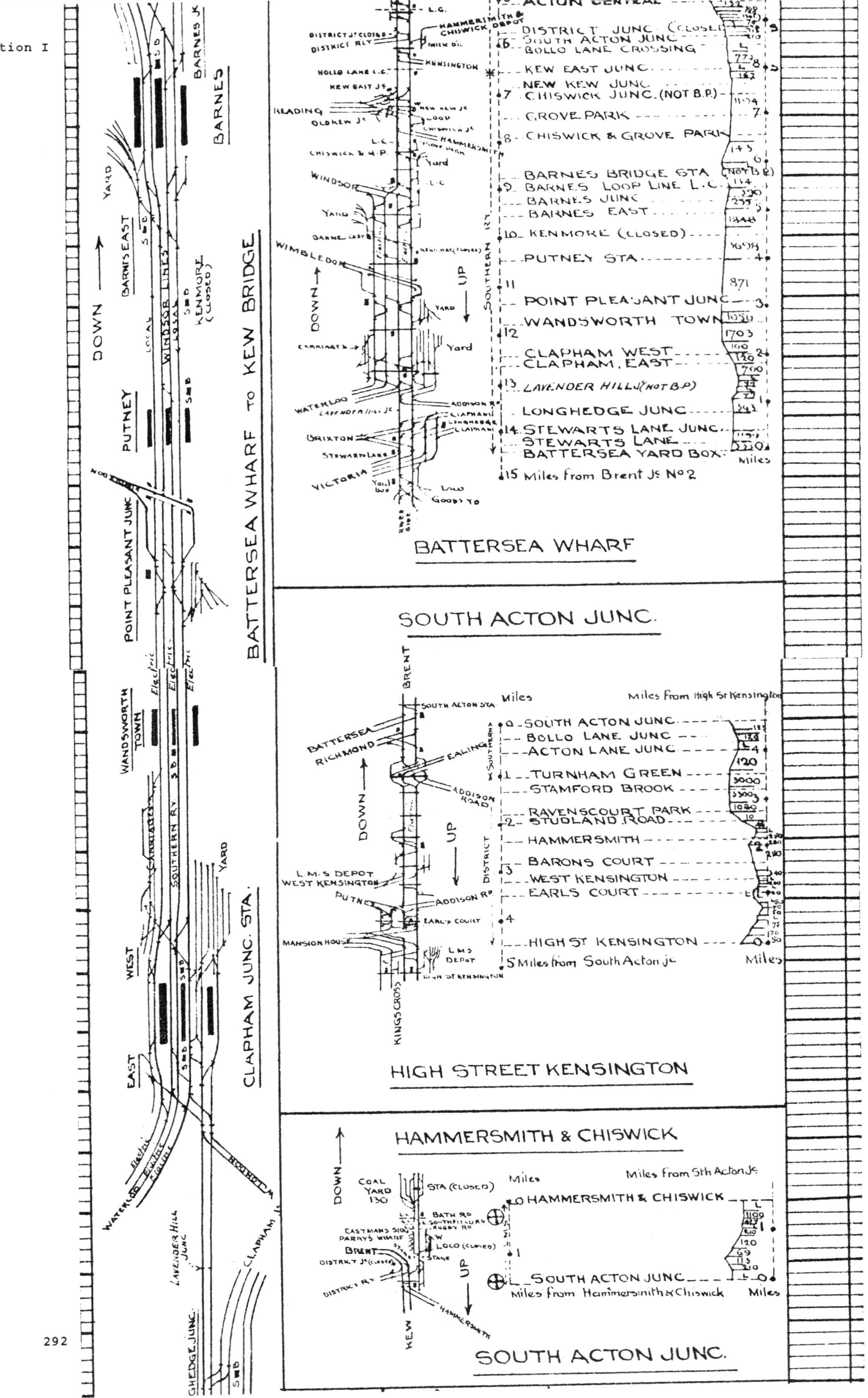
BATTERSEA WHARF TO KEW BRIDGE
CLAPHAM JUNC. STA.
BATTERSEA WHARF
SOUTH ACTON JUNC.
HIGH STREET KENSINGTON
HAMMERSMITH & CHISWICK
SOUTH ACTON JUNC.
15 Miles from Brent Jc No 2
5 Miles from South Acton jc
Miles from High St Kensington
Miles from Sth Acton Jc
Miles from Hammersmith & Chiswick

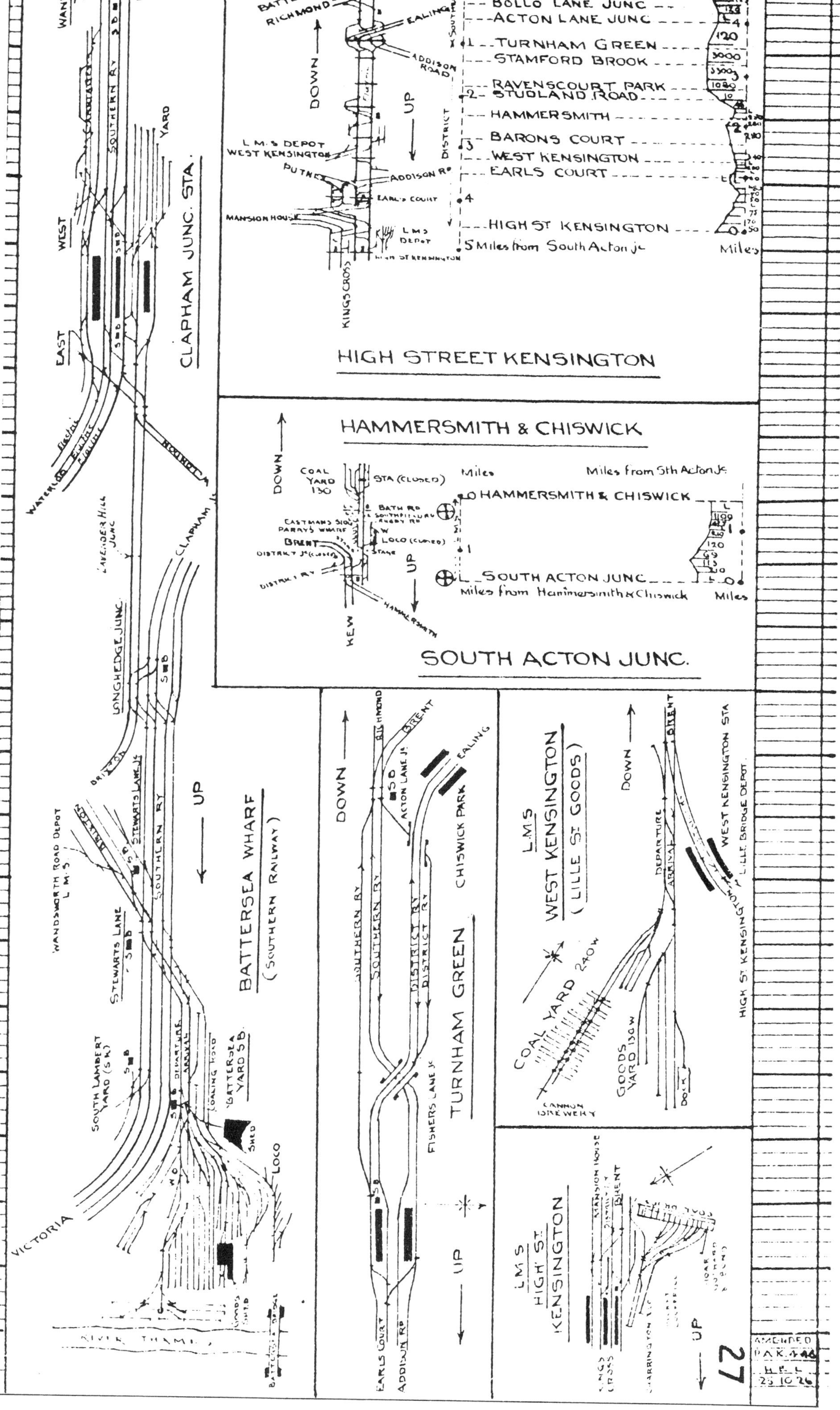
HIGH STREET KENSINGTON
BOLLO LANE JUNC
ACTON LANE JUNC
TURNHAM GREEN
STAMFORD BROOK
RAVENSCOURT PARK
STUDLAND ROAD
HAMMERSMITH
BARONS COURT
WEST KENSINGTON
EARLS COURT
HIGH ST KENSINGTON
5 Miles from South Acton jc
Miles
HAMMERSMITH & CHISWICK
Miles from Sth Acton Jc
HAMMERSMITH & CHISWICK
SOUTH ACTON JUNC
Miles from Hammersmith & Chiswick
SOUTH ACTON JUNC.
CLAPHAM JUNC. STA.
BATTERSEA WHARF
(SOUTHERN RAILWAY)
TURNHAM GREEN
L.M.S
WEST KENSINGTON
(LILLE ST GOODS)
L.M.S
HIGH ST.
KENSINGTON
COAL YARD 240w
GOODS YARD 130w
AMENDED
25 10 26
27

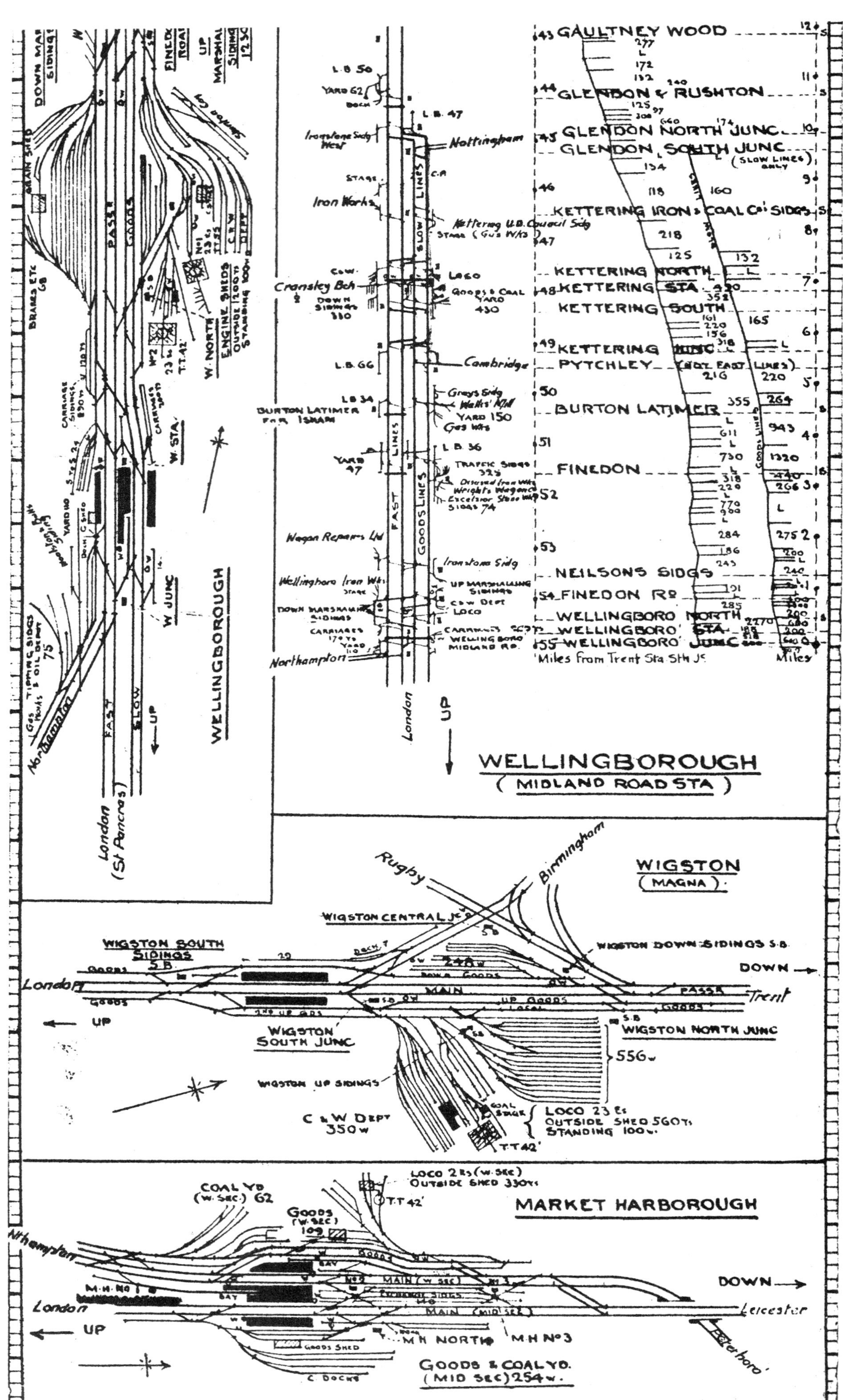
WELLINGBOROUGH
(MIDLAND ROAD STA)
GAULTNEY WOOD
GLENDON & RUSHTON
GLENDON NORTH JUNC
GLENDON SOUTH JUNC
KETTERING IRON & COAL Co. SIDGS
KETTERING NORTH
KETTERING STA
KETTERING SOUTH
KETTERING JUNC
PYTCHLEY
BURTON LATIMER
FINEDON
NEILSONS SIDGS
FINEDON RD
WELLINGBORO NORTH
WELLINGBORO STA
WELLINGBORO JUNC
Miles From Trent Sta Sth Jc
Miles
WIGSTON
(MAGNA)
WIGSTON CENTRAL Jc
WIGSTON SOUTH SIDINGS S.B.
WIGSTON DOWN SIDINGS S.B.
WIGSTON SOUTH JUNC
WIGSTON NORTH JUNC
WIGSTON UP SIDINGS
C & W DEPT 350w
LOCO 23 Es
OUTSIDE SHED 560Ts
STANDING 100w
T.T 42'
Rugby
Birmingham
London
Trent
DOWN
UP
MARKET HARBOROUGH
COAL YD (W. SEC.) 62
GOODS (W. SEC.) 109
LOCO 2 Es (W. SEC)
OUTSIDE SHED 330Ts
T.T 42'
M.H. NORTH
M.H No 3
GOODS & COAL YD. (MID SEC) 254w.
Leicester
London
H.E.L. 1929

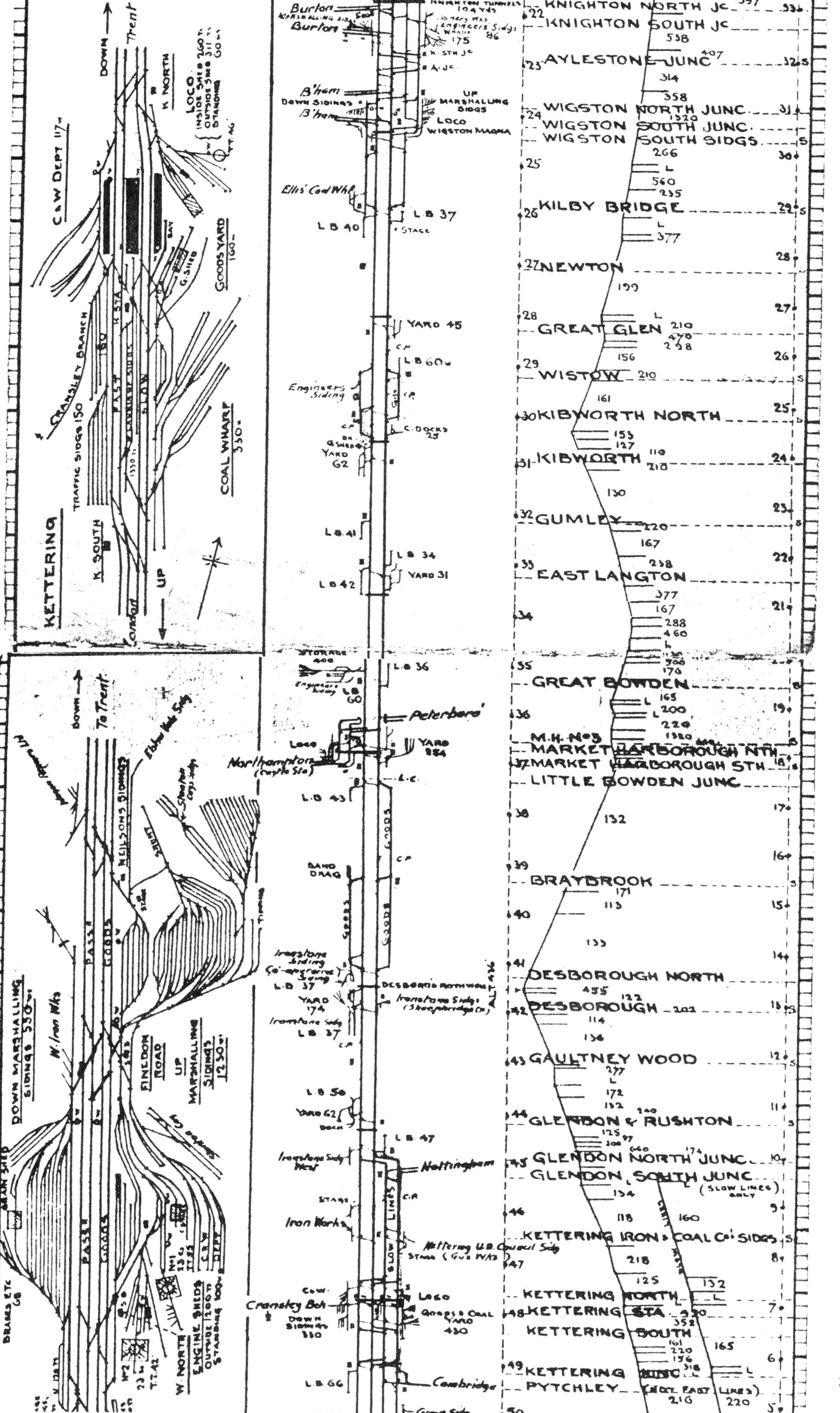
CATTLE MARKET SIDGS
KNIGHTON NORTH Jc
KNIGHTON SOUTH Jc
AYLESTONE JUNC
WIGSTON NORTH JUNC
WIGSTON SOUTH JUNC
WIGSTON SOUTH SIDGS
KILBY BRIDGE
NEWTON
GREAT GLEN
WISTOW
KIBWORTH NORTH
KIBWORTH
GUMLEY
EAST LANGTON
GREAT BOWDEN
M.H. No3
MARKET HARBOROUGH NTH
MARKET HARBOROUGH STH
LITTLE BOWDEN JUNC
BRAYBROOK
DESBOROUGH NORTH
DESBOROUGH
GAULTNEY WOOD
GLENDON & RUSHTON
GLENDON NORTH JUNC
GLENDON SOUTH JUNC
(SLOW LINES ONLY)
KETTERING IRON & COAL Co' SIDGS
KETTERING NORTH
KETTERING STA
KETTERING SOUTH
KETTERING JUNC
PYTCHLEY
(NOT FAST LINES)
Cattle Market
Burton
Burton
B'ham
B'ham
Ellis' Coal Whf
Peterboro'
Northampton
Nottingham
Cransley Bch
Cambridge
KETTERING
C & W DEPT 117
GOODS YARD 160
COAL WHARF 330
CRANSLEY BRANCH
TRAFFIC SIDGS 150
K. SOUTH
K. NORTH
LOCO
DOWN
UP
Trent
London
To Trent
DOWN MARSHALLING SIDINGS 350
UP MARSHALLING SIDINGS 1230
FINEDON ROAD
NEILSONS SIDINGS
W. Iron Wks
W. NORTH ENGINE SHEDS
MAIN SHED
BRAKES ETC 68

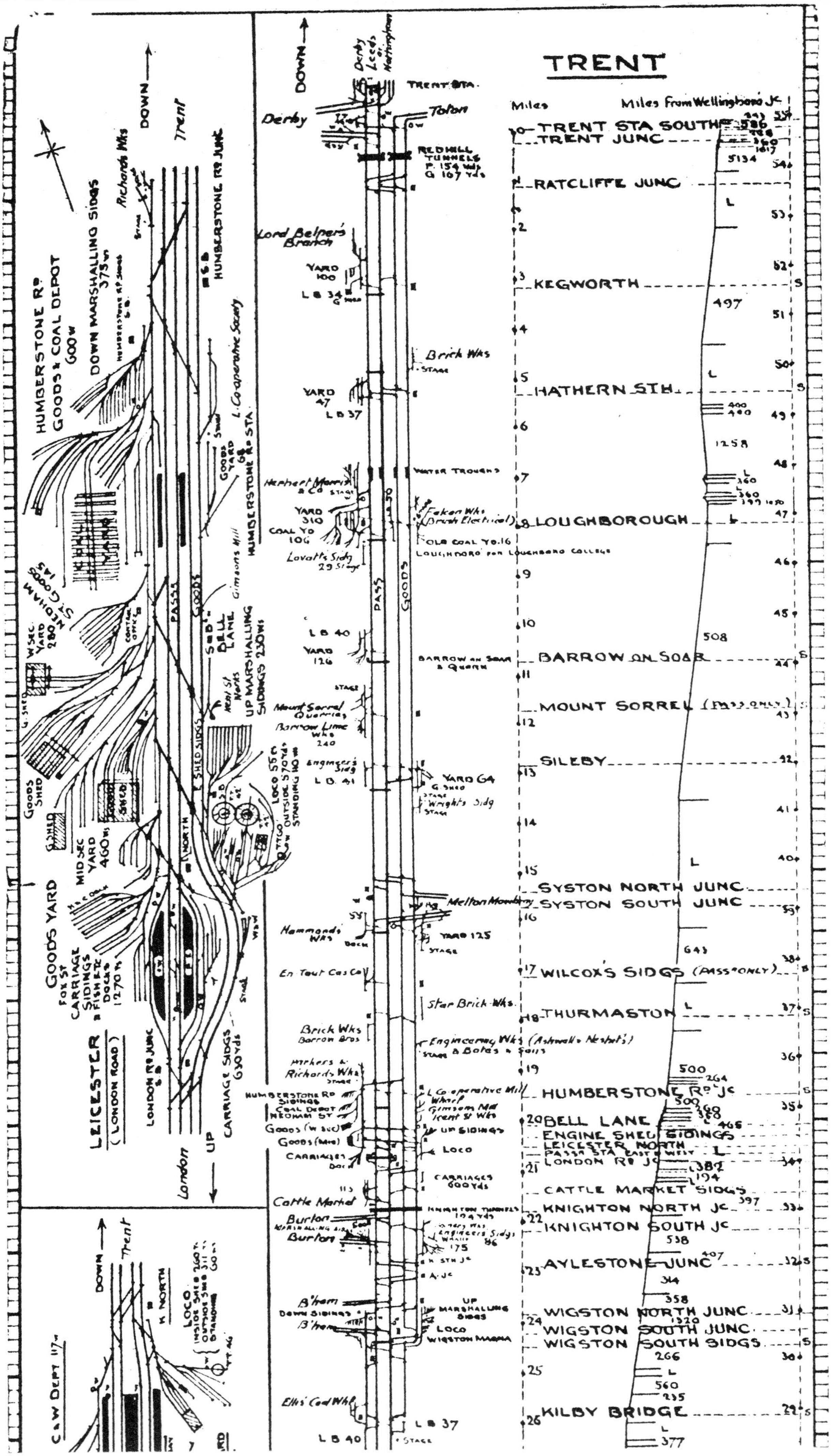

TRENT

DOWN → Derby, Leeds & Nottingham

Miles — Miles From Wellingboro Jc

Miles	Location	Miles from Wellingboro Jc
0	TRENT STA SOUTH	55
	TRENT JUNC	
		54
1	RATCLIFFE JUNC	
		53
2		
		52
3	KEGWORTH	
		51
4		
		50
5	HATHERN STH.	
		49
6		
		48
7		
		47
8	LOUGHBOROUGH	
		46
9		
		45
10		
	BARROW ON SOAR	44
11		
	MOUNT SORREL (PASS ONLY)	43
12		
	SILEBY	42
13		
		41
14		
		40
15		
	SYSTON NORTH JUNC	
	SYSTON SOUTH JUNC	39
16		
		38
17	WILCOX'S SIDGS (PASS ONLY)	
18	THURMASTON	37
		36
19		
	HUMBERSTONE Rᴰ Jc	
		35
20	BELL LANE	
	ENGINE SHED SIDINGS	
	LEICESTER NORTH	
	PASSR STA EAST & WEST	
	LONDON Rᴰ Jc	34
21		
	CATTLE MARKET SIDGS	
	KNIGHTON NORTH Jc	33
22	KNIGHTON SOUTH Jc	
23	AYLESTONE JUNC	32
		31
24	WIGSTON NORTH JUNC	
	WIGSTON SOUTH JUNC	
	WIGSTON SOUTH SIDGS	
25		30
26	KILBY BRIDGE	29

Derby — Toton — TRENT STA. — REDHILL TUNNELS P. 154 Yds G. 107 Yds

Lord Belper's Branch — YARD 100 — L B 34 — Brick Wks — YARD 47 — L B 37 — Herbert Morris & Co — WATER TROUGHS — YARD 310 — COAL YD 106 — Falcon Wks (Brush Electrical) — OLD COAL YD. 16 — Lovatt's Sidg 29 — LOUGHBORO' FOR LOUGHBORO COLLEGE — L B 40 — YARD 126 — BARROW ON SOAR & QUORN — Mount Sorrel Quarries — Barrow Lime Wks 240 — Engineers Sidg — L. B. 41 — YARD 64 — G. SHED — Wright's Sidg — Melton Mowbray — Hammonds Wks — YARD 125 — En Tout Cas Co — Star Brick Wks. — Brick Wks Barron Bros — Engineering Wks (Ashwell & Nesbit's) & Bates & Sons — Harkers & Richards Wks — L Co-operative Mill Wharf — Gimsons Mill — Trent St Wks — HUMBERSTONE Rᴰ SIDINGS COAL DEPOT — NEDHAM ST — Goods (W Sec) — Goods (Mid) — UP SIDINGS — Loco — CARRIAGES — CARRIAGES 600 Yds — Cattle Market — KNIGHTON TUNNELS 104 Yds — Burton Marshalling Sidgs — Burton — Engineers Sidgs — 175 — 86 — K STH Jc — A. Jc — B'ham Down Sidings — B'ham — UP MARSHALLING SIDGS — LOCO WIGSTON MAGNA — Ellis' Coal Whf — L B 37 — L B 40 — PASS — GOODS

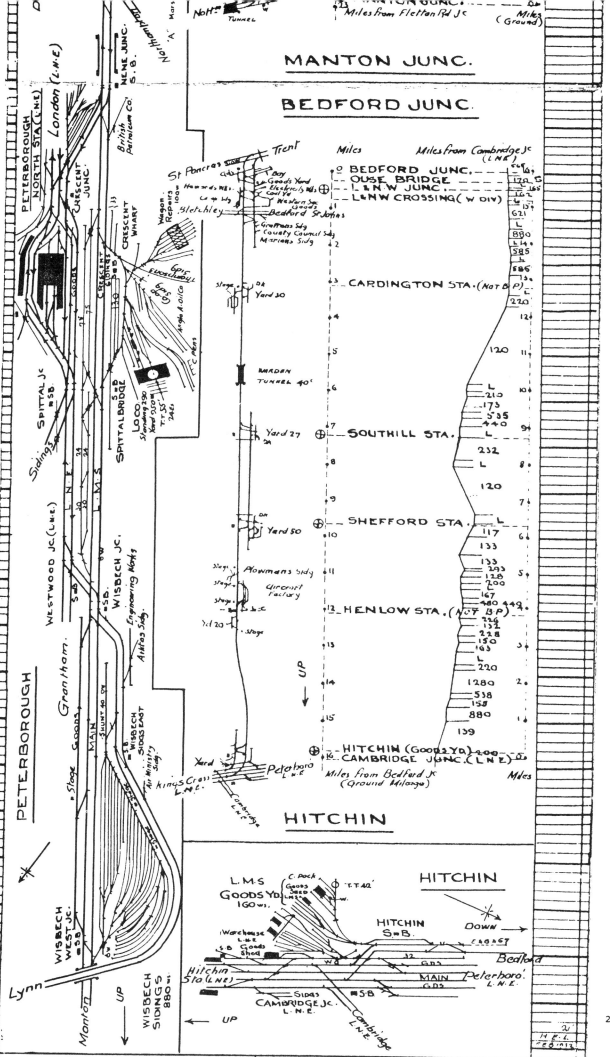

MANTON JUNC.

BEDFORD JUNC.

Miles — Miles from Cambridge Jc (L.N.E.)

- 0 BEDFORD JUNC.
- OUSE BRIDGE
- L & N W JUNC.
- L & N W CROSSING (W DIV)
- 3 CARDINGTON STA. (NOT B.P.)
- 7 SOUTHILL STA.
- 10 SHEFFORD STA.
- 12 HENLOW STA. (NOT B.P.)
- HITCHIN (GOODS YD.)
- 16 CAMBRIDGE JUNC. (L.N.E.)

Miles from Bedford Jc (Ground Mileage) — Miles

HITCHIN

PETERBOROUGH

LUFFENHAM

STAMFORD

NORTHAMPTON

OAKLEY JUNC.

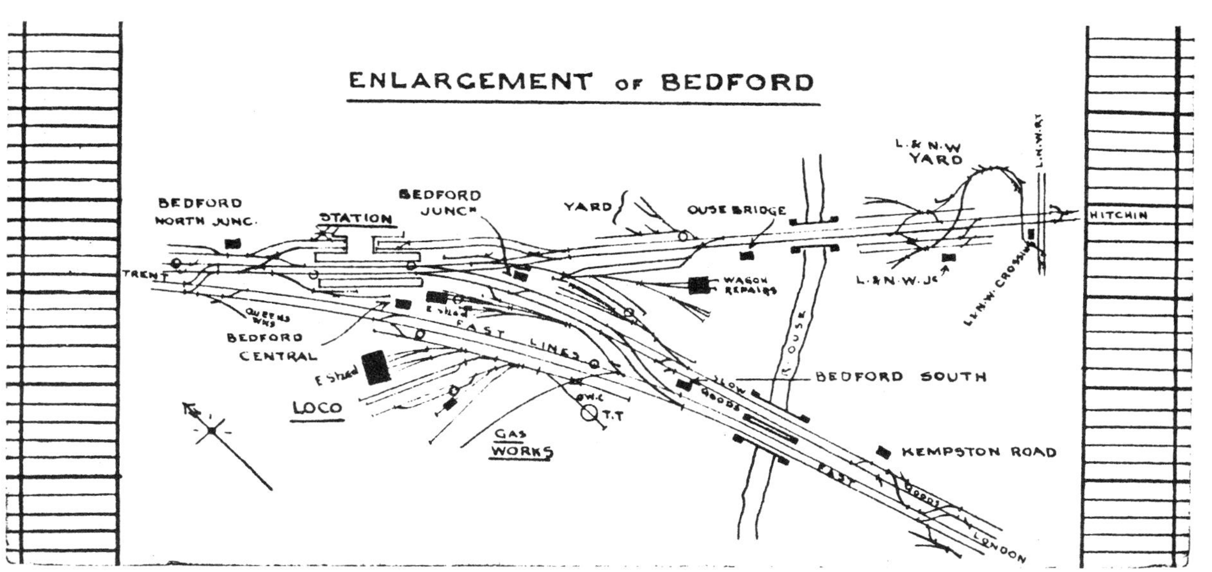

WELLINGBOROUGH

TRENT

LONDON

PETERBORO'

M.R.

L.&N.W.

DOWN UP

L.B. 49.

L.&N.W.

DOWN UP

OAKLEY J^C

M.R.

T.T.

NORTHAMPTON (L.&N.W.)

MID. GOODS

NORTHAMPTON STA

miles			miles from Hardingstone J^cn
0	WELLINGBORO JUNC^N	140	
		L	11
	MIDLAND JUNC^N	270	
1	LEVEL CROSSING	330	
			10
2		1625	
			9
3	HARDWATER CROSSING		8
		924	
4			
			7
5	CASTLE ASHBY STA.		
			6
6		1066	
			5
7		414	
			4
	BILLING STA.		
8		270	
	LITTLE HOUGHTON CROSSING		3
		309	
9			
		747	2
10			
	BEDFORD ROAD CROSSING	L	1
11		990	
	HARDINGSTONE JUNC^N		0

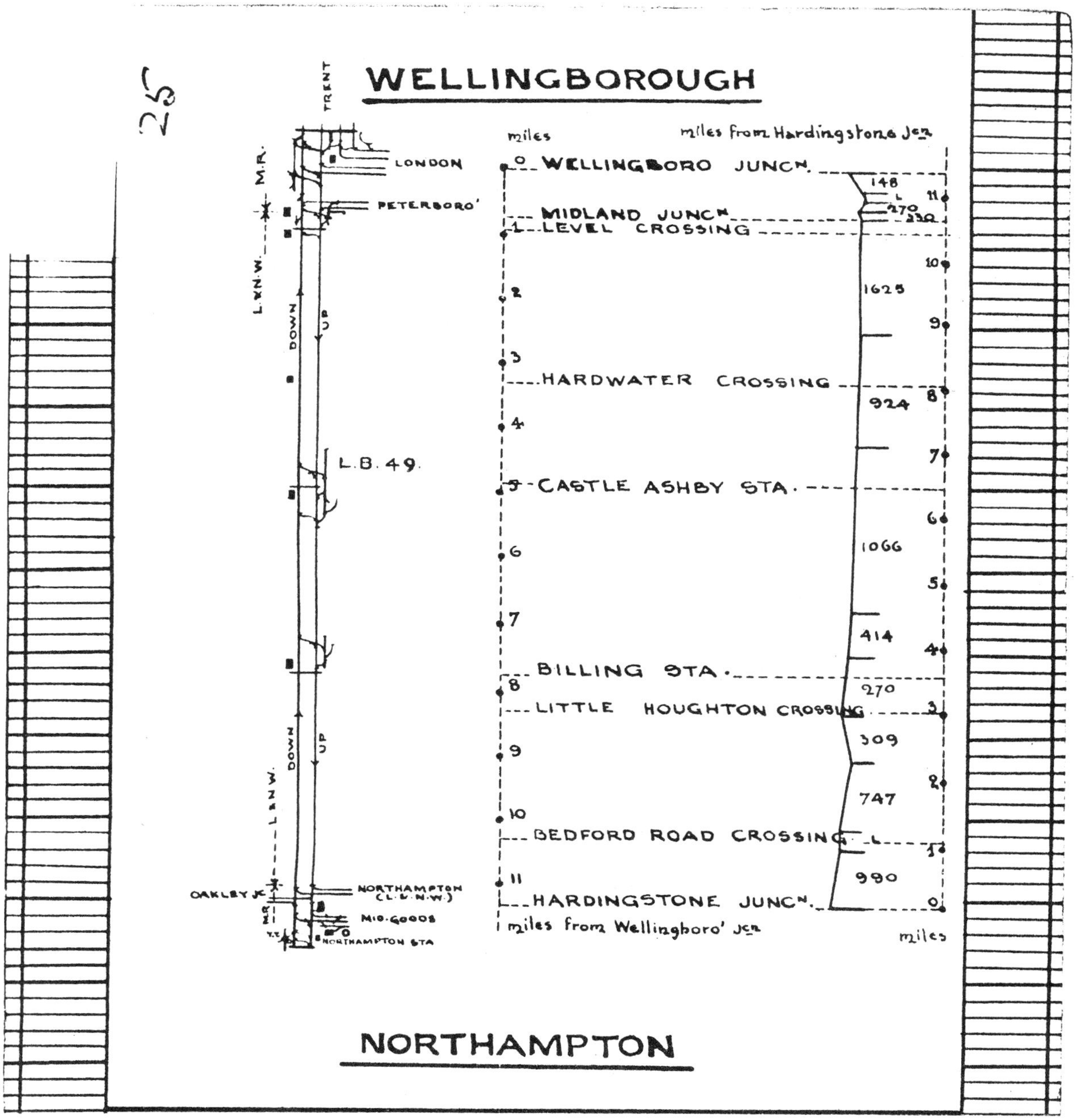

miles from Wellingboro' J^cn — miles

NORTHAMPTON

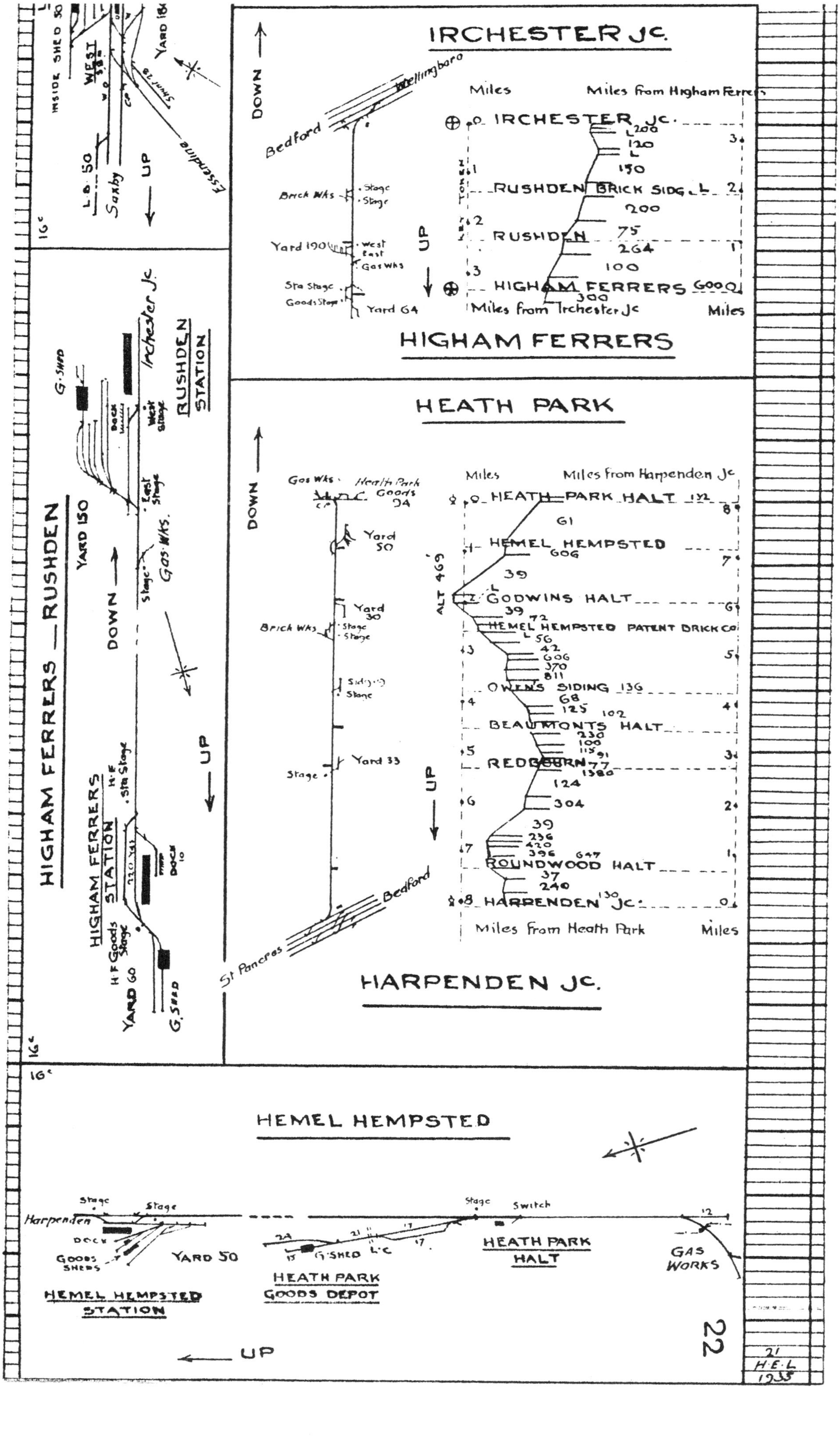

INSIDE SHED 30
WEST
Yard 184
Saxby
L.B. 50
UP
Essendine
16c

IRCHESTER Jc.

DOWN
Wellingboro
Bedford
Brick Wks
Stage
Stage
Yard 190
West
East
Gas Wks
Sta Stage
Goods Stage
Yard 64
UP

Miles | Miles from Higham Ferrers
0 IRCHESTER Jc. 200 L 120 L 150 3
1 RUSHDEN BRICK SIDG L 200 2
2 RUSHDEN 75 264 100 1
3 HIGHAM FERRERS 300 600 0
Miles from Irchester Jc | Miles

HIGHAM FERRERS

HIGHAM FERRERS — RUSHDEN

Irchester Jc
RUSHDEN STATION
G. SHED
DOCK
West Stage
East Stage
YARD 150
DOWN
Stage
GAS WKS.
UP
H.F. Sta Stage
HIGHAM FERRERS STATION
DOCK 10
H.F. Goods Stage
YARD 60
G. SHED
16c

HEATH PARK

DOWN
Gas Wks
Heath Park Goods 94
Yard 50
Yard 30
Brick Wks
Stage
Stage
Siding
Stage
Yard 33
Stage
UP
Bedford
St Pancras

Miles | Miles from Harpenden Jc
0 HEATH PARK HALT 192 8
61
1 HEMEL HEMPSTED 606 7
39
ALT 469
2 GODWINS HALT L 6
39 72
HEMEL HEMPSTED PATENT BRICK Co
L 56
3 42 606 370 811 5
OWENS SIDING 136
4 68 125 102 4
BEAUMONTS HALT 230 100 115 91
5 REDBOURN 77 1380 3
124
6 304 2
39 236 420
7 396 647 1
ROUNDWOOD HALT 37 240
8 HARPENDEN 130 Jc. 0
Miles from Heath Park | Miles

HARPENDEN Jc.

16c

HEMEL HEMPSTED

Stage
Stage
Harpenden
DOCK
GOODS SHEDS
YARD 50
HEMEL HEMPSTED STATION
24
15
G. SHED
21
L.C
17
17
HEATH PARK GOODS DEPOT
Stage
Switch
HEATH PARK HALT
12
GAS WORKS
UP

22

21
H.E.L
1935

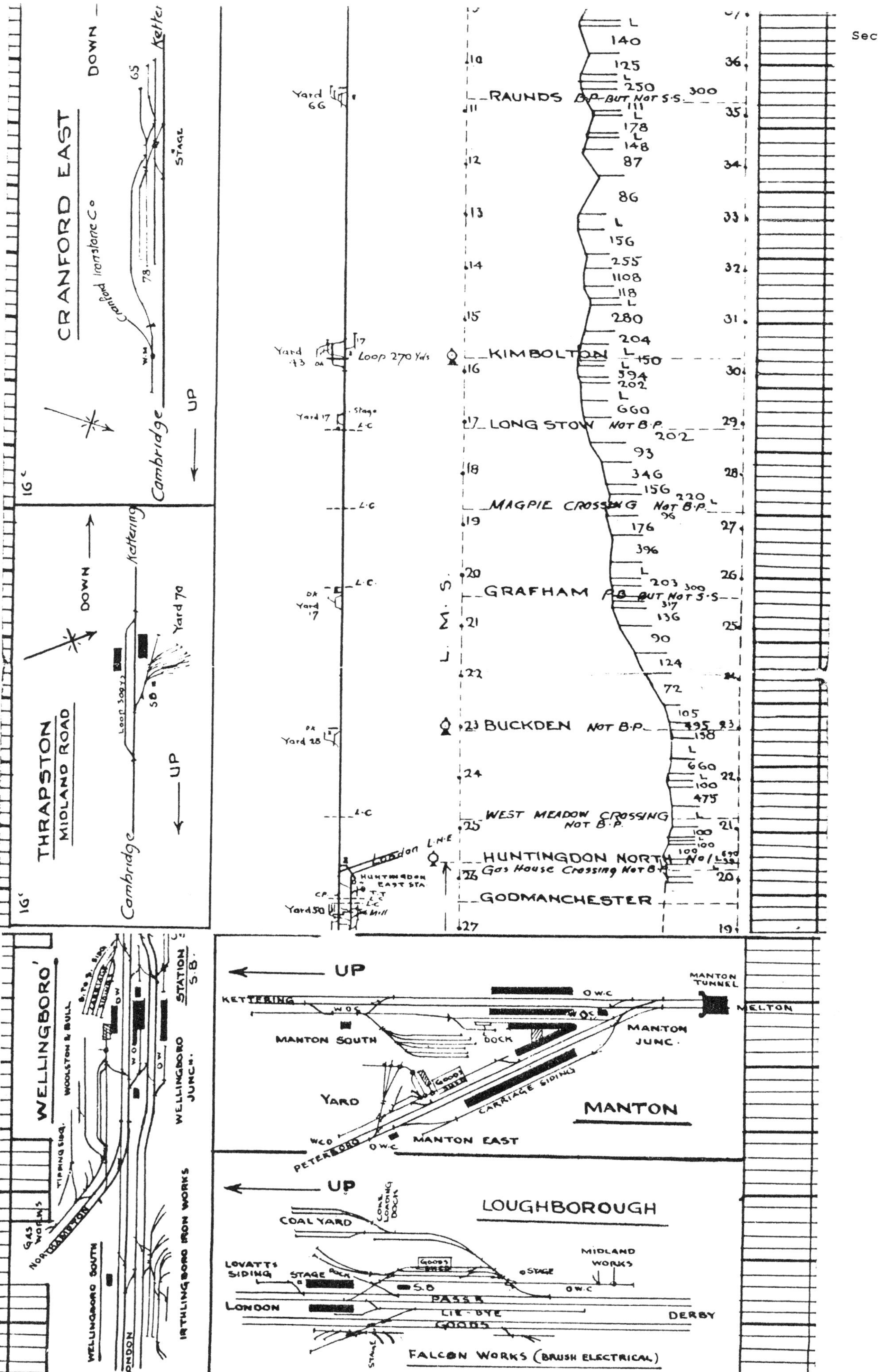
CRANFORD EAST
DOWN
UP
Cambridge
Kettering
Cranford Ironstone Co
STAGE
THRAPSTON
MIDLAND ROAD
Cambridge
Kettering
Yard 70
Loop 300 Yds
UP
DOWN
RAUNDS
KIMBOLTON
Loop 270 Yds
LONG STOW NOT B.P.
MAGPIE CROSSING NOT B.P.
GRAFHAM
BUCKDEN NOT B.P.
WEST MEADOW CROSSING NOT B.P.
HUNTINGDON NORTH
Gas House Crossing Not B.P.
GODMANCHESTER
L.M.S.
London L.N.E
HUNTINGDON EAST STA
WELLINGBORO'
STATION S.B.
WELLINGBORO JUNCN.
WOOLSTON & BULL
TIPPING SIDG.
GAS WORKS
NORTHAMPTON
WELLINGBORO SOUTH
LONDON
IRTHLINGBORO IRON WORKS
UP
KETTERING
MANTON TUNNEL
MELTON
MANTON SOUTH
DOCK
MANTON JUNC.
YARD
CARRIAGE SIDINGS
MANTON
MANTON EAST
PETERBORO
UP
LOUGHBOROUGH
COAL YARD
LOVATTS SIDING
STAGE
DOCK
GOODS SHED
S.B
MIDLAND WORKS
PASS'R
LONDON
LIE-BYE
GOODS
DERBY
FALCON WORKS (BRUSH ELECTRICAL)

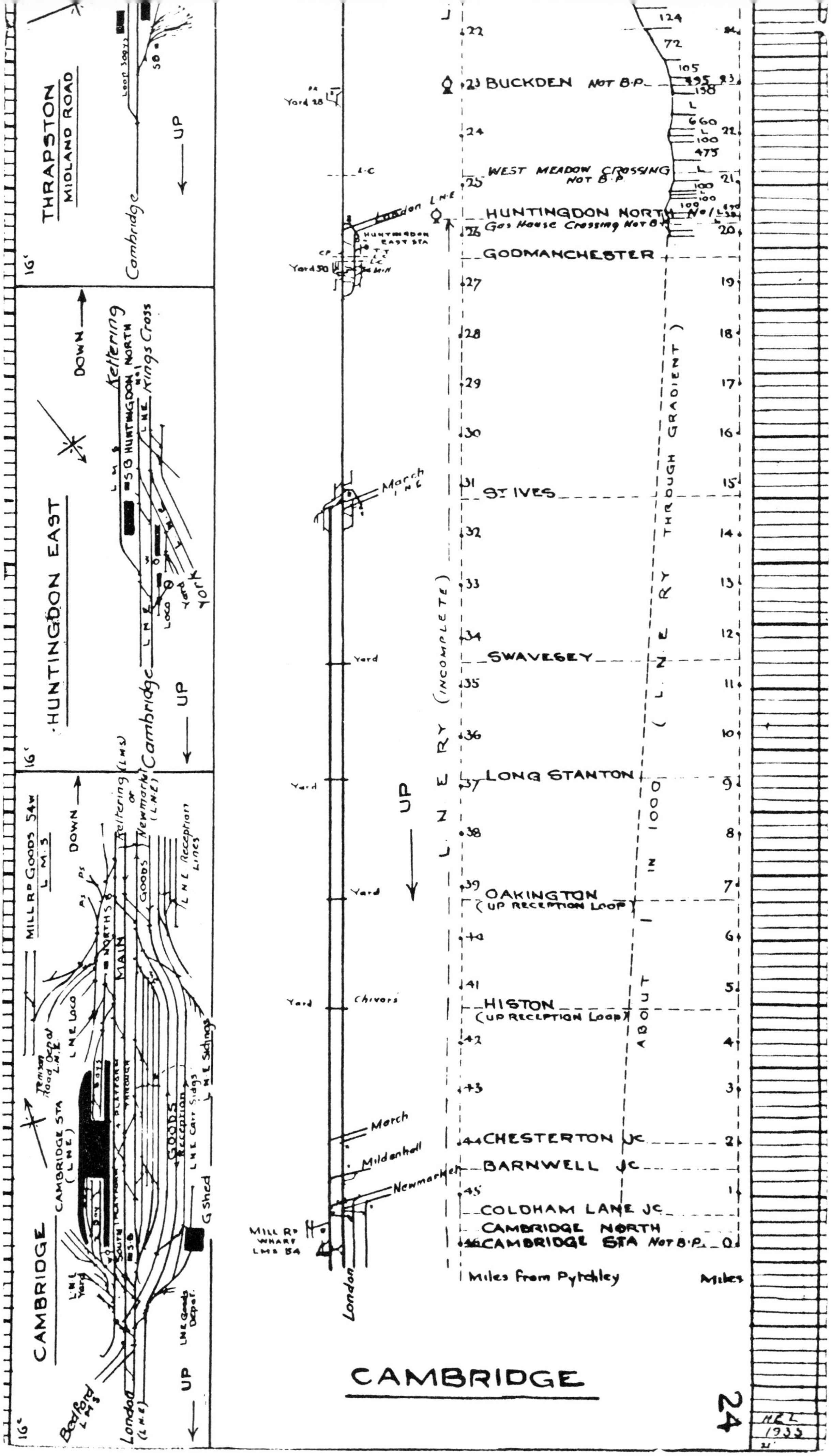

THRAPSTON
MIDLAND ROAD
Cambridge
UP
16c

HUNTINGDON EAST
DOWN
Kettering
HUNTINGDON NORTH No 1
Kings Cross
L M S
SB HUNTINGDON
L N E
York
Yard
Loco
Cambridge
UP
16c

CAMBRIDGE
MILL Rd GOODS 54W
L M S
DOWN
Kettering (LMS)
or
Newmarket (LNE)
L N E Reception Lines
NORTH
MAIN
GOODS
L N E Loco
Tenison Road Depot L.N.E.
CAMBRIDGE STA (L N E)
PLATFORM
THROUGH
GOODS
Reception
L N E Carr Sidgs
L N E Sidings
G Shed
L N E Yard
L N E Goods Depot
Bedford L M S
London (L N E)
UP
16c

22
23 BUCKDEN NOT B.P.
24
25 WEST MEADOW CROSSING NOT B.P.
HUNTINGDON NORTH No 1
26 Gas House Crossing Not B.P.
GODMANCHESTER
27
28
29
30
31 ST IVES
32
33
34
SWAVESEY
35
36
37 LONG STANTON
38
39 OAKINGTON (UP RECEPTION LOOP)
40
41 HISTON (UP RECEPTION LOOP)
42
43
44 CHESTERTON JC
BARNWELL JC
45
COLDHAM LANE JC
CAMBRIDGE NORTH
46 CAMBRIDGE STA NOT B.P.
Miles from Pytchley

L N E R Y (INCOMPLETE)
UP
(L N E R Y THROUGH GRADIENT)
ABOUT 1 IN 1000

124
72
105
195
150
L
660
L
100
475
L
100
100
100
L
24
23
22
21
20
19
18
17
16
15
14
13
12
11
10
9
8
7
6
5
4
3
2
1
0
Miles

Yard 28
L.C
London L N E
HUNTINGDON EAST STA
Yard 50
March L N E
Yard
Yard
Yard
Yard
Chivers
March
Mildenhall
Newmarket
MILL Rd WHARF LMS 54
London

CAMBRIDGE

24

H.E.L. 1933

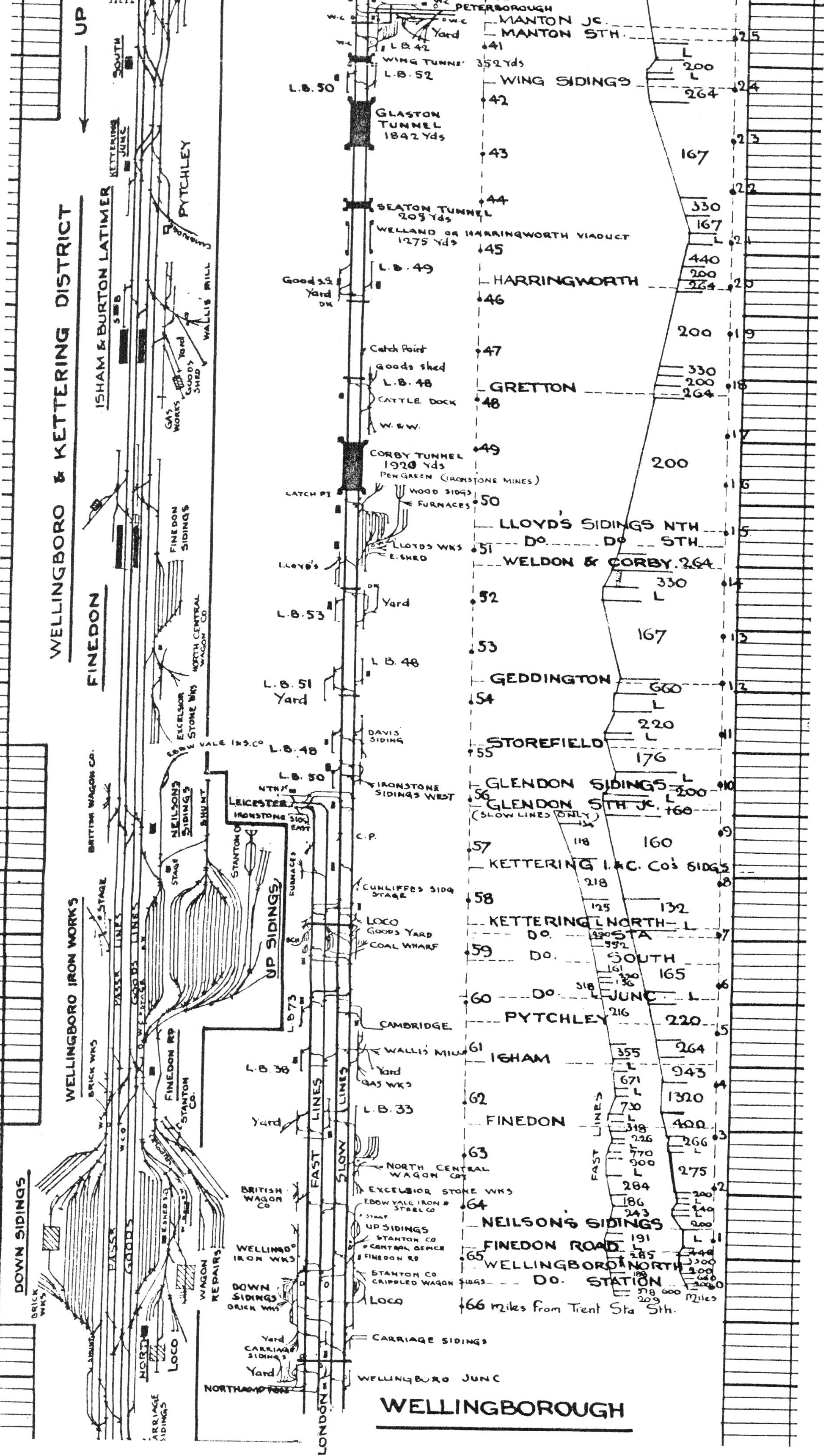
WELLINGBORO & KETTERING DISTRICT
PETERBOROUGH
MANTON JC.
MANTON STH
WING TUNNEL 352 Yds
WING SIDINGS
GLASTON TUNNEL 1842 Yds
SEATON TUNNEL 205 Yds
WELLAND OR HARRINGWORTH VIADUCT 1275 Yds
HARRINGWORTH
GRETTON
CORBY TUNNEL 1920 Yds
LLOYD'S SIDINGS NTH
WELDON & CORBY
GEDDINGTON
STOREFIELD
GLENDON SIDINGS
GLENDON STH. JC.
KETTERING I. & C. Co's SIDGS
KETTERING NORTH
PYTCHLEY
ISHAM
FINEDON
NEILSON'S SIDINGS
FINEDON ROAD
WELLINGBORO NORTH
66 miles from Trent Sta Sth.
KETTERING JUNC
ISHAM & BURTON LATIMER
FINEDON
WELLINGBORO IRON WORKS
DOWN SIDINGS
UP SIDINGS
FAST LINES
SLOW LINES
WELLINGBORO JUNC
NORTHAMPTON
LONDON
WELLINGBOROUGH

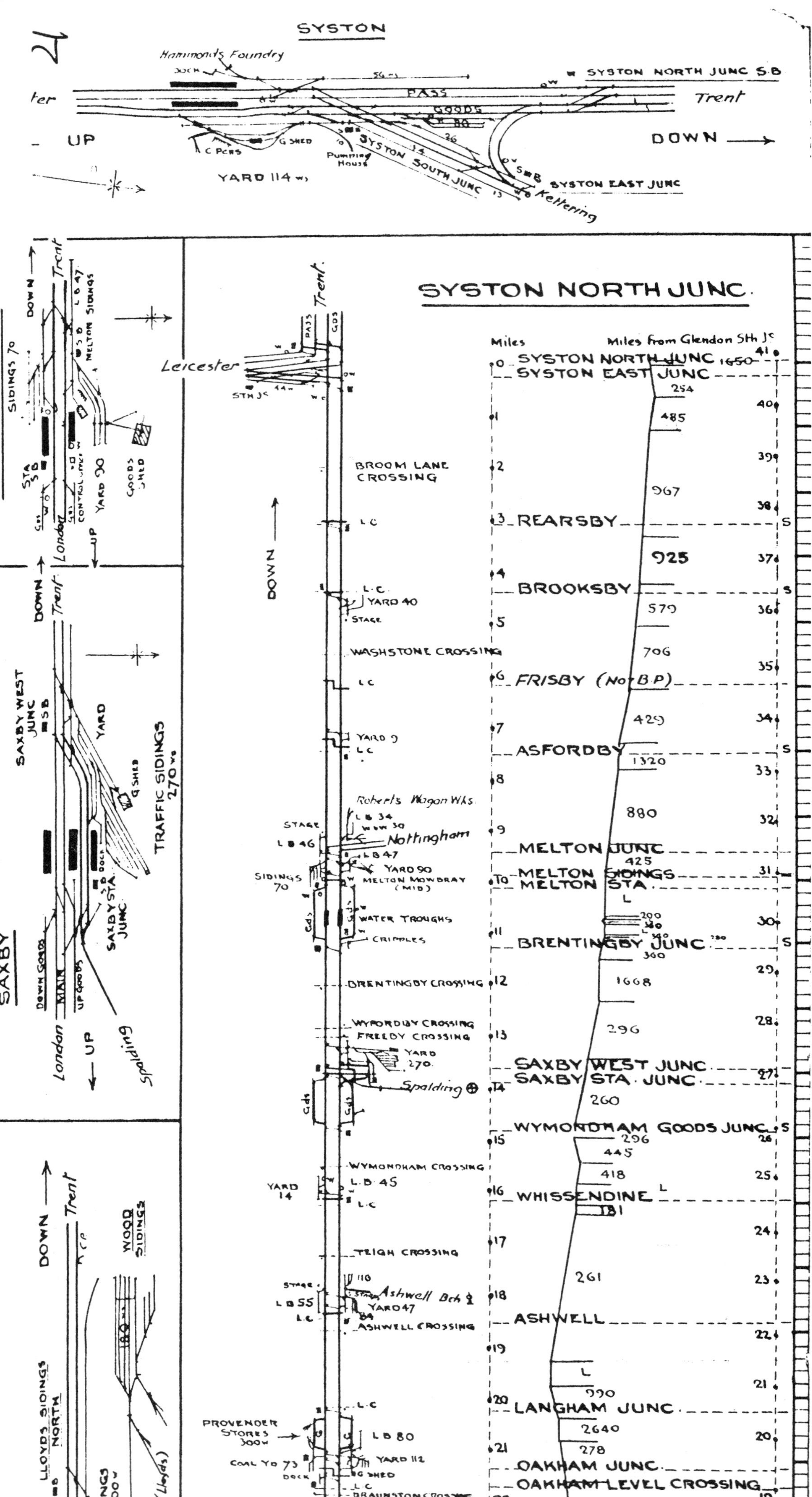
SYSTON
Hammonds Foundry
SYSTON NORTH JUNC S.B
PASS
GOODS
Trent
UP
DOWN
YARD 114 yds
SYSTON SOUTH JUNC
SYSTON EAST JUNC
Kettering
MELTON MOWBRAY
SIDINGS 70
YARD 90
GOODS SHED
SAXBY
SAXBY WEST JUNC
TRAFFIC SIDINGS 270 yds
SAXBY STA. JUNC
Spalding
London
Leicester
LLOYDS SIDINGS NORTH
WOOD SIDINGS
SYSTON NORTH JUNC.
Miles
Miles from Glendon Sth Jc
SYSTON NORTH JUNC
SYSTON EAST JUNC
BROOM LANE CROSSING
REARSBY
BROOKSBY
WASHSTONE CROSSING
FRISBY (No B.P)
ASFORDBY
Roberts Wagon Wks.
Nottingham
MELTON JUNC
MELTON SIDINGS
MELTON STA.
MELTON MOWBRAY (MID)
WATER TROUGHS
CRIPPLES
BRENTINGBY JUNC
BRENTINGBY CROSSING
WYFORDBY CROSSING
FREEBY CROSSING
SAXBY WEST JUNC
SAXBY STA. JUNC
WYMONDHAM GOODS JUNC
WYMONDHAM CROSSING
WHISSENDINE
TEIGH CROSSING
Ashwell Bch
ASHWELL
ASHWELL CROSSING
LANGHAM JUNC
PROVENDER STORES 300 yds
OAKHAM JUNC
OAKHAM LEVEL CROSSING
BRAUNSTON CROSSING

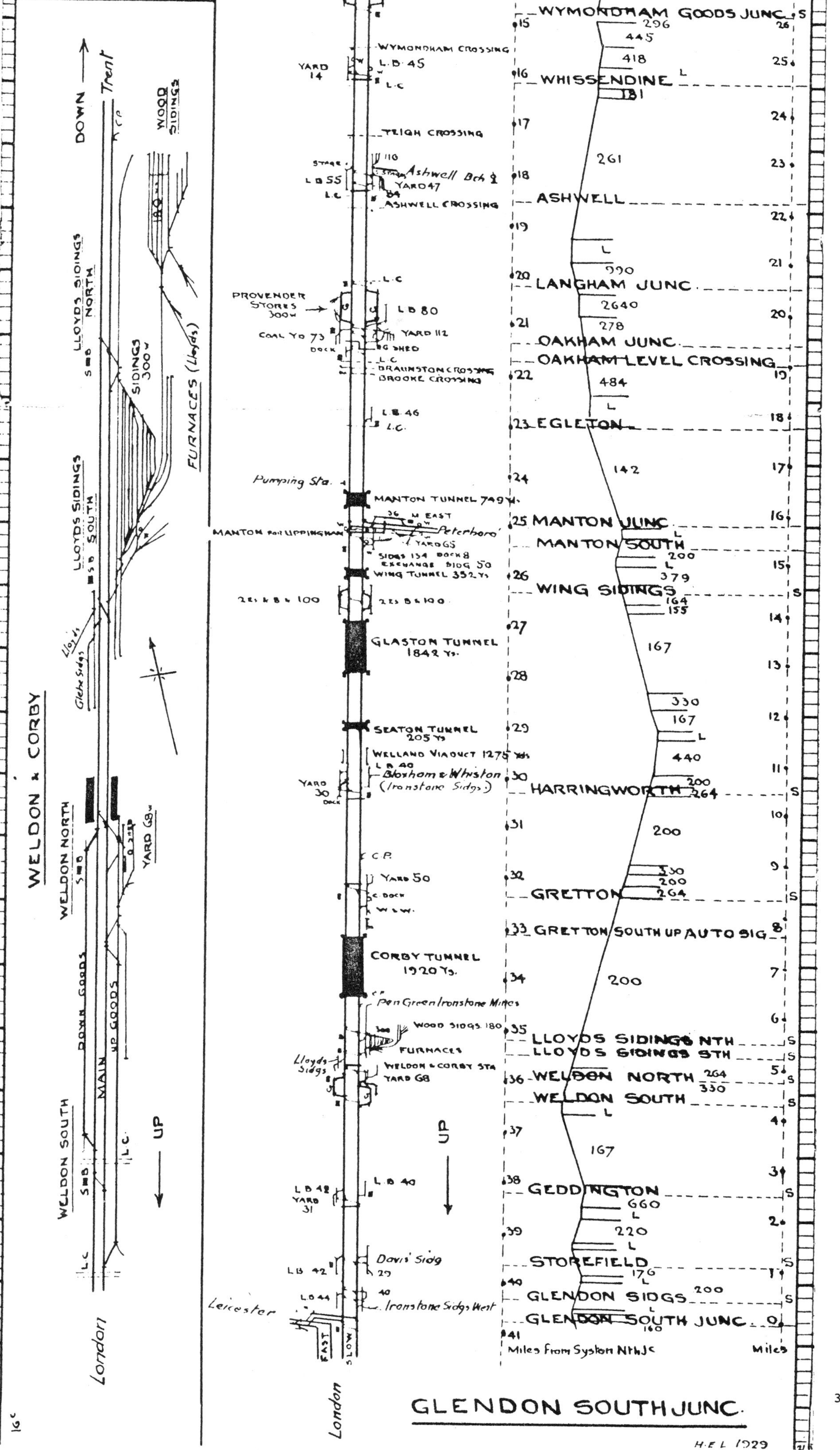
WEYMONDHAM GOODS JUNC
WYMONDHAM CROSSING
YARD 14
L.B. 45
L.C
WHISSENDINE
TEIGH CROSSING
Ashwell Bch
YARD 47
L.B 55
ASHWELL
ASHWELL CROSSING
LANGHAM JUNC
PROVENDER STORES 300w
L.B 80
COAL YD 73
YARD 112
OAKHAM JUNC
OAKHAM LEVEL CROSSING
BRAUNSTON CROSSING
BROOKE CROSSING
L.B. 46
EGLETON
Pumping Sta.
MANTON TUNNEL 749 Ys.
MANTON JUNC
MANTON FOR UPPINGHAM
Peterboro'
MANTON SOUTH
WING TUNNEL 352 Ys
WING SIDINGS
GLASTON TUNNEL 1842 Ys.
SEATON TUNNEL 205 Ys
WELLAND VIADUCT 1275 Yds
Bloxhom & Whiston (Ironstone Sidgs)
HARRINGWORTH
Yard 50
GRETTON
GRETTON SOUTH UP AUTO SIG
CORBY TUNNEL 1920 Ys.
Pen Green Ironstone Mines
WOOD SIDGS 180
FURNACES
WELDON & CORBY STA
YARD 68
LLOYDS SIDINGS NTH
LLOYDS SIDINGS STH
WELDON NORTH
WELDON SOUTH
L.B. 40
GEDDINGTON
Davis' Sidg
STOREFIELD
Ironstone Sidgs West
GLENDON SIDGS
GLENDON SOUTH JUNC
Leicester
FAST
SLOW
Miles From Syston Nth J^c
Miles
London
UP
GLENDON SOUTH JUNC.
H.E.L 1929
WELDON & CORBY
DOWN
Trent
WOOD SIDINGS
LLOYDS SIDINGS NORTH
SIDINGS 300w
FURNACES (Lloyds)
LLOYDS SIDINGS SOUTH
Glebe Sidgs
WELDON NORTH
YARD 68w
DOWN GOODS
MAIN
UP GOODS
WELDON SOUTH
UP
London
16^c

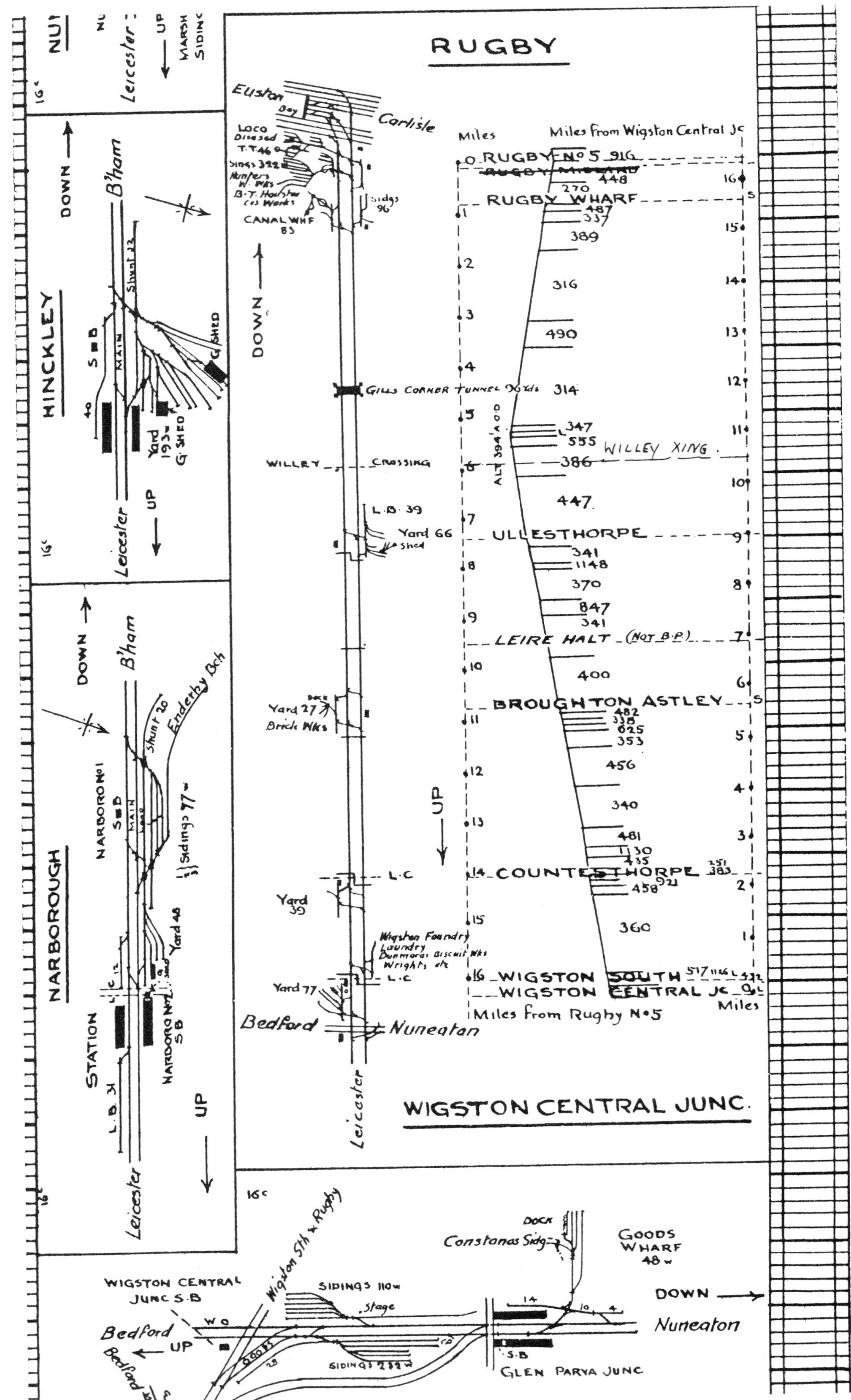
RUGBY
Euston
Carlisle
Miles
Miles from Wigston Central Jc
RUGBY No 5
RUGBY WHARF
GILLS CORNER TUNNEL
WILLEY XING
WILLEY CROSSING
ULLESTHORPE
LEIRE HALT (NOT B.P.)
BROUGHTON ASTLEY
COUNTESTHORPE
WIGSTON SOUTH
WIGSTON CENTRAL JC
Miles from Rugby No 5
Bedford
Nuneaton
Leicester
WIGSTON CENTRAL JUNC.
HINCKLEY
B'ham
Leicester
NARBOROUGH
Enderby Bch
STATION
WIGSTON CENTRAL JUNC S.B
SIDINGS 110w
GOODS WHARF
Constanas Sidg
GLEN PARVA JUNC
DOWN
UP

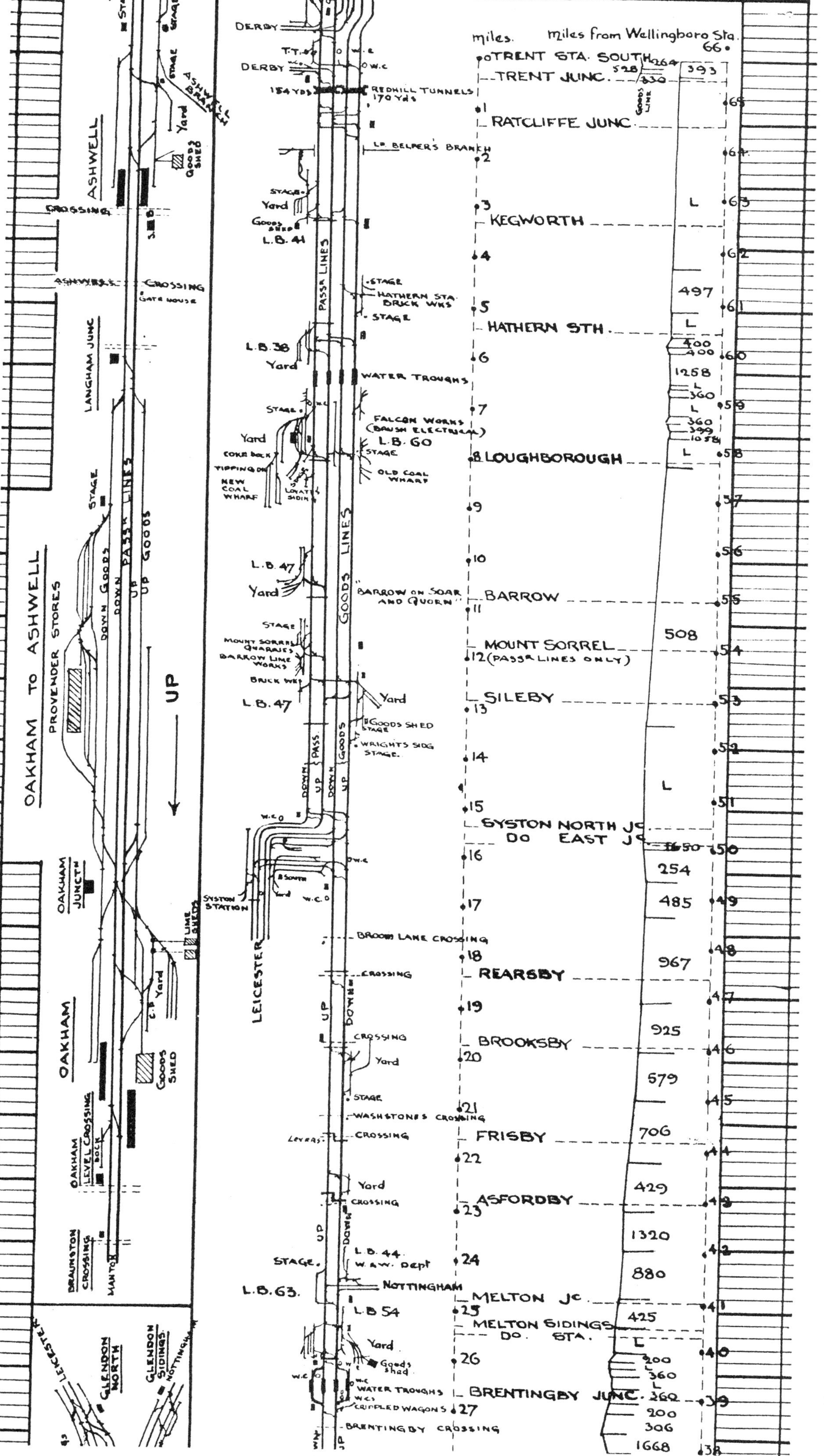

OAKHAM TO ASHWELL
ASHWELL
ASHWELL BRANCH
CROSSING
LANGHAM JUNC
PROVENDER STORES
DOWN GOODS
DOWN PASSR LINES
UP PASSR LINES
UP GOODS
UP
OAKHAM JUNCTN
LIME SHEDS
OAKHAM
GOODS SHED
OAKHAM LEVEL CROSSING
BRAUNSTON CROSSING
MANTON
LEICESTER
GLENDON NORTH
GLENDON SIDINGS
NOTTINGHAM
miles.
miles from Wellingboro Sta.
DERBY
TRENT STA. SOUTH
TRENT JUNC.
REDHILL TUNNELS 170 YDS
154 YDS
RATCLIFFE JUNC.
GOODS LINE
LD BELPER'S BRANCH
KEGWORTH
L.B. 41
PASSR LINES
HATHERN STA. BRICK WKS
HATHERN STN.
L.B. 38
WATER TROUGHS
FALCON WORKS (BRUSH ELECTRICAL)
L.B. 60
LOUGHBOROUGH
COKE DOCK
NEW COAL WHARF
OLD COAL WHARF
GOODS LINES
L.B. 47
"BARROW ON SOAR AND QUORN"
BARROW
MOUNT SORREL QUARRIES
BARROW LIME WORKS
MOUNT SORREL
12 (PASSR LINES ONLY)
SILEBY
GOODS SHED
WRIGHTS SIDG
SYSTON NORTH JC
DO EAST JC
SYSTON STATION
LEICESTER
BROOM LANE CROSSING
REARSBY
BROOKSBY
WASHSTONES CROSSING
FRISBY
ASFORDBY
L.B. 44
W.&W. Dept
NOTTINGHAM
L.B. 63.
MELTON JC
L.B. 54
MELTON SIDINGS
DO. STA.
WATER TROUGHS
CRIPPLED WAGONS
BRENTINGBY JUNC.
BRENTINGBY CROSSING

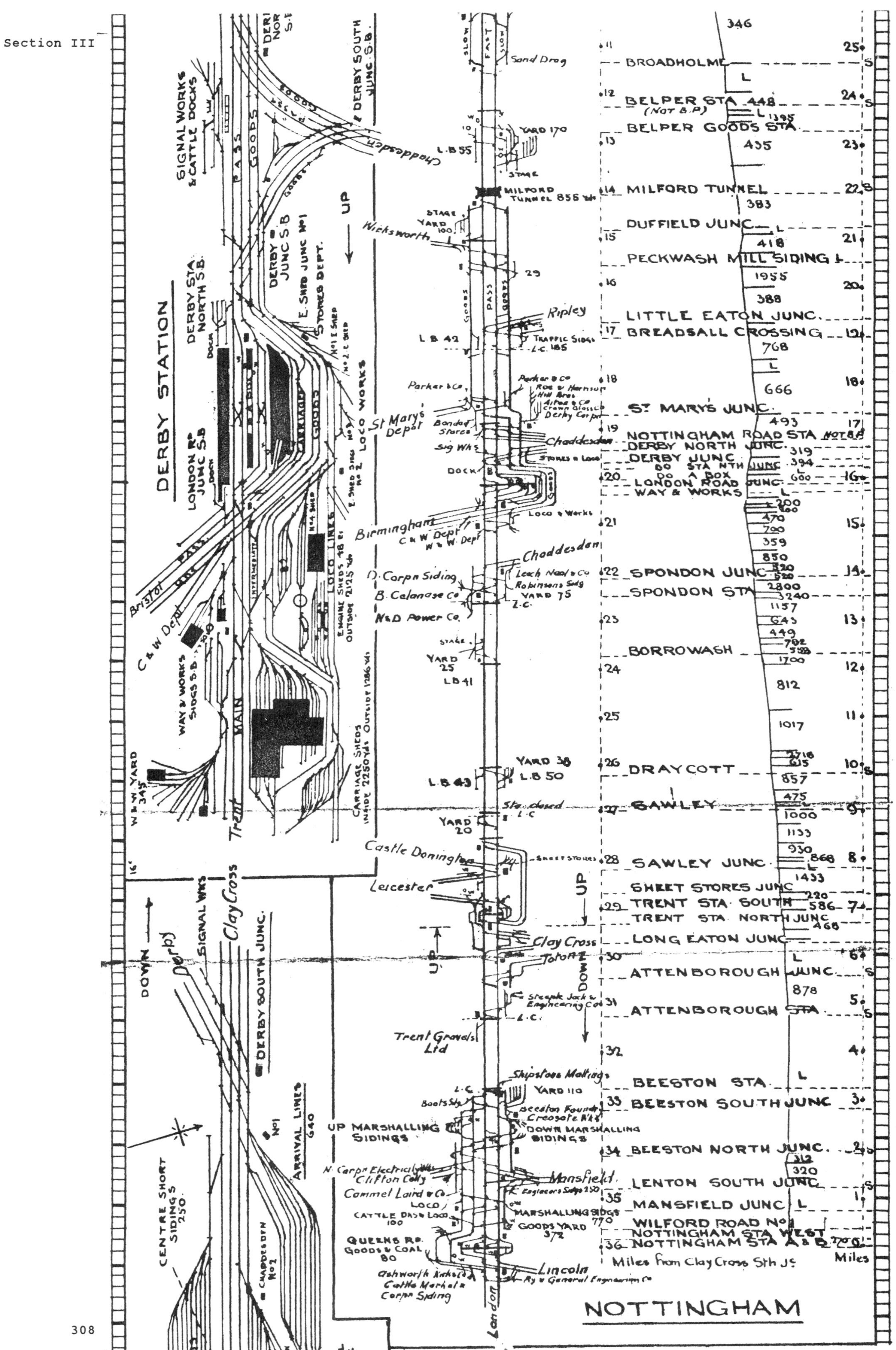
DERBY STATION
NOTTINGHAM
BROADHOLME
BELPER STA 448
(NOT B.P.)
BELPER GOODS STA
MILFORD TUNNEL
DUFFIELD JUNC
PECKWASH MILL SIDING
LITTLE EATON JUNC
BREADSALL CROSSING
ST MARY'S JUNC
NOTTINGHAM ROAD STA
DERBY NORTH JUNC
DERBY JUNC
LONDON ROAD JUNC
WAY & WORKS
SPONDON JUNC
SPONDON STA
BORROWASH
DRAYCOTT
SAWLEY
SAWLEY JUNC
SHEET STORES JUNC
TRENT STA SOUTH
TRENT STA NORTH JUNC
LONG EATON JUNC
ATTENBOROUGH JUNC
ATTENBOROUGH STA
BEESTON STA
BEESTON SOUTH JUNC
BEESTON NORTH JUNC
LENTON SOUTH JUNC
MANSFIELD JUNC
WILFORD ROAD No 1
NOTTINGHAM STA WEST
NOTTINGHAM STA A & B
Miles from Clay Cross Sth Jc
Miles
UP MARSHALLING SIDINGS
DOWN MARSHALLING SIDINGS
QUEENS RD GOODS & COAL 80
GOODS YARD 372
Lincoln
London
Chaddesden
Birmingham
Bristol
Castle Donington
Leicester
Clay Cross
Mansfield
Wirksworth
Ripley
MILFORD TUNNEL 855 Yds
SIGNAL WORKS & CATTLE DOCKS
DERBY SOUTH JUNC S.B.
DERBY STA NORTH S.B.
LONDON RD JUNC S.B.
LOCO WORKS
CARRIAGE SHEDS
ENGINE SHEDS
CENTRE SHORT SIDINGS 250
ARRIVAL LINES 640
DERBY SOUTH JUNC.
Trent Gravels Ltd
Shipstone Maltings
Boots Sdg
Cammel Laird & Co
Clifton Colly
UP
DOWN

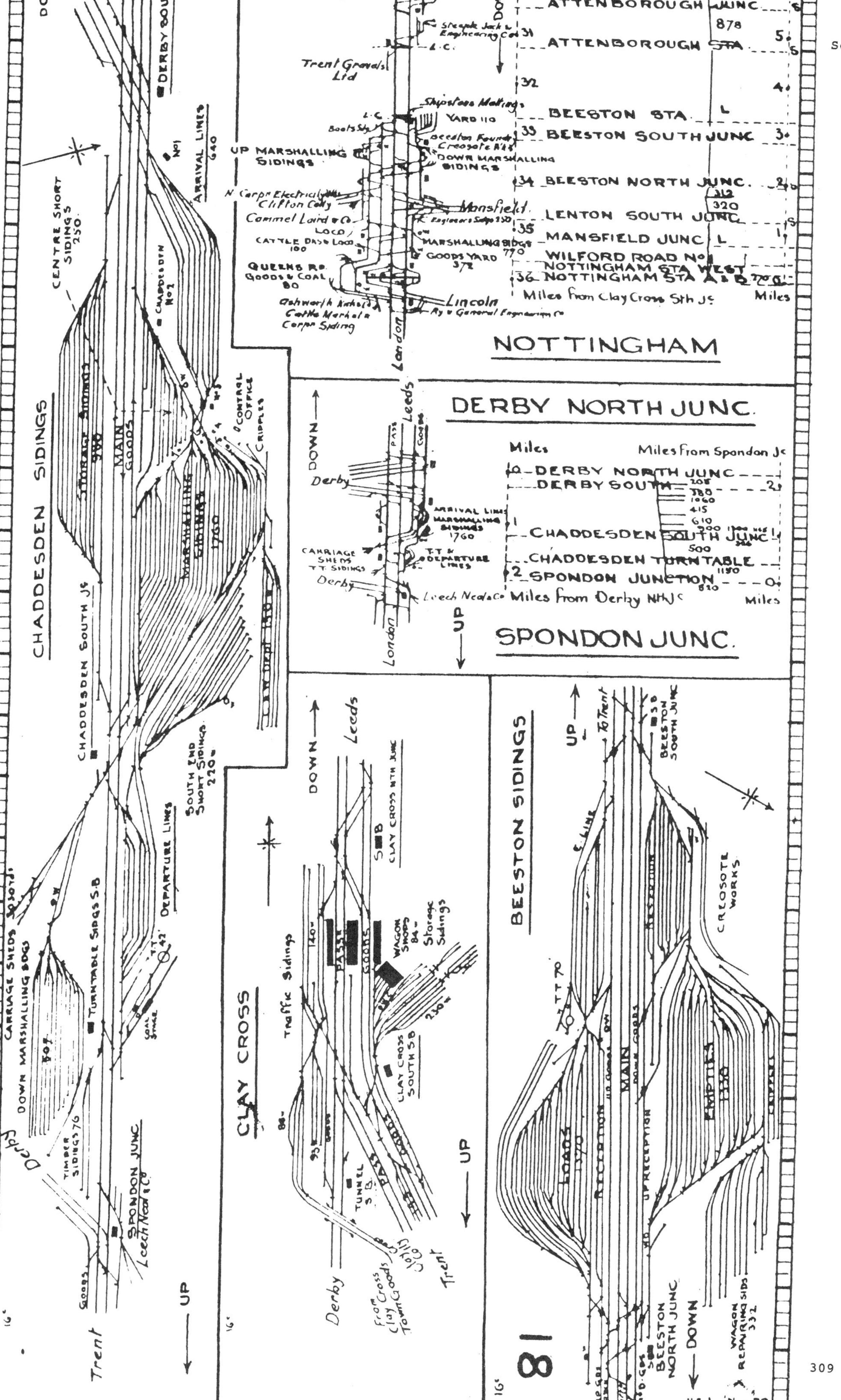
NOTTINGHAM
ATTENBOROUGH JUNC
ATTENBOROUGH STA
BEESTON STA
BEESTON SOUTH JUNC
BEESTON NORTH JUNC
LENTON SOUTH JUNC
MANSFIELD JUNC
WILFORD ROAD No
NOTTINGHAM STA WEST
NOTTINGHAM STA A & B
Miles from Clay Cross Sth Jc
Miles
Trent Gravels Ltd
UP MARSHALLING SIDINGS
DOWN MARSHALLING SIDINGS
Clifton Colly
Cammel Laird & Co
CATTLE DOCK LOCO
QUEENS RD GOODS & COAL
GOODS YARD
Mansfield
Lincoln
London
Leeds
DERBY NORTH JUNC.
Miles
Miles From Spondon Jc
DERBY NORTH JUNC
DERBY SOUTH
CHADDESDEN SOUTH JUNC
CHADDESDEN TURNTABLE
SPONDON JUNCTION
Miles from Derby Nth Jc
SPONDON JUNC.
DOWN
UP
Derby
ARRIVAL LINES
MARSHALLING SIDINGS
1760
DEPARTURE LINES
CARRIAGE SHEDS
T.T. SIDINGS
Leech Neal & Co
CHADDESDEN SIDINGS
CENTRE SHORT SIDINGS 250
ARRIVAL LINES
DERBY SOUTH
CHADDESDEN No 2
STORAGE SIDINGS
MAIN
GOODS
CONTROL OFFICE
CRIPPLES
CHADDESDEN SOUTH Jc
SOUTH END SHORT SIDINGS 220
DEPARTURE LINES
TURNTABLE SIDGS S.B.
CARRIAGE SHEDS
DOWN MARSHALLING SDGS
TIMBER SIDINGS
SPONDON JUNC
Leech Neal & Co
Trent
CLAY CROSS
Traffic Sidings
PASS
GOODS
CLAY CROSS NTH JUNC
WAGON SHOPS
Storage Sidings
CLAY CROSS SOUTH S.B.
TUNNEL S.B.
From Clay Cross Town Goods
BEESTON SIDINGS
To Trent
BEESTON SOUTH JUNC
CREOSOTE WORKS
RECEPTION
LOADS
MAIN
EMPTIES
CRIPPLES
UP RECEPTION
BEESTON NORTH JUNC
WAGON REPAIRING SIDS 332
18
H.R.L. Nov 29

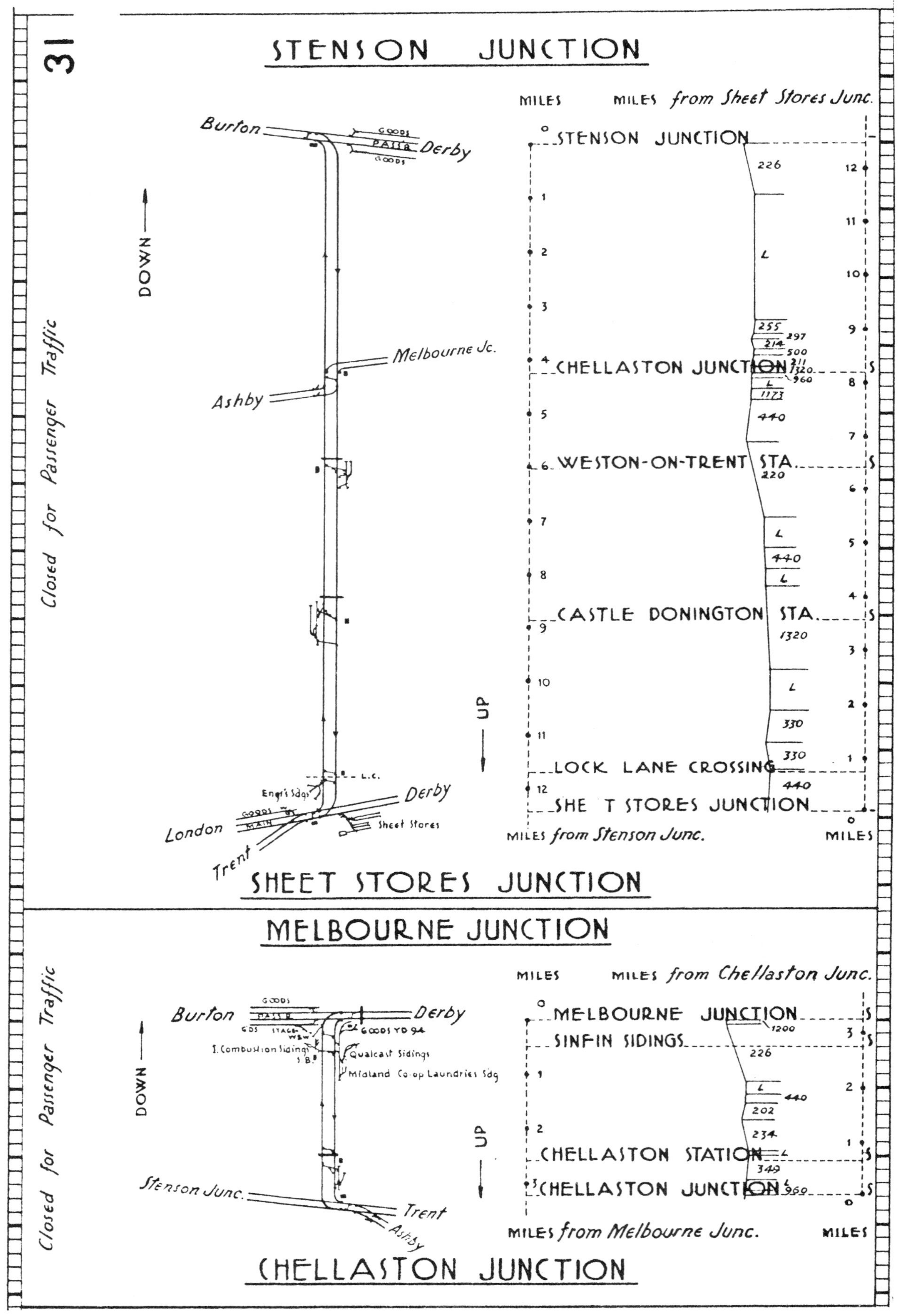
31
STENSON JUNCTION
Closed for Passenger Traffic
Burton
Derby
GOODS
PASS R
DOWN
UP
Melbourne Jc.
Ashby
L.C.
Engr's Sdgs
London
GOODS
MAIN
Trent
Sheet Stores
MILES
MILES from Sheet Stores Junc.
STENSON JUNCTION
CHELLASTON JUNCTION
WESTON-ON-TRENT STA.
CASTLE DONINGTON STA.
LOCK LANE CROSSING
SHEET STORES JUNCTION
MILES from Stenson Junc.
MILES
SHEET STORES JUNCTION
MELBOURNE JUNCTION
Closed for Passenger Traffic
Burton
Derby
GOODS
PASS R
GOODS YD 94
I. Combustion Sidings
S.B.
Qualcast Sidings
Midland Co-op Laundries Sdg
Stenson Junc.
Trent
Ashby
MILES
MILES from Chellaston Junc.
MELBOURNE JUNCTION
SINFIN SIDINGS
CHELLASTON STATION
CHELLASTON JUNCTION
MILES from Melbourne Junc.
MILES
CHELLASTON JUNCTION

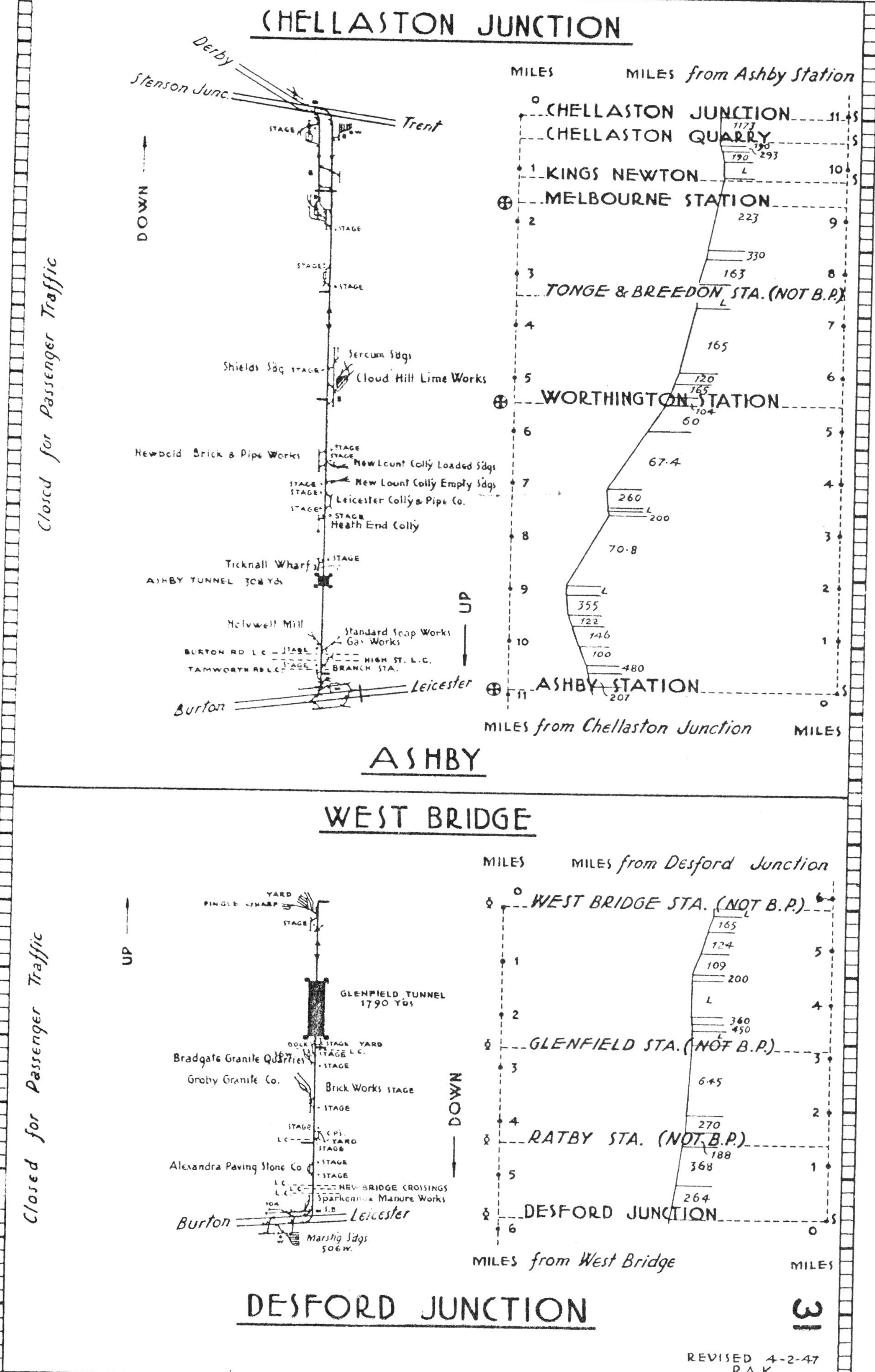
CHELLASTON JUNCTION
Derby
Stenson Junc.
Trent
DOWN
Closed for Passenger Traffic
Sercum Sdgs
Shields Sdg
Cloud Hill Lime Works
Newbold Brick & Pipe Works
New Lount Colly Loaded Sdgs
New Lount Colly Empty Sdgs
Leicester Colly & Pipe Co.
Heath End Colly
Ticknall Wharf
ASHBY TUNNEL 308 Yds
Hulwell Mill
Standard Soap Works
Gas Works
BURTON RD L.C.
TAMWORTH RD L.C.
HIGH ST. L.C.
BRANCH STA.
Leicester
Burton
UP
MILES
MILES from Ashby Station
CHELLASTON JUNCTION
CHELLASTON QUARRY
KINGS NEWTON
MELBOURNE STATION
TONGE & BREEDON STA. (NOT B.P.)
WORTHINGTON STATION
ASHBY STATION
MILES from Chellaston Junction
MILES
ASHBY
WEST BRIDGE
MILES
MILES from Desford Junction
UP
Closed for Passenger Traffic
GLENFIELD TUNNEL 1790 Yds
Bradgate Granite Quarries
Groby Granite Co.
Brick Works
Alexandra Paving Stone Co.
NEW BRIDGE CROSSINGS
Sparkenhoe Manure Works
Leicester
Burton
DOWN
WEST BRIDGE STA. (NOT B.P.)
GLENFIELD STA. (NOT B.P.)
RATBY STA. (NOT B.P.)
DESFORD JUNCTION
MILES from West Bridge
MILES
DESFORD JUNCTION
REVISED 4-2-47
P.A.K.

LEICESTER JUNC. (BURTON)

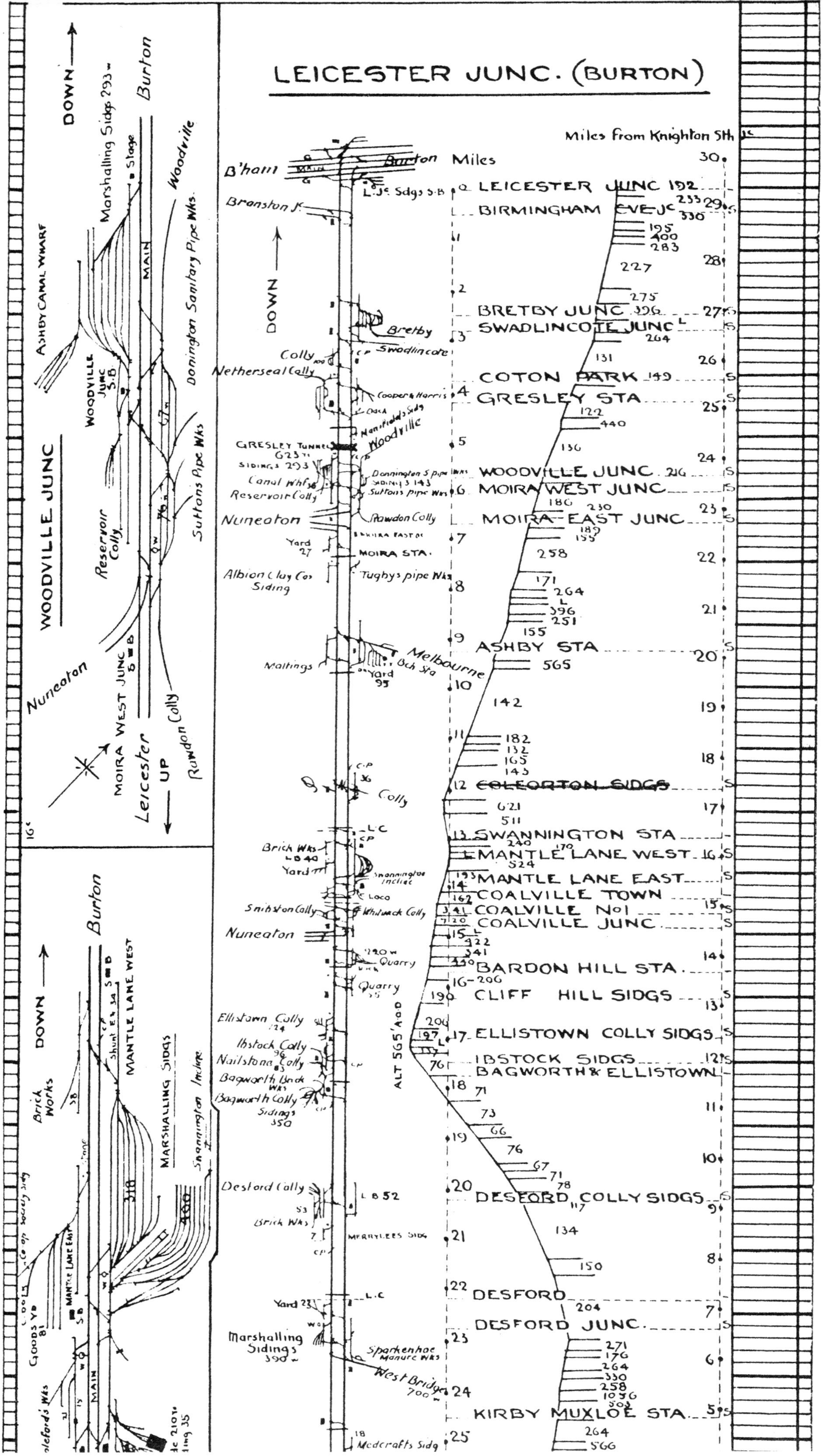

Miles from Knighton Sth Jc

Miles	Location	Miles from Knighton Sth Jc
0	LEICESTER JUNC 192	30
	BIRMINGHAM CVE JC	29
1		
		28
2		
	BRETBY JUNC	27
3	SWADLINCOTE JUNC	
		26
	COTON PARK	
4	GRESLEY STA	25
5		24
	WOODVILLE JUNC	
6	MOIRA WEST JUNC	
	MOIRA EAST JUNC	23
7		22
8		21
9	ASHBY STA	20
10		19
11		18
12	COLEORTON SIDGS	17
13	SWANNINGTON STA	
	MANTLE LANE WEST	16
14	MANTLE LANE EAST	
	COALVILLE TOWN	15
	COALVILLE No1	
15	COALVILLE JUNC	
	BARDON HILL STA	14
16	CLIFF HILL SIDGS	13
17	ELLISTOWN COLLY SIDGS	
	IBSTOCK SIDGS	12
18	BAGWORTH & ELLISTOWN	
		11
19		10
20	DESFORD COLLY SIDGS	9
21		8
22	DESFORD	7
	DESFORD JUNC.	
23		6
24	KIRBY MUXLOE STA	5
25		

ALT 565' A.O.D

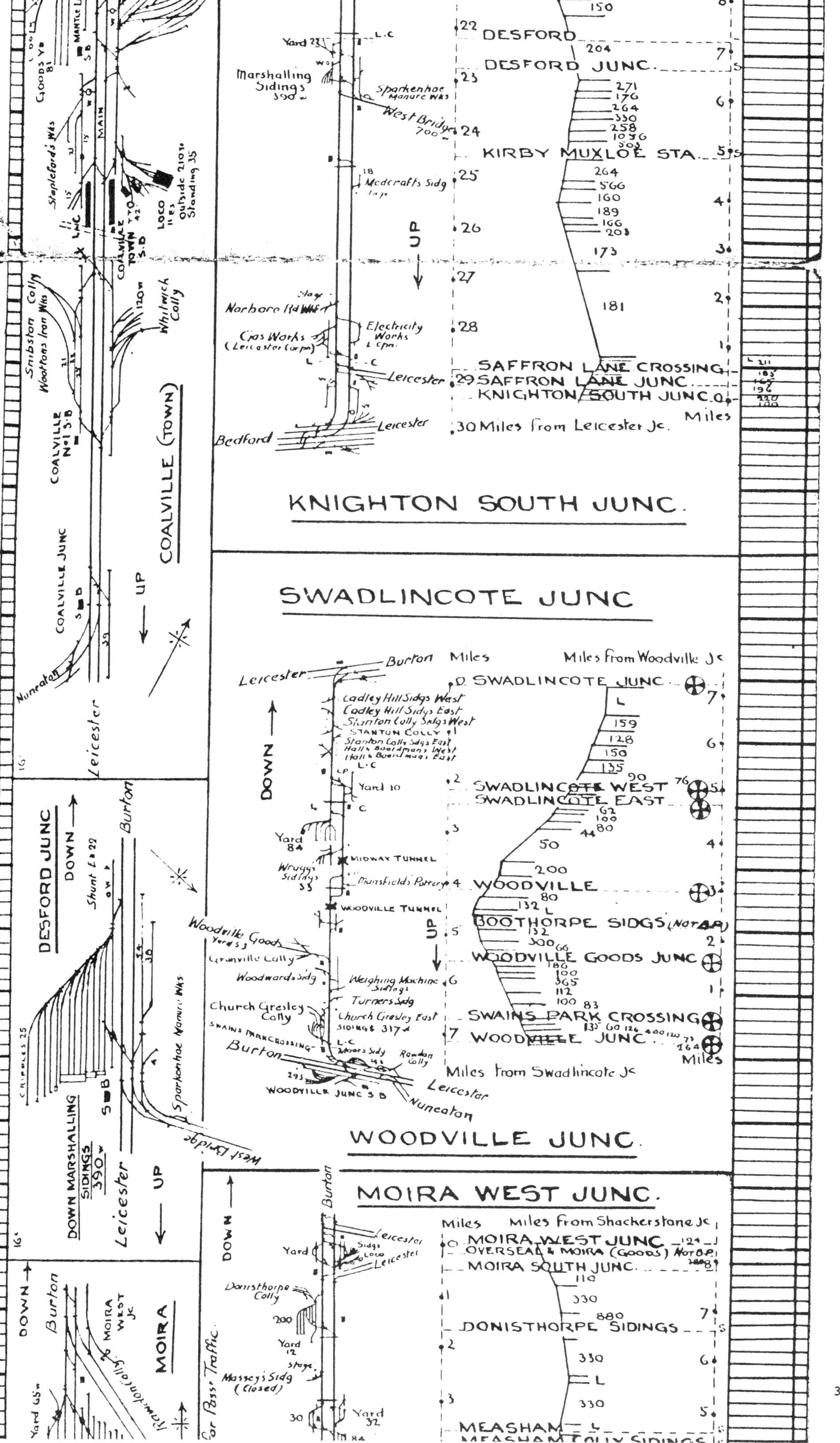
KNIGHTON SOUTH JUNC.
DESFORD
DESFORD JUNC.
KIRBY MUXLOE STA.
SAFFRON LANE CROSSING
SAFFRON LANE JUNC.
KNIGHTON SOUTH JUNC.
30 Miles from Leicester Jc.
Miles
SWADLINCOTE JUNC
Miles from Woodville Jc
SWADLINCOTE WEST
SWADLINCOTE EAST
WOODVILLE
BOOTHORPE SIDGS (NOT A.P.)
WOODVILLE GOODS JUNC
SWAINS PARK CROSSING
WOODVILLE JUNC.
Miles from Swadlincote Jc
WOODVILLE JUNC.
MOIRA WEST JUNC.
Miles from Shackerstone Jc
MOIRA SOUTH JUNC.
DONISTHORPE SIDINGS
MEASHAM
COALVILLE (TOWN)
COALVILLE JUNC
DESFORD JUNC
DOWN MARSHALLING SIDINGS 390w
MOIRA
Leicester
Burton
Nuneaton
UP
DOWN

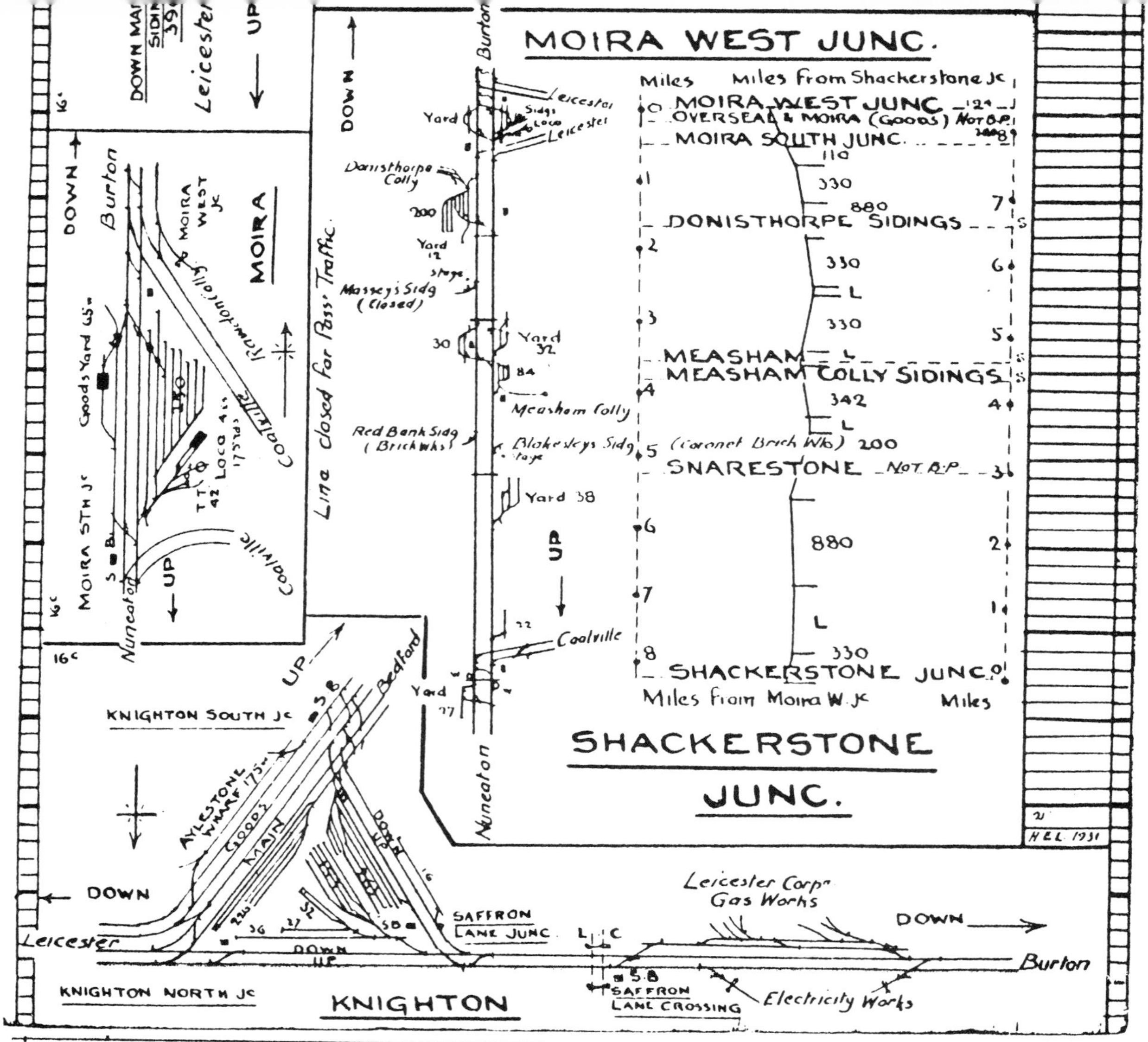
MOIRA WEST JUNC.
Miles
Miles from Shackerstone Jc
MOIRA WEST JUNC
OVERSEAL & MOIRA (GOODS) NOT B.P.
MOIRA SOUTH JUNC.
DONISTHORPE SIDINGS
MEASHAM
MEASHAM COLLY SIDINGS
(Coronet Brick Wks)
SNARESTONE NOT B.P.
SHACKERSTONE JUNC.
Miles from Moira W. Jc
Miles
SHACKERSTONE
JUNC.
HEL 1931
Donisthorpe Colly
Massey's Sidg (Closed)
Measham Colly
Red Bank Sidg (Brickwks)
Blakesleys Sidg
Coalville
Nuneaton
Burton
Leicester
DOWN
UP
Line closed for Pass' Traffic
MOIRA
MOIRA WEST Jc
MOIRA STH Jc
Goods Yard
Coalville
DOWN MAIN SIDINGS
KNIGHTON SOUTH Jc
AYLESTONE WHARF
GOODS
MAIN
Bedford
SAFFRON LANE JUNC.
Leicester Corpn Gas Works
Electricity Works
SAFFRON LANE CROSSING
KNIGHTON NORTH Jc
KNIGHTON

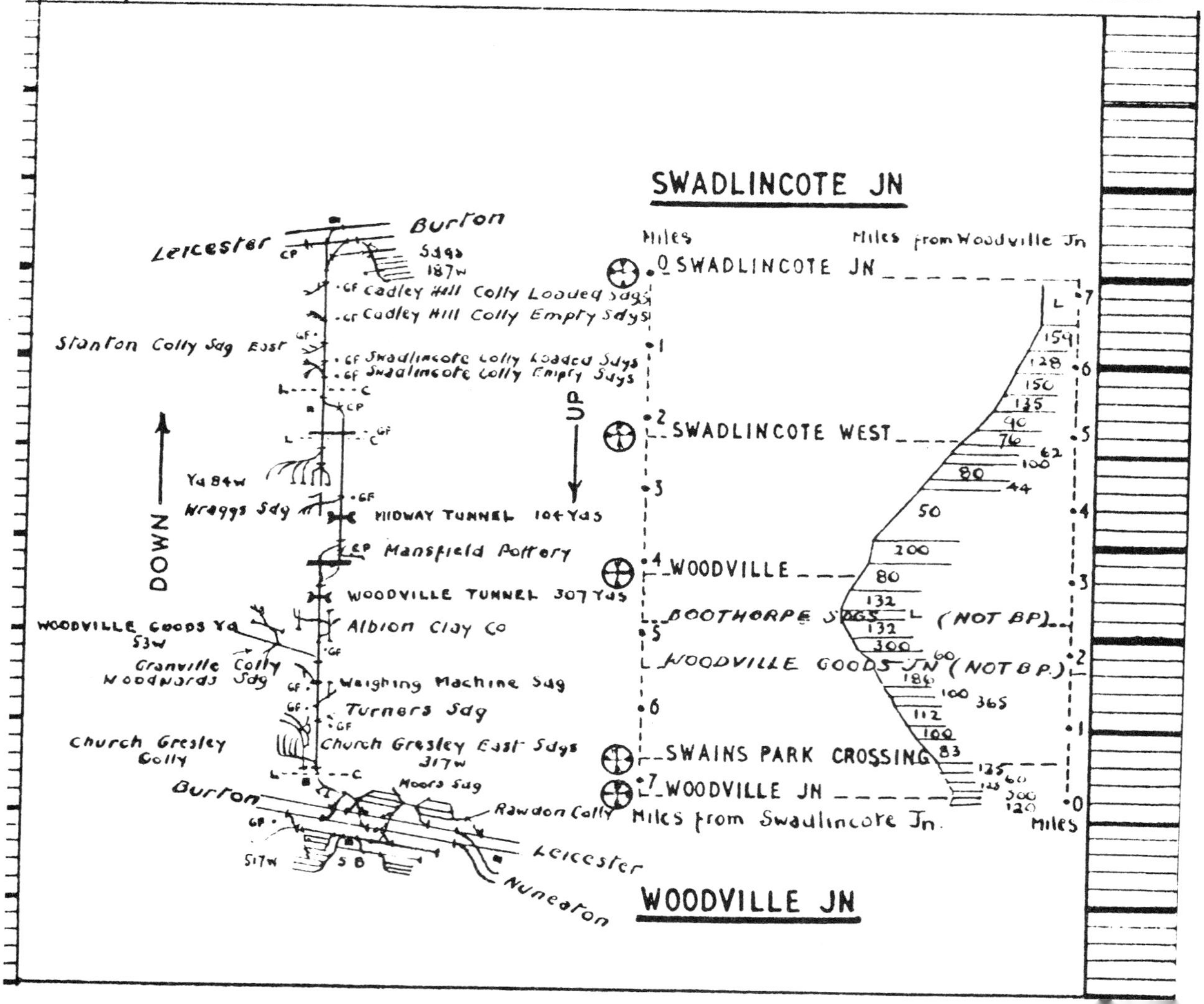
SWADLINCOTE JN
Miles
Miles from Woodville Jn
SWADLINCOTE JN
SWADLINCOTE WEST
WOODVILLE
BOOTHORPE SDGS (NOT BP)
WOODVILLE GOODS JN (NOT B.P.)
SWAINS PARK CROSSING
WOODVILLE JN
Miles from Swadlincote Jn.
Miles
Leicester
Burton
Cadley Hill Colly Loaded Sdgs
Cadley Hill Colly Empty Sdgs
Stanton Colly Sdg East
Swadlincote Colly Loaded Sdys
Swadlincote Colly Empty Sdys
Wraggs Sdg
MIDWAY TUNNEL 104 Yds
Mansfield Pottery
WOODVILLE TUNNEL 307 Yds
WOODVILLE GOODS Yd
Albion Clay Co
Granville Colly
Woodwards Sdg
Weighing Machine Sdg
Turners Sdg
Church Gresley Colly
Church Gresley East Sdys
Moors Sdg
Rawdon Colly
Nuneaton
DOWN
UP
WOODVILLE JN

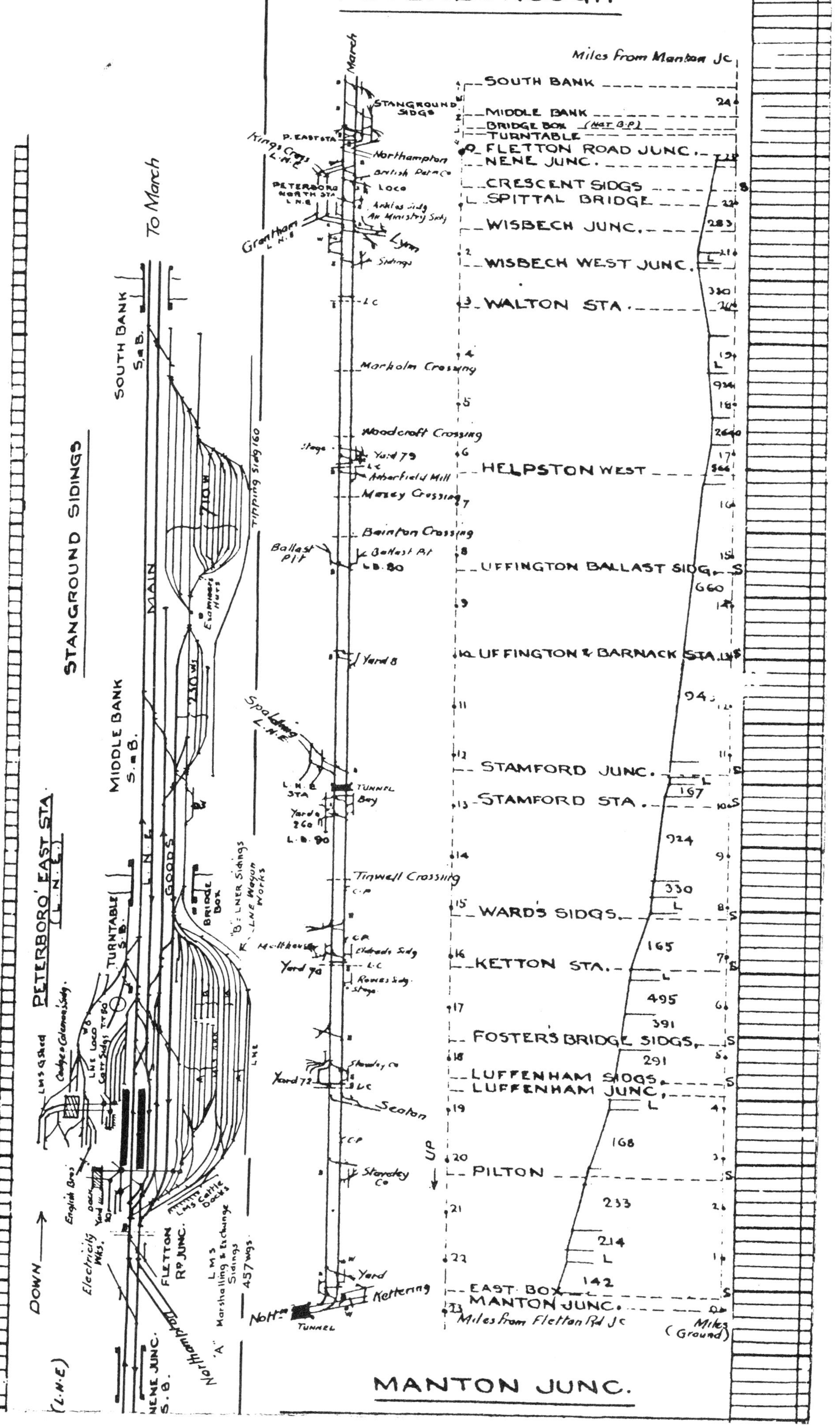
PETERBOROUGH
Miles from Manton Jc
SOUTH BANK
MIDDLE BANK
BRIDGE BOX (Not B.P.)
TURNTABLE
FLETTON ROAD JUNC.
NENE JUNC.
CRESCENT SIDGS
SPITTAL BRIDGE
WISBECH JUNC.
WISBECH WEST JUNC.
WALTON STA.
Marholm Crossing
Woodcroft Crossing
HELPSTON WEST
Maxey Crossing
Bainton Crossing
UFFINGTON BALLAST SIDG.
UFFINGTON & BARNACK STA.
STAMFORD JUNC.
STAMFORD STA.
Tinwell Crossing
WARD'S SIDGS.
KETTON STA.
FOSTER'S BRIDGE SIDGS.
LUFFENHAM SIDGS.
LUFFENHAM JUNC.
Seaton
PILTON
EAST BOX
MANTON JUNC.
Miles from Fletton Rd Jc
Miles (Ground)
Kettering
Tunnel
MANTON JUNC.
STANGROUND SIDINGS
SOUTH BANK S.B.
MIDDLE BANK S.B.
To March
MAIN
GOODS
L.N.E.
PETERBORO' EAST STA (L.N.E.)
TURNTABLE S.B.
BRIDGE BOX
FLETTON RD JUNC.
NENE JUNC. S.B.
DOWN
(L.N.E)
Electricity Wks.
English Bros
Tipping Sidg 160
LMS Marshalling & Exchange Sidings 457 wgs.
LMS Cattle Docks
Northampton
Kings Cross L.N.E
Grantham L.N.E
Spalding L.N.E
Northampton
British Petrol Co
Loco
PETERBORO NORTH STA L.N.E
Lynn
Sidings
Ballast Pit
Yard 79
Yard 8
Yard 72
Stanton Crossing
UP

SPALDING

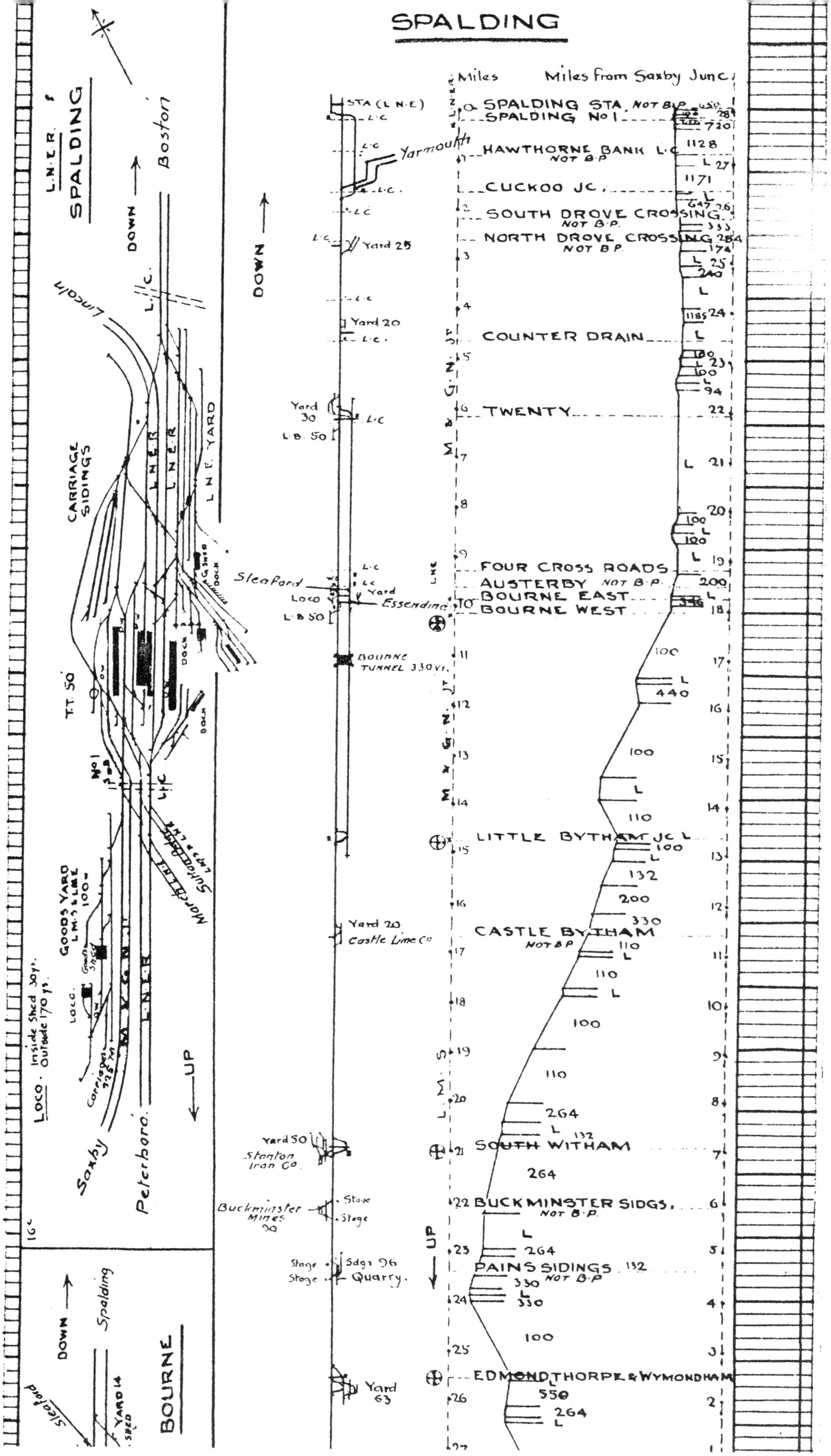

Miles | Miles from Saxby Junc.

Miles	Location	Miles from Saxby Junc.
0	SPALDING STA. NOT B.P.	28
	SPALDING No 1	
1	HAWTHORNE BANK L.C. NOT B.P.	27
	CUCKOO JC.	
2	SOUTH DROVE CROSSING NOT B.P.	26
	NORTH DROVE CROSSING NOT B.P.	
3		25
4		24
	COUNTER DRAIN	
5		23
6	TWENTY	22
7		21
8		20
9	FOUR CROSS ROADS	19
	AUSTERBY NOT B.P.	
	BOURNE EAST	
10	BOURNE WEST	18
11		17
12		16
13		15
14		14
15	LITTLE BYTHAM JC.	13
16		12
	CASTLE BYTHAM NOT B.P.	
17		11
18		10
19		9
20		8
21	SOUTH WITHAM	7
22	BUCKMINSTER SIDGS. NOT B.P.	6
23		5
	PAINS SIDINGS NOT B.P.	
24		4
25		3
	EDMONDTHORPE & WYMONDHAM	
26		2
27		1

Gradients: 650, 720, 1128, L, 1171, L, 647, 333, 264, 174, L, 240, L, 1185, L, 100, L, 100, L, 94, L, L, 100, L, 100, L, 200, L, 345, 100, L, 440, 100, L, 110, L, 100, L, 132, 200, 330, 110, L, 110, L, 100, 110, 264, L, 132, 264, L, 264, 132, 330, L, 330, 100, L, 550, 264, L

Line sections: L.N.E. ; M. & G.N. Jt. ; L.N.E. ; M. & G.N. Jt. ; L.M.S. ; UP

STA (L.N.E.), L.C., Yarmouth, L.C., Yard 25, DOWN, L.C., Yard 20, L.C., Yard 30, L.C., L.B. 50, Sleaford, L.C., Yard, Loco, Essendine, L.B. 50, BOURNE TUNNEL 330 Yds., Yard 20 Castle Lime Co., Yard 50 Stanton Iron Co., Buckminster Mines 90, Stage, Stage, Stage, Stage, Sdgs 96 Quarry, Yard 63

L.N.E.R. & SPALDING

DOWN, Boston, Lincoln, L.C., CARRIAGE SIDINGS, L.N.E.R., L.N.E.R., L.N.E. YARD, G.N.&G.E. DOCK, DOCK, DOCK, DOCK, T.T. 50', No 1, L.C., GOODS YARD L.M.S. & L.N.E. 100, Goods Shed, Loco, Loco. Inside Shed 30 yds. Outside 170 yds., Carriages 125 M, M & G.N. Jt., L.N.E.R., Saxby, Peterboro', UP, March, Sutton Bridge, Lynn, Lincs.

16c

BOURNE

DOWN, Spalding, Sleaford, YARD 14, SPED

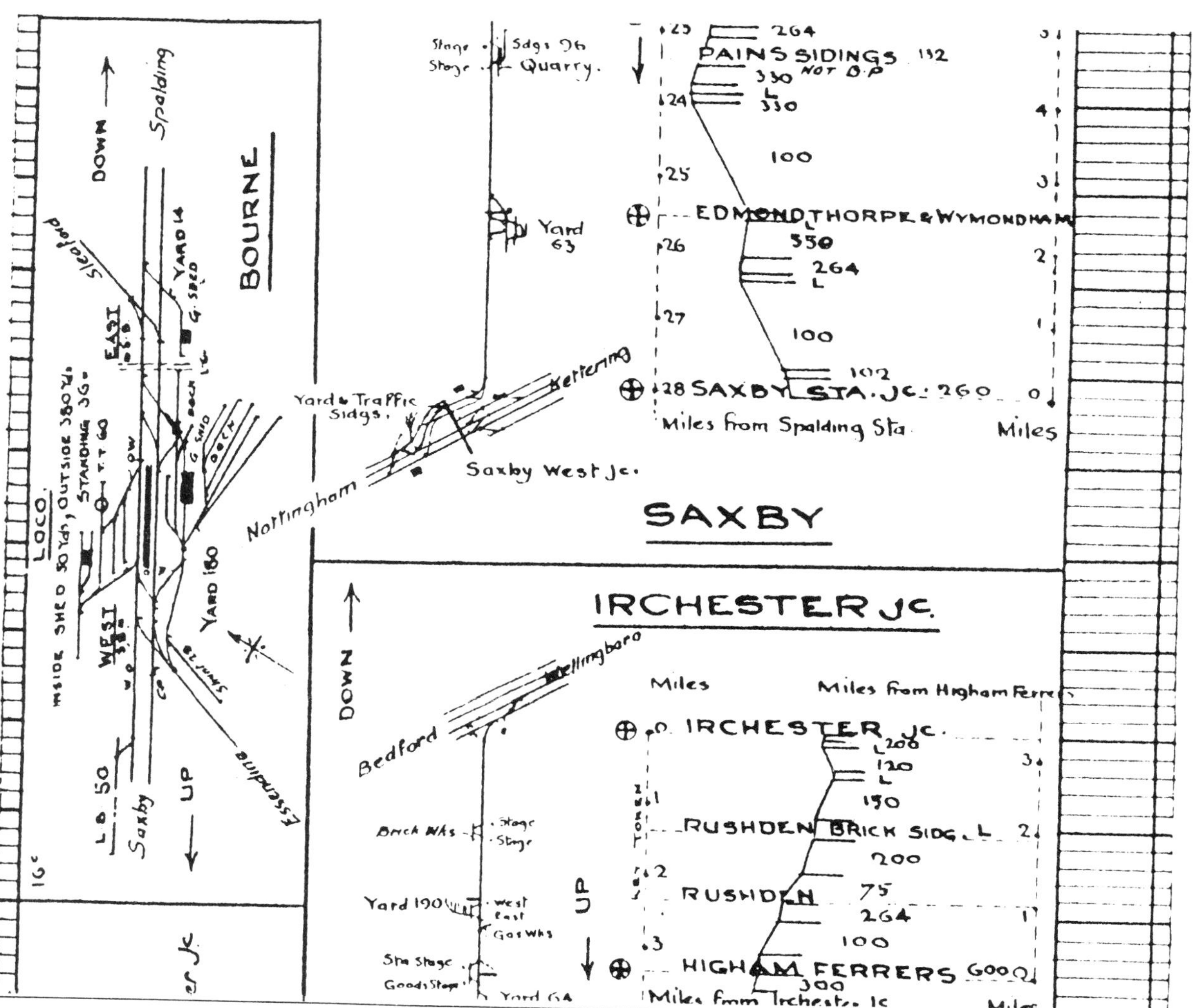
BOURNE
DOWN
UP
Spalding
Saxby
Sleaford
Essendine
Yard 14
Yard 180
LOCO
EAST
WEST
SAXBY
Stage
Sdgs 96
Quarry
Yard 63
Yard & Traffic Sidgs.
Kettering
Nottingham
Saxby West Jc.
PAINS SIDINGS
NOT O.P.
EDMONDTHORPE & WYMONDHAM
SAXBY STA. JC.
Miles from Spalding Sta.
Miles
IRCHESTER JC.
Wellingboro
Bedford
Brick Wks
Yard 190
Sta Stage
Goods Stage
Miles from Higham Ferrers
RUSHDEN BRICK SIDG
RUSHDEN
HIGHAM FERRERS
Miles from Irchester Jc

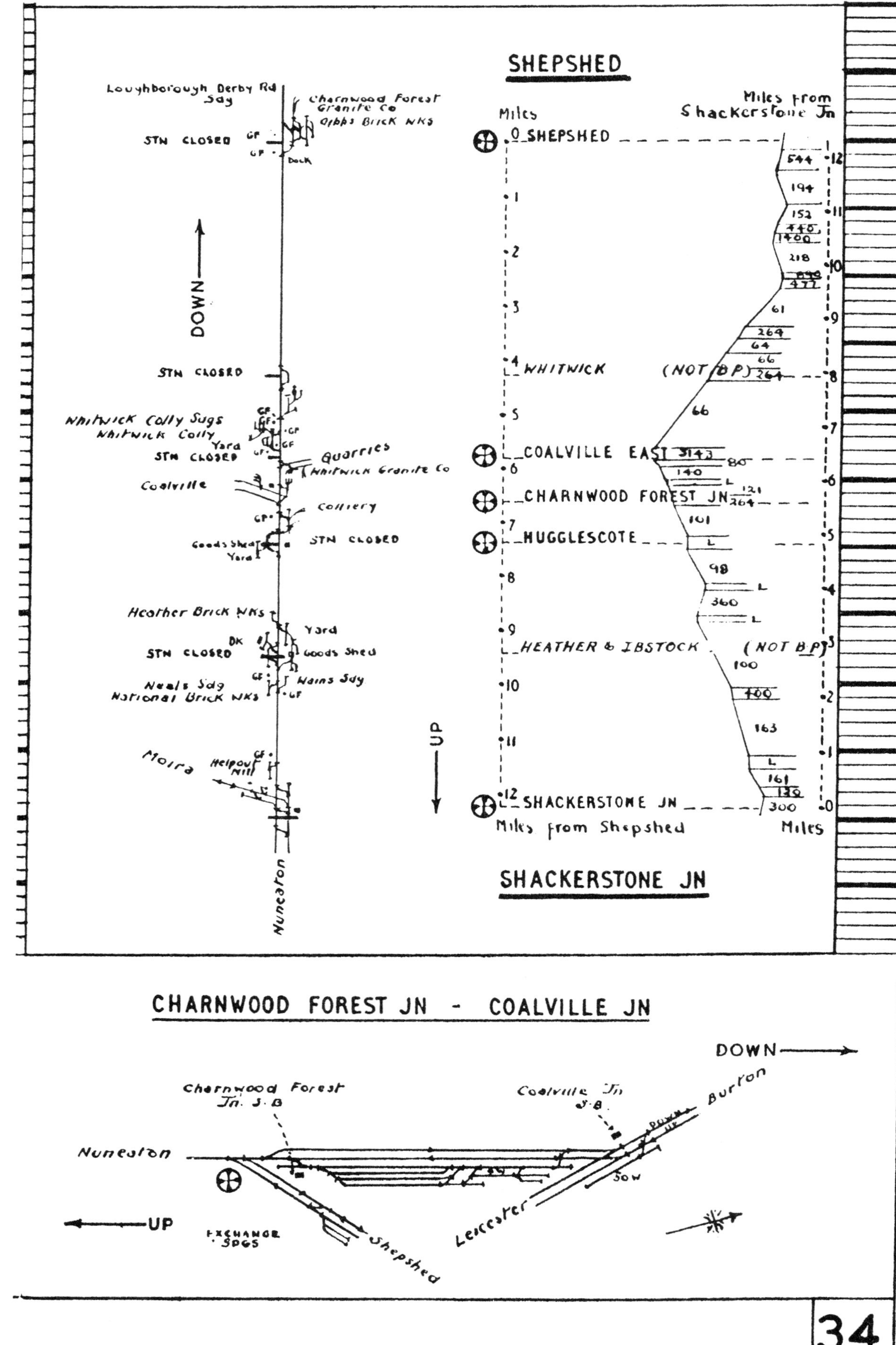
SHEPSHED
Loughborough Derby Rd Sdg
Charnwood Forest Granite Co
Gibbs Brick WKS
STN CLOSED
Dock
DOWN
Miles
Miles from Shackerstone Jn
0 SHEPSHED
WHITWICK (NOT B P)
COALVILLE EAST
CHARNWOOD FOREST JN
HUGGLESCOTE
HEATHER & IBSTOCK (NOT B P)
SHACKERSTONE JN
Miles from Shepshed
Miles
Whitwick Colly Sdgs
Whitwick Colly
Yard
Quarries
Whitwick Granite Co
Coalville
Colliery
Goods Shed
Heather Brick WKS
Goods Shed
Neals Sdg
National Brick WKS
Wains Sdy
Moira
Helpout Mill
UP
Nuneaton
SHACKERSTONE JN
CHARNWOOD FOREST JN - COALVILLE JN
DOWN
UP
Charnwood Forest Jn. S.B
Coalville Jn S.B
Nuneaton
Burton
Leicester
Shepshed
EXCHANGE SDGS
34
DRAWN. MAR. 58. V.L

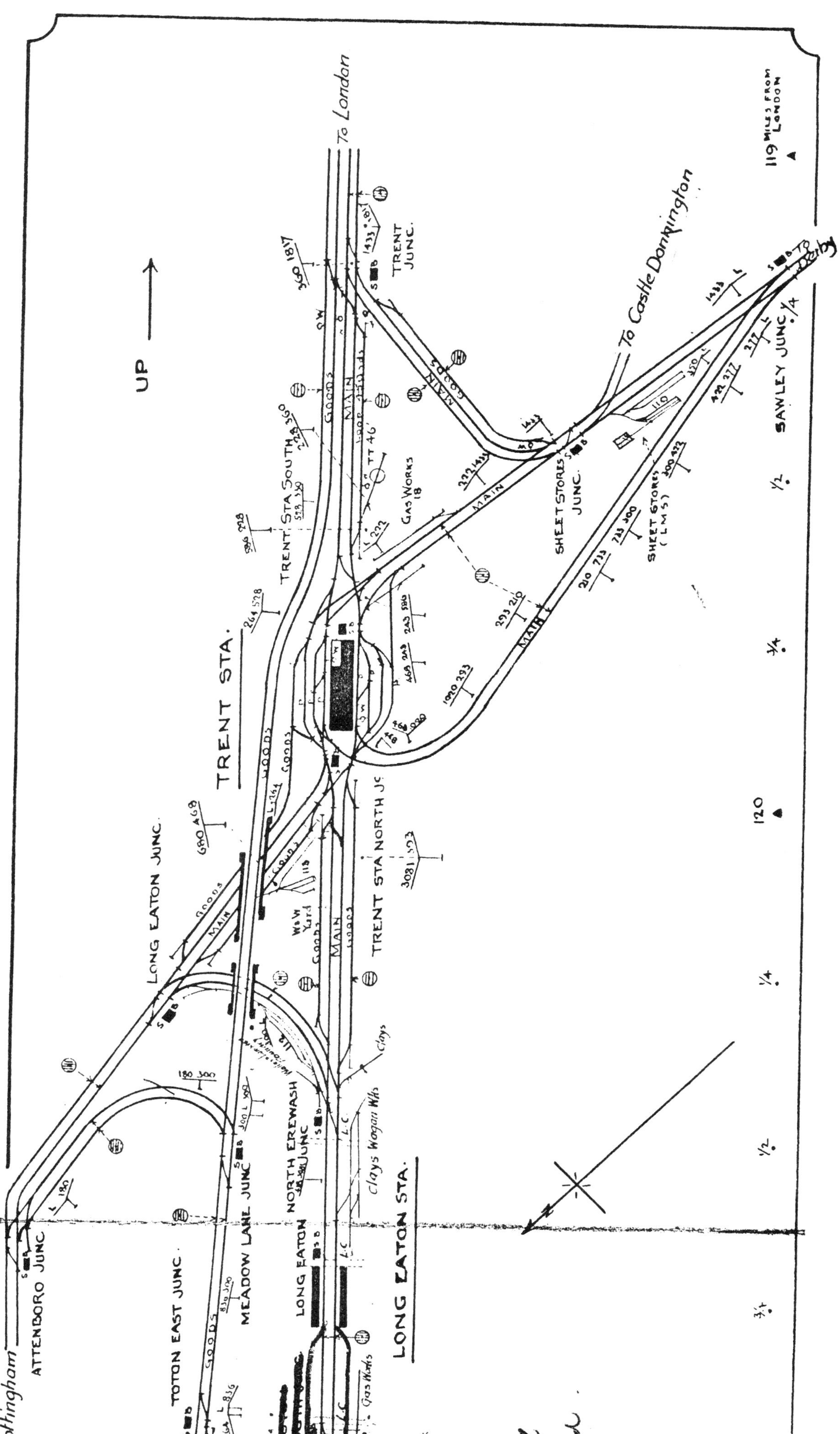
To London
UP
TRENT JUNC.
TRENT STA SOUTH
TRENT STA.
TRENT STA NORTH JC
GAS WORKS
SHEET STORES JUNC.
SHEET STORES (LMS)
To Castle Donington
To Derby
SAWLEY JUNC.
119 MILES FROM LONDON
120
LONG EATON JUNC
W&W Yard
NORTH EREWASH JUNC
MEADOW LANE JUNC
TOTON EAST JUNC
ATTENBORO JUNC
Nottingham
LONG EATON
LONG EATON STA.
Clays Wagon Wks
Clays
Gas Works
MAIN
GOODS

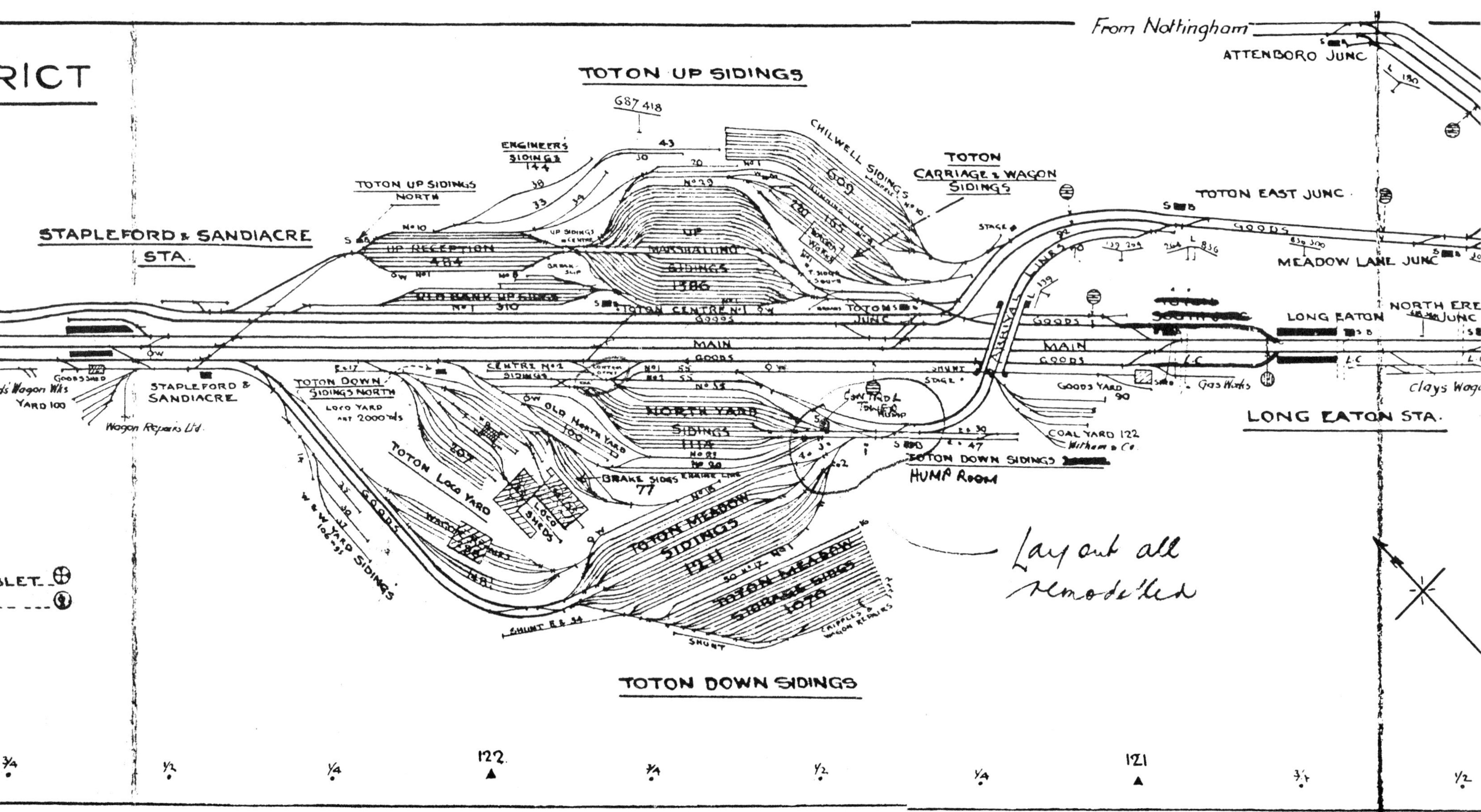
RICT
TOTON UP SIDINGS
From Nottingham
ATTENBORO JUNC
ENGINEERS SIDINGS 144
TOTON UP SIDINGS NORTH
CHILWELL SIDINGS
TOTON CARRIAGE & WAGON SIDINGS
TOTON EAST JUNC
MEADOW LANE JUNC
STAPLEFORD & SANDIACRE STA.
UP RECEPTION 484
UP MARSHALLING SIDINGS 1386
TOTON CENTRE No1
TOTON JUNC
LONG EATON
NORTH ERE JUNC
GOODS
MAIN
STAPLEFORD & SANDIACRE
TOTON DOWN SIDINGS NORTH
Wagon Repairs Ltd
OLD NORTH YARD
NORTH YARD SIDINGS 1114
CONTROL TOWER
Goods Yard 90
Gas Works
Clays Wagon
LONG EATON STA.
COAL YARD 122
TOTON DOWN SIDINGS
HUMP ROOM
TOTON LOCO YARD
LOCO SHEDS
BRAKE SIDGS 77
W & W YARD SIDINGS
TOTON MEADOW SIDINGS 1211
TOTON MEADOW STORAGE SIDGS 1070
Layout all remodelled
TOTON DOWN SIDINGS
122
121

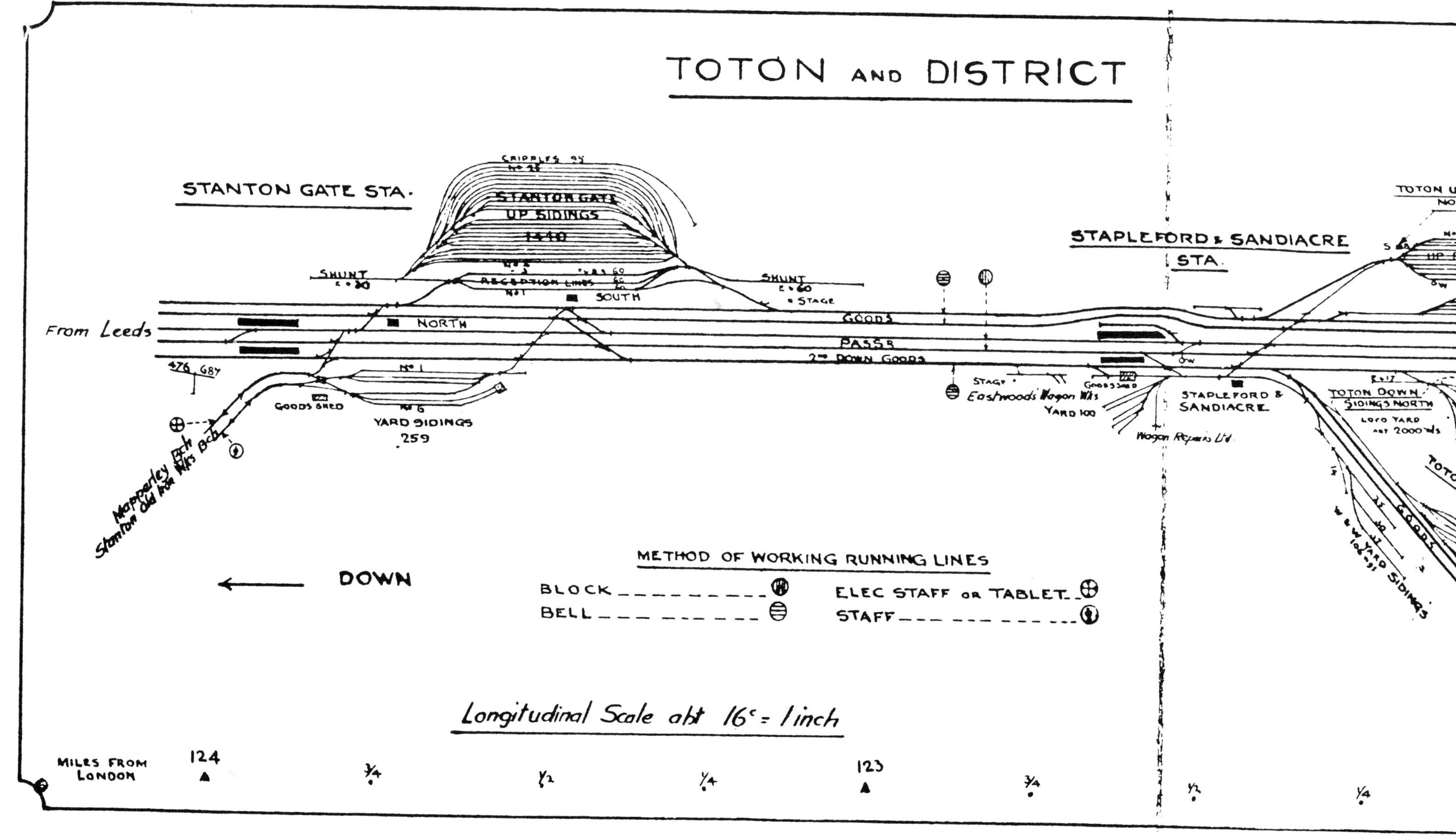
TOTON AND DISTRICT
STANTON GATE STA.
STANTON GATE UP SIDINGS 1440
RECEPTION LINES
SHUNT
SOUTH
NORTH
From Leeds
GOODS
PASSR
2ND DOWN GOODS
GOODS SHED
YARD SIDINGS 259
Mapperley Bch
Stanton Old Iron Wks Bch
STAPLEFORD & SANDIACRE STA.
Eastwoods Wagon Wks
YARD 100
STAPLEFORD & SANDIACRE
Wagon Repairs Ltd
TOTON DOWN SIDINGS NORTH
LOCO YARD abt 2000 Ws
TOTON UP SIDINGS NORTH
METHOD OF WORKING RUNNING LINES
BLOCK
BELL
ELEC STAFF OR TABLET
STAFF
DOWN
Longitudinal Scale abt 16c = 1inch
MILES FROM LONDON
124
¾
½
¼
123
¾
½
¼

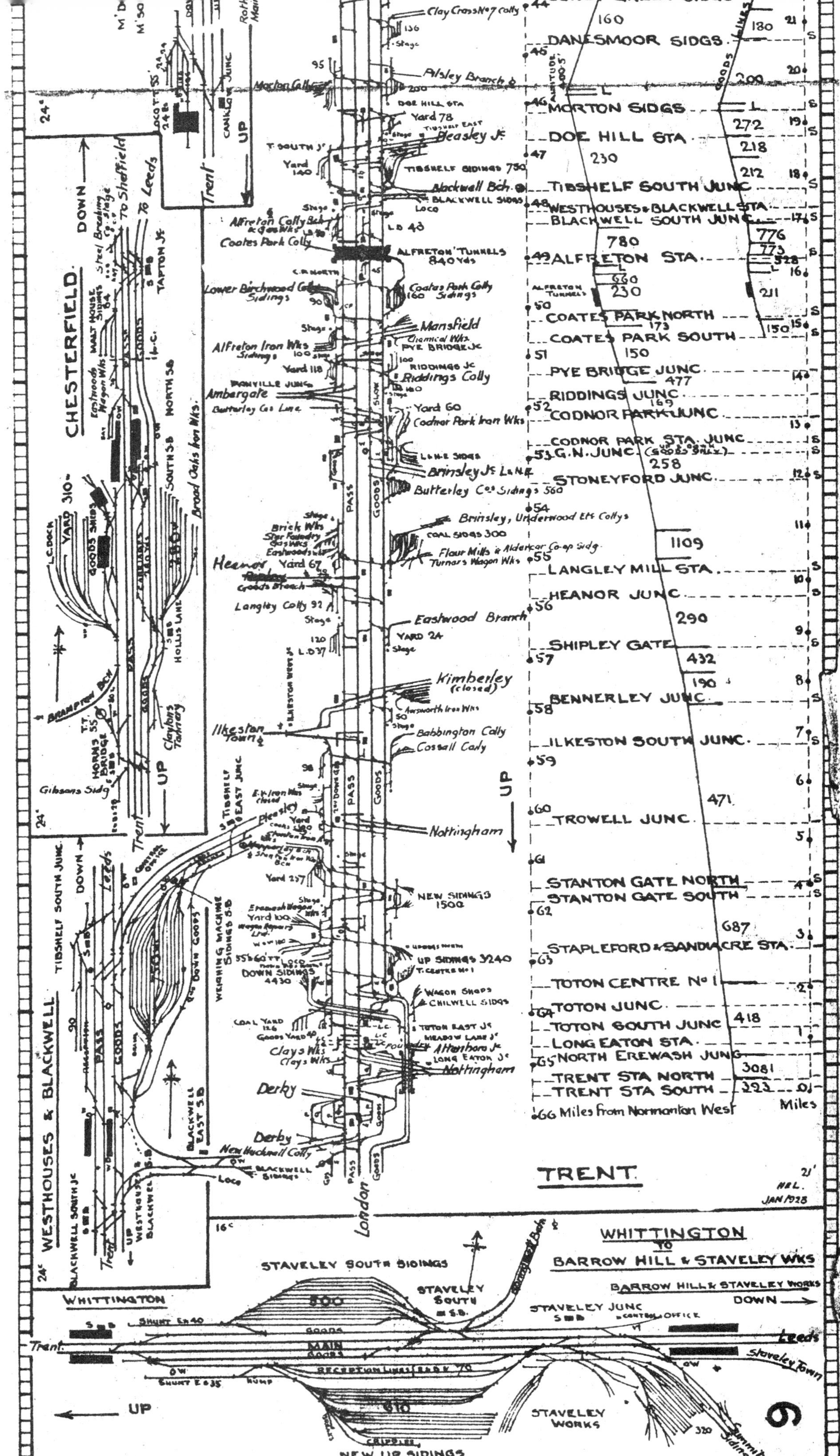
CLAY CROSS N°7 COLLY
DANESMOOR SIDGS
MORTON SIDGS
DOE HILL STA
TIBSHELF SOUTH JUNC
WESTHOUSES & BLACKWELL STA.
BLACKWELL SOUTH JUNC.
ALFRETON STA.
COATES PARK NORTH
COATES PARK SOUTH
PYE BRIDGE JUNC.
RIDDINGS JUNC
CODNOR PARK JUNC
CODNOR PARK STA. JUNC
G.N. JUNC.
STONEYFORD JUNC.
LANGLEY MILL STA.
HEANOR JUNC.
SHIPLEY GATE
BENNERLEY JUNC.
ILKESTON SOUTH JUNC.
TROWELL JUNC.
STANTON GATE NORTH
STANTON GATE SOUTH
STAPLEFORD & SANDIACRE STA.
TOTON CENTRE N° 1
TOTON JUNC.
TOTON SOUTH JUNC
LONG EATON STA.
NORTH EREWASH JUNC
TRENT STA NORTH
TRENT STA SOUTH
66 Miles from Normanton West
Miles
TRENT
H.E.L.
JAN 1928
CHESTERFIELD
WESTHOUSES & BLACKWELL
WHITTINGTON TO BARROW HILL & STAVELEY WKS
STAVELEY SOUTH SIDINGS
STAVELEY SOUTH
STAVELEY JUNC
STAVELEY WORKS
NEW UP SIDINGS
WHITTINGTON
BARROW HILL & STAVELEY WORKS
DOWN
UP
Leeds
Trent
London
Nottingham
Derby
Mansfield
Ambergate
Heanor
Ilkeston Town
Kimberley (closed)
Eastwood Branch
9

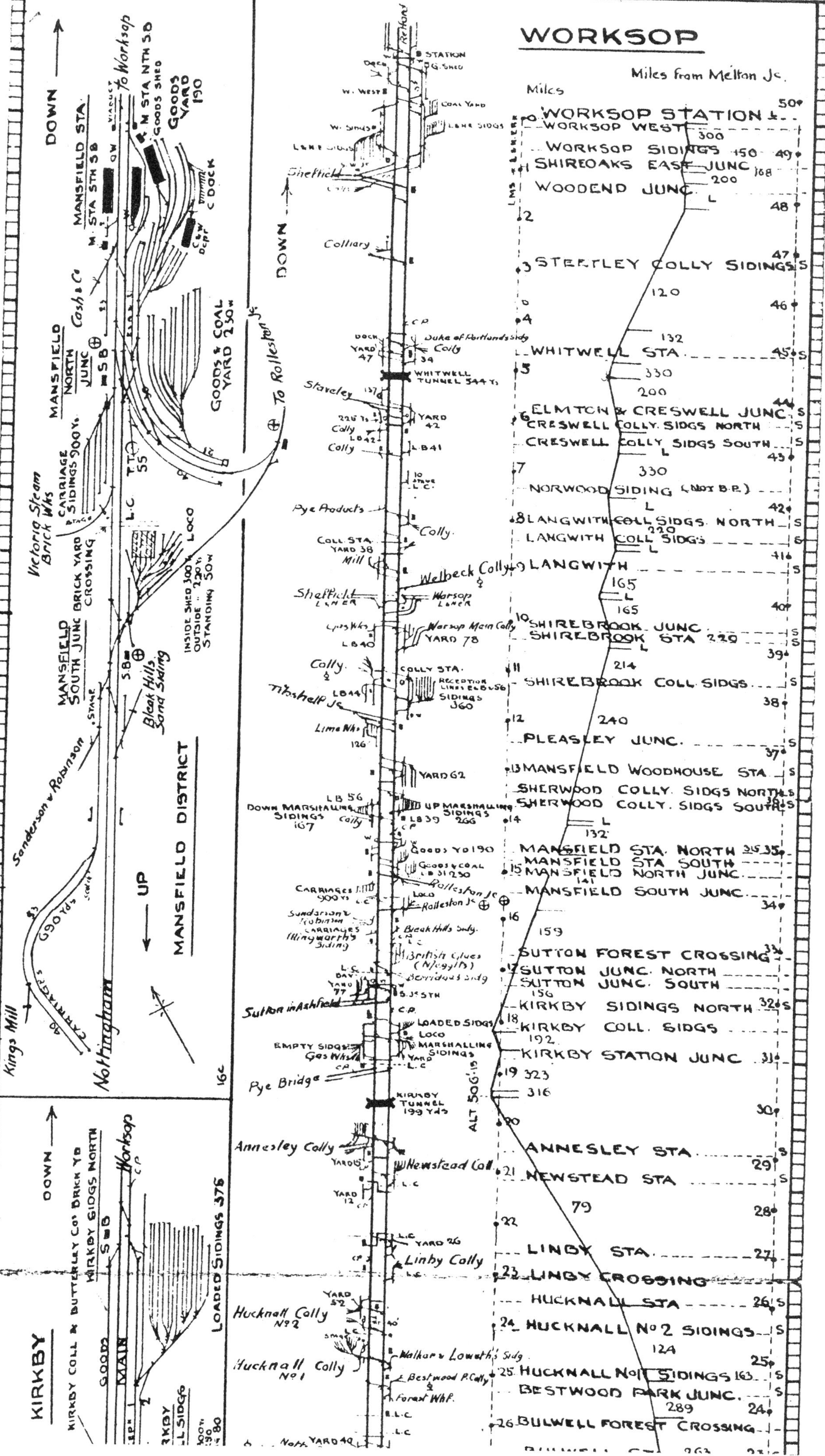
WORKSOP
Miles from Melton Jc.
Miles
WORKSOP STATION
WORKSOP WEST
WORKSOP SIDINGS
SHIREOAKS EAST JUNC
WOODEND JUNC
STEETLEY COLLY SIDINGS
WHITWELL STA
ELMTON & CRESWELL JUNC
CRESWELL COLLY SIDGS NORTH
CRESWELL COLLY SIDGS SOUTH
NORWOOD SIDING
LANGWITH COLL SIDGS NORTH
LANGWITH COLL SIDGS
LANGWITH
SHIREBROOK JUNC
SHIREBROOK STA
SHIREBROOK COLL SIDGS
PLEASLEY JUNC
MANSFIELD WOODHOUSE STA
SHERWOOD COLLY SIDGS NORTH
SHERWOOD COLLY SIDGS SOUTH
MANSFIELD STA NORTH
MANSFIELD STA SOUTH
MANSFIELD NORTH JUNC
MANSFIELD SOUTH JUNC
SUTTON FOREST CROSSING
SUTTON JUNC NORTH
SUTTON JUNC SOUTH
KIRKBY SIDINGS NORTH
KIRKBY COLL SIDGS
KIRKBY STATION JUNC
ALT 506·15
ANNESLEY STA
NEWSTEAD STA
LINBY STA
LINBY CROSSING
HUCKNALL STA
HUCKNALL No 2 SIDINGS
HUCKNALL No 1 SIDINGS
BESTWOOD PARK JUNC
BULWELL FOREST CROSSING
DOWN
Sheffield
Colliary
Duke of Portland's Sidg
WHITWELL TUNNEL 544 Yds
Staveley
Pye Products
Welbeck Colly
Worsop Main Colly
Tibshelf Jc
Rolleston Jc
Bleak Hills Sdg
British Glues
Sutton in Ashfield
Pye Bridge
KIRKBY TUNNEL 199 Yds
Annesley Colly
Newstead Coll
Linby Colly
Hucknall Colly No 2
Hucknall Colly No 1
Walker & Loweth's Sidg
Bestwood P. Colly
Forest Whf
MANSFIELD DISTRICT
DOWN
UP
To Worksop
MANSFIELD STA
MANSFIELD NORTH JUNC
MANSFIELD SOUTH JUNC
GOODS YARD 190
GOODS & COAL YARD 230 W
To Rolleston Jc
Cash & Co
Victoria Steam Brick Wks
CARRIAGE SIDINGS 900 Yds
BRICK YARD CROSSING
Bleak Hills Sand Siding
INSIDE SHED 300 W OUTSIDE 220 W STANDING 50 W
Sanderson & Robinson
690 Yds
Kings Mill
Nottingham
KIRKBY
KIRKBY COLL & BUTTERLEY Co's BRICK YD
KIRKBY SIDGS NORTH
Worksop
LOADED SIDINGS 376
GOODS
MAIN
DOWN

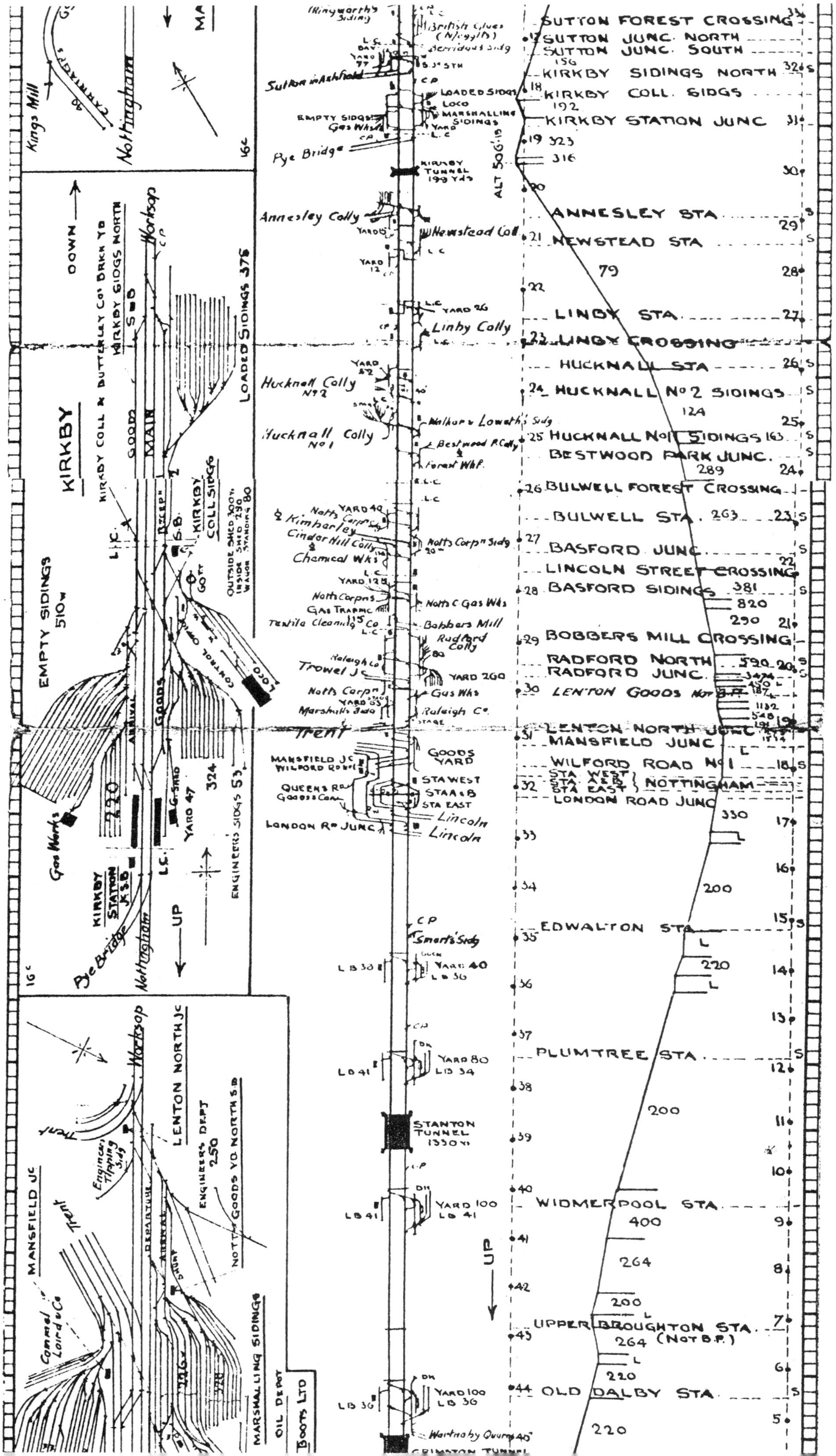

SUTTON FOREST CROSSING 33
SUTTON JUNC. NORTH
SUTTON JUNC. SOUTH
156
KIRKBY SIDINGS NORTH 32 S
18 KIRKBY COLL. SIDGS
192
KIRKBY STATION JUNC 31
19 323
316
ALT 506·15
30
20
ANNESLEY STA
29 S
21 NEWSTEAD STA
79
28
22
LINBY STA 27
23 LINBY CROSSING
HUCKNALL STA 26 S
24 HUCKNALL No 2 SIDINGS S
124
25
25 HUCKNALL No 1 SIDINGS 163 S
BESTWOOD PARK JUNC. S
289 24
26 BULWELL FOREST CROSSING
BULWELL STA. 263 23 S
27 BASFORD JUNC. S
22
LINCOLN STREET CROSSING
28 BASFORD SIDINGS 381 S
820
290 21
29 BOBBERS MILL CROSSING
RADFORD NORTH 590 20 S
RADFORD JUNC.
30 LENTON GOODS Not B.P.
LENTON NORTH JUNC
31 MANSFIELD JUNC
WILFORD ROAD No 1 18 S
32 STA WEST / STA A&B / STA EAST } NOTTINGHAM
LONDON ROAD JUNC
330
33 17
34 16
200
35 EDWALTON STA 15 S
L
220
36 14
L
37 13
PLUMTREE STA S
38 12
200
39 11
40 10
WIDMERPOOL STA
400
41 9
264
UP
42 8
200
L
43 UPPER BROUGHTON STA 7
264 (Not B.P.)
L
220 6
44 OLD DALBY STA S
220 5

(Ringworth's Siding)
British Glues (N/gyll'D)
L.C.
Berridge's Sidg
Yard 77
Sutton in Ashfield
C.P.
Loaded Sidgs
Loco
Marshalling Sidings
Empty Sidgs
Gas Wks
Yard
L.C.
C.P.
Pye Bridge
Kirkby Tunnel 199 Yds
Annesley Colly
Yard
Newstead Coll
L.C.
Yard 12
L.C.
Yard 26
C.P.
Linby Colly
L.C.
Yard 52
Hucknall Colly No 2
Walkers Loweth's Sidg
Hucknall Colly No 1
Bestwood P. Colly
Forest Whf.
L.C.
L.C.
Yard 40
Notts Corpn & Kimberley Sidg
Cinder Hill Colly & Chemical Wks
Notts Corpn Sidg
L.C.
Yard 125
Notts Corpns Gas Traffic
Notts C Gas Wks
Textile Cleaning Co
Bobbers Mill
L.C.
Radford Colly
Raleigh Co
Trowel Jc
Yard 260
Notts Corpn
Gas Wks
Yard 53
Marshalls Sidg
Raleigh Co.
Trent
Mansfield Jc / Wilford Road
Goods Yard
Sta West
Queens Rd Goods Con
Sta A & B
Sta East
London Rd Junc
Lincoln
Lincoln
C.P.
Smart's Sidg
LB 38
Yard 40
LB 36
C.P.
LB 41
Yard 80
LB 34
Stanton Tunnel 1330 Yds
C.P.
LB 41
Yard 100
LB 41
LB 36
Yard 100
LB 36
Wartnaby Quarry
Grimston Tunnel

Kings Mill
Carriages
Nottingham
MA
16C

DOWN
KIRKBY
Kirkby Coll & Butterley Co's Brkk Yd
Kirkby Sidgs North S.B.
Worksop
C.P.
Goods
Main
Loaded Sidings 376
L.C.
Kirkby Coll Sidgs
S.B.
Outside Shed 300T, Inside Shed 290, Wagon Standing 80
Empty Sidings 510W
Arrival
Goods
Control Office
Loco
Gas Works
220
Yard 47
324
Engineers Sidgs 53
G. Shed
Kirkby Station Jc S.B.
L.C.
Pye Bridge
Nottingham
UP
16C

Worksop
Trent
Lenton North Jc
Engineers Tipping Sidg
Engineers Dept 250
Notts Goods Yd North S.B.
Mansfield Jc
Trent
Departure
Arrival
Carrel Laird & Co
Marshalling Sidings
Oil Depot
Boots Ltd

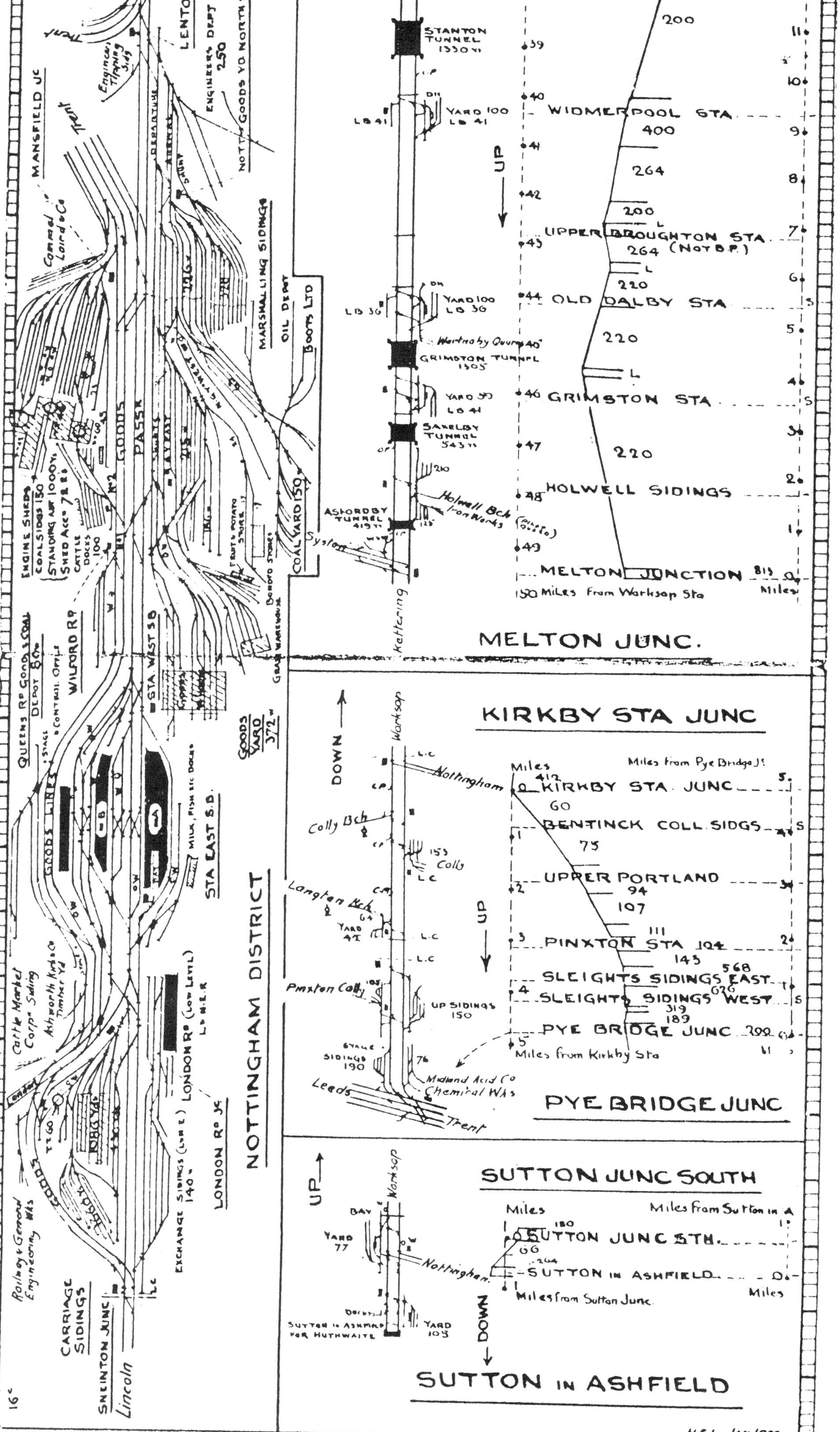
MELTON JUNC.
STANTON TUNNEL 1330 YDS
WIDMERPOOL STA
UPPER BROUGHTON STA (NOT B.P.)
OLD DALBY STA
GRIMSTON TUNNEL 1305
GRIMSTON STA
SAXELBY TUNNEL 543 YDS
HOLWELL SIDINGS
ASFORDBY TUNNEL 419 YDS
MELTON JUNCTION
150 Miles from Worksop Sta
Kettering
KIRKBY STA JUNC
Miles from Pye Bridge Jc
BENTINCK COLL SIDGS
UPPER PORTLAND
PINXTON STA
SLEIGHTS SIDINGS EAST
SLEIGHTS SIDINGS WEST
PYE BRIDGE JUNC
Miles from Kirkby Sta
PYE BRIDGE JUNC
SUTTON JUNC SOUTH
SUTTON JUNC STH.
SUTTON IN ASHFIELD
Miles from Sutton Junc
Miles from Sutton in A
SUTTON IN ASHFIELD FOR HUTHWAITE
SUTTON IN ASHFIELD
NOTTINGHAM DISTRICT
MANSFIELD JC
LENTON
ENGINEERS DEPT 250
NOTT'M GOODS YD NORTH S.B.
MARSHALLING SIDINGS
OIL DEPOT
BOOTS LTD
COAL YARD 150
ENGINE SHEDS
QUEENS Rd GOODS & COAL DEPOT 80
WILFORD Rd
STA WEST S.B.
STA EAST S.B.
GOODS YARD 372
LONDON Rd (LOW LEVEL) L & N.E.R.
LONDON Rd Jc
CARRIAGE SIDINGS
SNEINTON JUNC
Lincoln
H.E.L. JAN 1939.

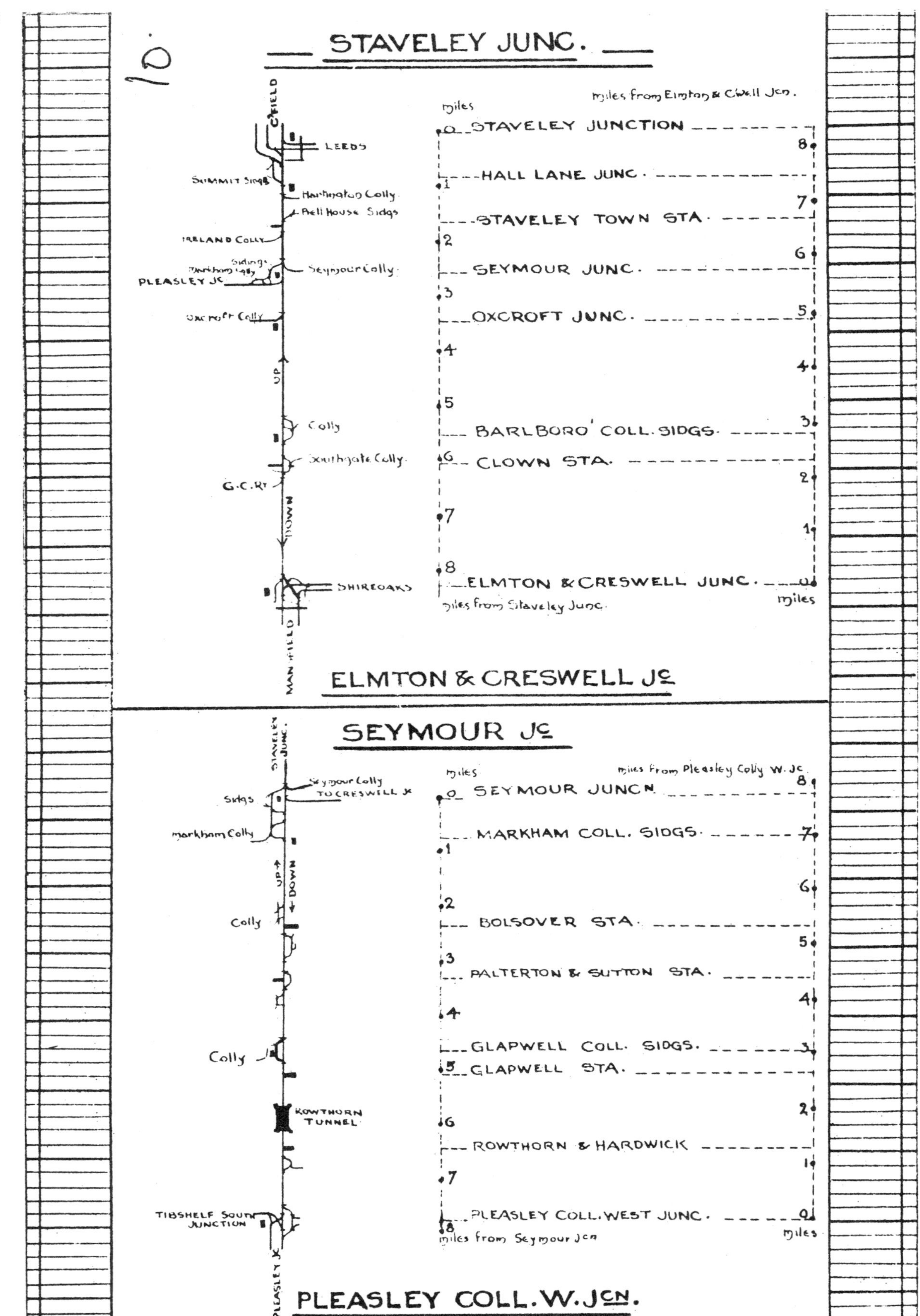
10
STAVELEY JUNC.
miles from Elmton & C'well Jcn.
miles
0 STAVELEY JUNCTION 8
HALL LANE JUNC. 1 7
STAVELEY TOWN STA.
2 SEYMOUR JUNC. 6
3 OXCROFT JUNC. 5
4 4
5 BARLBORO' COLL. SIDGS. 3
6 CLOWN STA. 2
7 1
8 ELMTON & CRESWELL JUNC. 0
miles from Staveley Junc.
miles
LEEDS
Summit Sidgs
Hartington Colly
Bell House Sidgs
IRELAND COLLY
Sidings
Markham Colly
Seymour Colly
PLEASLEY JC
Oxcroft Colly
UP
Colly
Southgate Colly
G.C.Ry
DOWN
SHIREOAKS
MANSFIELD
ELMTON & CRESWELL JC
SEYMOUR JC
miles
miles from Pleasley Colly W. Jc
0 SEYMOUR JUNCN. 8
MARKHAM COLL. SIDGS. 7
1
6
2 BOLSOVER STA.
5
3 PALTERTON & SUTTON STA.
4
4
GLAPWELL COLL. SIDGS. 3
5 GLAPWELL STA.
2
6
ROWTHORN & HARDWICK
1
7
8 PLEASLEY COLL. WEST JUNC. 0
miles from Seymour Jcn
miles
STAVELEY JUNC.
Seymour Colly
TO CRESWELL JC
Sidgs
Markham Colly
UP
DOWN
Colly
Colly
ROWTHORN TUNNEL
TIBSHELF SOUTH JUNCTION
PLEASLEY JC
PLEASLEY COLL. W. JCN.

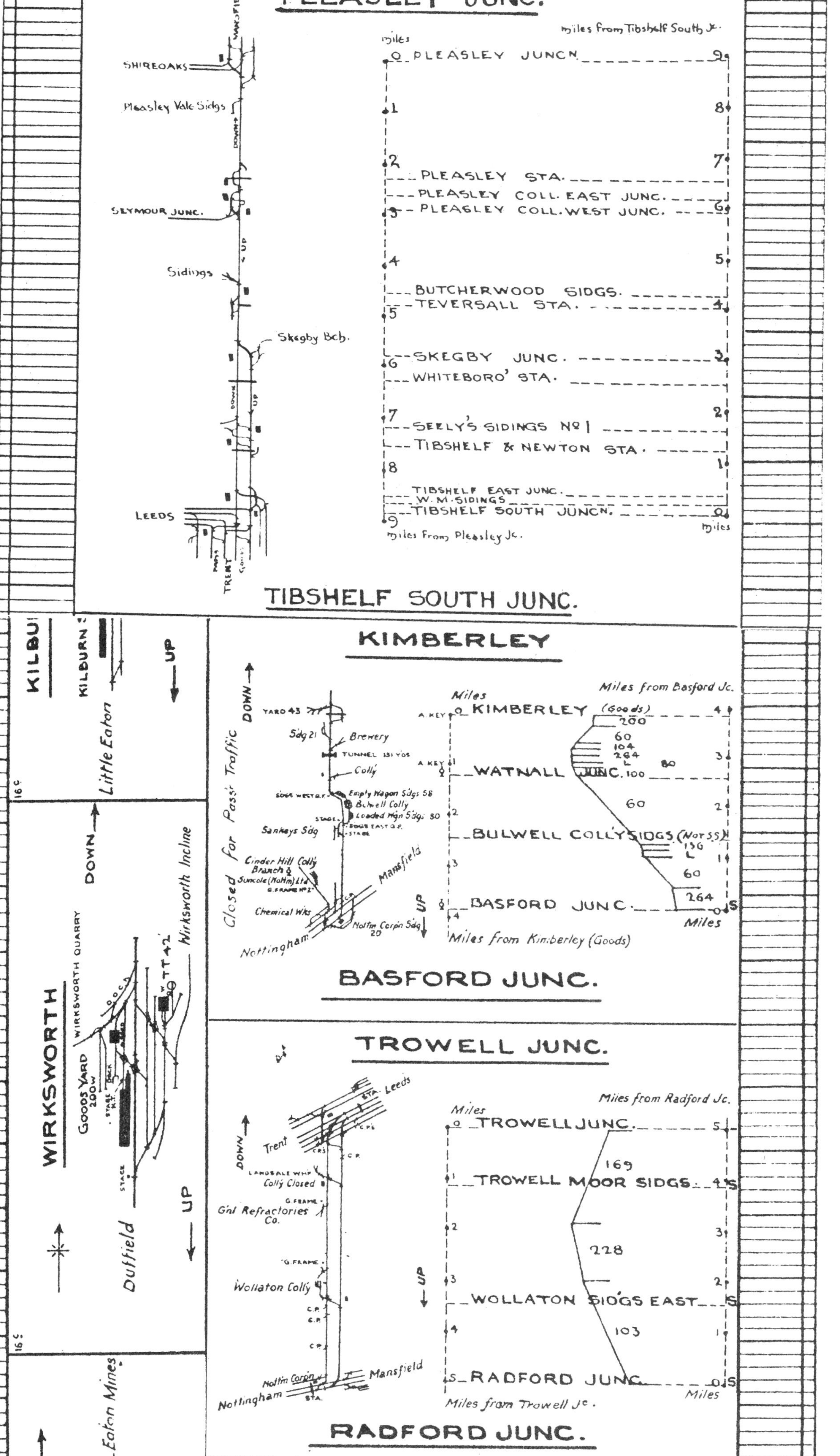
PLEASLEY JUNC.
TIBSHELF SOUTH JUNC.
KIMBERLEY
BASFORD JUNC.
TROWELL JUNC.
RADFORD JUNC.
WIRKSWORTH
KILBURN

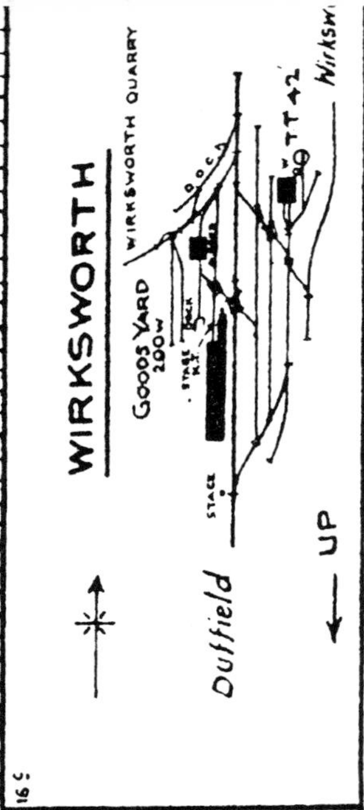

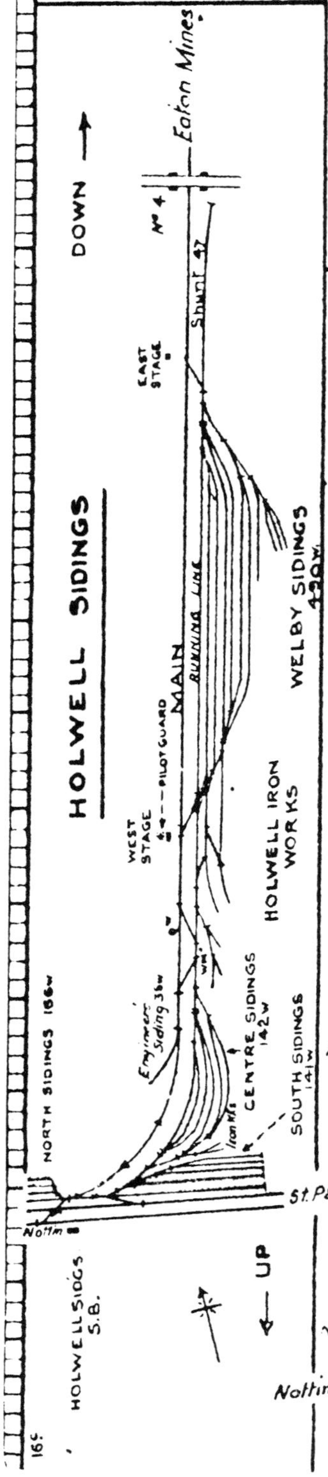

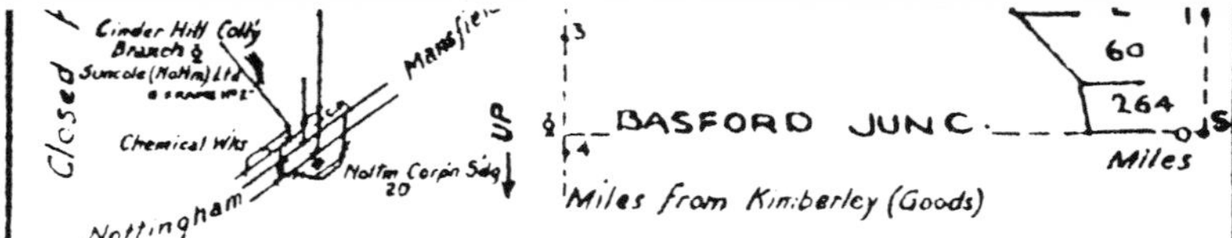

WIRKSWORTH

BASFORD JUNC.

TROWELL JUNC.

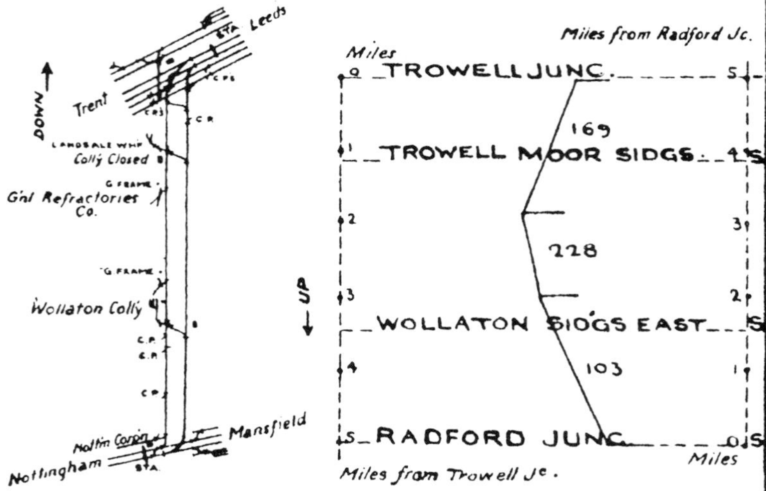

Miles from Radford Jc.

Miles	Location	Gradient	Miles
0	TROWELL JUNC.		5
		169	
1	TROWELL MOOR SIDGS.		4
2			3
		228	
3			2
	WOLLATON SIDGS EAST		
		103	
4			1
5	RADFORD JUNC.		0

Miles from Trowell Jc.

RADFORD JUNC.

HOLWELL BRANCH

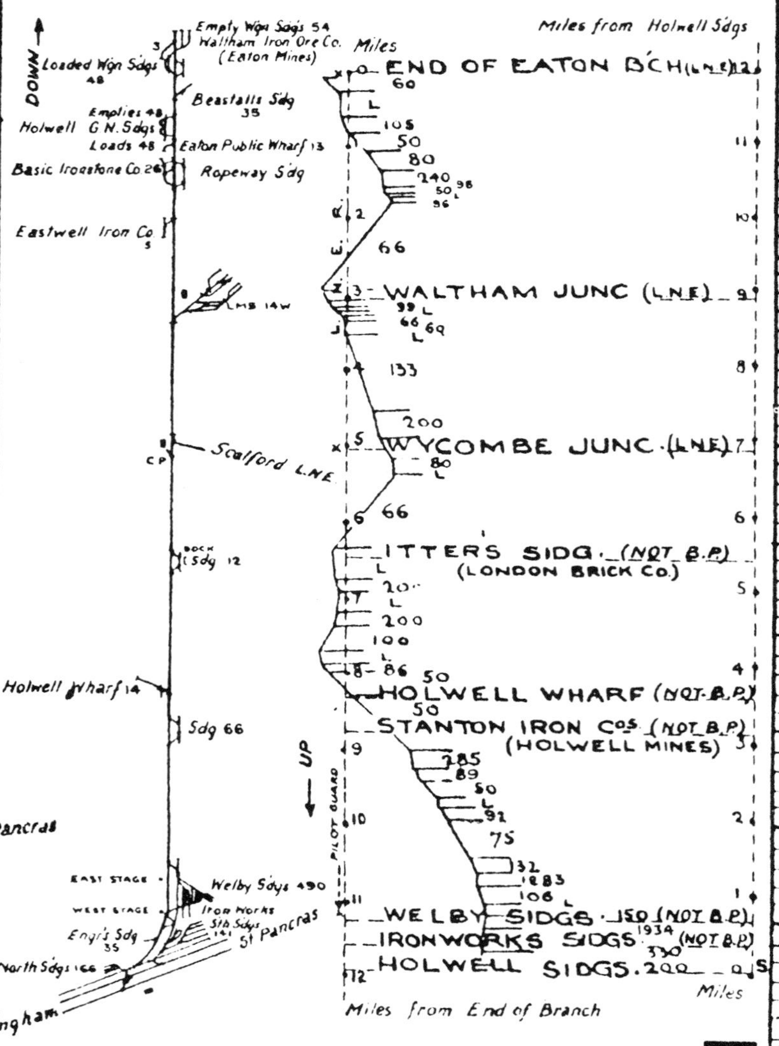

Miles from Holwell Sdgs

Miles	Location	Miles
0	END OF EATON B'CH (L.N.E.)	12
3	WALTHAM JUNC (L.N.E.)	9
5	WYCOMBE JUNC. (L.N.E.)	7
	ITTER'S SIDG. (NOT B.P.) (LONDON BRICK CO.)	
	HOLWELL WHARF (NOT B.P.)	
	STANTON IRON COS (NOT B.P.) (HOLWELL MINES)	
	WELBY SIDGS (NOT B.P.)	
	IRONWORKS SIDGS (NOT B.P.)	
12	HOLWELL SIDGS.	0

Miles from End of Branch

HOLWELL SIDINGS

HOLWELL SIDGS S.B.

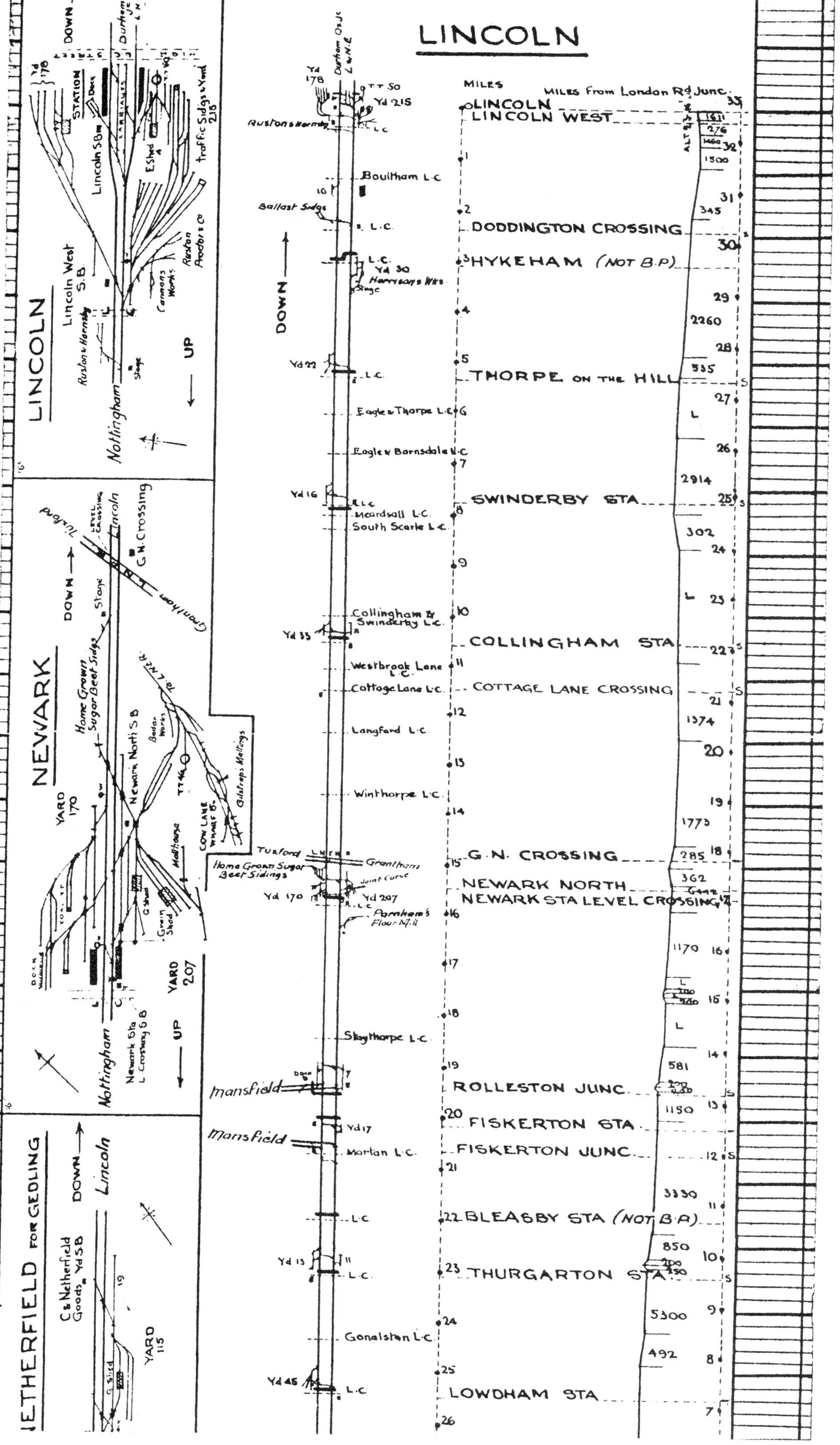
LINCOLN
MILES
MILES from London Rd Junc.
LINCOLN
LINCOLN WEST
DODDINGTON CROSSING
HYKEHAM (NOT B.P)
THORPE ON THE HILL
SWINDERBY STA
COLLINGHAM STA
COTTAGE LANE CROSSING
G.N. CROSSING
NEWARK NORTH
NEWARK STA LEVEL CROSSING
ROLLESTON JUNC.
FISKERTON STA
FISKERTON JUNC.
BLEASBY STA (NOT B.P)
THURGARTON STA
LOWDHAM STA
Boultham L.C.
Ballast Sdgs
Eagle & Thorpe L.C.
Eagle & Barnsdale L.C.
Meardsall L.C.
South Scarle L.C.
Collingham & Swinderby L.C.
Westbrook Lane L.C.
Cottage Lane L.C.
Langford L.C.
Winthorpe L.C.
Staythorpe L.C.
Morton L.C.
Gonalston L.C.
Mansfield
Mansfield
DOWN
LINCOLN
Lincoln West S.B.
Nottingham
UP
NEWARK
Newark North S.B.
G.N. Crossing
Grantham
Tuxford
YARD 170
YARD 207
Newark Sta L Crossing S.B
NETHERFIELD FOR GEDLING
C & Netherfield Goods Yd S.B
YARD 115
Lincoln

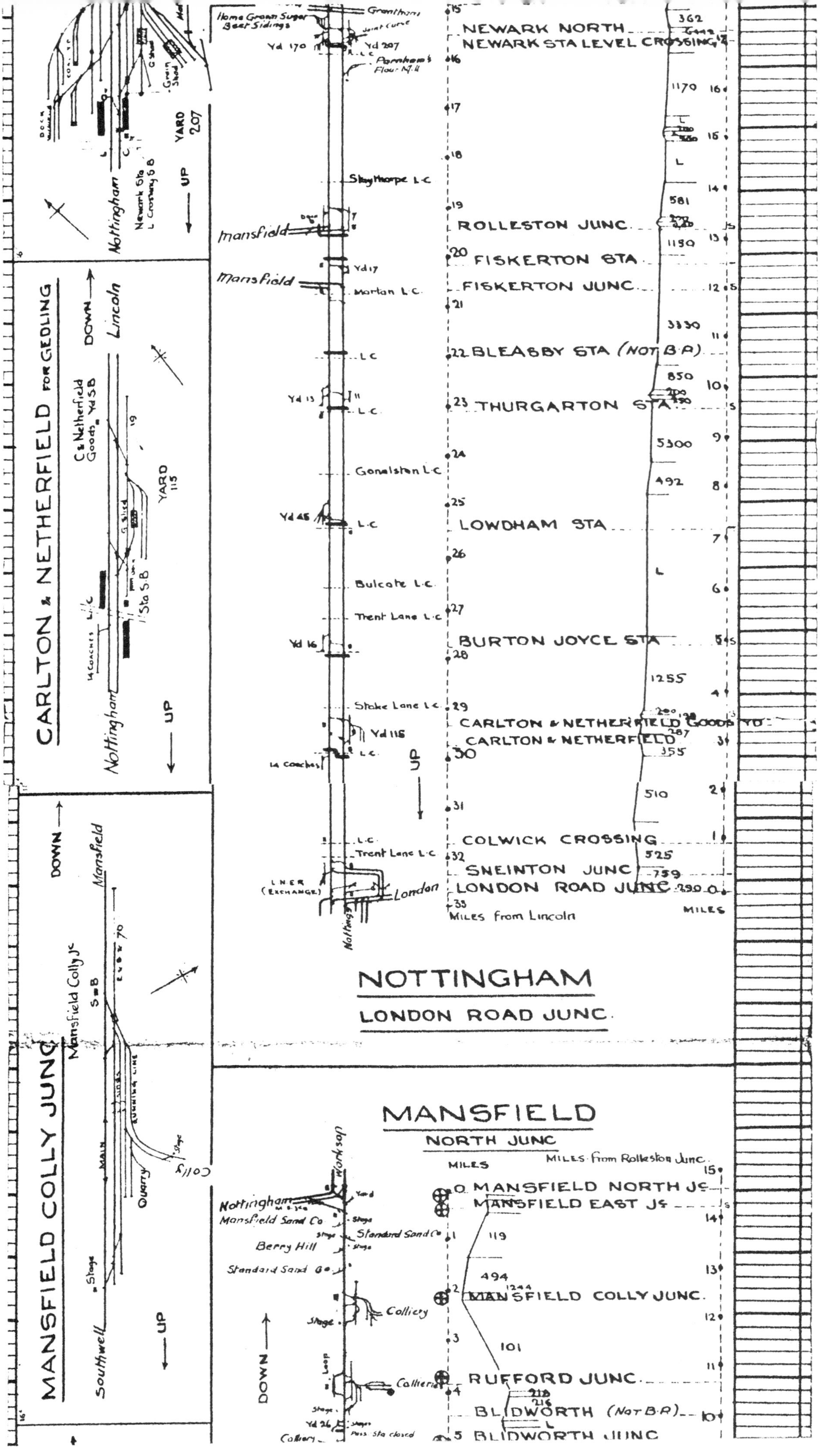
Home Grown Sugar Beet Sidings
Grantham
Yd 170
Yd 207
Parnham's Flour Mill
NEWARK NORTH
NEWARK STA LEVEL CROSSING
Staythorpe L.C.
Mansfield
ROLLESTON JUNC
Yd 17
FISKERTON STA
Mansfield
Morton L.C.
FISKERTON JUNC
BLEASBY STA (NOT B.R)
Yd 13
THURGARTON STA
Gonalston L.C.
Yd 45
LOWDHAM STA
Bulcote L.C.
Trent Lane L.C.
Yd 16
BURTON JOYCE STA
Stoke Lane L.C.
Yd 115
CARLTON & NETHERFIELD GOODS YD
CARLTON & NETHERFIELD
14 coaches
UP
Trent Lane L.C.
COLWICK CROSSING
SNEINTON JUNC
L.N.E.R (EXCHANGE)
London
LONDON ROAD JUNC
Nottingham
MILES from Lincoln
MILES
Nottingham
Newark Sta L Crossing S.B
YARD 207
UP
CARLTON & NETHERFIELD FOR GEDLING
DOWN
Lincoln
C & Netherfield Goods Yd S.B
YARD 115
Sta S.B
14 COACHES
Nottingham
UP
NOTTINGHAM
LONDON ROAD JUNC.
DOWN
Mansfield
Mansfield Colly Jc S.B
MANSFIELD COLLY JUNC
MAIN
RUNNING LINE
Quarry
Colly
Stage
Southwell
UP
MANSFIELD
NORTH JUNC
MILES
MILES from Rolleston Junc.
Worksop
Yard
Nottingham
Mansfield Sand Co
Standard Sand Co
Berry Hill
Standard Sand Co
MANSFIELD NORTH Jc
MANSFIELD EAST Jc
MANSFIELD COLLY JUNC.
Colliery
Stage
DOWN
Loop
Collieries
RUFFORD JUNC.
BLIDWORTH (Not B.R)
Yd 26
Pass. Sta closed
Colliery
BLIDWORTH JUNC

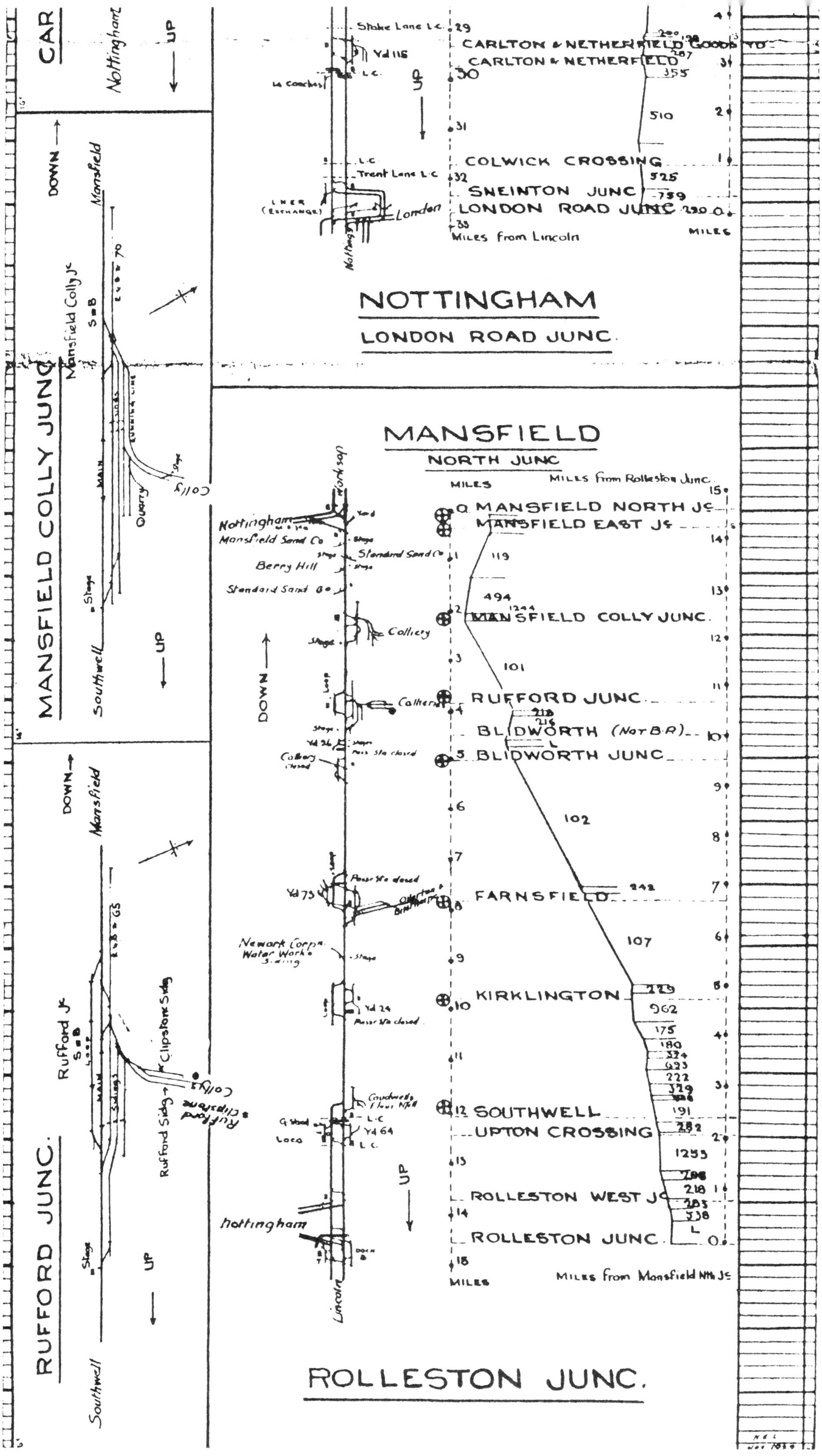

NOTTINGHAM
LONDON ROAD JUNC.

CARLTON & NETHERFIELD GOODS YD
CARLTON & NETHERFIELD
COLWICK CROSSING
SNEINTON JUNC
LONDON ROAD JUNC
MILES from Lincoln

MANSFIELD
NORTH JUNC

MILES — MILES from Rolleston Junc

0 MANSFIELD NORTH JC
MANSFIELD EAST JC
2 MANSFIELD COLLY JUNC.
RUFFORD JUNC
BLIDWORTH (NOT B.R.)
5 BLIDWORTH JUNC
FARNSFIELD
10 KIRKLINGTON
12 SOUTHWELL
UPTON CROSSING
ROLLESTON WEST JC
ROLLESTON JUNC
MILES — MILES from Mansfield Nth JC

ROLLESTON JUNC.

MANSFIELD COLLY JUNC

RUFFORD JUNC.

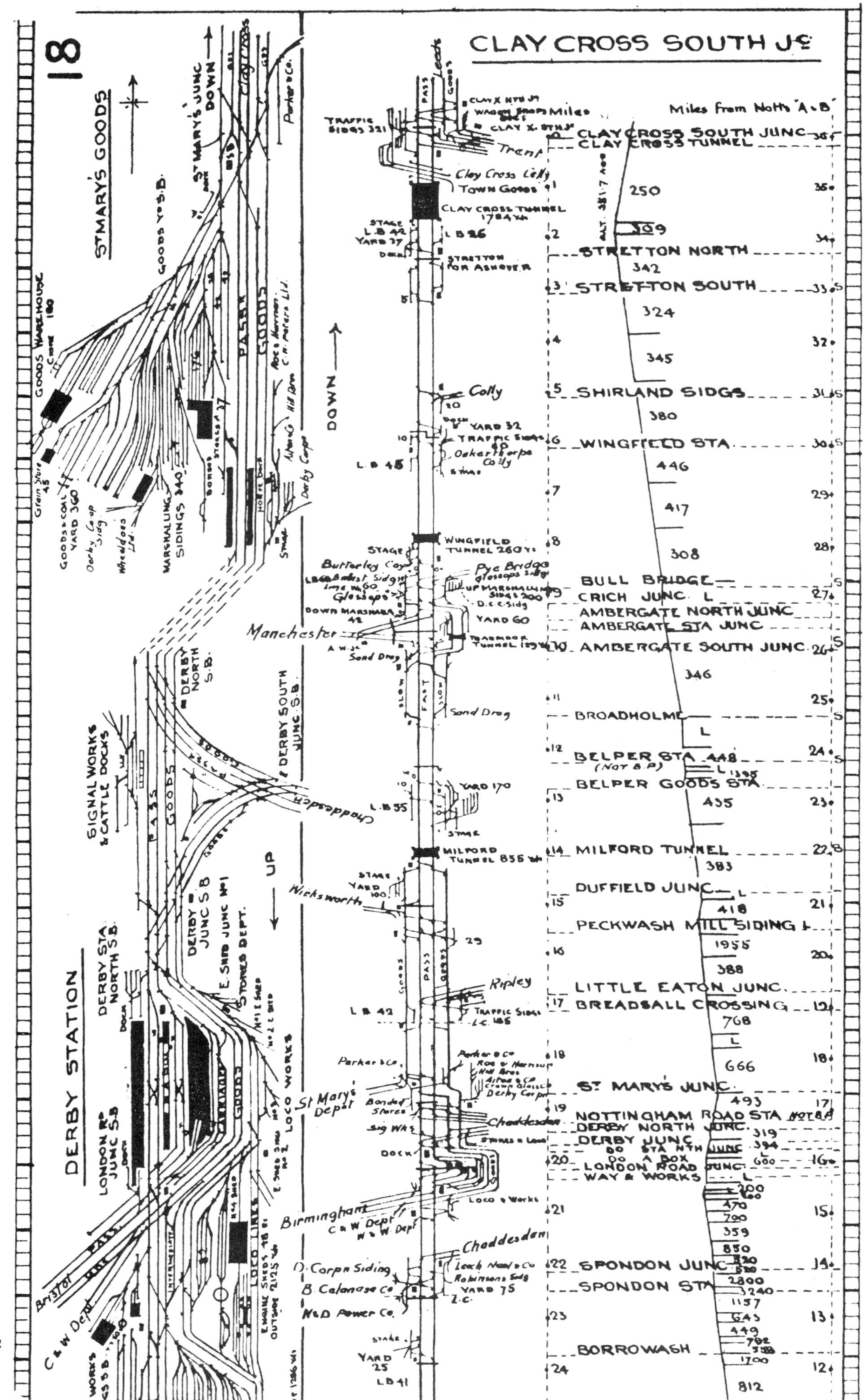

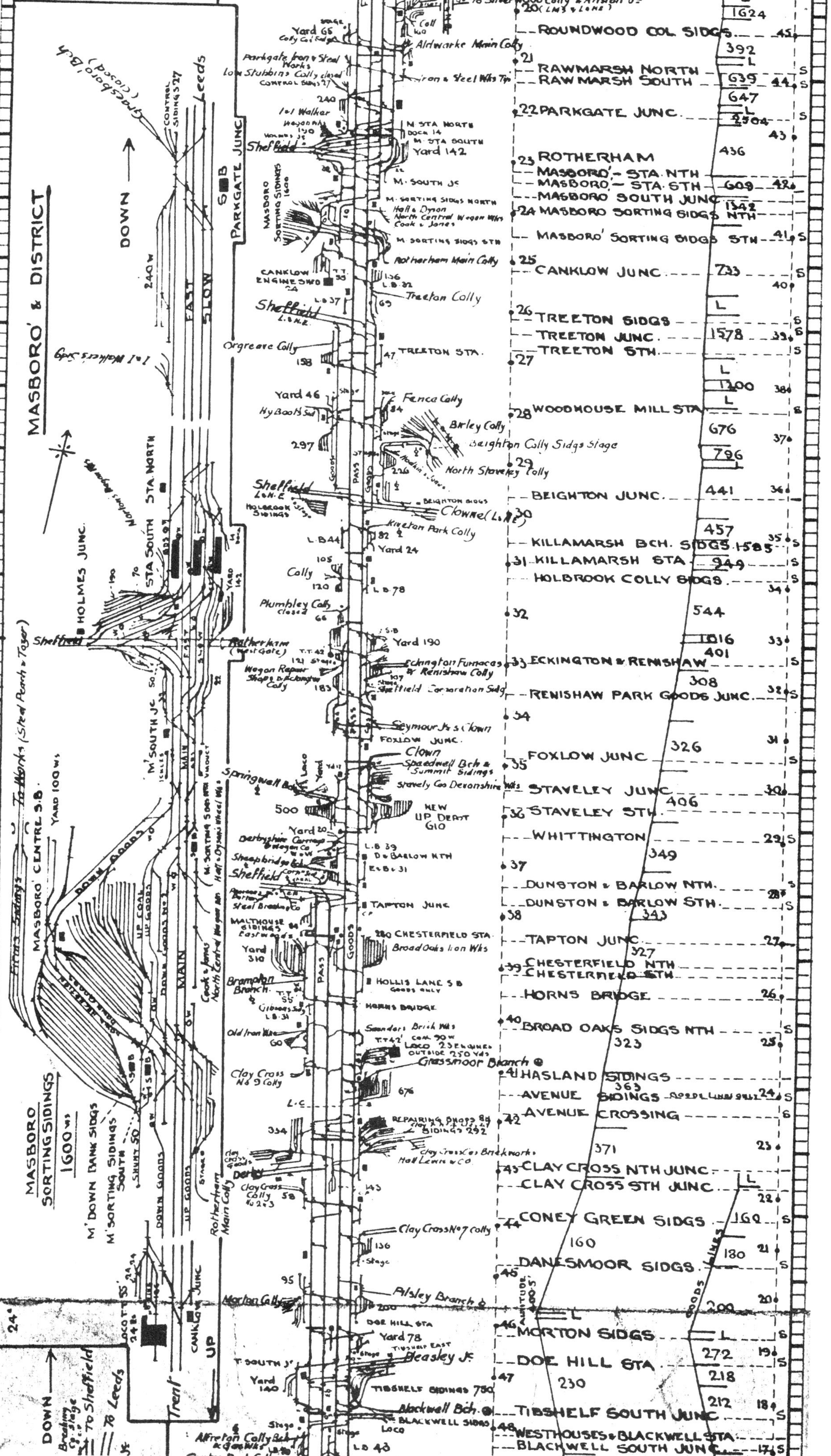
MASBORO' & DISTRICT
MASBORO SORTING SIDINGS 1600 ws
PARKGATE JUNC
ROUNDWOOD COL SIDGS
RAWMARSH NORTH
RAWMARSH SOUTH
PARKGATE JUNC.
ROTHERHAM
MASBORO' - STA NTH
MASBORO' - STA STH
MASBORO SOUTH JUNC
MASBORO SORTING SIDGS NTH
MASBORO' SORTING SIDGS STH
CANKLOW JUNC
TREETON SIDGS
TREETON JUNC.
TREETON STH.
WOODHOUSE MILL STA
BEIGHTON JUNC.
KILLAMARSH BCH. SIDGS
KILLAMARSH STA
HOLBROOK COLLY SIDGS
ECKINGTON & RENISHAW
RENISHAW PARK GOODS JUNC.
FOXLOW JUNC
STAVELEY JUNC
STAVELEY STH.
WHITTINGTON
DUNSTON & BARLOW NTH.
DUNSTON & BARLOW STH.
TAPTON JUNC
CHESTERFIELD NTH
CHESTERFIELD STH
HORNS BRIDGE
BROAD OAKS SIDGS NTH
HASLAND SIDINGS
AVENUE SIDINGS
AVENUE CROSSING
CLAY CROSS NTH JUNC.
CLAY CROSS STH JUNC.
CONEY GREEN SIDGS
DANESMOOR SIDGS
MORTON SIDGS
DOE HILL STA
TIBSHELF SOUTH JUNC
WESTHOUSES & BLACKWELL STA.
BLACKWELL SOUTH JUNC.

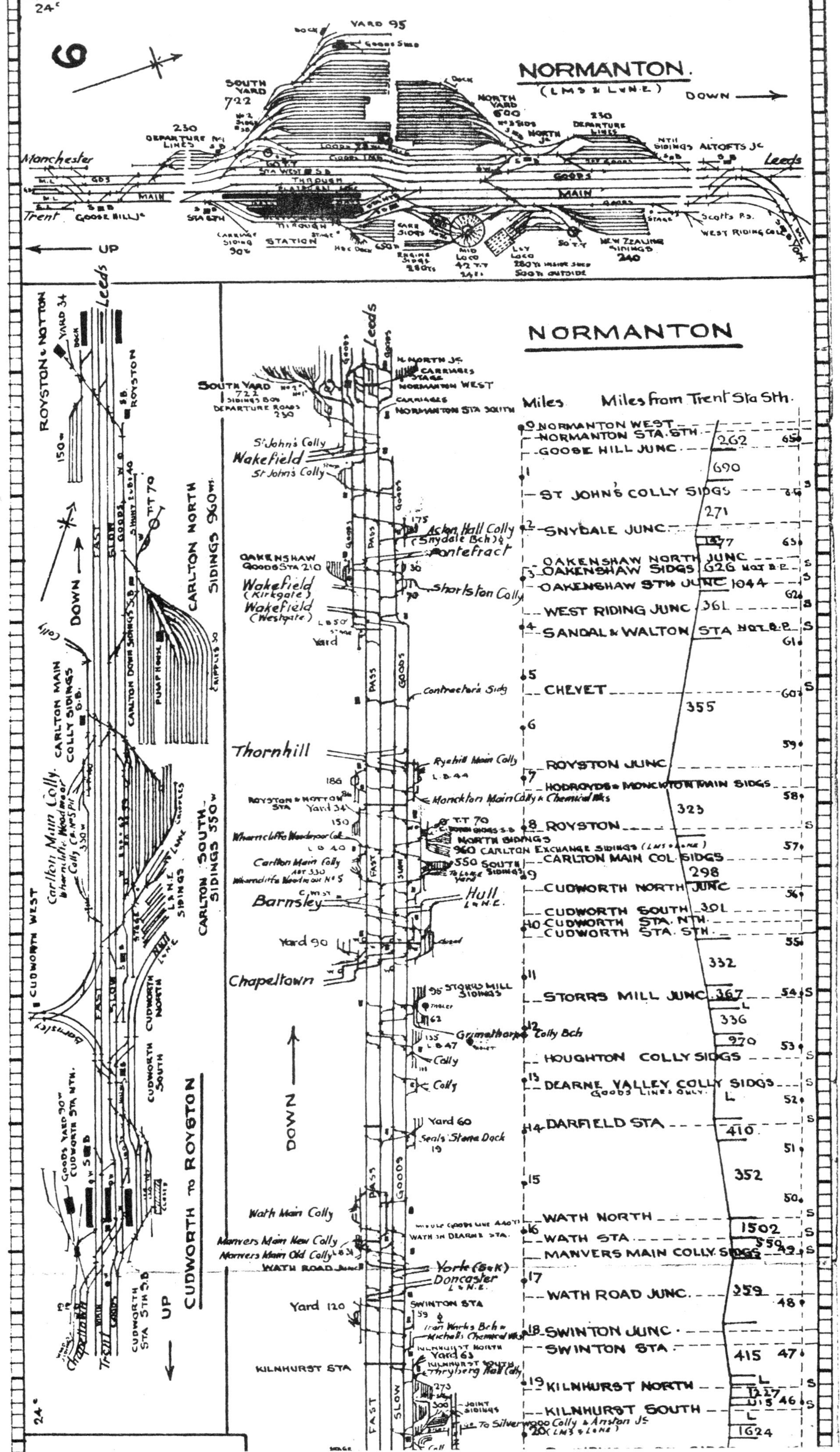
6
NORMANTON.
(LMS & LNE)
DOWN
UP
Manchester
Trent
Leeds
York
SOUTH YARD 722
NORTH YARD 600
YARD 95
GOOSE HILL JC
ALTOFTS JC
STATION
MAIN
GOODS
THROUGH
Scotts P.S.
WEST RIDING COLLY
NEW ZEALAND SIDINGS 240
NORMANTON
Miles
Miles from Trent Sta Sth
NORMANTON WEST
NORMANTON STA. STH
GOOSE HILL JUNC
ST JOHN'S COLLY SIDGS
SNYDALE JUNC
OAKENSHAW NORTH JUNC
OAKENSHAW SIDGS
OAKENSHAW STH JUNC
WEST RIDING JUNC
SANDAL & WALTON STA
CHEVET
ROYSTON JUNC
HODROYDS & MONCKTON MAIN SIDGS
ROYSTON
CARLTON EXCHANGE SIDINGS (LMS & LNE)
CARLTON MAIN COL. SIDGS
CUDWORTH NORTH JUNC
CUDWORTH SOUTH
CUDWORTH STA. NTH.
CUDWORTH STA. STH.
STORRS MILL JUNC
HOUGHTON COLLY SIDGS
DEARNE VALLEY COLLY SIDGS
DARFIELD STA
WATH NORTH
WATH STA
MANVERS MAIN COLLY SIDGS
WATH ROAD JUNC.
SWINTON JUNC
SWINTON STA
KILNHURST NORTH
KILNHURST SOUTH
Wakefield
Thornhill
Barnsley
Chapeltown
Hull
Doncaster
Pontefract
ROYSTON & NOTTON
CARLTON NORTH SIDINGS 960 WS.
CARLTON SOUTH SIDINGS 550 W
CUDWORTH TO ROYSTON
CUDWORTH WEST
FAST
SLOW
GOODS
PASS

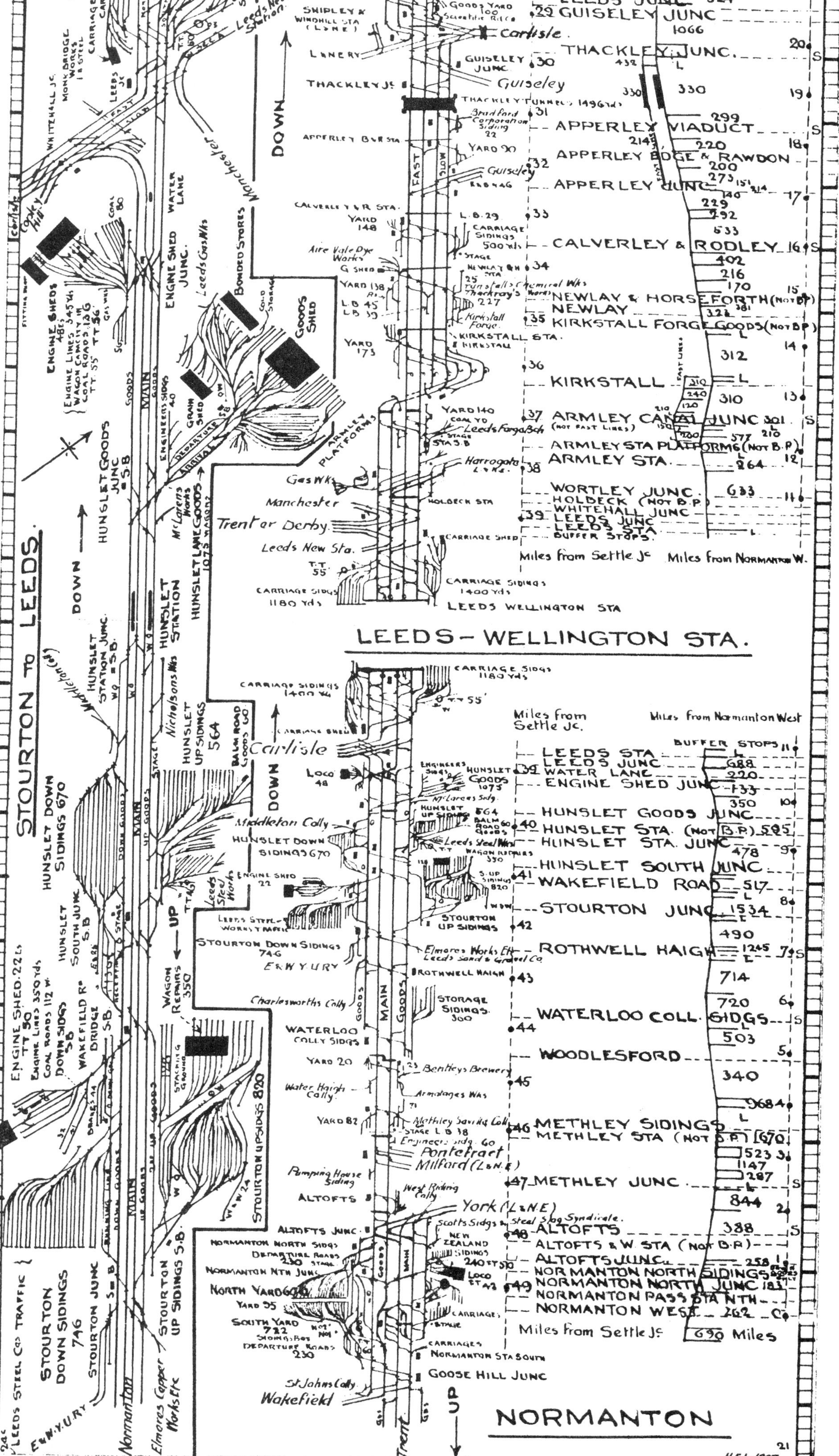
STOURTON TO LEEDS
LEEDS - WELLINGTON STA.
NORMANTON
DOWN
UP
FAST
SLOW
MAIN
GOODS
Carlisle
Guiseley
Manchester
Trent or Derby
Leeds New Sta.
Pontefract
Milford (L&N.E)
York (L&N.E)
Wakefield
Normanton
Trent
BRADFORD JUNC.
LEEDS JUNC
GUISELEY JUNC
THACKLEY JUNC.
APPERLEY VIADUCT
APPERLEY BDGE & RAWDON
APPERLEY JUNC
CALVERLEY & RODLEY
NEWLAY & HORSEFORTH (NOT BP)
NEWLAY
KIRKSTALL FORGE GOODS (NOT BP)
KIRKSTALL
ARMLEY CANAL JUNC
ARMLEY STA PLATFORMS (NOT B.P)
ARMLEY STA.
WORTLEY JUNC.
HOLBECK (NOT B.P)
WHITEHALL JUNC
LEEDS JUNC
LEEDS STA
BUFFER STOPS
Miles from Settle Jc
Miles from Normanton W.
LEEDS WELLINGTON STA
Miles from Settle Jc.
Miles from Normanton West
LEEDS STA
LEEDS JUNC
WATER LANE
ENGINE SHED JUNC
HUNSLET GOODS JUNC
HUNSLET STA. (NOT B.P)
HUNSLET STA. JUNC
HUNSLET SOUTH JUNC
WAKEFIELD ROAD
STOURTON JUNC
ROTHWELL HAIGH
WATERLOO COLL. SIDGS
WOODLESFORD
METHLEY SIDINGS
METHLEY STA (NOT B.P)
METHLEY JUNC
ALTOFTS
ALTOFTS & W. STA (NOT B.P)
ALTOFTS JUNC.
NORMANTON NORTH SIDINGS
NORMANTON NORTH JUNC
NORMANTON PASS STA NTH
NORMANTON WEST
Miles from Settle Jc
Miles
HUNSLET GOODS JUNC S.B
HUNSLET STATION
HUNSLET LANE GOODS 1075 WAGONS
HUNSLET UP SIDINGS 564
HUNSLET DOWN SIDINGS 670
HUNSLET SOUTH JUNC S.B
STOURTON DOWN SIDINGS 746
STOURTON UP SIDINGS 820
STOURTON UP SIDINGS S.B.
STOURTON JUNC
WAGON REPAIRS 350
ENGINE SHED 22 Ls
GOODS SHED
GRAIN SHED
BONDED STORES
ENGINE SHED JUNC
WATER LANE
GOOSE HILL JUNC
NORMANTON STA SOUTH
H.E.L. 1927.

14 UNSTONE COLLIERY SIDINGS 3 S
15 100 2
16 SHEEPBRIDGE STA 118 198 2 657 1328 677 1 S
17 TAPTON JUNC 296 0
Miles
Miles from Masboro' Sta Str Jc

TAPTON JUNCTION

WICKER GOODS TO BRIGHTSIDE

SHEFFIELD

HEELEY

JUNE 1928

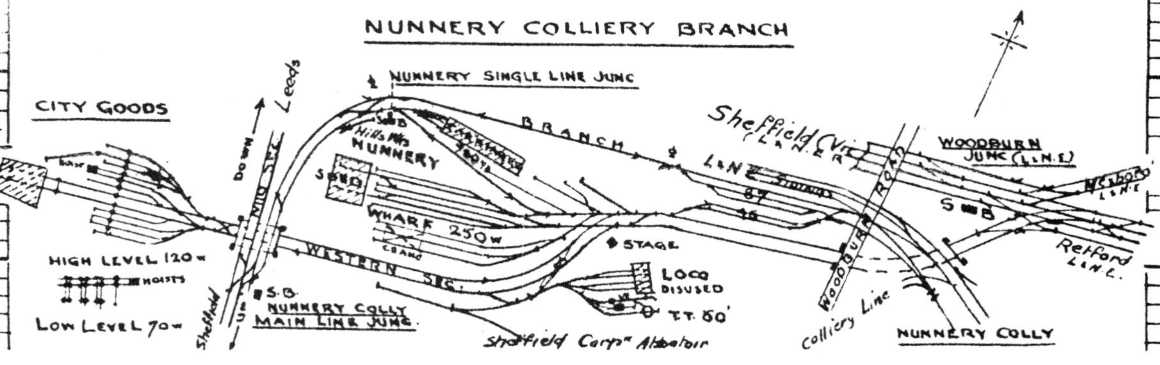

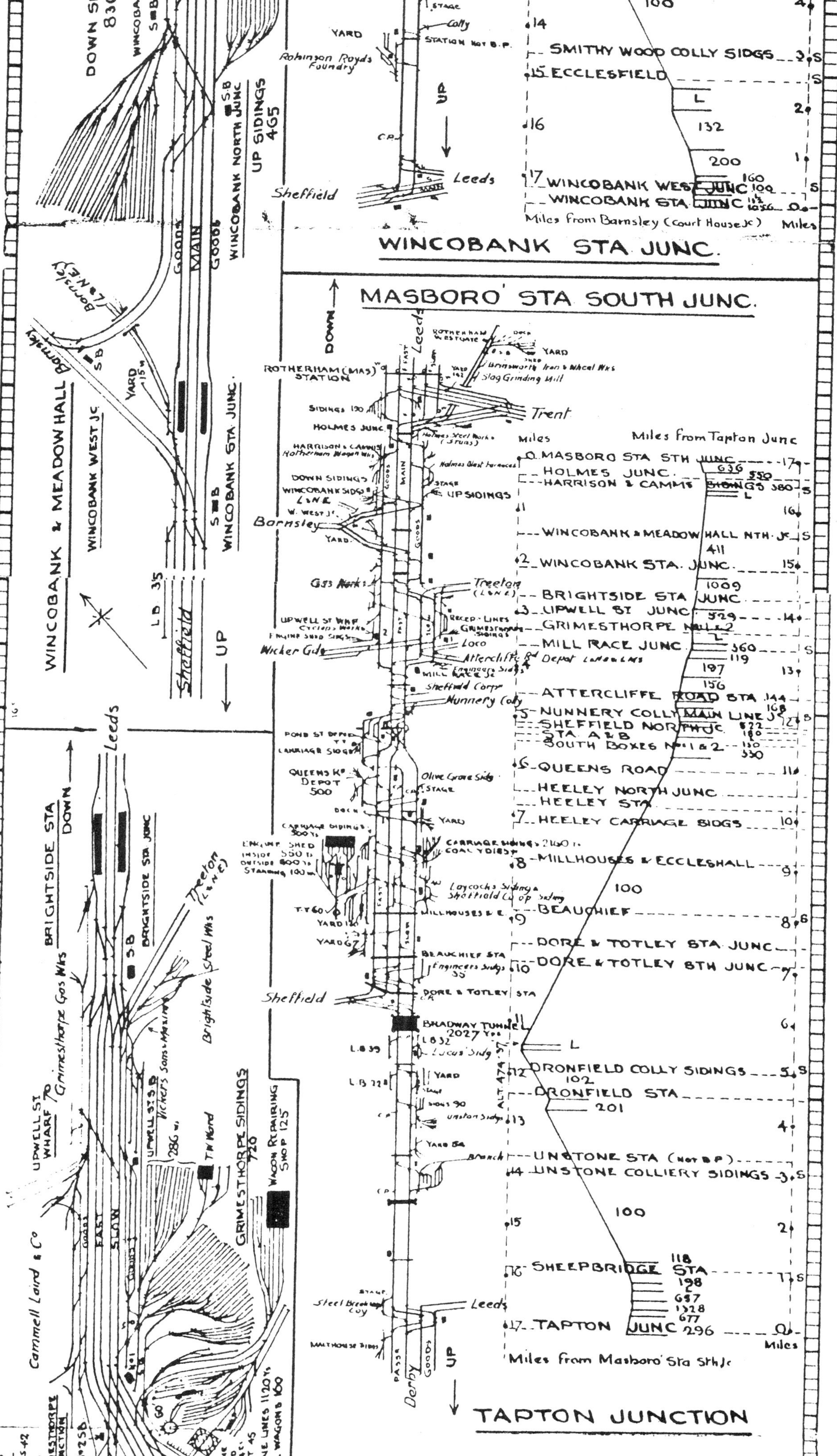
WINCOBANK STA JUNC.
SMITHY WOOD COLLY SIDGS
ECCLESFIELD
WINCOBANK WEST JUNC
WINCOBANK STA JUNC
Miles from Barnsley (Court House Jc)
Miles
MASBORO' STA SOUTH JUNC.
Miles from Tapton Junc
MASBORO STA STH JUNC
HOLMES JUNC.
HARRISON & CAMMS SIDINGS
WINCOBANK & MEADOW HALL NTH. JC
WINCOBANK STA. JUNC.
BRIGHTSIDE STA JUNC
UPWELL ST JUNC
GRIMESTHORPE
MILL RACE JUNC
ATTERCLIFFE ROAD STA
NUNNERY COLLY MAIN LINE
SHEFFIELD NORTH JC
STA A & B
SOUTH BOXES No 1 & 2
QUEENS ROAD
HEELEY NORTH JUNC
HEELEY STA
HEELEY CARRIAGE SIDGS
MILLHOUSES & ECCLESHALL
BEAUCHIEF
DORE & TOTLEY STA JUNC
DORE & TOTLEY STH JUNC
DRONFIELD COLLY SIDINGS
DRONFIELD STA
UNSTONE STA (NOT B.P.)
UNSTONE COLLIERY SIDINGS
SHEEPBRIDGE STA
TAPTON JUNC
Miles from Masboro' Sta Sth Jc
TAPTON JUNCTION
WINCOBANK & MEADOWHALL
WINCOBANK WEST JC
WINCOBANK STA. JUNC.
WINCOBANK NORTH JUNC
UP SIDINGS 465
DOWN SIDINGS 836
BRIGHTSIDE STA
BRIGHTSIDE STA JUNC
GRIMESTHORPE SIDINGS 720
WAGON REPAIRING SHOP 125
UPWELL ST. WHARF
Cammell Laird & Co
Leeds
Sheffield
Barnsley
Treeton
Trent
Derby
BRADWAY TUNNEL 2027 Yds

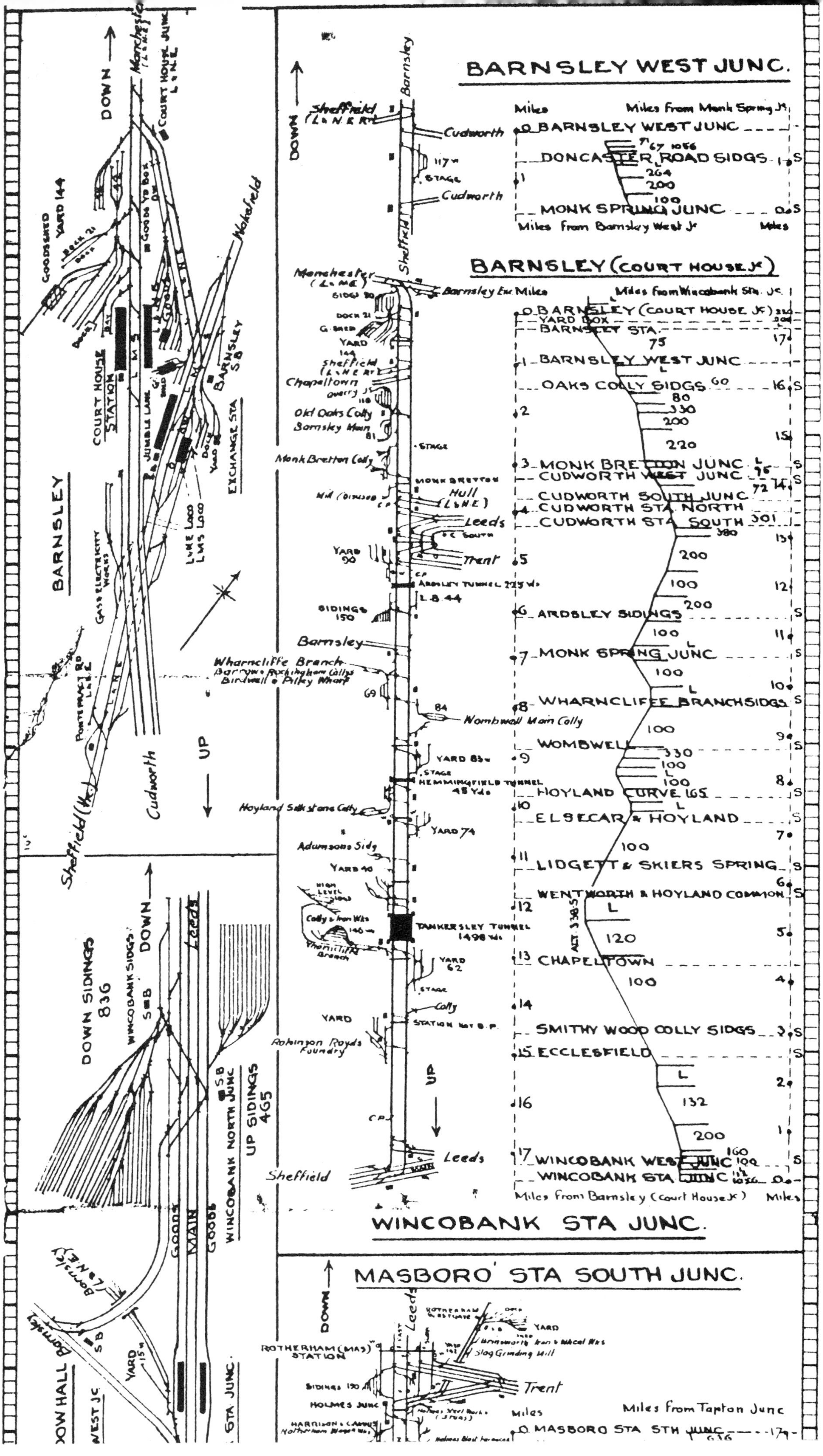

BARNSLEY WEST JUNC.

Miles | Miles From Monk Spring Jn.

- 0 BARNSLEY WEST JUNC.
- DONCASTER ROAD SIDGS — 1 S
- 1
- MONK SPRING JUNC. — 0 S

Gradients: 67, 1056, 264, 200, 100

Miles From Barnsley West Jn. | Miles

BARNSLEY (COURT HOUSE Jc)

Miles | Miles From Wincobank Sta. Jc.

- 0 BARNSLEY (COURT HOUSE Jc)
- YARD BOX
- BARNSLEY STA. — 17
- 1 BARNSLEY WEST JUNC.
- OAKS COLLY SIDGS — 16 S
- 2
- 15
- 3 MONK BRETTON JUNC. — S
- CUDWORTH WEST JUNC. — 14 S
- CUDWORTH SOUTH JUNC.
- 4 CUDWORTH STA. NORTH
- CUDWORTH STA. SOUTH
- 5 — 13
- 12
- 6 ARDSLEY SIDINGS — S
- 11
- 7 MONK SPRING JUNC. — S
- 10
- 8 WHARNCLIFFE BRANCH SIDGS — S
- WOMBWELL — 9 S
- 9
- HOYLAND CURVE — 8 S
- 10 ELSECAR & HOYLAND — S
- 7
- 11 LIDGETT & SKIERS SPRING — S
- WENTWORTH & HOYLAND COMMON — 6 S
- 12 ALT. 338.5
- 5
- 13 CHAPELTOWN
- 4
- 14
- SMITHY WOOD COLLY SIDGS — 3 S
- 15 ECCLESFIELD — S
- 2
- 16
- 1
- 17 WINCOBANK WEST JUNC. — S
- WINCOBANK STA JUNC. — 0

Gradients: 75, 60, 80, 330, 200, 220, 75, 72, 301, 380, 200, 100, 200, 100, 100, 100, 330, 100, 100, 165, 100, 120, 100, 132, 200, 160, 100, 1056

Miles From Barnsley (Court House Jc) | Miles

Diagram labels: Sheffield (L&NER), Barnsley, Cudworth, 117 Wa, Stage, Manchester (L&ME), Barnsley Exc., Sidgs 90, Dock 21, G. Shed, Yard 144, Sheffield (L&NER), Chapeltown Quarry 35, Old Oaks Colly, Barnsley Main 81, Stage, Monk Bretton Colly, Monk Bretton, Hull (L&NE), Leeds, Trent, Yard 90, Ardsley Tunnel 225 Yds, L.B. 44, Sidings 150, Barnsley, Wharncliffe Branch, Barrow & Rockingham Collys, Birdwell & Pilley Wharf, 69, 84, Wombwell Main Colly, Yard 83, Stage, Hemmingfield Tunnel 45 Yds, Hoyland Silkstone Colly, Yard 74, Adamsons Sidg, Yard 40, High Level Sidgs, Colly & Iron Wks, Tankersley Tunnel 1498 Yds, Wharncliffe Branch, Yard 62, Stage, Colly, Yard, Station, Robinson Royds Foundry, Down, Up, Leeds, Sheffield

WINCOBANK STA JUNC.

MASBORO' STA SOUTH JUNC.

Diagram labels: Down, Leeds, Rotherham Westgate, Yard, Rotherham (Mas.) Station, Slag Grinding Mill, Sidings 190, Trent, Holmes Junc, Harrison & Camm Rotherham Waggon Wks, Holmes Steel Works, Holmes Blast Furnaces

Miles | Miles From Tapton Junc

- 0 MASBORO STA STH JUNC — 17

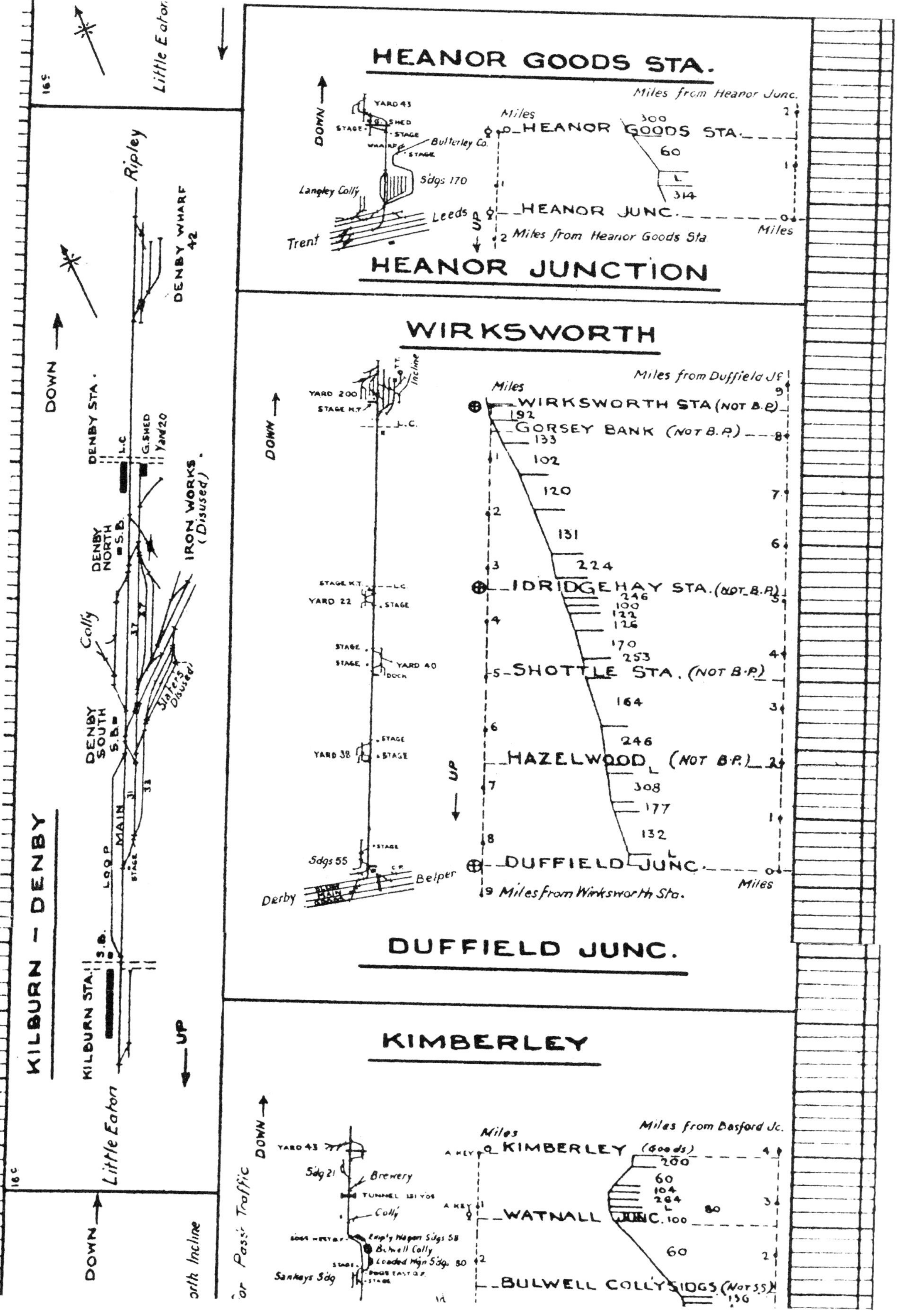
HEANOR GOODS STA.
Miles from Heanor Junc.
HEANOR GOODS STA.
HEANOR JUNC.
Miles from Heanor Goods Sta
HEANOR JUNCTION
WIRKSWORTH
Miles from Duffield Jc
WIRKSWORTH STA (NOT B.P.)
GORSEY BANK (NOT B.P.)
IDRIDGEHAY STA. (NOT B.P.)
SHOTTLE STA. (NOT B.P.)
HAZELWOOD (NOT B.P.)
DUFFIELD JUNC.
Miles from Wirksworth Sta.
DUFFIELD JUNC.
KIMBERLEY
Miles from Basford Jc.
KIMBERLEY (Goods)
WATNALL JUNC.
BULWELL COLLY SIDGS (Not 55)
KILBURN - DENBY
KILBURN STA.
DENBY SOUTH S.B.
DENBY NORTH S.B.
DENBY STA.
DENBY WHARF 42
IRON WORKS (Disused)
Ripley
Little Eaton

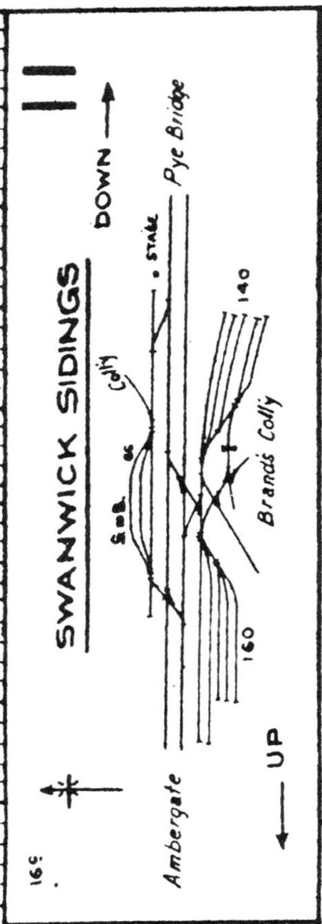

PYE BRIDGE (RIDDINGS JUNC.)

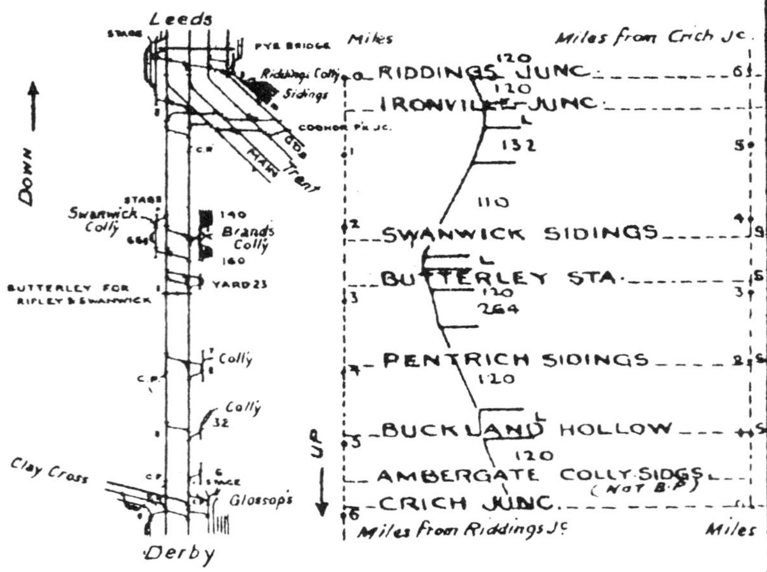

CRICH JUNC.

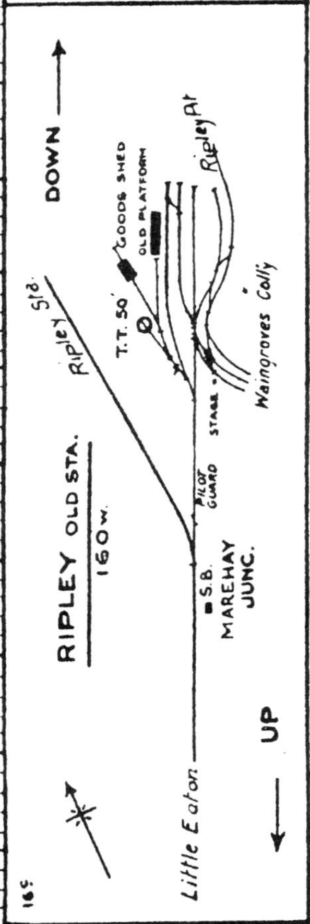

SWANWICK SIDINGS

RIPLEY

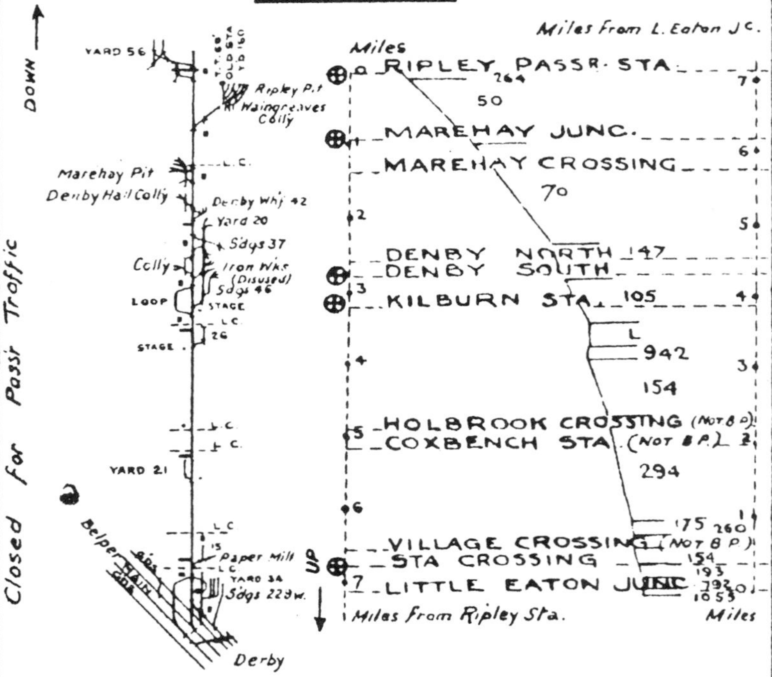

LITTLE EATON JUNC.

RIPLEY OLD STA. 160w.

HEANOR GOODS STA.

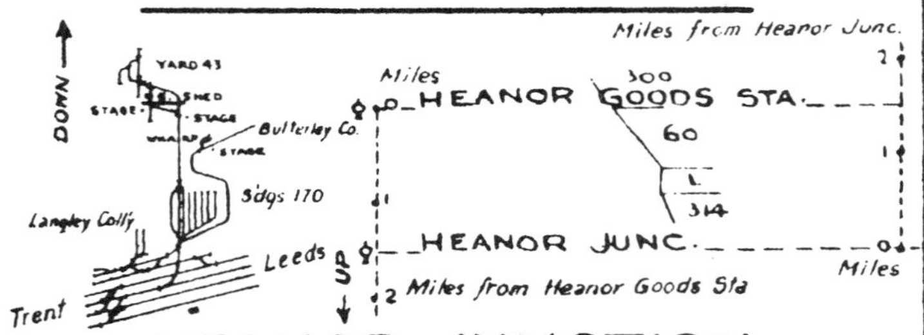

HEANOR JUNCTION

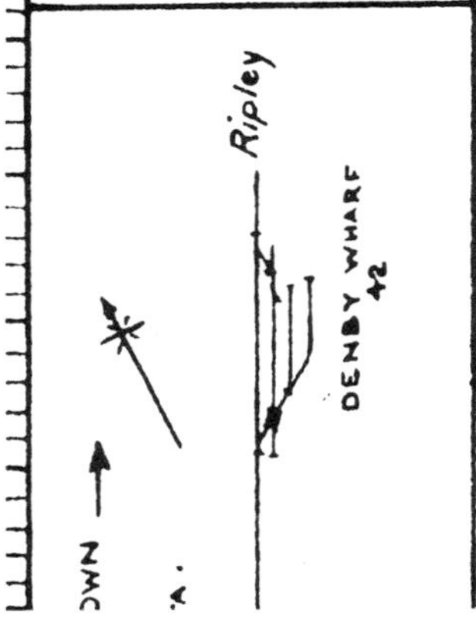

WIRKSWORTH

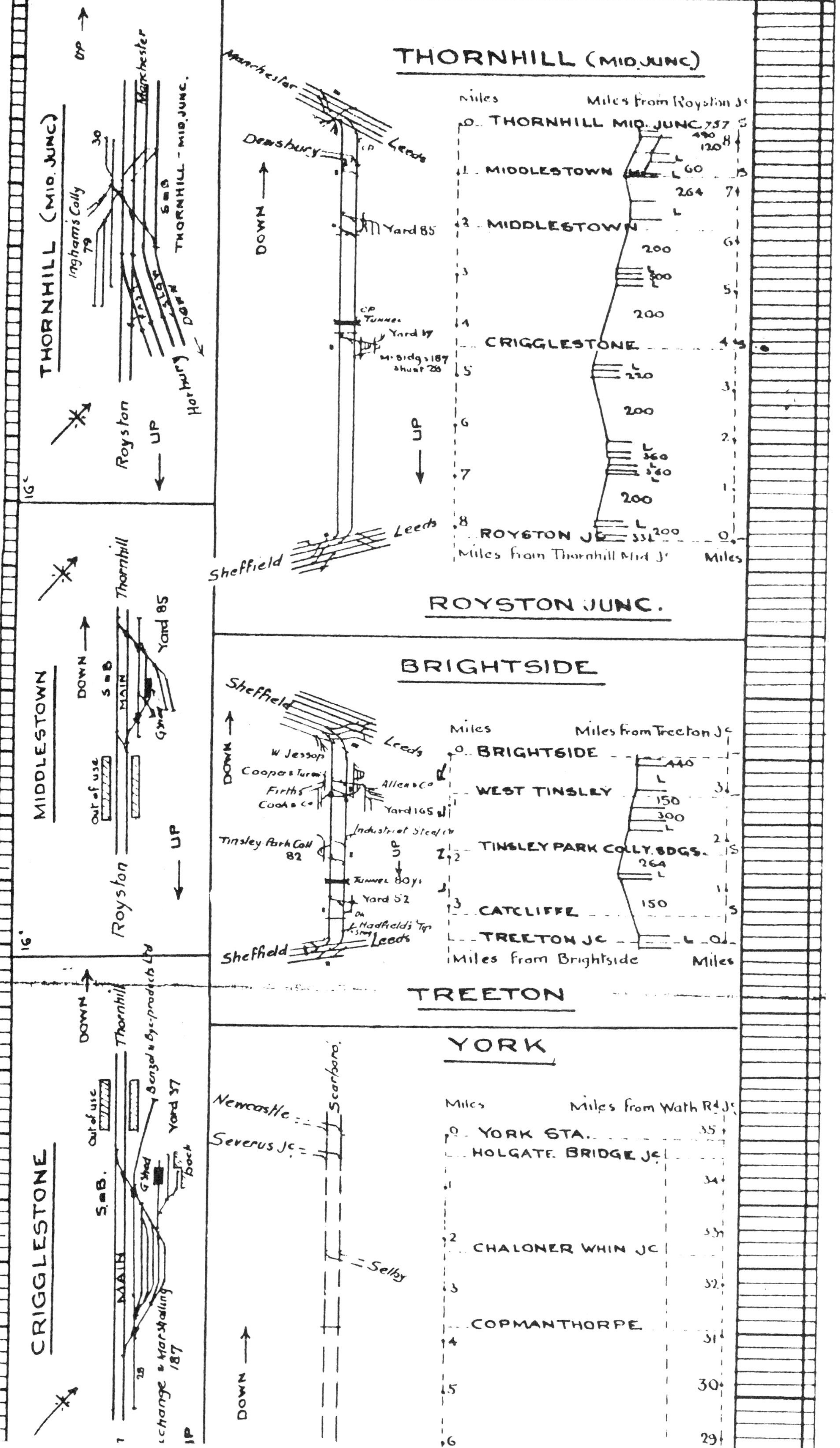
THORNHILL (MID. JUNC)
ROYSTON JUNC.
BRIGHTSIDE
TREETON
YORK
Miles
Miles from Royston Jc
THORNHILL MID. JUNC.
MIDDLESTOWN
CRIGGLESTONE
ROYSTON JC
Miles from Thornhill Mid Jc
Miles from Treeton Jc
BRIGHTSIDE
WEST TINSLEY
TINSLEY PARK COLLY. SDGS.
CATCLIFFE
TREETON JC
Miles from Brightside
Miles from Wath Rd Jc
YORK STA.
HOLGATE BRIDGE JC
CHALONER WHIN JC
COPMANTHORPE
THORNHILL (MID. JUNC)
MIDDLESTOWN
CRIGGLESTONE
Manchester
Leeds
Dewsbury
Sheffield
Newcastle
Scarboro'
Severus Jc
Selby
Royston
Horbury
Thornhill
DOWN
UP
Yard 85
Tunnel
Tinsley Park Coll 82
W. Jessop
Firths
Cooks & Co
Allen & Co
Yard 165
Yard 52
Hadfield's
out of use
Yard 37
G. Shed
Benzol & Bye-products Ltd

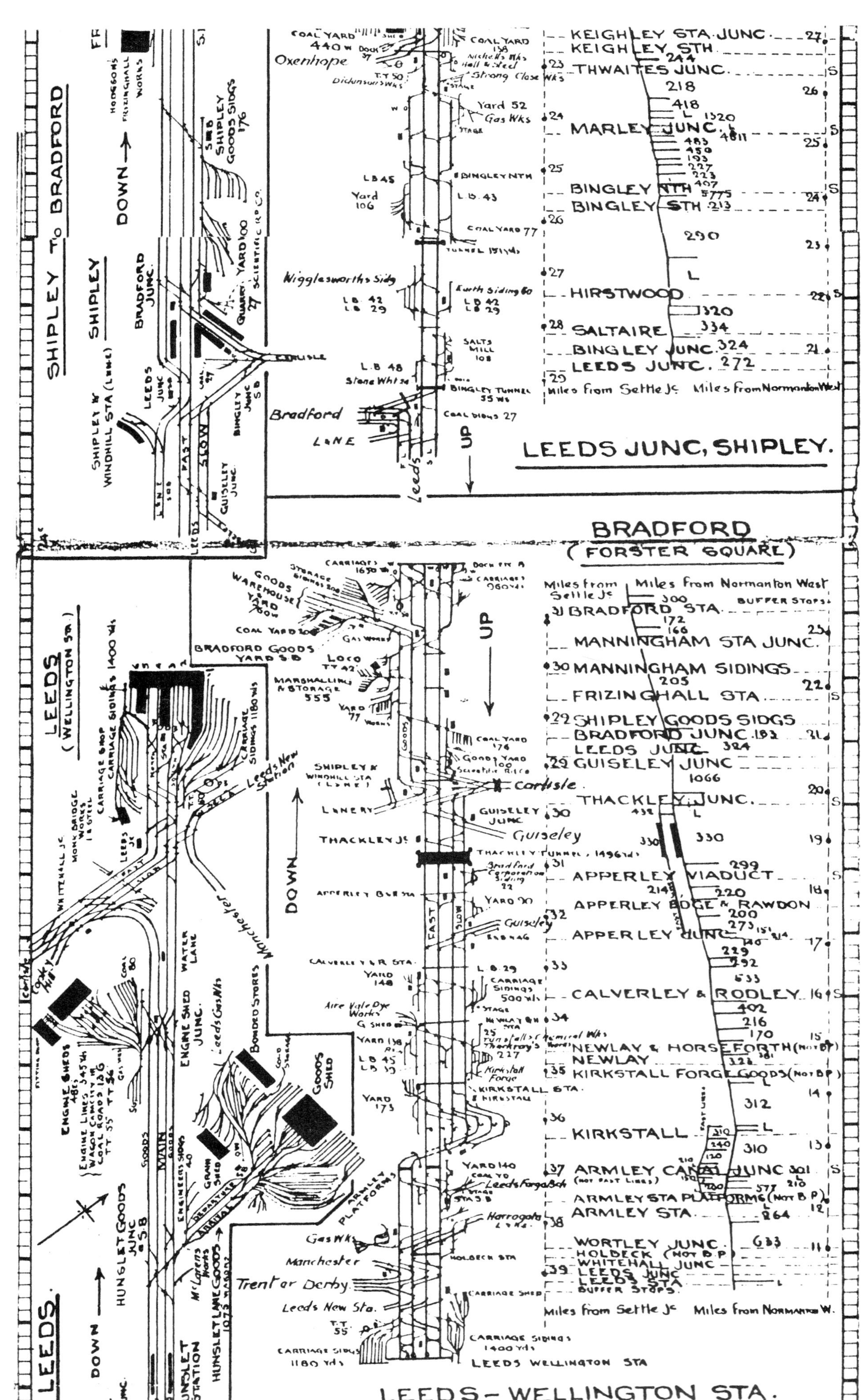
LEEDS JUNC, SHIPLEY.
BRADFORD (FORSTER SQUARE)
LEEDS - WELLINGTON STA.
SHIPLEY TO BRADFORD
LEEDS (WELLINGTON STA.)
LEEDS.
Miles from Settle Jc
Miles from Normanton West
KEIGHLEY STA. JUNC.
KEIGHLEY STH.
THWAITES JUNC.
MARLEY JUNC.
BINGLEY NTH
BINGLEY STH
HIRSTWOOD
SALTAIRE
BINGLEY JUNC.
LEEDS JUNC.
BRADFORD STA.
MANNINGHAM STA JUNC.
MANNINGHAM SIDINGS
FRIZINGHALL STA.
SHIPLEY GOODS SIDGS
BRADFORD JUNC.
LEEDS JUNC.
GUISELEY JUNC
THACKLEY JUNC.
APPERLEY VIADUCT
APPERLEY BDGE & RAWDON
APPERLEY JUNC.
CALVERLEY & RODLEY
NEWLAY & HORSEFORTH (NOT BP)
NEWLAY
KIRKSTALL FORGE GOODS (NOT BP)
KIRKSTALL
ARMLEY CANAL JUNC
ARMLEY STA PLATFORMS (NOT B P)
ARMLEY STA.
WORTLEY JUNC.
HOLBECK (NOT B.P.)
WHITEHALL JUNC
LEEDS JUNC
LEEDS STA
BUFFER STOPS
UP
DOWN

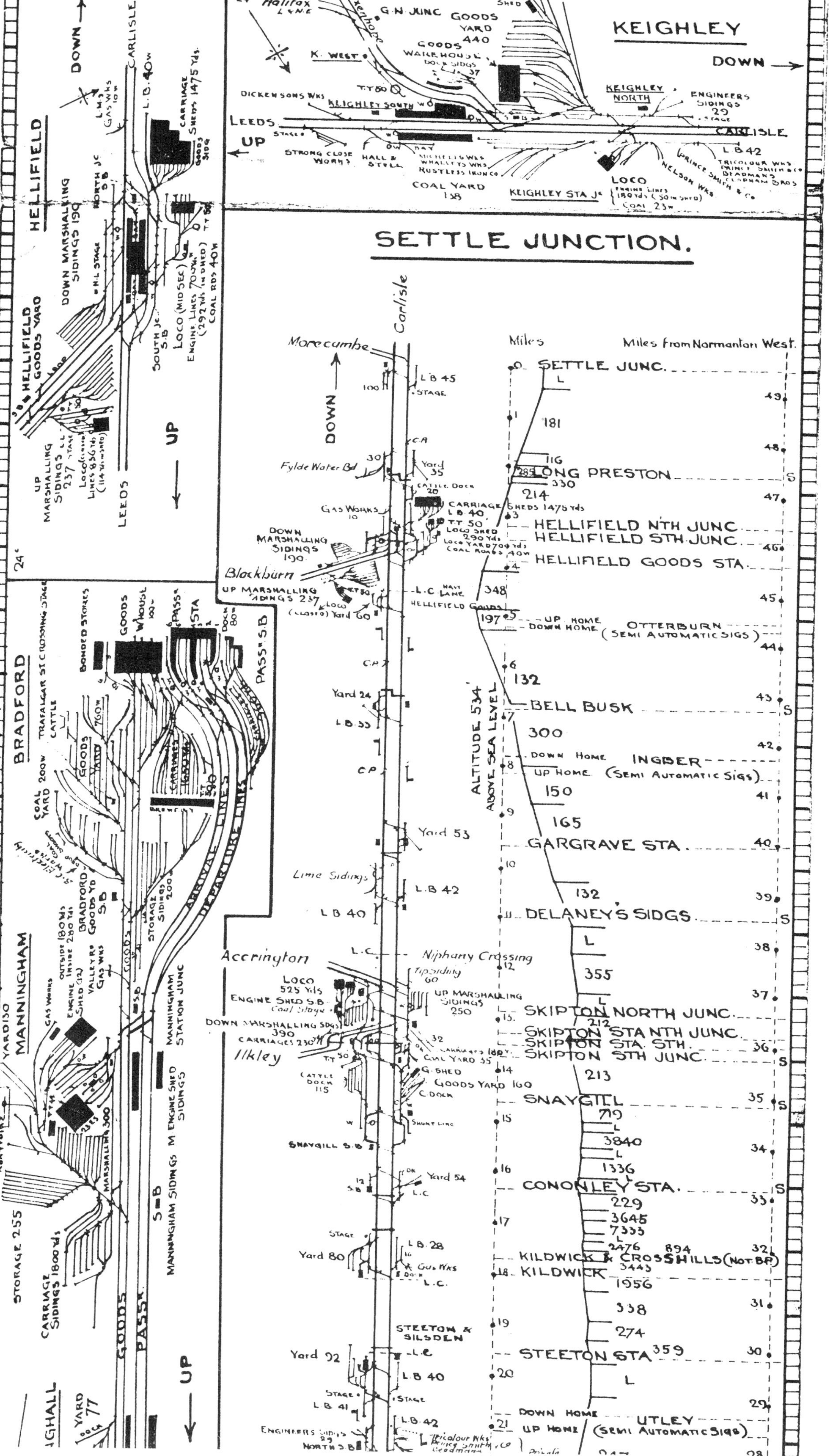
KEIGHLEY
DOWN
Halifax Line
G.N. JUNC
GOODS YARD 440
GOODS WAREHOUSE
K. WEST
DICKENSONS WKS
KEIGHLEY SOUTH
LEEDS
UP
STRONG CLOSE WORKS
HALL & STELL
COAL YARD 138
KEIGHLEY STA Jc
KEIGHLEY NORTH
ENGINEERS SIDINGS 29
CARLISLE
L.B 42
LOCO
NELSON WKS
PRINCE SMITH & Co
HELLIFIELD
DOWN MARSHALLING SIDINGS 190
UP MARSHALLING SIDINGS 237
HELLIFIELD GOODS YARD
NORTH Jc
SOUTH Jc S.B
LOCO (MID SEC)
CARRIAGE SHEDS 1475 Yds
CARLISLE
L.B. 40w
LEEDS
UP
DOWN
SETTLE JUNCTION.
Carlisle
Morecambe
DOWN
Miles
Miles from Normanton West.
SETTLE JUNC.
181
LONG PRESTON
214
HELLIFIELD N'TH JUNC.
HELLIFIELD STH. JUNC.
HELLIFIELD GOODS STA.
Fylde Water Bd
Gas Works
DOWN MARSHALLING SIDINGS 190
Blackburn
UP MARSHALLING SIDINGS 237
348
197
OTTERBURN
(SEMI AUTOMATIC SIGS)
132
BELL BUSK
300
ALTITUDE 534' ABOVE SEA LEVEL
INGBER
(SEMI AUTOMATIC SIGS)
150
165
GARGRAVE STA.
Lime Sidings
132
DELANEY'S SIDGS
Accrington
Niphany Crossing
355
SKIPTON NORTH JUNC.
SKIPTON STA NTH JUNC.
SKIPTON STA. STH.
SKIPTON STH JUNC.
Ilkley
213
SNAYGILL
CONONLEY STA.
KILDWICK & CROSSHILLS (NOT BR)
KILDWICK
1956
274
STEETON & SILSDEN
STEETON STA
UTLEY
(SEMI AUTOMATIC SIGS)
BRADFORD
COAL YARD 200w
GOODS YARD
BONDED STORES
GOODS W'HOUSE
PASS STA
PASS S.B
ARRIVAL LINES
DEPARTURE LINES
BRADFORD GOODS YD S.B
MANNINGHAM
MANNINGHAM STATION JUNC
MANNINGHAM SIDINGS
M ENGINE SHED SIDINGS
STORAGE 255
CARRIAGE SIDINGS 1800 Yds
GOODS
PASS
S-B
UP

BOLTON ABBEY

ADDINGHAM

ILKLEY

MENSTON JUNC.

OTLEY

GUISELEY JUNC.

ESHOLT JUNC.

APPERLEY JUNC.

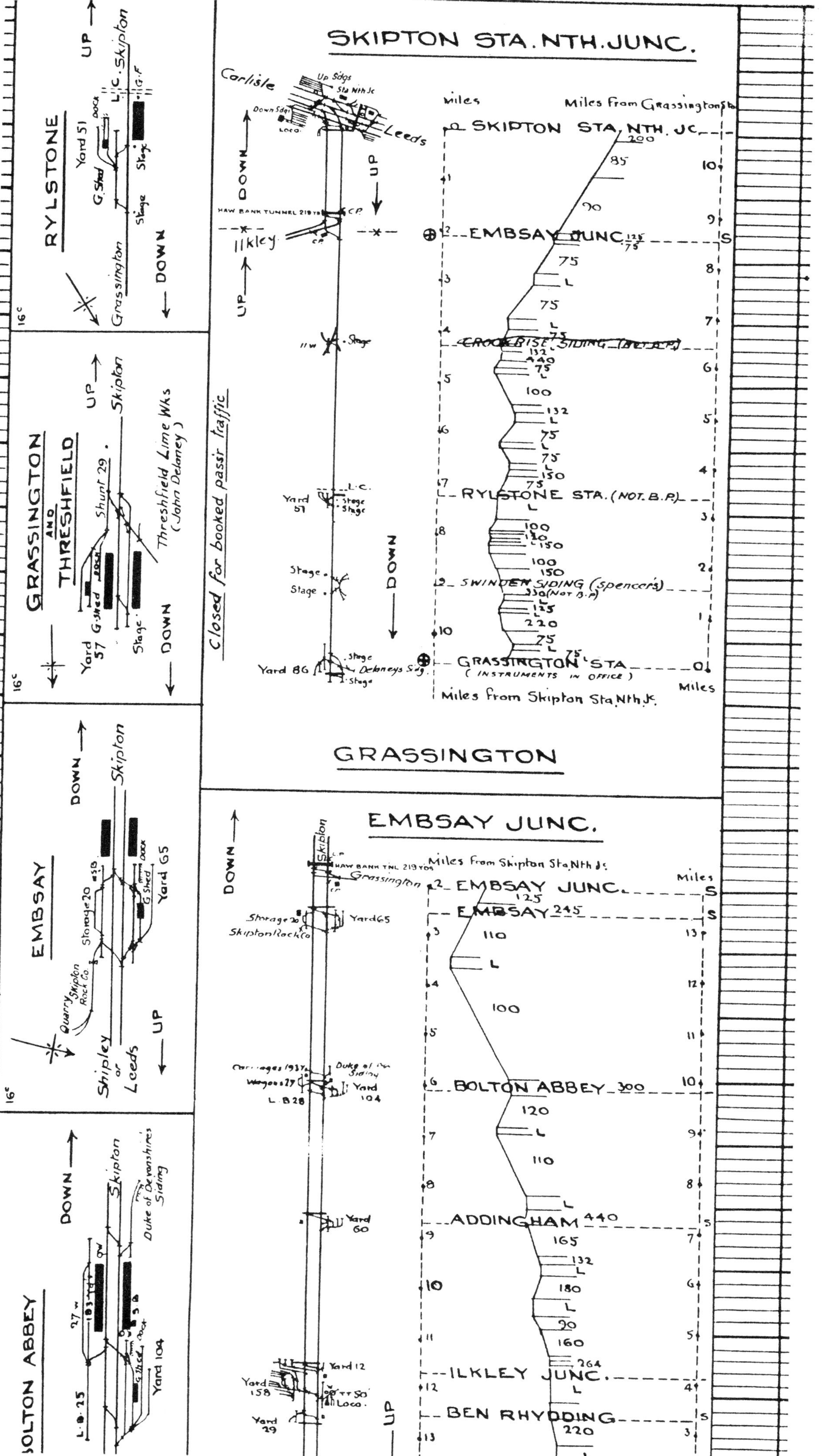
SKIPTON STA. NTH. JUNC.
Carlisle
Leeds
Ilkley
DOWN
UP
Miles
Miles from Grassington Sta.
SKIPTON STA. NTH. JC.
EMBSAY JUNC.
CRACKRISE SIDING
RYLSTONE STA. (NOT. B.P.)
SWINDEN SIDING (Spencer's)
GRASSINGTON STA
(INSTRUMENTS IN OFFICE)
Miles from Skipton Sta. Nth. Jc.
Closed for booked pass^r traffic
GRASSINGTON
EMBSAY JUNC.
Miles from Skipton Sta. Nth. Jc.
EMBSAY JUNC.
EMBSAY
BOLTON ABBEY
ADDINGHAM
ILKLEY JUNC.
BEN RHYDDING
RYLSTONE
GRASSINGTON AND THRESHFIELD
Threshfield Lime Wks (John Delaney)
EMBSAY
Skipton
Shipley or Leeds
BOLTON ABBEY
Duke of Devonshire's Siding

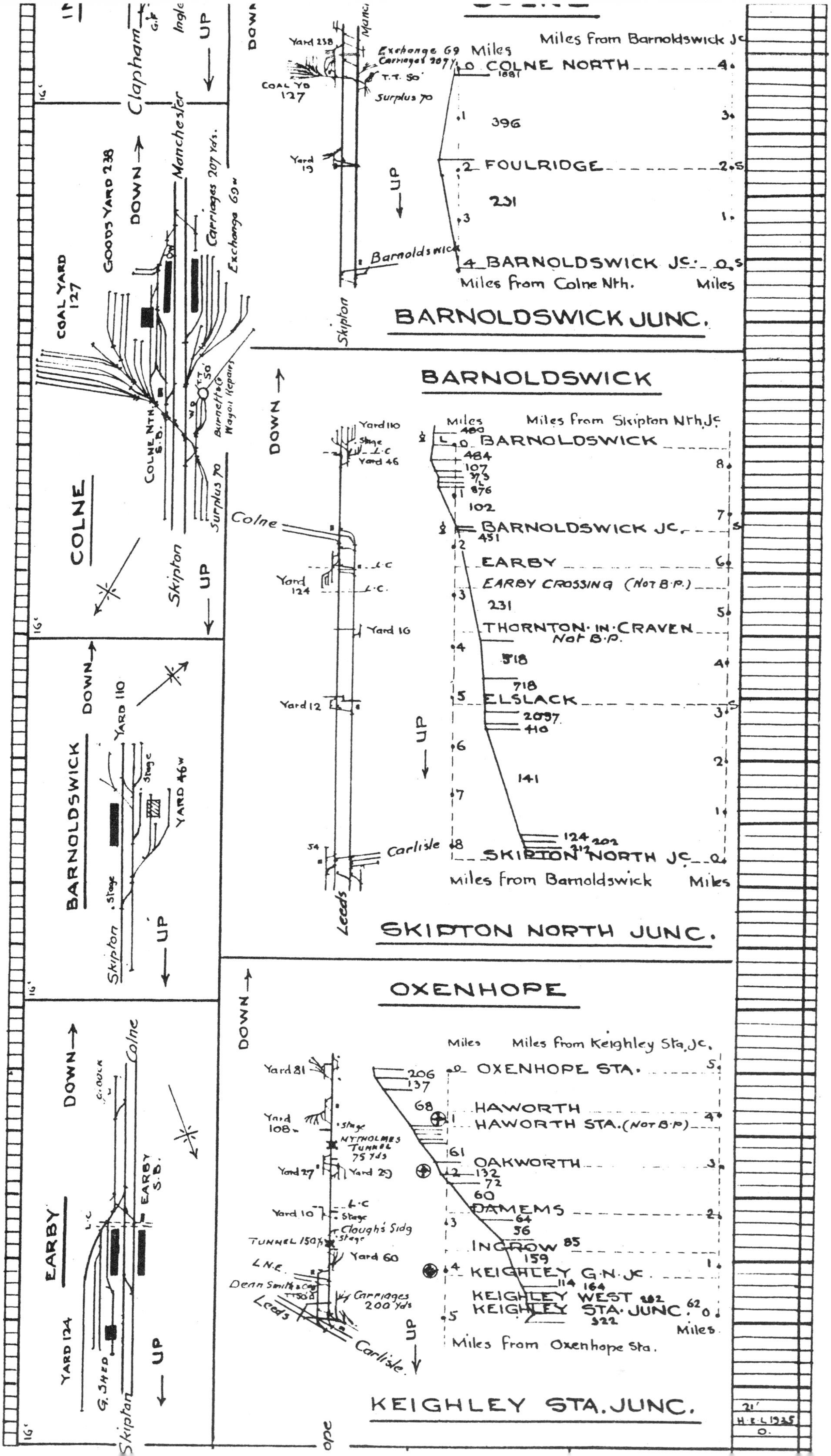

BARNOLDSWICK JUNC.

Miles from Barnoldswick Jc / Miles

Miles	Location	Miles
0	COLNE NORTH	4
1		3
2	FOULRIDGE	2.5
3		1
4	BARNOLDSWICK JC.	0.5

Miles from Colne Nth. / Miles

Gradients: 1881, 396, 231

Yard 238; Exchange 69; Carriages 207 yds; Coal Yd 127; T.T. 50'; Surplus 70; Yard 19; Barnoldswick; Skipton; UP; DOWN

BARNOLDSWICK

Miles / Miles from Skipton Nth. Jc.

Miles	Location	Miles
0	BARNOLDSWICK	
		8
		7
	BARNOLDSWICK JC.	
2	EARBY	6
	EARBY CROSSING (NOT B.P.)	
3		5
	THORNTON-IN-CRAVEN Not B.P.	
4		4
5	ELSLACK	3.5
6		2
7		1
8	SKIPTON NORTH JC.	0

Miles from Barnoldswick / Miles

Gradients: 480, 484, 107, 373, 876, 102, 451, 231, 518, 718, 2097, 410, 141, 124, 202, 312

Yard 110; Stage; L.C.; Yard 46; Colne; Yard 124; L.C.; Yard 16; Yard 12; 54; Carlisle; Leeds; DOWN; UP

SKIPTON NORTH JUNC.

OXENHOPE

Miles / Miles from Keighley Sta. Jc.

Miles	Location	Miles
0	OXENHOPE STA.	5
1	HAWORTH	4
	HAWORTH STA. (NOT B.P.)	
2	OAKWORTH	3
	DAMEMS	2
3	INGROW	
4	KEIGHLEY G.N. JC.	1
	KEIGHLEY WEST	
5	KEIGHLEY STA. JUNC.	0

Miles from Oxenhope Sta. / Miles

Gradients: 206, 137, 68, 61, 132, 72, 60, 64, 56, 85, 159, 114, 164, 282, 62, 322

Yard 81; Yard 108; Stage; Nythholmes Tunnel 75 yds; Yard 27; Yard 29; L.C.; Yard 10; Stage; Clough's Sidg; Stage; Tunnel 150 yds; Yard 60; L.N.E.; Dean Smith & Co; T.T. 50; Carriages 200 yds; Leeds; Carlisle; DOWN; UP

KEIGHLEY STA. JUNC.

21' H.E.L. 1935 O.

COLNE: Coal Yard 127; Goods Yard 238; Down; Manchester; Carriages 207 yds; Exchange 69W; T.T. 50'; W.B.; Burnett & Co Wagon Repairs; Colne Nth. S.B.; Surplus 70; Skipton; UP; Clapham; Ingleton

BARNOLDSWICK: Down; Yard 110; Stage; Yard 46W; Stage; Skipton; UP

EARBY: Down; Colne; G. Dock; Earby S.B.; L.C.; Yard 124; G. Shed; Skipton; UP

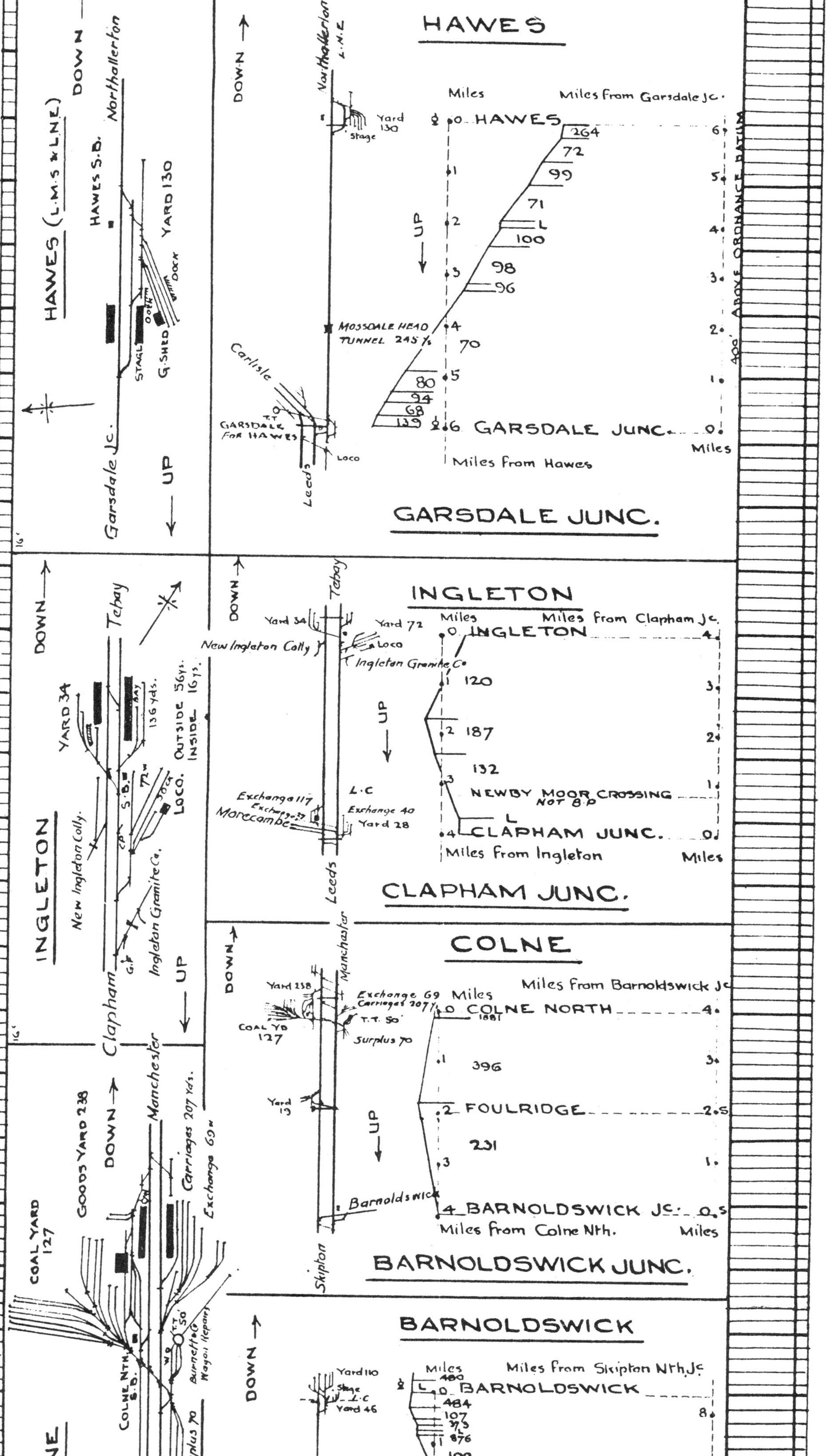
HAWES
GARSDALE JUNC.
Miles
Miles from Garsdale Jc.
0 HAWES
264
72
99
71
L
100
98
96
MOSSDALE HEAD TUNNEL 245 Yds
70
80
94
68
139
6 GARSDALE JUNC.
Miles from Hawes
Miles
ABOVE ORDNANCE DATUM
HAWES (L.M.S. & L.N.E.)
Northallerton
Garsdale Jc.
HAWES S.B.
YARD 130
DOCK
STAGE
G. SHED
DOWN
UP
Carlisle
Leeds
Loco
INGLETON
CLAPHAM JUNC.
Miles from Clapham Jc.
0 INGLETON
120
187
132
NEWBY MOOR CROSSING NOT B.P.
L
4 CLAPHAM JUNC.
Miles from Ingleton
Tebay
Yard 34
Yard 72
New Ingleton Colly
Ingleton Granite Co.
Exchange 117
Exchange 40
Yard 28
Morecambe
OUTSIDE 56 Yds.
INSIDE 16 Yds.
LOCO.
Clapham
COLNE
BARNOLDSWICK JUNC.
Miles from Barnoldswick Jc.
0 COLNE NORTH
1881
396
2 FOULRIDGE
231
4 BARNOLDSWICK Jc.
Miles from Colne Nth.
Manchester
Yard 238
Exchange 69
Carriages 207 Yds
T.T. 50
Surplus 70
COAL YD 127
Yard 19
Barnoldswick
Skipton
GOODS YARD 238
COAL YARD 127
COLNE NTH. S.B.
Burnett & Co Wagon Repairs
BARNOLDSWICK
Miles from Skipton Nth. Jc.
Yard 110
Stage
Yard 46
480
0 BARNOLDSWICK
484
107
37.3
876
102

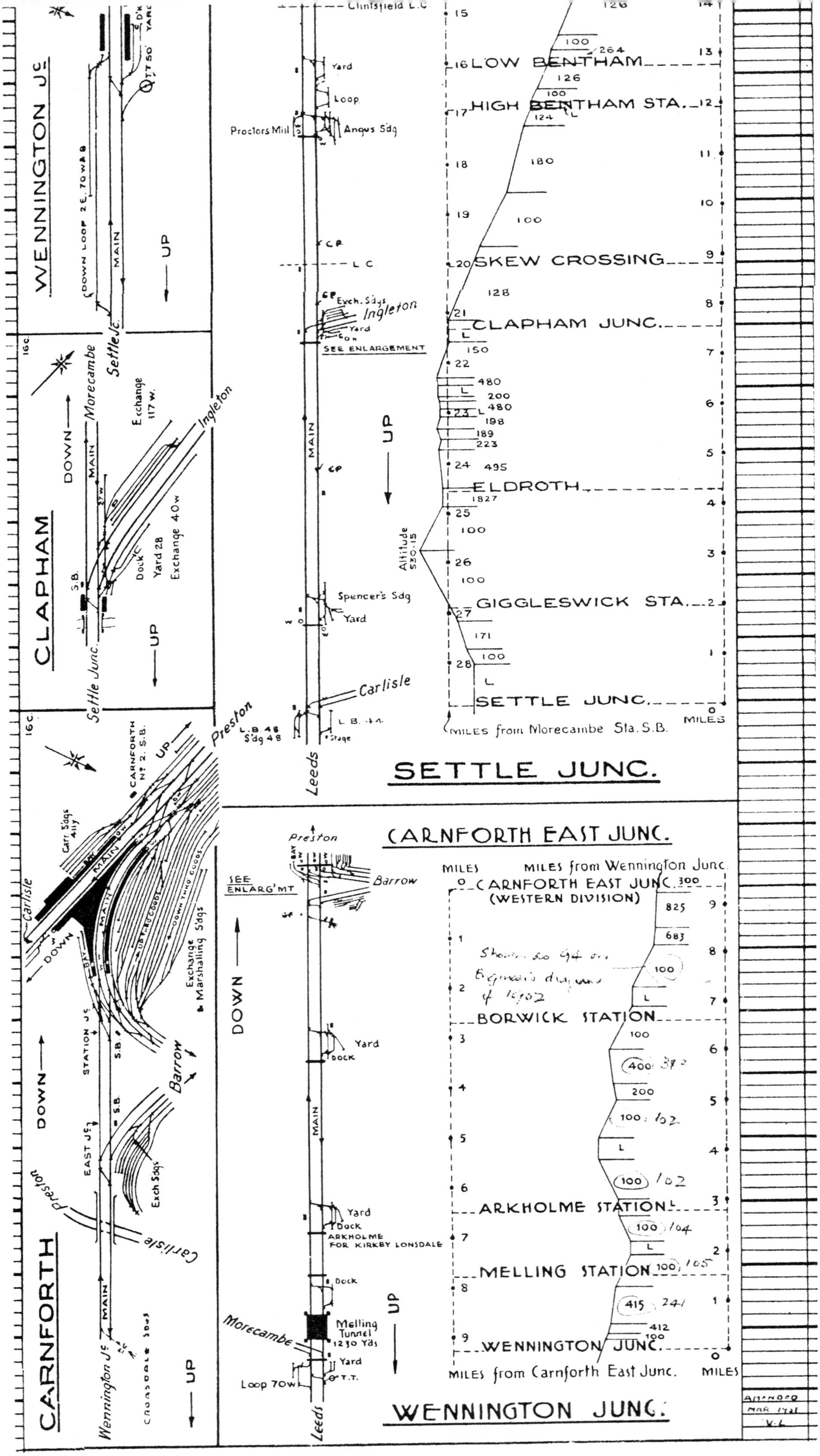
WENNINGTON Jc.
DOWN LOOP 2E. 70W & B
MAIN
UP
Settle Jc.
Yard
Loop
Proctors Mill
Angus Sdg
L.C.
Exch. Sdgs
Ingleton
SEE ENLARGEMENT
MAIN
UP
Spencer's Sdg
Yard
Carlisle
L.B. 48
Sdg 48
L.B. 44
Leeds
LOW BENTHAM
HIGH BENTHAM STA.
SKEW CROSSING
CLAPHAM JUNC.
ELDROTH
Altitude 530.15
GIGGLESWICK STA.
SETTLE JUNC.
MILES from Morecambe Sta. S.B.
MILES
SETTLE JUNC.
CLAPHAM
Morecambe
DOWN
MAIN
Exchange 117 W.
Ingleton
Exchange 40w
Yard 28
Dock
S.B.
Settle Junc.
UP
CARNFORTH
Carlisle
Preston
CARNFORTH No 2. S.B.
Carr. Sdgs
MAIN
DOWN
Exchange & Marshalling Sdgs
STATION Jc
S.B.
Barrow
EAST Jc
Exch Sdgs
Wennington Jc
UP
CARNFORTH EAST JUNC.
Preston
Barrow
SEE ENLARG'MT
DOWN
Yard
Dock
ARKHOLME FOR KIRKBY LONSDALE
Melling Tunnel 1230 Yds
Morecambe
Loop 70w
Leeds
UP
MILES
MILES from Wennington Junc.
CARNFORTH EAST JUNC.
(WESTERN DIVISION)
BORWICK STATION
ARKHOLME STATION
MELLING STATION
WENNINGTON JUNC.
MILES from Carnforth East Junc.
WENNINGTON JUNC.
AMENDED MAR 1931

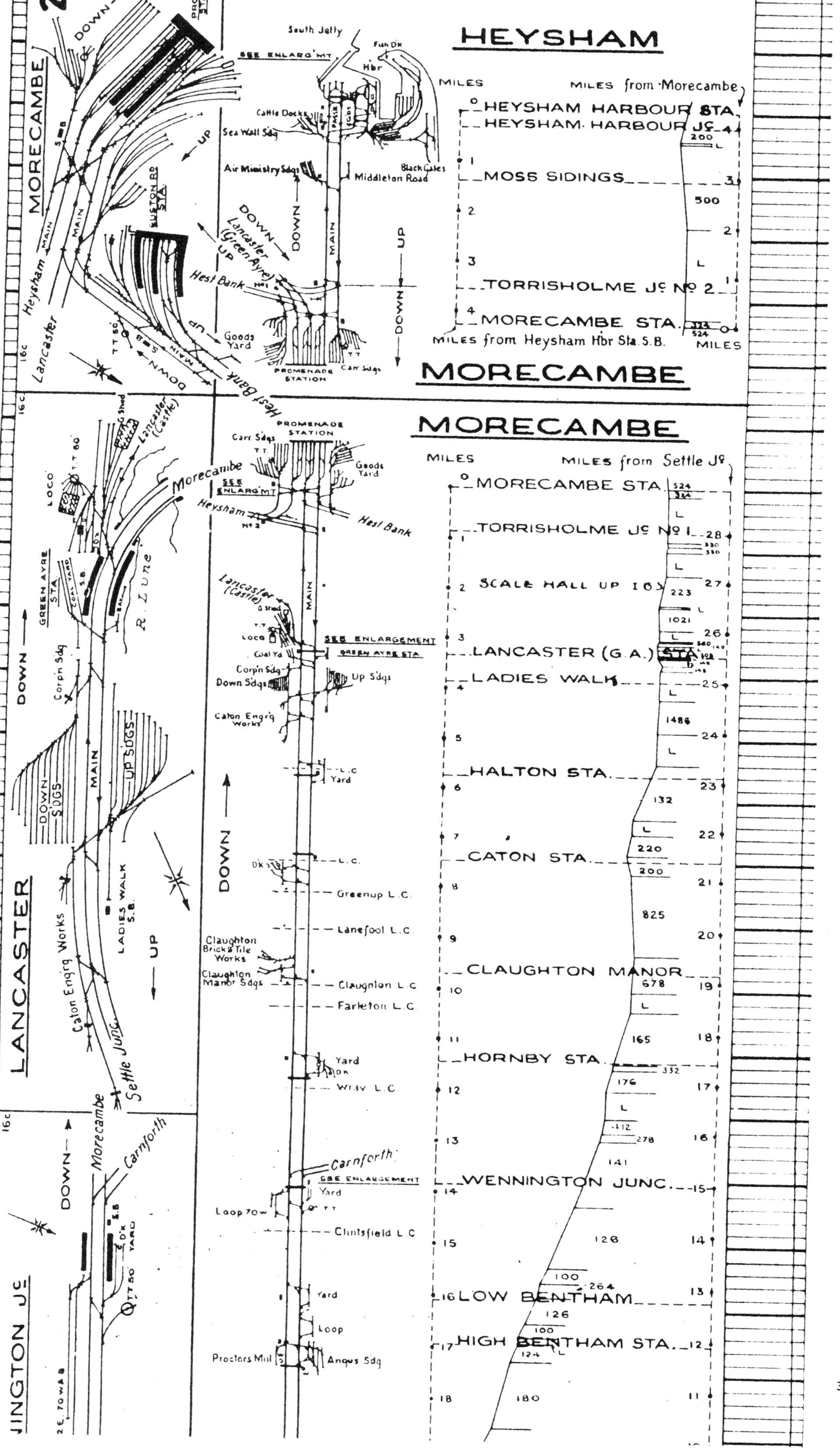
HEYSHAM
MILES
MILES from Morecambe
HEYSHAM HARBOUR STA.
HEYSHAM HARBOUR JC
MOSS SIDINGS
TORRISHOLME JC No 2
MORECAMBE STA.
MILES from Heysham Hbr Sta. S.B.
MILES
MORECAMBE
MORECAMBE
MILES
MILES from Settle Jc
MORECAMBE STA.
TORRISHOLME JC No 1
SCALE HALL UP
LANCASTER (G.A.) STA.
LADIES WALK
HALTON STA.
CATON STA.
CLAUGHTON MANOR
HORNBY STA.
WENNINGTON JUNC.
LOW BENTHAM
HIGH BENTHAM STA.
MORECAMBE
LANCASTER
South Jetty
Cattle Docks
Sea Wall Sdg
Air Ministry Sdgs
Middleton Road
Black Gates
Hest Bank
Goods Yard
PROMENADE STATION
Carr Sdgs
Heysham
Lancaster (Castle)
R. Lune
GREEN AYRE STA
Corp'n Sdg
Down Sdgs
Up Sdgs
Caton Engr'g Works
Greenup L.C.
Lanefoot L.C.
Claughton Brick & Tile Works
Claughton Manor Sdgs
Claughton L.C.
Farleton L.C.
Wray L.C.
Carnforth
Loop 70w
Clintsfield L.C.
Proctors Mill
Angus Sdg
Settle Junc
DOWN
UP
MAIN

HEYSHAM HARBOUR

Morecambe
HEYSHAM HARBOUR Jc
S.B.
OW
PASS'R
GOODS
UP
DOWN
SHOPS
PUMP STA
CATTLE LAIRS
CATTLE DOCKS
C.T. LAIRS
HEYSHAM HARBOUR STA.
S.B.
HEYSHAM HARBOUR STATION
WEST WALL
LIGHTHOUSE
SOUTH JETTY
GOODS SHED
SOUTH QUAY
HARBOUR
NORTH QUAY
FISH STAGE
Aviation Fuel Depot
ANEMOMETER TOWER
...ISH SEA
2

OXENHOPE

16c
DOWN
Keighley
UP
YARD 81
G.SHED
G.F
G.F

HAWORTH

16c
DOWN
YARD 108
G SHED
Keighley
Stage
S.B. HAWORTH
Oxenh
UP

OAKWORTH

16c
DOWN
Yard 27
S.B.
L.C
Keighley
Oxenhope
G.Shed
Dock
Yard 29
UP

INGROW

16c
DOWN
Keighley
Stage
Stage
Oxenhope
Robert Cloughs Grove Mills
DOCK
G.SHED
YARD 85
UP
3

BURLEY IN WHARFEDALE

16c
BURLEY Jc.
S.B.
Yard 34
Coal Drops
DOWN
Shipley or Leeds
Skipton
UP
G.Shed
DOCK
Yard 61
Otley

OTLEY

16c
Yard 171
G Shed
DOCK
Yard 16
Coal Drops
UP
Shipley or Leeds
L.N.E.R
GOODS S.B.
Exchange 62
10 3/4 Y's
STA.S.B.
B.P. Spirit Pump
DOWN

GUISELEY

16c
Yard 242
DOWN
G.Shed
Dock
S.B
Stage
Shipley or Leeds
Skipton
Moon & Son
Ings Mill
UP
4

AMENDED DEC. 38 P.A.K.
21'
H.E.L.
1935

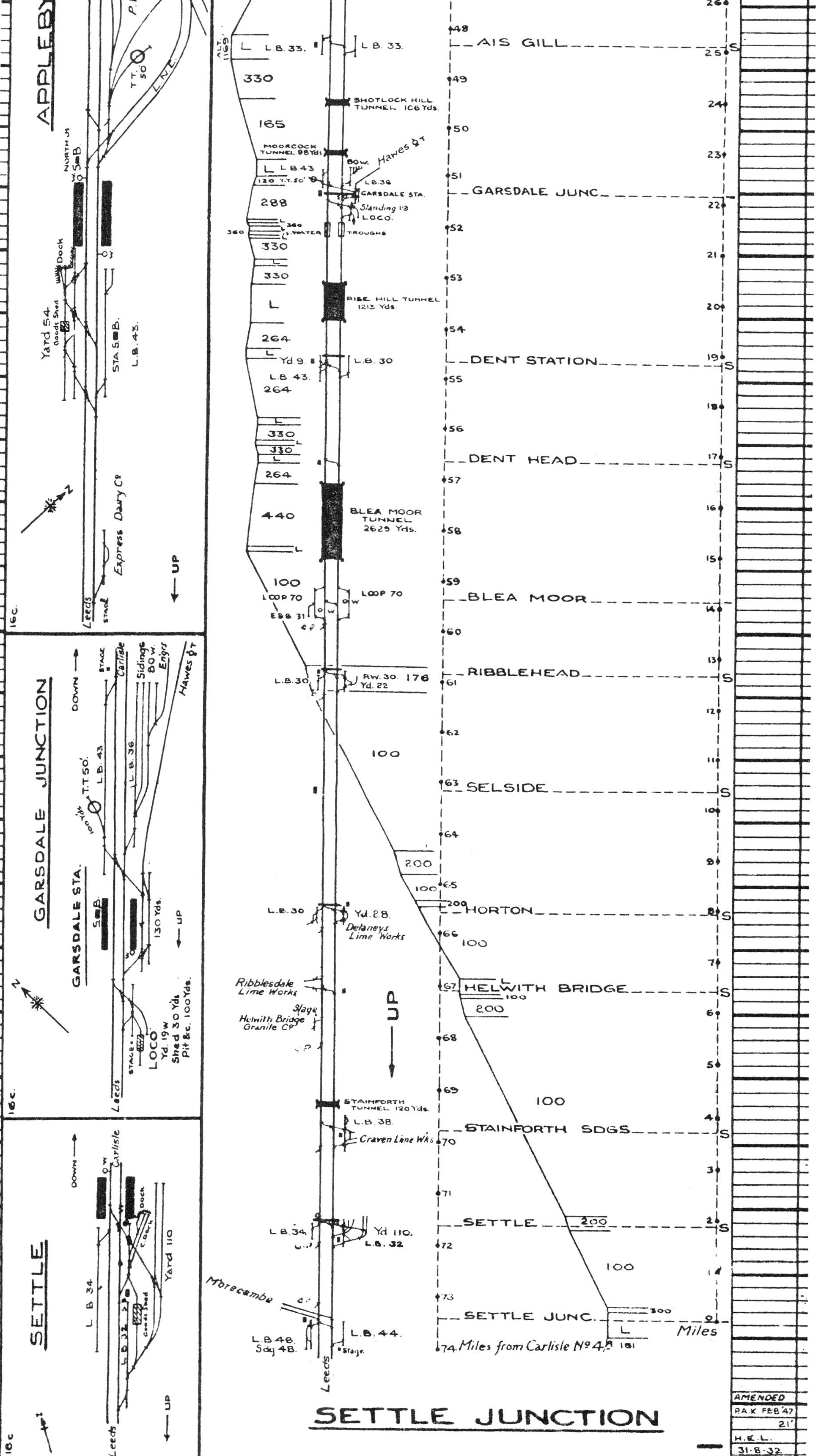
APPLEBY
GARSDALE JUNCTION
GARSDALE STA.
SETTLE
AIS GILL
GARSDALE JUNC.
DENT STATION
DENT HEAD
BLEA MOOR
RIBBLEHEAD
SELSIDE
HORTON
HELWITH BRIDGE
STAINFORTH SDGS
SETTLE
SETTLE JUNC.
SHOTLOCK HILL TUNNEL 106 Yds.
MOORCOCK TUNNEL 98 Yds.
RISE HILL TUNNEL 1213 Yds.
BLEA MOOR TUNNEL 2629 Yds.
STAINFORTH TUNNEL 120 Yds.
Delaneys Lime Works
Ribblesdale Lime Works
Helwith Bridge Granite Co
Craven Lime Wks
Express Dairy Co
Morecambe
Miles
74 Miles from Carlisle No 4
SETTLE JUNCTION
AMENDED
P.A.K. FEB '47
H.E.L.
31-8-32
P.A.K.

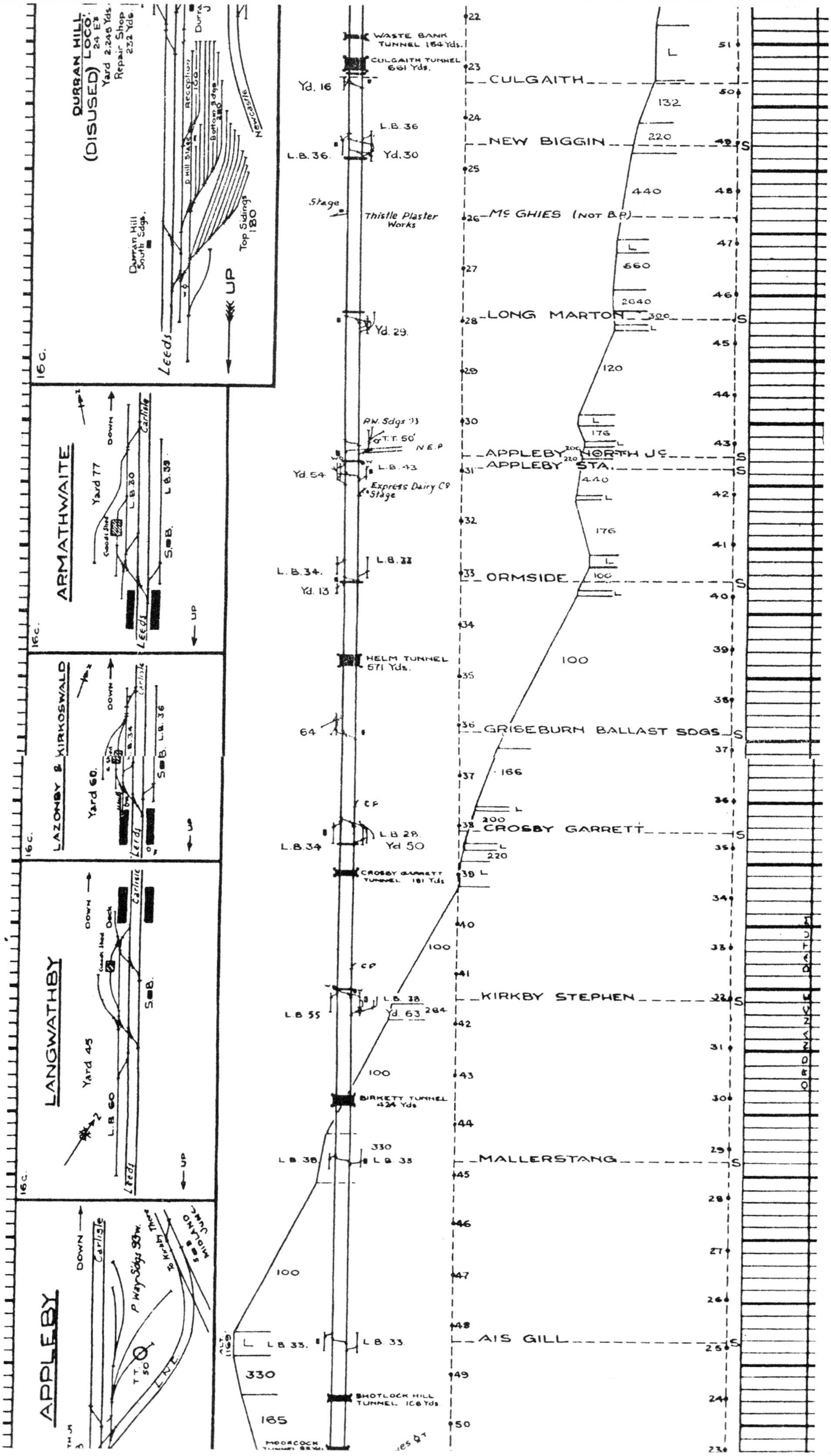

WASTE BANK TUNNEL 164 Yds.
CULGAITH TUNNEL 661 Yds.
Yd. 16
CULGAITH
L.B. 36
L.B. 36.
Yd. 30
NEW BIGGIN
Stage
Thistle Plaster Works
Mc GHIES (NOT B.P)
LONG MARTON
Yd. 29
RN. Sdgs 13
T.T. 50'
N.E.P.
L.B. 43
Yd. 54
APPLEBY NORTH Jc
APPLEBY STA.
Express Dairy Co Stage
L.B. 34.
L.B. 33
Yd. 13
ORMSIDE
HELM TUNNEL 571 Yds.
64
GRISEBURN BALLAST SDGS
CP
L.B. 34
L.B. 28
Yd. 50
CROSBY GARRETT
CROSBY GARRETT TUNNEL 181 Yds
CP
L.B. 55
L.B. 38
Yd. 63
KIRKBY STEPHEN
BIRKETT TUNNEL 424 Yds
L.B. 38
L.B. 33
MALLERSTANG
L.B. 33.
L.B. 33.
AIS GILL
SHOTLOCK HILL TUNNEL 106 Yds
MOORCOCK TUNNEL 98 Yds

Gradients: L, 132, 220, 440, L, 660, 2640, 300, 120, L, 176, L, 200, 220, 440, L, 176, L, 100, L, 100, 166, L, 200, L, 220, L, 100, 284, 100, 330, 100, L, 330, 165
ALT. 1169

Mileposts: 22, 23, 24, 25, 26, 27, 28, 29, 30, 31, 32, 33, 34, 35, 36, 37, 38, 39, 40, 41, 42, 43, 44, 45, 46, 47, 48, 49, 50

Datum scale: 51, 50, 49, 48, 47, 46, 45, 44, 43, 42, 41, 40, 39, 38, 37, 36, 35, 34, 33, 32, 31, 30, 29, 28, 27, 26, 25, 24, 23
ORDNANCE DATUM

DURRAN HILL (DISUSED) LOCO. 24 E3
Yard 2,248 Yds.
Repair Shop 232 Yds.
Reception 100
Bottom Sdgs 280
D. Hill Stage
Durran Hill South Sdgs.
Top Sidings 180
Newcastle
UP
Leeds
16c.

ARMATHWAITE
Yard 77
DOWN
Carlisle
L.B. 30
L.B. 33
Goods Shed
S.B.
Leeds
UP
16c.

LAZONBY & KIRKOSWALD
Yard 60.
DOWN
Carlisle
L.B. 34
L.B. 36
S.B.
Leeds
UP
16c.

LANGWATHBY
Yard 45
DOWN
Carlisle
Dock
Goods Shed
S.B.
L.B. 60
Leeds
UP
16c.

APPLEBY
DOWN
Carlisle
P. Way Sdgs 33w.
To Kirkby Thore
S.B. AND MIDLAND JUNC.
T.T. 50
L.N.E.

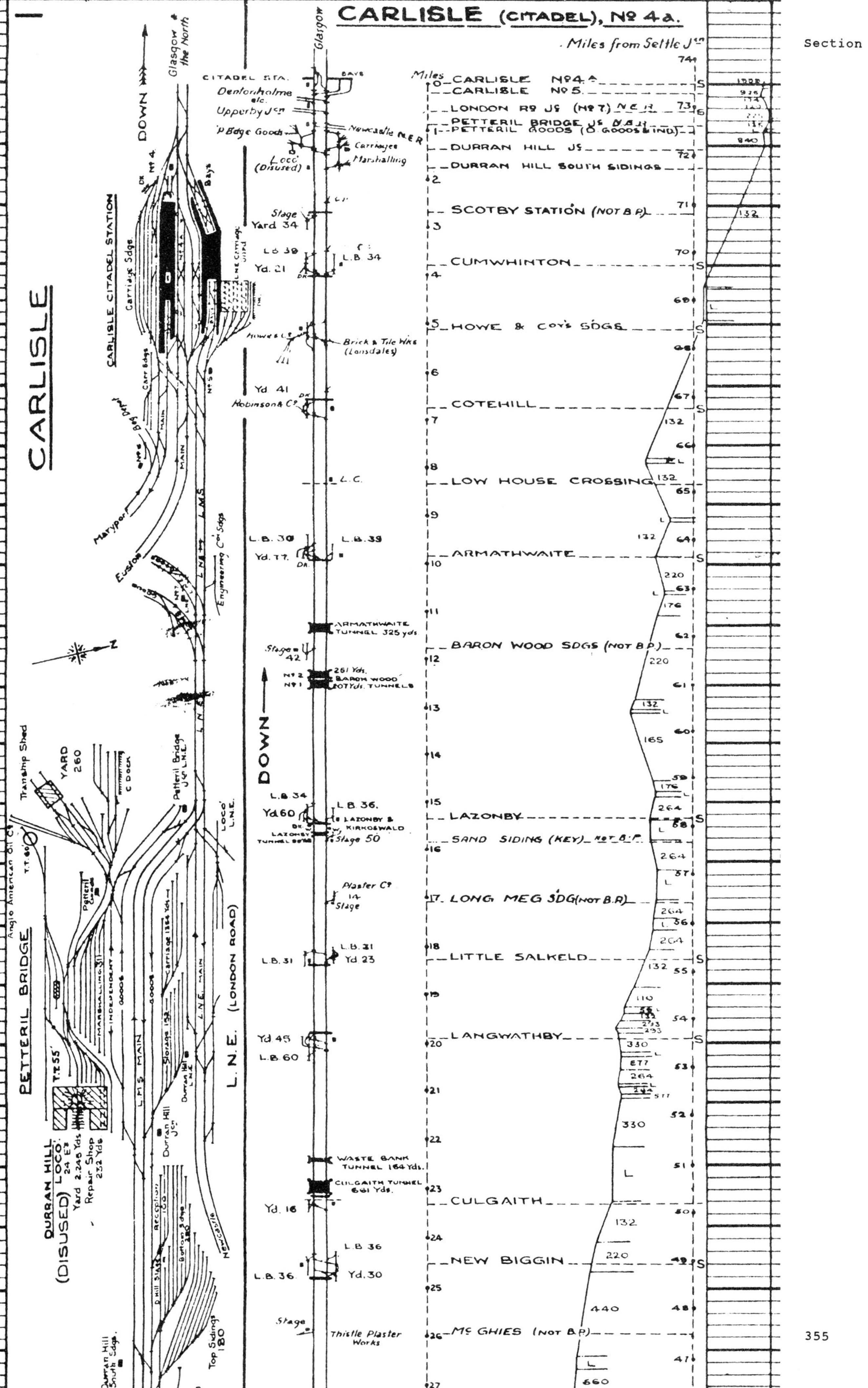
CARLISLE (CITADEL), Nº 4a.
Miles from Settle Jcn
CARLISLE Nº4A
CARLISLE Nº5
LONDON Rd Jc (Nº7) N.E.R.
PETTERIL BRIDGE Jc N.B.R.
PETTERIL GOODS (D. GOODS & IND.)
DURRAN HILL Jc
DURRAN HILL SOUTH SIDINGS
SCOTBY STATION (NOT B.P.)
CUMWHINTON
HOWE & COY'S SDGS
COTEHILL
LOW HOUSE CROSSING
ARMATHWAITE
ARMATHWAITE TUNNEL 325 yds
BARON WOOD SDGS (NOT B.P.)
261 Yds. BARON WOOD Nº2 Nº1 207 Yds. TUNNELS
LAZONBY
LAZONBY & KIRKOSWALD
SAND SIDING (KEY) NOT B.P.
LONG MEG SDG (NOT B.P.)
LITTLE SALKELD
LANGWATHBY
WASTE BANK TUNNEL 164 Yds.
CULGAITH TUNNEL 661 Yds.
CULGAITH
NEW BIGGIN
Mc GHIES (NOT B.P.)
Thistle Plaster Works
Glasgow
DOWN
CARLISLE
CARLISLE CITADEL STATION
Glasgow & the North
Maryport
Euston
PETTERIL BRIDGE
DURRAN HILL LOCO (DISUSED) 24 En Yard 2,245 Yds Repair Shop 232 Yds
L.N.E. (LONDON ROAD)
Newcastle
Top Sidings 180
Durran Hill South Sdgs
Transhp Shed
YARD 260
Anglo American Oil Co.

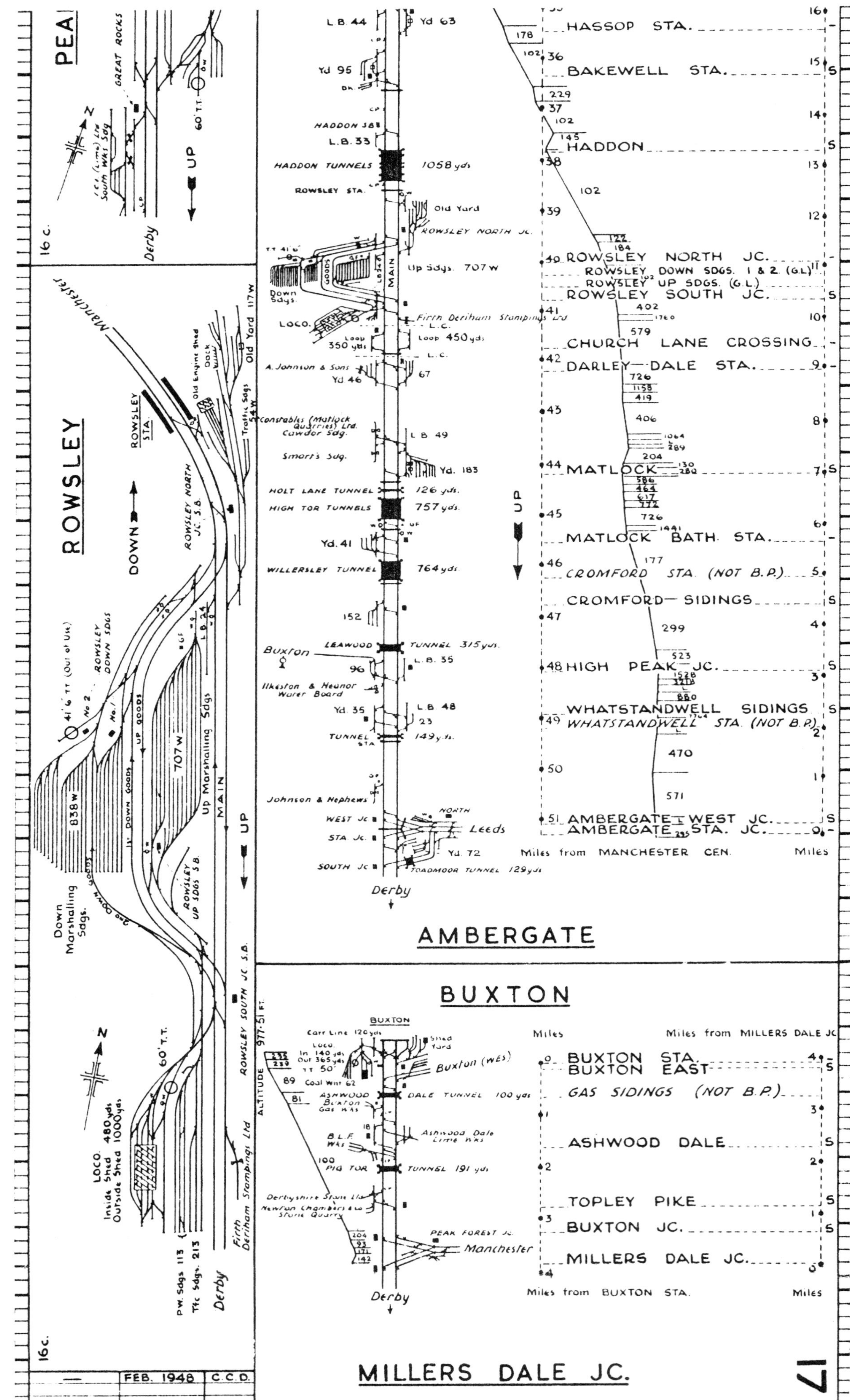

ROWSLEY
AMBERGATE
BUXTON
MILLERS DALE JC.
HASSOP STA.
BAKEWELL STA.
HADDON
ROWSLEY NORTH JC.
ROWSLEY DOWN SDGS. 1 & 2. (G.L.)
ROWSLEY UP SDGS. (G.L.)
ROWSLEY SOUTH JC.
CHURCH LANE CROSSING
DARLEY DALE STA.
MATLOCK
MATLOCK BATH STA.
CROMFORD STA. (NOT B.P.)
CROMFORD SIDINGS
HIGH PEAK JC.
WHATSTANDWELL SIDINGS
WHATSTANDWELL STA. (NOT B.P.)
AMBERGATE WEST JC.
AMBERGATE STA. JC.
Miles from MANCHESTER CEN.
HADDON TUNNELS 1058 yds
HOLT LANE TUNNEL 126 yds.
HIGH TOR TUNNELS 757 yds.
WILLERSLEY TUNNEL 764 yds.
LEAWOOD TUNNEL 315 yds.
TOADMOOR TUNNEL 129 yds
Derby
Leeds
BUXTON STA.
BUXTON EAST
GAS SIDINGS (NOT B.P.)
ASHWOOD DALE
TOPLEY PIKE
BUXTON JC.
MILLERS DALE JC.
Miles from MILLERS DALE JC.
Miles from BUXTON STA.
DALE TUNNEL 100 yds
PIG TOR TUNNEL 191 yds
Manchester
Buxton (WES)
PEAK FOREST JC.
ALTITUDE 977.51 FT.
Manchester
DOWN
UP
MAIN
Up Marshalling Sdgs
Down Marshalling Sdgs.
ROWSLEY NORTH JC. S.B.
ROWSLEY SOUTH JC. S.B.
ROWSLEY UP SDGS S.B.
LOCO. Inside Shed 480 yds Outside Shed 1000 yds
Firth Derihams Stampings Ltd
GREAT ROCKS
FEB. 1948
C.C.D.
16c.
17

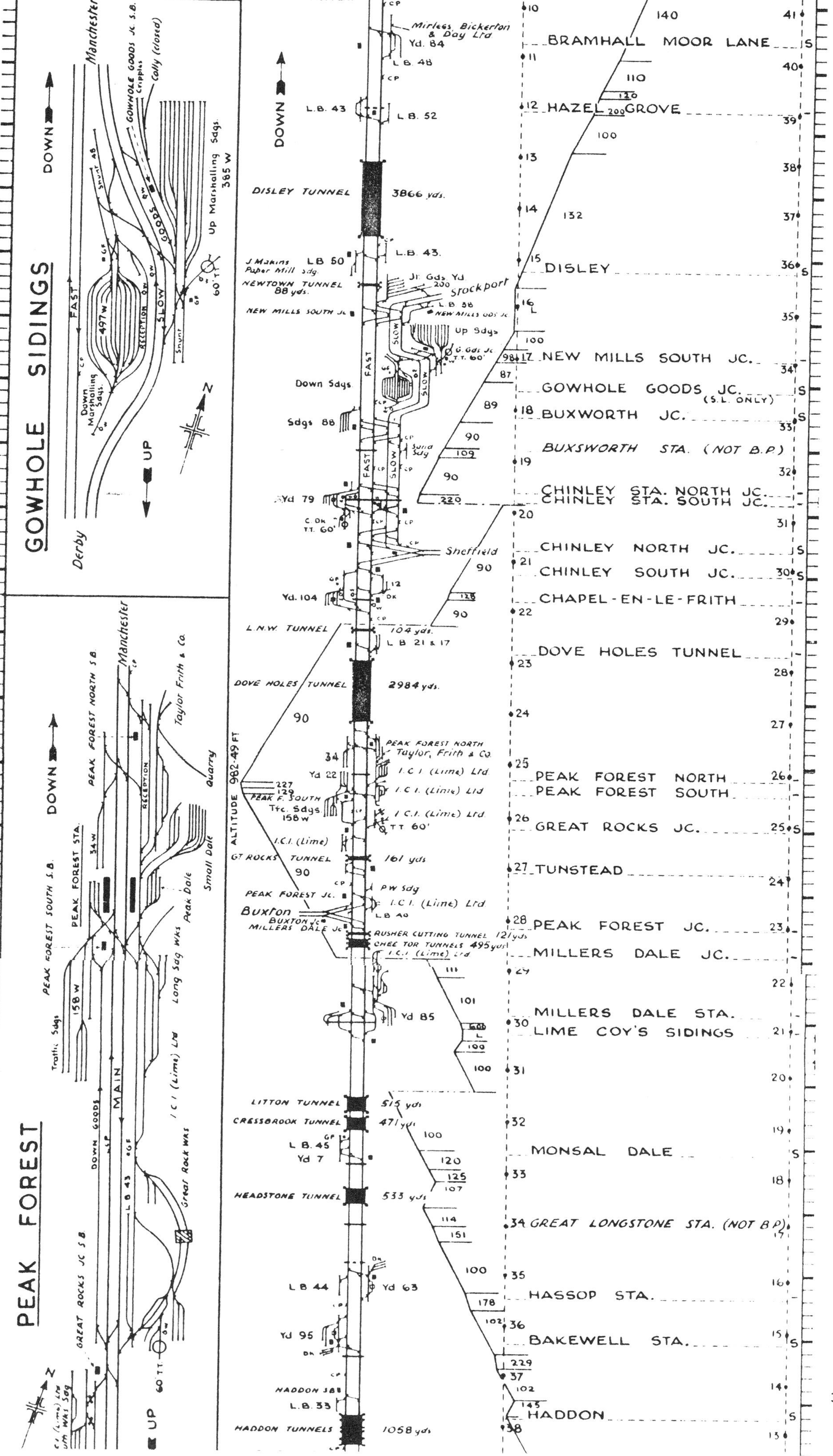
GOWHOLE SIDINGS
PEAK FOREST
BRAMHALL MOOR LANE
HAZEL GROVE
DISLEY
DISLEY TUNNEL
3866 yds.
NEW MILLS SOUTH JC.
GOWHOLE GOODS JC. (S.L. ONLY)
BUXWORTH JC.
BUXSWORTH STA. (NOT B.P.)
CHINLEY STA. NORTH JC.
CHINLEY STA. SOUTH JC.
CHINLEY NORTH JC.
CHINLEY SOUTH JC.
CHAPEL-EN-LE-FRITH
DOVE HOLES TUNNEL
2984 yds.
PEAK FOREST NORTH
PEAK FOREST SOUTH
GREAT ROCKS JC.
TUNSTEAD
PEAK FOREST JC.
MILLERS DALE JC.
MILLERS DALE STA.
LIME COY'S SIDINGS
MONSAL DALE
GREAT LONGSTONE STA. (NOT B.P.)
HASSOP STA.
BAKEWELL STA.
HADDON
LITTON TUNNEL 515 yds
CRESSBROOK TUNNEL 471 yds
HEADSTONE TUNNEL 533 yds
HADDON TUNNELS 1058 yds
Stockport
Sheffield
Buxton
Manchester
Derby
ALTITUDE 982·49 FT

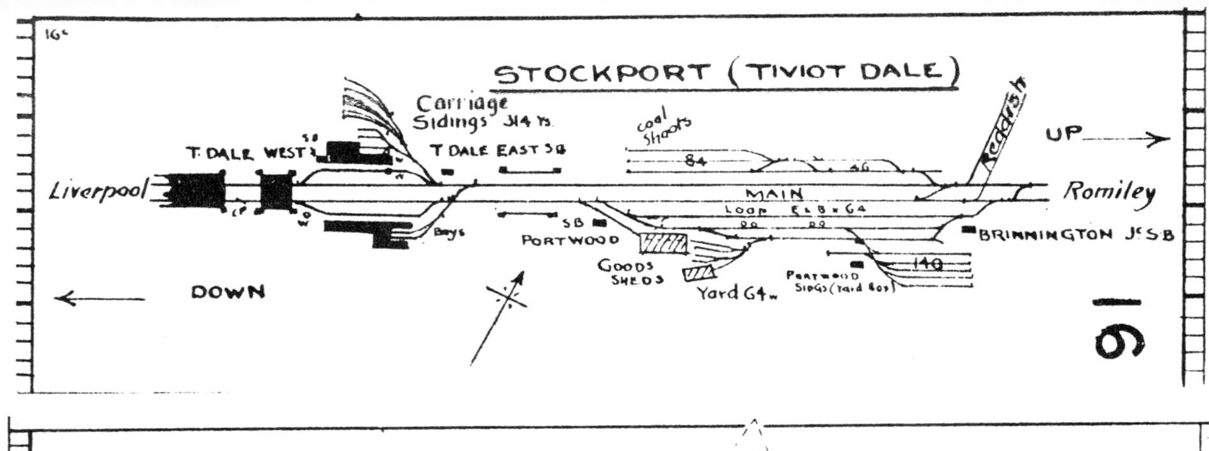

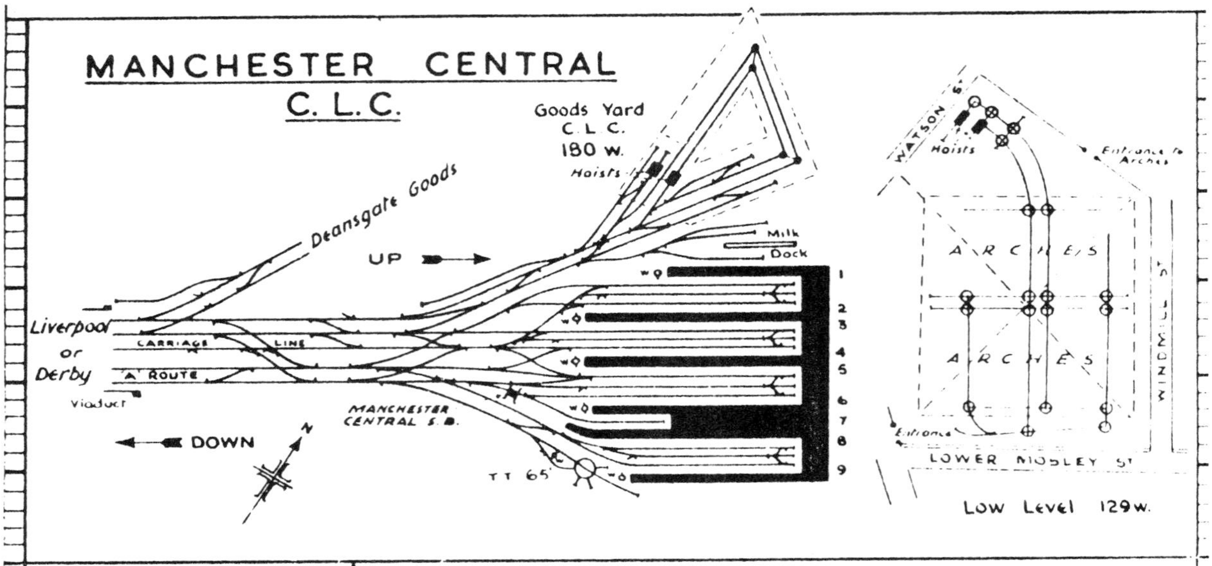

MANCHESTER CENTRAL
C. L. C.

Goods Yard C.L.C. 180 w.

Hoists

Deansgate Goods

Milk Dock

UP

Liverpool or Derby

CARRIAGE LINE

'A' ROUTE

Viaduct

MANCHESTER CENTRAL S.B.

DOWN

TT 65'

1 2 3 4 5 6 7 8 9

WATSON St

Hoists

Entrance to Arches

ARCHES

ARCHES

WINDMILL St

Entrance

LOWER MOSLEY St

Low Level 129w.

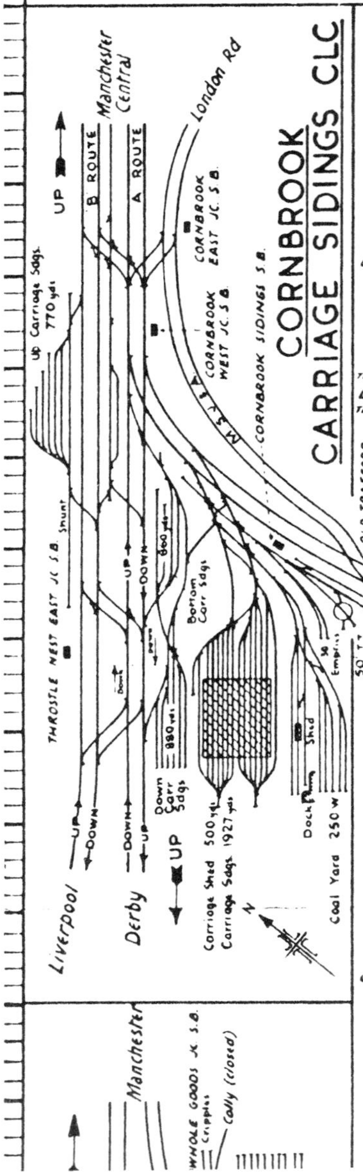

CORNBROOK CARRIAGE SIDINGS CLC

Manchester Central

London Rd

UP

B ROUTE

A ROUTE

CORNBROOK EAST JC S.B.

CORNBROOK WEST JC S.B.

CORNBROOK SIDINGS S.B.

OLD TRAFFORD JC S.B.

Up Carriage Sdgs 770 yds

THROSTLE NEST EAST JC S.B.

Shunt

Bottom Carr Sdgs

880 yds

Down Carr Sdgs

Altrincham

SB Empties

Corn Sdg

Shed

Dock

Coal Yard 250 w

Carriage Shed 500 yds

Carriage Sdgs 1927 yds

UP

DOWN

Liverpool

Derby

Manchester

WHOLE GOODS JC S.B.

Cripples

Cally (closed)

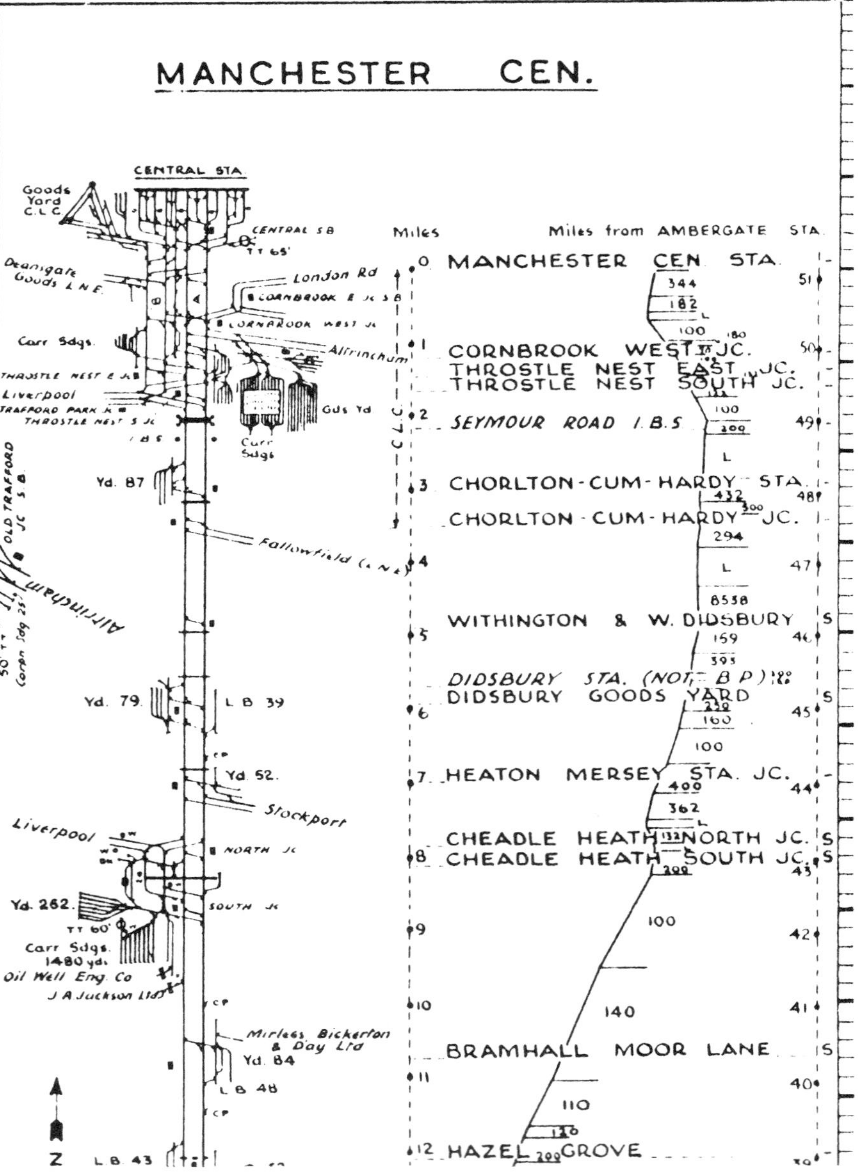

MANCHESTER CEN.

CENTRAL STA.

Goods Yard C.L.C.

CENTRAL SB

TT 65'

Deansgate Goods L.N.E.

London Rd

CORNBROOK E JC S.B

CORNBROOK WEST JC

Carr Sdgs.

Altrincham

THROSTLE NEST E JC

Liverpool

TRAFFORD PARK JC

THROSTLE NEST S JC

I.B.S.

Gds Yd

Carr Sdgs

Yd. 87

Fallowfield (L.N.E.)

Yd. 79

L B 39

Yd. 52

Stockport

Liverpool

NORTH JC

SOUTH JC

Yd. 262

TT 60'

Carr. Sdgs. 1480 yds

Oil Well Eng. Co

J A Jackson Ltd

CP

Mirlees Bickerton & Day Ltd

Yd. 84

L B 48

L B 43

N

CLC

Miles	Station	Miles from AMBERGATE STA.
0	MANCHESTER CEN STA.	51
1	CORNBROOK WEST JC. / THROSTLE NEST EAST JC. / THROSTLE NEST SOUTH JC.	50
2	SEYMOUR ROAD I.B.S	49
3	CHORLTON-CUM-HARDY STA. / CHORLTON-CUM-HARDY JC.	48
4		47
5	WITHINGTON & W. DIDSBURY	46 S
6	DIDSBURY STA. (NOT B P) / DIDSBURY GOODS YARD	45 S
7	HEATON MERSEY STA. JC.	44
8	CHEADLE HEATH NORTH JC. / CHEADLE HEATH SOUTH JC.	43 S S
9		42
10		41
	BRAMHALL MOOR LANE	S
11		40
12	HAZEL GROVE	39

Gradients: 344, 182, L, 100, 180, 100, 300, L, 432, 300, 294, L, 8538, 159, 393, 180, 180, 250, 160, 100, 400, 362, L, 132, 200, 100, 140, 110, 120, 200

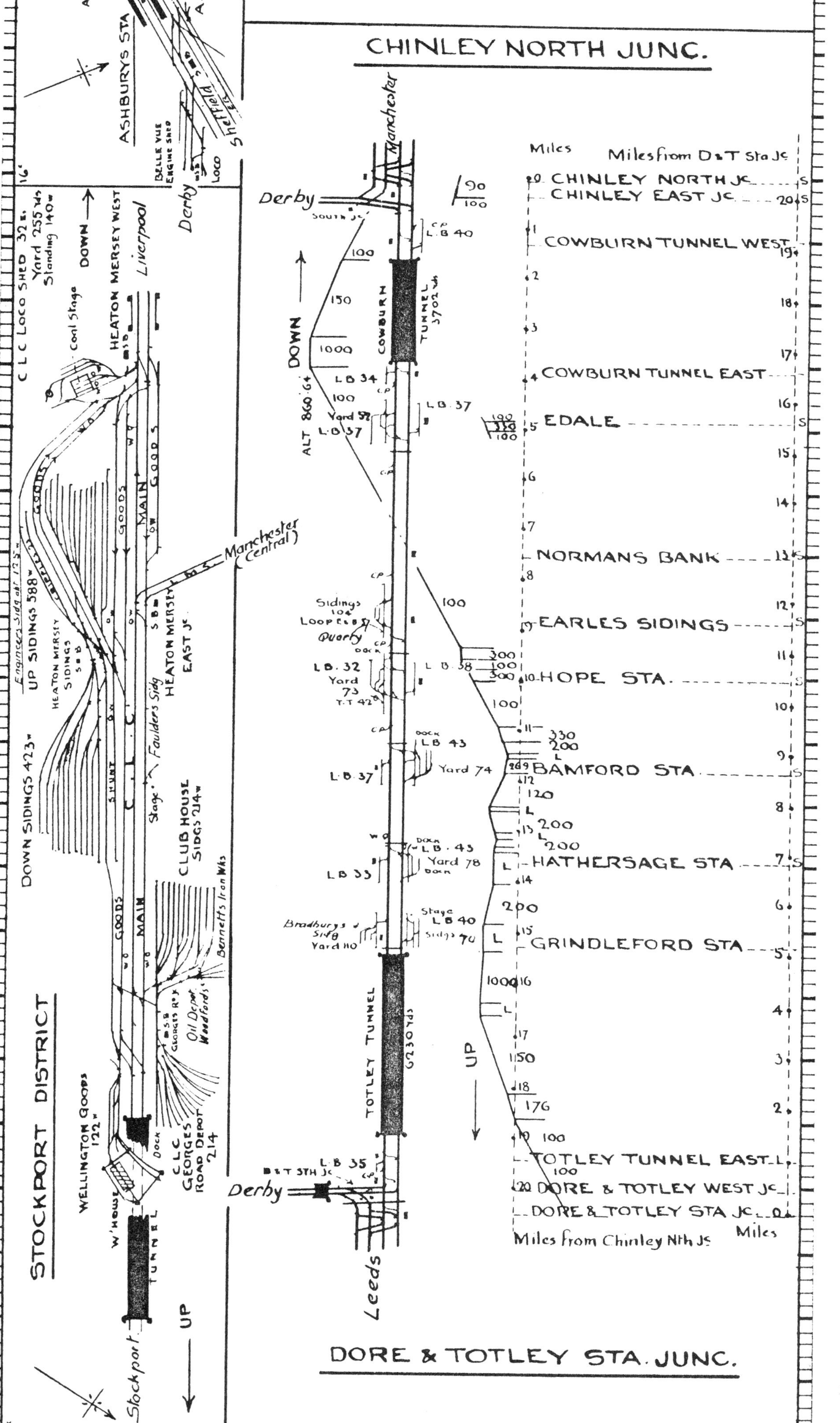
CHINLEY NORTH JUNC.
Miles
Miles from D & T Sta Jc
CHINLEY NORTH Jc
CHINLEY EAST Jc
COWBURN TUNNEL WEST
COWBURN TUNNEL EAST
EDALE
NORMANS BANK
EARLES SIDINGS
HOPE STA.
BAMFORD STA
HATHERSAGE STA
GRINDLEFORD STA
TOTLEY TUNNEL EAST
DORE & TOTLEY WEST Jc
DORE & TOTLEY STA Jc
Miles from Chinley Nth Jc
Miles
DORE & TOTLEY STA. JUNC.
Manchester
Derby
Leeds
COWBURN TUNNEL 3702 yds
TOTLEY TUNNEL 6230 yds
DOWN
UP
ALT 860.64
STOCKPORT DISTRICT
ASHBURYS STA
HEATON MERSEY WEST
HEATON MERSEY EAST Jc
C L C LOCO SHED
Liverpool
Manchester (Central)
DOWN SIDINGS 423
UP SIDINGS 588
CLUB HOUSE SIDGS 214
WELLINGTON GOODS 122
C L C GEORGES ROAD DEPOT 214
Stockport
H.E.L 1930

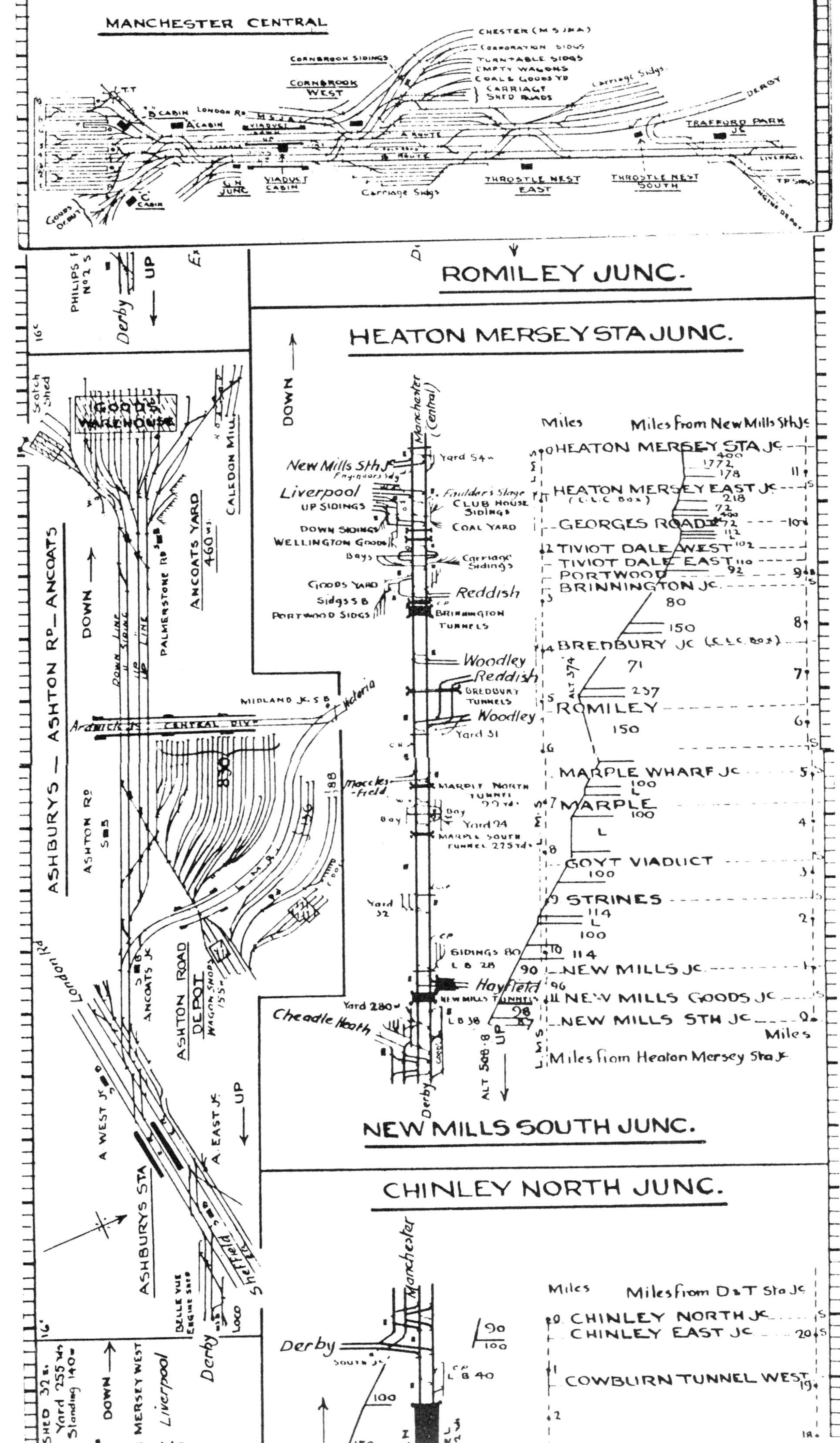
MANCHESTER CENTRAL
CORNBROOK SIDINGS
CORNBROOK WEST
CHESTER (M S J & A)
CORPORATION SIDGS
TURNTABLE SIDGS
EMPTY WAGONS
COAL & GOODS YD
CARRIAGE SHED ROADS
Carriage Sidgs
DERBY
TRAFFORD PARK JC
THROSTLE NEST EAST
THROSTLE NEST SOUTH
VIADUCT CABIN
C.N. JUNC
Carriage Sidgs
ROMILEY JUNC.
HEATON MERSEY STA JUNC.
Miles
Miles from New Mills Sth Jc
HEATON MERSEY STA JC
HEATON MERSEY EAST JC
GEORGES ROAD
TIVIOT DALE WEST
TIVIOT DALE EAST
PORTWOOD
BRINNINGTON JC
BREDBURY JC
ROMILEY
MARPLE WHARF JC
MARPLE
GOYT VIADUCT
STRINES
NEW MILLS JC
NEW MILLS GOODS JC
NEW MILLS STH JC
Miles from Heaton Mersey Sta Jc
NEW MILLS SOUTH JUNC.
CHINLEY NORTH JUNC.
Miles from D&T Sta Jc
CHINLEY NORTH JC
CHINLEY EAST JC
COWBURN TUNNEL WEST
ASHBURYS — ASHTON RD — ANCOATS
GOODS WAREHOUSE
ANCOATS YARD 460 wgs
CALEDON MILL
PALMERSTONE RD
ASHTON ROAD DEPOT
ASHBURYS STA
Ardwick Jc
CENTRAL DIVN
MIDLAND JC S.B
Victoria
London Rd
Sheffield
Derby
Liverpool
DOWN
UP

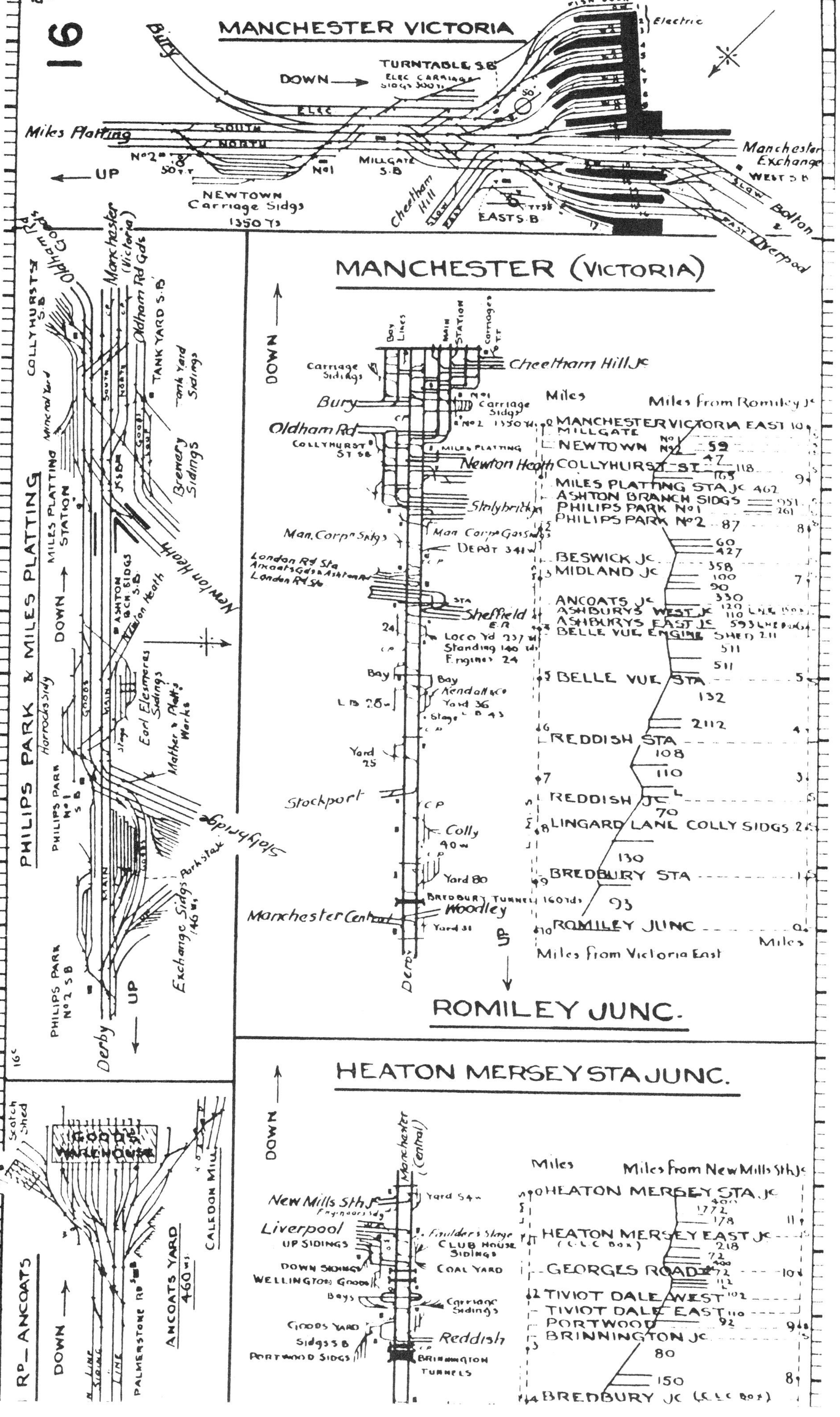
16
MANCHESTER VICTORIA
MANCHESTER (VICTORIA)
ROMILEY JUNC.
PHILIPS PARK & MILES PLATTING
Rd_ANCOATS
HEATON MERSEY STA JUNC.
Miles from Romiley Jc
Miles from Victoria East
Miles from New Mills Sth Jc
MANCHESTER VICTORIA EAST
MILLGATE
NEWTOWN
COLLYHURST ST
MILES PLATTING STA Jc
ASHTON BRANCH SIDGS
PHILIPS PARK No1
PHILIPS PARK No2
BESWICK Jc
MIDLAND Jc
ANCOATS Jc
ASHBURYS WEST Jc
ASHBURYS EAST Jc
BELLE VUE ENGINE SHED
BELLE VUE STA
REDDISH STA
REDDISH Jc
LINGARD LANE COLLY SIDGS
BREDBURY STA
ROMILEY JUNC
HEATON MERSEY STA Jc
HEATON MERSEY EAST Jc
GEORGES ROAD
TIVIOT DALE WEST
TIVIOT DALE EAST
PORTWOOD
BRINNINGTON Jc
BREDBURY Jc
GOODS WAREHOUSE
ANCOATS YARD
CALEDON MILL
PALMERSTONE Rd

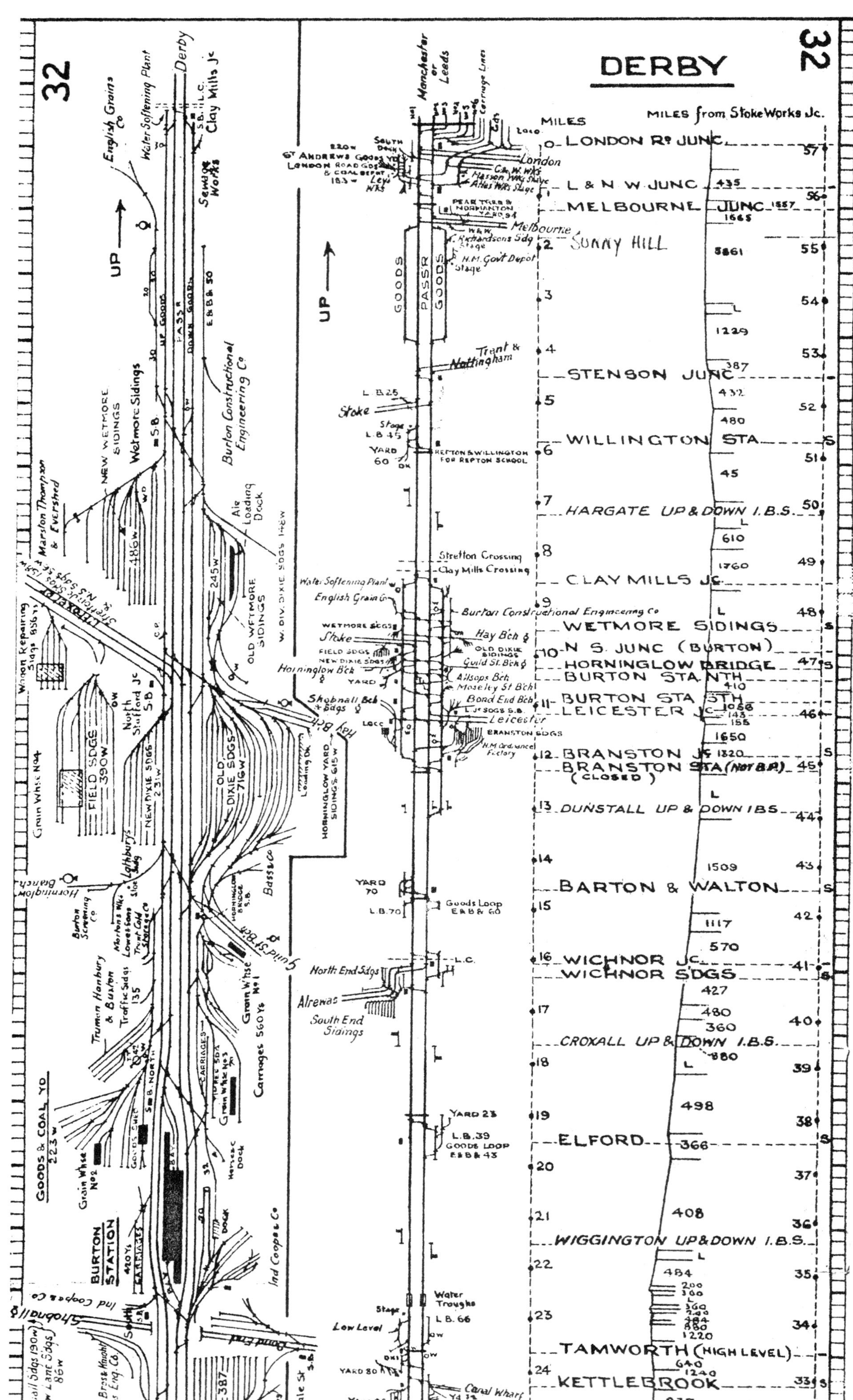

32
DERBY
MILES from Stoke Works Jc.
MILES
LONDON Rd JUNC
L & N W JUNC
MELBOURNE JUNC
SUNNY HILL
STENSON JUNC
WILLINGTON STA
HARGATE UP & DOWN I.B.S.
CLAY MILLS Jc
WETMORE SIDINGS
N S JUNC (BURTON)
HORNINGLOW BRIDGE
BURTON STA NTH
BURTON STA STH
LEICESTER Jc
BRANSTON Jc
BRANSTON STA (NOT B.P.)
(CLOSED)
DUNSTALL UP & DOWN IBS
BARTON & WALTON
WICHNOR Jc
WICHNOR SDGS
CROXALL UP & DOWN I.B.S.
ELFORD
WIGGINGTON UP & DOWN I.B.S.
TAMWORTH (HIGH LEVEL)
KETTLEBROOK
GOODS
PASSR
GOODS
UP
BURTON STATION

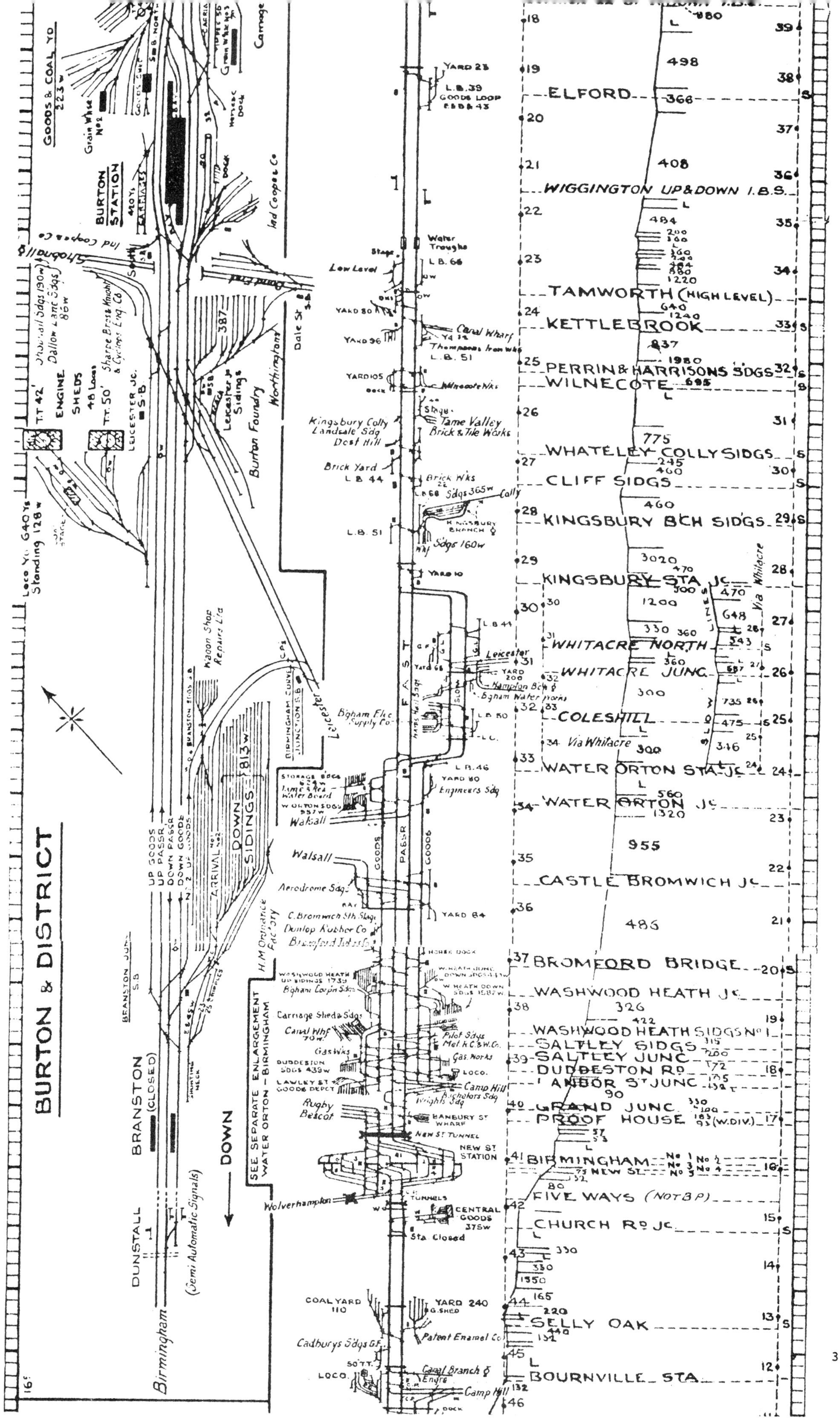

BURTON & DISTRICT

GOODS & COAL YD 223w
Grain Whse No 2
BURTON STATION
440 Yds
Carriage
Ind Coope & Co
Shobnall Sdgs (190w)
Dallow Lane Sdgs 86w
Sharpe Bros & Knight & Cyclops Eng. Co
Dale St S.B.
Worthingtons
387
Leicester Jc Sidings
Burton Foundry
ENGINE SHEDS 48 Locos
T.T. 42'
T.T. 50'
LEICESTER JC. S.B.
Loco Yd 640 Yds Standing 128w
Waggon Shop Repairs Ltd
BRANSTON SIDGS
DOWN SIDINGS 813w
ARRIVAL
BIRMINGHAM CURVE JUNCTION S.B.
Leicester
UP GOODS
UP PASSR
DOWN PASSR
DOWN GOODS
N 2 UP GOODS
BRANSTON JUNC S.B.
BRANSTON (CLOSED)
DUNSTALL
(Semi Automatic Signals)
DOWN
Birmingham
SHUNTING NECK
H.M. Ordnance Fac'try
SEE SEPARATE ENLARGEMENT WATER ORTON – BIRMINGHAM
16c

YARD 23
L.B. 39
GOODS LOOP
Water Troughs
Low Level
L.B. 66
YARD 80
YARD 96
Canal Wharf
Thompsons Iron Wks
L.B. 51
YARD 105
Wilnecote Wks
Kingsbury Colly Landsale Sdg
Dost Hill
Stage
Tame Valley Brick & Tile Works
Brick Yard
L.B. 44
Brick Wks
L.B. 68
Sdgs 365w
Colly
KINGSBURY BRANCH
L.B. 51
Wh Sdgs 160w
YARD 10
L.B. 44
Leicester
YARD 200
Hampton Bch
Bigham Water Works
Bigham Elec Supply Co
L.B. 50
L.B. 46
YARD 80
Engineers Sdg
Tame & Rea Water Board
W. ORTON SDGS 957w
Walsall
Walsall
FAST
SLOW
GOODS
PASSR
GOODS
Aerodrome Sdg
C. Bromwich Sth. Stage
Dunlop Rubber Co
Bromford Tubes Co
YARD 84
HORSE DOCK
WASHWOOD HEATH UP SIDINGS 1739
Bigham Coop'n Sidgs
W. HEATH JUNC DOWN SIDINGS
W HEATH DOWN SDGS 1587w
Carriage Sheds Sdgs
Canal Whf 70w
Pilot Sdgs
Met. R.C. & W. Co.
Gas Wks
Gas Works
DUDDESTON SDGS 439w
LAWLEY ST GOODS DEPOT
LOCO
Camp Hill
Bachelors Sdg
Wrights Sdg
Rugby
Bescot
BANBURY ST WHARF
NEW ST TUNNEL
NEW ST STATION
Wolverhampton
TUNNELS
CENTRAL GOODS 375w
Sta. Closed
COAL YARD 110
YARD 240
G. SHED
Patent Enamel Co
Cadburys Sdgs
LOCO
Canal Branch
Camp Hill
DOCK

18 (39) 880
19 (38) 498
ELFORD 366
20 (37)
21 (36) 408
WIGGINGTON UP & DOWN I.B.S.
22 (35) 484 200 100 160 200 484 880 1220
23 (34)
TAMWORTH (HIGH LEVEL) 640 1240
24 (33) KETTLEBROOK 837
25 (32) 1980 PERRIN & HARRISONS SDGS
WILNECOTE 695
26 (31) 775
WHATELEY COLLY SIDGS 245 460
27 (30) CLIFF SIDGS 460
28 (29) KINGSBURY BCH SIDGS
29 (28) 3020 470
KINGSBURY STA JC 300 470
30 (27) 1200 648 SLOW LINES Via Whitacre
31 330 360 WHITACRE NORTH 543
31 (26) 360 WHITACRE JUNC 687
32 300 735
32 (25) 33 COLESHILL 475
34 Via Whitacre 300 346
33 (24) WATER ORTON STA JC
34 (23) WATER ORTON JC 560 1320
955
35 (22) CASTLE BROMWICH JC
36 (21) 485
37 (20) BROMFORD BRIDGE
WASHWOOD HEATH JC 326
38 (19) 422
WASHWOOD HEATH SIDGS No 1
SALTLEY SIDGS 315 200
39 SALTLEY JUNC 172
(18) DUDDESTON RD 175 132
LANDOR ST JUNC 90
40 GRAND JUNC 330 100
(17) PROOF HOUSE 183 93 (W. DIV.) 57 53
41 (16) BIRMINGHAM NEW ST No 1 No 2 No 3 No 4 75 132
80 FIVE WAYS (NOT B P)
42 (15) CHURCH RD JC
43 (14) 330 330 1350
44 165 220
(13) SELLY OAK 440 132
45 (12) BOURNVILLE STA 132
46

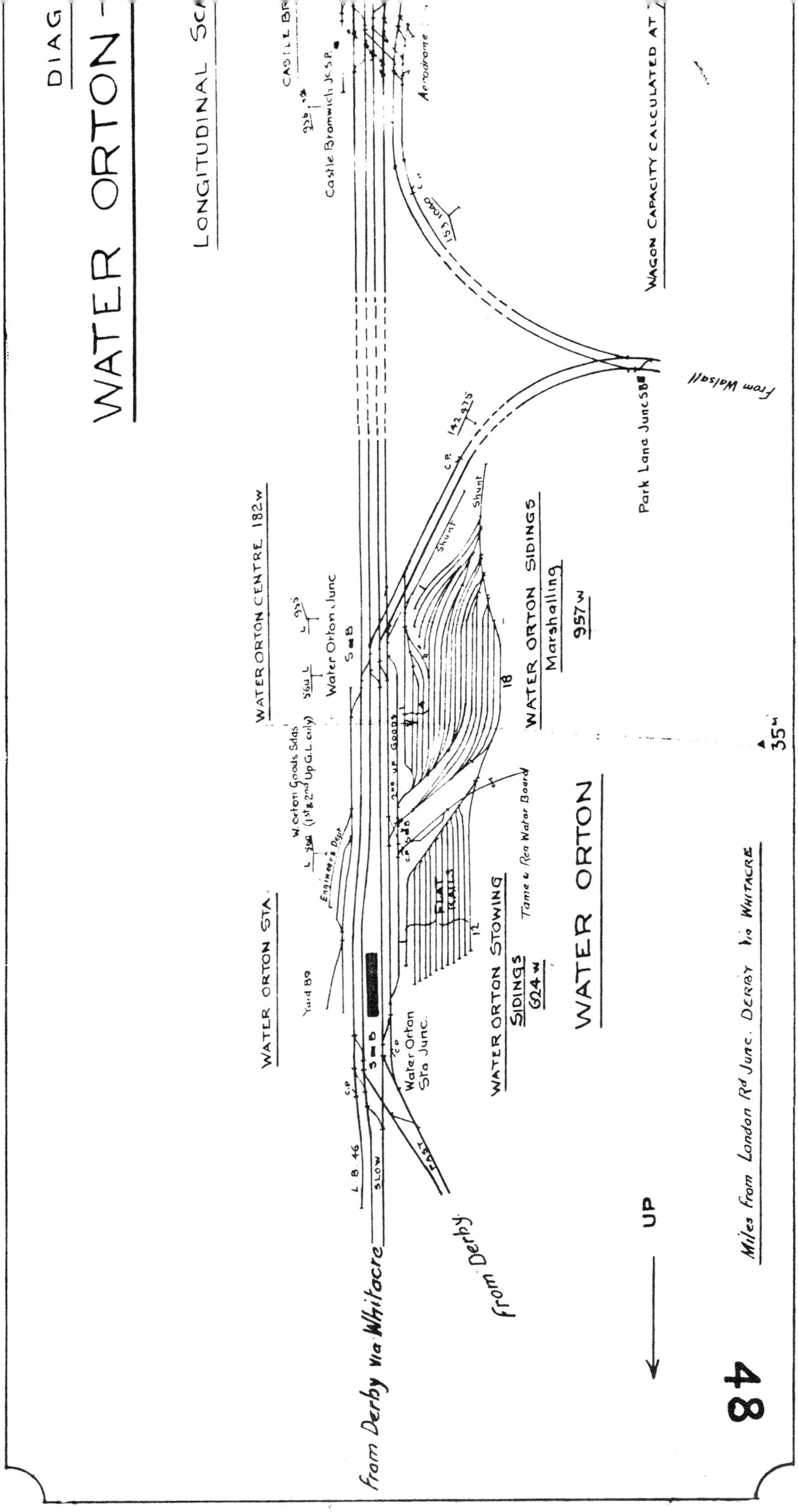

DIAG

WATER ORTON –

LONGITUDINAL SC

WATER ORTON STA.

WATER ORTON CENTRE 182w

CASTLE BR

Yard 80

W. Orton Goods Sdgs (1st & 2nd Up G.L. only)

L 960

Engineers Dept

560 L

L 955

Water Orton Junc

S B

956

Castle Bromwich Jc S.B.

L B 46

C.P

From Derby via Whitacre

SLOW

S B

Water Orton Sta Junc.

C.P

FAST

From Derby

2nd UP GOODS

C.P. S B

FLAT RAILS

12

18

Shunt

Shunt

C.P.

142 975

153 1040

Aerodrome

WATER ORTON STOWING SIDINGS 624 w

Tame & Rea Water Board

WATER ORTON SIDINGS Marshalling 957 w

WATER ORTON

Park Lane Junc SB

WAGON CAPACITY CALCULATED AT

← UP

From Walsall

48

Miles from London Rd Junc. DERBY via WHITACRE

35m

DIAGRAM

RTON — BIRMINGHAM

ITUDINAL SCALE ABT 5IN = 1MILE

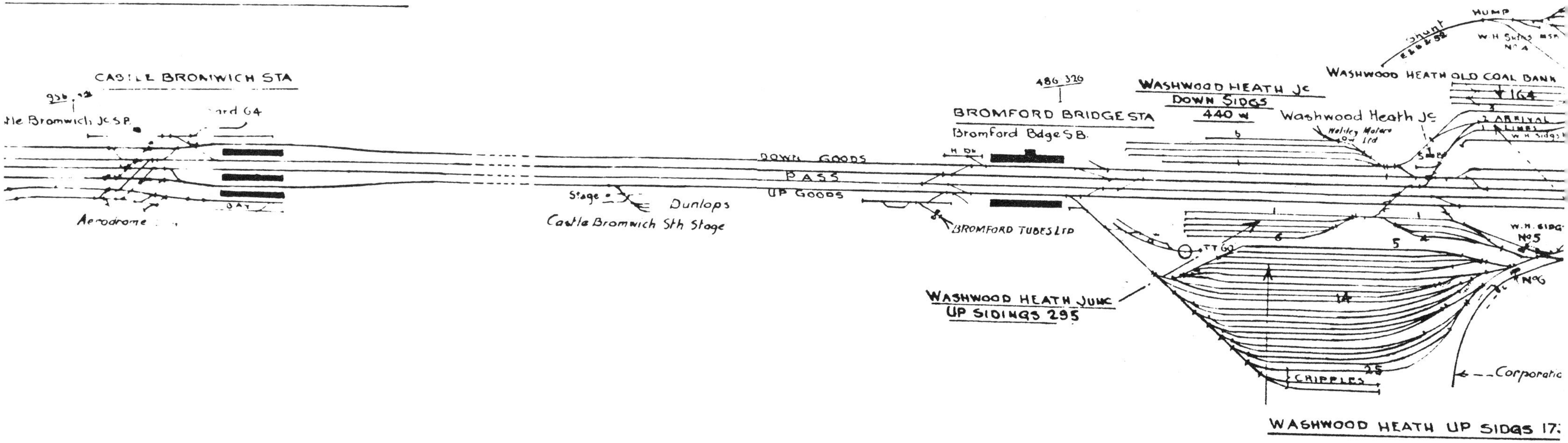

Y CALCULATED AT 7YDS TO 1 WAGON

WASHWOOD HEATH

CASTLE BROMWICH STA

tle Bromwich Jc S.B.

ard 64

Aerodrome

Stage

Dunlops

Castle Bromwich Sth Stage

DOWN GOODS

PASS

UP GOODS

486 326

BROMFORD BRIDGE STA

Bromford Bdge S.B.

BROMFORD TUBES LTD

WASHWOOD HEATH Jc DOWN SIDGS 440 W

Washwood Heath Jc

Wolseley Motors Ltd

WASHWOOD HEATH OLD COAL BANK 164

ARRIVAL LINES

W.H. Sidgs

HUMP

W.H. Sidgs No 4

W.H. SIDGS No 5

No 6

TT 60

WASHWOOD HEATH JUNC UP SIDINGS 295

CRIPPLES

Corporation

WASHWOOD HEATH UP SIDGS 17:

37M

38M

39M

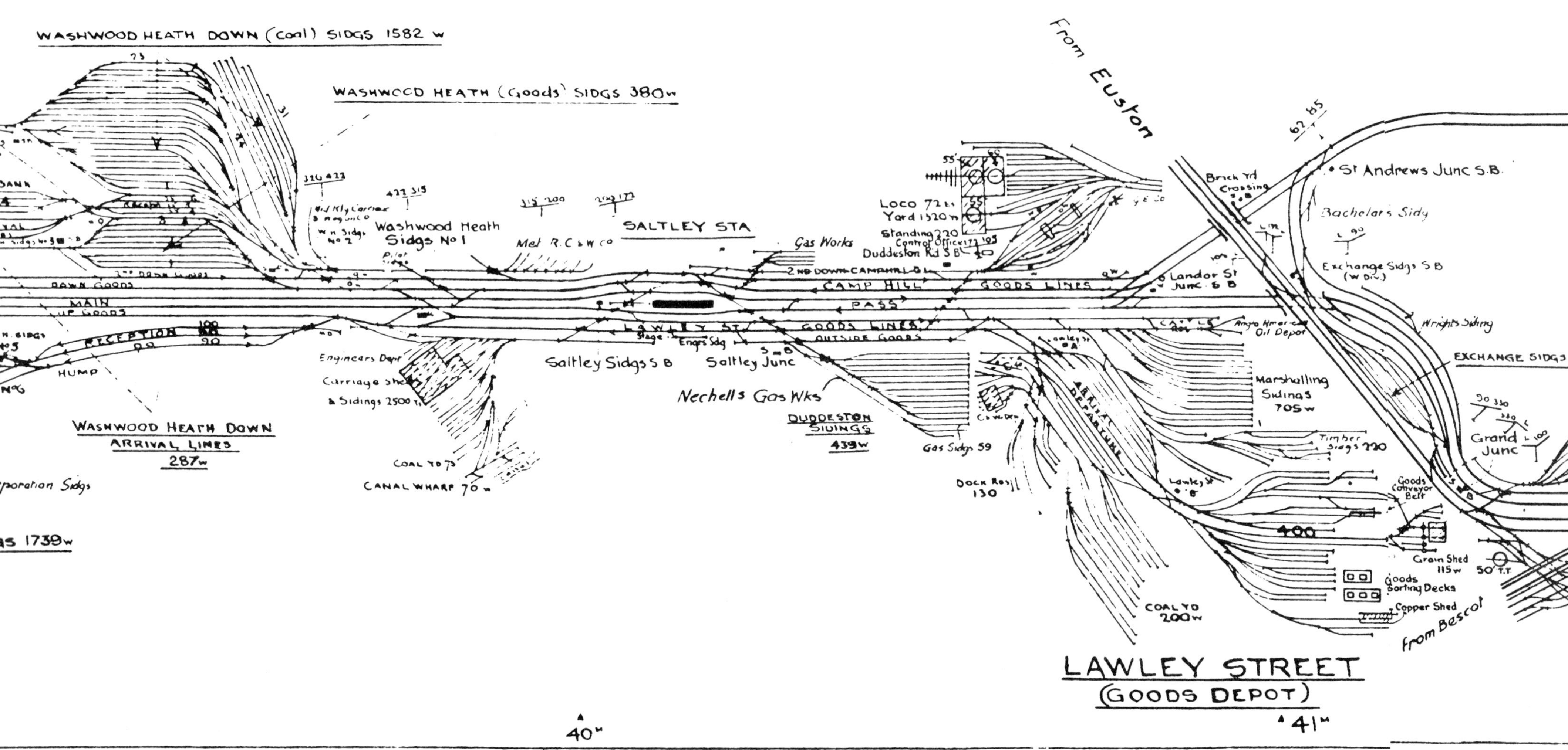
LAWLEY STREET
(GOODS DEPOT)
41m
40m
From Euston
From Bescot
St Andrews Junc S.B.
Bachelors Sidy
Exchange Sidgs S B (W Div)
Wrights Siding
EXCHANGE SIDGS
Grand Junc
Brick Yd Crossing
Landor St Junc S B
Marshalling Sidings 705w
Timber Sidgs 220
Grain Shed 115w
Goods Sorting Decks
Copper Shed
COAL YD 200w
Gas Sidgs 59
Dock Rd 130
Duddeston Rd S B
GOODS LINES
CAMP HILL
PASS
Gas Works
DUDDESTON SIDINGS 439w
Nechells Gas Wks
Saltley Junc
SALTLEY STA
Saltley Sidgs S B
Met R C & W Co
Washwood Heath Sidgs No 1
Engineers Dept
Carriage Shed
COAL YD 75
CANAL WHARF 70w
WASHWOOD HEATH (Goods) SIDGS 380w
WASHWOOD HEATH DOWN (Coal) SIDGS 1582 w
WASHWOOD HEATH DOWN ARRIVAL LINES 287w
MAIN
HUMP

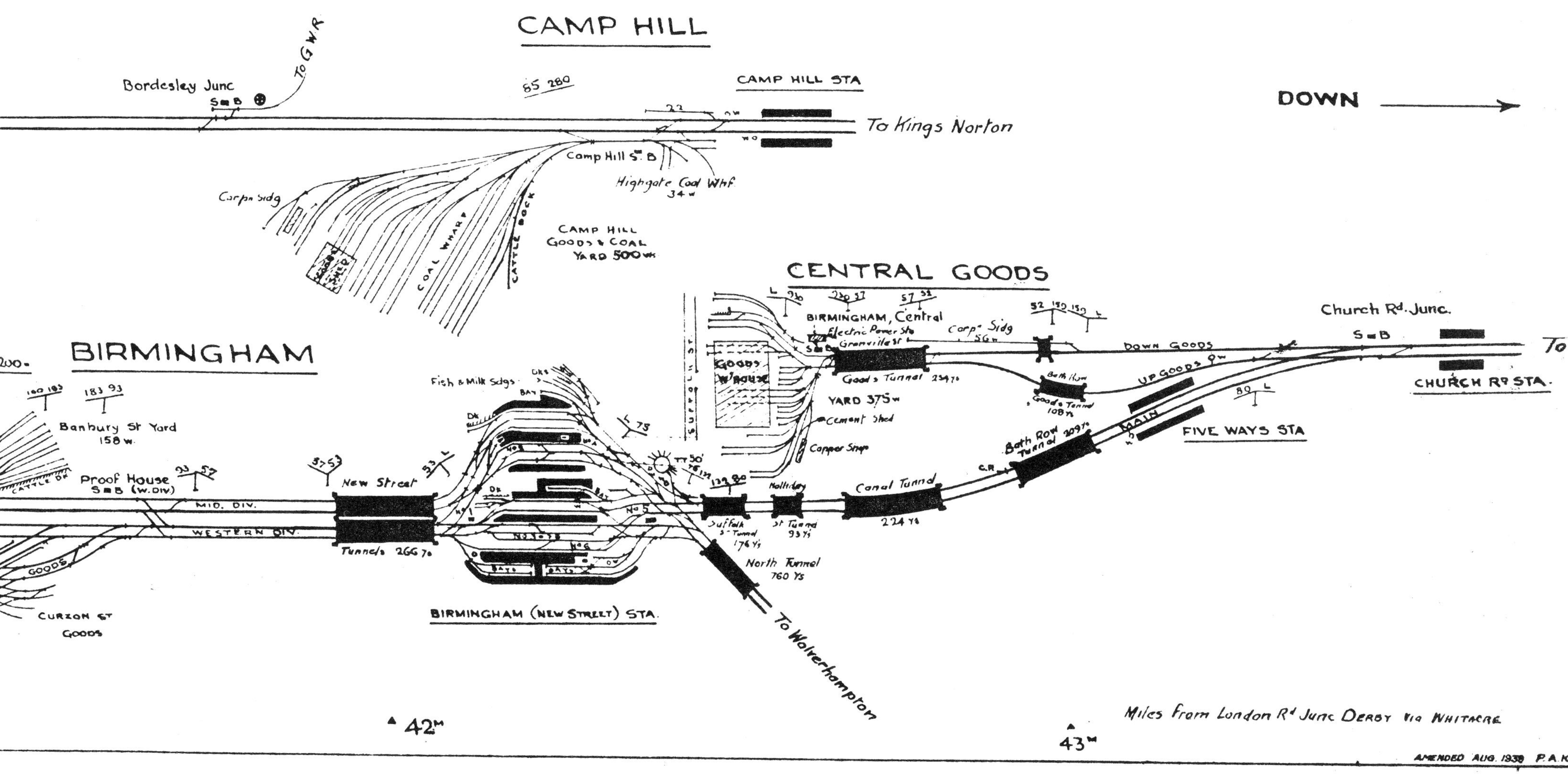
CAMP HILL
Bordesley Junc S B
To G W R
CAMP HILL STA
To Kings Norton
DOWN
Camp Hill S B
Highgate Coal Whf 34w
Corpn Sidg
COAL WHARF
CATTLE DOCK
CAMP HILL GOODS & COAL YARD 500w
CENTRAL GOODS
BIRMINGHAM, Central
Electric Power Sta
Granville St
Corpn Sidg
Church Rd. Junc.
S B
CHURCH RD STA.
DOWN GOODS
UP GOODS
MAIN
FIVE WAYS STA
Goods Tunnel 234 yds
YARD 375w
Cement Shed
Copper Shop
GOODS W'HOUSE
SUFFOLK ST
Bath Row Tunnel 209 yds
Canal Tunnel 224 yds
BIRMINGHAM
Fish & Milk Sdgs
Banbury St Yard 158w
Proof House S B (W. DIV)
MID. DIV.
WESTERN DIV.
New Street
Tunnels 266 yds
GOODS
CURZON ST GOODS
BIRMINGHAM (NEW STREET) STA.
Suffolk St Tunnel 176 yds
St Tunnel 93 yds
North Tunnel 760 yds
To Wolverhampton
42M
43M
Miles from London Rd Junc Derby via Whitacre
AMENDED AUG. 1938 P.A.K.

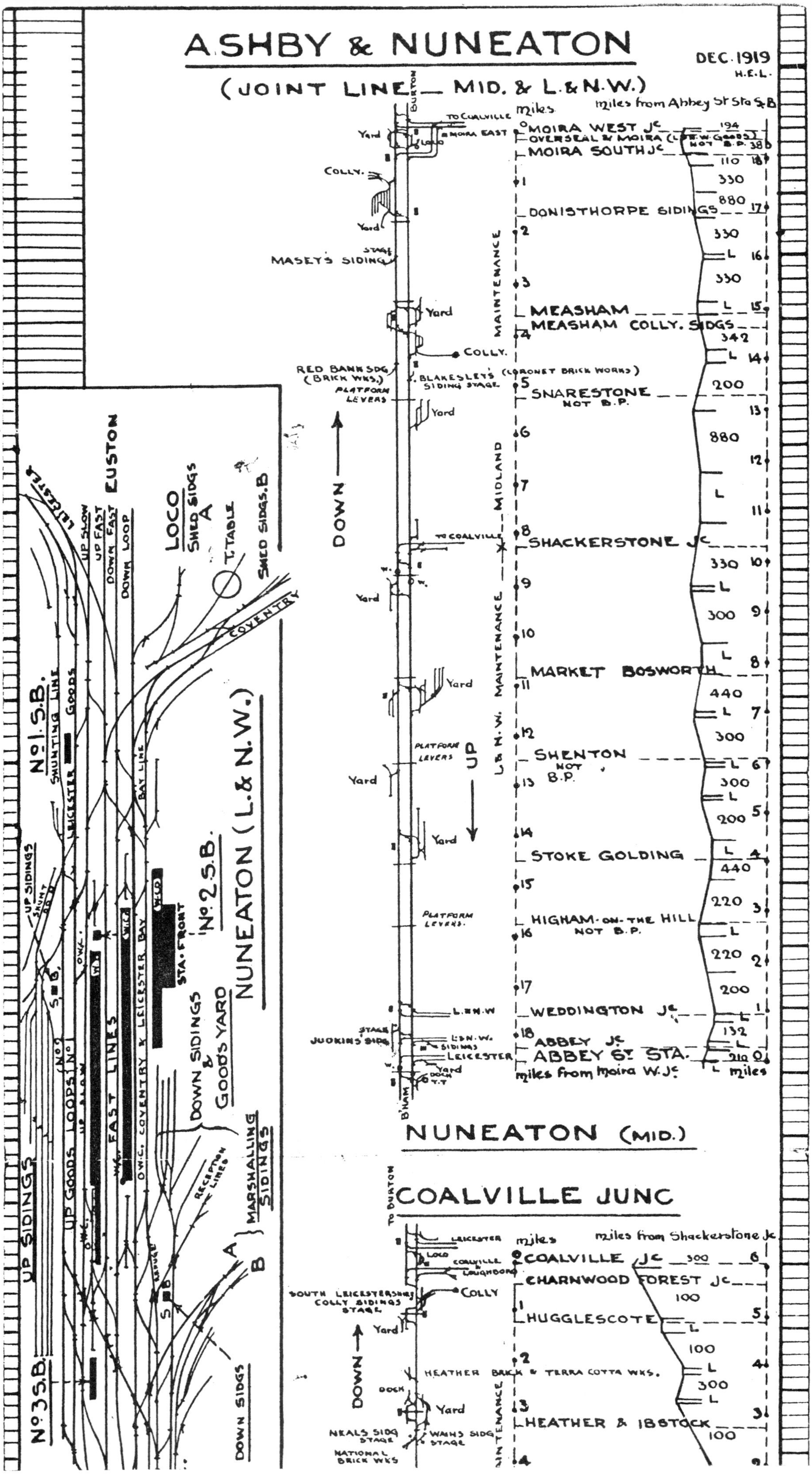

ASHBY & NUNEATON

(JOINT LINE — MID. & L.&N.W.)

DEC. 1919
H.E.L.

miles | miles from Abbey St Sta S.B.

MOIRA WEST J^{c}
OVERSEAL & MOIRA (L.&N.W. GOODS) NOT B.P.
MOIRA SOUTH J^{c}
DONISTHORPE SIDINGS
MASEY'S SIDING
MEASHAM
MEASHAM COLLY. SIDGS
RED BANK SDG (BRICK WKS.)
BLAKESLEY'S (CORONET BRICK WORKS) SIDING STAGE
SNARESTONE NOT B.P.
SHACKERSTONE J^{c}
MARKET BOSWORTH
SHENTON NOT B.P.
STOKE GOLDING
HIGHAM-ON-THE HILL NOT B.P.
WEDDINGTON J^{c}
JUDKINS SIDG
ABBEY J^{c}
ABBEY S^{t} STA.
miles from Moira W. J^{c} | miles

MIDLAND MAINTENANCE
L.&N.W. MAINTENANCE
DOWN
UP

NUNEATON (MID.)

NUNEATON (L.&N.W.)

EUSTON
LEICESTER
COVENTRY
LOCO
SHED SIDGS A
SHED SIDGS B
T. TABLE
No 1 S.B.
No 2 S.B.
No 3 S.B.
SHUNTING LINE
LEICESTER GOODS
UP SLOW
UP FAST
DOWN FAST
DOWN LOOP
BAY LINE
FAST LINES
O.W.C. COVENTRY & LEICESTER BAY
STA. FRONT
UP SIDINGS
UP GOODS LOOPS
DOWN SIDINGS & GOODS YARD
MARSHALLING SIDINGS
RECEPTION LINES
DOWN SIDGS

COALVILLE JUNC

miles | miles from Shackerstone J^{c}

COALVILLE J^{c}
CHARNWOOD FOREST J^{c}
SOUTH LEICESTERSHIRE COLLY SIDINGS STAGE
HUGGLESCOTE
HEATHER BRICK & TERRA COTTA WKS.
HEATHER & IBSTOCK
NEALS SIDG STAGE
WAINS SIDG STAGE
NATIONAL BRICK WKS

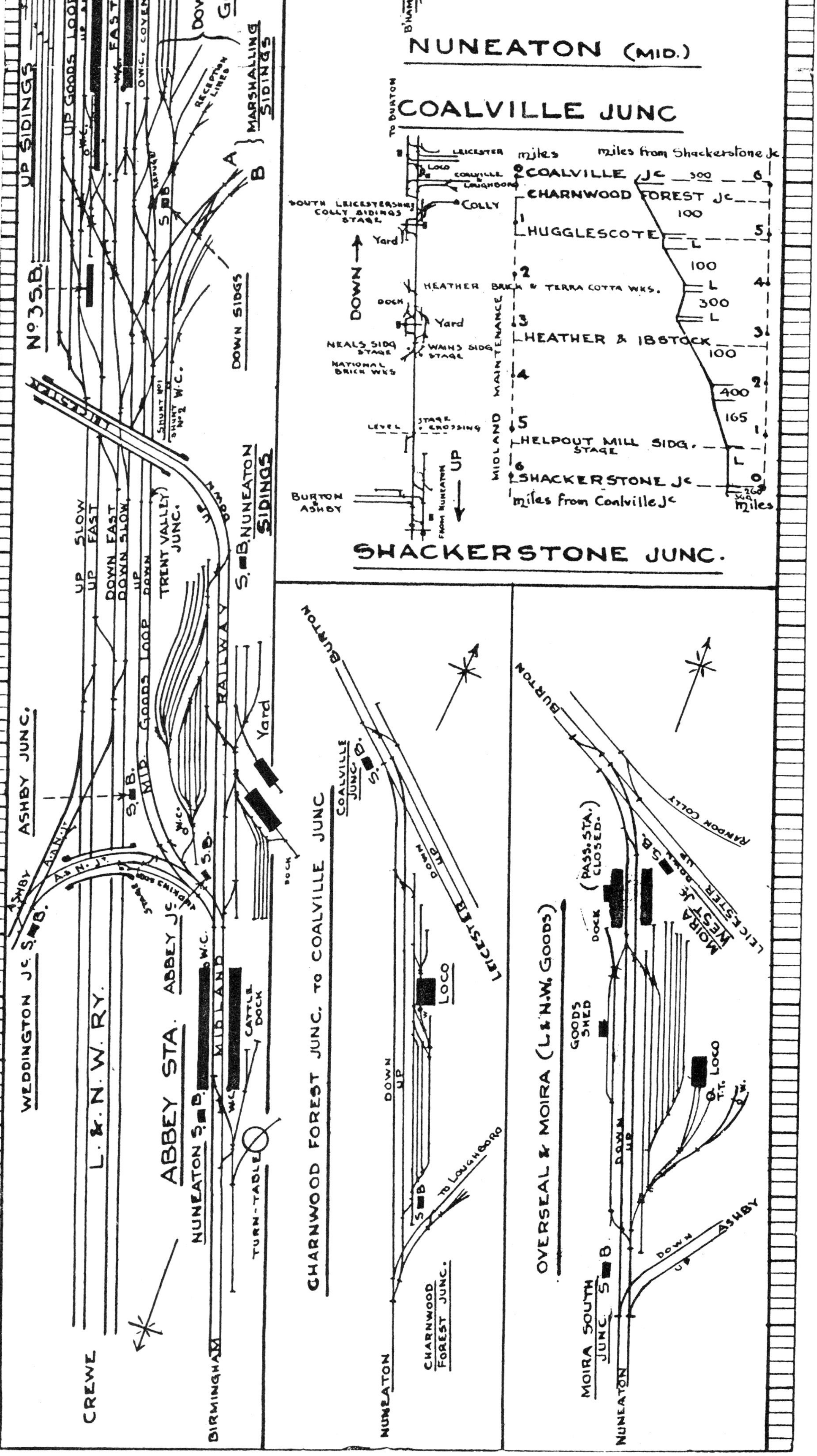
NUNEATON (MID.)
COALVILLE JUNC
TO BURTON
LEICESTER
LOCO
COALVILLE & LOUGHBORO
COLLY
SOUTH LEICESTERSHIRE COLLY SIDINGS STAGE
Yard
DOWN
HEATHER BRICK & TERRA COTTA WKS.
DOCK
NEALS SIDG STAGE
WAINS SIDG STAGE
NATIONAL BRICK WKS
LEVEL STAGE CROSSING
BURTON & ASHBY
UP
FROM NUNEATON
MIDLAND MAINTENANCE
miles
miles from Shackerstone Jc
COALVILLE Jc
CHARNWOOD FOREST Jc
HUGGLESCOTE
HEATHER & IBSTOCK
HELPOUT MILL SIDG. STAGE
SHACKERSTONE Jc
miles from Coalville Jc
miles
SHACKERSTONE JUNC.
UP SIDINGS
UP GOODS LOOP
MARSHALLING SIDINGS
RECEPTION LINES
No. 3 S.B.
DOWN SIDGS
NUNEATON SIDINGS
TRENT VALLEY JUNC.
UP SLOW
UP FAST
DOWN FAST
DOWN SLOW
UP
DOWN
GOODS LOOP
MID. RAILWAY
ASHBY JUNC.
WEDDINGTON Jc S.B.
L. & N. W. RY.
ABBEY STA.
ABBEY Jc
NUNEATON S.B.
MIDLAND
CATTLE DOCK
TURN-TABLE
CREWE
BIRMINGHAM
CHARNWOOD FOREST JUNC. TO COALVILLE JUNC
COALVILLE JUNC. S.B.
BURTON
LEICESTER
LOCO
TO LOUGHBORO
CHARNWOOD FOREST JUNC.
NUNEATON
OVERSEAL & MOIRA (L & N.W. GOODS)
MOIRA WEST Jc S.B.
(PASS. STA. CLOSED.)
RAWDON COLLY
DOCK
GOODS SHED
LOCO
MOIRA SOUTH JUNC. S.B.
ASHBY
NUNEATON

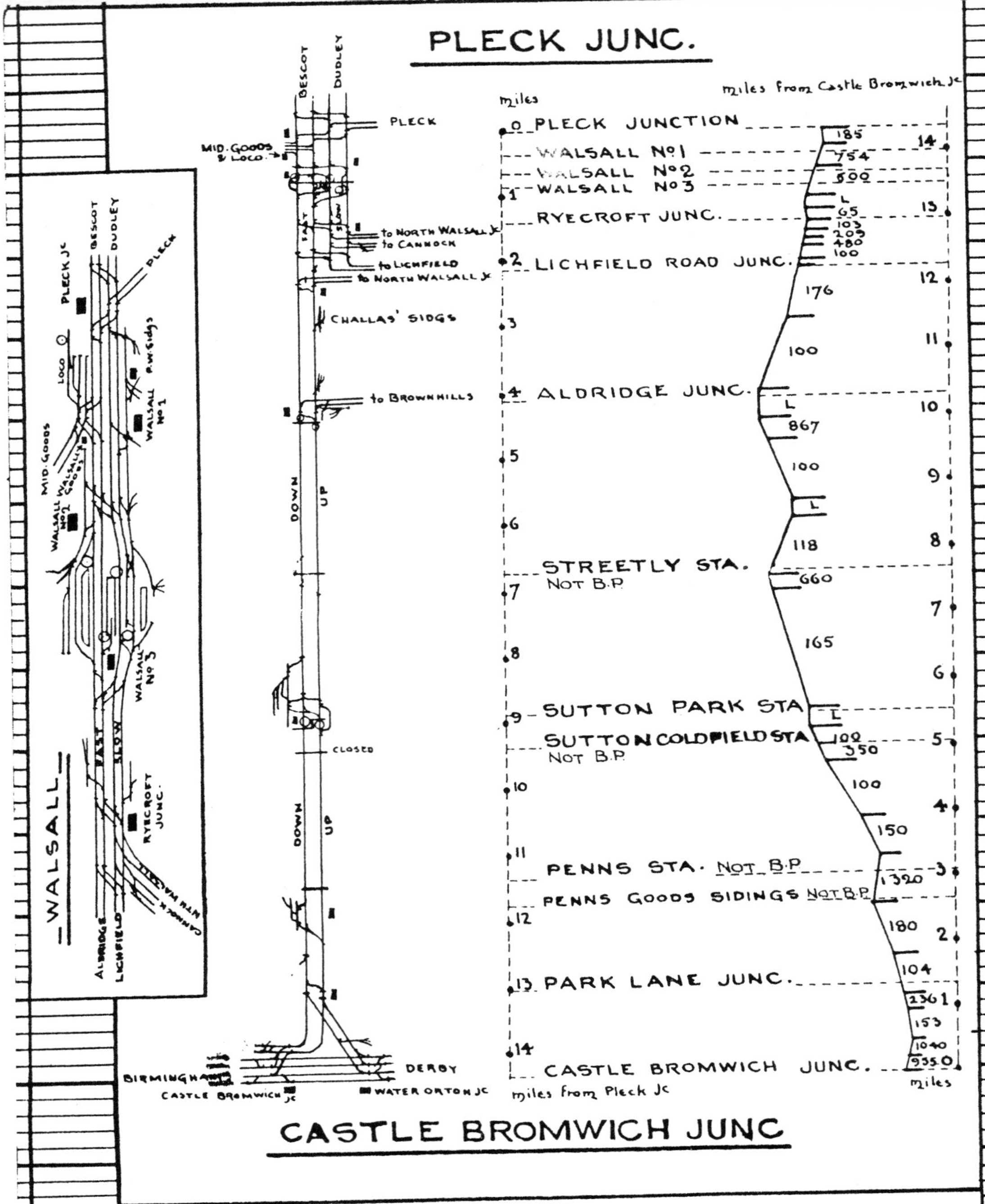

PLECK JUNC.

miles — miles from Castle Bromwich Jc

0 PLECK JUNCTION — 14

WALSALL No 1

WALSALL No 2

1 WALSALL No 3 — 13

RYECROFT JUNC.

2 LICHFIELD ROAD JUNC. — 12

3 — 11

4 ALDRIDGE JUNC. — 10

5 — 9

6 — 8

STREETLY STA. NOT B.P.

7 — 7

8 — 6

9 SUTTON PARK STA

SUTTON COLDFIELD STA NOT B.P. — 5

10 — 4

11 PENNS STA. NOT B.P — 3

PENNS GOODS SIDINGS NOT B.P.

12 — 2

13 PARK LANE JUNC. — 1

14 CASTLE BROMWICH JUNC. — 0

miles from Pleck Jc — miles

Gradients: 185, 754, 600, L, 65, 103, 209, 480, 100, 176, 100, L, 867, 100, L, 118, 660, 165, L, 100, 350, 100, 150, 1320, 180, 104, 2361, 153, 1040, 935

BESCOT, DUDLEY, PLECK, MID. GOODS & LOCO, FAST, SLOW, to NORTH WALSALL Jc, to CANNOCK, to LICHFIELD, to NORTH WALSALL Jc, CHALLAS' SIDGS, to BROWNHILLS, DOWN, UP, CLOSED, DOWN, UP, BIRMINGHAM, CASTLE BROMWICH Jc, DERBY, WATER ORTON Jc

WALSALL

PLECK Jc, BESCOT, DUDLEY, PLECK, LOCO, P.W. Sidgs, WALSALL No 1, MID. GOODS, WALSALL GOODS, WALSALL No 2, WALSALL No 3, FAST, SLOW, RYECROFT JUNC., NTH WALSALL, CANNOCK, ALDRIDGE, LICHFIELD

CASTLE BROMWICH JUNC

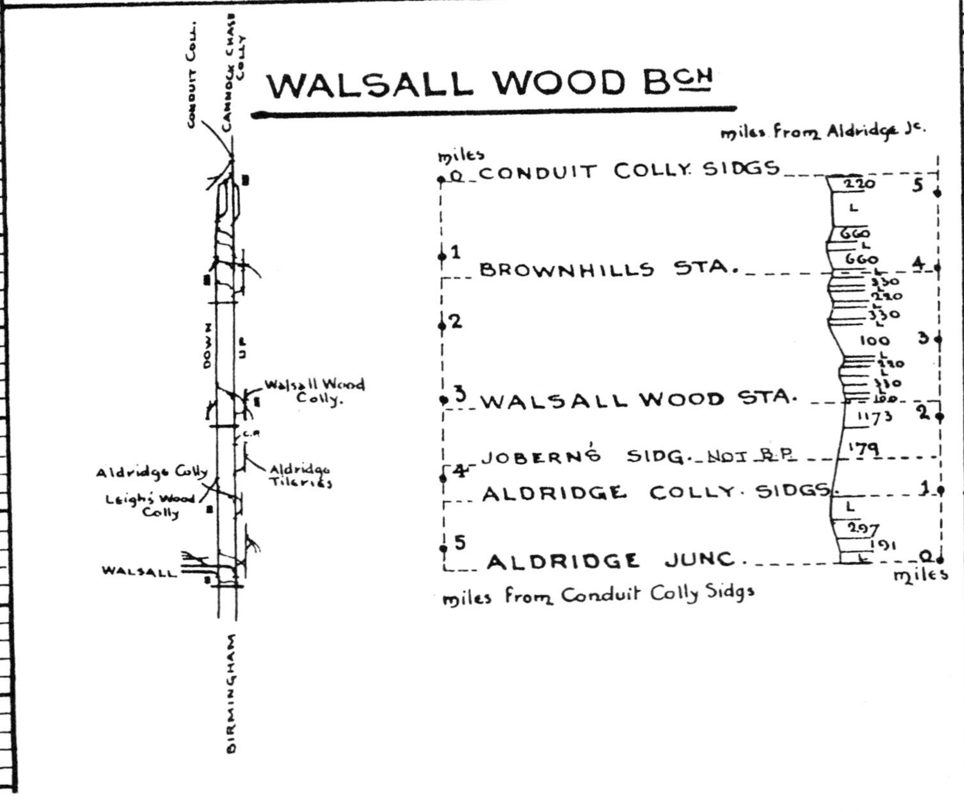

WALSALL WOOD Bch

miles — miles from Aldridge Jc.

0 CONDUIT COLLY SIDGS — 5

1 BROWNHILLS STA. — 4

2 — 3

3 WALSALL WOOD STA. — 2

JOBERN'S SIDG. NOT B.P.

4 ALDRIDGE COLLY. SIDGS — 1

5 ALDRIDGE JUNC. — 0

miles from Conduit Colly Sidgs — miles

Gradients: 220, L, 660, L, 660, 330, 220, 330, 100, 220, 330, 100, 1173, 179, L, 297, 191, L

CONDUIT COLL., CANNOCK CHASE COLLY, DOWN, UP, Walsall Wood Colly., C.R., Aldridge Colly, Aldridge Tileries, Leigh's Wood Colly, WALSALL, BIRMINGHAM

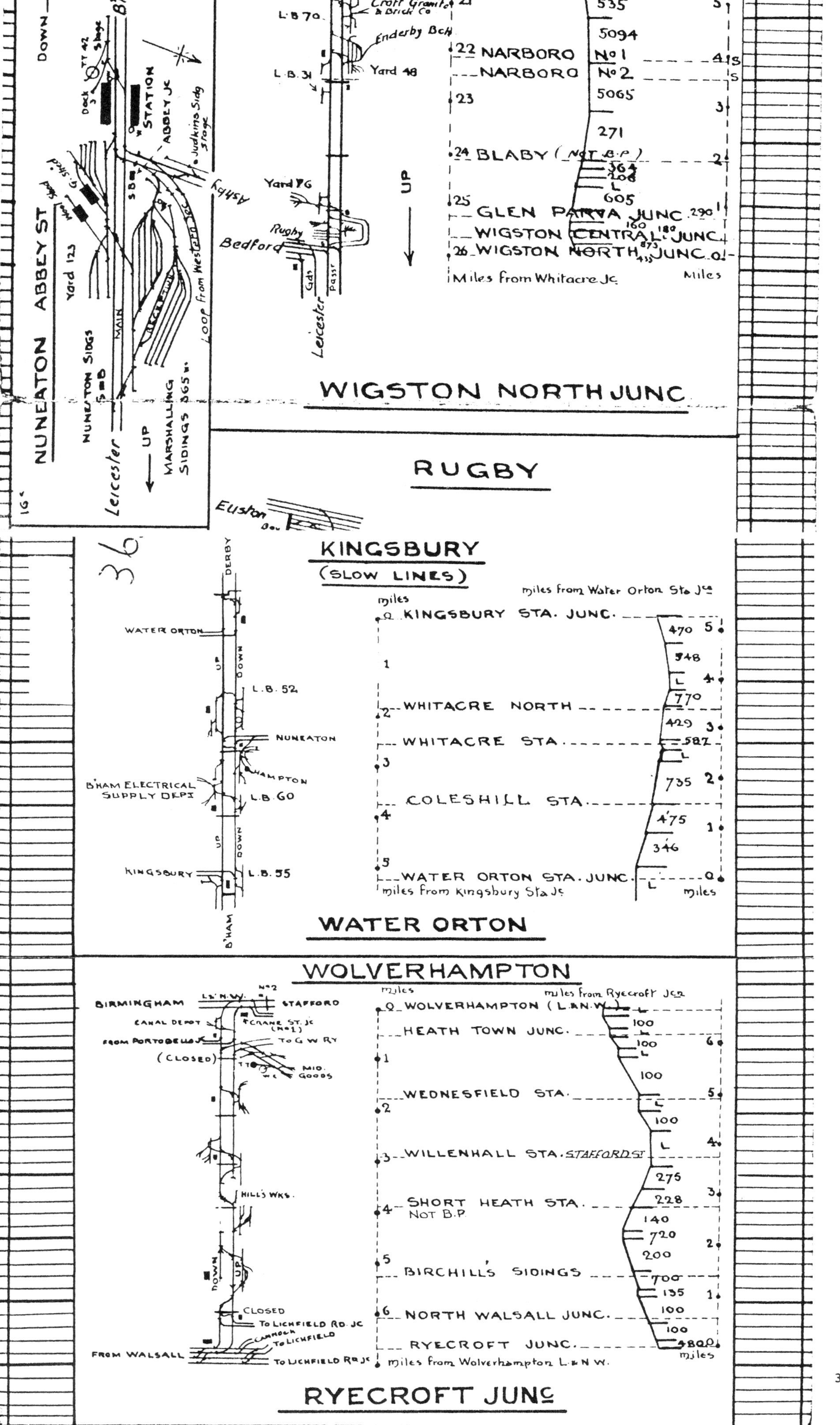
NUNEATON ABBEY ST
DOWN
UP
B'ham
Leicester
STATION
ABBEY JC
Judkins Sidg
Ashby
Yard 123
NUNEATON SIDGS
MARSHALLING SIDINGS
MAIN
Loop from Western Jc
CROFT SIDINGS
L.B. 55
L.B. 70
L.B. 31
Croft Granite & Brick Co
Enderby Bch
Yard 48
Yard 76
Rugby
Bedford
Leicester
NARBORO No 1
NARBORO No 2
BLABY (NOT B.P.)
GLEN PARVA JUNC
WIGSTON CENTRAL JUNC
WIGSTON NORTH JUNC
Miles from Whitacre Jc
Miles
WIGSTON NORTH JUNC
RUGBY
Euston
KINGSBURY
(SLOW LINES)
miles from Water Orton Sta Jc
miles
KINGSBURY STA. JUNC.
WHITACRE NORTH
WHITACRE STA.
COLESHILL STA.
WATER ORTON STA. JUNC.
miles from Kingsbury Sta Jc
DERBY
WATER ORTON
L.B. 52
NUNEATON
HAMPTON
B'HAM ELECTRICAL SUPPLY DEPT
L.B. 60
KINGSBURY
L.B. 55
B'HAM
WATER ORTON
WOLVERHAMPTON
miles from Ryecroft Jcn
WOLVERHAMPTON (L.&N.W.)
HEATH TOWN JUNC.
WEDNESFIELD STA.
WILLENHALL STA. STAFFORD ST
SHORT HEATH STA.
NOT B.P.
BIRCHILLS SIDINGS
NORTH WALSALL JUNC.
RYECROFT JUNC.
miles from Wolverhampton L.&N.W.
BIRMINGHAM
STAFFORD
CANAL DEPOT
CRANE ST. JC (No 1)
FROM PORTOBELLO
(CLOSED)
TO G W RY
MID. GOODS
HILL'S WKS.
CLOSED
To LICHFIELD RD. JC
CANNOCK
To LICHFIELD
FROM WALSALL
To LICHFIELD RD JC
RYECROFT JUNC

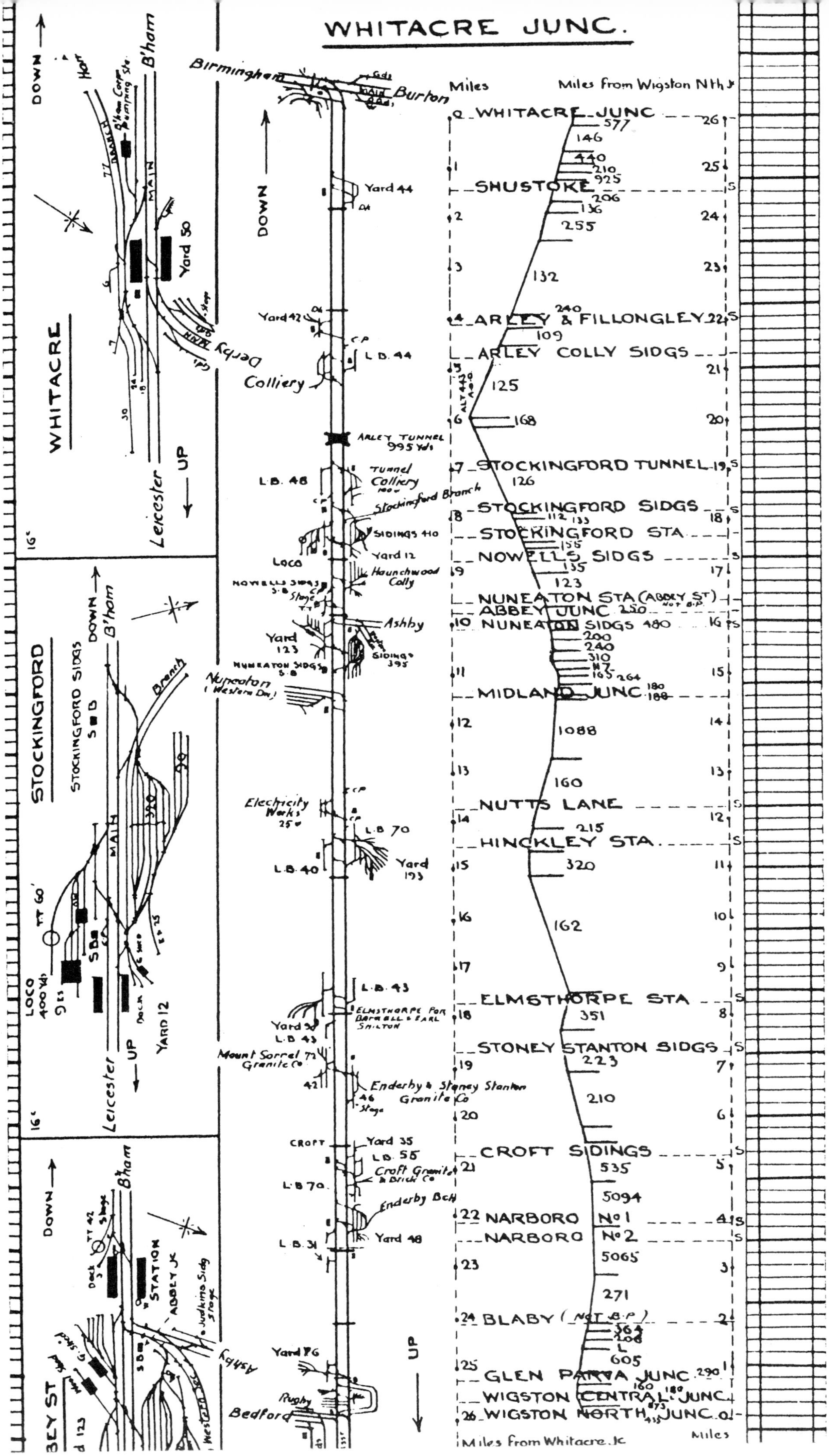

WHITACRE JUNC.

Birmingham — Burton

Miles		Miles From Wigston Nth Jc
0	WHITACRE JUNC.	26
1	SHUSTOKE	25
4	ARLEY & FILLONGLEY	22
	ARLEY COLLY SIDGS	
7	STOCKINGFORD TUNNEL	19
8	STOCKINGFORD SIDGS	18
	STOCKINGFORD STA	
	NOWELLS SIDGS	17
	NUNEATON STA (ABBEY ST)	
	ABBEY JUNC (NOT B.P.)	
10	NUNEATON SIDGS 480	16
	MIDLAND JUNC	
	NUTTS LANE	12
14	HINCKLEY STA.	
	ELMSTHORPE STA	8
	STONEY STANTON SIDGS	7
	CROFT SIDINGS	5
22	NARBORO No 1	4
	NARBORO No 2	
24	BLABY (NOT B.P.)	2
25	GLEN PARVA JUNC	1
	WIGSTON CENTRAL JUNC	
26	WIGSTON NORTH JUNC	0

Miles From Whitacre Jc — Miles

Gradients: 577, 146, 440, 210, 925, 206, 136, 255, 132, 240, 109, 125, 168, 126, 112, 133, 155, 135, 123, 250, 200, 240, 310, 147, 165, 264, 180, 188, 1088, 160, 215, 320, 162, 351, 223, 210, 535, 5094, 5065, 271, 364, 206, L, 605, 290, 160, 180, 873, 435

DOWN ↑ — UP ↓

Yard 44; Yard 42; L.B. 44; Colliery; ALT 420 / 440; ARLEY TUNNEL 995 Yds; L.B. 48; Tunnel Colliery 100W; Stockingford Branch; Sidings 410; Yard 12; Loco; Haunchwood Colly; Nowells Sidgs S.B.; Stage; T.T.; Ashby; Yard 123; Sidings 395; Nuneaton Sidgs S.B.; Nuneaton (Western Div); Electricity Works 25W; L.B. 70; L.B. 40; Yard 193; L.B. 43; Elmsthorpe for Barwell & Earl Shilton; Yard 50; L.B. 43; Mount Sorrel Granite Co 71; 42; Enderby & Stoney Stanton Granite Co; 46 Stage; Croft; Yard 35; L.B. 55; Croft Granite & Brick Co; L.B. 70; Enderby Bch; Yard 48; L.B. 31; Yard 76; Rugby; Bedford

WHITACRE

DOWN ↑ Ham; B'ham Corp. Pumping Sta.; B'ham; BRANCH; MAIN; Yard 50; Derby Main; Gds; Leicester; UP ↓; 16c

STOCKINGFORD

DOWN → B'ham; STOCKINGFORD SIDGS S.B.; Branch; MAIN; TT 60'; LOCO 400 Yds; S.B.; Dock; YARD 12; Leicester; UP ↓; 16c

ABBEY ST

DOWN ↑ B'ham; TT 42; Stage; Dock; STATION; ABBEY JC; Judkins Sidg Stage; Ashby; S.B.; Western Jc; Yard 123

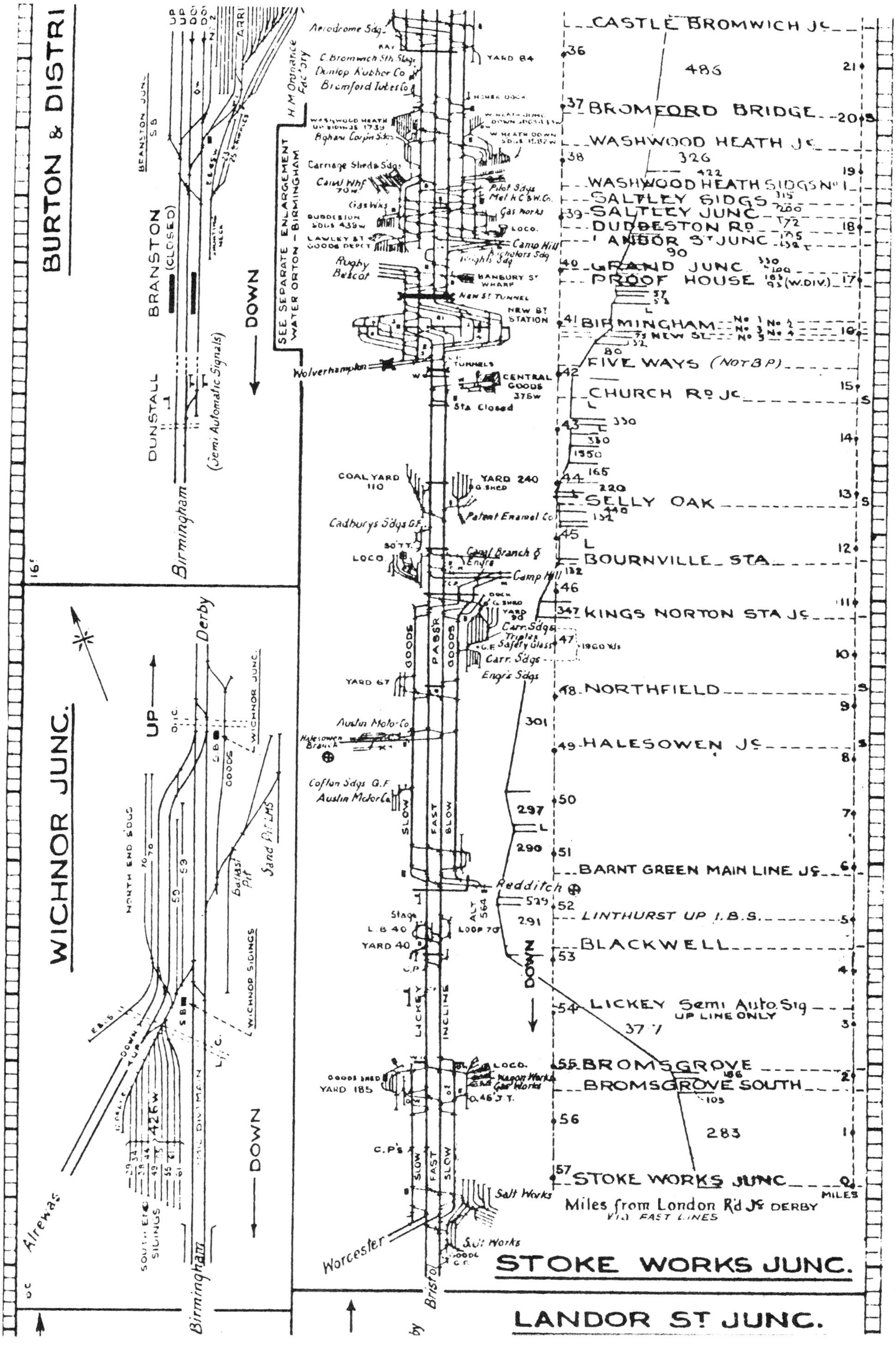
BURTON & DISTRI
BRANSTON (CLOSED)
DUNSTALL
(Semi Automatic Signals)
Birmingham
DOWN
WICHNOR JUNC.
WICHNOR JUNC.
WICHNOR SIDINGS
NORTH END SDGS
Ballast Pit
Sand Pit LMS
Derby
UP
DOWN
Alrewas
Birmingham
SEE SEPARATE ENLARGEMENT WATER ORTON - BIRMINGHAM
H M Ordnance Fac'try
Aerodrome Sdg.
C. Bromwich Sth Sdgs
Dunlop Rubber Co
Bromford Tubes Co
Carriage Sheds Sdgs
Canal Whf
Gas Wks
Rugby
Bescot
NEW ST TUNNEL
NEW ST STATION
Wolverhampton
CENTRAL GOODS 375w
Sta Closed
COAL YARD 110
YARD 240
Cadburys Sdgs G.F.
Patent Enamel Co
Canal Branch & Engrs
Camp Hill
Carr. Sdgs
Triplex Safety Glass
Engrs Sdgs
YARD 67
GOODS
PASSR
GOODS
Austin Motor Co
Halesowen Branch
Coften Sdgs G.F.
Austin Motor Co
SLOW
FAST
SLOW
Redditch
LICKEY
INCLINE
YARD 40
YARD 185
C.P's
Salt Works
Worcester
Bristol
CASTLE BROMWICH JC
36
486
21
37 BROMFORD BRIDGE 20
WASHWOOD HEATH JC
38
326
19
WASHWOOD HEATH SIDGS No 1
SALTLEY SIDGS
39 SALTLEY JUNC
DUDDESTON RD 18
LANDOR ST JUNC
90
40 GRAND JUNC
PROOF HOUSE (W.DIV.) 17
41 BIRMINGHAM No 1 No 2 No 3 No 4 No 5
NEW ST
16
80
42 FIVE WAYS (NOT B P)
CHURCH RD JC 15
43
14
44
SELLY OAK 13
45
BOURNVILLE STA 12
46
11
47 KINGS NORTON STA JC
10
48 NORTHFIELD
9
301
49 HALESOWEN JC 8
50
297
7
290
51
BARNT GREEN MAIN LINE JC 6
52
LINTHURST UP I.B.S. 5
291
BLACKWELL
53
4
DOWN
54 LICKEY Semi Auto.Sig UP LINE ONLY
377
3
55 BROMSGROVE 2
BROMSGROVE SOUTH
56
283
1
57 STOKE WORKS JUNC 0
MILES
Miles from London Rd Jc DERBY VIA FAST LINES
STOKE WORKS JUNC.
LANDOR ST JUNC.

STOKE WORKS JUNC.

Miles from Bristol West

MILES		Miles from Bristol West
0	STOKE WORKS JUNC.	73
2	DROITWICH RD (GOODS)	70
4½	DUNHAMPSTEAD (GOODS)	68
8½	SPETCHLEY (GOODS)	64
11	ABBOTTS WOOD JUNC.	62
12½	WADBOROUGH STA NOT B.P.	60
13	PIRTON SIDINGS (GOODS)	60
16	DEFFORD	57
17	ECKINGTON	56
20	BREDON	53
22	ASHCHURCH LEVEL CROSSING	51
22	ASHCHURCH JUNC	51

ASHCHURCH

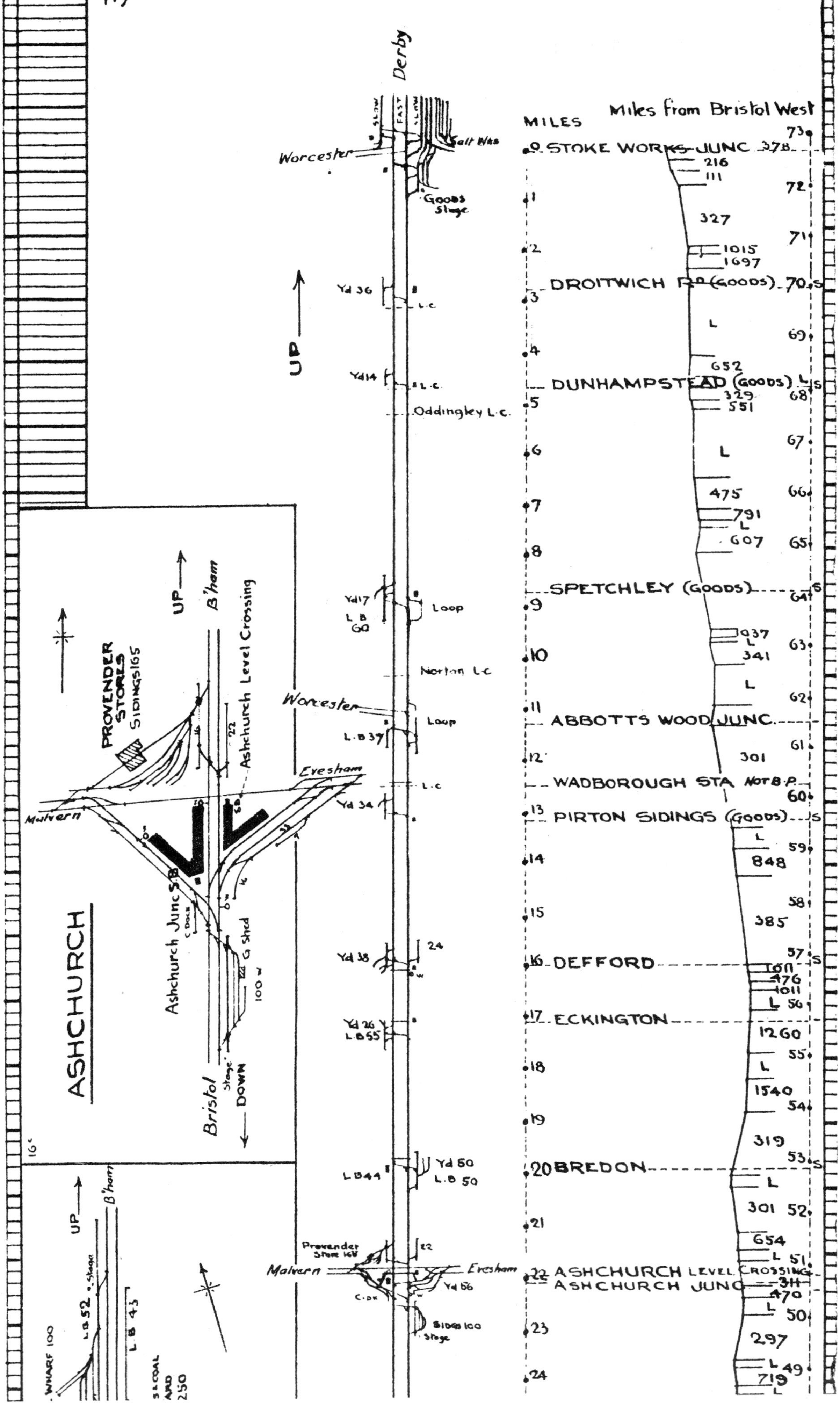

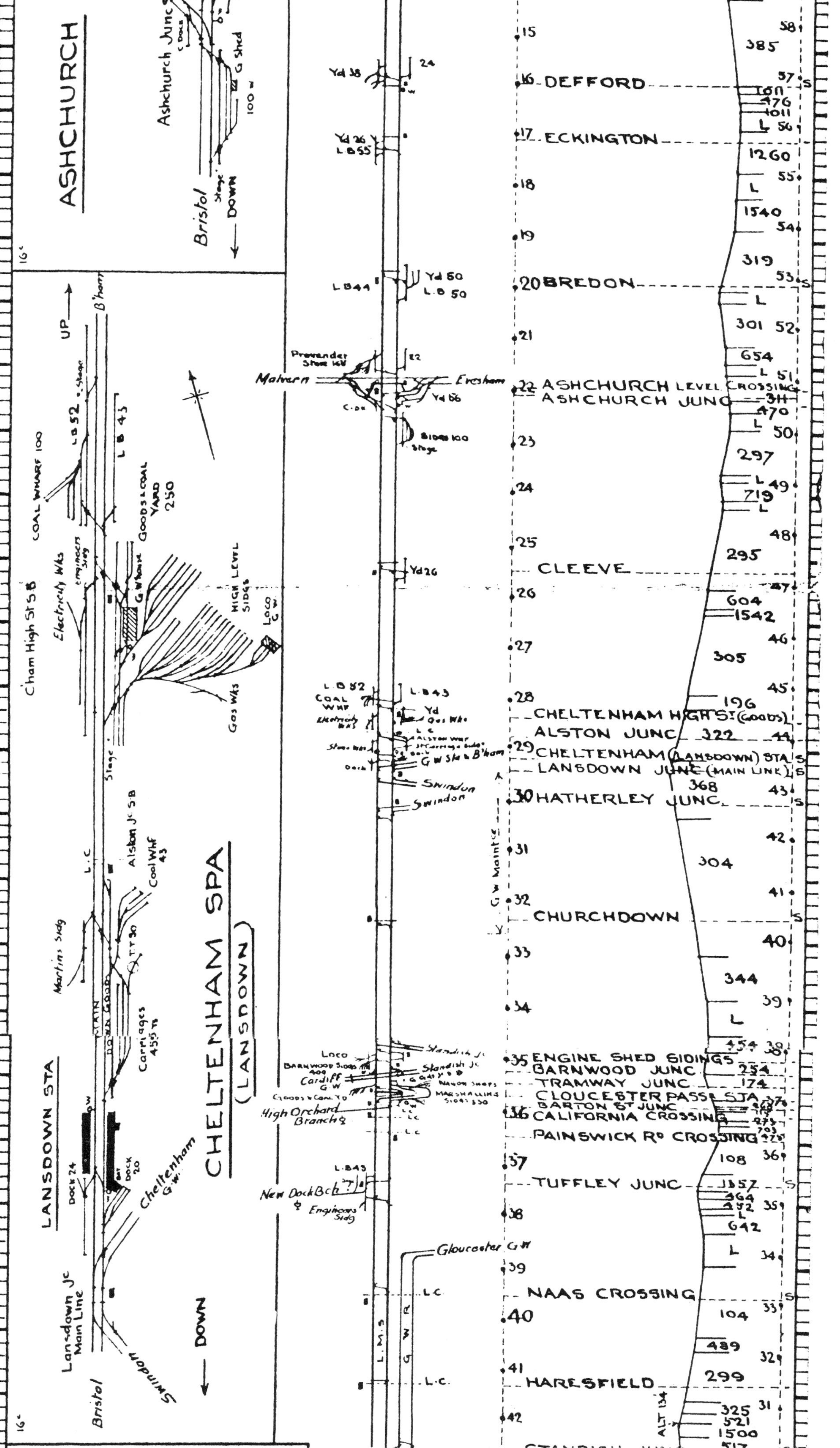
ASHCHURCH
Ashchurch Junc SB
G Shed
Bristol
DOWN
UP
CHELTENHAM SPA
(LANSDOWN)
LANSDOWN STA
Cham High St SB
Electricity Wks
COAL WHARF 100
GOODS & COAL YARD 250
HIGH LEVEL SIDGS
Gas Wks
Alston Jc SB
Coal Whf 43
Martins Sidg
Carriages
Cheltenham G.W.
Lansdown Jc Main Line
Bristol
Swindon
Malvern
Evesham
Provender Store
High Orchard Branch
New Dock Bch
Engineers Sidg
Gloucester G.W.
L.M.S.
G.W.R.
G.W. Maint
15
16 DEFFORD
17 ECKINGTON
18
19
20 BREDON
21
22 ASHCHURCH LEVEL CROSSING
ASHCHURCH JUNC
23
24
25
CLEEVE
26
27
28
CHELTENHAM HIGH ST (GOODS)
ALSTON JUNC
29 CHELTENHAM (LANSDOWN) STA
LANSDOWN JUNC (MAIN LINE)
30 HATHERLEY JUNC
31
32 CHURCHDOWN
33
34
35 ENGINE SHED SIDINGS
BARNWOOD JUNC
TRAMWAY JUNC
GLOUCESTER PASS STA
BARTON ST JUNC
36 CALIFORNIA CROSSING
PAINSWICK Rd CROSSING
37
TUFFLEY JUNC
38
39
NAAS CROSSING
40
41 HARESFIELD
42
385
1011
1260
1540
319
301
654
470
297
719
295
604
1542
305
196
322
368
304
344
454
108
642
104
489
299
325
1500

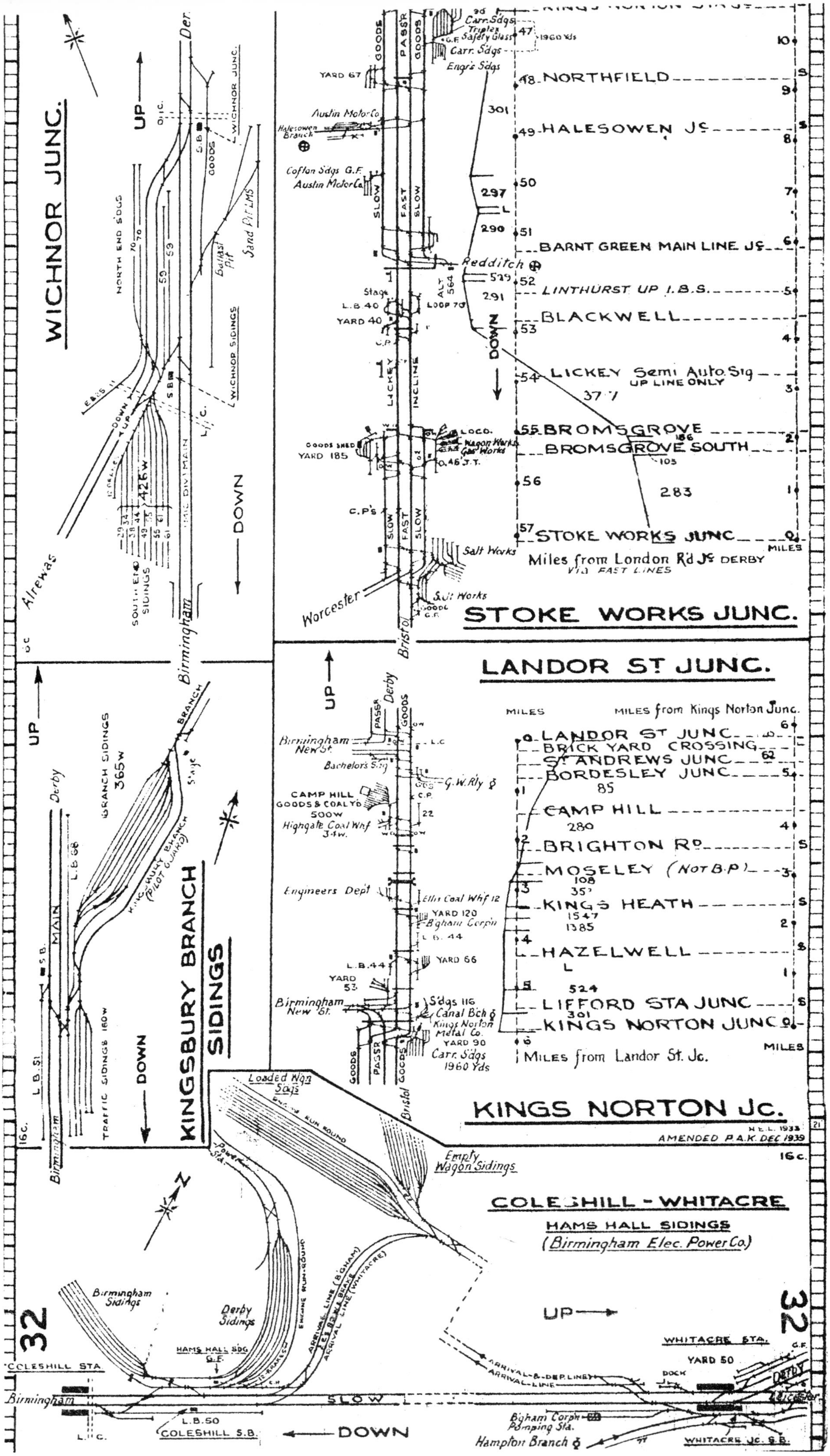

WICHNOR JUNC.

UP
DOWN
Der.
Birmingham
Alrewas
WICHNOR JUNC.
S.B.
GOODS
NORTH END SDGS
Ballast Pit
Sand Pit LMS
WICHNOR SIDINGS
B'HAM DIV MAIN
426w
SOUTH END SIDINGS

STOKE WORKS JUNC.

GOODS
PASSR
GOODS
Carr. Sdgs
Triplex Safety Glass
Carr. Sdgs
Engrs Sdgs
YARD 67
Austin Motor Co.
Halesowen Branch
Cofton Sdgs G.F.
Austin Motor Co.
SLOW
FAST
SLOW
Redditch
Stage
L.B. 40
YARD 40
LOOP 79
LICKEY
INCLINE
DOWN
LOCO.
Wagon Works
Gas Works
GOODS SHED
YARD 185
C.P's
Salt Works
Worcester
Bristol

47		10
48	NORTHFIELD	9
49	HALESOWEN Jc	8
50		7
51	BARNT GREEN MAIN LINE Jc	6
52	LINTHURST UP I.B.S.	5
53	BLACKWELL	4
54	LICKEY Semi Auto Sig UP LINE ONLY	3
55	BROMSGROVE	2
	BROMSGROVE SOUTH	
56		1
57	STOKE WORKS JUNC	0 MILES

Miles from London Rd Jc DERBY via FAST LINES

LANDOR St JUNC.

KINGS NORTON Jc.

UP
Derby
PASSR
GOODS
Birmingham New St.
Bachelors Sdg
G.W. Rly
CAMP HILL GOODS & COAL YD. 500W
Highgate Coal Whf 3-1w.
Engineers Dept
Ellis Coal Whf 12
YARD 120
B'gham Corpn
L.B. 44
YARD 66
L.B.44
YARD 53
Birmingham New St.
Sdgs 116
Canal Bch
Kings Norton Metal Co.
YARD 90
Carr. Sdgs 1960 Yds
GOODS
PASSR
GOODS
Bristol

MILES — MILES from Kings Norton Junc.

0	LANDOR St JUNC	6
	BRICK YARD CROSSING	
	St ANDREWS JUNC	
	BORDESLEY JUNC	5
1	CAMP HILL	4
2	BRIGHTON Rd	
	MOSELEY (NOT B.P.)	3
3	KINGS HEATH	
		2
4	HAZELWELL	1
5	LIFFORD STA JUNC	
	KINGS NORTON JUNC	0
6		MILES

Miles from Landor St. Jc.

H.E.L. 1933
AMENDED P.A.K. DEC 1939

KINGSBURY BRANCH SIDINGS

UP
DOWN
Derby
MAIN
L.B. 88
S.B.
L.B. 51
Birmingham
BRANCH SIDINGS 365w
KINGSBURY BRANCH (PILOT GUARD)
BRANCH
Stage
TRAFFIC SIDINGS 160w

COLESHILL - WHITACRE

HAMS HALL SIDINGS

(Birmingham Elec. Power Co.)

Loaded Wgn Sdgs
ENGINE RUN ROUND
Empty Wagon Sidings
Power Sta.
Birmingham Sidings
Derby Sidings
HAMS HALL SDG G.F.
ENGINE RUN-ROUND
ARRIVAL LINE (B'GHAM)
ARRIVAL LINE (WHITACRE)
UP
COLESHILL STA
Birmingham
SLOW
L.B. 50
COLESHILL S.B.
DOWN
WHITACRE STA.
YARD 50
ARRIVAL & DEP. LINE
ARRIVAL LINE
DOCK
DERBY
Leicester
B'gham Corpn Pumping Sta.
Hampton Branch
WHITACRE Jc. S.B.

16c.
32
32

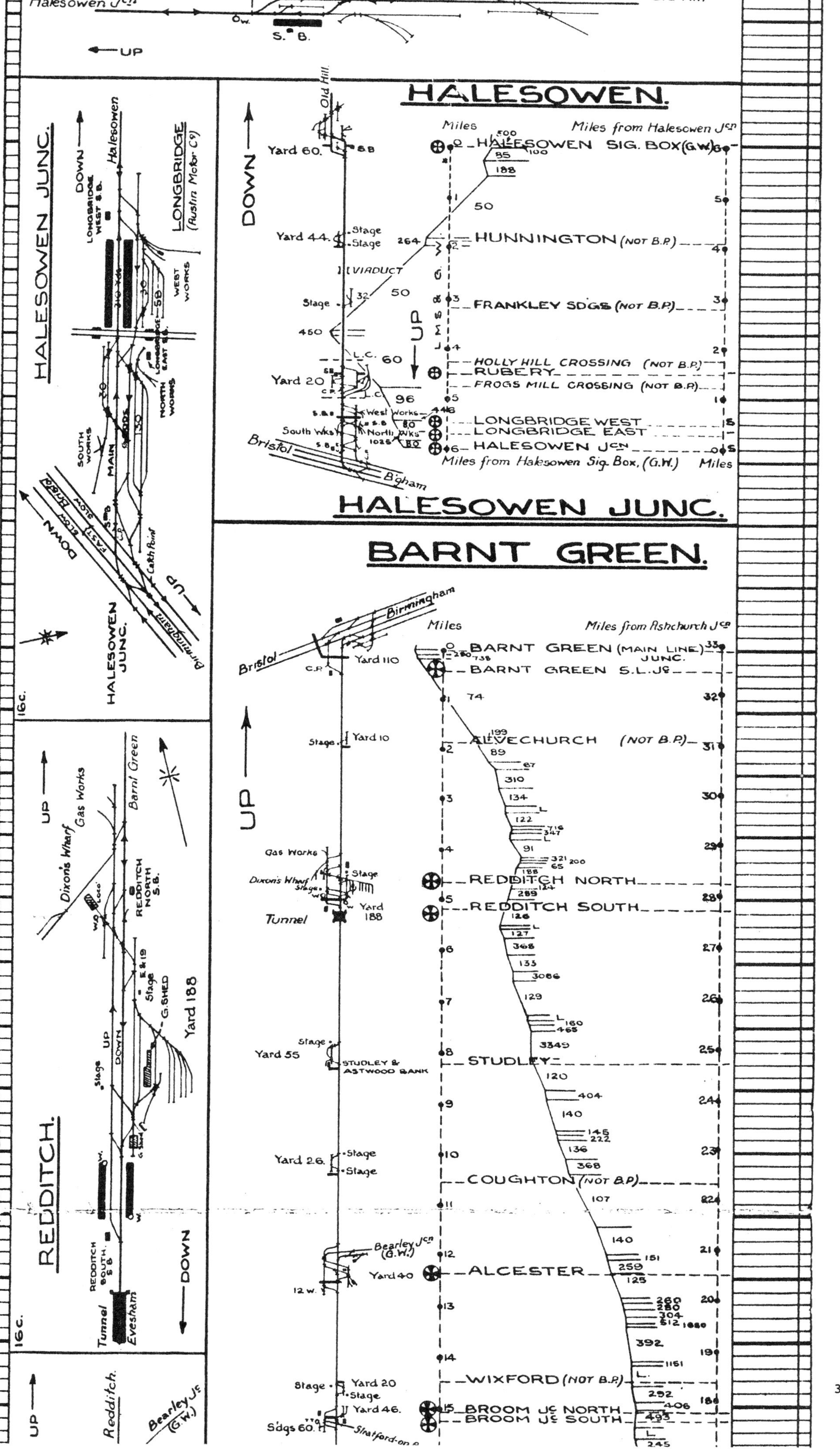
HALESOWEN.
Miles
Miles from Halesowen Jcn
HALESOWEN SIG. BOX (G.W.)
HUNNINGTON (NOT B.P.)
FRANKLEY SDGS (NOT B.P.)
HOLLY HILL CROSSING (NOT B.P.)
RUBERY
FROGS MILL CROSSING (NOT B.P.)
LONGBRIDGE WEST
LONGBRIDGE EAST
HALESOWEN JCN
Miles from Halesowen Sig. Box, (G.W.)
HALESOWEN JUNC.
HALESOWEN JUNC.
LONGBRIDGE (Austin Motor Co)
BARNT GREEN.
Miles
Miles from Ashchurch Jcn
BARNT GREEN (MAIN LINE) JUNC.
BARNT GREEN S.L.JC
ALVECHURCH (NOT B.P.)
REDDITCH NORTH
REDDITCH SOUTH
STUDLEY
COUGHTON (NOT B.P.)
ALCESTER
WIXFORD (NOT B.P.)
BROOM JC NORTH
BROOM JC SOUTH
REDDITCH.
16c.

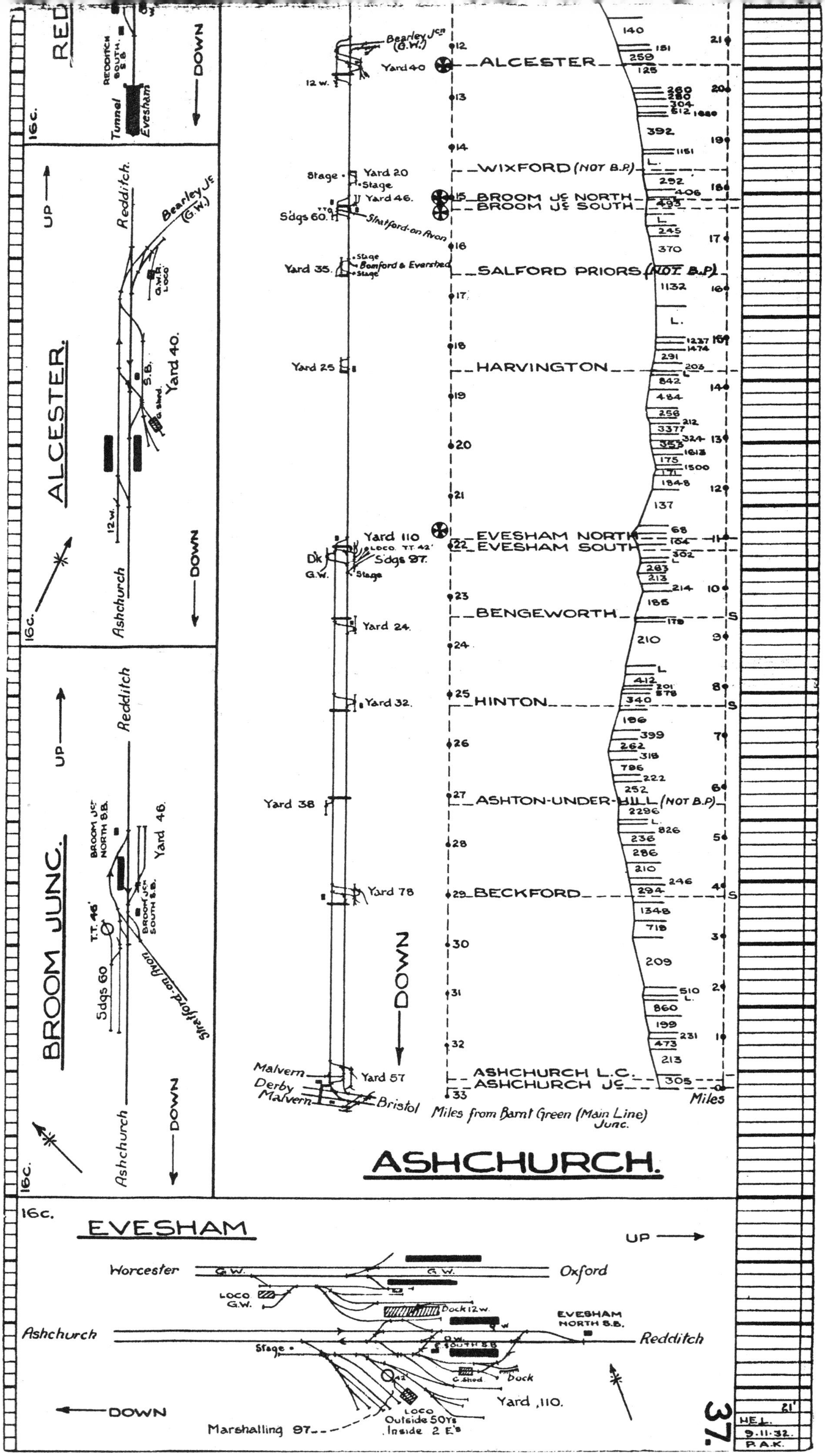

RED

Redditch South S.B.
Tunnel
Evesham
DOWN
16c.

Bearley Jcn (G.W.)
Yard 40
12 w.
12 ALCESTER 140 151 259 125 21
13 260 280 304 512 1080 20
392
14 1151 19
WIXFORD (NOT B.P.) L.
Stage Yard 20 Stage 252 406
15 BROOM Jc NORTH 18
BROOM Jc SOUTH 495
Yard 46.
Sdgs 60. Stratford-on-Avon L. 245
16 370 17
Stage Bomford & Evershed Stage
Yard 35. SALFORD PRIORS (NOT B.P.) 1132 16
17 L.
18 1237 1474 15
291
Yard 25 HARVINGTON 203 L.
842 484
19 14
256 212
3377 324
20 353 1613 13
175 1500
171
184-8
21 12
137
Yard 110 EVESHAM NORTH 68 11
Loco T.T. 42' 22 EVESHAM SOUTH 104
Dk Sdgs 97. 302 L.
G.W. Stage 283 213
23 214 10
185
BENGEWORTH 178 S
Yard 24.
24 210 9
L.
412 201 578
25 Yard 32. HINTON 340 8 S
186
26 399 7
262 318
786
222
27 Yard 38 ASHTON-UNDER-HILL (NOT B.P.) 252 6
2296 L.
28 826 5
236
286
210
29 Yard 78 BECKFORD 246 4 S
294
1348
719
30 3
209
31 510 L. 2
860
199
32 231 1
473
213
ASHCHURCH L.C.
33 Malvern Derby Malvern Bristol Yard 57 ASHCHURCH Jc 305 0
Miles from Barnt Green (Main Line) Junc. Miles
DOWN

ASHCHURCH.

ALCESTER.

UP
Redditch.
Bearley Jc (G.W.)
G.W.R. LOCO
S.B.
G. Shed
Yard 40.
12 w.
Ashchurch
DOWN
16c.

BROOM JUNC.

UP
Redditch
Broom Jc North S.B.
Broom Jcn South S.B.
Yard 46
T.T. 46'
Sdgs 60
Stratford-on-Avon
Ashchurch
DOWN
16c.

16c.

EVESHAM

UP

Worcester G.W. G.W. Oxford
LOCO G.W.
Dock 12 w.
Evesham North S.B.
Ashchurch Redditch
G.W. G. South S.B.
Stage
42 G. Shed Dock
LOCO Outside 50 Ys Inside 2 E's
Yard 110.
DOWN
Marshalling 97

37.

21'
H.E.L.
9.11.32.
P.A.K.

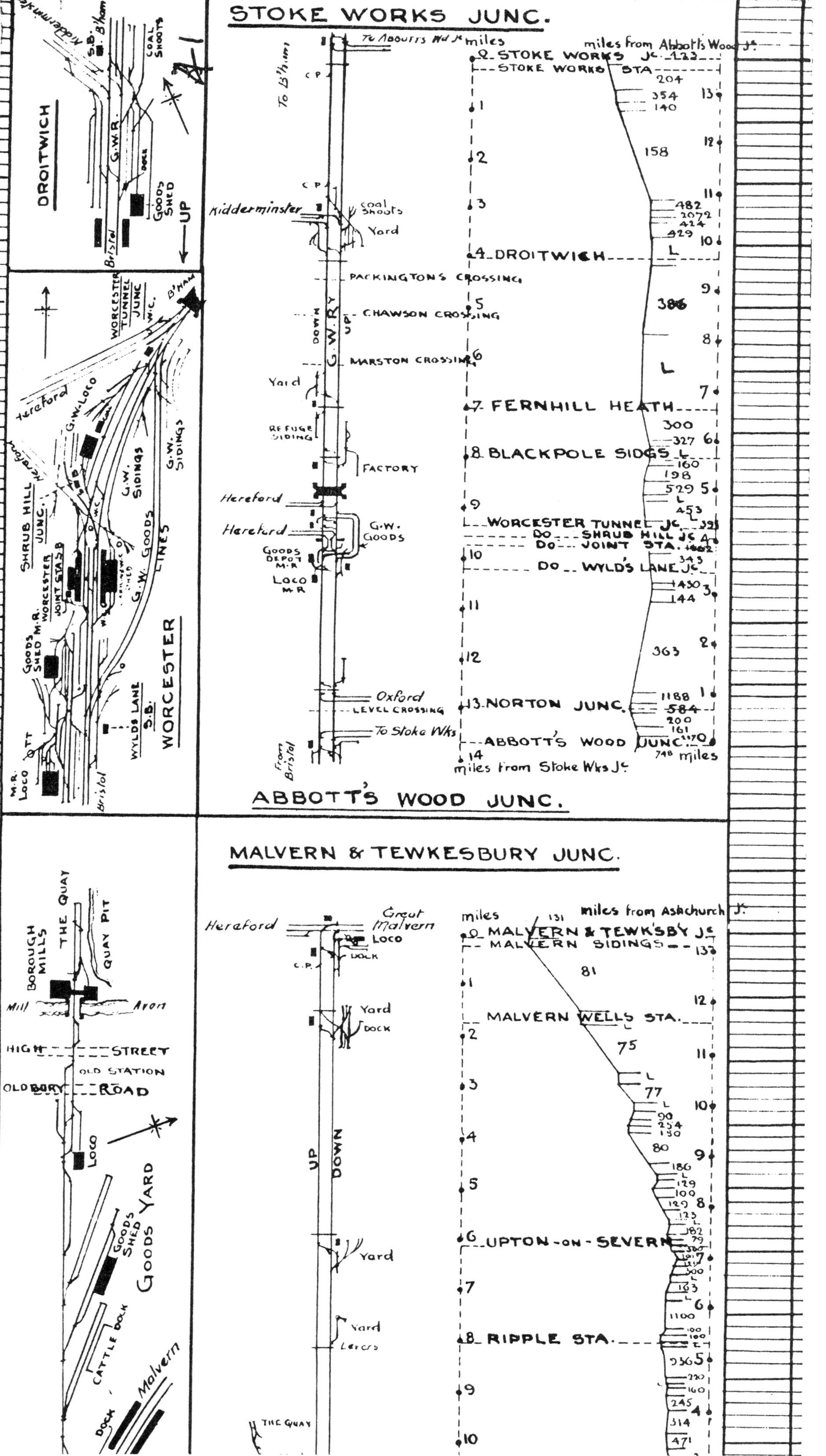
STOKE WORKS JUNC.
DROITWICH
Kidderminster
S.B.
B'ham
COAL SHOOTS
G.W.R.
DOCK
GOODS SHED
Bristol
UP
To B'ham
C.P.
Coal Shoots
Yard
PACKINGTONS CROSSING
CHAWSON CROSSING
MARSTON CROSSING
DOWN
G.W.R'Y
UP
REFUGE SIDING
FACTORY
Hereford
G.W. GOODS
GOODS DEPOT M.R.
Loco M.R.
Oxford
LEVEL CROSSING
To Stoke Wks
From Bristol
miles
miles from Abbott's Wood Jc.
0 STOKE WORKS Jc.
STOKE WORKS STA.
4 DROITWICH
7 FERNHILL HEATH
8 BLACKPOLE SIDGS
WORCESTER TUNNEL Jc.
DO SHRUB HILL Jc.
DO JOINT STA.
DO WYLD'S LANE Jc.
13 NORTON JUNC.
ABBOTT'S WOOD JUNC.
miles from Stoke Wks Jc.
miles
ABBOTT'S WOOD JUNC.
WORCESTER TUNNEL JUNC
W.C.
B'HAM
Hereford
G.W. LOCO
G.W. SIDINGS
SHRUB HILL JUNC.
M.R. WORCESTER JOINT STA. S.B.
G.W. GOODS LINES
GOODS SHED M.R.
WYLDS LANE S.B.
WORCESTER
M.R. LOCO
Bristol
MALVERN & TEWKESBURY JUNC.
Hereford
Great Malvern
Loco
DOCK
C.P.
Yard
DOCK
UP
DOWN
Yard
Yard
Levers
THE QUAY
miles
miles from Ashchurch Jc.
0 MALVERN & TEWK'SBY Jc.
MALVERN SIDINGS
MALVERN WELLS STA.
6 UPTON-ON-SEVERN
8 RIPPLE STA.
BOROUGH MILLS
THE QUAY
QUAY PIT
Mill
Avon
HIGH STREET
OLD STATION
OLDBURY ROAD
LOCO
GOODS SHED
GOODS YARD
CATTLE DOCK
DOCK
Malvern

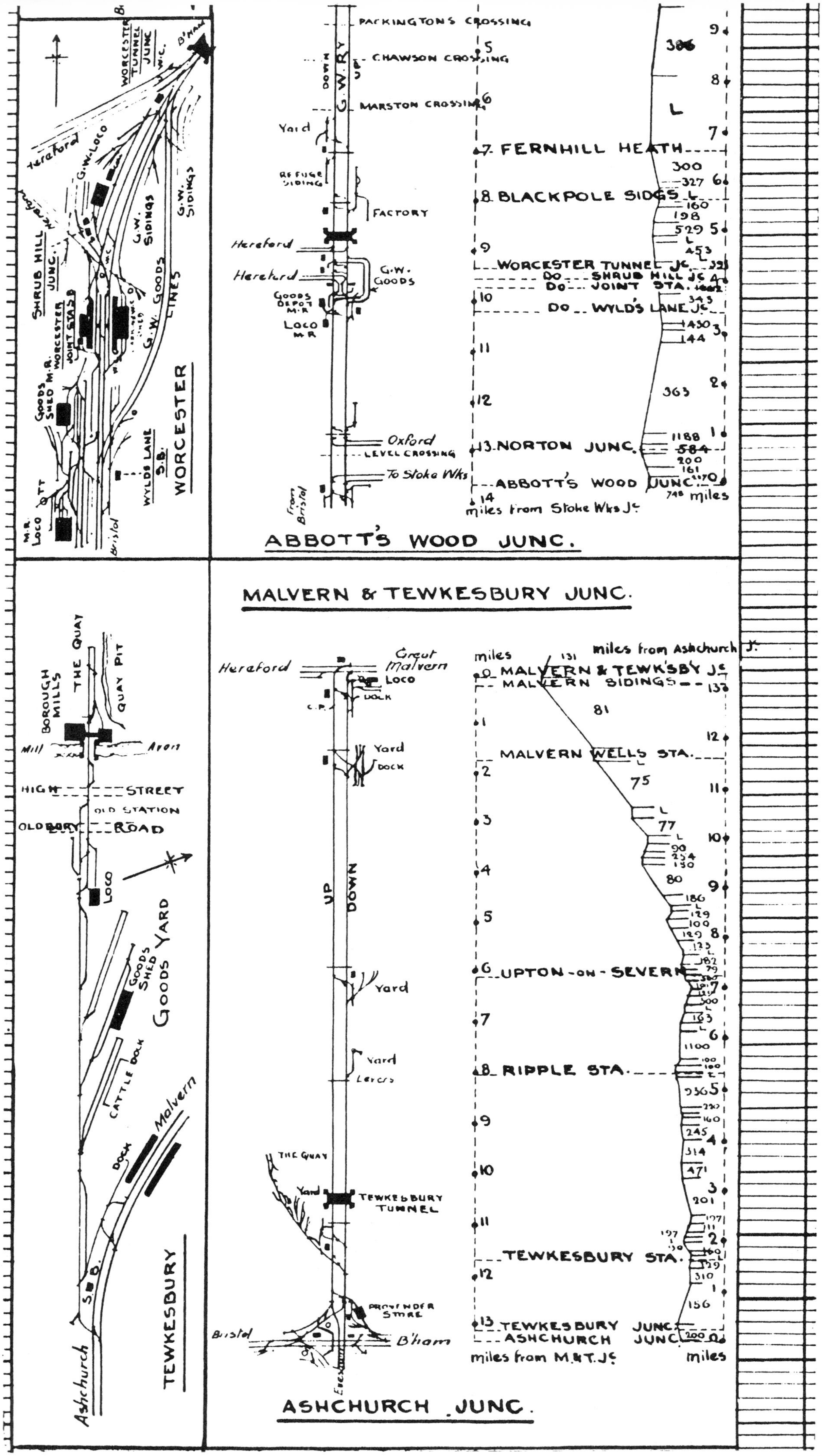

WORCESTER

ABBOTT'S WOOD JUNC.

PACKINGTON'S CROSSING

5 CHAWSON CROSSING

6 MARSTON CROSSING

7 FERNHILL HEATH

8 BLACKPOLE SIDGS

9

WORCESTER TUNNEL JC.

DO SHRUB HILL JC.

DO JOINT STA.

10 DO WYLD'S LANE JC.

11

12

13 NORTON JUNC.

ABBOTT'S WOOD JUNC.

14

miles from Stoke Wks Jc.

MALVERN & TEWKESBURY JUNC.

miles — miles from Ashchurch Jc.

0 MALVERN & TEWK'SBY Jc.

MALVERN SIDINGS — 13

1

MALVERN WELLS STA. — 12

2

3

4

5

6 UPTON-ON-SEVERN

7

8 RIPPLE STA.

9

10

11

TEWKESBURY STA.

12

13 TEWKESBURY JUNC.

ASHCHURCH JUNC. — 0

miles from M.&T. Jc. — miles

TEWKESBURY

ASHCHURCH JUNC.

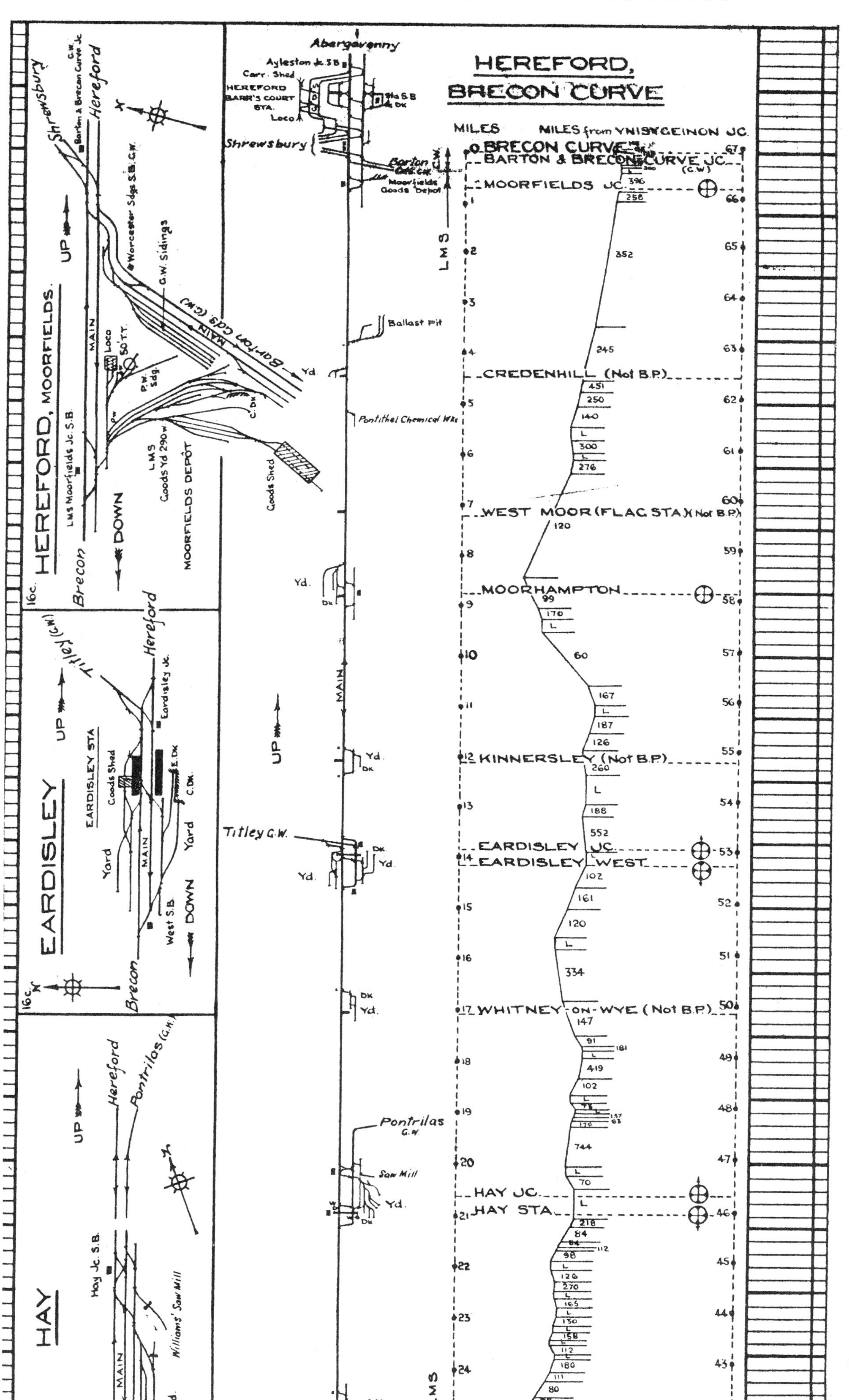
HEREFORD, BRECON CURVE
MILES
MILES from YNISYGEINON JC.
BRECON CURVE
BARTON & BRECON CURVE JC. (G.W.)
MOORFIELDS JC.
CREDENHILL (Not B.P.)
WEST MOOR (FLAG STA.) (Not B.P.)
MOORHAMPTON
KINNERSLEY (Not B.P.)
EARDISLEY JC.
EARDISLEY WEST
WHITNEY-ON-WYE (Not B.P.)
HAY JC.
HAY STA.
GLASBURY-ON-WYE (Not B.P.)
LMS
Abergavenny
Shrewsbury
Ballast Pit
Pontithel Chemical Wks
Titley G.W.
Pontrilas G.W.
Saw Mill
HEREFORD, MOORFIELDS
Barton Gds (G.W.)
Goods Shed
MOORFIELDS DEPOT
EARDISLEY
EARDISLEY STA
HAY
Williams' Saw Mill

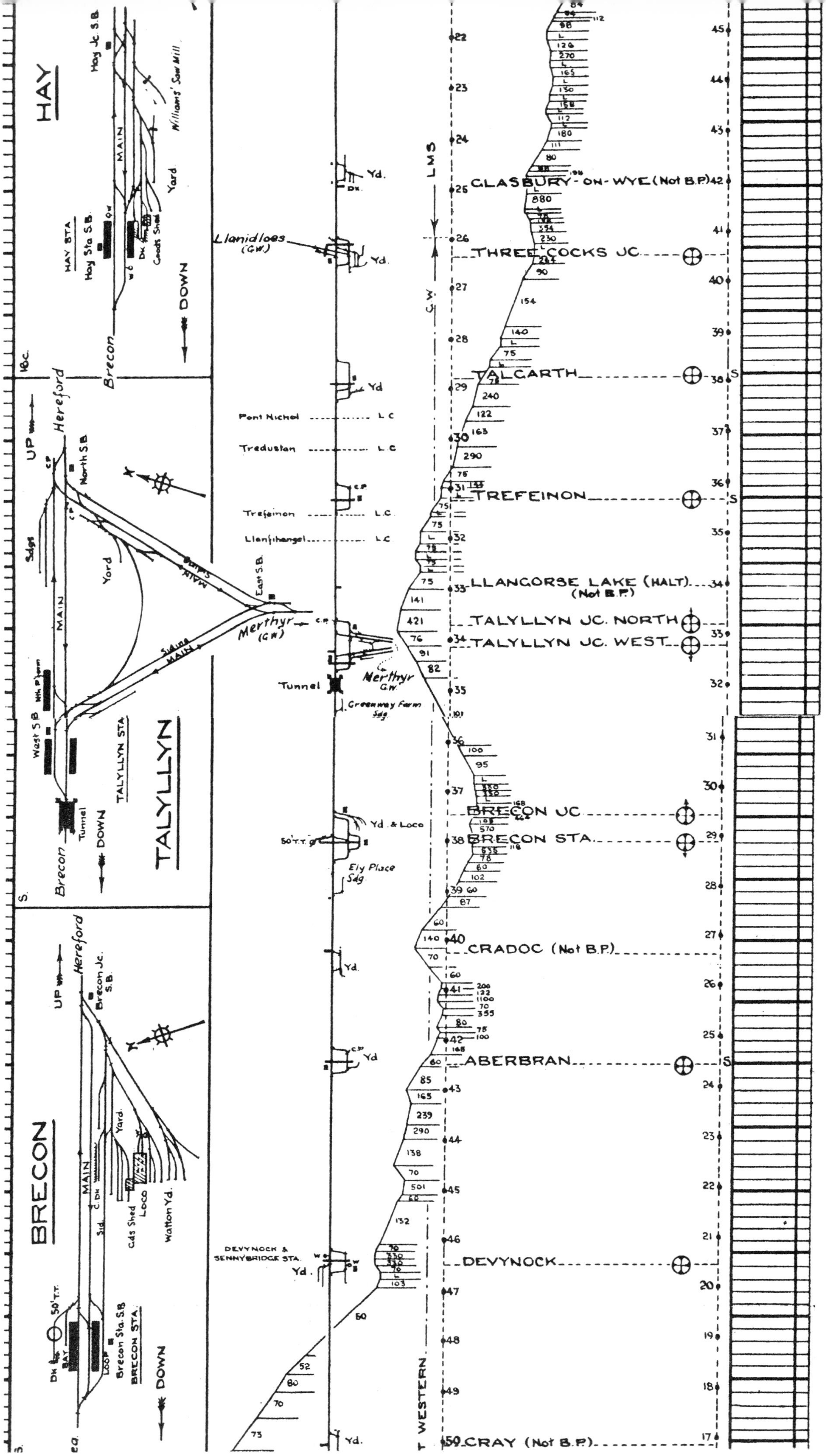

22

23

24

LMS

Yd.

25 GLASBURY-ON-WYE (Not B.P.) 42

Llanidloes (G.W.)

26 Yd.

THREE COCKS JC. 41

G.W.

27 40

28 39

Yd.

TALGARTH 38 S

29

Pont Nichol .... L.C.

Treduston .... L.C.

30 37

C.P.

31 TREFEINON 36 S

Trefeinon .... L.C.

Llanfihangel .... L.C.

32 35

33 LLANGORSE LAKE (HALT) (Not B.P.) 34

C.P.

TALYLLYN JC. NORTH

34 TALYLLYN JC. WEST 33

Merthyr G.W.

Tunnel

Greenway Farm Sdg.

35 32

36 31

37 30

Yd. & Loco

BRECON JC.

50' T.T.

38 BRECON STA. 29

Ely Place Sdg.

39 28

40 CRADOC (Not B.P.) 27

Yd.

41 26

42 25

C.P. Yd.

ABERBRAN 24 S

43

44 23

45 22

46 21

DEVYNOCK & SENNYBRIDGE STA. Yd.

DEVYNOCK 20

47

48 19

49 18

Yd.

WESTERN

50 CRAY (Not B.P.) 17

HAY

Hay Jc. S.B.

Williams' Saw Mill

MAIN

Yard

HAY STA

Hay Sta S.B.

Goods Shed

Brecon

DOWN

TALYLLYN

Hereford

UP

North S.B.

Sdgs

Yard

MAIN

East S.B.

Merthyr (G.W.)

Siding

West S.B.

TALYLLYN STA

Tunnel

Brecon

DOWN

BRECON

Hereford

UP

Brecon Jc. S.B.

MAIN

Yard

Loco

Gds Shed

Watton Yd.

50' T.T.

BAY

LOOP

Brecon Sta. S.B.

BRECON STA.

DOWN

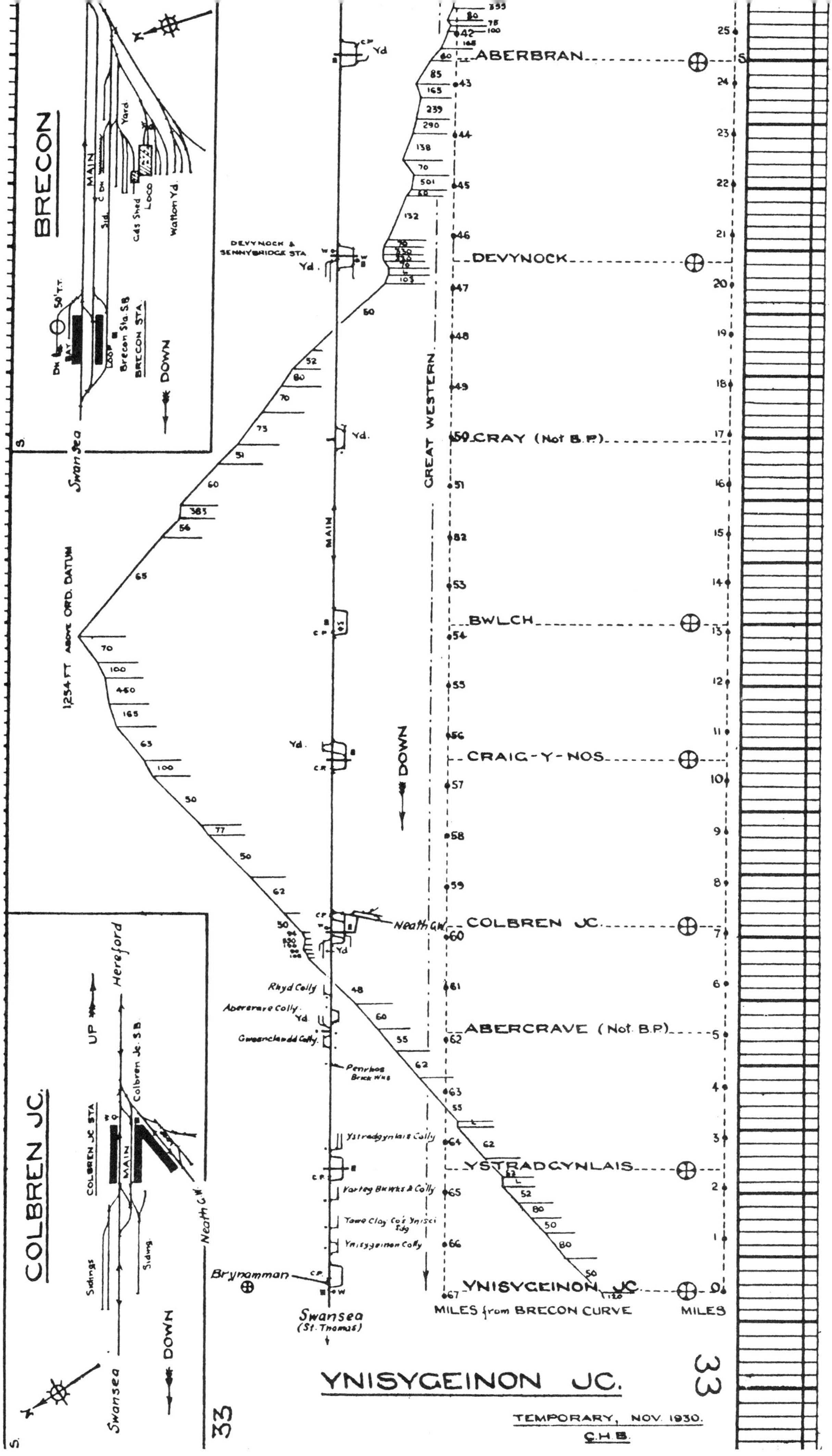

YNISYGEINON JC.

TEMPORARY, NOV. 1930.
C.H.B.

33

BRECON

Swansea
DOWN
BRECON STA.
Brecon Sta. S.B.
50' T.T.
BAY
LOOP
MAIN
Sid.
C. Dn
Yard
Gds Shed
Loco
Watton Yd.

COLBREN JC.

UP
Hereford
Colbren Jc. S.B.
COLBREN JC. STA.
MAIN
Neath G.W.
Sidings
Siding
Swansea
DOWN

1,234 FT ABOVE ORD. DATUM

GREAT WESTERN

MAIN

DOWN

DEVYNOCK & SENNYBRIDGE STA

Neath G.W.

Rhyd Colly
Abercrave Colly
Gwaenclawdd Colly
Penrhos Brick Wks
Ystradgynlais Colly
Varteg Bk Wks & Colly
Tawe Clay Co's Ynisci Sdg
Ynisygeinon Colly
Brynamman

Swansea (St. Thomas)

ABERBRAN
DEVYNOCK
CRAY (Not B.P.)
BWLCH
CRAIG-Y-NOS
COLBREN JC.
ABERCRAVE (Not B.P.)
YSTRADGYNLAIS
YNISYGEINON JC.

MILES from BRECON CURVE

MILES

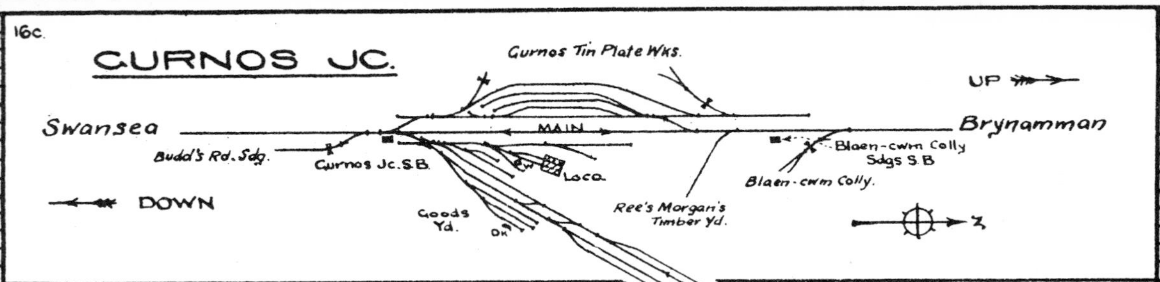
16c.
GURNOS JC.
Gurnos Tin Plate Wks.
UP
Swansea
MAIN
Brynamman
Budd's Rd. Sdg.
Gurnos Jc. S.B.
Loco
Blaen-cwm Colly Sdgs S.B
Blaen-cwm Colly.
DOWN
Goods Yd.
Ree's Morgan's Timber Yd.
Clayphon Goods

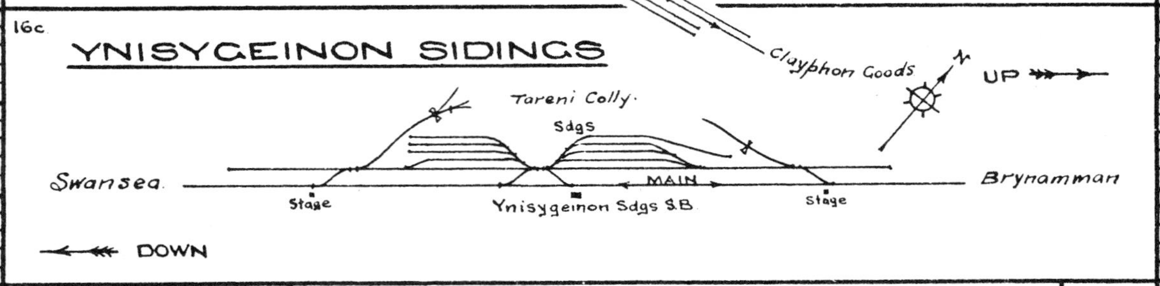
16c
YNISYGEINON SIDINGS
UP
Tareni Colly.
Sdgs
Swansea
MAIN
Brynamman
Stage
Ynisygeinon Sdgs S.B
Stage
DOWN

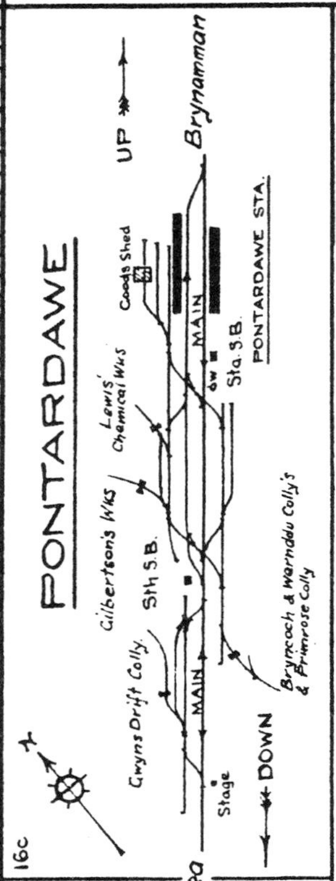
PONTARDAWE
UP
Brynamman
PONTARDAWE STA.
Goods Shed
MAIN
Sta. S.B.
Lewis' Chemical Wks
Gilbertson's Wks
Sth S.B.
Bryncoch & Wernddu Colly's & Primrose Colly
Gwyns Drift Colly
MAIN
DOWN
Stage
16c
Swansea

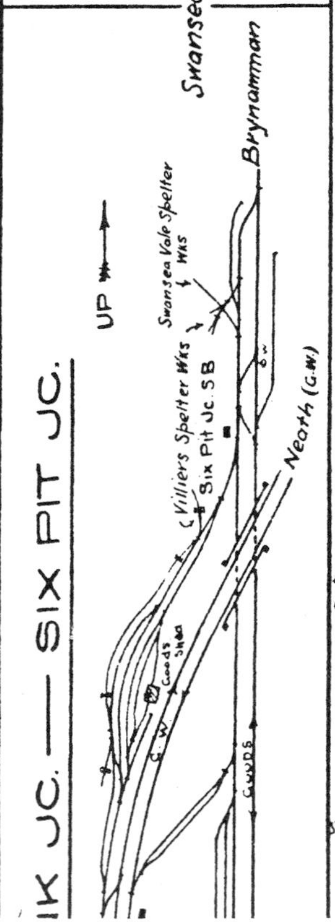
Brynamman
Swansea Vale Spelter Wks
UP
Villiers Spelter Wks
Six Pit Jc. S.B
Neath (G.W.)
SIX PIT JC.
Goods Shed
G.W.
GOODS

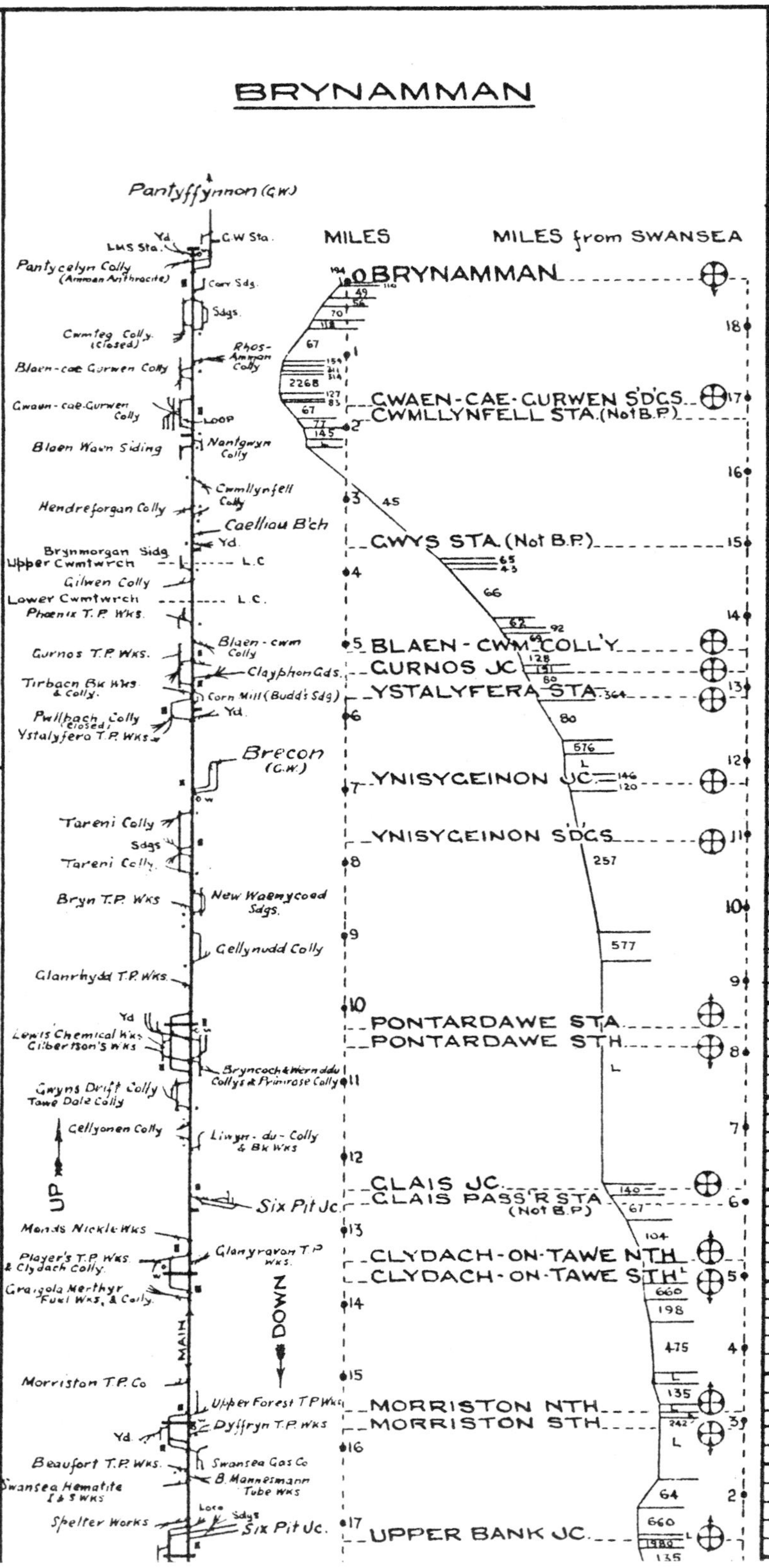
BRYNAMMAN
Pantyffynnon (G.W.)
MILES
MILES from SWANSEA
0 BRYNAMMAN
CWAEN-CAE-GURWEN SDGS.
CWMLLYNFELL STA. (Not B.P.)
GWYS STA. (Not B.P.)
BLAEN-CWM COLL'Y
GURNOS JC
YSTALYFERA STA.
YNISYGEINON JC.
YNISYGEINON SDGS.
PONTARDAWE STA.
PONTARDAWE STH.
CLAIS JC.
CLAIS PASS'R STA (Not B.P.)
CLYDACH-ON-TAWE NTH.
CLYDACH-ON-TAWE STH.
MORRISTON NTH.
MORRISTON STH.
UPPER BANK JC.
Pantycelyn Colly (Amman Anthracite)
Cwmteg Colly. (Closed)
Blaen-cae Gurwen Colly
Gwaun-cae-Gurwen Colly
Blaen Waun Siding
Hendreforgan Colly
Brynmorgan Sidg
Upper Cwmtwrch
Gilwen Colly
Lower Cwmtwrch
Phoenix T.P. Wks.
Gurnos T.P. Wks.
Tirbach Bk Wks & Colly.
Pwllbach Colly (Closed)
Ystalyfera T.P. Wks.
Brecon (G.W.)
Tareni Colly
Sdgs
Tareni Colly
Bryn T.P. Wks
New Waenycoed Sdgs.
Gellynudd Colly
Glanrhyd T.P. Wks.
Lewis Chemical Wks
Gilbertson's Wks
Bryncoch & Wernddu Collys & Primrose Colly
Gwyns Drift Colly
Tawe Dale Colly
Gellyonen Colly
Llwyn-du-Colly & Bk Wks
Six Pit Jc.
Monds Nickle Wks
Player's T.P. Wks. & Clydach Colly.
Glanyravon T.P. Wks.
Graigola Merthyr Fuel Wks, & Colly.
Morriston T.P. Co
Upper Forest T.P. Wks
Dyffryn T.P. Wks
Beaufort T.P. Wks.
Swansea Gas Co
B. Mannesmann Tube Wks
Swansea Hematite I & S Wks
Spelter Works
Six Pit Jc.
MAIN
UP
DOWN

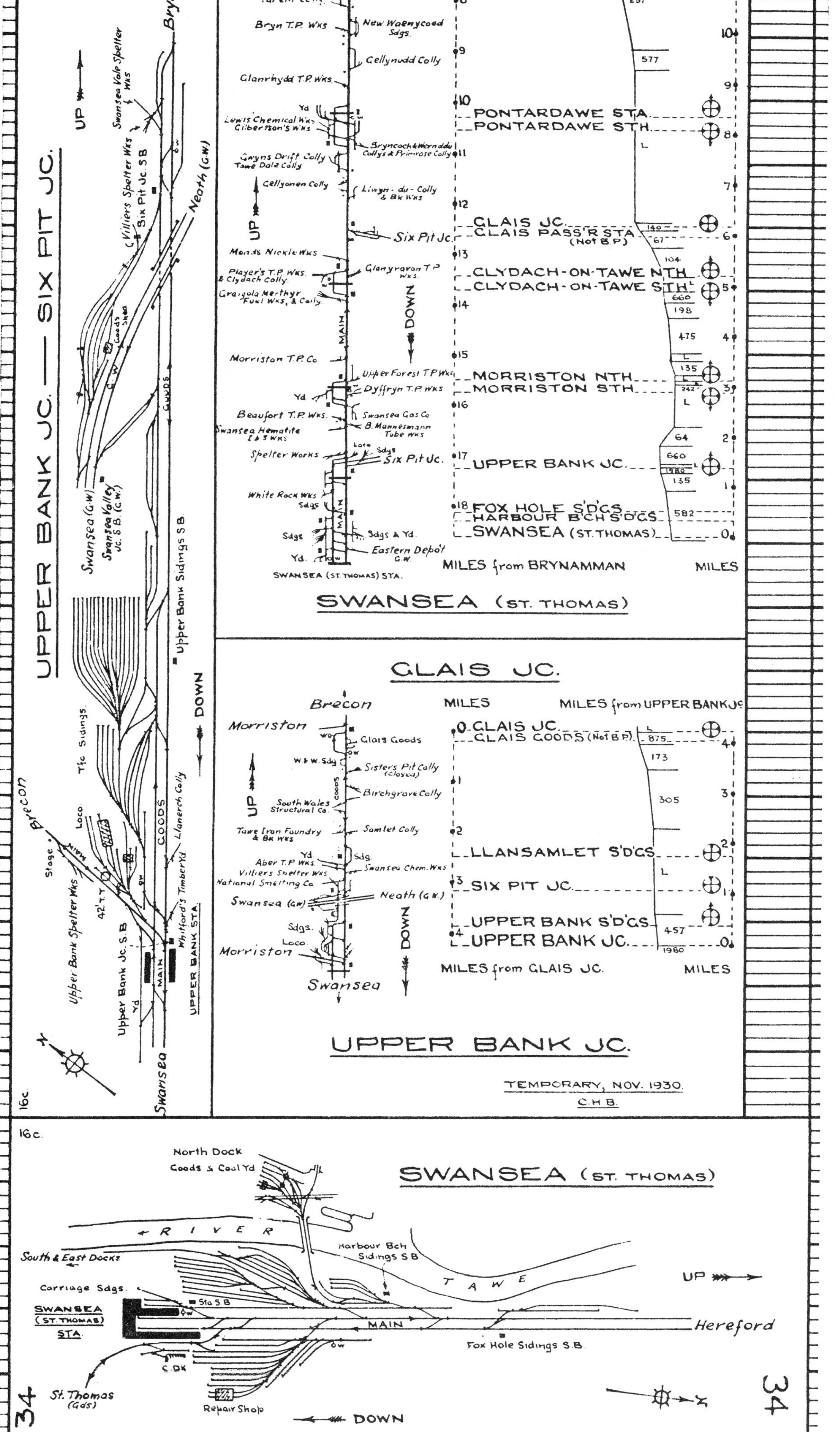

SWANSEA (ST. THOMAS)
MILES from BRYNAMMAN
MILES
YNISYGEINON SDGS
PONTARDAWE STA
PONTARDAWE STH
GLAIS JC.
GLAIS PASS'R STA (Not B.P.)
CLYDACH-ON-TAWE NTH
CLYDACH-ON-TAWE STH
MORRISTON NTH
MORRISTON STH
UPPER BANK JC.
FOX HOLE S'D'GS
HARBOUR B'CH S'D'GS
SWANSEA (ST. THOMAS)
GLAIS JC.
MILES
MILES from UPPER BANK JC
GLAIS JC.
GLAIS GOODS (Not B.P.)
LLANSAMLET S'D'GS
SIX PIT JC.
UPPER BANK S'D'GS
UPPER BANK JC.
MILES from GLAIS JC.
UPPER BANK JC.
TEMPORARY, NOV. 1930.
C.H.B.
UPPER BANK JC. — SIX PIT JC.
16c.
SWANSEA (ST. THOMAS)
North Dock Goods & Coal Yd
RIVER
TAWE
South & East Docks
Harbour Bch Sidings S.B.
Carriage Sdgs.
SWANSEA (ST. THOMAS) STA.
MAIN
Hereford
Fox Hole Sidings S.B.
UP
DOWN
St. Thomas (Gds)
Repair Shop
34

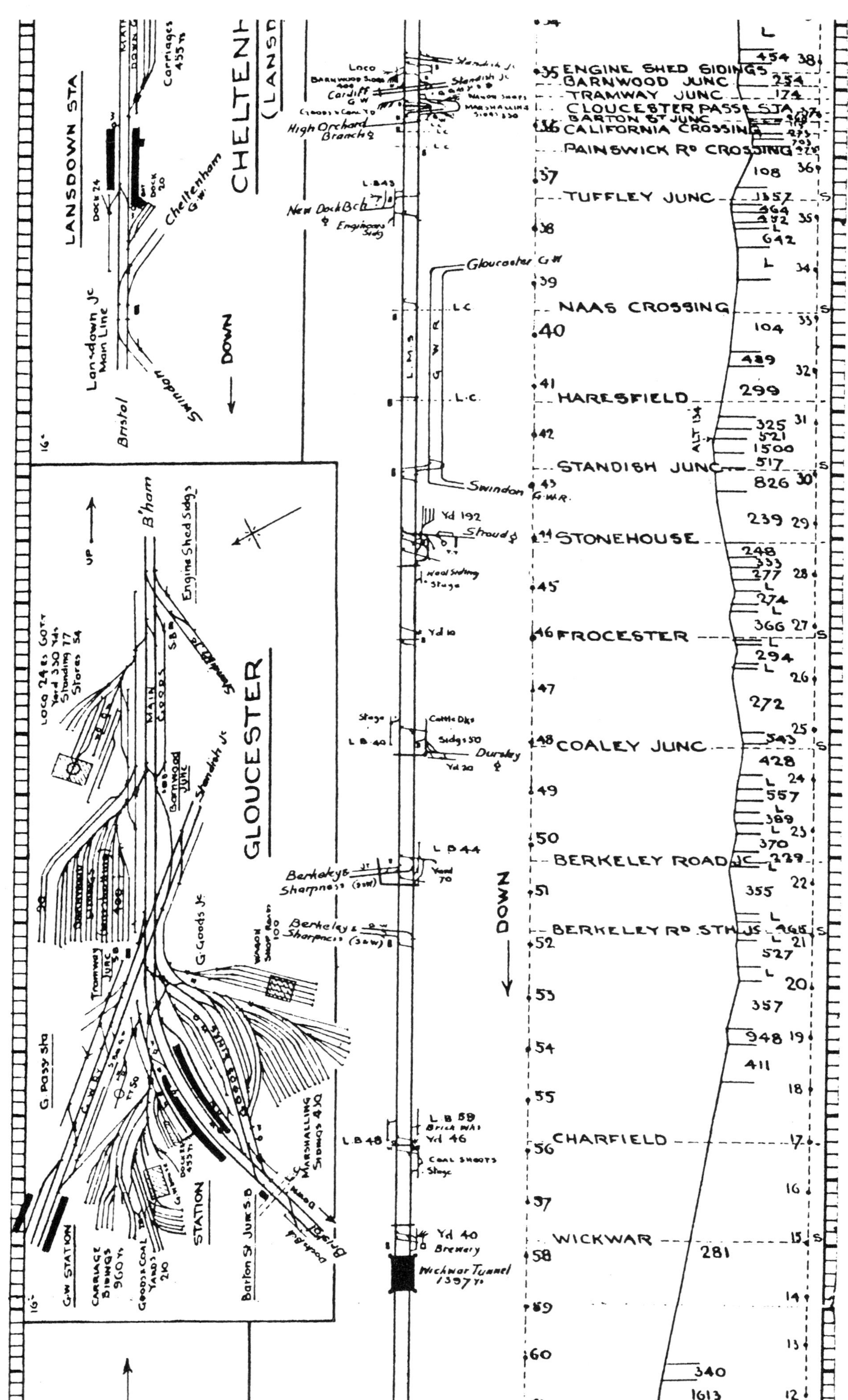

LANSDOWN STA
CHELTENHAM (LANSDOWN)
Cheltenham G.W.
Lansdown Jc Main Line
Bristol
Swindon
DOWN
GLOUCESTER
UP
B'ham
Engine Shed Sidgs
G. Goods Jc
G.W STATION
STATION
Barton St Junc S.B
Marshalling Sidings 430
ENGINE SHED SIDINGS
BARNWOOD JUNC
TRAMWAY JUNC
GLOUCESTER PASS. STA
BARTON ST JUNC
CALIFORNIA CROSSING
PAINSWICK Rᴰ CROSSING
TUFFLEY JUNC
NAAS CROSSING
HARESFIELD
STANDISH JUNC
STONEHOUSE
FROCESTER
COALEY JUNC
BERKELEY ROAD JC
BERKELEY Rᴰ STH JC
CHARFIELD
WICKWAR
High Orchard Branch
New Dock Bch
Gloucester G.W.
Swindon G.W.R.
Stroud
Dursley
Berkeley & Sharpness
Wickwar Tunnel 1397 Yds
DOWN

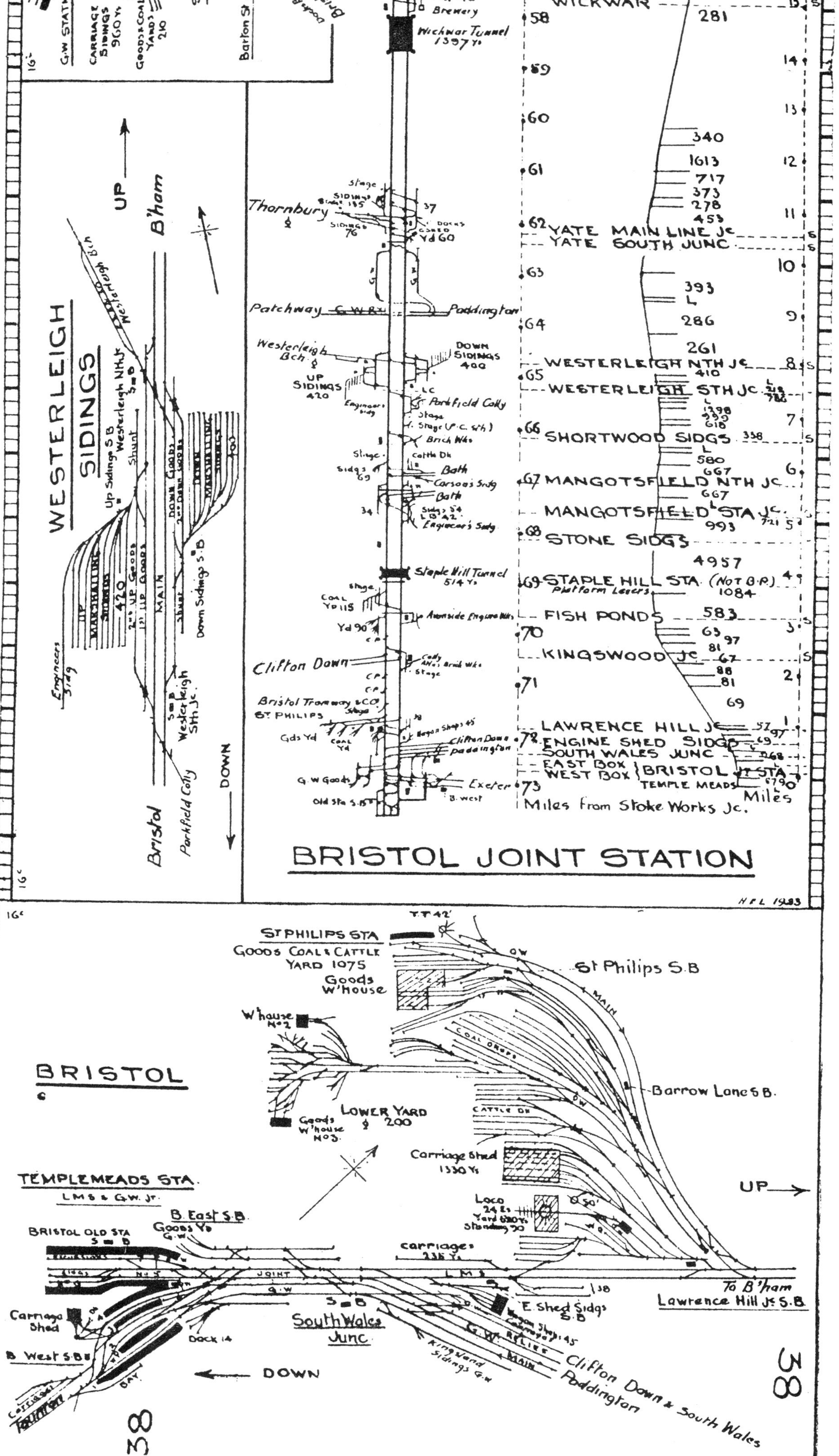
WESTERLEIGH SIDINGS
BRISTOL JOINT STATION
BRISTOL
WICKWAR
YATE MAIN LINE JC
YATE SOUTH JUNC
WESTERLEIGH NTH JC
WESTERLEIGH STH JC
SHORTWOOD SIDGS
MANGOTSFIELD NTH JC
MANGOTSFIELD STA JC
STONE SIDGS
STAPLE HILL STA (NOT B.R.)
FISH PONDS
KINGSWOOD JC
LAWRENCE HILL JC
ENGINE SHED SIDGS
SOUTH WALES JUNC
EAST BOX
WEST BOX
BRISTOL JT STA
TEMPLE MEADS
Miles from Stoke Works Jc.
Miles
Wickwar Tunnel 1397 Yds
Staple Hill Tunnel 514 Yds
Thornbury
Patchway G.W.R.
Paddington
Westerleigh Bch
Clifton Down
Bristol Tramway & Co
ST PHILIPS
Exeter
ST PHILIPS STA
GOODS COAL & CATTLE YARD 1075
St Philips S.B
Barrow Lane S.B.
LOWER YARD 200
Carriage Shed 1330 Yds
TEMPLEMEADS STA.
LMS & G.W. Jt.
B. East S.B.
BRISTOL OLD STA
South Wales Junc
E. Shed Sidgs S.B
To B'ham
Lawrence Hill Jc S.B.
Clifton Down & South Wales
Paddington
UP
DOWN
B. West S.B
HFL 1933
38

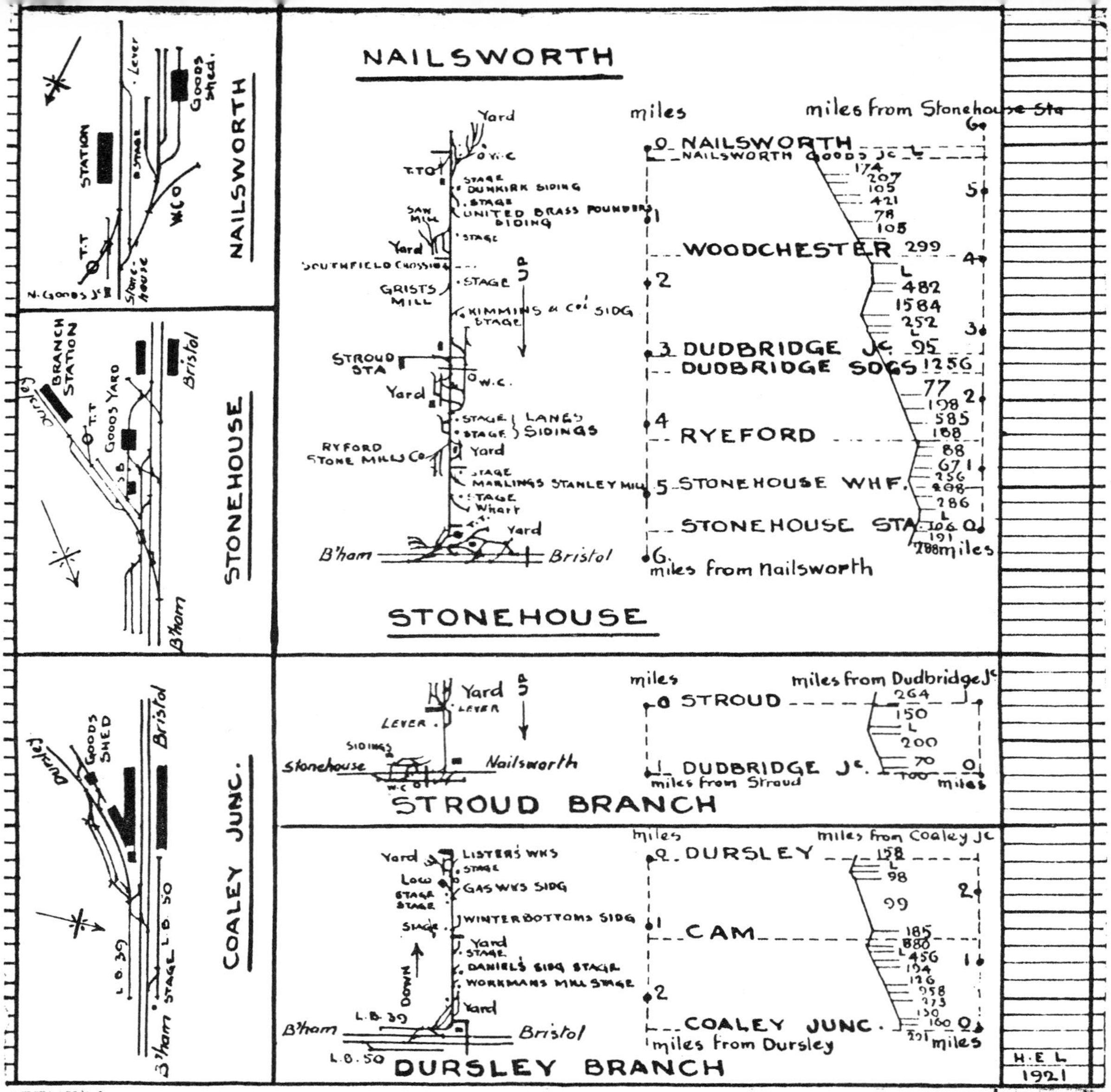
NAILSWORTH
STATION
Goods Shed
W.C.O.
N. Goods Jc
Stonehouse
STONEHOUSE
BRANCH STATION
Goods Yard
Bristol
B'ham
NAILSWORTH
miles
miles from Stonehouse Sta
0 NAILSWORTH
NAILSWORTH GOODS Jc
WOODCHESTER
3 DUDBRIDGE Jc
DUDBRIDGE SDGS
4 RYEFORD
5 STONEHOUSE WHF.
STONEHOUSE STA
miles from Nailsworth
Yard
DUNKIRK SIDING
UNITED BRASS FOUNDERS SIDING
SOUTHFIELD CROSSING
GRISTS MILL
KIMMINS & Co's SIDG
STROUD STA
RYFORD STONE MILLS Co
LANGS SIDINGS
MARLINGS STANLEY MILL
Wharf
B'ham
Bristol
STONEHOUSE
COALEY JUNC.
Goods Shed
Dursley
L.B. 39
L.B. 50
STAGE
miles
miles from Dudbridge Jc
0 STROUD
1 DUDBRIDGE Jc
miles from Stroud
Yard
LEVER
Stonehouse
Nailsworth
STROUD BRANCH
miles
miles from Coaley Jc
0 DURSLEY
1 CAM
COALEY JUNC.
miles from Dursley
LISTERS WKS
GAS WKS SIDG
WINTERBOTTOMS SIDG
DANIELS SIDG STAGE
WORKMANS MILL STAGE
DURSLEY BRANCH
H.E.L. 1921

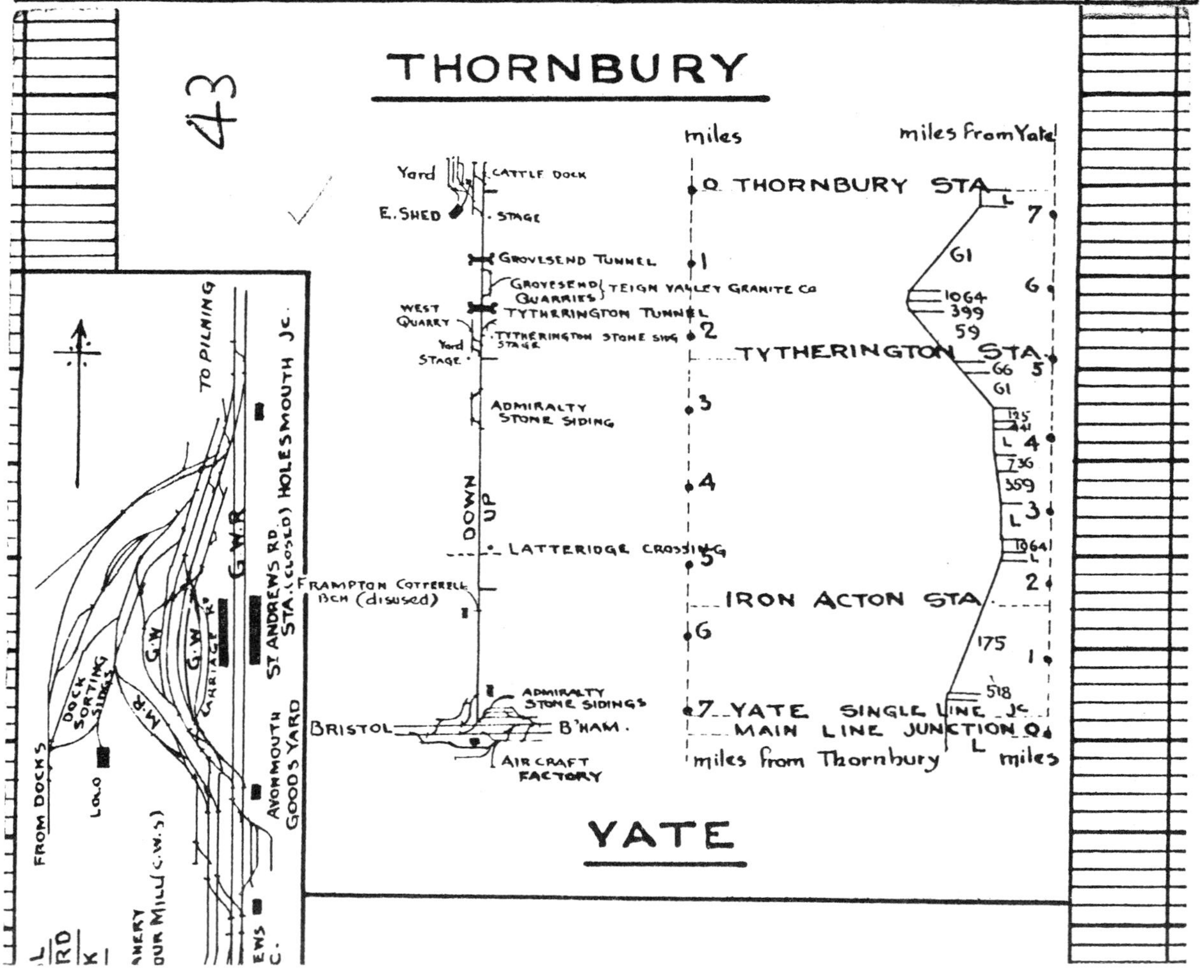
43
THORNBURY
miles
miles from Yate
0 THORNBURY STA
TYTHERINGTON STA
IRON ACTON STA
7 YATE SINGLE LINE Jc
MAIN LINE JUNCTION
miles from Thornbury
Yard
CATTLE DOCK
E. SHED
GROVESEND TUNNEL
GROVESEND QUARRIES
TEIGN VALLEY GRANITE Co
WEST QUARRY
TYTHERINGTON TUNNEL
TYTHERINGTON STONE SIDG
ADMIRALTY STONE SIDING
LATTERIDGE CROSSING
FRAMPTON COTTERELL BCH (disused)
ADMIRALTY STONE SIDINGS
BRISTOL
B'HAM.
AIRCRAFT FACTORY
YATE
TO PILNING
HOLESMOUTH Jc
ST ANDREWS RD. STA. (CLOSED)
G.W.R.
DOCK SORTING SIDINGS
FROM DOCKS
LOCO
AVONMOUTH GOODS YARD

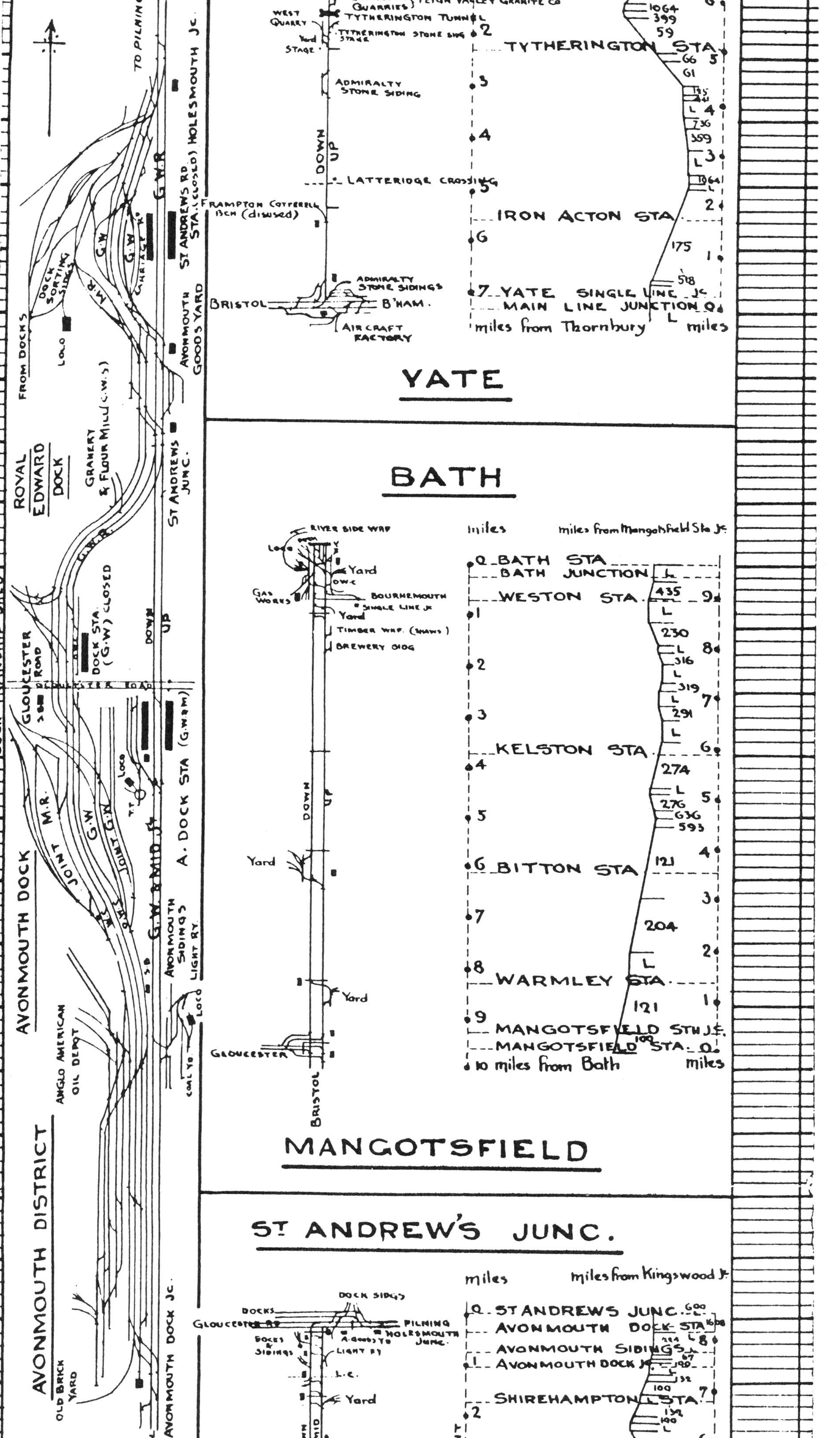
YATE
BATH
MANGOTSFIELD
ST ANDREW'S JUNC.
AVONMOUTH DISTRICT
TYTHERINGTON STA
IRON ACTON STA
YATE SINGLE LINE Jc
MAIN LINE JUNCTION
miles from Thornbury
BATH STA
BATH JUNCTION
WESTON STA
KELSTON STA
BITTON STA
WARMLEY STA
MANGOTSFIELD STH Jc
MANGOTSFIELD STA
miles from Bath
miles from Mangotsfield Sta Jc
ST ANDREWS JUNC
AVONMOUTH DOCK STA
AVONMOUTH SIDINGS
AVONMOUTH DOCK Jc
SHIREHAMPTON STA
miles from Kingswood Jc
ROYAL EDWARD DOCK
AVONMOUTH DOCK
DOCK TRANSHIP SHED
TO PILNING
FROM DOCKS
DOCK SORTING SIDGS
ST ANDREWS RD. STA. (CLOSED)
HOLESMOUTH Jc
AVONMOUTH GOODS YARD
ST ANDREWS JUNC.
GRANERY & FLOUR MILL (C.W.S)
DOCK STA (G.W) CLOSED
GLOUCESTER ROAD
A. DOCK STA (G.W.&M)
AVONMOUTH SIDINGS LIGHT RY.
ANGLO AMERICAN OIL DEPOT
OLD BRICK YARD
AVONMOUTH DOCK Jc.

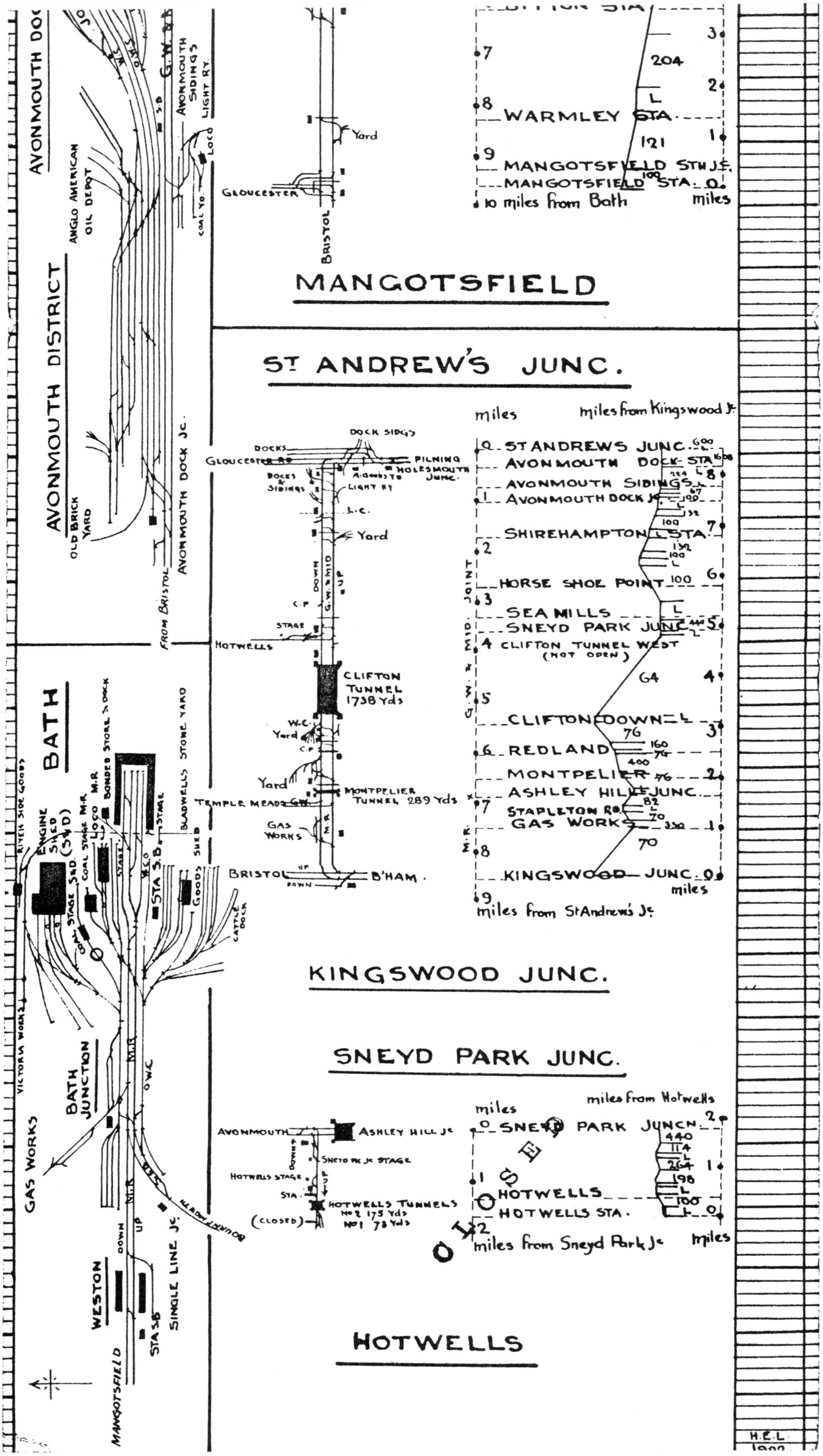

WARMLEY STA.
MANGOTSFIELD STH JC.
MANGOTSFIELD STA.
10 miles from Bath
miles
204
121
L
100
GLOUCESTER
Yard
BRISTOL

MANGOTSFIELD

ST ANDREW'S JUNC.

miles
miles from Kingswood Jc.

0 ST ANDREWS JUNC.
AVONMOUTH DOCK STA.
AVONMOUTH SIDINGS
1 AVONMOUTH DOCK Jc.
SHIREHAMPTON STA.
2
HORSE SHOE POINT
3 SEA MILLS
SNEYD PARK JUNC.
4 CLIFTON TUNNEL WEST (NOT OPEN)
5
CLIFTON DOWN
6 REDLAND
MONTPELIER
ASHLEY HILL JUNC.
7 STAPLETON RD.
GAS WORKS
8
KINGSWOOD JUNC. 0
9 miles from St Andrew's Jc.
miles

G.W. & MID. JOINT
M.R.

DOCK SIDGS
DOCKS
GLOUCESTER RD
PILNING
HOLESMOUTH JUNC.
DOCKS & SIDINGS
LIGHT RY
L.C.
Yard
DOWN
G.W. & MID
UP
C.P.
STAGE
HOTWELLS
CLIFTON TUNNEL 1738 Yds
W.C.
Yard
Yard
MONTPELIER TUNNEL 289 Yds
TEMPLE MEADS GW
GAS WORKS
BRISTOL
B'HAM.

KINGSWOOD JUNC.

SNEYD PARK JUNC.

miles
miles from Hotwells
0 SNEYD PARK JUNCN. 2
1
HOTWELLS
HOTWELLS STA. 0
2 miles from Sneyd Park Jc.
miles
440
114
264
198
100
L

CLOSED

AVONMOUTH
ASHLEY HILL Jc.
SNEYD PK Jc STAGE
HOTWELLS STAGE
STA.
HOTWELLS TUNNELS No 2 175 Yds No 1 78 Yds
(CLOSED)

HOTWELLS

AVONMOUTH DOCK
AVONMOUTH DISTRICT
ANGLO AMERICAN OIL DEPOT
OLD BRICK YARD
AVONMOUTH DOCK Jc.
FROM BRISTOL
AVONMOUTH SIDINGS
LIGHT RY
COAL YD.
LOCO
S.B.
G.W.

BATH
RIVER SIDE GOODS
ENGINE SHED (S&D)
COAL STAGE M.R.
LOCO M.R.
BONDED STORE & DOCK
BLADWELLS STONE YARD
STA. S.B.
GOODS
CATTLE DOCK
VICTORIA WORKS
GAS WORKS

BATH JUNCTION
M.R.
S.&D.

WESTON
STA. S.B.
SINGLE LINE Jc.
MANGOTSFIELD
DOWN
UP
BOURNEMOUTH

H.E.L. 1902

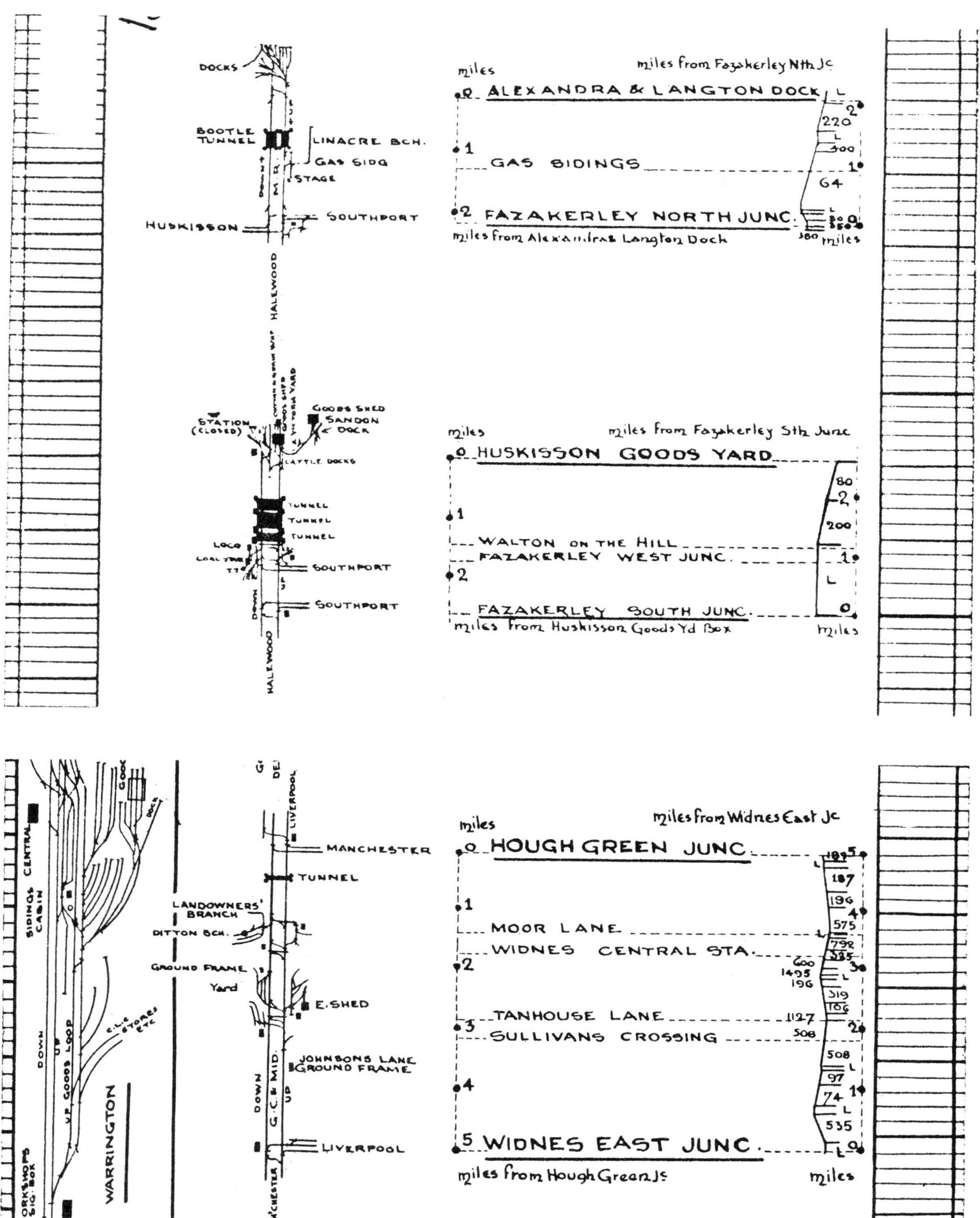
miles
miles from Fazakerley Nth Jc
0 ALEXANDRA & LANGTON DOCK
1
GAS SIDINGS
2 FAZAKERLEY NORTH JUNC.
miles from Alexandra & Langton Dock
miles
miles
miles from Fazakerley Sth Junc
0 HUSKISSON GOODS YARD
1
WALTON ON THE HILL
FAZAKERLEY WEST JUNC.
2
FAZAKERLEY SOUTH JUNC.
miles from Huskisson Goods Yd Box
miles
miles
miles from Widnes East Jc
0 HOUGH GREEN JUNC.
1
MOOR LANE
WIDNES CENTRAL STA.
2
TANHOUSE LANE
3
SULLIVANS CROSSING
4
5 WIDNES EAST JUNC.
miles from Hough Green Jc
miles
DOCKS
BOOTLE TUNNEL
LINACRE BCH.
GAS SIDG
STAGE
HUSKISSON
SOUTHPORT
HALEWOOD
STATION (CLOSED)
GOODS SHED
SANDON DOCK
CATTLE DOCKS
TUNNEL
LOCO
SOUTHPORT
MANCHESTER
TUNNEL
LANDOWNERS' BRANCH
DITTON BCH.
GROUND FRAME
Yard
E. SHED
JOHNSONS LANE GROUND FRAME
G.C. & MID.
LIVERPOOL
WARRINGTON
SIDINGS CENTRAL CABIN
UP GOODS LOOP
WORKSHOPS SIG. BOX

CORRECTIONS

28.	WALWORTH ROAD DEPOT was temporarily closed for reconstruction between 1 April 1958 and 21 September 1959.		
32.	BARKING goods depot was replaced by the new RIPPLE LANE goods depot on 1 April 1957.		
64.	Humberstone Road Jcn: a ladder junction with its south end in the down-side reception line replaced the connections at Bell Lane	... ...	30.9.1979
65.	LOUGHBOROUGH TOWN altered to LOUGHBOROUGH MIDLAND and altered to LOUGHBOROUGH NOTTINGHAM ROAD	Passenger Goods	9.7.1923 1.7.1950
65.	Kegworth to Kingston Mine	Tfc. ceased	17.4.1971
90.	Cossall Colliery Branch	Closed	1.3.1967
97.	Swanwick Sidings (Adamson-Butterley Siding) to Ironville Jcn: although closure was on 30 April 1979, the last train ran on 17 May 1979.		
101.	PLEASLEY altered to PLEASLEY WEST	... ...	1.7.1950
101.	Nottingham East to Sneinton Jcn: up goods line	t.o.u.	2.1986
104.	The new lines at Lincoln were opened, and the line from Boultham Crossing to St Mark's station was closed, on 12 May 1985, as all Sunday trains ran via Lincoln Central and the curve. St Mark's station was closed at 2345 on the Saturday evening.		
105, 106, 107, 201.	The first Public Time Table to use the altered named BASFORD VERNON, BULWELL MARKET, HUCKNALL BYRON, and REDDISH NORTH is the summer issue of 1953, valid from 8 June 1953.		
154.	Wincobank North Jcn to Harrison & Camm's Sidings: up and down goods lines taken out of use as through lines	... ...	21.3.1971
171.	SHIPLEY: new No. 5 platform brought into use for down trains	... ...	14.5.1979
184.	KIRKBY STEPHEN WEST altered to KIRKBY STEPHEN	... ...	6.5.1968
224.	Overseal to Moira West Jcn	t.o.u.	27.1.1985
262.	Stroud branch and STROUD station	RO(P)	29.1.1917